Theoretical and Practical Advances in Information Systems Development:
Emerging Trends and Approaches

Keng Siau
University of Nebraska–Lincoln, USA

Information Science
REFERENCE

Senior Editorial Director:	Kristin Klinger
Director of Book Publications:	Julia Mosemann
Editorial Director:	Lindsay Johnston
Acquisitions Editor:	Erika Carter
Development Editor:	Michael Killian
Production Coordinator:	Jamie Snavely
Typesetters:	Jennifer Romanchak, Milan Vracarich, and Michael Brehm
Cover Design:	Nick Newcomer

Published in the United States of America by
Information Science Reference (an imprint of IGI Global)
701 E. Chocolate Avenue
Hershey PA 17033
Tel: 717-533-8845
Fax: 717-533-8661
E-mail: cust@igi-global.com
Web site: http://www.igi-global.com/reference

Library of Congress Cataloging-in-Publication Data

Theoretical and practical advances in information systems development: emerging trends and approaches / Keng Siau, editor.   p. cm.
  Includes bibliographical references and index. Summary: "This book contains fundamental concepts, emerging theories, and practical applications in database management, systems analysis and design, and software engineering"-- Provided by publisher.
  ISBN 978-1-60960-521-6 (hardcover) -- ISBN 978-1-60960-522-3 (ebook) 1. Information technology. 2. System design. I. Siau, Keng, 1964-
  T58.5.T497 2011
  658.4'038011--dc22
                        2011001624

British Cataloguing in Publication Data
A Cataloguing in Publication record for this book is available from the British Library.

All work contributed to this book is new, previously-unpublished material. The views expressed in this book are those of the authors, but not necessarily of the publisher.

Table of Contents

Section 4

Detailed Table of Contents

Section 1

Chapter 1
Andrew Gemino, Simon Fraser University, Canada
Drew Parker, Simon Fraser University, Canada

The Unified Modeling Language, UML has been evolving as a standard approach to Systems Analysis and Design. Use cases are a de facto standard tool, and corresponding use case diagrams offer visual support for this tool. The Cognitive Theory of Multimedia Learning suggests that the visual nature of use case diagrams would enhance understanding, particularly for novice users, by providing visual cues to focus relevant information. This chapter describes an experiment to test this theory, offering use cases with and without supporting use case diagrams. Retention, comprehension, and problem solving tasks were tested and measured. As hypothesized, the results find that users had a significantly higher level of understanding, measured by problem solving tasks, if they were provided with use case diagrams accompanying the use cases. These results are promising support that use cases and use case diagrams could be considered important boundary objects in systems analysis.

Chapter 2
Debra VanderMeer, Florida International University, USA
Kaushik Dutta, Florida International University, USA

The Unified Modeling Language has been shown to be complex and difficult to learn. The difficulty of learning to build the individual diagrams in the UML, however, has received scant attention. In this chapter, we consider the case of the UML sequence diagram. Despite the fact that these diagrams are among the most frequently used in practice, they are difficult to learn to build. In this chapter, we consider the question of why these diagrams remain so difficult to learn to build. Specifically, we analyze the process of learning to build sequence diagrams in the context of cognitive complexity theory. Based on this analysis, and drawing on the theory of learner-centered design, we develop a set of recommendations for presenting the sequence diagram building task to the student analyst to reduce the complexity of learning how to build them.

Chapter 3

Joerg Evermann, Memorial University of Newfoundland, Canada
Yair Wand, The University of British Columbia, Canada

An important step in developing the requirements for an information system is analyzing the application domain. In this step, conceptual models are used for representing an application domain. However, while languages for software design are available and widely used, no generally accepted language exists for conceptual modeling. This work suggests the use of object-oriented software modeling languages also for conceptual modeling. Such use can support a more accurate transition from domain models to software models. As software-modeling languages were not intended for modeling application domains, their constructs lack the required semantics. While previous chapters addressed the representation of structural elements of domains using object concepts, this chapter addresses behavioral aspects, related to change and interaction. The proposed semantics are based on a mapping between ontological concepts that describe behavior and object-oriented constructs related to dynamics. Based on these mappings, modeling rules are proposed to guide the modeler in creating ontologically well-formed models. The mappings and rules are exemplified using UML and are demonstrated using a case study

Section 2

Chapter 4

Aykut Firat, Northeastern University, USA
Lynn Wu, Massachusetts Institute of Technology, USA
Stuart Madnick, Massachusetts Institute of Technology, USA

Modern database management systems are supporting the inclusion and querying of non-relational sources within a data federation environment via wrappers. Wrapper development for Web sources, however, is a convolution of code with extraction and query planning knowledge and becomes a daunting task. We use IBM DB2 federation engine to demonstrate the challenges of incorporating Web sources into a data federation. We, then, present a practical and general strategy for the inclusion and querying of Web sources without requiring any changes in the underlying data federation technology. This strategy separates the code and knowledge in wrapper development by introducing a general-purpose capabilities-aware mini query-planner and a data extraction engine. As a result, Web sources can be included in a data federation system faster, and maintained easier.

The acquisition and use of personal information by large corporations continues to be a leading issue in the age of virtual communication and collaboration. This research reviews and analyzes the privacy policies of large US companies to evaluate the substance and quality of their stated information practices. Six factors are identified that indicate the extent to which a firm is dependent upon consumer personal information, and therefore, more likely to develop high quality privacy statements. The study's findings provide practical and theoretical implications for information privacy issues, particularly for consumers who need to decide whether to disclose their personal identifying information to firms. The research also highlights the complexity and challenges of managing personal private information.

Extensible markup language, XML has become a standard for persistent storage and data interchange via the Internet due to its openness, self-descriptiveness, and flexibility. This chapter proposes a systematic approach to reverse engineer arbitrary XML documents to their conceptual schema–extended DTD graphs?which is a DTD graph with data semantics. The proposed approach not only determines the structure of the XML document, but also derives candidate data semantics from the XML element instances by treating each XML element instance as a record in a table of a relational database. One application of the determined data semantics is to verify the linkages among elements. Implicit and explicit referential linkages are among XML elements modeled by the parent-children structure and ID/IDREF(S respectively. As a result, an arbitrary XML document can be reverse engineered into its conceptual schema in an extended DTD graph format.

Over the past few years, there have been an increasing number of Web applications that exchange various types of data on the Internet. In this chapter, we propose a technique for building efficient and scalable XML publish/subscribe applications. In particular, we look at the problem of processing streaming XML data efficiently against a large number of branch XPath queries. To improve the performance of XML data processing, branch queries that have similar query characteristics are grouped, and common paths between queries in the same group are identified. Then, these groups of queries are checked against XML schema to validate query structures. After performing structural matching of queries, queries are organized in a way that multiple queries can be evaluated simultaneously in the post-processing phase. In the post-processing phase, join operations are executed in a pipeline fashion, and intermediate join results are shared amongst the queries in the same group. The benefit of this approach is that, the total number of join operations performed in the post-processing phase is significantly reduced. In addition, we also present how to efficiently return all matching elements for each matching branch query. Experiments show that our proposal is efficient and scalable compared to previous works.

Section 3

Chapter 8

Baoning Niu, Taiyuan University of Technology, China & Queen's University, Canada
Patrick Martin, Queen's University, Canada
Wendy Powley, Queen's University, Canada

Workload management is the discipline of effectively managing, controlling and monitoring work flow across computing systems. It is an increasingly important requirement of database management systems, DBMSs in view of the trends towards server consolidation and more diverse workloads. Workload management is necessary so the DBMS can be business-objective oriented, can provide efficient differentiated service at fine granularity and can maintain high utilization of resources with low management costs. We see that workload management is shifting from offline planning to online adaptation. In this chapter we discuss the objectives of workload management in autonomic DBMSs and provide a framework for examining how current workload management mechanisms match up with these objectives. We then use the framework to study several mechanisms from both DBMS products and research efforts. We also propose directions for future work in the area of workload management for autonomic DBMSs.

Chapter 9

Kamal Taha, The University of Texas at Arlington, USA

There has been extensive research in XML Keyword-based and Loosely Structured querying. Some frameworks work well for certain types of XML data models while fail in others. The reason is that the proposed techniques overlook the context of elements when building relationships between the elements. The context of a data element is determined by its parent, because a data element is generally a characteristic of its parent. Overlooking the contexts of elements may result in relationships between the elements that are semantically disconnected, which lead to erroneous results. We present in this chapter a context-driven search engine called XTEngine for answering XML Keyword-based and Loosely Structured queries. XTEngine treats each set of elements consisting of a parent and its children data elements as one unified entity, and then uses context-driven search techniques for determining the relationships between the different unified entities. We evaluated XTEngine experimentally and compared it with three other search engines. The results showed marked improvement.

Chapter 10

Fredrik Karlsson, Örebro University, Sweden
Pär J. Ågerfalk, Uppsala University, Sweden & University of Limerick, Ireland

Method configuration is a specific type of Method Engineering, ME that takes an existing organization-wide Information Systems Development Method, ISDM as its point of departure. Existing assembly-based ME approaches are not well suited to this task. As an alternative, this chapter suggests a meta-method approach to tailoring organization-wide ISDMs. We refer to this approach as the Method for Method Configuration, MMC. MMC takes into account the need to combine structure, which is one reason for choosing an organization-wide ISDM in the first place, with flexibility, which is essential for making the chosen ISDM fit actual projects. The metamethod is built using a three-layered reuse model comprising method components, configuration packages, and configuration templates. These concepts are combined efficiently to produce a situational method and thereby to facilitate the work of method engineers.

Chapter 11

Sherif Sakr, University of New South Wales, Australia

Recently, the use of XML continues to grow in popularity, large repositories of XML documents are going to emerge, and users are likely to pose increasingly more complex queries on these data sets. In 2001 XQuery is decided by the World Wide Web Consortium (W3C) as the standard XML query language. In this chapter, we describe the design and implementation of an efficient and scalable purely relational XQuery processor which translates expressions of the XQuery language into their equivalent SQL evaluation scripts. The experiments of this chapter demonstrated the efficiency and scalability of our purely relational approach in comparison to the native XML/XQuery functionality supported by conventional RDBMSs and has shown that our purely relational approach for implementing XQuery processor deserves to be pursued further.

Section 4

Chapter 12

Anteneh Ayanso, Brock University, Canada
Paulo Goes, University of Arizona, USA
Kumar Mehta, George Mason University, USA

Relational databases have increasingly become the basis for a wide range of applications that require efficient methods for exploratory search and retrieval. Top-k retrieval addresses this need and involves finding a limited number of records whose attribute values are the closest to those specified in a query. One of the approaches in the recent literature is query-mapping which deals with converting top-k queries into equivalent range queries that relational database management systems (RDBMSs) normally support. This approach combines the advantages of simplicity as well as practicality by avoiding the need for modifications to the query engine, or specialized data structures and indexing techniques to handle top-k queries separately. This chapter reviews existing query-mapping techniques in the literature and presents a range query estimation method based on cost modeling. Experiments on real world and synthetic data sets show that the cost-based range estimation method performs at least as well as prior methods and avoids the need to calibrate workloads on specific database contents.

This chapter presents DSQL, a conservative extension of SQL, as an ad-hoc query language for XML. The development of DSQL follows the theoretical foundations of first order logic, and uses common query semantics already accepted for SQL. DSQL represents a core subset of XQuery that lends well to query optimization techniques; while at the same time allows easy integration into current databases and applications that use SQL. The intent of DSQL is not to replace XQuery, the current W3C recommended XML query language, but to serve as an ad-hoc querying frontend to XQuery. Further, the authors present proofs for important query language properties such as complexity and closure. An empirical study comparing DSQL and XQuery for the purpose of ad-hoc querying demonstrates that users perform better with DSQL for both flat and tree structures, in terms of both accuracy and efficiency.

Chapter 14

In this chapter, the authors propose to use the grid file to store multi-dimensional data cubes and answer range-sum queries. The grid file is enhanced with a dynamic splitting mechanism to accommodate insertions of data. It overcomes the drawback of the traditional grid file in storing uneven data while enjoying its advantages of simplicity and efficiency. The space requirement grows linearly with the dimension of the data cube, compared with the exponential growth of conventional methods that store pre-computed aggregate values for range-sum queries. The update cost is $O(1)$, much faster than the pre-computed data cube approaches, which generally have exponential update cost. The grid file structure can also respond to range queries quickly. They compare it with an approach that uses the R*-tree structure to store the data cube. The experimental results show that the proposed method performs favorably in file size, update speed, construction time, and query response time for both evenly and unevenly distributed data.

Preface

The field of information systems development is constantly evolving. New techniques and tools are continuously being introduced. In this volume "Theoretical and Practical Advances in Information Systems Development: Emerging Trends and Approaches", we are proud to present a compilation of excellent cutting-edge research from world-class researchers around the world. The volume is targeted at researchers in the areas as well as professionals in the industry.

The following are the short descriptions of each chapter:

Chapter 1, "*Visual Support for Use Case Modeling: An Experiment to Determine the Effectiveness of Use Case Diagrams*" discusses the advancement of Unified Modeling Language, UML as a customary approach to Systems Analysis and Design. It explores the Cognitive Theory of Multimedia Learning, and describes an experiment conducted in order to analyze this theory. The results provide considerable support that cases and use case diagrams may be significant boundary objects in systems analysis.

Chapter 2, "*Applying Learner-Centered Design Principles to UML Sequence Diagrams*" explores the sophistication and difficulty of learning to shape individual diagrams in the Unified Modeling Language. This chapter also analyzes the procedure of learning to build sequence diagrams and provides suggestions for presenting the sequence diagram construction with the purpose of condensing the difficulty of the learning process.

Chapter 3, "*Ontology Based Object-Oriented Domain Modeling: Representing Behavior*" presents issues regarding analyzing the application domain, and conceptual models involved. This chapter further discusses the use of object-oriented software modeling languages to support a more precise conversion from domain models to software models. It addresses behavioral matters relating to change and interaction, based upon mappings between ontological concepts. Modeling rules formed are used in creating ontologically well-formed models.

Chapter 4, "*General Strategy for Querying Web Sources in a Data Federation Environment*" focuses the support for inclusion and querying of non-relational sources within a data federation setting using wrappers. IBM DB2 federation engine is used to reveal the challenges of integrating Web sources into a data federation. A strategy is presented which detaches the code and knowledge in wrapper development, causing Web sources to be included promptly in a data federation system.

Chapter 5, "*Information Privacy: Understanding How Firms Behave Online*" proposes the idea concerning the acquisition and use of personal information by large corporations. The privacy policies of large US firms are analyzed in order to assess the content and value of their stated information practices. The study provides findings regarding factors that influence a firm's independence upon consumer personal information, and implications for information privacy issues. The complication and disputes of managing personal private information are also adequately addressed.

Chapter 6, "*Reverse Engineering from an XML Document into an Extended DTD Graph*" relates to Extensible Markup Language (XML) which has become a benchmark for consistent storage and data exchange through the Internet. A systematic solution to reverse engineer arbitrary XML documents to their conceptual schema–extended DTD graphs is proposed, which determines the organization of the XML document, and derives candidate data semantics from the XML element instances to validate the linkages among elements. Because implicit and explicit referential linkages are among XML elements, an arbitrary XML document can be reverse engineered into its theoretical schema.

Chapter 7, "*Scalable XML Filtering for Content Subscriptions*" presents ideas relating to a technique for building efficient and scalable XML publish/subscribe applications. This chapter looks at the trouble of processing streaming XML data efficiently against a large number of branch XPath queries, and ways to improve the performance of XML data processing. This section also introduces ways to organize queries and execute join operations in a pipeline fashion. As a result, the number of join operations is reduced and all matching elements are efficiently returned.

Chapter 8, "*Towards Autonomic Workload Management in DBMSs*" provides insight into workload management as a requirement of database management systems, which is necessary for DBMS to be business-objective oriented, providing efficient differentiated service at fine granularity and maintaining high utilization of resources with low management costs. This chapter suggests that there is a shift in workload management from offline planning to online adaptation, where the objectives of workload management in autonomic DBMSs are discussed. A framework for examining current workload management mechanisms is used to study several mechanisms from both DBMS products and research efforts.

Chapter 9, "*XTEngine: A Twin Search Engine for XML*" proposes that the reason some frameworks work well for certain types of XML data models while fail in others is that the proposed techniques overlook the context of elements when building relationships between the elements. This division suggests that context of a data element is determined by its parent because a data element is generally a characteristic of its parent. A context-driven search engine called XTEngine for answering XML Keyword-based and Loosely Structured queries, is introduced in this chapter. It treats each set of elements consisting of a parent and its children data elements as one unified entity, and then uses context-driven exploration techniques for determining the relationships between the different unified entities.

Chapter 10, "*Towards Structured Flexibility in Information Systems Development: Devising a Method for Method Configuration*" introduces Method configuration as a specific type of Method Engineering. This chapter suggests that a metamethod approach (Method for Method Configuration, MMC) be used to cater towards organization-wide ISDMs. MMC considers the need to combine structure with flexibility, and is built with a three-layered reuse model. With these concepts united in an effective manner, a situational method is produced, facilitating the work of method engineers.

Chapter 11, "*On Efficient Evaluation of XML Queries*" discusses that W3C be used as the standard XML query language, as decided by the World Wide Web Consortium. This chapter explains the design and implementation of an efficient and scalable purely relational XQuery processor. The efficiency and scalability of our purely relational approach in comparison to the native XML/XQuery functionality is clearly exhibited, and results show that further research concerning purely relational approach for implementing XQuery processor is indeed necessary.

Chapter 12, "*Cost Modeling and Range Estimation for Top-k Retrieval in Relational Databases*" introduces Top-k retrieval which fulfills the need for efficient methods for exploratory search and retrieval. This chapter further describes the query-mapping approach that deals with converting top-k queries into equivalent range queries, combining the advantages of simplicity as well as practicality. It also reviews current query-mapping techniques, and presents a range query estimation method based on cost modeling. Real-world experiments and synthetic data sets prove that the cost-based range evaluation means performs as well as prior methods and avoids the need to regulate workloads on specific database contents.

Chapter 13, *"Document SQL, DSQL: A Conservative Extension to SQL as an Ad-hoc Querying Frontend for XQuery"* presents DSQL, a conservative extension of SQL, as a query language for XML, and its development process. The chapter further discusses DSQL as a core subset of XQuery that lends well to query optimization techniques, allowing easy integration into current databases and applications that use SQL. Significant query language properties and an experimental study are also presented to display the influence of DSQL in terms of precision and effectiveness.

Chapter 14, *"Range-Sum Queries over High Dimensional Data Cubes Using a Dynamic Grid File"* proposes the use of grid file to store multi-dimensional data cubes and answer range-sum queries, with the grid file being enhanced with a dynamic splitting mechanism to accommodate insertions of data. This chapter debates about the drawbacks which are overcome by the use of grid file, and its various benefits of ease and competence. This part further introduces topics regarding the space requirement, update costs, and structure of grid files. Experimental outcome shows that the proposed method performs favorably in file size, update speed, construction time, and query response time for both evenly and unevenly distributed data.

Keng Siau
University of Nebraska-Lincoln, USA
Editor-in-Chief, Journal of Database Management

Section 1

Chapter 1
Visual Support for Use Case Modeling:
An Experiment to Determine the Effectiveness of Use Case Diagrams

Andrew Gemino
Simon Fraser University, Canada

Drew Parker
Simon Fraser University, Canada

ABSTRACT

The Unified Modeling Language (UML) has been evolving as a standard approach to Systems Analysis and Design. Use cases are a de facto standard tool, and corresponding use case diagrams offer visual support for this tool. The Cognitive Theory of Multimedia Learning suggests that the visual nature of use case diagrams would enhance understanding, particularly for novice users, by providing visual cues to focus relevant information. This paper describes an experiment to test this theory, offering use cases with and without supporting use case diagrams. Retention, comprehension, and problem solving tasks were tested and measured. As hypothesized, the results find that users had a significantly higher level of understanding, measured by problem solving tasks, if they were provided with use case diagrams accompanying the use cases. These results are promising support that use cases and use case diagrams could be considered important boundary objects in systems analysis.

DOI: 10.4018/978-1-60960-521-6.ch001

INTRODUCTION

The Unified Modeling Language (UML) offers a language specification to support an object-oriented approach to systems analysis and design. The use case is a text-based description defined in the UML that provides a structured sequence of processes within a system (Jacobsen et. al., 1994). Use cases are a popular modeling technique amongst UML practitioners (Batra, 2008; Dobing & Parsons, 2008) and use cases have received significant research attention (Burton-Jones & Meso, 2006; Siau & Loo, 2006). While text is a rich, familiar and expressive modeling tool, the exclusive use of text across multiple use cases may be difficult for users to conceptualize, particularly as the size of the modeled system increases.

Given the popularity of use cases, it seems reasonable to consider whether a diagram in support of use case modeling, specifically in this case the use case diagram, provides a more effective method for communicating system analysis information than text-based use cases alone. Dobing and Parsons (2000) found that while use case narratives and use case diagrams were the UML tools most likely to be used in interacting with users, that 42% of respondents indicated that use case diagrams provide insufficient value to justify their cost. In a subsequent survey, Dobing and Parsons (2008) found that the use case diagram seems to be gaining popularity: for client validation, implementation, documentation, and clarification, respondents believed the use case diagram to be at least moderately useful.

Communication of analysis information is recognized as an important factor in information system development success. The oft-quoted CHAOS report (Standish Group, 1994) and more recent reports (Charette, 2005) suggest that poorly defined system requirements and poor communication with users remain important inhibitors to development success. A primary challenge of effective systems analysis is to find ways to integrate knowledge across user and technical communities in a way that develops a high quality of pragmatic understanding. In her study of shared work contexts, Bechky (2003) noted that a lack of a shared work context leads to poor communication because members of the different communities will describe elements of the work system in different ways using context most familiar to them. She labeled this issue "de-contextualization" and suggested that: "decontextualization occurred when people from different groups met to discuss a problem, and brought different understandings of the problem to their discussion," the result of which was a "situation was presented in language that was assumed to be universal and unproblematic, but in fact the words were incomprehensible to those who did not share an understanding of the context of the situation" (Bechky 2006). While the context of operational work in Bechky (2006) differs for that of work system analysis, the notion of decontextualization clearly rings true when considering the communities in conceptual modeling.

One method to bridge the knowledge gap across communities is to find an appropriate boundary object that can be understood by members of both communities (Star et al. 1989). According to Star et al. (1989, p. 393), boundary objects:

"...may be abstract or concrete. They have different meanings in different social worlds but their structure is common enough to more than one world to make them recognizable means of translation. The creation and management of boundary objects is key in developing and maintaining coherence across intersecting social worlds."

Given this definition, and a recognition that the quality of a conceptual model is realized by the effective communication that is made through the model (Lindland et al. 1994), it can be argued that a use case serves as a potential boundary object for the stakeholder and analyst communities in systems analysis and design..

This paper hypothesizes that understanding of text-based tools such as use cases could be significantly enhanced by incorporating diagrams conveying the information in a graphical format. This would make the Use Case and related Use Case Diagram a potential boundary object for the analysis and design process. The Cognitive Theory of Multimedia Learning (CTML) developed by Mayer (2009) recognizes that both graphical and textual cognitive channels are involved in developing understanding and supports this assertion. The CTML provided the theoretical core of the argument in this paper.

An experiment was undertaken to compare the effectiveness of use cases with and without supporting use case diagrams in conceptual modeling. To accomplish this, we take the view that techniques should be compared on how well they support the development of an understanding of the domain they represent (Gemino & Wand, 2003). The CTML (Mayer, 2009) is used to hypothesize that diagrams improve the effectiveness of use case delivery by providing visual cues aiding model viewers in selecting and integrating relevant domain information into effective cognitive representations. To test understanding, we use a problem solving task (Bodart et. al., 2001; Burton-Jones & Meso, 2006; Gemino, 1999) that requires reasoning about the domain and focuses attention on higher levels of understanding.

BACKGROUND

The term "use case" refers to a complete sequence of events in the system as understood from a user's perspective. In other words, a use case represents the actions associated with an actor's "use" of the system (Jacobson et. al., 1994). The use case has become an important part of object-oriented analysis methods (Siau and Cao, 2001) and is prevalent in early requirements analysis (Dobing & Parsons, 2008).

Kobryn (1999) has argued that use cases include simple and natural notations that are easy to understand for stakeholders, analysts and designers. This simplicity makes use cases ideal tools for interacting with users. A key to the success of the use case remains the lack of formalism enabling stakeholders and analysts to communicate (Jacobson et. al., 1999). Improving the effective communication between designers, analysts and users addresses a primary factor in system development failure and increases the chances the resulting system will address the business challenges it was intended to support.

Previous Research in UML Use Case Modeling

A significant amount of research has studied the UML (Agarwal, De, & Sinha, 2003; Burton Jones & Meso, 2006; Evermann & Wand, 2005; Fedorowicz & Villeneuve, 1999; Siau & Cao, 2001; Siau & Loo, 2006). Much of the focus has been placed on theoretical work relating to diagramming techniques (Douglass, 1998; Halpin & Bloesch, 1999; Mellor, 2002). While much has been said regarding the potential benefits of use case modeling (Jacobson et. al., 1999; Kobryn, 1999), surprisingly little empirical research has considered these claims. For example, Dobing and Parsons (2006) found little or no empirical research on the effectiveness of use case modeling.

While UML modeling is popular, it also has critics. Douglass (1998) and Siau *et al* (2005) have suggested that the UML is large and can be complex for users. Halpin and Bloesch (1999) suggested UML models are designed for software engineering and are less suitable for validation of conceptual models. Dori (2002) and Shoval and Kabeli (2005) have suggested that it is difficult in UML to integrate structural and process elements of system designs. In regard to use cases, Dobing and Parsons (2006) suggested that use case modeling faces two significant challenges. One challenge is that use cases tend to isolate stakeholders from object class models. This results in a lack of information on classifications and categories within the system. They argue that information in the Class Diagram is valuable in developing understanding and is not provided by use cases. A second challenge is the lack of formalism, which allows use cases to mix conceptual, design and implementation details in the same description. This mixture of design and conceptual elements may cause confusion for stakeholders and reduce the effectiveness of the stakeholder/analyst communication. Both of these challenges offer an opportunity to extend understanding with a diagram. These criticisms suggest the need for empirical evidence (Johnson, 2002; Wand and Weber, 2002).

Separating Conceptual Modeling from Requirements Engineering

To understand how uses cases support conceptual modeling, it is important to outline basic elements in system development process. The information system development process can be viewed as a series of increasingly formal representations ending in machine executable code (Wand & Weber, 1993). This process is depicted in Figure 1.

Three generic roles involved in this development process include stakeholders, analysts and developers as shown in Figure 2. The least formal representations of the system are the concepts held by stakeholders. Analysts can be portrayed as interacting with stakeholders to develop initial

representations of the system, which are referred to here as conceptual models (Everman, 2005; Wand & Weber, 2002). It should be noted that software engineering practices, such as Agile Development, that do not aim to develop structured requirements would not assume a separation between developer and analyst nor separate conceptual modeling from software development (Angioni et al, 2006; Meso & Jain, 2006). Still, the evolution of this formalization would hold true. An iterative process produces conceptual models then can serve as a foundation for the development of more formal requirements in a process of requirements engineering. Analysts develop formal requirements primarily to communicate system details with developers. Developers can then use formalized requirements as an input for the software construction process to develop the eventual machine code for the system (the system artifact).

The role of the analyst in this process is to communicate system details in such a way as to develop a common understanding of the system between developers, analysts and stakeholders. This view suggests analysts are involved in two distinct processes. The first involves interacting with stakeholders to develop an understanding of the system. This is conceptual modeling (CM). CM involves eliciting initial ideas about the system, representing them, and then having stakeholders interpret and validate these requirements. The second process formalizes this conceptual

Figure 1. System development as a process of increasingly formal representations

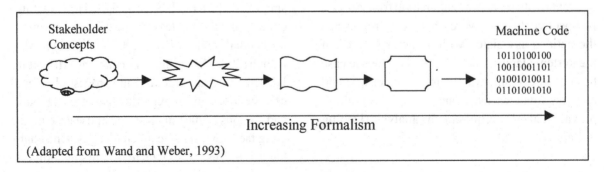

Stakeholder Concepts

Machine Code

10110100100
10011001101
01001010011
01101001010

Increasing Formalism

(Adapted from Wand and Weber, 1993)

Figure 2. Roles and interaction in the analysis and design process

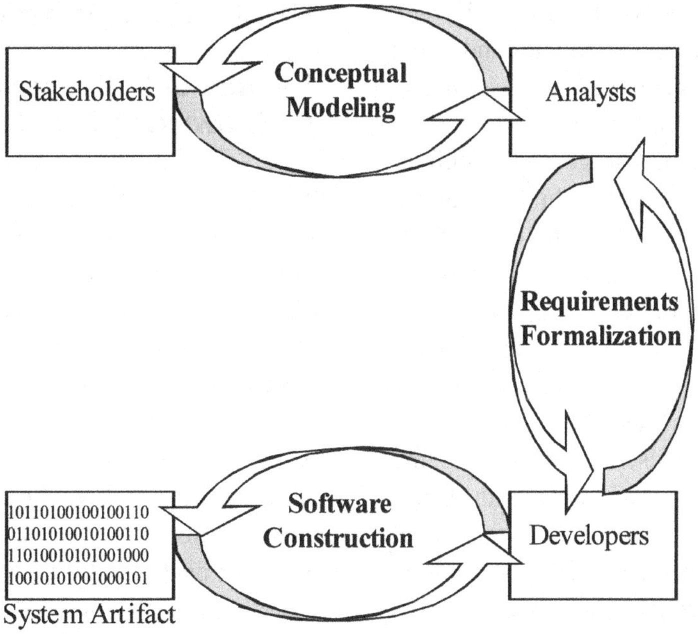

understanding into a set of requirements. This second process is defined here as requirements formalization (RF).

CM and RF are related processes that facilitate the common objective to reason and communicate about a domain.

Because the processes are related, the same techniques are often suggested for use in both CM and RF. The target audiences for CM and RF, however, differ in both experience with the system and experience with formal modeling languages such as the UML. It is not clear that the same modeling techniques will be useful for both audiences. Use cases have often been suggested as useful tools for interacting with stakeholders, and hence could support CM, but they can also inform developers about process issues. In this study, the focus is placed on use cases as they pertain to the process of conceptual modeling and the interaction between analysts and stakeholders.

THEORETICAL FOUNDATIONS

CM involves the elicitation and collection of domain information to develop understanding and support communication and can be viewed as a process of learning (Gemino and Wand, 2003). This is true for the person developing the model as well as the person viewing it. The design of CM techniques may be informed, therefore, by theories of how humans develop understanding from the graphics and words they are presented with. Mayer (2009) suggests two contrasting views of learning –information acquisition and knowledge construction. These views are discussed briefly below.

Information Acquisition and Knowledge Construction

Learning as information acquisition suggests learning is adding to long-term memory. The person looking at the model can be viewed as an "empty vessel" that can be filled with the information provided in the model. The model creator presents information to model viewers. The model viewer receives information and stores it in memory. The responsibility for learning in this view rests on the model creator to deliver appropriate information. The goal is to deliver required information efficiently. In the information acquisition view, the conceptual model is a standard vehicle for efficient information delivery to people viewing the model.

An alternative view of the learning process is that of knowledge construction. This view suggests knowledge is personally constructed. Two model viewers presented with the same conceptual model may come away with different learned outcomes. This occurs as the model viewers attempt to make sense of the information presented, There is a process where model viewers integrate new information provided by the model with information that has each person has available in long term memory. It is at this integration point where knowledge is constructed. Knowledge construction suggests the model viewer is an active sense maker rather than a passive receiver of information. The model creator's role in the knowledge construction view is to assist the model viewer in their sense-making by not only presenting information but also determining what

information to pay attention to and how to better relate the information to prior experience.

A Model of Conceptual Modeling as Knowledge Construction

We use the model of knowledge construction as a framework for reasoning about conceptual modeling (Gemino & Wand, 2003). The model viewer, in this framework, is constructing knowledge by actively organizing and integrating newly presented information with previous experiences. Three antecedents of the process are suggested: (1) content, (2) presentation method, and (3) model viewer characteristics. The content represents the domain information to be communicated. The presentation method is the way in which content is presented to the viewer. Viewer characteristics are attributes of the person viewing the model prior to viewing the content. These characteristics include knowledge and experience with the domain and with the modeling methods used to present information. This model is depicted in Figure 3.

The construction process is where the sense making activity is hypothesized to occur. The results of knowledge construction are encoded into the long-term memory. This new knowledge is termed the learning outcome. The learning outcome modifies the model viewer's character-

Figure 3. Elements of learning process in conceptual modeling (Gemino & Wand, 2003, p. 82)

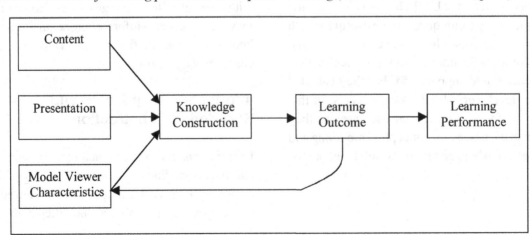

istics as shown in Figure 3. Learning outcomes can then be observed, only indirectly, through learning performance tasks.

The Cognitive Theory of Multimedia Learning

Conceptual modeling techniques often combine graphical symbols with words. Messages that combine graphics and words are defined by Mayer (2009) as "multimedia messages". He defines multimedia based on presentation modes (verbal and visual) of the person receiving this information rather than on the media used to present this information (video, written word, speaker, etc.). The Cognitive Theory of Multimedia Learning (CTML) provides a theoretical perspective for considering the level of understanding developed by a person viewing explanative material, such as an analysis diagram in conceptual model validation. The theory is based on work by Baddeley (1992) and Paivio (1986) and has been developed using over two decades of empirical work (Mayer, 1989; Mayer, 2009).

The theory is focused on the interaction between a person and the information presented to him or her. The CTML suggests there are two pathways in cognition, verbal and visual. While independent, these channels communicate in working memory. When a person views presented material, relevant information from the verbal and

visual channels is selected into working memory. This information is organized to create separate visual and verbal models in working memory. These two visual and verbal models then interact and are subsequently integrated with prior knowledge in long-term memory to develop new knowledge. An overview is provided in Figure 4.

In the CTML, an understanding of verbal and visual information is developed through three stages of memory. In the first stage, *sensory memory*, information is selected into one of the two dual coding pathways. This first stage of memory requires viewers to pay attention to appropriate pieces of information and filter other irrelevant or less relevant information out. This stage is a process of selecting information. Experts and novices are likely to have different abilities to select appropriate information so the amount of cognitive activity required to select appropriate information will vary between individuals. The selected information is then incorporated into visual and verbal models in the second stage of memory called *working memory*. Working memory is used to organize the selected information. There is the opportunity for some interaction between the visual and verbal models in working memory. These linkages help to increase the sophistication of the cognitive model and can improve the integration process. In the final stage of memory, the verbal and visual models from working memory are integrated with *long-term*

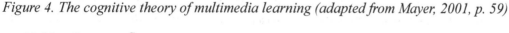

Figure 4. The cognitive theory of multimedia learning (adapted from Mayer, 2001, p. 59)

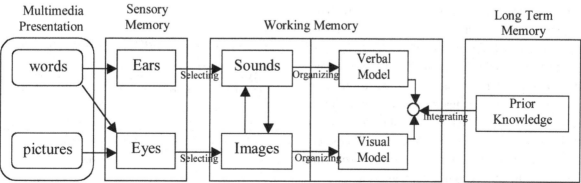

memory. This integration results in the level of understanding developed by the person viewing the content. This three-stage memory process describes what we will refer to here as the knowledge construction process.

There are two additional important considerations in the knowledge construction process. The first is that the three memory stages described above occur simultaneously and continuously during cognitive processing. Information is continually being selected, organized and integrated and all three of these memory stages must be supported at the same time. The second consideration is that human beings have limited cognitive resources. Only a limited amount of processing power is available to support each of the three stages. If, for example, the content is presented in a confusing way for the viewer, it is likely that more cognitive activity must be shifted to the memory selection stage, thereby slowing down or limiting the ability to of the viewer to organize and integrate the selected information. The attention for new content competes against the other stages of memory required for organizing and integrating previously received information. To develop understanding, it is therefore important to provide information that is not only easily recognized but also easily assimilated.

Learning Outcomes and Performance

The CTML has enabled the development of principles relating to the effective design of multimedia messages. The theory suggests the most effective communication occurs when verbal and visual pathways are utilized simultaneously. Mayer (2009) suggests three outcomes when presenting explanative material to people: (1) no learning, (2) rote learning and (3) meaningful learning. These outcomes are based on measures of retention and problem solving. Retention is the comprehension over time of material being presented. Problem solving is the ability to use knowledge gained to answer related problems not directly answerable from presented material. For example, if presented with an explanation of how a car's brake system works, a retention question might be "*List the components of a braking system*," but a problem solving question would be "*What could be done to make brakes more reliable?*" These problem solving task have been used by Bodart *et al* (2001); Burton-Jones and Meso (2006); Gemino (1999; 2004) and Gemino and Wand (2005).

No learning occurs were retention and problem solving are low. Rote learning occurs where retention is high; however, problem solving measures are low. This indicates that although the material has been selected and received, the material has not been well integrated with prior knowledge. Meaningful learning occurs where retention and problem solving are high. This is summarized in Table 1.

This section has described a theory, the CTML, which suggests that combining graphic and textual information can lead to increased learning outcomes. We have argued above that increased learning outcomes are equivalent to higher levels of meaningful learning as measured by the combination of retention/comprehension and problem solving instruments. The CTML has provided a path for a better learning environment, but has yet to be used and tested in the Systems Analysis literature. In the section that follows, we will outline an experiment and hypotheses that suggest that the use of a summary graphic, such as a use case diagram, along with a set of primarily text based use cases will provide model viewers with

Table 1. Describing types of learning outcomes

Type of Learning	Scores on Retention/ Comprehension Tasks	Scores on Problem Solving Tasks
No Learning	Low	Low
Rote Learning	High	Low
Meaningful Learning	High	High

a significantly higher level of meaningful learning. The level of meaningful learning will be measured by a combination of retention/comprehension and problem solving questions. Meaningful learning will occur when comprehension levels are equal to or greater than the group provided with no diagram and where problem solving measures are significantly higher in the group provided with the diagram.

EXPERIMENTAL DESIGN AND HYPOTHESES

Overview of Experimental Design

In the application of CTML to this study, three dependent variables (comprehension, retention and problem solving) were measured. Other variables measured included prior knowledge of the domain, knowledge of the modeling method, and participant demographics. A treatment group was compared to a control group using a single case. The control group was provided with a set of five use cases describing a simple bus reservation system. The treatment group was provided the same set of use cases along with a one-page use case diagram. The only difference between the two groups was that the treatment group had the use case diagram. The single page use case diagram shows the interaction between use cases and actors in the system as well as any interactions among use cases in the system.

The following statement provides the underlying logic for conducting this experiment: If a participant is presented with a) a set of use cases and b) a set of use cases and a use case diagram relating these use cases, then the participant will develop a significantly higher level of understanding of the domain being presented with b) than with a). Since use case diagrams in this context are supplements to use cases, the only combination of treatments that makes sense is the use case

alone or the use case supplemented by a use case diagram.

Hypotheses

Mayer's (2009) multimedia principle suggests individuals learn better from words and pictures than words alone. When words and graphics are presented together, learners have the opportunity to develop verbal and visual models and build connections between them. When presented with only words, individuals are less likely to develop visual models. As a result, the connections between the verbal and visual models may be lost. The use case diagram may provide a foundation for the selection and integration of information across the use cases. Since cognitive resources are limited, the use case diagram may serve as a effective framework for organizing information and hence allow additional cognitive resources for developing a more sophisticated model of the domain being represented. This suggests a potential for higher levels of understanding derived from use cases supported with a use case diagram as opposed to use cases alone.

The multimedia principle therefore enables us to suggest the following hypotheses. Participants viewing a set use cases with an associated use case diagram will:

H1: achieve scores on comprehension tasks that are equal to or greater than the group of participants viewing use cases alone.
H2: achieve scores on retention tasks that are equal to or greater than the group of participants viewing use cases alone.
H3: achieve scores on problem solving tasks that are greater than the group of participants viewing use cases alone.

METHOD

An empirical procedure was developed to test the hypotheses. The procedure of collecting comprehension, retention, and problem solving measures is based on work by Mayer (1989, 2009). This procedure has been used in the area of system analysis by others including Gemino (1999), Bodart *et al* (2001), Burton-Jones and Meso (2006), Gemino (1999, 2004) and Gemino and Wand (2005).

Participants

Forty-nine upper level business students took part in the study. All students had taken a system analysis course and had basic familiarity with use case models. Females accounted for 20 of the 49 participants (41%) of participants. Participation was voluntary. An incentive of $15 was provided for the top four performers. The average time to complete the study was 45 minutes. All participants were at an introductory level in business process design, and had no particular experience with object oriented analysis or the UML. An instrument was provided before the experimental tasks to collect experience with system analysis and the business domain used in the analysis as well as other demographic variables.

Materials

One case including five use cases and one use case diagram was used in the experiment. The materials are provided in the Appendix. The use cases and use case diagram were created using an approach described in Dennis and Wixom (2000). The text description was provided by the Voyager Bus company case in Bodart *et al* (2001).

An important note must be made in regard to informational and computational equivalence of the control and treatment groups. The use cases provided to both groups were exactly the same. The level of detail in the uses cases was very general and provided little information in regards to how the system was designed (other than you log onto the system). We argue that with regard to informational equivalence, the control and treatments can be viewed as providing similar information content. The use case diagram provides no additional information that could not be derived from the use cases. The information about the actors involved with the system is available in the use cases. The actors interacting with the each use case are noted. The interaction type (external or temporal) was also noted.

While we argue there are no informational differences between the cases, we recognize that there is likely computational inequivalence. The use case diagram provides no new information, however, the use case diagram does organize the available information differently than the use cases. This organization may help viewers improve their understanding because it provides an understandable graphic. This would represent a computational advantage. The question of whether the computational advantage is significant is what is addressed by the experiment.

Procedure

Participants were randomly assigned into two treatment groups (with or without diagram). An envelope was given to each participant containing a pre-test, five use cases (plus diagrams if necessary), experimental tasks (comprehension, retention and problem solving) and a posttest. Participants worked independently and first completed the pre-test followed by the three experimental tasks and finally the post-test.

The three experimental tasks were completed in a specific order. The first task was a twelve question multiple choice comprehension task (True, False, Uncertain). After the comprehension task, participants were instructed to put away the use cases and diagram (if provided). Participants were than given 6 minutes to complete a retention task, which asked participants to write down everything they knew about the processes in the use cases. This task was followed by four problem-solving questions used by Bodart *et al*. (2001). Participants were given 2 minutes to write as many answers as possible to each problem solving question.

Measures

Learning performance was measured using three variables: comprehension, retention and problem solving. Comprehension was the number of correct answers out of a possible of 12 (true/false/ uncertain) questions. Retention and problem solving scores were coded by two individuals. The retention score was created by giving one mark for each complete and correct idea statement expressed by the participant. There was a maximum of 20 idea statements identified in the use cases. The problem solving score was created by giving participants one point for each acceptable response to the problem solving questions. The Pearson correlation between coders for retention was 0.88 and for problem solving questions 0.90. Differences between independent ratings were then discussed, and a final score for retention and problem solving was established.

RESULTS

Since the sample size was relatively small, it is important to establish the homogeneity of variances before ANOVA analysis. Table 2 provides the Levene statistics for each of the dependent measures. As shown in the table, the hypothesis of equal variances is not rejected across any of the variables at the 0.05 level.

Domain and modeling experience were collected in the pre-test survey and used as covariates in an ANCOVA analyses. Both domain and modeling method experience were found to have insignificant influences on the dependent variables. This result may be due to the uniformly low levels of experience held by participants. While it seems likely prior domain experience and modeling method experience are related to the dependent measures (Khatri et al., 2006), the factors, as

Table 2. Test for homogeneity of variances for dependent measures

Measure	Levene Statistic	df1	df2	Sig.
Comprehension	0.349	1	47	0.558
Retention	0.375	1	47	0.543
Problem solving	0.236	1	47	0.630

measured in this study, had no significant effect in this study and were excluded in further analysis.

Results

The means and standard deviations of the dependent measures (comprehension, retention and problem solving) across the two treatment groups are provided in Table 3. The results show little difference across treatment groups for comprehension measures. Note that participants had full access to use cases during the comprehension test. Since the information was available in either treatment, the diagram had little effect in basic comprehension. This result suggests that no systematic information advantage was noted between the two experimental groups.

Retention measures showed differences in the anticipated direction. The size of the effects was approximately 22%. This is measured by dividing the difference between the "with" and "without" diagram scores and then dividing the result by the score for the without diagram group.

More importantly, the problem solving measures showed significant differences in the anticipated direction. The size of the effects was approximately 20% which was again created by dividing the difference between the "with" and "without" diagram scores and then dividing the result by the score for the without diagram group.

An ANOVA was applied to test the significance of these differences and to test hypotheses H1a, b and c. Results, provided in the final column

Table 3. Means and Std. Dev. across treatments for dependent measures

Dependent Measure	Case: Voyager Bus				
	Treatment Groups				
	Without Diagram n=25 Means (SD)	With Diagram n=24 Means (SD)	Difference between means (With-Without)	Effect Size as % of Without Diagram	Sig.
Comprehension	7.627 (.321)	8.139 (.328)	.512	6.7%	0.271
Retention	7.877 (.541)	9.670 (.552)	1.793	22%	0.025*
Problem solving	12.174 (.824)	14.568 (.841)	2.394	20%	0.045*

* significant at the 0.05 level

of Table 2, suggests no significant different in comprehension. This confirms hypothesis H1. The results also imply that there seemed to be no systematic informational bias towards the group provided with the diagram.

In addition, significant differences were observed for both retention and problem solving measures at $\alpha = 0.05$ level. These results support both H2 and H3. These results suggest that although the informational content across treatments was essentially the same, the organization provided by the use case diagram enabled participants with access to the diagram to build a more sophisticated mental model and establish more meaningful learning. This was revealed in higher scores in the problem solving task. Note that although the sample size is relatively small, the effect size is relatively large.

These results suggest that diagrams, even simple diagrams such as the use case diagram provided in this experiment, can have measurable effects on viewer understanding. While use case modeling may be a step forward in requirements determination, it should be noted that text-only use cases may perform significantly better when a corresponding use case diagram is also provided. This occurs because the use case diagram provides a pictorial view of the relations between use cases. The pictorial view provides clues for

selecting and integrating important information from text descriptions thereby preserving cognitive processing for increased integration of the material presented in later memory stages.

DISCUSSION

This article used the CTML to hypothesize that the inclusion of a use case diagram can make use case modeling significantly more effective in developing understanding of the system domain among novice users. This would make the combination of use cases and use case diagram a potentially effective boundary objet for the analysis process. Use case modeling is a widely used technique to communicate systems models. If the models used to represent systems can be improved to lead to more effective communication and learning about the system being represented, perhaps the failure rate of systems projects could be favorably affected. Charette (2005) states that one of the 'most common' reasons for the failure of IT projects is: 'Poor communication among customers, developers, and users.'

For practitioners who choose to communicate using use cases alone, the results suggest a relatively simple approach of combining text and graphics will improve meaningful learning about the system. These results help to explain the results in Dobing and Parsons (2008) which show the relatively high use of use case diagrams in interaction with clients, second only to the use case narrative. While the use case diagram does not seem to add new information, and hence may not be worth the cost of development, the graphic does seem to provide a cognitive framework that helps users better understand sets of uses cases. This is likely the reason why practitioners continue to use the use case diagrams in interactions with clients. For those practitioners and researchers who suggest combining use cases with UML diagrams, this study provides tangible proof that the combination of text and diagrams can make for significantly improved levels of understanding.

Pictures representing domain constructs are a natural form of communication. The results of this experiment provide evidence that participants developed a higher level of domain understanding when viewing UML use cases with the support of a use case diagram. The hypothesis that a use case diagram has a significant positive effect on level of understanding developed by a person viewing use cases was therefore supported. This result also supports our assertion that use cases augmented with a use case diagram provides a more effective communication of system information than use cases alone. The implications for researchers and practitioners are to include use case diagrams with use cases when possible. Practitioners in particular should note the effectiveness of graphical models when used in conjunction with use case models.

This article provides the first evidence that the authors are aware of showing use case diagrams can effectively support use case modeling. In addition, the article provides support for the Cognitive Theory of Multimedia Learning and the multimedia principle that the theory suggests in the realm of systems analysis and design. This use of theory answers a call for more theory-based approaches to the investigation of analysis methods (Wand & Weber, 2002). The results reaffirm the importance of diagrams and visual information in developing understanding. The results also suggest that practitioners utilizing uses cases without some form of visual overview may not be getting the full effect of use case modeling.

When considering the results, it should also be noted that the use case diagram is not the only graphic model available to researchers and practitioners. While this study has shown a significant effect from including a use case diagram, further improvements may be possible by adding or substituting other UML diagrams (e.g. class model, sequence diagram, activity diagram) This experiment has provided evidence that relevant graphic information improved understanding above that provided by text based uses cases alone. The results of this experiment do not show that the use case diagram is the "best" diagram to be used with uses cases. For example, a class diagram may offer additional insight for model viewers. Future research can be directed more closely on what diagram elements are most effective in supporting use cases. In addition, more empirical evidence is required to understand the effectiveness of use case modeling. While the text based approach has some excellent features and has appealed to practitioners, it is clear that diagrams are an important component for communication. More needs to be understood about this relationship if we are to make use case modeling an even more effective communication tool for stakeholders and developers.

CONCLUSION

The addition of a graphic representation to the text-based use case can significantly enhance understanding of a system among novice modelers. This result is important, since 'the modeling technique should facilitate learning by employing the limited cognitive resources of a novice analyst.' (Batra, 2009, ii). The combination of use cases and use case diagram therefore should be considered a potentially effective boundary object that could be used in the analysis process. The combination of text and graphic elements should improve the communication across the technical and user-based communities hence improving the level of understanding of the system being analyzed. This result has promise for systems analysts trying to explain complex systems to users. The Cognitive Theory of Multimedia Learning has been shown as a potential theory to support and test systems analysis techniques. The results of this experiment support the use of a combination of text and visual models to communicate complex systems information.

ACKNOWLEDGMENT

The authors wish to thank Liliana Petrescu for her work in collecting and coding experimental data. This research was supported by the National Science and Engineering Research Council of Canada.

REFERENCES

Agarwal, R., De, P., & Sinha, A.P., A.P. (2003). Object Oriented Modeling with UML: A Study of Developer Perceptions. *Communications of the ACM*, *46*(9), 248–256. doi:10.1145/903893.903944

Angioni, M., Carboni, D., Pinna, S., Sanna, R., Serra, N., & Soro, A. (2006). Integrating XP project management in development environments. *Journal of Systems Architecture*, *52*(11), 619–626. doi:10.1016/j.sysarc.2006.06.006

Baddeley, A. D. (1992). Working Memory. *Science*, *255*, 556–559. doi:10.1126/science.1736359

Batra, D. (2008). Unified Modeling Language (UML) Topics: The Past, the Problems, and the Prospects. Guest Editorial Preface. *Journal of Database Management*, *19*(1), i–vii.

Batra, D. (2009). Devising Information Systems Modeling Techniques Using the Cognitive Load Theory. Guest Editorial Preface. *Journal of Database Management*, *20*(1), i–vi.

Bechky, B. A. (2003). Sharing Meaning Across Occupational Communities: The Transformation of Understanding on a Production Floor. *Organization Science*, *14*(3), 312–330. doi:10.1287/orsc.14.3.312.15162

Bechky, B. A. (2006). Talking About Machines, Thick Description, and Knowledge Work. *Organization Studies*, *27*(12), 1757–1768. doi:10.1177/0170840606071894

Bodart, F., Patel, A., Sim, M., & Weber, R. (2001). Should Optional Properties Be Used in Conceptual Modelling? A Theory and Three Empirical Tests. *Information Systems Research*, *12*(4), 384–405. doi:10.1287/isre.12.4.384.9702

Burton-Jones, A., & Meso, P. (2006). Conceptualizing Systems for Understanding: An Empirical Test of Decomposition Principles in Object-Oriented Analysis. *Information Systems Research*, *17*(1), 38–60. doi:10.1287/isre.1050.0079

Charette, R. (2005) Why Software Fails. *IEEE Spectrum Online*. http://www.spectrum.ieee.org/sep05/1685 Accessed September 11, 2007.

Dennis, A., & Wixom, B. (2000). *System Analysis and Design: An Applied Approach*. New York: John Wiley and Sons.

Dobing, B., & Parsons, J. (2000). Understanding the role of use cases in UML: A review and research agenda. *Journal of Database Management*, *11*(4), 28–36. doi:10.4018/jdm.2000100103

Dobing, B., & Parsons, J. (2008). Dimensions of UML Diagram Use: A Survey of Practitioners. *Journal of Database Management*, *19*(1), 1–18. doi:10.4018/jdm.2008010101

Dori, D. (2002). Why Significant UML Change is Unlikely. *Communications of the ACM, 45*(11), 82–85. doi:10.1145/581571.581599

Douglass, B. (1998). UML for Systems Engineering. *Computer Design's. Electronic Systems Technology & Design, 37*(11), 44–49.

Evermann, J. (2005). Thinking Ontologically - Conceptual versus Design Models in UML. In: Rosemann, M. and Green, P. (eds.) *Ontologies and Business Analysis.* Idea Group Publishing, 82-104.

Evermann, J., & Wand, Y. (2005). Ontology-Based Object-Oriented Business Modelling: Fundamental Concepts. *Requirements Engineering Journal, 10*(2), 146–160. doi:10.1007/s00766-004-0208-2

Fedorowicz, J., & Villeneuve, A. (1999). Surveying Object Technology Usage and Benefits: A Test of Conventional Wisdom. *Information & Management, 35*(6), 331–345. doi:10.1016/S0378-7206(98)00098-6

Gemino, A. (1999). *Empirical Comparison of System Analysis Techniques*, Ph.D. Thesis, University of British Columbia, Vancouver, British Columbia.

Gemino, A. (2004)... *Empirical Comparisons of Animation and Narration in Requirements Validation Requirements Engineering Journal, 9*(3), 153–168.

Gemino, A., & Wand, Y. (2003). Evaluating Modeling Techniques Based on Models of Learning. *Communications of the ACM, 46*(10), 79–84. doi:10.1145/944217.944243

Gemino, A., & Wand, Y. (2004). Dimensions in Experimental Evaluation of Conceptual Modeling Techniques. *Requirements Engineering Journal, 9*(4), 248–260. doi:10.1007/s00766-004-0204-6

Gemino, A., & Wand, Y. (2005). Simplicity versus Clarity: An Empirical Comparison of Mandatory and Optional Properties in Conceptual Modeling. *Data & Knowledge Engineering, 55*, 301–326. doi:10.1016/j.datak.2004.12.009

Halpin, T., & Bloesch, A. (1999). Data modeling in UML and ORM: A Comparison. *Journal of Database Management, 10*(4), 4–13.

Jacobson, I., Booch, G., & Rumbaugh, J. (1999). *The Unified Software Development Process.* Reading, MA: Addison Wesley.

Jacobson, I., Ericsson, M., & Jacobson, A. (1994). *The Object Advantage: Business Process Reengineering with Object Technology.* Reading, MA: Addison-Wesley.

Johnson, R. (2002). Object-Oriented System Development: A Review of Empirical Research. *Communications of the Association for Information Systems, 8*, 65–81.

Khatri, V., Vessey, I., Ramesh, V., Clay, P., & Park, S.-J. (2006). Understanding Conceptual Schemas: Exploring the Role of Application and IS Domain Knowledge. *Information Systems Research, 17*(1), 81–99. doi:10.1287/isre.1060.0081

Kobryn, C. (1999). A Standardization Odyssey. *Communications of the ACM, 42*(10), 29–38. doi:10.1145/317665.317673

Lindland, O. I., Sindre, G., & Solvberg, A. (1994). Understanding quality in conceptual modeling. *IEEE Software, 11*(2), 42–49. doi:10.1109/52.268955

Mayer, R. (1989). Models for Understanding. *Review of Educational Research, 59*(1), 43–64.

Mayer, R. (2009). *Multimedia Learning* (2nd ed.). New York: Cambridge University Press.

Mellor, S. (2002). Make models be assets. *Communications of the ACM, 45*(11), 76–78. doi:10.1145/581571.581597

Meso, P., & Jain, R. (2006). Agile Software Development: Adaptive System Principles and Best Practices. *Information Systems Management, 23*(5), 19–29. doi:10.1201/1078.10580530/46108.23.3.20060601/93704.3

Paivio, A. (1986). *Mental representations: A Dual Coding Approach.* Oxford, England: Oxford University Press.

Shoval, P., & Kabeli, J. (2005) Essentials of Functional and Object-Oriented Methodology. *Encyclopedia of Information Science and Technology II,* 1108-1115.

Siau, K., & Cao, Q. (2001). Unified Modeling Language (UML) - a complexity analysis. *Journal of Database Management, 12*(1), 26–34. doi:10.4018/jdm.2001010103

Siau, K., Erickson, J., & Lee, L. (2005). Theoretical vs. Practical Complexity: The Case of UML. *Journal of Database Management, 16*(3), 40–57. doi:10.4018/jdm.2005070103

Siau, K., & Loo, P. (2006). Identifying Difficulties in Learning UML. *Information Systems Management, 23*(3), 43–51. doi:10.1201/1078.10580530/46108.23.3.20060601/93706.5

Standish Group. (1994). *Chaos Report.* http://standishgroup.com/sample_research/ chaos_1994_1.php Accessed September 11, 2007.

Star, S., & Griesemer, J. (1989). Institutional ecology,'translations' and boundary objects: Amateurs and professionals in Berkeley's Museum of Vertebrate Zoology, 1907-39. *Social Studies of Science, 19*(3), 387–420. doi:10.1177/030631289019003001

Wand, Y., & Weber, R. (1993). On the Ontological Expressiveness of Information Systems Analysis and Design Grammars. *Journal of Information Systems, 3,* 217–237. doi:10.1111/j.1365-2575.1993.tb00127.x

Wand, Y., & Weber, R. (2002). Information Systems and Conceptual Modeling: a Research Agenda. *Information Systems Research,* 203–223.

APPENDIX

FIVE USE CASES (SEE BELOW)

1. User Login
2. Purchase Ticket
3. Organizing a Trip
4. Assign Driver to Trip
5. Assign Bus to Trip

Figure 5. Use case diagram

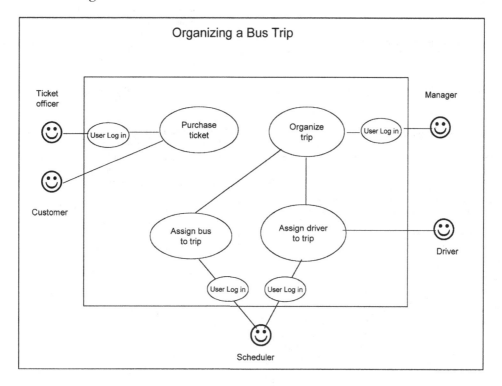

Table 4. Use case Description

Use case Name: User Login			ID Number: 1
Use case Description: This describes how the users accesses the Voyager system			
Trigger: Employee needs to access the system Type: **External** / Temporal			
Major Inputs: Description Source		Major Outputs: Description Destination	
User Login ID Password	Em- ployee Em- ployee	Employee accesses the system	System function-ality
Major Steps Performed 1. User needs to access the Voyager system and enters login ID, then password in order to perform specific tasks in the system.		Information for Steps User ID User password	

Table 5. Use case Description

Use case Name: Purchase ticket			ID Number: 2
Use case Description: This describes the ways that can be used to book travel with Voyager, namely through reservation or direct purchase.			
Trigger: Person decides to go on a trip with Voyager Type: **External** / Temporal			
Major Inputs: Description Source		Major Outputs: Description Destination	
Destination of trip Desired date of the trip Traveler's name Traveler's address Traveler's phone number	Passen-ger Passen-ger Passen-ger Passen-ger Passen-ger Passen-ger	Passenger reser-vation date Passenger boarding date	Passenger Bus trip attendance Passenger Bus trip attendance
Major Steps Performed 1. Passenger requests a reservation on a trip, by providing name, address and tele-phone number and payment method. • Or, passenger directly purchases a ticket at the boarding gate for an unreserved seat, also providing name, address and telephone number. 2. Passengers with a reservation are as-signed a reservation date and confirmation number. Passengers without a reservation are assigned a boarding date and a ticket.		Information for Steps Passenger Bus trip at-tendance Passenger Bus trip at-tendance	

Table 6. Use case Description

Use case Name: Organizing a trip			ID Number: 3
Use case Description: This describes how a trip is created us-ing route segments.			
Trigger: Manager receives go ahead to enter a trip into system Type: **External** / Temporal			
Major Inputs: Description Source		Major Outputs: Description Destination	
Route segment's start town Route segment's finish town Trip start town Trip finish town Trip start time Trip finish time	Route segment Route segment Town list Town list Trip sched-ule Trip sched-ule	Trip with as-sociated number, event name if applicable, start town and finish town	Trip
Major Steps Performed 1. To enter a new trip, a manager enters a unique trip number, a start and finish town as well as a start and finish date. 2. Each trip is made up of route segments. A manager assigns route segments to the trip number. Route segments are defined by a segment number with a start and finish town. 3. Manager assigns maximum and minimum number of passengers for the trip. Trips do not run unless they have a minimum number of passengers.		Information for Steps Route segment Daily route segment Bus trip	

Table 7. Use case Description

Use case Name: Assign driver to trip			ID Number: 4
Use case Description: This describes the procedure of assigning available bus drivers to trips			
Trigger: Manager enters new trip Type: External / **Temporal**			
Major Inputs: Description Source		Major Outputs: Description Destination	
Driver's name Driver's address Driver's employee number Driver's absence status	Drivers records Drivers records Drivers records Drivers records	Driver(s) choice for bus trip is made	Driver's schedule
Major Steps Performed 1. When the daily bus trip has been defined, scheduler receives trip details. 2. Drivers' profiles (including availability) are viewed in order to assign one or more drivers to the trip. 3. If a driver has a record of frequent absences, then the scheduler must verify availability with driver before scheduling. 4. At the end of each week, a report of the drivers' schedules is created for the coming week. 5. The scheduler posts this schedule for the coming week.		Information for Steps Drivers records Drivers records Bus trips Drivers records	

Table 8. Use case Description

Use case Name: Assign bus to trip			ID Number: 5
Use case Description: This describes the process of assigning a bus to a daily trip, after checking the maintenance status of the bus			
Trigger: Driver is assigned by scheduler Type: External / **Temporal**			
Major Inputs: Description Source		Major Outputs: Description Destination	
Make of bus Model of bus Registration number of bus Date of last maintenance Average daily kilometers	Bus records Bus records Bus records Bus records Bus records	Bus choice is made	Bus trip
Major Steps Performed 1. When the bus trip has been defined and a driver has been selected, buses' records are reviewed in order to assign a bus to the daily trip. 2. Maintenance status for each bus is verified. If maintenance status is up-to-date and in good standing, the bus is considered for the trip. 3. Once maintenance records have been approved, the bus with the lowest kilometers that meets the maximum number of passengers required for the trip is selected and assigned to the trip. 4. Once a vehicle is assigned to a particular trip number and route segment, it cannot be assigned to another trip number.		Information for Steps Bus records Bus records Bus records	

Chapter 2
Applying Learner–Centered Design Principles to UML Sequence Diagrams

Debra VanderMeer
Florida International University, USA

Kaushik Dutta
Florida International University, USA

ABSTRACT

The Unified Modeling Language has been shown to be complex and difficult to learn. The difficulty of learning to build the individual diagrams in the UML, however, has received scant attention. In this paper, we consider the case of the UML sequence diagram. Despite the fact that these diagrams are among the most frequently used in practice, they are difficult to learn to build. In this paper, we consider the question of why these diagrams remain so difficult to learn to build. Specifically, we analyze the process of learning to build sequence diagrams in the context of cognitive complexity theory. Based on this analysis, and drawing on the theory of learner-centered design, we develop a set of recommendations for presenting the sequence diagram building task to the student analyst to reduce the complexity of learning how to build them.

INTRODUCTION

Object-oriented analysis and design (OOAD) is the dominant software design method among practitioners. The Unified Modeling Language (UML) is an ISO standard graphical modeling language

DOI: 10.4018/978-1-60960-521-6.ch002

used in OOAD (International Organization for Standardization, 2005). The UML consists of a set of diagrams and associated notations, where each diagram represents a different view of a software analysis and design model -- structure, interaction, or state (Blaha & Rumbaugh, 2005Dori, 2002). In the OOAD process, analysts develop a set of *objects*, where each object has a set of *attributes* (data that the object knows about) and *behaviors* (operations that the object can perform). Objects interact by invoking one another's operations to fulfill the high-level behaviors required of the system, representing the business logic of the to-be software system. The analyst captures this logic in a set of UML *sequence diagrams* (SDs). Figure 1 shows an example of such a diagram (all diagrams in this paper were developed using Visual Paradigm, a software tool from Visual Paradigm International).

SDs are a crucial building block in system design. Analyst errors in building them lead to significant rework efforts or serious software defects at implementation time, which in turn leads to increased costs. Thus, it is critical that

analysts have the skills to produce high-quality SDs. *While sequence diagrams are among the most widely used diagrams in the UML in practice* (Dobing & Parsons, 2006; *Dobing & Parsons, 2008*; Fowler, 1997) *and are critical to the design process, they are difficult to learn to build* (Bolloju & Leung, 2006; Siau & Loo, 2006).

The OOAD process consists of five basic steps: (1) developing high-level requirements, (2) use case analysis, (3) domain data modeling, and (4) building sequence diagrams (George, Batra, Valacich & Hoffer, 2006), and (5) building a class diagram. In steps (1) and (2), the analyst develops a description of *what the system should do*. In step (3), the analyst develops the *structure* of the system from a data perspective and, in step (4),

Figure 1. Example UML sequence diagram

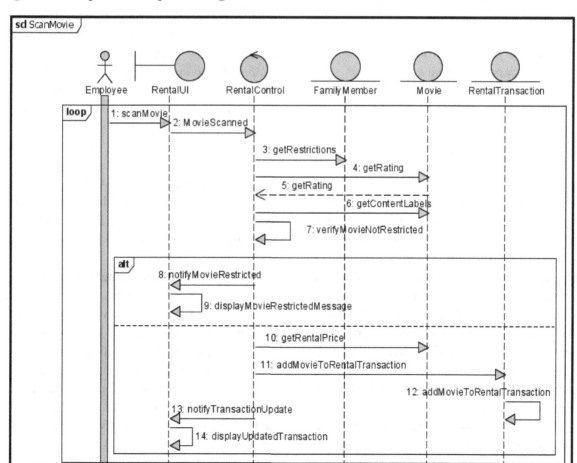

defines *how the system should achieve the behaviors required*. In step (5), the analyst refines the structure of the system to include both data and behavior. Good, clear techniques and heuristics are available for steps (1), (2), (3) and (5) through many textbooks and other sources. Textbooks covering OOAD (George, et al., 2006), as well as other sources (Fowler, 1997), offer a sizeable set of advice on step (4). Even with so many useful guidelines and heuristics, however, learning to build these diagrams remains difficult.

In this paper, we consider the task of learning to build SDs. Although much thinking has been done on the problem of developing guidelines and heuristics for building a good SD, and much work has been done on the difficulties of learning OOAD, there has not been much discussion of the process of learning to build SDs in particular. This is our focus in this paper. Specifically, we concentrate on two questions:

- *What are the complexity factors inherent in the process of learning to build SDs?*
- *How can these factors be mitigated to minimize the cognitive load of learning to build SDs?*

In this paper, we apply Reeves' Learner-Centered Design *(LCD) framework* (Reeves, 1999) *to the task of learning to build SDs.* We chose this framework for two major reasons. First, it provides both a way to describe the *cognitive complexity of learning to perform a task*, in this case learning to build SDs, as well as several *learner models* and *recommendations* for reducing cognitive loads for each learner type -- making it directly applicable to our research question. Second, it is grounded in more than thirty years of research in cognitive science, information systems, and design theory, and thus provides a strong theoretical foundation for our work.

The two main contributions of this paper are as follows: (1) *we present a qualitative analysis of cognitive complexity of learning to build SDs* to identify the characteristics of the task that increase its difficulty; and (2) *we develop a set of recommendations for mitigating the complexity of the task of learning to build SDs, based on the theory of LCD.* These recommendations focus primarily on how to present the SD-building task to beginners, rather than on redesigning the actual SD-building task itself.

Example

We present an example based on a video rental store scenario. This serves as the basis for examples throughout the paper. Suppose a portion of the requirements reads as follows:

The rental chain allows families to give separate membership cards to all family members, and to restrict a given family member's access to movies by movie rating, e.g., a child in the family cannot rent an 'R' rated movie on his own, or content, e.g., a child in the family cannot rent a movie that is labeled with an 'L' for potentially objectionable language. At rental time, the software must enforce any restrictions associated with the family member presenting his membership card.

Based on these requirements, one might write a use case narrative similar to the one shown in Figure 2, and develop a partial class diagram similar to the one shown in Figure 3. Based on these diagrams, Figure 1 shows one possible solution SD for this scenario.

The remainder of this paper is organized as follows. We first describe related work, and then provide an overview of cognitive complexity and learner-centered design. We then present an analysis of the cognitive complexity of learning to build sequence diagrams, and propose a set provide a set of recommendations aimed at reducing the complexity of learning to build SDs based on LCD principles. Finally, we conclude the paper and describe future work.

Figure 2. Example use case narrative

User	System
1. For each movie the cardholder wishes to rent, the Employee scans the movie's barcode	2. For each movie, the System checks the cardholder's restriction set for any holds based on rating or content
	3. For each movie, the System retrieves the cost of rental for the movie, adds the movie to the rental transaction, and updates the total transaction cost
Exceptions: Step 2. If the desired movie violates the restrictions associated with the customer's membership card, the system displays a message "unable to rent this movie", along with the reason (which restrictions the movie violates). A movie violating the customer's restrictions is not added to the rental transaction list in step 3.	

Figure 3. Example UML class diagram

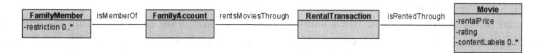

RELATED WORK

Compared to structural techniques (developed prior to OO methods), OOAD is cited as a more natural method of design (Rosson & Alpert, 1990). Booch (Booch, 1986) proposed one of the earliest generalized OO design methods, providing a starting point for the development of what we know today as OOAD. Others refined and expanded these notions, defining key OO concepts, e.g., reusability (Johnson & Fotte, 1988; Micallef, 1988). To support the OOAD process, several early modeling languages were proposed, e.g., (Rumbaugh, Blaha, Premerlani & Lorensen, 1991); over time, these languages were assimilated together and extended by others to produce the current UML specification (International Organization for Standardization, 2005).

Since we are interested in the complexity of UML SDs in this work, it is useful to consider other work describing UML complexity and related difficulties. As a language, UML is known to be complex (Siau & Cao, 2001; Siau, Erickson & Lee, 2005), as well as difficult to learn (Bol-

loju & Leung, 2006; Siau & Loo, 2006) and use (Agarwal & Sinha, 2003).

Siau & Cao (2001) present a quantitative analysis of the theoretical mathematical complexity of UML. This study considered both individual diagrams as well as the UML in aggregate, comparing both the diagrams and the aggregate UML to other OO methods. This analysis concluded that, while individual diagrams are approximately as complex as other OO methods, the UML as a whole is 2 to 11 times more complex than other OO methods. In a follow-on study (Siau, et al., 2005), the authors begin to consider the comparative complexity among pairs of diagrams, looking specifically at class diagrams and use case diagrams, and finding that class diagrams are more complex than use case diagrams. Our work differs from this work in two ways. First, we are interested in the cognitive complexity of the task of learning to build SDS, rather than the structural complexity (defined mathematically) of the diagrams themselves. Second, we are interested in the complexity of SDs, rather than class or use case diagrams, or the UML as a whole.

Siau & Loo (2006) present the results of an empirical study aimed at identifying the factors that make learning UML difficult. This study surveyed students in OOAD courses to identify what they found difficult, using concept mapping to categorize the results. This study identifies several specific areas students found difficult in building SDs as well as other UML diagrams. In (Bolloju & Leung, 2006), the authors study a set of projects produced by OOAD students in a university setting to identify the typical mistakes that novices make in building the four most commonly-used diagrams in UML.

In (Sheetz, 2002), the author presents the results of an empirical study examining the difficulties professional developers experience when using OO techniques. This study surveyed several groups of developers, from novices to experts, to determine what aspects of OO development they found difficult. The subject matter scope of this study is much larger than our scope – this study considers not only technical issues (e.g., analysis, design, implementation), but also managerial and organizational issues (e.g., project estimation, managing user expectations, stakeholder buy-in), whereas our focus is on novice-level analysts learning to build SDs. The results detail specific aspects of OO development that specific experience groups found difficult (i.e., what novices found difficult, what intermediates found difficult, etc.), and what aggregated groups found difficult (i.e., what novices and intermediates found difficult, what intermediates and experts found difficult, etc.).

In (Agarwal & Sinha, 2003), the authors present a survey-based study of developers, focused on questions of UML usability and ease-of-use. Of particular interest here are the results for novice developers, which indicate that this class of developers found the UML diagrams difficult to use. This study advocates simplifying the UML to make it more user-friendly.

Work on teaching OOAD and UML is also related. In (Beck & Cunningham, 1989), the authors introduce one of the earliest studies of teaching OO techniques to students, focusing on OO thinking. More recent research (Burton & Bruhn, 2004; Brewer & Lorenz, 2003) considers how teaching UML along with OOAD can improve learning in OOAD overall. Tabrizi, Collins, Ozan & Li (2004) extend this work by proposing that OO concepts and UML should be integrated into beginning programming courses. In a similar vein, Wei, Moritz, Parvez & Blank (2005) advocate an automated tutoring method to provide immediate feedback to students while learning OOAD and programming.

Our work differs from these efforts in its focus and method. These studies focus on identifying *what is difficult within OOAD and UML* and *how OOAD education in general can be improved*, while we focus on *why it is difficult to learn, with a specific focus on SDs*. These studies are complementary to our work in that they identify the difficulties we will consider in our analysis of the cognitive complexity of learning to build sequence diagrams.

COGNITIVE COMPLEXITY AND LEARNER-CENTERED DESIGN

We base our analysis of the cognitive complexity of learning to build sequence diagrams on the Reeves model (Reeves, 1999) and develop our recommendations for reducing the complexity of learning to build SDs on LCD theory. We provide overviews of cognitive complexity and LCD in this section.

Cognitive Complexity

Reeves' model of cognitive complexity considers different sources of complexity in learning to perform a task with the aim of identifying the concrete factors that make it difficult to understand. By exposing these factors, we can then modify the task to reduce the complexity of learning to perform it using the principles of learner-centered design.

Reeves' model considers multiple different potential sources of cognitive complexity, some of which, e.g., metasocial forces, are not relevant to the topic at hand, and are omitted from this discussion. We consider each of the relevant potential sources of complexity.

Information about the task. The information available regarding a task falls into two categories: (1) *process-related information* about how to perform the task in general; and (2) *domain-specific information* about the task at hand. In the context of learning to build SDs, process-related information refers to the specific steps to follow in building an SD, while domain-specific information refers to the actual problem scenario to be modeled, as described in a high-level requirements document.

The level of cognitive complexity arising from information sources is dependent on the *quantity* of information as compared to the *utility* of the information presented. Not all information-based complexity is bad – considering additional complexifying information can lead to a higher-quality design. However, complexifying information that the task performer cannot use to improve the design is simply noise, where increasing noise leads to increasing difficulty in selecting the useful information, and hence additional cognitive complexity.

The design of the task. We consider the difficulties introduced by the task itself, in terms of the process steps and guidelines provided to lead the analyst from the problem formulation to the goal solution. Generally, the design of a task introduces cognitive complexity if it exhibits one or more of the following characteristics.

- The task process does not provide enough information for task performer to build a complete mental model. A mental model of a task is a framework that allows the task performer to deduce new information about the task or predict the future effects of a choice made during the task. With an incomplete mental model, the task performer may make incorrect inferences about the task.

- The next step in the process is not always evident. If a task process is not sufficiently detailed, and the task performer must guess at the next step in the process, the probability of error is high.

- A lack of constraints among choices forces the task performer to choose from too many options. As the number of possible choices increases, the task performer must attempt to search through the option space for the optimal choice. As the size of the option space increases, the difficulty for the task performer in finding the optimal choice increases significantly.

In each of these cases, the task performer is forced to make decisions without an adequate basis for the choice, making each decision more difficult and thus introducing cognitive complexity.

Problem solving within the task. Problem-solving refers to the process of transforming a problem formulation into a goal solution. In the context of this paper, the problem faced by the novice analyst is to produce an SD that is both correct and of a high quality. The complexity of solving a problem can be defined along multiple dimensions, where a problem formulation can vary from simple to complex along each dimension. A problem becomes less complex as:

- Sufficient information is provided about the problem. A lack of crucial information increases the cognitive complexity of solving a problem. The simplifying aspect of additional information applies only so far as the added information is useful (as described above).
- The goal is defined more precisely. The less clearly the expected solution is defined, the

more difficult it is for the learner to work toward the goal solution.

- There are fewer variables, and fewer interrelationships and dependencies among them. Larger numbers of variables and increasing numbers of relationships among those variables leads to increased numbers of decisions the problem-solver must make in working toward a goal solution, increasing the potential for errors.

- Significant expertise is not required to solve the problem. The more experience a problem-solver requires to reach a quality solution to a problem formulation, the more complex it is for the novice to approach. Essentially, the novice must develop expertise before being able to confidently produce quality solutions.

- There are fewer possible solutions. A larger number of potential solutions makes a problem more difficult to solve, particularly when some solutions are of higher quality than others, or when there is a trade-off between competing priorities.

- Logic and known patterns/expertise from other domains can be applied to solve the problem. The applicability of existing expertise from other domains tends to simplify the problem-solving task.

Learner-Centered Design

Learner-Centered Design theory presents a set of design principles aimed at reducing the cognitive complexity of learning how to perform a task through the redesign of the task itself. Once we have determined the root causes of complexity, we can apply the relevant LCD principles to ensure that the learner experiences as little confusion as possible.

In his LCD theory, Reeves (Reeves, 1999) proposes several models of learners, classified by the goal of the learning process at hand. For example, the *learner as categorizer* model con-siders ways to help learners filter and categorize large amounts of information, while the *learner as searcher* model suggests ways to help learners search through an information space to identify high-quality, useful and relevant information. For each model, he then proposes a set of techniques for reducing cognitive complexity for tasks that fit the model.

The learner model most useful to the problem of helping beginner analysts learn to build SDs is the *learner as expert problem solver* model. Effectively, we can think of the analyst's progress from novice to intermediate to expert SD-builder as one of *building expertise*.

Reeves (1999) defines the characteristic difference between an expert problem solver and a novice problem solver can be summarized as follows: novices have small amounts of information of varying quality in a loose organization, while experts have a high quantity of highly relevant information in an intricate web of interconnections. Empirical studies (Wiedenbeck, Fix & Scholtz, 1993; Wiedenbeck, Ramalingam, Sarasamma & Corritore, 1999) show that the mental models for novice and expert programmers differ significantly, where an expert typically has built an intricate, pattern-oriented mental model that the novice lacks.

The question that arises in terms of LCD for the task of building SDs is this: *How can we help the novice analyst (a) build a strong knowledge base; (b) filter out low-quality information; and (c) build a mental model of the task with high-quality relationships among information elements?*

To help reduce the complexity of developing expertise in problem solving, Reeves suggests several recommendations for organizing the relevant material:

Provide scaffolding. We can think of the "scaffolding" here as providing a knowledge framework upon which a learner can learn while gaining expertise, as a way to help the user climb the learning curve. This suggests organizing content to build on the learner's accumulated knowledge.

Decompose and recompose. Smaller problems are easier for the learner to solve than larger ones. Solving a large problem becomes easier if it can be broken down into smaller problems, where the solutions to the smaller problems can be combined into a complete solution.

Use examples and exercises extensively. A novice develops expertise by reasoning from the specific to the abstract. Exercises and examples, provided each exposes some new information or variation, add new knowledge to the learner's mental model of the task. The larger the number of exercises and examples the novice encounters, the more opportunities there will be to build a better abstract task model, and the greater the resulting expertise level will be.

Engage the learner actively. Engaging learners actively, through spoken questions and interactive exercises, forces them to "think on their feet", which helps the learner actively construct a mental model of the task. This type of interaction not only motivates the learner to think in the desired direction, but it also allows the educator/mentor to determine the learner's current level of expertise and provide feedback in real time.

ANALYSIS OF THE COGNITIVE COMPLEXITY OF LEARNING TO BUILD UML SEQUENCE DIAGRAMS

In this section, we enumerate several characteristics of the SD-building task that make learning to build SDs difficult for the beginner analyst. These characteristics were drawn primarily from work in identifying typical errors and difficulties in OOAD and programming, as described in our earlier discussion of related work.

For the purpose of this analysis, we consider the beginner to be a student with no prior knowledge of OOAD or programming experience (a worst-case scenario). We also assume that the student has progressed in the course to the point where SDs arise – after use case analysis and domain

data modeling discussions. For students with some prior experience, some parts of this discussion may not apply. We also assume that the learner has the basic building blocks for an SD (i.e., requirements, use case narratives, domain data model) in place at the start of the SD building task.

For each characteristic, we: (1) describe why it makes the task difficult; (2) identify the type of cognitive complexity associated with the difficulty, and (3) discuss whether the complexity stems from the design process in general, or from SDs in particular. We then apply the LCD principles to recommend ways to mitigate the complexity associated with these characteristics.

Unfamiliar Metaphors

A number significant metaphor in SD syntax and semantics refers to OO programming, including concepts such as message passing, parameters, and returns. However, not every student learning OOAD techniques has been exposed to programming.

Students without prior programming experience increased complexity in learning SDs, primarily coming from problem-solving complexity - knowledge from domains other than programming cannot be applied; rather some level of expertise is required. This complexity is not related to the design process, but is introduced by the SDs themselves.

Working with SD Syntax

SDs have a detailed and very specific syntax. At every step in the SD-building process, the student's choice of syntactic element makes a specific statement about the design of the to-be software. Message arrows are a good example of this – should the arrow line be solid or dashed? Each has its own specific meaning, respectively, message call or return. A solid-line arrow placed on an angle has yet another meaning. Modeling alternative flows is another example. SDs are inherently linear diagrams, but if-then-else branching is a very common software structure in practice. One method of handling this within the SD syntax is to use alt boxes. If the logic within each branch is complex, these alt boxes quickly become large and very cumbersome.

Working with the SD syntax creates a combination of task design complexity and information complexity: the student must apply a complex set of syntax rules from the very outset of learning to build SDs. This complexity stems from SD syntax, not the overall design process.

Omitting Explicit Returns

The notion of flow of control through the logic is not evident in an experienced analyst's SDs, since explicit return notations are often omitted to reduce clutter and fit more logic into a given space. If returns are added to the diagram, one can trace the flow of logic through the SD with a pencil as the focus of control moves from one object to another.

A student who omits these returns may mistakenly leave the focus of control at the recipient object, rather than returning it to the calling object, once processing is complete. As a result, the novice will often mistakenly assign responsibility for initiating some processing (i.e., sending a message to another object), to an inappropriate object.

For example, Figure 4 shows a fragment of an SD representing the first few interactions of the main video store checkout SD (shown in Figure 3). Here, after the *RentalControl* object asks the *FamilyMember* object for its restriction set, rather than implicitly returning its restriction set and the focus of control back to the caller object, the *FamilyMember* object instead sends a message to the *Movie* object asking for its rating. While this is not necessarily incorrect, this places the responsibility for obtaining the movie's rating on the *FamilyMember* object. This is likely not the analyst's intention, given that the *FamilyMember* object was only asked to return its restriction set, and no more.

The requirement that the focus of control should return to the calling object comes directly from programming, where an explicit return call at the end of each method returns the focus of control to the caller. A student, however, may have little

Figure 4. Focus of control remains on the called object

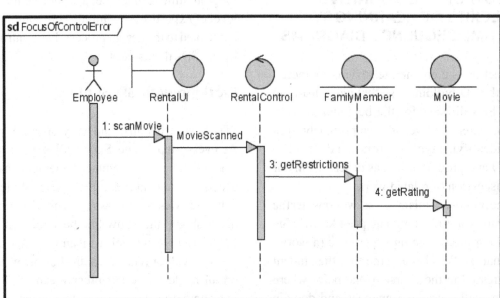

or no exposure to coding. When building the first few SDs, then, a novice who is not advised to explicitly include returns may apply a more familiar "connect-the-dots" metaphor.

Here, we can see problem-solving cognitive complexity issues arising: the novice analyst cannot apply familiar metaphors; rather, some domain-specific knowledge of programming is required. Task design complexity is also evident: without this domain knowledge, the novice cannot build an appropriate mental model of the task, so the next step the novice should take is not evident. This complexity is due to SD-building conventions in practice, and not to OO design in general.

Decomposing High-Level Requirements into Logic Steps

For a given step in the use case narrative, the analyst must decompose the system-side requirements into more detailed responsibilities to define the step-by-step business logic. For example, consider the use case narrative fragment for step 2 as presented in Figure 2. Here, some object in the system must be responsible for (1) obtaining the movie's rating and content labels, (2) obtaining the restriction set for the cardholder, and (3) comparing the movie rating and content labels to the cardholder's restriction set to determine if the cardholder should be permitted to rent the movie.

This is a logical jump in abstraction from a lower granularity of detail to a higher granularity of detail, where the student analyst must add detail not explicitly provided in the requirements document or use case narrative. This can seem like making up information. A more experienced analyst, however, will recognize that the design process inherently involves adding new detail at each stage, and that not all detail can be mapped directly back to explicit statements from documents developed earlier in the OOAD process.

Here, we can see cognitive complexity arising from the design of the SD-building task in two ways. First, the next step in assigning responsi-

bilities is not always obvious, since the high-level requirements often do not explicitly enumerate the low-level steps of the business logic. Second, this lack of explicit step-by-step logic leaves the analyst free to choose among all available options with very few constraints. This complexity is part of the design process, as has been noted in previous work (Sheetz, 2002), but arises noticeably in SD-building process.

Choosing to Centralize or Decentralize Responsibility Assignments

While the responsibilities for knowing information are relatively easy to assign (e.g., the *Movie* object should be responsible for answering queries about its own rating), it is less obvious which object should be responsible for initiating processing.

We consider step 2 in Figure 2, where we can decompose the required behavior of the system into three responsibilities: (1) obtaining the movie's rating and content labels, (2) obtaining the restriction set for the cardholder, and (3) comparing the movie rating and content labels to the cardholder's restriction set to determine if the cardholder should be permitted to rent the movie.

Which object should be responsible for initiating this processing? Many introductory texts suggest assigning this responsibility to a centralized controller object, which contains the main flow of logic for responding to a specific external event, and make all other objects responsible only for providing information about their attributes or doing simple calculations. Figure 1 shows an example of centralization of responsibility for initiating processing, where the *RentalControl* object is assigned these responsibilities.

Centralization doesn't necessarily represent good OO design because it places virtually all the responsibility for initiating processing on a single object (the controller object). When implemented, the code for the centralized controller class would likely be significantly more complicated than that of other objects. Assigning entity objects responsibility for initiating messages is not necessarily incorrect. In fact, such messaging assignments can lead to a more decentralized assignment of responsibilities.

Consider, for example, Figure 5, which shows a decentralized logic flow. Here, the *RentalControl* object asks the *FamilyMember* object to determine whether or not the movie is acceptable to rent based on the movie's ID code. This places the responsibility for obtaining the movie's rating and content information, as well as checking this information against the cardholder's restriction set, on the *FamilyMember* object, rather than the controller object.

This freedom presents the beginner with a wide spectrum of choices from which to choose, increasing the problem-solving complexity in terms of the design of the task. This complexity is a part of OO design in general, but arises mainly in the specific context of SDs.

Choosing among Multiple Candidate Solutions

The large number of choices available when assigning responsibilities results in a large number of candidate solutions. While many of these solutions might be incorrect in terms of syntax or semantics, many will also be acceptable as solution SDs. The fact that multiple solutions are possible introduces problem-solving complexity into the SD-building task in that the goal is not precisely defined – there are no specific guidelines in the literature that will guarantee that the analyst will be able to narrow the candidate solution pool to a single SD, particularly when there is more than one acceptable solution. Here, the novice analyst may recognize that there are multiple possible acceptable solutions, but may lack the expertise to recognize that one solution is better than another, or that two solutions are equally good. The lack of a precise goal definition introduces uncertainty into the process. This issue is due to both the characteristics of SDs as well as the overall

Figure 5. Decentralization example

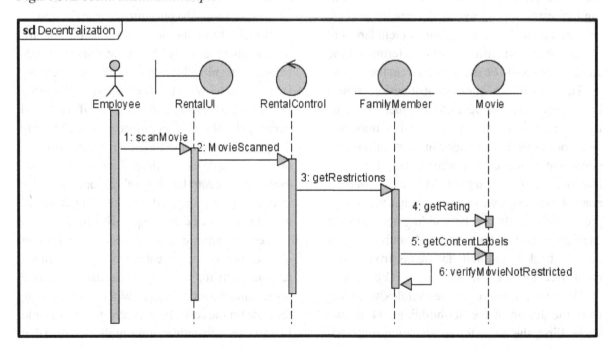

design process. Design, by its very nature, does not presuppose a goal. This is further complicated by the fact that minor differences in SD syntax choice can lead to major quality and correctness differences between candidate solutions, where a novice may have difficulty identifying the most correct or highest quality design.

Rate of Information Presentation

Most OOAD texts provide a wealth of information about SDs. As noted in the previous sections, many characteristics of the SD-building process are sources of cognitive complexity. The beginner analyst must digest a large amount of SD-building information in a short time. Here, information is a significant source of cognitive complexity, in the sense that the novice analyst is unlikely to be able to internalize and make use of all the information on building SDs at the same time.

For example, an analyst building a first SD might be able to model only a very simple scenario using a few guidelines. At this level of expertise, providing sophisticated SD-building heuristics introduces significant cognitive complexity because the novice is not prepared to incorporate them, but feels as though it is required.

With more experience in building SDs, the student becomes better prepared to apply more complicated techniques and model more detailed scenarios. While the new information does increase the complexity of the task, this complexity is useful because it will generally result in more detailed and higher quality SDs, and better overall designs. This complexity is due primarily to the overall complexity of SD building, rather than design in general.

Designing for Quality

The quality of an SD is difficult for a novice to evaluate. For example, the notions of coupling and cohesion, which refer to the quality of an overall design (encompassing not only SDs, but also class and other diagrams), are often introduced in texts, e.g., (Stumpf & Teague, 2005) aimed at the beginner analyst in the course of the discussion of building SDs. These concepts are difficult for the novice to apply, especially early in the analyst's introduction to OOAD. These concepts are subject to the "too much information too quickly" cognitive complexity issue.

Once the analyst is prepared to approach coupling and cohesion, there is additional complexity introduced by the relationship between the two concepts. Designing for low coupling tends to increase responsibility assignments to an object, while designing for high cohesion tends to reduce them. Thus, there is a clear trade-off between coupling and cohesion – reducing coupling tends to increase cohesion and vice versa. This introduces interrelationship and dependency-based problem-solving complexity in that the novice analyst must find a good balance between the two properties. Generally, quality is an issue for the overall design process, but the issue is exacerbated by the complexities associated with building SDs.

The Cumulative Effect

To see the overall effect of these complexity factors, let us consider what happens when a student analyst is actually building an SD. At each step, the student must be able to answer several questions:

- What is the next bit of behavior/processing required?
- Have I broken down the use case narrative step into sufficient detail, or have I glossed over something important? Have I missed any dependencies?
- Where is the focus of control right now? Is it in the correct place? Have I incorporated all returns required?
- Does the current focus of control match the next caller object? If not, how do I get the focus to the correct object?

- When I add the message for the next bit of behavior, am I using the correct syntax and semantics? Dashed or solid line arrow? Many syntax-related questions are possible here.
- Have I given the message an appropriate name, one that fully describes and limits the scope of responsibility? Does the called object fully perform that scope of responsibility, and no more?
- Does the next bit of behavior represent the start of if-then-else processing (needing an alt box)?
- If the current focus of control is inside an alternative within an alt box, does the next bit of behavior belong inside or outside the alt box?

At this point, the student is rapidly approaching Miller's (Miller, 1956) "seven plus or minus two" limit on information processing capacity, but hasn't yet considered the full scope of possible syntax- and semantics-related questions, or considered design quality.

OVERCOMING THE COGNITIVE COMPLEXITY OF BUILDING SEQUENCE DIAGRAMS

We introduce a set of recommendations aimed at reducing the cognitive complexity of learning to build SDs based on the LCD principles described earlier.

Build on the learner's knowledge level. As described earlier, information presented to the novice analyst before it can be processed and applied is not useful; however, as the student gains experience, additional information can be helpful and increase the quality of SDs.

In the context of learning to build SDs, we suggest focusing on different dimensions of SD-quality separately, from simpler to more complicated measures of SD-quality. Here, we

suggest thinking about the quality of an SD using a (partially) language-based model similar to that described in Lindland, Sindre & Solvberg (1994). Specifically, we can think of the quality of an SD as varying along three general dimensions:

1. **Syntax quality:** how well an SD conforms to the rules for using SD notation.
2. **Semantic quality:** how well an SD conforms to the scenario described in the high-level requirements, use case narratives, and any domain knowledge available.
3. **Design quality:** how well an SD can be executed in a high-quality software implementation (e.g., using concepts like coupling and cohesion).

In order to reduce the complexity associated with giving the beginner too much information too quickly, we suggest that SD-related information be presented first focusing on syntax, then on semantics, and finally on quality. Here, syntactic quality provides a foundation for the other quality dimensions - if the SD's syntax is not correct, it will never have high semantic or design quality. Similarly, once the novice has mastered SD syntax, if the SD does not match the requirements document (semantic quality), there is no point in thinking about design quality.

This recommendation makes use of the LCD principle of *scaffolding* to directly address the cognitive complexity associated with the rate of information presentation and evaluating design quality, and help to address the other issues by assuring that information is not presented before the learner is ready to use it.

Provide a wide variety of exercises for each stage. To support the development of varying dimensions of quality (syntax, semantic, and design quality), we can reduce the complexity of developing skills in each area by providing focused exercises specific to each dimension of quality.

For example, an exercise focusing on syntax may provide both an ordered set of logical steps, as well as a mapping that describes which object should perform each step, and ask the novice to simply draw the diagram. Similarly, an exercise focusing on semantics may provide a flowchart of the logic and a set of objects participating in the SD, and ask the student to assign responsibilities to objects. A design quality-focused exercise might ask a student to compare and contrast two SDs in terms of coupling and cohesion, or to modify an SD to improve its design quality.

This recommendation makes use of the LCD principles of *scaffolding* and *extensive use of exercises* to address the cognitive complexity associated with many of the SD-building complexity issues, including unfamiliar metaphors, working with SD syntax, omitting returns, decomposing high-level requirements, choosing between centralization and decentralization, choosing among candidate solutions, and quality evaluation.

Consider intermingling the OOAD and OO programming learning experiences. The programming roots of some SD syntax and semantic elements introduce complexity for some students, particularly those with little or no previous exposure to programming. This is a bit of a chicken-and-egg problem – the student needs to become familiar with these concepts, but the question arises: teach programming or design first? One proposal (Tabrizi, et al., 2004) suggests incorporating design and programming into single cohesive learning experience. This allows the student to see the goal of the design process - finished software (and all that it takes to turn design into implementation) – while concurrently building expertise in design.

This uses a form of scaffolding, making the end goal clear, and potentially enabling the student to foresee the consequences of design decisions in the implemented software, and helps to address the cognitive complexity associated with unfamiliar metaphors, working with SD syntax, omitting returns, decomposing high-level requirements, and choosing between centralization and decentralization.

Separate logical flow design from responsibility assignment. Many SD-building guidelines suggest working through the logic required for a use case and assigning responsibility for these logical steps at the same time. This requires the analyst to have a clear view of both the data structure of the to-be software as well as a strong sense of the detailed logic required to satisfy the use case scenario, and to be able to map these logical steps to the objects that will be responsible for them – all at once.

One way of reducing the complexity associated with this is for the beginner analyst to separate out the task of detailed logical flow development from that of responsibility assignment. This is useful when the use case steps require further decomposition into system-internal logic steps, because it allows the novice analyst decompose a less-detailed logic description in the use case into more detailed logical steps without worrying immediately about which object will be responsible for a given step.

Many texts (Fowler, 2004; George, et al., 2006) suggest taking advantage of any available useful tools in building analysis and design models, even if those tools are not part of the UML. In separating logic from responsibility assignment, a useful tool for the novice analyst is the familiar *flowchart*. This allows the analyst to map out individual logical steps, including conditional and repeating logic, without thinking about specific objects. Once this is done, the student can then consider responsibility assignment for each step.

This recommendation makes use of the LCD principles of *scaffolding* and *decomposition and recomposition*, by suggesting the separation of logic and structure, to address the cognitive complexity associated with decomposing high-level requirements into logic steps.

Actively think the problem through. Another potential mechanism for reducing the complexity of the responsibility-assignment task, one that would work best primarily in an educational setting, is to have a group of students role-play to work through which object should be responsible for which logical steps. Here, each student is assigned a role as an object, and given a list of the object's attributes. A token of some sort represents the focus of control, and students must ask one another to perform tasks, passing around the token, to fulfill the requirements of a particular use case. (The authors have applied this technique in the classroom with good results.)

This approach allows multiple student analysts to contribute to the group's common model of the logic flow and responsibility assignment set, reducing the cognitive load on any given individual, while simultaneously ensuring that all students are engaged in the learning process.

For a large group of students, it is possible to ask the larger group to break the problem into smaller pieces. Smaller groups can then attack each sub-problem, and the group as a whole can then integrate the solutions to the sub-problems into a larger solution to the whole problem.

This recommendation makes use of the LCD principles of *engaging the learner actively*, *using exercises extensively*, and *decomposition and recomposition* to address the cognitive complexity associated with several of our SD complexity characteristics: decomposing high-level requirements into logic steps, choosing among multiple candidate solutions, assigning responsibilities, and choosing between centralization and decentralization.

Document and use patterns. Applying a pattern is a well-known way of reusing previous work and reducing the overall workload of a task. Patterns can reduce the cognitive complexity of the SD-building process for an analyst who has mastered SD syntax and semantics by providing a starting point of a known quality design for a standard organizational scenario (e.g., the workflow for processing paychecks). While a pattern might not apply completely to a given scenario, it can still provide a modifiable starting point to the analyst that would otherwise have required significant thought to produce from scratch.

Design patterns have been discussed in the literature (France, Kim, Ghosh & Song, 2004), and are cited in some textbooks, e.g., (Stumpf & Teague, 2005). These abstract patterns provide a basis for solving particular design patterns (e.g., using a singleton class to represent an interface), and are meant to provide the experienced designer with generally applicable solutions. For a novice, however, applying these patterns presents a major challenge: the patterns are described at a level of abstraction that makes it difficult for the novice to recognize where they can be applied, partially due to the fact that these patterns have their origins in coding design patterns.

Fowler (1997) introduced the idea of detailed domain-specific analysis patterns. This book contains a set of highly-detailed analysis patterns describing common situations from accounting and health-care domains, and provides data and behavior models for each situation. This book was written prior to the development of UML, so the models in this book are not built using the familiar UML syntax. However, the idea of reuse of detailed analysis-stage models holds. The availability of a set of tried-and-true analysis patterns, covering a large number of domains, could significantly reduce the complexity of designing logic for a frequently-encountered domain.

This recommendation makes use of the LCD principle of the *use of examples* to address the cognitive complexity associated with several SD-building complexity issues: omitting returns, decomposing high-level requirements, choosing objects when assigning responsibilities, choosing between centralization and decentralization, and quality evaluation.

CONCLUSION

In this paper, we have considered the question of why SDs are difficult to learn to build. We have described a set of characteristics of the SD-building task that add complexity to the task, and identified why each of these adds difficulty using concepts from cognitive complexity theory. Further, we developed a set of recommendations aimed at reducing the difficulty associated with the task of learning to build SDs by applying concepts from the theory of LCD. We believe these recommendations will be of interest to educators, experienced analysts mentoring novices, and others.

Future work includes empirical testing to determine the efficacy of our recommendations in practice, as well as developing a set of reusable foundation SDs that provide novice analysts with a strong starting point for learning to build their own SDs.

REFERENCES

Agarwal, R., & Sinha, A. (2003). Object-Oriented Modeling with UML: A Study of Developers' Perceptions. *Communications of the ACM, 49*(9), 248–256. doi:10.1145/903893.903944

Beck, K., & Cunningham, W. (1989). A Laboratory for Teaching Object Oriented Thinking. *Proceedings of the 1989 ACM OOPSLA Conference on Object-Oriented Programming*, (pp. 1-6).

Blaha, M., & Rumbaugh, J. (2005). *Object-Oriented Modeling and Design with UML* (2nd ed.). Pearson Prentice Hall.

Bolloju, N., & Leung, F. S. (2006). Assisting the Novice Analyst in Developing Quality Conceptual Models with UML. *Communications of the ACM, 49*(7), 108–112. doi:10.1145/1139922.1139926

Booch, G. (1986). Object-Oriented Development. *IEEE Transactions on Software Engineering, 12*(2), 211–221.

Brewer, J., & Lorenz, L. (2003). Using UML and Agile Development Methodologies to Teach Object-Oriented Analysis and Design Tools and Techniques. *Proceedings of the 4th Conference on Information Technology Education*, (pp. 54-57).

Burton, P., & Bruhn, R. (2004). Using UML to Facilitate the Teaching of Object-Oriented Systems Analysis and Design. *Journal of Computing Sciences in Colleges, 19*(3), 278–290.

Dobing, B., & Parsons, J. (2006). How UML is Used. *Communications of the ACM, 49*(5), 109–113. doi:10.1145/1125944.1125949

Dobing, B., & Parsons, J. (2008). Dimensions of UML Diagram Use: A Survey of Practitioners. *Journal of Database Management, 19*(1), 1–18. doi:10.4018/jdm.2008010101

Dori, D. (2002). Why Significant UML Change is Unlikely. *Communications of the ACM, 45*(11), 82–85. doi:10.1145/581571.581599

Fowler, M. (1997). *Analysis Patterns: Reusable Object Models*. Addison-Wesley Pearson Education.

Fowler, M. (2004). *UML Distilled Third Edition: A Brief Guide to the Standard Object Modeling Language*. Addison-Wesley Pearson Education.

France, R., Kim, D.-K., Ghosh, S., & Song, E. (2004). A UML-based Pattern Specification Technique. *IEEE Transactions on Software Engineering, 30*(3), 193–206. doi:10.1109/TSE.2004.1271174

George, J. F., Batra, D., Valacich, J. S., & Hoffer, J. A. (2006). *Object-Oriented Systems Analysis and Design* (2nd ed.). Prentice Hall.

International Organization for Standardization. (2005, April). *ISO/IEC 19501:2004 -- Unified Modeling Language (UML)*. Retrieved from http://www.iso.org.

Johnson, R. E., & Fotte, B. (1988). Designing Reusable Classes. *Journal of Object-Oriented Programming, 1*(2), 22–35.

Lindland, O., Sindre, G., & Solvberg, A. (1994). Understanding Quality in Conceptual Modeling. *IEEE Software, 11*(2), 42–49. doi:10.1109/52.268955

Micallef, J. (1988). Encapsulation, Reusability, and Extensibility in Object-Oriented Programming Languages. *Journal of Object-Oriented Programming, 1*(1), 12–36.

Miller, G. (1956). The Magical Number Seven, Plus Or Minus Two: Some Limits On Our Capacity For Processing Information. *Psychological Review, 63*(2), 209–227. doi:10.1037/h0043158

Reeves, W. (1999). *Learner-Centered Design: A Cognitive View of Managing Complexity in Product, Information, and Environmental Design.* Sage Publications.

Rosson, M. B., & Alpert, S. R. (1990). The Cognitive Consequences of Object-Oriented Design. *Human-Computer Interaction, 5*(4), 345–379. doi:10.1207/s15327051hci0504_1

Rumbaugh, J., Blaha, M., Premerlani, W., & Lorensen, W. (1991). *Object-Oriented Modeling and Design.* Englewood Cliffs, NJ: Prentice Hall.

Sheetz, S. (2002). Identifying the Difficulties of Object-Oriented Development. *Journal of Systems and Software, 64*(1), 23–36. doi:10.1016/S0164-1212(02)00019-5

Siau, K., & Cao, Q. (2001). Unified Modeling Language (UML) -- A Complextiy Analysis. *Journal of Database Management, 12*(1), 26–34. doi:10.4018/jdm.2001010103

Siau, K., Erickson, J., & Lee, L. (2005). Theoretical vs. Practical Complexity: The Case of UML. *Journal of Database Management, 16*(3), 40–57. doi:10.4018/jdm.2005070103

Siau, K., & Loo, P.-P. (2006). Identifying Difficulties in Learning UML. *Information Systems Management, 23*(3), 43–51. doi:10.1201/1078.1 0580530/46108.23.3.20060601/93706.5

Stumpf, R., & Teague, L. (2005). *Object-Oriented Systems Analysis and Design with UML.* Pearson Prentice Hall.

Tabrizi, M., Collins, C., Ozan, E., & Li, K. (2004). Implementation of Object-Orientation Using UML in Entry Level Software Development Courses. *Proceedings of the 5th Conference on Information Technology Education,* (pp. 128-131).

Visual Paradigm International. (2006). Retrieved from Visual Paradigm for UML: http://www. visual-paradigm.com.

Wei, F., Moritz, S., Parvez, S., & Blank, G. (2005). A Student Model for Object-Oriented Design and Programming. *Journal of Computing Sciences in Colleges, 20*(5), 260–273.

Wiedenbeck, S., Fix, V., & Scholtz, J. (1993). Characteristics of the Mental Representations of Novice and Expert Programmers: an Empirical Study. *International Journal of Man-Machine Studies, 39*(5), 793–812. doi:10.1006/imms.1993.1084

Wiedenbeck, S., Ramalingam, V., Sarasamma, S., & Corritore, C. (1999). A Comparison of the Comprehension of Object-oriented and Procedural Programs by Novice Programmers. *Interacting with Computers, 11*(3), 255–282. doi:10.1016/S0953-5438(98)00029-0

This work was previously published in Journal of Database Management (JDM) 20(1), edited by Keng Siau, pp. 25-47, copyright 2009 by IGI Publishing (an imprint of IGI Global).

Chapter 3
Ontology Based Object–Oriented Domain Modeling:
Representing Behavior

Joerg Evermann[1]
Memorial University of Newfoundland, Canada

Yair Wand
The University of British Columbia, Canada

ABSTRACT

An important step in developing the requirements for an information system is analyzing the application domain. In this step, conceptual models are used for representing an application domain. However, while languages for software design are available and widely used, no generally accepted language exists for conceptual modeling. This work suggests the use of object-oriented software modeling languages also for conceptual modeling. Such use can support a more accurate transition from domain modes to software models. As software-modeling languages were not intended for modeling application domains, their constructs lack the required semantics. While previous papers addressed the representation of structural elements of domains using object concepts, this paper addresses behavioral aspects, related to change and interaction. The proposed semantics are based on a mapping between ontological concepts that describe behavior and object-oriented constructs related to dynamics. Based on these mappings, modeling rules are proposed to guide the modeler in creating ontologically well-formed models. The mappings and rules are exemplified using UML and are demonstrated using a case study.

DOI: 10.4018/978-1-60960-521-6.ch003

INTRODUCTION

A good understanding of the application domain is necessary to develop the requirements for information systems (IS). Such understanding can be facilitated with the use of conceptual models. Conceptual modeling is the "activity of formally describing some aspects of the physical and social world for the purpose of understanding" (Mylopoulos, 1992).

Despite possible benefits to IS development of using conceptual models, no widely used formal or semi-formal language for conceptual modeling exists. In contrast, formal and semi-formal languages, notably object-oriented languages, are commonly used in software design. As reported in (Dobing & Parsons, 2006, 2008) and also found in our case study (Sec. 8), practitioners, for lack of a language specific to conceptual modeling, have been using software design languages for this purpose. However, this often occurs in an unguided way, possibly leading to confusion and difficulties in understanding. Without guidance, the support of UML for describing domains other than software is poor and this can lead to miscommunication (Smolander & Rossi, 2008).

Adopting widely used and well-accepted object-oriented languages, usually employed for software design, in a guided way and with clearly specified semantic for conceptual modeling, has several potential benefits: (1) It can provide a shared language to support better communication between analysts and software designers. (2) It can help mitigate translation problems between the conceptual and the software models, (also called "impedance mismatch" (Cilia *et al.*, 2003; Kolp *et al.*, 2002; Roe, 2003; Rozen & Shasha, 1989). More specifically, because the domain model is specified in the same language as software, the domain model can also serve as an initial model of the software system (Coad & Yourdon, 1991), which can subsequently be adapted to particular technologies. Such technology-driven refactoring is beyond the scope of this paper. The discussion in Section 9 will revisit this point in more detail. (3) A clear representation of application aspects can reduce possible confusion of business and implementation aspects in conceptual models (Parsons & Wand, 1997). (4) Assigning semantics to language constructs for domain representation purposes can provide modeling rules (Evermann & Wand, 2005a).

Because object-oriented languages were not developed for conceptual modeling, they lack application domain semantics. For example, while language constructs such as "Method" or "Operation" have clear meaning for software design, it less clear what they represent in the application domain. However, assigning application domain semantics to language constructs, while necessary for their use in application domain modeling, is insufficient. It is also desirable to identify *modeling rules* to ensure that the created models represent only really possible situations in the application domain. Modeling rules can improve the ability to communicate and reason about the domain by restricting the possible interpretations of a model (Hadar & Soffer, 2006), and hence can support convergence of the domain understanding among different stakeholders, a pre-requisite for development and implementation success. Therefore, such rules can improve the effectiveness of the created models as ways to communicate and reason about the domain (Reinhartz-Berger & Sturm, 2008).

Previous research (Evermann & Wand, 2005b) proposed the use of object-oriented design languages for modeling the structural aspects of application domains. That research proposed specific application domain semantics for the static structure constructs found in UML class diagrams, and suggested modeling rules to develop well-formed and meaningful (with respect to perceptions of the real world application domain) models. The present work addresses the behavioral aspects of conceptual modeling, focusing on constructs to describe change and interaction. We exclude use case related constructs as they describe external interactions with a system, whereas the remaining UML constructs describe the system itself.

Our approach is based on the use of ontology, a specification of concepts that exist in a domain. Previously, ontologies have been used mostly to *evaluate* modeling languages (Green & Rosemann, 2000; Opdahl & Henderson-Sellers, 2002; Opdahl *et al.*, 1999). This work extends the ontological approach to *prescribe* modeling rules for using constructs related to dynamic to model behavioral aspects of a domain. We use the Unified Modeling Language UML (OMG, 2005) as a specific instantiation of object-oriented software design languages, due to its wide acceptance (Dobing & Parsons, 2006, 2008).

The paper is organized as follows. Section 2 presents the research methodology, followed by an introduction to ontology and the specific ontology used for this research (Sec. 3). These introductions are limited to the analysis of behavior and interactions. The main sections (Sec. 4-7) develop the proposed semantics and modeling rules. The paper closes with a presentation of case study research that provides empirical support for the proposed semantics and rules (Sec. 8).

RESEARCH METHODOLOGY

To assign application domain semantics to object-oriented language constructs, we create mappings between language constructs and domain concepts. Domain concepts are specified in terms of an ontology. Ontology as an area of study is "that branch of philosophy which deals with the order and structure of reality in the broadest sense possible" (Angeles, 1981). A particular ontology specifies what exists and how things behave in a domain. Ontological mappings are established by the following two steps (Wand & Weber, 1993):

1. Representation mapping: Assign each ontological concept a language construct with which to *represent* it.

2. Interpretation mapping: Assign each language construct an ontological *interpretation*.

Once ontological mappings have been established, the transfer of ontological assumptions and constraints to the language generates modeling rules. This transfer is based on the principle that relationships between ontological concepts should also hold between the language constructs that are used to represent them.

Our analysis is guided by the principle that the mappings should retain the existing relationships between language constructs, so as not to affect its software design semantics. For example, as associations can relate UML classes, there should be something that relates the ontological concepts to which UML classes are mapped. If this condition cannot be satisfied, then the assignment of semantics to object constructs cannot be accomplished without violating some fundamental design language aspects. Given this requirement, the mapping of one language construct has implications for the possible mapping of other, related ones. We address these interdependencies by using an iterative method, changing our perspective repeatedly between the representation mapping and the interpretation mapping. We begin by proposing an initial representation mapping for core ontological concepts (Section 4). Based on this mapping, we propose an interpretation mapping for related, as yet unmapped, language constructs (Section 5). We repeat this for a second time to cover all remaining ontological concepts and language constructs (Sections 6, 7). In this way, we ensure a mapping that is internally consistent and respects the existing dependencies between language constructs as much as possible.

This iterative methodology also addresses the problem of "correct" interpretation of the ontology and the language syntax. As both specifications are texts that must be read and interpreted, the iterative methodology follows the hermeneutic cycle (Gadamer, 1976; Ricoeur, 1976), recognized as essential in interpretive IS research (Boland, 1985;

Chalmers, 2004; Myers, 1995; Prasad, 2002). This prevents premature assignment of meaning and allows the entire meaning of the language and ontology specifications to emerge.

Our work has the following limitations. First, it is not our purpose to suggest modeling rules for software design. The derived rules are appropriate for conceptual modeling but may not be so for software design. However, models that conform to our rules are valid software models, as we do not violate the existing software semantics of the language. Second, our rules do not guide us in how to perceive the world. Thus, we might suggest rules on how to use modeling constructs such as objects and classes, but not on how to identify them in the domain. For example, we do not offer rules that tell the modeler how to identify things in the domain. Instead, our rules are of the kind that, given the modeler has already identified a thing, the rules tell her how to model it in object-oriented terms. Third, it is beyond the scope of a single paper to examine all UML constructs, as several hundreds UML constructs exist. We restrict ourselves to the basic constructs commonly seen in UML diagrams. Furthermore, some language constructs serve a purely syntactic purpose or only have meanings in the software context and cannot be assigned any domain semantics (e.g. Pseudo State, Stub State). We consider these constructs not relevant for conceptual modelling. We also exclude use case related constructs, as they describe external interactions with a system, whereas the remaining UML constructs describe the system itself.

ONTOLOGY

The term *ontology* has seen increasing use in such areas as information systems, artificial intelligence, and knowledge engineering (Gruninger & Lee, 2002; Noy & Hafner, 1997; Uschold & Gruninger, 1996). The present research takes up the call for a return to philosophical ontology (Guarino & Welty, 2002; Smith & Welty, 2001).

An ontology is taken to be a commitment to the belief in the existence of certain entities in external reality, e.g. the business and organizational world. A specific ontology is a set of assumptions about what exists or is perceived to exist in a domain. Adopting an ontology is a fundamental philosophical choice that cannot be justified *a-priori*. As any philosophy, it is the framework that enables one to carry out research (Kuhn, 1996), and the merits of its adoption can only be assessed based on the results of that research. Some reasons for our choice of ontology, based on previous research results, are given below.

The Bunge-Ontology

The specific ontology chosen for our purposes is based on the work of Mario Bunge (Bunge, 1977, 1979). We use this particular ontology for pragmatic reasons:

- It is based on ontological work done over a long period (Bunge, 1977, pg. xiii).
- It is an axiomatic system and formally represented in set theory notation.
- It has not been developed specifically for use in software development, but is instead based on "the ontological presuppositions of contemporary scientific research" (Bunge, 1977, pg. xiii). Thus, its use can help distinguish between domain and software concepts.
- It has been shown to provide a good benchmark for the evaluation of modeling languages and methods (Dussart *et al.*, 2004; Evermann & Wand, 2005b; Opdahl & Henderson-Sellers, 2001; Parsons & Wand, 1997; Rosemann & Green, 2000; Soffer *et al.*, 2001; Wand *et al.*, 1999; Wand & Weber, 1989, 1993; Weber & Zhang, 1996).
- It has been used to assign ontological meaning to object concepts (Wand, 1989).

Table 1. Concepts of the Bunge ontology

Ontological Concept	Explanation
Thing	Fundamental concept. The world consists of things and only of things.
Property	Things have properties.
Intrinsic Property	Property of one thing.
Mutual Property	Property of two or more things.
Law	Restriction of or relation on properties.
Composition	Things can be composed to form composite things.
Emergent Property	Property of a composite thing that is not a property of one of its components.
State Function	Function describing a property of a thing. Synonymous with attribute.
Functional Schema (Model)	Set of state functions describing things. A model of things that are similar in some ways.
State	Value vector of state functions of a functional schema.
Natural Kind	Set of things adhering to same laws (common behavior).
Quantitative Change	Change of state of a thing.
Qualitative Change	Change of natural kind of a thing by loss or acquisition of properties.
Event	Change of state.
Process	Ordered set of events of one thing.
Lawful Transformation	Path in state space between an initial and a final state, where all points on the path are lawful states.
History	The states a thing traverses over time.
Action	A thing A acts on a thing B iff the state history of B depends on the existence of A.
Interaction	Two or more things acting on each other.

- It has been empirically shown to lead to useful outcomes (Bodart *et al.*, 2001; Cockroft & Rowles, 2003; Evermann & Wand, 2006; Gemino, 1999; Weber & Zhang, 1996).

The following paragraphs introduce the ontological concepts of Bunge's work (Bunge, 1977, 1979). This is necessarily an incomplete exposition of the entire ontology, including only the concepts relevant to this paper. A brief synopsis is presented in Table 1.

The world is made up of substantial *things* that exist physically in the world. Things can combine to form a *composite* thing. Things possess (substantial) *properties*. Properties in general are those possessed by a set of things, e.g. "color", "speed", "salary", etc. Individual properties, i.e. properties of an individual thing, can be considered values

of properties in general, (e.g. a specific thing is blue in color, and is traveling at a speed of 100 mph; a specific thing is a person earning a salary of $50000). Intrinsic properties are those that a thing possesses by itself, whereas mutual properties exist between two or more things. Composites possess *emergent* properties, i.e. properties not possessed by any component. A *law* is any restriction on the properties of a thing.

Any thing can be described by a set of *attributes,* which (Bunge, 1977) also calls *state functions*. A set of state functions is called a *functional schema* or *model*. A thing can be described by many different schemata. For example, a person may be described by height and weight, or described by location and organizational unit. The *state* of a thing is defined as the set of values of *all* state functions comprising a particular model. The *lawful state space* of a thing is defined by constraining the values of the state functions to those values consistent with the laws the thing adheres to.

All things change, and every change is a change of things. A change may be *quantitative*, in which case the values of one or more state functions (and individual properties) are changed, or it may be *qualitative*, in which case state functions (and general properties) are acquired or lost. Concurrent with loss or acquisition of properties is the loss or acquisition of behavior as things lose or gain possible ways in which they can change. Change always involves the change of state of some thing. Since all things are changeable, every lawful state space contains at least two distinct states.

A discrete change is termed an *event*. An event can be described as an ordered pair of states. An event is defined for the state space of a *single* thing. A change in one thing may also be a change in another (e.g. changes of mutual properties). This is an interaction consisting of two distinct events in the two things. If the state space is non-denumerable, i.e. for continuous change, a change is represented by a triple (s_i, s_f, g) representing the initial state, the final state and a function g, the *lawful transformation*, which represents the path in the state space that the thing traverses. All possible changes must be in accordance with laws.

Interaction is defined through the state history of a thing: If the state history of one thing depends on the existence of another thing then the second is said to *act on* the first. Things interact, if each acts upon the other. Everything acts on, and is acted on, by other things. Changes occur as a consequence of laws: If two properties are lawfully related and one changes, then the other may also change, depending on the laws that relate them. Since laws relate properties of one thing only, for a thing A to act on a thing B as the result of laws, there must exist a mutual property of A and B which is lawfully related to (intrinsic) properties of A and B. Furthermore, interaction may give rise to mutual properties. The interaction of a person enrolling at a university to become a student would give rise to the mutual property

"tuition fee balance". Hence, some properties necessarily exist prior to interaction and some others may exist post interaction (Evermann, 2005).

REPRESENTATION MAPPING

We base our mapping process on the mapping of some fundamental concepts in existing research (Evermann & Wand, 2005b). These fundamental mappings are in agreement also with other work on UML and Bunge's ontology (Dussart et al., 2004; Evermann, 2005; Opdahl & Henderson-Sellers, 2001, 2002). Table 2 shows these mappings. With these fundamental mapping of Table 2 in mind, we begin our mapping of concepts related to change and behavior.

States and State Transitions

The central concepts of behavior in Bunge's ontology are states and state transitions. Object-oriented languages such as UML also provide states and state transition. We propose to represent ontological states by object-states and ontological state transitions by object-state transitions. Some consequences follow from this mapping.

In Bunge's ontology, a state is the *complete* assignment of values to the state functions, i.e. a vector of the values of *all* state functions. While the object-oriented literature has noted the connection between attributes and states (Booch, 1994; Coad & Yourdon, 1990; Jacobson, 1992; Rumbaugh, 1991), UML does not support modeling this connection. We therefore propose the following rule to preserve the ontological relationship between states and properties also in object-oriented languages:

Rule 1: *Every object-state must be defined by a specific assignment of values to a set of attributes of the object for which the state is defined.*

Table 2. Prior mappings of fundamental concepts

Ontological Concept	Object Construct in UML	Remarks
Thing	Object	
Property	Attribute	
Intrinsic Property	Attribute of 'ordinary' class	
Mutual Property	Attribute of association class	
Emergent Property	Class attribute	Attribute of an aggregate made of class instances.
Functional Schema	Class	
Natural Kind	Set of objects (extension of class)	Described by class.
Composition	Aggregation	
	Composition	Does not have an ontological equivalence. In ontology things exist independent of whether they are components or not.
	Association	Does not have an ontological equivalence. Implies interaction (Evermann, 2005).
A collection of mutual properties that are generated together	Association class	

This rule ensures that appropriate attributes are modeled to be able to fully represent the dynamics allowed by the state space and the transitions within this space. For example, if a student in a university domain has two states, "passed" or "failed", this must be modeled using some attributes (for example "Course Credits" with different number of course credits defining each state, "passed" or "failed").

Ontologically, every change of state changes the value of at least one state function. For example, when a student passes a course (transitions from "failed" to "passed" standing), the changed value would be that of the attribute "Course Credits". Hence, from Rule 1 follows:

Corollary 1: *An object's state transition must change the value of at least one of its attributes.*

5. INTERPRETATION MAPPING (1ST ITERATION)

Sub-States

Object-oriented languages like UML allow the definition of a state hierarchy in which a state may contain sub-states. An object in a sub-state is also in the super-state containing that sub-state. In Bunge's ontology, states do not have sub-states. Hence, we must find an ontological interpretation for this object-oriented "shorthand" notation.

Ontologically, sub-states can be interpreted using two different functional schemata of the represented thing, spanning two different state spaces. For example, let a telephone answering machine have a state "Passive" and a composite state "Active" with sub-states "Greeting Recording", "Message Recording", and "Message Playback". States "Active" and "Passive" can be characterized by an attribute "Tape Speed" (zero - for "Passive" and greater than zero "Active"). This is one model of the answering machine. Distinguishing among the sub-states of "Active" requires additional state functions, e.g. "Recording Source" (with values "Microphone" or "Telephone Line"), and "Mode" (with values "Recording" or "Playback"). Thus, the second model is defined by three attributes. In this model it is possible to distinguish between states such as "Message Recording" ("Tape Speed > zero", "Recording Source=Telephone Line" and "Mode=Recording"), and "Greeting Recording" ("Tape Speed > zero", "Recording Source=Microphone" and "Mode-recording").

Formally, let state x (defined by a set of state variables $a=a_1$) be a point in state space sp_x, spanned by attribute a. Let sub-state y be a point in state space sp_y, spanned by attribute set a and a set of additional attributes b. Multiple points in sp_y, e.g. $<a=a_1, b=b_1>$, $<a=a_1, b=b_2>$, etc. can be mapped to a single point x in sp_x. State space sp_x is a *projection* of sp_y onto attribute set a. Based on the above example and this formal discussion we propose the following rule and corollary:

Rule 2: *Object-oriented sub-states are defined using attributes in addition to those defining the super-state.*

Corollary 2: *For an object transitioning among sub-states, the values of only those attributes change, that are not used to define the super-state.*

In object-oriented languages, two or more sub-states of the same super-state may be concurrent. In addition to the conditions on the super- and sub-states expressed by Rule 2 and Corollary 2 we require that, for two sub-states of a common super-state to be concurrent, the two higher-dimensional state spaces are independent:

Corollary 3: *Concurrent sub-states require mutually disjoint sets of additional attributes in the class description.*

The rules proposed in this section help to ensure that the attribute definitions for object classes are sufficient to support the desired behavioral characteristics of the object as expressed in state charts. Specifically, in UML, the proposed language rules relate elements of state charts with those of class diagrams.

Active States

Some object-oriented languages allow modeling of object states during which the object undergoes a change. In UML 1.x, these were called action states. In UML 2.0, actions and activities are separated from states. However, the notion of a state during which changes occur remains, as behavior can be associated with states in the form of a "DoActivity". This is incompatible with the ontological notion that a state is an assignment of values to attributes at a specific instance in time. Again, we must identify the proper ontological interpretation of this object-oriented "shorthand notation".

We build on our interpretation of object-oriented sub-states: If a change occurs while a thing is in a certain state, there must exist a state variable not employed for the state definition and that state variable may change. Hence, action states can be represented by means of sub-states:

Rule 3: *Action states are composite states comprising a set of sub-states. The object transitions among the sub-states while in the action state. State charts and class diagrams must reflect this.*

For example, the situation in Figure 1A is equivalent to that in Figure 1B. An item that is in the action state of "being shipped" undergoes state transitions while being in that state, e.g. from state "On Shelf" to a new state "In Packing System" etc.

Operations

Bunge's ontology provides no construct that is equivalent to methods or operations in object-oriented languages. It has been suggested that these are software related constructs, i.e. without relevance for real-world models (Parsons & Wand, 1991, 1997) and thus need not be interpreted ontologically. However, as operations feature prominently in object-oriented modelling, this section shows how operations are related to state transitions, thereby gaining an ontological interpretation and derives rules for their use in conceptual modeling.

Whereas operations specify behavior only in abstract terms, a method provides a specific implementation of an operation[2]. As Bunge's ontology expresses dynamics through states and

Figure 1. Action-States

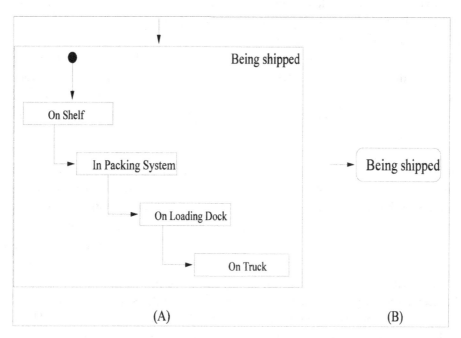

(A)   (B)

transitions, we must use these concepts to assign domain semantics to methods and operations.

We note that in the object approach, the *entire* range of behavior of an object (except creation and reclassification, i.e. qualitative change) is determined by its set of operations. Ontologically, *every* change of a thing is describable in terms of state transitions. We therefore propose:

Rule 4: *The quantitative behavior of objects of a particular class (for each model) is entirely describable by a top-level state chart SC_0 associated with the class.*

Since the behavior of objects is limited to the operations defined on the object:

Rule 5: *Every object-oriented state-transition in SC_0 must correspond to an operation modeled for the class of objects that SC_0 is associated with and vice versa.*

Since in our ontology everything is able to change, we propose the following:

Corollary 4: *Every object must have at least one operation.*

Bunge's ontology, as adapted in (Wand & Weber, 1993, 1995), distinguishes among *stable* and *unstable* states. A thing can only leave a stable state due to interaction. In object-oriented descriptions, an object remains in a particular state until an operation is invoked on it. An operation reflects the complete response to this invocation; the object then awaits another operation to be invoked. Since we have proposed that operations are realizations of top-level state transitions, we add now the rule that top-level state transitions are transitions from and to stable states:

Corollary 5: *States in SC_0 represent stable states.*

The above rules and corollaries allow the modeler to identify operations that may have been missed in constructing the class diagram, or identify operations for which there are no corresponding state transitions. Such operations would be redundant. Figure 2 shows an example.

Consider a car that can be in three states, engine "Stopped", engine "Running" and going "Forward". Assume the states of a car are defined as in Table 3. Then the class definition in Figure 2 (A) is consistent with the top-level state chart SC_0 depicted in Figure 2 (B).

Explicitly modeling the link between operations and state transitions provides the operation and method designer a way of ensuring that the full state description of a system is realized. It also helps ensure that operations do not implement change beyond that in the state description.

Behavior

In object-oriented languages such as UML, state charts may be used to specify the behavior that implements an operation. These state charts must follow some rules. In general, behavior represents lawful transformations that describe in greater detail the state transition represented by an operation. Hence, the beginning and end of the path in state space represented by a particular state chart must match the initial and final states of the operation whose behavior this state chart describes:

Corollary 6: *A state chart describing an operation must begin and end with the initial and final state of the transition in SC_0 that corresponds to the operation.*

Corollary 7: *The behavior represented by a state chart must modify the attribute values of the object in a way that corresponds to the values defined for the initial and the final state of the state chart.*

These rules and corollaries allow the modeler to identify incomplete state charts. If a state chart describing a particular behavior does not begin and end with the proper states, it may be incomplete. Corollary 7 can help to design behavior specifications that conform to the state description by providing pre- and post-conditions of a method. For example, let the answering machine switch from state "Message Recording" to state "Passive". The initial state is characterized by attributes and values "Tape Speed > 0", "Recording Source = Telephone Line", and "Mode = Recording" while the final state is defined by "Tape Speed = 0". A method implementing an operation corresponding to this state transition should assume the object representing the answering machine is in a state possessing attributes according to the initial state and must ensure the assignment of object attributes according to the final state.

Figure 2. Class definition and state chart

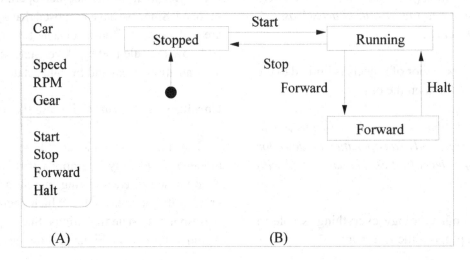

(A)   (B)

Table 3. Example state definitions

Stopped	(Speed = 0, RPM = 0)
Running	(Speed = 0, RPM = 1000, Gear = 0)
Forward	(Speed = 50, RPM = 3000, Gear = 1)

REPRESENTATION MAPPING

In Bunge's ontology, interaction is represented by state transitions, rather than message-passing, as in object-oriented modeling. Ontologically, interaction arises because things adhere to laws that must be satisfied at all times: When an event in thing A changes a property that is lawfully related to a property of thing B (this relation must be via mutual properties), the property of thing B may need to adjust so that the law remains satisfied. Hence, interactions can, in theory, be derived from the knowledge of the laws, e.g. by means of constraint solving (Mackworth, 1977) or constraint programming (Van Hentenryck, 1989). We say 'in theory' because these methods are not generally applicable and, except for special cases, not computationally efficient.

It is the object-oriented system designer's task to ensure that the modeled message-passing pattern satisfies all application domain laws (often termed business rules). It is often the case that such laws are only implicitly understood by analysts, rather than being explicitly stated and modeled. A rigorous ontological analysis of the domain can help explicate the existence of laws or constraints and suggest possible ways how laws (business rules) can be implemented via interactions (message passing).

The discussion of Bunge's ontology in Section 3 suggests that since laws constrain the state variables of only a single thing, changes between two things must happen by virtue of mutual properties. Thus, a change of a mutual property in one thing does not lead to a change in another thing

but *is* a change in a property of another thing. Since mutual properties are mapped to association class attributes (see Table 2), we derive the following rule:

Rule 6: *For every two classes of objects between which message passing is declared, there exists an association class with at least one attribute.*

This rule can help the modeler to identify which messages need to be shown in a model and between which two objects an association class needs to be identified. This in turn can provide for a richer analysis of the application domain. The case study in Section 8 demonstrates that this is feasible as the number of relevant messages, and therefore the number of association classes, typically remains manageable.

The scope of the model and level of abstraction determines whether a particular thing and its mutual properties should be modeled. Clearly, one does not wish to model individual atoms and molecules even though they are ultimately the connected things. Scope and level of abstraction are determined based on the model purpose prior to modeling. For example, intermediate communication mechanisms such as communication systems are typically outside the scope of a model of a business (but not a technical) domain: A telephone line between two people possesses mutual properties with both the speaker and the listener. It is these mutual properties and the properties of the phone line (voltage, waveform, etc.) that undergo change. However, as the telephone line is typically outside of the model scope, it and its properties will not be included in the model. Instead, the interaction between the two individuals will be considered using properties shared directly between the individuals, such as shared beliefs, goals, etc. that may be affected by the interaction.

In Bunge's ontology everything acts on and is acted upon by other things. Hence, there should be interactions originating from and terminating on the thing:

Rule 7: *Every object must be the receiver and sender of, or responder to, some message.*

This rule shows the need to critically examine the interactions or information flows. One could argue that things in the environment of a system may only send but not receive messages, e.g. a customer ordering a product, a student registering for a course, etc. Nevertheless, even for these examples, the actions of ordering and registering are pointless unless the customer and the student also receive messages. This could be order acknowledgements or shipping details for the customer. For the student, the messages may involve tuition fee billing or textbook requirement messages. Neither customers nor students will only send messages without expecting to receive any. This rule also illustrates differences between software and domain models. Consider a LineItem object in a transaction application that might in a software model be shown as only receiving messages. However, as we wish to describe the domain, rather than the software, we require an interpretation of what a LineItem object represents. For example, it might represent a particular product being ordered by a particular customer. In that case, it is not a thing, but an event or activity, and should not be modeled as an object.

Often, a thing is made up of parts. In such cases, it is sufficient for any of its parts receive and send some message to satisfy rule 7. The receiving and sending must not necessarily be done by the same part. For example, assume an object A with parts P_1 and P_2. If P_1 receives messages (is acted upon) but does not send any messages (acts on), and P_2 sends messages but does not receive any, we consider rule 7 to be satisfied, as the object A both receives and sends messages. In this case, some interaction necessarily exists between the parts P_1 and P_2 (which is not shown on the level of the composite object).

A specific instance of such a composite object is the domain environment. The necessarily limited scope of any model leads to some things interacting with things beyond the model scope, i.e. with the environment. Rather than showing the individual objects comprising the environment (which are outside the scope), the modeler may instead choose to designate one thing as the environment, with the understanding that it is a composite object and subject to message passing amongst its parts.

In summary, while we suggest that message passing is not ontologically real, we advocate its use in conceptual modeling to represent interaction, with the understanding that the ontologically real interaction occurs by mutual properties and therefore requires association classes.

7. INTERPRETATION MAPPING (2ND ITERATION)

Message passing is one of the core concepts of the object-oriented approach. It is the mechanism by which object interaction is realized. Messages can be interpreted in two ways, depending on the ontological status we ascribe to them:

- Messages are not things in the world. They are abstract concepts that serve as descriptions, illustrations, abstractions or representations of interaction (Wand, 1989).
- Messages are substantive things in the world. They are ontologically real.

There are two arguments against the second interpretation (Evermann, 2005). First, the message passing mechanism for interaction has previously been examined with respect to Bunge's ontology and found to be an unsuitable construct or mechanism for describing real world business domains (Parsons & Wand, 1991, 1997; Wand & Weber, 1993). Consider the following examples:

- The machine sends a message to the machined item to move itself to a new location.

- The general ledger sends a message to an office desk to depreciate its value.
- A truck sends a message to the crate to load itself onto the loading dock.

While acceptable in software specifications, such messages are not likely to be observed between these things in the real world. Clearly, a machine does not send messages to machined items to move them. Instead, an operator moves the items to and from the machine.

Second, if messages did represent real things in the world, they should be represented as objects (see Table 2). Instead of two objects interacting directly, one object would have to interact with a message object, which in turn would need to interact with the second object. This would lead to an infinite regress. Based on these two reasons, we interpret messages as abstract expressions of interaction, not as things. Consequently, they are mapped to the ontological concept of interaction, not to things.

In UML, messages are associated with value specifications (their arguments). Specifying message arguments implies that interaction occurs through changes to the value of properties represented by the message parameters. However, message arguments do not refer to attributes of either the sending or receiving object, and are therefore not interpreted as (mutual) properties.

To summarize, messages and their arguments do not have a direct ontological interpretation, but express interaction. In turn, Sect. 6 proposed that interpretation should be expressed using association class attributes.

CASE STUDY

A case study was conducted to examine the feasibility of the proposed modeling rules in practical situations. The organization under study was a large North American university. The project under study was the provision of an opportunity for prospective students to assess their likelihood of admittance[3]. This project was chosen as the basis for the case study for two reasons. (1) The main stakeholders and informants of the analysis were still available for interviews. Their involvement with the project and the analysis was recent so that rich data could still be gathered. (2) The project team had used UML for an initial model of the organizational domain. UML class diagrams were used specifically for understanding the organizational domain. The project leader confirmed there was no intention to use them for later software design and all coding would be done independent of any generated UML model. It was hoped that additional insight could be gained by comparing the project team's UML model with that developed as part of this case study. When this case study was begun, the project was almost at the beginning of the implementation stage. Figure 3 shows the class diagram developed by the project team.

As part of the case study, an independent business analysis was undertaken by the first author in order to model the domain of student admissions and assessment. This served two purposes: (1) It tested the applicability of the proposed modeling rules and (2) produced an alternative model with ontological semantics, which could be compared to the original one created by the project team. Interviews were conducted with stakeholders and informants who contributed to the project. All interviews were conducted on-site using open-ended questions. The following interviews were conducted for purposes of domain analysis and model creation:

- Approx 1-hour interview with director, student systems, IT services
- Approx 1.5-hour interview with a high school student recruiter
- Approx 2-hour interview with an admissions officer
- 3 approx 1-hour interviews with three first year university students

Figure 3. UML class diagram developed by project team

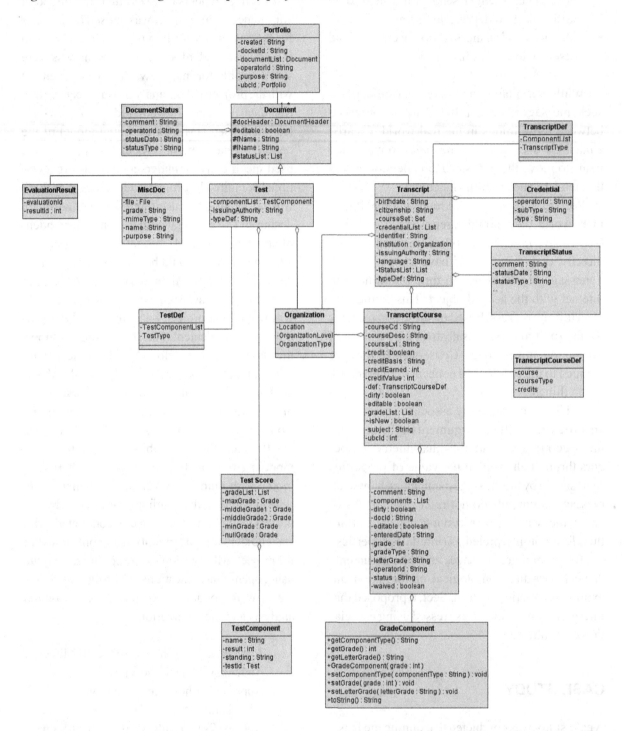

- 3 approx 1 hour interviews with lead analyst of the project

In addition, access was provided to all project
documentation, mainly requirements documents
generated from a prior business process reengi-

neering project. Moreover, frequent email contact was maintained with the lead analyst of the project for clarification and discussion of details. For purposes of evaluating and comparing the independently generated model, more interviews were conducted:

- Approx. 2-hour interview with the project leader
- Approx. 2-hour interview with the lead developer

For preparation for these interviews, the entire set of independently created diagrams was provided two weeks prior to the interview with a request to carefully examine these for correctness, usefulness, usability and to compare these to the project's own UML model. The interviewees were made aware of these aims before the interviews commenced.

The process of analyzing the domain and modeling it according to the proposed ontological semantics and rules showed that all produced diagrams were valid UML models, and adhered to all UML syntactic rules. The models were neither trivial nor overly complex. Hence, use of the rules was found to be at least feasible in this practical setting. The independently generated model consisted of the following diagrams:

- 20 class diagrams showing 35 classes and 14 association classes,
- 8 sequence diagrams showing 37 messages, representing interactions that occur through changes to the attributes of the 14 association classes,
- 2 state charts showing 7 states and sub-states.

An excerpt of the class model is shown in Figure 5 below. In the model, application is not a thing (it is not represented as a class, but as an association class). Its attributes reflect mutual properties, the result of an interaction between the university and the applicant. Either the applicant or the university can modify these mutual properties, which would be further interaction between university and the applicant. Similarly, acknowledgement is not a thing (it is not represented as a class, but as an association class). Its attributes reflect mutual properties, the results of the application event/activity and can be changed by either the university or the applicant. Such changes are interactions. Note further that while the domain describes student admissions, there is no admission object. Instead, in the state chart in Figure 4, "accepted" is a state that the university can have with respect to a student. One may model acceptance as a state transition to this state, i.e. a change in the university object.

The process of business analysis and modeling showed that at various stages in the process the rules and proposed semantics led the modeler to include information in the model that was not necessary for building software, but that was important to domain understanding.

With respect to action and interaction, the general absence of detailed state charts in the independent business re-analysis indicated mostly *qualitative* interactions (e.g. a student enrolling, a student being admitted, etc.). This might not be surprising, as non-technical, human organizational systems appear to generally involve more qualitative than quantitative change.

When quantitative change was modeled (e.g. as a transition between the states "Not Admissible", "Conditionally Admitted", and "Unconditionally Admitted" based on revisions to the required grades), application of the rules led to a fundamental insight into the domain. Instead of assigning states such as "on hold", "pending", "admitted", etc. to the student, the rules led us to assign such states to the university (Figure 4). The student's state cannot change without interaction, and changes to admission criteria by the university do not affect the student *per se*, but only the student's admissibility with respect to the university. Hence, it was concluded that

Figure 4. Example state chart diagram from the case study

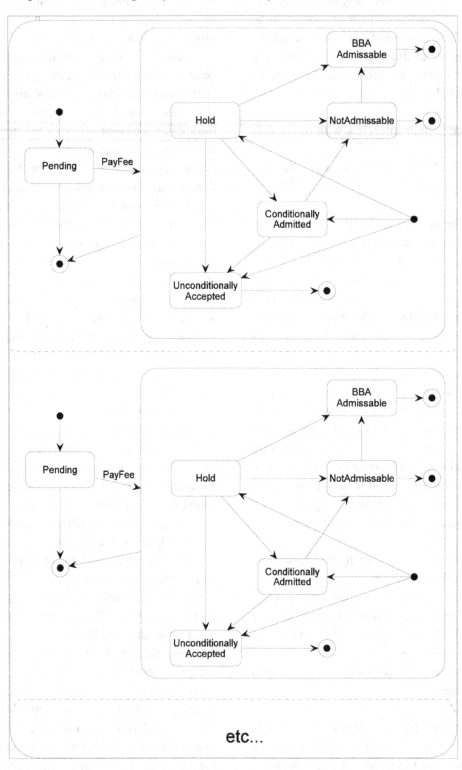

these states were states of the university, defined using mutual properties of the university and the student. Consequently, the university possesses an independent sub-state machine for each student. This observation confirms the notion that in the real world it is the university that can change the state of the students (i.e. those aspects of state related to the university), and it is the university that holds the state information. Thus, modeling the admission domain with the view that admission information is part of the university state leads to a more realistic model. However, this may not be intuitively obvious to software designers or programmers.

The initial models created by the project team did not provide any operations. Attributes were assumed to be provided with accessor operations. Either approach hides the semantics of the changes inside any behavior implementations. Hence, this information might not be „visible" for the domain understanding and conceptual modeling process, and might be implicitly assumed by the software designer.

The newly developed models included operations for all object classes, developed based on the requirements to express qualitative and quantitative change. The former was derived from the different sub-classes that students can be in, the latter as expressed in state charts. In this way, the

capabilities of an object of a given class become explicit and clear. Moreover, as these operations are related to external stimuli, modeled as messages in the sequence diagrams (e.g. Figure 6), the ordering of the changes expressed by methods can be deduced. For example (Figures 5 & 6), it is clear that an In-Province Student (students refer to high-school, rather than university students in this domain) can become an applicant. The university can then process the application of the applicant and the Ministry of Education can administer exams for the In-Province Student. This information was lacking in the model developed by the project team. Explicating it in the conceptual model improved understanding and allowed critique and assessment of the correctness of the information about the application domain.

Subsequent discussion with two project team members, the project lead (LF) and the lead developer (CH) of the project, were undertaken to corroborate and confirm these observations. Both suggested that the newly developed models indeed included more information about the domain under study. Both team members commented on the fact that the original model contained many hidden and implicit assumptions:

Figure 5. Excerpt of the case study class diagram

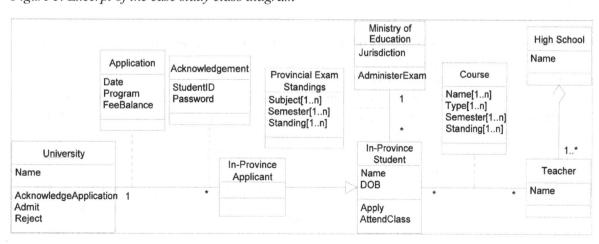

Figure 6. Excerpt of the case study sequence diagram

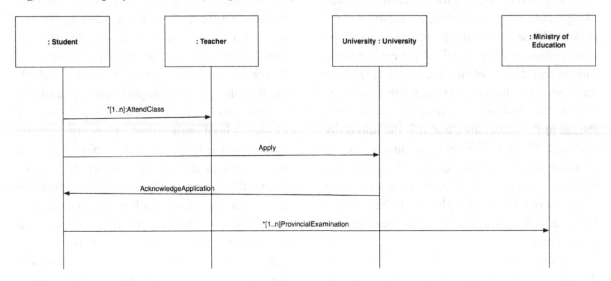

"We relied a lot on assumptions that were never written down in the model... yours is more comprehensive." (CH - lead developer)

"Ours [models] have all sorts of stuff around that is assumed but not modeled" (LF - project lead)

This may be in part due to the additional information included in the model. Note that this is contextual information, i.e. information about aspects of the domain that would not be reflected in the design of the software. As such, this information would be useful in allowing team members and stakeholders to discover *why* the design for the information system is defined one way or another, even though the information does not itself constitute or directly affect the software design.

The second important purpose for a conceptual model besides the representation of a real world domain is the starting point for software design. The alternative model was seen as appropriate for this purpose:

"I don't see any reason why you couldn't just take these [the models] and run with them." (CH)

During the discussion with the project lead, it also became clear that the use of UML without any guidelines was a substantial challenge in the project. Some analysts were aware of the subtle differences between possible interpretation and the difficulties associated with them:

"It's normally difficult to model a course object, because it is a relationship... What do you mean by a course? The curriculum, the interaction, the grade?" (LF)

Another interesting finding is that the extensive use of sequence diagrams and modeling of interactions, which is a central aspect of the proposed ontological semantics and rules, was viewed as something that should be included more often in projects but is not done.

"They don't get done as official project documents. When developers meet, two thirds of them will use in-official sequence diagrams... That makes things much clearer." (CH)

This observation suggests that the interaction-centered perspective enforced by the proposed guidelines can make a positive contribution to understanding. Interactions are not officially documented, yet interaction diagrams appear as unofficial tools. This seems to indicate that explicit modeling of interactions, as prescribed by the proposed rules, can help with understanding of the model and the domain. This demonstrates the importance of interactions in analyzing a real-world domain.

When the modeling rules were revealed at the end of the case study, the project lead and lead developer agreed that modeling rules were necessary and helpful, both for guiding the modeling process and for ensuring model quality and consistency:

"Such rules would have helped in our groups. The rules would tell whether a model is good and can help answer some questions. They seemed like a lot of valid questions to ask." (CH)

"Rules can force the modelers to think deeper about what they're modeling" (LF)

In summary, the case study supported the use of the proposed rules and confirmed their potential usefulness in understanding the domain and communicating that understanding through conceptual models.

9. DISCUSSION

The objective of this work was to extend the use of object-oriented languages from software design to conceptual modeling of an application domain. This required that domain semantics be assigned to language constructs, which was done by defining mappings between language constructs and ontological concepts (Table 4). The paper began by examining the central ontological concepts related to change and interaction and mapped them to object-oriented constructs. The ontological elements used include states, state transitions and lawful transformations. With this representation mapping in mind, object-oriented

constructs such as sub-states, activity states and partitions were examined. We then re-examined ontological interaction and discussed the object-oriented concept of message passing.

Table 4 shows that most of the basic ontological concepts can be assigned an object-oriented equivalent. This mapping is either a one-to-one relation by definition or has been made so by our proposed modeling rules. This indicates that object-oriented languages can be used to model application domains.

Based on the proposed mappings, the paper explored the consequences of transferring ontological assumptions to the language, resulting in a set of rules. These rules are applicable to object-oriented languages when they are used for conceptual modeling. However, they may not be applicable to, nor are they intended for, using object-oriented languages for software design. Yet, the rules do not contradict existing rules for using object constructs for software design.

These results extend well-known and widely used object-oriented languages into the domain of business analysis and conceptual modeling. The use of the same language for both domain modeling and software design can bridge the gap between system analysis and software design, often called

Table 4. Summary of interpretations related to behavior and interaction

Ontological Concept	Object-Oriented Construct	Remarks
State	State	Connection with attributes of objects made.
State	Sub-state	
State	Action State	Action states are composite states.
Transition	Transition	
Transition	Operation	
Lawful Transformation	Method	
Interaction	Message	Not a substantial thing.

"impedance mismatch" (Cilia et al., 2003; Kolp et al., 2002; Roe, 2003; Rozen & Shasha, 1989). Traditionally, the use of different languages required either a translation of the conceptual model to the software design model, or a relatively independent development of the software model based on the designer's understanding of the problem. Using the same language eliminates the translation step (Evermann & Wand, 2005a). Thus, it can eliminate a possible source of errors, inadvertent alterations, omissions, etc. Figure 7 shows the traditional process. The domain is represented in a domain model, using a domain modeling language (1). This is then translated, a potentially error-prone step, to a software model in different language (2), which is then transformed to software (3).

Figure 8 shows software development without translating between modeling languages. The modeling language elements are interpreted with respect to the domain (1) and used to represent the domain using a common modeling language (2). Then, the semantics of the modeling language are assumed with respect to software (3) and the same model is interpreted as a software design model (4).

Domain analysts as well as software developers can use the same familiar language to communicate not only amongst themselves but also between the two groups, reducing the potential for misunderstandings and misinterpretation of diagrams.

Additionally, the use of the modeling rules leads to further benefits. Application of ontological modeling rules have been shown to reduce the variability in conceptual models (Hadar & Soffer, 2006). A reduction in the range of possible models of a domain allows easier and more effective stakeholder communication and can improve the consensus of stakeholders on how to describe the domain. It can also promote convergence of model interpretations, thus helping to ensure that stakeholders share the same problem and domain understanding.

Figure 7. Traditional process using model translations, from (Evermann & Wand, 2005a)

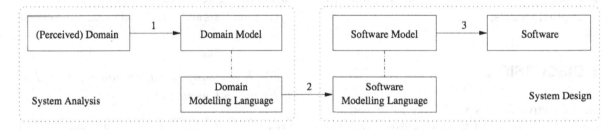

Figure 8. Process without model translation, using common modeling language, from (Evermann & Wand, 2005a)

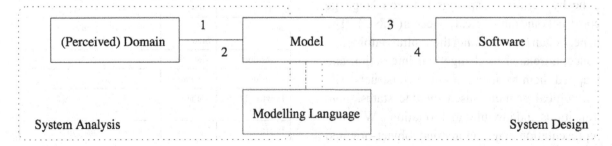

10. CONCLUSION

The research results were tested on a case study that demonstrated the feasibility and applicability of the proposed semantics and modeling rules for medium size projects. The resulting models were found to be helpful and the modeling rules useful in the construction of the domain model.

Finally, we note that the results depend on the ontological model assumed. Thus, their validity can only be demonstrated by empirical methods. Such methods would include in particular, controlled experiments and realistic case studies. While experiments can test the usability of the rules and clarity of the resulting models (Evermann & Wand, 2006), case studies are required to examine the applicability and usefulness of the method.

REFERENCES

Angeles, P. (1981). *Dictionary of philosophy.* New York: Harper Perennial.

Bodart, F., Patel, A., Sim, M., & Weber, R. (2001). Should optional properties be used in conceptual modelling? A theory and three empirical tests. *Information Systems Research, 12*(4). doi:10.1287/isre.12.4.384.9702

Boland, R. (1985). Phenomenology: A preferred approach to research in information systems. In Mumford, E., Hirschheim, R., Fitzgerald, G., & Wood-Harper, T. (Eds.), *Research methods in information systems.* Elsevier.

Booch, G. (1994). *Object oriented analysis and design with applications.* Redwood City, CA: Benjamin/Cummings.

Bunge, M. A. (1977). *Ontology i: The furniture of the world (Vol. 3).* Dordrecht, Holland: D. Reidel Publishing Company.

Bunge, M. A. (1979). *Ontology ii: A world of systems* (Vol. 4). Dordrecht, Hallond: D. Reidel Publishing Company.

Chalmers, M. (2004). Hermeneutics, information, and representation. *European Journal of Information Systems, 13,* 210–220. doi:10.1057/palgrave.ejis.3000504

Cilia, M., Haupt, M., Mezini, M., & Buchmann, A. (2003). *The convergence of aop and active databases: Towards reactive middleware.* Paper presented at the International Conference on Generative Programming and Component Engineering GPCE.

Coad, P., & Yourdon, E. (1990). *Object-oriented analysis.* Englewood Cliffs, NJ: Yourdon Press.

Coad, P., & Yourdon, E. (1991). *Object-oriented design.* Englewood Cliffs, New Jersey: Prentice-Hall, Inc.

Cockroft, S., & Rowles, S. (2003). *Ontological evaluation of health models: Some early findings.* Paper presented at the 7th Pacific Asia Conference on Information Systems PACIS, Adelaide, Australia.

Dobing, B., & Parsons, J. (2006). How the UML is used. *Commmunications of the ACM, 49*(5).

Dobing, B., & Parsons, J. (2008). Dimensions of UML diagram use: A survey of practitioners. *Journal of Database Management, 19*(1). doi:10.4018/jdm.2008010101

Dussart, A., Aubert, B. A., & Patry, M. (2004). An evaluation of inter-organizational workflow modeling formalisms. *Journal of Database Management, 15*(2), 74–104. doi:10.4018/jdm.2004040104

Evermann, J. (2005). *The association construct in conceptual modeling - an analysis using the bunge ontological model.* Paper presented at the 17th International Conference on Advanced Information Systems Engineering, Porto, Portugal.

Evermann, J., & Wand, Y. (2005a). Ontological semantics and formal syntax. *IEEE Transactions on Software Engineering, 31*(1), 21–37. doi:10.1109/TSE.2005.15

Evermann, J., & Wand, Y. (2005b). Ontology-based object-oriented business modelling: Fundamental concepts. *Requirements Engineering, 10*(2), 146–160. doi:10.1007/s00766-004-0208-2

Evermann, J., & Wand, Y. (2006). Ontological modelling rules for UML: An empirical assessment. *Journal of Computer Information Systems, 47*(1).

Gadamer, H.-G. (1976). *Philosophical hermeneutics*. University of California Press.

Gemino, A. (1999). *Empirical comparisons of systems analysis modeling techniques*. Unpublished PhD Thesis, The University of British Columbia, Vancouver, BC.

Green, P., & Rosemann, M. (2000). Ontological analysis of integrated process modelling. *Information Systems, 25*(2). doi:10.1016/S0306-4379(00)00010-7

Gruninger, M., & Lee, J. (2002). Ontology applications and design. *Commmunications of the ACM, 45*(2).

Guarino, N., & Welty, C. (2002). Evaluating ontological decisions with ontoclean. *Communications of the ACM, 45*(2), 61–65. doi:10.1145/503124.503150

Hadar, I., & Soffer, P. (2006). Variations in conceptual modeling: Classification and ontological analysis. *Journal of the AIS, 7*(8).

Jacobson, I. (1992). *Object-oriented software engineering: A use case driven approach*. Wokingham, MA: Addison-Wesley.

Kolp, M., Giorgini, P., & Mylopoulos, J. (2002). *Information systems development through social strcutures*. Paper presented at the International Conference on Software Engineering and Knowledge Engineering SEKE.

Kuhn, T. (1996). *The structure of scientific revolutions*. Chicago, IL: The University of Chicago Press.

Mackworth, A. K. (1977). Consistency in networks of relations. *Artificial Intelligence*, 99–118. doi:10.1016/0004-3702(77)90007-8

Myers, M. (1995). Dialectical hermeneutics: A theoretical framework for the implementation of information systems. *Information Systems Journal, 5*, 51–70. doi:10.1111/j.1365-2575.1995.tb00089.x

Mylopoulos, J. (1992). Conceptual modeling and telos. In Locoupoulos, P., & Zicari, R. (Eds.), *Conceptual modeling, databases, and cases*. New York, NY: John Wiley & Sons, Inc.

Noy, N. F., & Hafner, C. D. (1997). The state of the art in ontology design: A survey and compartive review. *AI Magazine, 18*(3), 53–74.

OMG. (2005). *Unified modeling language: Superstructure, version 2.0 (No. formal/05-07-04)*. The Object Management Group.

Opdahl, A., & Henderson-Sellers, B. (2001). Grounding the oml meta-model in ontology. *Journal of Systems and Software, 57*(2), 119–143. doi:10.1016/S0164-1212(00)00123-0

Opdahl, A., & Henderson-Sellers, B. (2002). Ontological evaluation of the UML using the bunge-wand-weber model. *Software and Systems Modeling, 1*(1), 43–67.

Opdahl, A., Henderson-Sellers, B., & Barbier, F. (1999). An ontological evaluation of the oml metamodel. In Falkenberg, E., & Lyytinen, K. (Eds.), *Information system concepts: An integrated discipline emerging*. IFIP/Kluwer.

Parsons, J., & Wand, Y. (1991). *The object paradigm - two for the price of one?* Paper presented at the Workshop on Information Technology and Systems WITS.

Parsons, J., & Wand, Y. (1997). Using objects for systems analysis. *Communications of the ACM, 40*(12), 104–110. doi:10.1145/265563.265578

Prasad, A. (2002). The contest over meaning: Hermeneutics as an interpretive methodology for understanding texts. *Organizational Research Methods, 5*, 12–33.

Reinhartz-Berger, I., & Sturm, A. (2008). Enhancing UML models: A domain analysis approach. *Journal of Database Management, 19*(1). doi:10.4018/jdm.2008010104

Ricoeur, P. (1976). *Interpretation theory: Discourse and the surplus of meaning.* Fort Worth, TX: The Texas Christian University Press.

Roe, P. (2003). *Distributed xml objects.* Paper presented at the Joint Modular Languages Conference JMLC.

Rosemann, M., & Green, P. (2000). Integrated process modelling: An ontological analysis. *Information Systems, 25*(2), 73–87. doi:10.1016/S0306-4379(00)00010-7

Rozen, S., & Shasha, D. (1989). Using a relational systm on wall street: The good, the bad, the ugly, and the ideal. *Communications of the ACM, 32*(8), 988–993. doi:10.1145/65971.65977

Rumbaugh, J. (1991). *Object oriented modeling and design.* Englewood Cliffs, NJ: Prentice Hall.

Smith, B., & Welty, C. (2001). *Ontology: Towards a new synthesis.* Paper presented at the Second International conference on Formal Ontology and Information Systems FOIS, Qgunquit, Maine.

Smolander, K., & Rossi, M. (2008). Conflicts, compromises, and political decisions: Methodological challenges of enterprise-wide e-business architecture creation. *Journal of Database Management, 19*(1). doi:10.4018/jdm.2008010102

Soffer, P., Golany, B., Dori, D., & Wand, Y. (2001). Modelling off-the-shelf information systems requirements: An ontological approach. *Requirements Engineering, 6*(3), 183–199. doi:10.1007/PL00010359

Uschold, M., & Gruninger, M. (1996). Ontologies: Principles, methods, and applications. *The Knowledge Engineering Review, 11*(2). doi:10.1017/S0269888900007797

Van Hentenryck, P. (1989). *Consistency techniques in logic programming.* Cambridge, MA: MIT Press.

Wand, Y. (1989). A proposal for a formal model of objects. In Kim, W., & Lochovsky, F. (Eds.), *Object-oriented concepts, languages, applications and databases* (pp. 537–559). ACM Press/Addison-Wesley.

Wand, Y., Storey, V., & Weber, R. (1999). An ontological analysis of the relationship construct in conceptual modeling. *ACM Transactions on Database Systems, 24*(4), 494–528. doi:10.1145/331983.331989

Wand, Y., & Weber, R. (1989). An ontological evaluation of systems analysis and design methods. In Falkenberg, E., & Lindgreen, P. (Eds.), *Information system concepts: An in-depth analysis.* Elsevier Science Publishers, B.V.

Wand, Y., & Weber, R. (1993). On the ontological expressiveness of information systems analysis and design grammars. *Journal of Information Systems, 3*, 217–237. doi:10.1111/j.1365-2575.1993.tb00127.x

Wand, Y., & Weber, R. (1995). On the deep structure of information systems. *Information Systems Journal*, (5): 203–223. doi:10.1111/j.1365-2575.1995. tb00108.x

Weber, R., & Zhang, Y. (1996). An analytical evaluation of niam's grammar for conceptual schema diagrams. *Information Systems Journal*, *6*(2), 147–170. doi:10.1111/j.1365-2575.1996. tb00010.x

ENDNOTES

[1]   The first author was with the School of Information Management, Victoria University of Wellington, Wellington, New Zealand for the duration of this research.

[2]   The terminology changed in UML 2.0. Here, operations are associated with behavior. Opaque behavior is a special class of behavior and represents what was called a method in UML 1.5.

[3]   Bunge's ontology is applicable to this domain comprising a university, high schools and other composite objects. According to Bunge (1977), certain things are composed of other things (composite things, pg. 114, Definition 3.4). Furthermore, if the parts of things interact, the composite thing is known as a system (Bunge, 1979, pg. 6, definition 1.1). Moreover, Bunge (1979) expounds a hierarchy of systems (ontological levels) that includes psychological and social/technical systems. For example, a university department is neither a simple (basic) thing, nor a mere composite, but a system with interacting ("connected") parts. The BWW ontology has been applied to a diverse range of domains, such as enterprise systems, workflows and business processes, etc., showing that it is applicable to organizational and social phenomena.

This work was previously published in the Journal of Database Management (JDM) 20(1), edited by Keng Siau, pp. 48-77, copyright 2009 by IGI Publishing (an imprint of IGI Global).

Section 2

Chapter 4
General Strategy for Querying Web Sources in a Data Federation Environment

Aykut Firat
Northeastern University, USA

Lynn Wu
Massachusetts Institute of Technology, USA

Stuart Madnick
Massachusetts Institute of Technology, USA

ABSTRACT

Modern database management systems are supporting the inclusion and querying of non-relational sources within a data federation environment via wrappers. Wrapper development for Web sources, however, is a convolution of code with extraction and query planning knowledge and becomes a daunting task. We use IBM DB2 federation engine to demonstrate the challenges of incorporating web sources into a data federation. We, then, present a practical and general strategy for the inclusion and querying of web sources without requiring any changes in the underlying data federation technology. This strategy separates the code and knowledge in wrapper development by introducing a general-purpose capabilities-aware mini query-planner and a data extraction engine. As a result, Web sources can be included in a data federation system faster, and maintained easier.

INTRODUCTION

Federated databases offer information integration on demand in dynamic environments, where data warehousing approaches are not feasible (Sheth and Larson 1990, Geer 2003). In modern relational database management systems, even non-relational sources can be included in a data federation via "wrappers" so that they can be queried as if they are part of a single large database (Somani, Choy, & Kleewein 2002; Thiran, Hainaut, Houben, & Benslimane 2006). Wrappers are mechanisms by which the federated server interacts with non-relational data sources by performing operations

DOI: 10.4018/978-1-60960-521-6.ch004

such as connecting to a data source and retrieving data from it iteratively.

Retrieving data from web sources, however, is complicated because data is semi-structured and web sources may have requirements (e.g. they may require forms to be filled before returning data); thus general-purpose wrappers for arbitrary web pages are not provided in data federation systems. Instead the user needs to implement a custom wrapper for each web source by coding data extraction patterns and parts of the federated query planning protocol in a low-level programming language such as C. This convolution of code with the data extraction and planning knowledge turns wrapper development into a daunting task, results in code duplication, and slows down the data federation process.

Within the last decade or so, many research projects (Papakonstantinou, Gupta, & Haas 1998; Levy, Rajaraman, & Ordille 1996; Li, & Chang 2000; Zadorozhny, Bright, Vidal, Raschid, & Urhan 2002; Li 2003; Pentaris, & Ioannidis 2006) offered algorithmic solutions to "query planning with source restrictions". The goal of these studies was to offer an expressive language to specify source restrictions, and let the federated query planner come up with an optimal plan using this knowledge. These approaches do not need any cooperation from the individual data sources other than knowing about their limitations. Had they found their way into commercial systems, they would eliminate part of the code and knowledge convolution problem: the wrapper developer would only need to code the data extraction knowledge and not worry about the query planning aspects. Yet the separation of code and knowledge would still not be satisfactorily achieved in non-cooperative federated query planners. For this study, we have chosen to work with IBM DB2's cooperative federated query planner, which poses more challenges than the non-cooperative ones. Our focus is on improving the usability and maintenance aspects of the wrapper development process without requiring

any changes in its underlying data federation technology. We do not offer yet another proposal to rewrite a state of the art distributed query planner (Kossmann 2000), or create an independent infrastructure for querying Internet data sources (Braumandl et al. 2001, Suciu 2002), but provide a non-intrusive approach that works with what is available today with minimal effort.

We have tested our prototype implementation with numerous web sites. A moderate user with no programming experience can include a typical web site into a data federation in less than an hour. The process often takes much longer when the existing procedural coding approach is used by an experienced programmer. Furthermore, explaining, learning and tutoring wrapper development become much easier, as the task changes from writing and debugging a *program* to specifying and debugging *knowledge*.

In the rest of this paper, we start with a motivational example that illustrates the need for data federation involving web sources. We then provide some background on data federation with non-relational data sources and describe the current architectural difficulties of incorporating a web source. Next, we describe our approach to wrapper development, and the algorithms used to perform planning and optimization for web sources with capability restrictions. We end with an overview of related work and future research issues.

MOTIVATIONAL EXAMPLE

Consider, first, finding the *military expenditure per capita* of countries in the world using the CIA world fact book web site. This information is scattered inside the world fact book (see Figure 1), and first needs to be located and extracted. By using the web wrapper, Cameleon# (Firat, Madnick, Yahaya, Kuan., & Bressan 2005; Firat, Madnick, & Siegel 2000) and its accompanied visual helper, Cameleon# Studio, we can wrap the CIA world fact book site using simple regular

Figure 1. Available data in CIA World Fact Book site

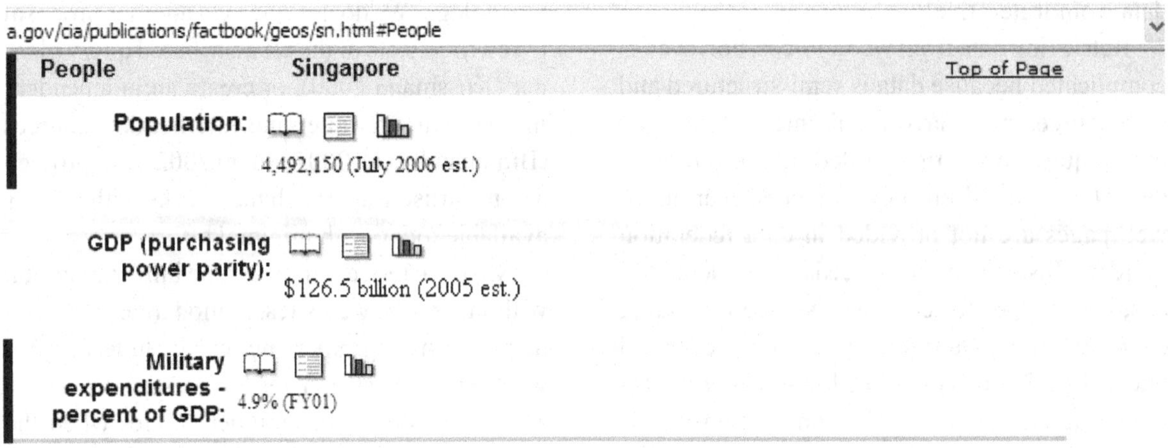

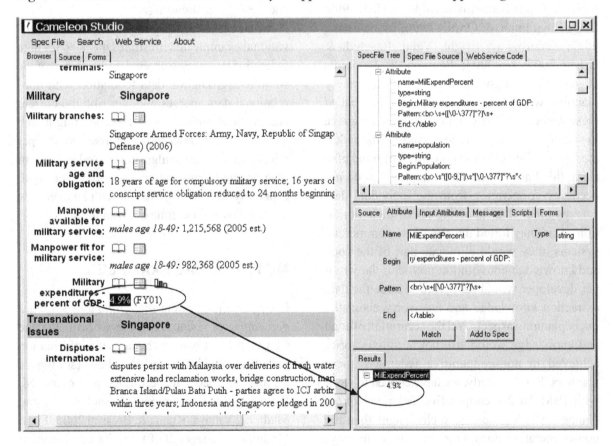

Figure 2. CIA World Fact Book site is visually wrapped with Cameleon# Wrapper Engine

Figure 3. Simple SQL Query against the wrapped CIA World Fact Book

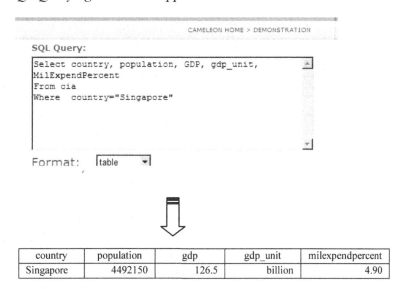

country	population	gdp	gdp_unit	milexpendpercent
Singapore	4492150	126.5	billion	4.90

expressions and treat it as a very simple relational table as illustrated in Figures 2 and 3.

The Cameleon# wrapper engine's main functionality is, however, extraction and thus is only able to answer SQL queries involving a single source, with required inputs bound to a single set of values at a time. For that reason, we decided to use the powerful query planning, optimizing and execution capabilities of a commercial data federation engine to handle more complex query situations. Using the extended architecture to be described later on, we define a nickname for our web source in DB2 as shown below:

```
CREATE NICKNAME CIA (
country char(20),
population dec(10,1),
GDP dec(10, 2),
GDP_unit char(20),
MilExpendPercent dec(9,4) for server
Cameleon#_server
options(SERVER_NAME 'http://inter-
change.mit.edu/Cameleon_sharp/cam-
serv.aspx?',
PREDICATES 'country')
```

The options in the above description indicate the location of Cameleon# information extraction server; and the required input column *country*. We are then able to treat the CIA Fact book like a relational table and issue the following query using DB2:

```
Q1: SELECT country, population, GDP,
gdp_unit, MilExpendPercent
    FROM cia
    WHERE country IN
("Singapore", "Israel", "United
States", "United Kingdom", "Malay-
sia")(see Table 1)
```

Since we want to calculate the *military expenditure per capita*, we need to perform the appropriate calculation with a mathematical expression. In addition, we must perform unit conversions (e.g., adjust for the fact that some GDP values are in billions and some in trillions) with the auxiliary database table scalefactor: (see Table 2)

This is achieved by joining the non-relational CIA web source with the relational scalefactor table using the following query:

Table 1.

COUNTRY	POPULATION	GDP	GDP_UNIT	MILEXPENDPERCENT
Singapore	4492150	126.5	billion	4.90
Israel	6352117	156.9	billion	7.70
United States	298444215	12.31	trillion	4.06
United Kingdom	60609153	1.81	trillion	2.40
Malaysia	24385858	287	billion	2.03

```
Q2: SELECT country, (MilExpendPercent
* GDP * scalefactor.scale / popula-
tion)
AS MilExpPerCapita
    FROM cia, scalefactor
    WHERE scalefactor.text=cia.gdp_
unit AND country IN
("Singapore", "Israel", "United
States", "United Kingdom", "Malay-
sia") (see Table 3)
```

Finally, we would like to obtain the *military expenditure per soldier* by creating another NICK-NAME for a Wikipedia web source that has the sizes of armed forces and formulating a federated query joining multiple web sources, as shown in Figure 4.

Table 2.

TEXT	SCALE
Billion	1000000000
Trillion	1000000000000

Table 3.

COUNTRY	MilExpPerCapita
Singapore	1379.85
Israel	1901.93
United States	1674.64
United Kingdom	716.72
Malaysia	238.91

As this simple example shows, querying web sources using a data federation offers many operational benefits. One can take advantage of the relational database technology in processing semi-structured web data. For example, web sources can be joined with each other and with other sources, calculations and set operations can be performed, and queries can be optimized. Currently, however, even setting up this motivational example is extremely difficult, if not impossible using one of the data federation engines. The most direct solution offered by DB2 requires coding a custom wrapper for each web-source, but even then those web sources cannot be joined with each other on the required input attributes (DB2 Information Center 2006).

We designed and implemented a new architecture that drastically accelerates the inclusion and querying of web sources in a data federation. The motivational example, for instance, can be set up in less than an hour without any low-level programming. Users only need to locate and specify the information they want to use on the web with Cameleon# Studio, a point and click helper tool, and define the web sources with data definition statements similar to classical "CREATE TABLE" statements. Before explaining the details of our extended architecture, we provide background on the typical operation of data federation systems by using DB2 and its Request-Reply-Compensate protocol as an example.

Figure 4. Available data in Wikipedia

List of countries by size of arme

From Wikipedia, the free encyclopedia

This **list of countries by size of armed forces** displays n and aircrafts. This list is indicative only, as strict comparisc forces might include administative or paramilitary functions the below figures

Rank ⊠	⊠	Country ⊠	Active troops ('000s) ⊠	Reserve troops ('000s) ⊠
1		People's Republic of China **	2255	0800
2		United States **	1426	0858
3		India **	1325	1155
4		North Korea **	1106	4700
5		Russia **	1037	2400
6		South Korea	0687	4500
7		Pakistan **	0619	0528
8		Iran	0545	0350
9		Turkey	0514	0378
10		Vietnam	0484	3000
11		Egypt	0450	0254

```
CREATE NICKNAME ARMFORCES (
country char(15),
armed_forces integer)
for server Cameleon#_server
options(SERVER_NAME
'http://interchange.mit.edu/Cameleon#_sharp/camserv.aspx?',
PREDICATES 'country')
```

```
Q3: SELECT cia.country, armed_forces,
       (MilExpendPercent*GDP*scalefactor.unit)/
       (armed_forces*1000) AS milpersoldier
FROM cia, armforces, scalefactor
WHERE cia.country IN ('Singapore', 'Israel',
       'United States', 'United Kingdom') AND
       armforces.country = cia.country AND
       scalefactor.text=cia.gdp_unit
```

COUNTRY	ARMED_FORCES	MILPERSOLDIER
Singapore	60	103308.33
Israel	168	71912.50
United States	1426	350481.07
United Kingdom	190	228631.58
Malaysia	110	52964.54

QUERYING NON-RELATIONAL SOURCES IN A DATA FEDERATION

The goal of a data federation system is to allow clients to access diverse and distributed data sources, regardless of location, format, or access language, from a single interface. While data federation may have a slower access performance compared to data consolidation (as in data warehousing), it has the benefits of (i) *reduced implementation and maintenance costs*, (ii) *access to current data from the source of record*, and (iii) *combining traditional data with mixed format data* (DB2 Information Center 2006; Haas, Lin, & Roth 2002).

As shown in Figure 5, a data federation system uses wrappers to access non-relational data sources such as flat files, XML pages, and Web Services. After the user submits a query, the federated server collaborates with the wrapper for each data source to generate an optimized access plan for the query

and then evaluates it. Such a plan might call for parts of the query to be processed by the wrappers, by the federated server, or partly by the wrappers and partly by the federated server. The federated server chooses among the plans primarily on the basis of cost.

Upon receiving the *request*, the wrapper indicates which sub-pieces of the query fragment it can evaluate, and puts this information in the *reply* to the request. Request properties such as cost, cardinality and ordering properties can also be included. For a typical request, a wrapper could return zero or more reply objects. Each reply represents a different accepted fragment. By the end of query planning, the federated server will weigh all the cost estimations and determine a query execution plan incorporating some set of the accepted fragments offered up by the wrapper in response to requests. During query execution, the federated server will ask the wrapper to ex-

Figure 5. IBM DB2 data federation architecture (Adopted from DB2 Information Center, 2006)

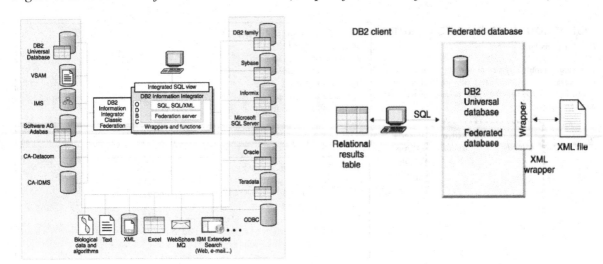

ecute these query fragments. The federated server can also *compensate* for any query fragments which have not been accepted. Examples of this include a complex predicate or sorting that is beyond the capability of the data source in question. This protocol is therefore called a *request-reply-compensate protocol* in IBM DB2.

Consider Figure 6 as an example. The query fragment (SELECT Name, Rate + Tax FROM Hotels WHERE Stars=3 AND Rate < 120) is passed to the wrapper as a request by indicating the head expressions (HXPs), table name, and

the predicates. In this case, we assume that the wrapper cannot handle the complete request as it cannot do the Rate + Tax calculation and it cannot do two predicates at a time, so replies with two separate parts, which when combined in the federated server answers the original query.

The request-reply-compensate protocol offers a generic framework allowing the federated server to communicate with non-relational data sources through a black box wrapper. Among the built in wrappers that comes with IBM DB2, there are two that are particularly relevant to querying

Figure 6. Request-reply-compensate protocol example (Adopted from DB2 Information Center, 2006)

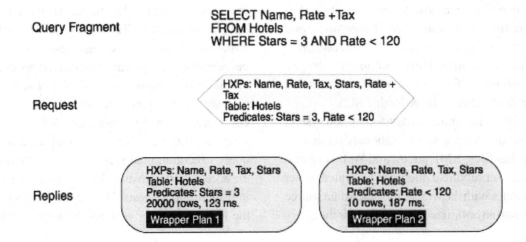

web sources: XML and Web Services wrappers. These wrappers can be used if web sources can be turned into XML format, or Web Services. Neither of these, however, satisfies our desire to include an arbitrary web source in a data federation and query them without artificial restrictions. The XML wrapper, for instance, does not have the concept of a required input attribute: the XML page should be accessible with a fixed address. Many web sources are dynamically generated based on input attributes, which precludes the use of XML wrapper as it is. The Web Services wrapper, on the other hand, has artificial query restrictions such as *"no IN or OR predicates are allowed for input columns"* (DB2 Information Center 2006). For instance, even our simplest query Q1 cannot be handled by the Web Services wrapper assuming our web source was somehow turned into a Web Service.

THREE-TIER ARCHITECTURE FOR QUERYING WEB SOURCES IN A DATA FEDERATION

The solution we offer for the inclusion and querying of web sources in a data federation involves extending the existing two-tier custom wrapper architecture into a three-tier architecture while separating the generic and custom aspects of wrapper development as shown in Figure 7. This new architecture separates code and knowledge, minimizes redundancy, and complements the central query planner when incorporating web sources in a data federation by following the wrapper development protocol specified in DB2 Information Integrator Wrapper Developer's Guide (2004).

In the first tier of our solution we have a general-purpose mini planner-wrapper responsible for planning queries involving web sources. We call it a mini-planner because web sources

Figure 7. Comparison of Architectures. The extended architecture separates data extraction and capability handling functionalities. Furthermore the primary wrapper is responsible for planning queries posed against web sources with capability restrictions

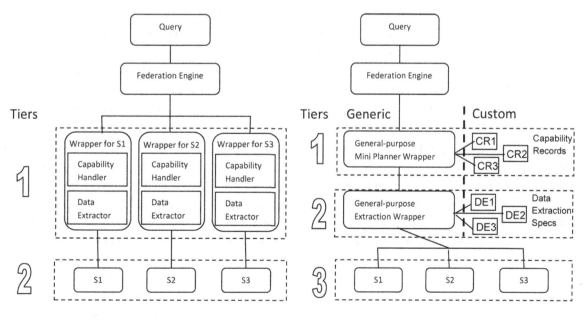

a) Existing two-tier architecture   b) Extended three-tier architecture

have characteristics that limit the query planning space; therefore we do not have to deal with the complexity of a traditional query planner. Our mini planner, in most cases, only needs to handle query planning for a single web source, leaving complex planning involving multiple sources to the federated server. The mini planner can run web source queries in parallel, and order them intelligently when they are joined, while respecting their capabilities. Web source capabilities are expressed using simple capability records, which indicate the required input attributes, and whether input attributes can be bound to more than one value at a time. For example, the capability record [b(1), f, f, f, f] for the CIA nickname means that the first attribute *country* needs to be bound with one value at a time (b(1)), and the rest of the attributes must be free (f). In general b(N) indicates that the attribute can be bound with up to N values; "f" indicates that the attribute must be free; and "?" indicates that the attribute can be either bound or free. These capability records are implemented for each source using the nickname definition, right after the predicate keyword. The second-tier is a general-purpose data extraction engine responsible for retrieving data from a Web source and presenting it in the format expected by the data federation engine. For this task, any capable general-purpose data extraction engine can be used. We used the data extraction engine, Cameleon#, which uses declarative rules based on regular expressions to extract data from web pages. Cameleon# Studio can be used to help generate the necessary specification file. An example specification file is shown in Figure 8.

The second-tier extraction wrapper accepts these specification files as input to extract data from any web source without any procedural coding. Next, we provide the details of the mini query planner for web sources with capability restrictions.

MINI QUERY PLANNER FOR WEB SOURCES

The mini query planner creates a plan that can efficiently retrieve remote data while satisfying query restrictions. Generally, a query planning engine needs to decompose the original query into component subqueries (CSQ), such that each CSQ can be answered using a single data source (Alatovic, 2001; Fynn 1997). Our mini query planning engine does not need to perform the decomposition since the federated database engine already divides the original query into CSQs, known as requests where each request can be processed by a single data source. In addition to query decomposition, a query planning engine also needs to maintain the CSQ execution order. Typically, independent CSQs are executed first, followed by dependent CSQs that can be answered using prior results. Thus, detecting the dependencies among the CSQs is crucial to successful planning. Our query planning engine uses both the federated engine and capability records to analyze CSQ dependencies. When the CSQ dependency can be determined using query semantics, our query planning engine uses the federated database engine. When a CSQ does not meet all the capability restrictions of a source, however, the query planning engine will determine if information from other parts of the query can be used to satisfy the capability restrictions. If the restrictions can be satisfied, the CSQ will be modified with the required information so that it can be answered by the native data source.

The simplest case for a query execution plan (QEP) is when all CSQs meet the capability restrictions imposed by their native data sources, and they can be executed independently and in parallel. In this case, the federated engine simply decomposes the original query into CSQs and sends them to the native sources through wrappers. After receiving all processed row sets from the native sources, the federated engine aggregates the data and returns the final result.

Figure 8. Example Specification File For the CIA Web Source

```
<?xml version="1.0" encoding="UTF-8" ?>
- <RELATION name="cia">
  - <SOURCE URI="https://www.cia.gov/cia/publications/factbook/index.html">
    - <ATTRIBUTE name="Link" type="string">
      - <BEGIN>
          <![CDATA[ <body ]]>
        </BEGIN>
      - <PATTERN>
          <![CDATA[ <option value="([^"]*)"[^>]*>#Country# ]]>
        </PATTERN>
      - <END>
          <![CDATA[ </[Bb][oO][dD][yY]> ]]>
        </END>
      </ATTRIBUTE>
    </SOURCE>
  - <SOURCE URI="https://www.cia.gov/cia/publications/factbook/#Link#">
    - <ATTRIBUTE name="MilExpendPercent" type="string">
      - <BEGIN>
          <![CDATA[ Military expenditures - percent of GDP: ]]>
        </BEGIN>
      - <PATTERN>
          <![CDATA[ <br>\s+([\0-\377]*?)\s+ ]]>
        </PATTERN>
      - <END>
          <![CDATA[ </table> ]]>
        </END>
      </ATTRIBUTE>
    - <ATTRIBUTE name="population" type="string">
      - <BEGIN>
          <![CDATA[ Population: ]]>
        </BEGIN>
      - <PATTERN>
          <![CDATA[ <br>\s*([0-9,]*)\s*[\0-\377]*?\s*< ]]>
        </PATTERN>
      - <END>
          <![CDATA[ </tr> ]]>
        </END>
      </ATTRIBUTE>
    - <ATTRIBUTE name="GDP" type="string">
      - <BEGIN>
          <![CDATA[ purchasing\s*power\s*parity ]]>
        </BEGIN>
      - <PATTERN>
          <![CDATA[ <br>\s+[$]*([,0-9\.]*)[\0-\377]*?\s*</td> ]]>
        </PATTERN>
      - <END>
          <![CDATA[ </tr> ]]>
        </END>
      </ATTRIBUTE>
    - <ATTRIBUTE name="GDP_unit" type="string">
      - <BEGIN>
          <![CDATA[ purchasing\s*power\s*parity ]]>
        </BEGIN>
      - <PATTERN>
          <![CDATA[ <br>\s+[$]*[,0-9\.]*([\0-\377]*?)\s*\( ]]>
        </PATTERN>
      - <END>
          <![CDATA[ </tr> ]]>
        </END>
      </ATTRIBUTE>
    </SOURCE>
  </RELATION>
```

Input Attribute

Output Attribute

Regular Expressions

When a CSQ cannot be executed by itself, however, it is necessary to determine if the CSQ can still be processed using results from other CSQs. Two procedures are used to determine the dependencies: the first method relies on detecting dependencies using query semantics; the second method employs the capability records to meet any unsatisfied restrictions using information from other processed CSQs. The next two sections describe in detail how the two procedures work and how they compensate for each other.

Dependencies Detected via Query Semantics

In Figure 9, we show an example dependency between CSQs that can be detected using the query semantics. In this example, the original query is decomposed into an inner-select CSQ, which can be executed independently, and an outer-select CSQ, which depends on the data returned by the inner-select CSQ. The federated engine facilitates the detection of this dependency by tagging country attribute with a type called *"unbound kind"* to signal to the wrapper that the binding values

would be available after the inner-select CSQ is executed. Once the result from the inner-select CSQ is returned, the wrapper needs to create a new set of CSQs by replacing the "unbound kind" tag in the original CSQ with the returned value(s). In this example as illustrated in Figure 9, since country names are returned from the inner-select CSQ; (e.g., Albania, Andorra, Austria, Belarus, etc.), new CSQs are formed after binding each country name to the country attribute. The wrapper then needs to send this new set of CSQs to the native data source. Once the native source processes the CSQs, the wrapper needs to assemble the results and return them to the federation engine. In this example, the wrapper sends the queries to the CIA web source, retrieves the GDP values and returns them to the federated engine.

Dependencies Implied by Capability Restrictions

Some CSQ dependencies may be not be detected via query semantics, but are implied by capability restrictions. Consider for example query Q5, which asks for the GDP and armed-force size of

Figure 9. An example query dependency that can be detected by query semantics

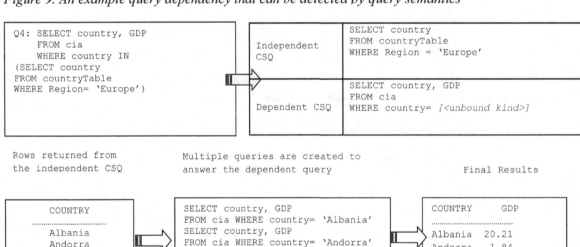

countries that are ranked in the top 10 both in terms of highest GDP and largest armed-force size. Like in the previous example, *countryTable* is a relational source that has the list of countries and their regions.

```
Q5: SELECT cia.country, armed_forc-
es, GDP
FROM countryTable,
(SELECT GDP
 FROM cia
 ORDER BY GDP DESC FETCH FIRST 10
ROWS ONLY) cia,
(SELECT armed_forces
 FROM armforces
 ORDER BY armed_forces DESC FETCH
FIRST 10 ROWS ONLY) armforces
WHERE cia.country = countryTable.
country AND
armforces.country = countryTable.
```

country

To process this query, the query planning engine needs to invoke the countryTable relation to retrieve the list of all countries, and then pass them to the cia and armed_forces relations to obtain the requested data. In order to answer this query, however, the federated engine creates the following two CSQs on web sources:

```
CSQ1: SELECT GDP
 FROM cia
CSQ2: SELECT armed_forces
 FROM armforces
```

Since none of the CSQs has unbound parameters, the federated engine assumes that they can be executed independently by using the native data sources. Both web sources, however, require that *country* must be bound before they can return any results. Thus, we cannot produce an answer

Figure 10. An example query dependency implied by capability restrictions

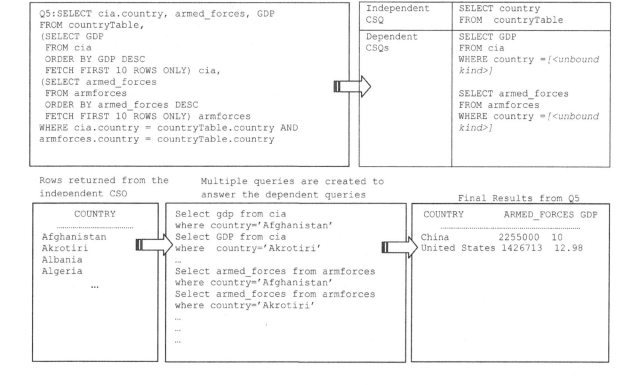

to the query by only using query semantics. If we consider the capability information, however, it is possible to process both CSQs by finding the missing information from other parts of the query. Using the join conditions "cia.country = countryTable.country" and "armforces.country = countryTable.country" we can rewrite CSQ1 and CSQ2 into CSQ3 and CSQ4 by providing the values for the country attribute from the countryTable relation:

```
CSQ3:SELECT GDP
FROM cia
WHERE country IN
(SELECT country FROM countryTable)
CSQ4:SELECT armed_forces
FROM armforces
WHERE country IN
(SELECT country FROM countryTable)
```

With this added condition, CSQ3 and CSQ4 satisfy the capability restrictions and thus can be processed by the native sources. Although CSQ3 depends on the result from countryTable, this dependency can now be resolved via query semantics with the help of the federation engine as in Figure 10.

The Query Execution Plan (QEP) algorithm, which uses capability records to process CSQs, is presented in Figure 11. The algorithm is based on finding independently executable CSQs in the query and processing them before any dependent CSQs. In most cases, the CSQs that cannot be executed independently lack at least one binding restriction. Once such a CSQ is detected, the algorithm determines if the CSQ can still be executed by searching for the missing binding from other CSQs. If the algorithm finds the missing binding, it is incorporated into the CSQ so that it can be processed by the native source.

There are two non-trivial steps in this algorithm: a) determining if a CSQ can be independently executed (step 3), and b) deciding whether a CSQ can be processed using join bindings from a set of executed CSQs (step 8). The details of these two steps are illustrated in the following sections.

Determining Independently Executable CSQs

Figure 12 shows the algorithm for determining whether a CSQ is independently executable. The algorithm uses the capability restrictions to detect

Figure 11. QEP generation algorithm supporting binding query restrictions

```
Input: Single Query q
Output: Query Execution Plan (QEP)

QEP Generation Algorithm:
1.    initialize set S to an empty set
2.    for all CSQs c in S
3.        if c is independently executable
4.            add c to set S
5.            add entry 0:c to QEP
6.    repeat until no more CSQs are added to S
7.        for all CSQs c outside of S
8.            if CSQ c can be executed using bindings from CSQs in S
9.                add an entry for c to QEP including all join bindings of c
10.               add CSQ c to set S
11.   if S does not contain all CSQs in a query
12.       throw exception "query cannot be executed"
13. return QEP
```

Figure 12. Algorithm for determining whether a CSQ is independently executable

```
Independently Executable CSQ:
1. for all binding specifiers bs of c's underlying relation r
2.      for all attribute specifiers as of bs
3.         if as is of type bound and there is no binding in CSQ c for corresponding attribute
4.                  continue 1
5.              else
6.                  continue 2
7.      end for
8.      return true
9.   end for
10.  return false
```

any missing binding in the CSQ, and if they exist, the algorithm determines if these binding conditions can still be satisfied.

Determining Whether a CSQ is Executable Given a Set of Executed CSQs

The algorithm for determining whether a CSQ is executable, given a set of CSQs that have already been executed, is depicted in Fig. 13. Consider the earlier example in Figure 10 once more. Although the cia and armforces CSQs cannot be executed independently, they can still be processed by finding the missing binding through the use of join

conditions in the query. This algorithm detects this class of CSQs that are missing bindings, but can still be executed using information made available through executing other parts of the query. For the specific example of Figure 10, upon finding the attribute country to be unbound, the algorithm discovers a joint binding, countryTable. country=cia.country, that can provide the missing values to the attribute *country*. After modifying the cia CSQ with the new joint binding, the cia CSQ can be executed. Similarly, the binding for armforces CSQ is discovered from the country-Table.country=armforces.country predicate; the CSQ is modified and executed.

Figure 13. Algorithm for determining whether a CSQ is executable given a set of executed CSQs

```
Input:    set of executed CSQs S, new CSQ n
Output:   if n cannot be executed given join bindings from CSQs in S
                 returns null
               else
                         returns list of join bindings for CSQ n
CSQ Executable:
1.   for all binding specifiers bs of CSQ n
2.        initialize list of join bindings to an empty list jbl
3.        for all attribute specifiers as of bs
4.            if as is of type bound and CSQ n does not contain binding
                     for attribute matching as
5.                if there is a join binding jb from n's attribute
                              matching as to one of CSQs in S
6.                    add jb to jbl
7.                    continue 3
8.              else
9.                    continue 1
10.       return jbl
11.  return null
```

Handling Key-at-a-Time Query Restriction

Many web sources require a single key value to be provided at a time. Consider for example the query Q1 again. (Cia web source has b(1) – one binding at a time – restriction on the attribute country):

```
Q1: SELECT country, population, GDP,
gdp_unit, MilExpendPercent
    FROM cia
    WHERE country IN
("Singapore", "Israel", "United
States", "United Kingdom", "Malay-
sia")
```

In order to answer this query, the mini-planner needs to change the query into a union of four one-key-at-a-time queries, and perform the union operations locally in parallel. In general, web sources may have b(N) – N binding at a time – restriction. The short algorithm, shown in Figure 14, handles the general case by recursively rewriting the original query into subqueries. Finally, the algorithm returns the result by performing the union operator on the results of all the sub-queries.

Cost Statistics Generation

Cost statistics are especially important for federated queries (Kache, Han, Markl, Raman, & Ewen 2006). The mini planner wrapper can also return cost statistics for web sources to the federated engine to aid in query optimization. These cost statistics, as described in DB2 Information Center, are:

1. The cardinality of a nickname. This is defined as the number of rows contained in the nickname. (default 1000 rows)
2. The setup cost for a nickname. Setup cost represents the typical time, in milliseconds, that it takes a wrapper to get a query fragment ready to submit to the remote source. (default 25 milliseconds.)
3. The submission cost for a nickname. Submission cost represents the typical time, in milliseconds, that it takes a wrapper to submit a query fragment to the remote source. (default 2000 milliseconds.)
4. The advance cost for a nickname. This is the typical time, in milliseconds, that it takes to fetch a single row for the nickname. (default 50 milliseconds).

Among these cost statistics, the set up and submission cost can be easily figured out, but the cardinality and the advance cost for a nickname are not easy to calculate for dynamic web sources. We can, however, estimate the cardinality and advance cost for a nickname by keeping time statistics and cardinality information of previously executed CSQs on the same underlying relation. The estimation process can be initiated by starting with a conservative default time estimate and then improving on it using time statistics on recently executed CSQs on the same underlying relation.

Figure 14. Algorithm to relax key-at-a-time query restrictions

```
KAT (key-at-a-time) rewriting algorithm:
1. for every key-at-a-time-restricted attribute in CSQ
2. if attribute is bound to more values than allowed by query restriction then
3. rewrite the CSQ as union of 2 KAT queries:
4. first KAT query with the attribute bound to the maximum allowed number of
       values
5.    second KAT query with the attribute bound to the remaining values
6.    call KAT algorithm recursively on both KAT queries
```

RELATED WORK AND DISCUSSION

Our general strategy for querying web sources in a data federation system fundamentally differs from other studies (see Florescu, Levy and Mendelzon 1998 for a review) in the same area for two reasons:

1. We clearly separate knowledge from code in wrapper development, and improve wrapper development speed and ease of maintenance.
2. We do not assume that we have the liberty to recode the existing federated database systems; thus we focus on improving the process of including and querying web sources in cooperation with the existing data federation planners.

Majority of the studies in the area are concerned with query planning under source capability restrictions, and we find two types of approaches in the existing literature: 1) the black-box approach of pushing the capability handling to the wrapper level, and 2) the central planning approach by using a complex declarative language to describe capability restrictions. The IBM DB2 follows the first approach: handling capability restrictions is pushed down to the wrapper layer and it relies on Request-Reply-Compensate protocol to communicate with the wrappers. Although this is a generic framework to incorporate many different sources, coding a different wrapper every time for a website with different capability restrictions can be extremely wasteful and error-prone, since most of the code between these wrappers will be common.

There are projects that follow the second approach by describing capability restrictions with a declarative yet complex language. Examples of research projects, which more or less take this route, are Garlic Project at IBM (Roth & Schwarz 1997; Papakonstantinou, Gupta & Hass 1998, Hass, Kossman, Wimmers, & Yang 1997), TSIMMIS Project at Stanford (Chawathe, Garcia-Molina, Hammer, Ireland, Papakonstantinou, Ullman, & Widom 1994), Information Manifold (Levy, Rajaraman, & Ordille 1996), and DISCO (Tomasic, Raschid, & Valduriez 1998). While this approach is more generic, it has not found its way into existing data federation technologies – perhaps due to its complexity.

The approach we take is a hybrid of these two. As in the black box approach, we push the capability handling to the wrapper level, and like the central planning approach we use declarative capability records. Yet these capability records are designed only to handle web source access limitations and are not as general as the approaches found in the literature. This restriction simplifies the development of the query planner. Furthermore, our mini query planner creates query plans in cooperation with the central federated query planner, thus differs from the central planning approach, which does not cooperate with the individual sources.

Another major difference we present is the clear separation of extraction and planning knowledge from the code. This is summarized in Table 4. The wrapper developer only deals with the task of specifying extraction and capability knowledge, and is not involved with low level coding as in other approaches.

Table 4. Code and knowledge separation in web wrapper development

	Extraction knowledge	Planning knowledge
Cooperative Planning Approach	Embedded in code	Embedded in code
Central Planning Approach	Embedded in code	Declarative
Our approach	Declarative	Declarative

Do not Web Services Solve the Problem?

It may be mistakenly thought that the solution offered here would not be needed if the web sources were Web Services returning XML. In fact, we are able to create virtual web services from any semi-structured web source by using a version of the Cameleon# web wrapping tool. The capability restrictions, however, are still valid problems for web services, which often require input attributes before returning any results (Petropoulos, Deutsch, Papakonstantinou, & Katsis 2007). There is an extra benefit of using Web Services, as the capability restrictions could be automatically deduced from the Web Service Description Language (WSDL) document instead of declaring them in the nickname statements. All the query dependency issues for arbitrary web sources, however, equally apply to Web Services as well. In fact, the built-in IBM wrapper for Web Services prohibits the formulation of queries where dependencies create problems. Our solution is more general and can be used for Web Services without artificial restrictions.

CONCLUSION

The web is undoubtedly the largest and most diverse repository of data; unfortunately it was not designed to offer the capabilities of traditional data base management systems. Modern databases promise to include web sources in a data federation via "wrappers" so that they can be queried as if they are part of a single large database. There are still, however, significant hurdles to fulfilling this promise. With this study we introduced an improved way of dealing with web source wrappers in federated database applications. With this new general-strategy not only do we accelerate the inclusion of web sources in federated databases, but also we are able to eliminate unnecessary query restrictions. Our contribution is not only at a conceptual level, but also has been implemented using IBM's commercial database engine DB2. Most importantly, all of this has been achieved via extensions allowed by the federation engine, and without requiring any implementation changes in the existing data federation technology.

REFERENCES

Alatovic, T. (2001). *Capabilities aware, planner, optimizer, executioner for Context Interchange project.* Unpublished master's thesis, Massachusetts Institute of Technology, Cambridge, MA, USA.

Braumandl, R., Keidl, M., Kemper, A., Kossmann, D., Kreutz, A., Seltzsam, S., & Stocker, K. (2001). ObjectGlobe: Ubiquitous query processing on the Internet. *The VLDB Journal, 10*(1), 48–71.

Chawathe, S. S., Garcia-Molina, H., Hammer, J., Ireland, K., Papakonstantinou, Y., Ullman, J. D., & Widom, J. (1994). The TSIMMIS project: Integration of heterogeneous information sources. *Proceedings of the 16th Meeting of the Information Processing Society of Japan*, 7–18.

DB2 Information Center. (2006, March 14). Retrieved January, 31, 2007 from http://publib.boulder.ibm.com/infocenter/db2luw/v8//index.jsp.

DB2 Information Integrator Wrapper Developer's Guide. (2004, September 8). Retrieved January, 31, 2007 from http://publibfp.boulder.ibm.com/epubs/pdf/c1891740.pdf

Firat, A., Madnick, S., Yahaya, N., Kuan, C., & Bressan, S. (2005). Information aggregation using the Caméléon# web wrapper. *Lecture Notes in Computer Science, 3590*(1), 76–86.

Firat, A., Madnick, S., & Siegel, M. (2000). The Caméléon web wrapper engine. *In Proceedings of the VLDB2000 Workshop on Technologies for E-Services*, 1-9.

Florescu, D., Levy, A., & Mendelzon, A. (1998). Database techniques for the World-Wide Web: A Survey. *SIGMOD Record, 27*(3), 59–74.

Fynn, K. (1997). *A planner/optimizer/executioner for context mediated queries*. Unpublished master's thesis, Massachusetts Institute of Technology, Cambridge, MA, USA.

Geer, D. (2003). Federated Approach Expands Database-Access Technology. *Computer, 36*(5), 18–20. doi:10.1109/MC.2003.1198230

Haas, L. M., Kossmann, D., Wimmers, E. L., & Yang, J. (1997). Optimizing Queries Across Diverse Data Sources. In *Proceedings of the 23rd international Conference on Very Large Data Bases*. M. Jarke, M. J. Carey, K. R. Dittrich, F. H. Lochovsky, P. Loucopoulos, and M. A. Jeusfeld, Eds. Very Large Data Bases. Morgan Kaufmann Publishers, San Francisco, CA, 276-285.

Haas, L. M., Lin, E. T., & Roth, M. A. (2002). Data integration through database federation. *IBM Systems Journal, 41*(4), 578–596.

Kache, H., Han, W., Markl, V., Raman, V., & Ewen, S. (2006). POP/FED: progressive query optimization for federated queries in DB2. In *Proceedings of the 32nd international Conference on Very Large Data Bases*. U. Dayal, K. Whang, D. Lomet, G. Alonso, G. Lohman, M. Kersten, S. K. Cha, and Y. Kim, Eds. Very Large Data Bases. VLDB Endowment, 1175-1178.

Kossmann, D. (2000). The state of the art in distributed query processing. *ACM Computing Surveys, 32*(4), 422–469. doi:10.1145/371578.371598

Levy, A. Y., Rajaraman, A., & Ordille, J. J. (1996). Querying Heterogeneous Information Sources Using Source Descriptions. In *Proceedings of the 22th international Conference on Very Large Data Bases*. T. M. Vijayaraman, A. P. Buchmann, C. Mohan, and N. L. Sarda, Eds. Very Large Data Bases. Morgan Kaufmann Publishers, San Francisco, CA, 251-262.

Li, C., & Chang, E. (2000). Query Planning with Limited Source Capabilities. In *Proceedings of the 16th international Conference on Data Engineering*, ICDE, IEEE Computer Society, Washington, DC, 401.

Li, C. (2003). Computing complete answers to queries in the presence of limited access patterns. *The VLDB Journal, 12*(3), 211–227. doi:10.1007/s00778-002-0085-6

Papakonstantinou, Y., Gupta, A., & Haas, L. (1998). Capabilities-based query rewriting in mediator systems. *Distributed and Parallel Databases, 6*(1), 73–110. doi:10.1023/A:1008646830769

Pentaris, F., & Ioannidis, Y. (2006). Query optimization in distributed networks of autonomous database systems. *ACM Transactions on Database Systems, 31*(2), 537–583. doi:10.1145/1138394.1138397

Petropoulos, M., Deutsch, A., Papakonstantinou, Y., & Katsis, Y. (2007). Exporting and interactively querying web service-accessed sources: The CLIDE system. *ACM Transactions on Database Systems, 32*(4), 22. doi:10.1145/1292609.1292612

Roth, M. T., & Schwarz, P. M. (1997). Don't scrap it, wrap it! A wrapper architecture for legacy data sources. In *Proceedings of the 23rd international Conference on Very Large Data Bases*. M. Jarke, M. J. Carey, K. R. Dittrich, F. H. Lochovsky, P. Loucopoulos, and M. A. Jeusfeld, Eds. Very Large Data Bases. Morgan Kaufmann Publishers, San Francisco, CA, 266-275.

Sheth, A. P., & Larson, J. A. (1990). Federated database systems for managing distributed, heterogeneous, and autonomous databases. *ACM Computing Surveys, 22*(3), 183–236. doi:10.1145/96602.96604

Suciu, D. (2002). Distributed query evaluation on semistructured data. *ACM Transactions on Database Systems, 27*(1), 1–62. doi:10.1145/507234.507235

Somani, A., Choy, D., & Kleewein, J. C. (2002). Bringing together content and data management systems: Challenges and opportunities. *IBM Systems Journal, 41*(4), 686–696. doi:10.1147/sj.414.0686

Thiran, P., Hainaut, J., Houben, G., & Benslimane, D. (2006). Wrapper-based evolution of legacy information systems. *ACM Transactions on Software Engineering and Methodology, 15*(4), 329–359. doi:10.1145/1178625.1178626

Tomasic, A., Raschid, L., & Valduriez, P. (1998). Scaling access to heterogeneous data sources with DISCO. *IEEE Transactions on Knowledge and Data Engineering, 10*(5), 808–823. doi:10.1109/69.729736

Zadorozhny, V., Raschid, L., Vidal, M. E., Urhan, T., & Bright, L. (2002). Efficient evaluation of queries in a mediator for web sources. In *Proceedings of the 2002 ACM SIGMOD international Conference on Management of Data*. SIGMOD '02. ACM, New York, NY, 85-96.

This work was previously published in the Journal of Database Management (JDM) 20(2), edited by Keng Siau, pp. 1-18 , copyright 2009 by IGI Publishing (an imprint of IGI Global).

Chapter 5

Information Privacy:
Understanding How Firms Behave Online

Gerald Kane
Boston College, USA

Kathy Stewart Schwaig
Kennesaw State University, USA

Veda Storey
Georgia State University, USA

ABSTRACT

The acquisition and use of personal information by large corporations continues to be a leading issue in the age of virtual communication and collaboration. This research reviews and analyzes the privacy policies of large US companies to evaluate the substance and quality of their stated information practices. Six factors are identified that indicate the extent to which a firm is dependent upon consumer personal information, and therefore, more likely to develop high quality privacy statements. The study's findings provide practical and theoretical implications for information privacy issues, particularly for consumers who need to decide whether to disclose their personal identifying information to firms. The research also highlights the complexity and challenges of managing personal private information.

INTRODUCTION

Identification is ever important in the online world with identity-related crime a related, growing problem (Koops et al., 2009). Much more information is being digitized, increasing the ability of companies to use and analyze this data. People are sharing more information than ever before via social networking sites and other means, and companies are increasingly using this information to improve their ability to both relate and market to consumers. People are sharing increasingly personal types of information in niche social media communities. For instance, on an online social network called *PatientsLikeMe*, people with chronic – often terminal – diseases share their disease progress and treatments used (Kane et al, 2010). New forms of personal information are increasingly becoming available automatically with the development of new technological

DOI: 10.4018/978-1-60960-521-6.ch005

capabilities, such as location-aware computing (Xu et al., 2009).

Companies are increasingly dependent on consumer information, and the degree to which they can collect and use that information without alienating or angering the customer increases the company's ability to engage in effective customer relationships (Son and Kim 2008). In this age of e-commerce, real time enterprises, and globalization, firms collect consumer information to provide customized services, identify buying trends, and target goods and services for specific markets (Kobsa, 2007; Chellappa & Sin, 2005). Although privacy is highly valued, most people believe that absolute privacy is not attainable. Consumers make choices with respect to how much and what type of privacy they are willing to give up in exchange for outcomes that are valuable to them (Diney & Hart, 2006).

Increased globalization means that companies not only need to consider US privacy policies, but also the privacy policies of other countries. With globalization, a company can be registered in one country, hosted in another, and do business with consumers anywhere in the world (Jensen et al., 2007). In some cases, consumers and privacy advocates protest the use of personal identifying information by asserting the right of any individual to control the way companies collect, store, and use their personal information (Culnan, 1995; 2000). Stakeholders include those who have privacy interests in a system (Preibusch et al., 2007).

Although the use of individual personal information is regulated in some industries, the majority of information privacy protection is voluntary. Extending protection to consumers, however, is not without costs. First, companies promise to limit their use of consumer information in particular ways and, presumably, surrender some of the potential value of the information compared to unrestricted collection, storage, and use. Second, since privacy protection is voluntary, most companies are subject to legal repercussions *only* after they develop privacy promises. Thus,

although companies are not required to make any privacy guarantees to consumers, once companies do make such promises, they are legally bound to deliver on the promises made (Chan, et. al., 2004). Finally, the direct cost of addressing information privacy concerns is high. Writing and enforcing a privacy policy as well as implementing other privacy enhancing mechanisms are time-consuming and costly. Providing information privacy protection is a complex issue. Privacy is an important determinant in customer behavior (Castañeda & Montoro, 2007, Tang et al. 2007, Yao et al., 2007). Yet, as companies are increasingly dependent upon consumer information for customization and target marketing purposes, they seek control over such information.

A strong, consumer-oriented privacy position may mean that the direct and indirect costs of addressing privacy concerns could lead to self-imposed restrictions that limit the firm's future actions. On the other hand, a proactive stance makes the firm appear more consumer-focused in the eyes of the consumer, privacy advocates, and potential government regulators. It is, therefore, important to understand why some firms extend privacy protection to their customers as well as the extent of the privacy protection they afford. The objective of this research, then, is to address the following research question:

What factors explain a firm's willingness to develop high quality privacy policies when these protections appear to limit the firm's ability to leverage consumer information to its advantage?

Specifically, this research seeks to provide insight into the motivation for privacy policies and to assess the extent of information privacy protection provided by large corporations.

Identifying the factors that lead firms to extend privacy protection to consumers benefits both the companies and their customers. First, companies can assess their business need to provide privacy protection to consumers as a function of their dependency on consumer personal information. Second, consumers benefit by knowing the characteristics of firms that are more likely to protect their privacy. The task of examining the privacy policies of each company every time a customer provides personally identifying information is onerous. Understanding the general characteristics of firms that are likely to protect personal information provides the customer with a better understanding of the overall information privacy landscape and helps them make better decisions about disclosing their personal data. For the purposes of this research, *privacy statement quality* is defined as the degree of privacy protection promised to a consumer by a company in the privacy statement of that company. Since a firm is expected to adhere to the promises it extends to its customers, it is important to understand whether specific firm characteristics can explain, in part, the quality of a firm's privacy policy.

BACKGROUND

This paper examines online privacy policies and the dynamics that lead to their formation. The research is motivated by the desire to understand why firms voluntarily adapt privacy policies and the extent to which these firms develop high-quality privacy policies. For legislators and policy makers, it is important to understand the impact of policy decisions in order to craft effective rules and legislation and to enforce them once adopted. Consumers must understand their risks, including occurrences of undesirable or dubious security and privacy practices, so they can make better decisions about whom to trust. For researchers, it is important to know what problems and practices need to be analyzed (Jensen et al., 2007).

Information Privacy

Privacy is defined as the ability of the individual to control the conditions under which personal information is acquired and used (Van der Heijden, 2003) or, simply, "the right to be left alone" (Warren & Brandeis, 1890). Information privacy continues to be an important issue in today's information society (Berendt et al., 2005; Traynor et al., 2006) with data spills, advances in data mining and awareness of the need for personal information privacy management (Thuraisingham, 2005). In fact, the number of breaches continues to grow. One privacy group reports that nearly 500 million personal records have been compromised in the approximately 1,700 data breaches made public between 2005 - 2010.[1] Privacy concerns have been cited as a major factor hindering the increasing "informating" of the healthcare industry (Angst & Agarwal, 2009).

Issues related to information privacy are debated by corporations, online discussion groups, privacy advocates, government legislative bodies, and international organizations (Berendt et al., 2005; Traynor et al., 2006). It is no longer becoming the exclusive purview of formal organizational policies at the macro-organizational level, but increasingly becoming infused with managerial responsibility at every level of the organization (Culnan & Williams, 2010). Arguments are based on national security, liberty, consumer rights, security, technology, cost savings and individual rights. Tension exists between the benefits of increased personal information disclosure by consumers to businesses and law enforcement agencies and the costs of disclosure to the individual. Privacy advocates prefer increased legislation; businesses prefer minimal government intrusion and self-regulation.

The information privacy debate presents a conflicting set of issues even for the consumer. On the cost side, consumers are faced with a loss of autonomy or individuality. Economic injury is a threat due to identity theft or unwarranted denial of credit based on inaccurate information. On the benefits side, consumers have unprecedented access to shopping, financial and credit services, and educational resources. In fact, many of these systems or processes work efficiently *because* sensitive consumer information is used by businesses *without* the individual's permission. Credit agencies and online retailers, for example, routinely buy, sell, and share sensitive financial data about consumers without their permission. By doing so, they facilitate the seamless transactions that so many consumers depend upon in their daily lives such as the buying and financing of homes, cars, and an array of consumer goods.

For companies, costs savings, increased sales, and customer retention are the primary motivators for using consumers' personal information. The capabilities of information technologies in an increasingly competitive marketplace make the use of consumers' personal information part of a cost-effective strategy. To succeed, however, most companies have to determine the extent to which they plan to address the privacy concerns of their external constituents.

Fair Information

Fair Information Practices (FIP) identify the important dimensions of privacy and are often cited as a de facto standard. The FIP have been widely adopted by agencies such as the Federal Trade Commission to assess how well private sector firms regulate themselves. Some studies of online information privacy polices used the FIP as an evaluation guide (Milne & Culnan, 2002).

The FIP are defined as representing the "global principles that fairly balance the need for business to collect and use personal information with the le-gitimate privacy interest of consumers to exercise control over the disclosure and subsequent uses of their personal information" (Milne & Culnan, 2002; p.3). In essence, the FIP are intended to provide individuals with control over the collection and disclosure of personal information and to govern the relationship between consumers and firms (Culnan & Bies, 2003). FIP guide the formulation and enforcement of privacy law and regulation. In addition, FIP seek to balance the competing interests of corporations and individuals. Many companies require their licensees to abide by posted privacy policies in accordance with Fair Information Practices (Liu et al., 2005). Table 1 provides the Fair Information Practices.

Online Disclosures

Fundamental differences exist between those who support a consumer's right to information privacy and those who recognize a firm's need to use consumer personal information for legitimate business purposes. Government regulation is largely reactive to a publicized problem within a specific industry. Hence, the most common way to address consumer protection is through self-regulation (Swire, 1997). Firms develop information practices that *should* be influenced by both the Fair Information Practices and acceptable industry standards.

Many companies communicate their information privacy practices through privacy policies or statements linked from their websites (Jensen & Potts, 2004). While posting a policy does not

Table 1. Fair information practices

Notice/Awareness: Consumers have a right to know if personal information is being collected and how it will be used.
Choice/consent: Consumers have choices about whether or not information collected for one purpose will be used for other purposes and about whether or not information will be shared with third parties unless it is required by law.
Access/Participation: Consumers have a right to access information and to correct errors.
Integrity/Security: Organizations should protect personal information from unauthorized access during transmission and storage.
Enforcement/redress: Consumers have a right to ensure that organizations comply with these core privacy principles either through external regulation (audits) or certification programs.

guarantee compliance with FIP, its absence indicates that a company fails to observe "notice," the most fundamental Fair Information Practice. Surveys of web privacy disclosures have been used to assess the effectiveness of self-regulation and compliance to FIP (Culnan, 2000; Culnan & Bies, 2003; Milne & Gordon, 1993). These studies focused on sampling websites based on the amount of traffic the sites received. The results reveal that the quality of online privacy disclosures tends to improve over time, although questions remain regarding the motivation of firms to post policies that comply to FIP. The degree of compliance is important because it is indicative of the strength and quality of the policy.

Resource Dependency Theory

This research seeks to understand why firms choose a certain degree of quality in their online privacy disclosures. To achieve this, Resource Dependency Theory (RDT) is applied because it is a powerful theory that addresses how organizations survive in complex environments. It has been used in prior research to better understand online privacy disclosures (Greenway & Chan, 2005) and, more recently, how firms make sourcing decisions about important information technology assets (e.g., Straub et al., 2008). In essence, RDT states that firms survive to the extent that they are effective. Firms, in turn, are effective based upon their ability to acquire and maintain resources (Pfeffer & Salancik, 1978).

According to RDT, firms are embedded in networks of interdependencies and social relationships. The need for specific resources—ranging from human to financial to informational—is dependent upon the environment, rendering the firm dependent on *external* sources for resources needed to survive and to be effective. RDT views an organization as constrained by its environment. Greater external constraints limit the firm's ability to respond to changes in its environment and impact its ability to negotiate its position within

these constraints. When a firm tries to control its environment, it encounters new constraints, resulting in more negotiations. As patterns of interdependency change and the various players maneuver for advantage, organizations, environments and interorganizational relationships form and evolve.

RDT recognizes the complexity of the social context within which a firm operates. In fact, RDT presumes that the best way to understand organizational choice and action is to focus on the firm's context and the pressures and constraints present (Pfeffer & Salancik, 1978). RDT also purports that management of environmental dependence and negotiation of favorable positions requires some degree of managerial discretion. Interestingly, dependencies are often reciprocal, resulting in *interdependencies* between the firm and external players. In terms of privacy, a strong privacy policy may limit a firm's control over customer information in the short term. As customers feel protected, however, they may trust the website more and be willing to provide more information in the future. Hence, in the long run, a strong privacy policy will help firms gain access to and control over more customer information.

Explaining Privacy Policy Quality via Resource Dependency Theory

RDT provides an appropriate theory for examining why organizations develop different information privacy disclosures. Firms are dependent upon consumers to the extent that the customer controls the information that is important to the firm for its survival (Hann et al. 2007). Furthermore, firms are constrained by the need to address consumers' privacy concerns, those of privacy advocates, and the need to keep potential, and even more constraining, government regulation away. The dependency, however, is reciprocal. Consumers, privacy advocates, and government regulators are dependent on firms to produce relevant goods and services and for providing jobs and a strong economy. Government regulators and consumers recognize the economic benefit of firms' ethical and appropriate use of personal information (Tang et al., 2007).

The social actors in this debate negotiate in light of this interdependency. Privacy disclosures are a major negotiation tool; firms disclose their information practices, and consumers respond by either providing or withholding their information. Consumers, regulators, and privacy advocates evaluate the appropriateness of a firm's policy in light of the Fair Information Practices. Companies recognize that compliance is costly and will comply only to the extent that their effectiveness and success is dependent upon the information resource (Pfeffer & Salancik, 1978).

Considerable research exists on both the degree of compliance to FIP and the evolution of information privacy policies in general (Culnan 1995; 2000; Culnan & Armstrong, 1999; Culnan & Bies, 2003). However, research is lacking that focuses on why certain companies choose to implement strong privacy policies in terms of the Fair Information Practices whereas others do not. Resource Dependency Theory suggests that companies are influenced by their environment to seek and to exercise greater control over the resources upon which they are dependent. Companies that are more dependent upon consumer personal information, therefore, are more likely to voluntarily craft and abide by strong privacy policies in an effort to exercise control over that information.

ENVIRONMENTAL FACTORS LEADING TO DEPENDENCY

The relationship between firms and their use of consumer personal information indicates that firms which are more dependent upon consumer information as a key resource should attempt to protect that resource more. Within the context of this study, such firms are more likely to establish strong privacy policies. Furthermore, certain environmental factors are likely to be indicative of a firm's dependence on consumer personal information and, therefore, impact the quality of a company's online privacy policy.

These six factors are: (1) firms engaged in business-to-consumer relationships, (2) firms engaged in e-commerce transactions, (3) firms in the technology industry, (4) firms in informational industries, (5) firms with heavily trafficked websites, and (6) large firm size. Each variable provides important information to both firms and consumers. Variables 1 and 2 address the type of information a website collects. Variables 3 and 4 reflect industry characteristics whereas variables 5 and 6 capture firm characteristics. Each category – information collected, industry, and firm characteristics -- provides insight into a different aspect of the firm's environment.

Firms Engaged in Business-to-Consumer Relationships (Informational)

A business-to-consumer website can afford an informational relationship between a firm and its customers (Tang et al., 2008). The website provides information on products or services to which consumers can respond and provide feedback, allowing users to submit information requests without performing actual transactions. These firms use their websites to actively interact with consumers and are more likely to be dependent on consumer information. This interaction may take the form of providing customized information about products or services offered by the company. The web sites may have a strong influence on a customer's impression of a company's legitimacy and the degree to which it cares about its customers (Winter, et. al., 2003). Thus, for these firms, a website is an important part of a company's public image, and the information it conveys can have major implications on the consumer's perceptions.

Consumers regard customized website more favorably (Palmer 2002; Murthi & Sarkar, 2003). Customization includes information regarding location, preferences, most valued information, and identity. Information load and emotional responses are equally powerful factors in explaining a customer's experience (Huang, 2003). Companies that collect customer information can personalize their websites to provide the most relevant information to a specific customer. For example, websites may request a customer's zip code to provide regional product information. Perceived visual attractiveness is also an important indication of the degree to which customers will interact with a website and how they will report their experience (Van der Heijden, 2003).

Companies that engage in business-to-consumer relationships through their website to provide information to potential customers are likely to be more dependent upon customer information. The ability of a firm to customize its website to individual customers is directly dependent on the availability of consumer information. In most cases, personal information customizes the website experience (Albert, et. al. 2004). Because of this dependency upon consumer information for website customization, companies that engage in business-to-consumer relationships are more likely to provide higher quality privacy policies.

H1: *Firms that engage in business-to-consumer relationships via their websites are more likely to develop high-quality online privacy policies.*

Firms Engaged in E-Commerce (Transactional)

Business-to-consumer websites can be classified into two general forms—informational and transactional (Teo & Pian, 2004). Informational sites are intended to provide valuable information to a firm's customers or potential customers. Transactional sites conduct business transactions with a firm's customers (and have a shopping cart).

Although both informational and transactional sites provide value, transactional sites are likely to provide greater value because of the direct revenue generated (Ngai & Wat, 2002). For this reason, companies that conduct business transactions over their websites are likely to be more dependent upon customer information than sites that provide information alone. The information collected in a business transaction is used to facilitate the transaction as well as to improve the likelihood of the transaction occurring.

If a company is able to collect and track information about particular customers, the company is better able to assess customers' value and target particular goods and services to them based on that value (Wheeler, 2002). Companies can leverage consumer information by tracking customers and directly marketing to them, based upon their preferences. For example, customers may differ in their shopping intentions, whether they have the product in mind they intend to buy or are simply "browsing". The degree to which a company can optimize the website experience to target these different shoppers provides value to the company (Moe & Fader, 2004). Firms can also develop entirely new marketing strategies by targeting consumers that "almost" bought an item and offering a comparable or better deal based on the information gained in the shopping experience (Pinker, et. al., 2003). Numerous factors influence online buying behavior, including individual personality traits (Jahng, et. al., 2002), trust (Bhattercherjee, 2002; Gefen, et. al., 2003; McKnight, et. al., 2002; Pavlou, 2002), and ease of use (Deveraj, et. al., 2002). Companies can customize their websites to address each of these factors. Customization, however, is heavily dependent upon the availability of reliable customer information.

Companies that engage in financial transactions via their websites (as opposed to just exchanging information) are dependent upon customer information to succeed and are more likely to develop high-quality privacy policies to protect the resources upon which these efforts depend.

H2: *Firms that conduct e-commerce transactions via their websites are more likely to develop high-quality privacy policies.*

Firms in the Technology Industry

Technology companies, for the purposes of this research, are those companies engaged in the information technology industry such as hardware, software, and telecommunications firms. Their dependency on consumer personal information is indirect, and derived from their customer base. If firms realize the value of technology-enabled marketing opportunities, they are more likely to invest in the hardware, software, and telecommunication infrastructures that leverage these opportunities. Technology companies, therefore, have a vested interest in promoting the Internet as a safe, viable platform for conducting business because of the benefit of other companies buying their products and services for engaging in online activities.

Technology companies, thus, are likely to be concerned with ethical and societal issues that limit the widespread use of information technologies. They are more likely to support third-party assurance or privacy-seal programs than other firms (Stewart-Schwaig, et. al., 2005). Technology companies have a vested interest in issues surrounding the use of information technology, so they are dependent on the successful deployment and use of these technologies by their customers. This makes them likely to advocate strong privacy protection.

H3: *Information technology firms have higher-quality privacy policies than non-information technology firms.*

Firms in Information-Intensive E-Industries

Previous research has investigated the value of information technology in informational industries, arguing that companies that obtain greater benefits from information as a resource are more likely to benefit from the investment in and implementation of information technology (Chatterjee, et. al., 2002; Chatterjee, et. al., 2001; Dos Santos, 1993; Im, et. al. 2001). This logic can be extended to the privacy-policy argument. Specifically, companies that are more dependent upon information are also going to be more dependent upon customer information. Thus, companies in information-intensive industries are more likely to extend higher-quality policies to consumers.

H4: *Companies in information-intensive industries have higher-quality privacy policies than companies in non-information-intensive industries.*

Firms with Heavily Trafficked Websites

Most online firms are intensely interested in the amount and type of traffic to their websites. Highly trafficked websites are inherently more valuable, assuming that the purpose of the website is to exchange information that is of some value to the company. More highly trafficked sites, therefore, are more likely to be dependent upon the information gleaned from the website.

Website traffic can be identified or classified into "types" and tracked (Lynne, 1999). Certain types of traffic may be more valuable than others. Knowing and leveraging this traffic for optimal purposes depends on customer information (Gupta, et. al., 2000). Furthermore, online advertising is a major source of revenue for companies operating high traffic websites (Dewan, et. al., 2002). Online advertising can be tailored to the preferences of the customer based on prior contact.

Thus, the ability to collect, store, and track consumer information is essential to successful online advertising. High-traffic websites are valuable advertising spaces largely enabled by consumer information. Therefore, website traffic is likely to be an environmental characteristic that reveals a company's dependence upon consumer information and result in higher-quality privacy policies.

H5: *Companies with heavily trafficked websites have higher-quality privacy policies than companies with lower traffic.*

Firm Size

Company size may also be an environmental characteristic that contributes to a company's dependence on customer information (Sarathy & Robertson, 2003). First, larger firms, presumably, have more valuable customers, either in terms of sheer number or in terms of profitability. Thus, the ability of a firm to leverage information about its customers will likely be more valuable to a larger firm. Second, larger firms may be the most dependent upon the effective handling of customer information. Larger firms are more often under media scrutiny, and, therefore, will likely have greater detrimental effects if customer information is mishandled. Larger firms may be more likely to be the target of customer complaints and/or lawsuits simply because they are a bigger and more lucrative target. For these reasons, larger companies are more dependent on customer information and more likely to develop higher quality privacy policies.

H6: *Larger companies will have higher-quality privacy policies than smaller companies.*

METHODOLOGY

The study used a modified version of an instrument used in prior studies by Culnan (2000) and the Federal Trade Commission. A portion of the instrument is in the appendix.

Sample

The Fortune 500 companies were selected because they represent some of the US's largest and most successful businesses and are often considered to be leaders in their industries. The Fortune 500 has been used as an effective sample in previous research (McLeod & Rogers, 1982; Liu, et. al., 1997). In addition, the Fortune 500 represents a relatively balanced cross-section of industries, a wide range of emphases upon the company's Internet presence, and varying degrees of dependency upon information for business advantage. Choosing the Fortune 500 is useful for two reasons. First, most prior research on online privacy disclosures includes samples based on website traffic. The assumption of this study is that the quality of a privacy statement is more a business issue than it is an Internet issue. Because the research questions focus on the business reasons for privacy statements, the sample provides greater variation in order to explore these questions (McLeod & Rogers, 1982).

Second, these companies have, in many ways, been successful in understanding their environments, constraints, and dependencies. One would expect them to take a leadership role in dealing with personal privacy issues. With the maturing and incorporation of e-commerce practices, privacy concerns for the Fortune 500 are of increasing importance as consumers continue to engage in e-commerce activities in which personal information is collected. As a result, the Fortune 500 companies are scrutinized closely by privacy advocates, by the government, and by international trade partners as possible violators of the Fair Information Practices.

Although the Fortune 500 are U.S.-based firms, it is reasonable to assume that the vast majority of these firms are engaged in global commerce and are, therefore, concerned about protecting the information privacy of citizens of other countries as well as those in the United States.

Data Collection

The researchers used the links found on the Fortune website to access each firm's site. One researcher surveyed all 500 websites of the Fortune 500. Two other researchers independently reviewed a random sample of the 500 sites and then performed inter-rater reliability checks conducted on 10% of the data; an 89.23% inter-rater reliability was recorded. This approach also enabled the researchers to record qualitative observations during their analysis (e.g., the only place to opt out was at the checkout). Using the links from the Fortune website, a researcher accessed each website and examined the site for a privacy policy. If a policy was found, the survey was completed; otherwise, only the first five demographic questions were answered. Each privacy policy was captured and indexed in electronic format. This facilitated a software-assisted keyword analysis and a qualitative comparison of the language and style of privacy policies.

Independent and Dependent Variables

The independent variables: business-to-consumer relationships, ecommerce, technology companies, informational industries, and traffic are coded as dichotomous variables. A site is considered business-to-consumer (**con**) if the site contains any form of feedback that the consumer can use to respond to information on the website. If the site is used to actually conduct ecommerce business over the Internet as evidenced by a "shopping cart" or other functionality through which customers can order and pay for products or services directly from the website, it is considered an electronic commerce site (**ec**). Third, a technology company (**tech**) is any company belonging to the computer

hardware, software, or telecommunications industries, as defined by Fortune.

Industries are classified as informational, non-informational, or semi-informational (Zhu and Kraemer, 2002). *Informational* firms are firms whose business does not involve physical goods (e.g., finance, insurance, and advertising). *Non-informational* firms are involved in producing, manufacturing, or handling physical goods (e.g., mining, construction, and apparel). *Semi-informational* firms are firms whose primary business is a mix of physical goods and information (e.g., airlines, retail, and utilities). Since the hypothesis relates only to informational industries, both semi-informational and non-informational companies are coded identically to ensure that only informational industries are coded as such, reducing bias.

Traffic data (**Top 5000**) was obtained from the Jupiter Media Metrix on the 5,000 most heavily trafficked websites for the time period during which the survey was conducted. The traffic variable indicates whether a company's website is included in the top 5,000 most heavily trafficked sites. Company size (**lnMktCap**) is assessed by overall market capitalization of the firm. Since this variable does not conform to the linearity assumptions of OLS regression, the natural log of market capitalization is used in the data analysis.

Control Variables

Two key control variables exist in the study. First, since the F500 is defined by revenue, it is important to control for company revenue. The natural log of revenue is used to control for a possible bias introduced by our sample and to transform the variable to meet the normality assumptions of regression. Also, certain industries are regulated by the government and must, by law, provide certain privacy protections to consumers. Thus, a second control is introduced into the analysis dealing with whether or not a firm is in a regulated industry.

Dependent Variable

The dependent variable is an aggregate measure constructed from the survey of the Fair Information Practices. A similar approach is used to analyze the quality of websites (Zhu & Kraemer, 2002). This methodology is extended for the current study.

First, as the base for the dependent variable, questions regarding Fair Information Practices used extensively in prior studies are incorporated into this study design (Culnan & Armstrong, 1999). This results in a ten-question measure of privacy-policy quality that balances the influences of the four FIP categories.

Second, due to continued business focus on the Internet and the privacy debate, three other questions are included. One question is added to the notice section of this scale that assessed whether the website uses cookies. The use of cookies has been the subject of considerable research and merits inclusion. Another measure of FIP (redress) is not included in prior studies. It is addressed in this research by assessing whether or not a firm participates in a privacy seal or third-party assurance program. Because the appearance of a privacy seal signals that the privacy practices of the firm have been audited by an external third party, it constitutes an effective proxy for enforcement, an often-overlooked fifth component of FIP. Finally, a question regarding whether the site afforded any special protections for children is included to assess whether firms are responding to legislation regarding the Children's Online Privacy Protection Act (COPPA).

The resulting scale, then, consists of 13 dichotomous variables intended to serve as a robust measure of the quality of an online privacy policy. Following a method similar to that of Zhu and Kramer (2002), these 13 dichotomous measures are combined into a single scale, resulting in a single continuous variable suitable for quantitative analysis.

RESULTS

Because of the nature of the dependent variable as a fairly robust continuous variable, OLS regression is appropriate for the analysis of the data. Since the dependent variable is constructed through count, however, some argument could be made that Poisson regression would be a more appropriate approach to data analysis. To ensure that the findings are not an artifact of the data analysis method chosen, a Poisson regression is used in addition to the OLS regression. In all instances, the interpretation of the OLS and the Poisson regression models are identical. Thus, the results of the OLS regression are reliable for the data at hand. In addition, the variance inflation factors (VIF) is assessed to ensure that multicollinearity did not pose a significant problem in the analysis. None of the VIFs are above 3, which is well below even the most conservative recommendations for VIF thresholds of 5, suggesting that multicollinearity is not a problem in the model. Table 2 provides descriptive statistics and a correlation matrix; The results of the OLS regression are reported in Table 3.

The overall model is significant with the R-square suggesting that the four factors explained approximately 27% of the variance in the model. The results of the model are strong in that most variables are highly significant ($p < .01$ or better).

Hypothesis 1 stated that companies that used their website to market, but not sell, products or services to customers are more likely to have higher-quality privacy policies. Results from the model show that this hypothesis is supported. Companies that cultivate direct relationships with their customers via their websites are more likely to develop higher-quality privacy policies.

Hypothesis 2 suggests that companies that conduct ecommerce via their websites by selling goods or services are also likely to have higher-quality privacy policies. Hypothesis 2 is also supported. Companies that sell goods or services are more likely to have higher-quality policies, over

Table 2. Descriptive statistics and correlation matrix

	mean	SD	1	2	3	4	5	6	7	8	9
1. Con	0.775	0.418	1.00	0.23*	0.22*	0.24*	0.15*	0.32*	0.22*	0.14*	0.34*
2. EC	0.891	0.312	0.23*	1.00	0.11	0.10	0.16*	0.18*	0.27*	0.19*	0.28*
3. Tech	0.180	0.385	0.22*	0.11	1.00	0.75*	0.38*	0.17*	0.26*	0.09	0.18*
4. Reg	0.234	0.424	0.24*	0.10	0.75*	1.00	0.52*	0.07*	0.25*	0.11	0.19*
5. Info	0.504	0.500	0.15*	0.16*	0.38*	0.52*	1.00	0.25*	0.21*	0.08	0.29*
6. Top 5000	0.288	0.453	0.32*	0.18*	0.17*	0.07	0.25*	1.00	0.29*	0.27*	0.41*
7. lnMkt Cap	8.846	1.615	0.22*	0.27*	0.26*	0.25*	0.21*	0.29*	1.00	0.59*	0.31*
8. lnRev	9.117	0.877	0.14*	0.19*	0.09	0.11	0.08	0.27*	0.59*	1.00	0.20*
9. Quality	6.44	4.467	0.34*	0.28*	0.18*	0.19*	0.29*	0.41*	0.31*	0.20*	1.00

Con (business-to-consumer); EC (conduct ecommerce); tech (technology company); Info (information industry); Top 5000 (most heavily trafficked websites)

and above companies that simply market, but do not sell, to consumers.

Hypothesis 3 stated that technology companies are more likely to have higher-quality privacy policies. Hypothesis 3 is not supported. This hypothesis suggested that technology companies might be *indirectly* dependent because the companies, which are their customers, are dependent upon their customer information. Therefore, the greater the dependencies these companies have on their customers' information, the greater the impact for the technology companies. Apparently, however, this indirect dependency does not result in higher quality policies.

Hypothesis 4 stated that firms in information-based industries are more likely to be dependent on customer data because their inherent business model is information based. Hypothesis 4 is supported; informational industries *are* more likely to provide higher-quality policies on their websites.

Hypothesis 5 suggested that companies with more heavily trafficked websites are more likely to provide higher-quality privacy policies. Hypothesis 5 is also supported and is highly significant.

Table 3. Regression summary for dependent variable

		B	S.E.	t	p	Hypothesis Supported?
	Intercept	-0.750	1.756	-0.427	0.669207	
H1	B2C Relationship	1.594***	0.427	3.731	0.000214	Supported
H2	Ecommerce Relationship	2.037***	0.551	3.700	0.000241	Supported
H3	Technology Company	-0.225	0.648	-0.345	0.728967	Not Supported
H4	Information Intensive Ind.	1.200**	0.394	3.045	0.002453	Supported
H5	Website Traffic	2.535***	0.410	6.182	0.000000	Supported
H6	Firm Market Cap (log)	0.293*	0.132	2.223	0.026678	Supported
	Regulated Industries	0.443	0.647	0.685	0.493670	
	Firm Revenue (log)	-0.011	0.226	-0.050	0.960442	

R^2=.29 Model F=24.575***
n= 497, + * p<.05 ** p<.01 ***p<.001

Heavily trafficked websites represent a much more valuable resource to the company that maintains them. Thus, these companies are more likely to offer higher-quality privacy policies in order to protect that resource.

Hypothesis 6 stated that larger companies provide higher-quality privacy policies. These companies are more dependent on customer information since they are more vulnerable to a mishandling of that information. Previous qualitative analysis suggests that some major companies employ the opposite strategy, protecting themselves by offering virtually no protection (Stewart-Schwaig, et. al., 2005). However, the current study suggests that larger companies protect their information and other resources by extending higher-quality policies.

DISCUSSION

The current research examined the privacy policies of Fortune 500 companies to assess the substance and quality of their stated information practices. Resource Dependency Theory was applied to understand why companies are more likely to develop higher-quality privacy policies. Basically, firms do so as a function of the degree to which they are dependent upon consumer information. Most companies create strong privacy policies to protect the *long-term* viability of consumer information as a resource. Otherwise, the possibility of a consumer revolt or government intervention becomes a real threat. A high-quality privacy policy provides greater control over the consumer information resource for two reasons. First, high-quality privacy protection helps management to either prevent or to more effectively manage a negative privacy incident. In most cases, the public mismanagement of private information typically compromises a firm's ability to leverage that information in the future (Culnan & Williams 2009). For example, a public revelation that one of the leading banks in Canada grossly mishandled privacy information

severely limited that company's ability to collect and use customer information (Chan, et. al., 2004). Second, mismanagement of private information increases the likelihood that governments will intervene with regulation resulting in significantly less control over how the information resource is used (Tang et al., 2008).

The question of why certain companies choose to self-impose strong privacy policies is important. First, early online privacy research embraces either self-regulation or governmental regulation as the main plausible routes to improved FIP compliance in online disclosures (Culnan, 2000). Self-regulation, however, may be effective in some environments more so than in others. The efficacy of self-regulation may be more dependent upon a company's environment and the degree to which the company is dependent upon consumer information as a resource. The environmental characteristics that motivate firms to create high-quality privacy policies are likely to be the same factors that make self-regulation a viable option.

Second, RDT suggests that companies that are dependent upon consumers' personal information should voluntarily establish strong privacy policies to retain effective control over the resource. Strong privacy policies are costly to draft and implement and expose a company to additional risk. Understanding the degree to which a firm is dependent upon consumer information, therefore, is important information in determining how much to invest in developing strong privacy policies and practices. Thus, by connecting privacy policy development with RDT, the issue of consumer privacy becomes an important strategic resource allocation issue.

Third, it is important to understand the environmental factors that lead to higher-quality policies. In the past, mechanisms for assessing whether a company provides strong privacy protection did not exist. Consumers were required to read and analyze these policies on a case-by-case basis (Stewart-Schwaig, et. al., 2002). Understanding the types of companies and environments that provide greater privacy protections will help consumers identify environmental contexts that are more likely to be trustworthy.

The study of the privacy policies of the Fortune 500 provides strong evidence for interpreting privacy-policy quality based on resource dependency theory. Five of the six hypotheses were supported, suggesting that businesses dependent upon customer information are more likely to extend higher-quality policies to consumers. Whether or not a firm belongs to a regulated industry was not a significant factor in the discussion. However, the results suggest that government regulation may not explain as much variation in privacy-policy quality as the degree to which the company is dependent upon consumer information as a resource.

The results provide insight into the quality variance that exists across firms. Consumers can use this study to assess the likelihood of a firm protecting their privacy, without having to read each company's policy before providing any information. The results may be somewhat counter-intuitive. Some customers may believe that firms that heavily use consumer personal information are more likely to abuse that information. Interestingly, the results of this study indicate the opposite: the more dependent a firm is on consumer personal information, the more likely it is to provide strong privacy protection. In contrast, perhaps firms that are less dependent on customer information should be viewed with greater scrutiny by customers, because they can afford to use that information for short-term gain at the expense of the customer's privacy.

CONCLUSION

This research examined online privacy disclosures to understand how firms determine the extent of privacy protection they will provide. The results show that companies that are information dependent have stronger policies. As a result, they can protect their information resource from negative publicity, consumer backlash and government intervention. Further research is needed to analyze related privacy issues by industry and to understand the impact of potential and realized privacy breaches. Since privacy policies are often in flux, a longitudinal analysis might reveal other dynamics not captured in this study. Finally, it might be useful to compare the short-term versus long-term impact of strong privacy policies on the control of customer information and the factors that influence this relationship.

ACKNOWLEDGMENT

This research is supported by Kennesaw State University, Boston College and Georgia State University.

REFERENCES

Albert, T. C., Goes, P. B., & Gupta, A. (2004). GIST: A model for design and management of content and interactivity of customer-centric web sites. *Management Information Systems Quarterly, 2*(28), 161–182.

Angst, C. M., & Agarwal, R. (2009). Adoption Of Electronic Health Records In The Presence Of Privacy Concerns: The Elaboration Likelihood Model And Individual Persuasion. *Management Information Systems Quarterly, 33*(2), 339–370.

Berendt, B., Günther, O., & Spiekermann, S. (2005). Privacy in e-commerce: stated preferences vs. actual behavior. *Communications of the ACM,* (48): 4.

Bhattacherjee, A. (2002). Individual trust in online firms: scale development and initial test. *Journal of Management Information Systems, 19*(1), 211–241.

Castañeda, J. A., & Montoro, F. J. (2007). The effect of internet general privacy concern on customer behavior. *Electronic Commerce Research, 7*(2), 117–141. doi:10.1007/s10660-007-9000-y

Chan, Y., Culnan, M., Laden, G., Levin, T., & Smith, J. (2004). Panel: information privacy management: proactive versus reactive approaches. *Proceedings of the Twenty-Fifth Annual International Conference on Information Systems,* Washington, D.C., 12-15.

Chatterjee, D., Pacini, C., & Sambamurthy, V. (2002). The shareholder-wealth and trading-volume effects of information-technology infrastructure investments. *Journal of Management Information Systems, 2*(19), 7–42.

Chatterjee, D., Richardson, V. J., & Zmud, R. W. (2001). Examining the shareholder wealth effects of announcements of newly created CIO positions. *Management Information Systems Quarterly, 1*(25), 43–70. doi:10.2307/3250958

Chellappa, R. K., & Sin, R. G. (2005). Personalization versus privacy: an empirical examination of the online consumer's dilemma. *Information Technology Management, 6*(2-3), 181–202. doi:10.1007/s10799-005-5879-y

Cranor, L. F., Guduru, P., & Arjula, M. (2006). User interfaces for privacy agents. [TOCHI]. *ACM Transactions on Computer-Human Interaction, 13*(2). doi:10.1145/1165734.1165735

Culnan, M. J. (1995). Consumer awareness of name removal procedures: implications for direct marketing. *Journal of Direct Marketing,* (9), 10-15.

Culnan, M. J. (2000). Protecting privacy online: is self-regulation working? *Journal of Public Policy & Marketing, 1*(19), 20–26. doi:10.1509/jppm.19.1.20.16944

Culnan, M. J., & Armstrong, P. K. (1999). Information privacy concerns, procedural fairness, and impersonal trust: an empirical investigation. *Organization Science, 1*(10), 104–116. doi:10.1287/orsc.10.1.104

Culnan, M. J., & Bies, R. J. (2003). Consumer privacy: balancing economic and justice considerations. *The Journal of Social Issues, 2*(59), 323–342. doi:10.1111/1540-4560.00067

Culnan, M. J., & Williams, C. C. (2009). How Ethics Can Enhance Organizational Privacy Lessons from the Choicepoint and Tjx Data Breaches. *Management Information Systems Quarterly, 33*(4), 673–687.

Devaraj, S., Fan, M., & Kohli, R. (2002). Antecedents of b2c channel satisfaction and preference: validating e-commerce metrics. *Information Systems Research, 3*(13), 316–333. doi:10.1287/isre.13.3.316.77

Dewan, R. M., Freimer, M. L., & Zhang, H. (2002). Management of valuation of advertisement-supported web sites. *Journal of Management Information Systems, 3*(19), 87–98.

Diney, T., & Hart, P. (2006). An extended privacy calculus model for e-commerce transactions. *Information Systems Research, 17*(1), 2006.

Dos Santos, B. L., Peffers, K., & Mauer, D. C. (1993). The impact of information technology investment announcements on the market value of the firm. *Information Systems Research, 1*(4), 1–23. doi:10.1287/isre.4.1.1

Federal Trade Commission. (2000, May). *Self-regulation and privacy online: a report to congress.* [Online]. Available: http://www.ftc.gov/privacy.

Gefen, D., Karahanna, E., & Straub, D. W. (2003). Trust and tam in online shopping: an integrated model. *Management Information Systems Quarterly, 1*(27), 51–90.

Greenaway, K. E., & Chan, Y. E. (2005). Theoretical explanations for firms' information privacy behaviors. *Journal of the Association for Information Systems*, (6): 6.

Gupta, A., Jukic, B., Stahl, D. O., & Whinston, A. B. (2000). Extracting consumers' private information for implementing incentive-compatible internet traffic pricing. *Journal of Management Information Systems*, *1*(17), 9–29.

Hann, H., Hui, K. L., Lee, S. Y. T., & Png, I. P. L. (2008). Consumer privacy and marketing avoidance: A static model. *Management Science*, *54*(6), 1094–1103. doi:10.1287/mnsc.1070.0837

Huang, M. H. (2003). Modeling virtual exploratory and shopping dynamics: an environmental psychology approach. *Information & Management*, *1*(41), 39–47. doi:10.1016/S0378-7206(03)00024-7

Im, K. S., Dow, K. E., & Grover, V. (2001). Research report: a reexamination of it investment and the market value of the firm - an event study methodology. *Information Systems Research*, *1*(12), 103–117. doi:10.1287/isre.12.1.103.9718

Jahng, J. J., Jain, H., & Ramamurthy, K. (2002). Personality traits and effectiveness of presentation of product information in e-business systems. *European Journal of Information Systems*, *3*(11), 181–195. doi:10.1057/palgrave.ejis.3000431

Jensen, C., & Potts, C. (2004, April). Privacy policies as decision-making tools: an evaluation of online privacy notices. *Proceedings of the SIGCHI conference on Human factors in computing systems CHI '04, ACM Press*.

Jensen, C., Sarkar, C., Jensen, C., & Potts, C. (2007). Tracking website data-collection and privacy practices with the iWatch web crawler. *Proceedings of the 3rd Symposium on Usable Privacy and Security*, Pittsburgh, Pennsylvania. 29-40.

Kane, G. C., Fichman, R. G., Gallaugher, J., & Glaser, J. (2009). Community Relations 2.0: With the rise of real-time social media, the rules about community outreach have changed. *Harvard Business Review*, *87*(11), 45–50.

Kobsa, A. (2007). Privacy-enhanced Personalization. *Communications of the ACM*, *50*(8), 24–33. doi:10.1145/1278201.1278202

Koops, B.-J., Leenes, R., Meints, M., van der Meulen, N., & Jaquet-Chiffelle, D.-O. (2009, February). A Typology of Identify-Related Crime: Conceptual, Technical, and Legal Issues. *Information Communication and Society*, *12*(1), 1–24. doi:10.1080/13691180802158516

Liu, C., Arnett, K. P., Capella, L., & Beatty, B. (1997). Web sties of the fortune 500 companies: facing customers through home pages. *Information & Management*, *1*(31), 335–345. doi:10.1016/S0378-7206(97)00001-3

Liu, C., Marchewka, J. T., Lu, J., & Yu, C.-S. (2005). Beyond concern—a privacy-trust-behavioral intention model of electronic commerce. *Information & Management*, *42*(2), 289–304. doi:10.1016/j.im.2004.01.003

Lynne, D. (1999). Web site stats: tracking hits and analyzing traffic. *Database*, *3*(22), 87–87.

McKnight, D. H., Choudhury, V., & Kacmar, C. (2002). Developing and validating trust measures for e-commerce: An integrative typology. *Information Systems Research*, *3*(13), 334–359. doi:10.1287/isre.13.3.334.81

McLeod, R., & Rogers, J. C. (1982). Marketing information systems: uses in the fortune 500. *California Management Review*, *25*(3), 106–118.

Milne, G. R., & Culnan, M. J. (2002). Using the content of online privacy notices to inform public policy: a longitudinal analysis of the 1998-3001 U.S. web surveys. *The Information Society*, (18): 345–359. doi:10.1080/01972240290108168

Milne, G. R., & Gordon, M. E. (1993). Direct mail privacy-efficiency trade-offs within an implied social contract framework. *Journal of Public Policy & Marketing*, (12): 206–215.

Moe, W. W., & Fader, P. S. (2004). Dynamic conversion behavior at e-commerce sites. *Management Science*, *3*(50), 326–335. doi:10.1287/mnsc.1040.0153

Murthi, B. P. S., & Sarkar, S. (2003). The role of the management sciences in research on personalization. *Management Science*, *10*(49), 1344–1362. doi:10.1287/mnsc.49.10.1344.17313

Ngai, E. W. T., & Wat, F. K. T. (2002). A literature review and classification of electronic commerce research. *Information & Management*, *5*(39), 415–429. doi:10.1016/S0378-7206(01)00107-0

Palmer, J. W. (2002). Web site usability, design, and performance metrics. *Information Systems Research*, *2*(13), 151–167. doi:10.1287/isre.13.2.151.88

Pavlou, P. A. (2002). Institution-based trust in interorganizational exchange relationships: the role of online B2B marketplaces on trust formation. *The Journal of Strategic Information Systems*, *3-4*(11), 215–243. doi:10.1016/S0963-8687(02)00017-3

Pfeffer, J., & Salancik, G. R. (1978). *The external control of organizations: a resource dependency perspective*. Stanford, California: Stanford Business Classics, Stanford Business Books.

Pinker, E. J., Seidmann, A., & Vakrat, Y. (2003). Managing online auctions: current business and research issues. *Management Science*, *11*(49), 1457–1484. doi:10.1287/mnsc.49.11.1457.20584

Preibusch, S., Hoser, B., Gürses, S., & Berendt, B. (2007). Ubiquitous social networks – opportunities and challenges for privacy-aware user modeling. *Proceedings of the Data Mining for Knowledge Discovery Workshop*.

Sarathy, R., & Robertson, C. J. (2003). Strategic and ethical considerations in managing digital privacy. *Journal of Business Ethics*, *46*(2). doi:10.1023/A:1025001627419

Son, J. Y., & Kim, S. S. (2008). Internet users' information privacy-protective responses: A taxonomy and a nomological model. *Management Information Systems Quarterly*, *32*(3), 503–529.

Stewart-Schwaig, K., Kane, J., & Storey, V. C. (2005). Privacy, fair information practices and the fortune 500: the virtual reality of compliance. *Database*, *36*(1), 49–63.

Straub, D., Weill, P., & Schwaig, K. S. (2008). Strategic dependence on the IT resource and outsourcing: a test of the strategic control model. *Information Systems Frontiers*, *10*(2), 195–210. doi:10.1007/s10796-008-9064-9

Swire, P. P. (1997). *Markets, self-regulation, and government enforcement in the protection of personal information. Privacy and Self-Regulation in the Information Age* (pp. 3–20). Washington, D.C.: U.S. Department of Commerce.

Tang, Z. L., Hu, Y., & Smith, M. D. (2008). Gaining trust through online privacy protection: Self-regulation, mandatory standards, or Caveat Emptor. *Journal of Management Information Systems*, *24*(4), 153–173. doi:10.2753/MIS0742-1222240406

Teo, T. S. H., & Pian, Y. (2004). A model for web adoption. *Information & Management*, *4*(41), 457–468. doi:10.1016/S0378-7206(03)00084-3

Thuraisingham, B. (2005). Privacy-preserving data mining: development and directions. *Journal of Database Management*, *16*(1), 75–87. doi:10.4018/jdm.2005010106

Van der Heijden, H. (2002). Factors influencing the usage of websites: The case of a generic portal in the Netherlands. *Information & Management, 40*(6), 541–549. doi:10.1016/S0378-7206(02)00079-4

Warren, S., & Brandeis, L. (1890). The right of privacy. *Harvard Law Review, 5*(4), 193–220. doi:10.2307/1321160

Westin, A. (1967). *Privacy and Freedom*. New York: Athenaeum.

Wheeler, B. C. (2002). NEBIC: A dynamic capabilities theory for assessing net- enablement. *Information Systems Research, 13*(2), 125–146. doi:10.1287/isre.13.2.125.89

Winter, S. J., Saunders, C., & Hart, P. (2003). Electronic window dressing: impression management with websites. *European Journal of Information Systems, 4*(12), 309–322. doi:10.1057/palgrave.ejis.3000470

Xu, H., Teo, H. H., Tan, B. C. Y., & Agarwal, R. (2009). The Role of Push-Pull Technology in Privacy Calculus: The Case of Location-Based Services. *Journal of Management Information Systems, 26*(3), 135–173. doi:10.2753/MIS0742-1222260305

Yao, M. Z., Rice, R. E., & Wallis, K. (2007). Predicting user concerns about online privacy. *Journal of the American Society for Information Science and Technology, 58*(5), doi:10.1002/asi.20530

Zhu, K., & Kraemer, K. L. (2002). E-commerce metrics for net-enhanced organizations: assessing the value of e-commerce to firm performance in the manufacturing sector. *Information Systems Research, 3*(13), 275–295. doi:10.1287/isre.13.3.275.82

ENDNOTE

[1]   http://www.privacyrights.org/data-breach

APPENDIX: SURVEY INSTRUMENT

For each question, give the privacy a statement a 1 for each question in which the privacy statement scores a "yes" and a 0 for each question in which the privacy statement scores a "no."

Enforcement/ Redress

Q1   Is a PRIVACY SEAL posted on this domain

Notice/ Awareness

Q2   Does the Privacy Policy/Information Practice Statement say anything about what specific personal information the domain collects from consumers?

Q3   Does the Privacy Policy/ Information Practice Statement say anything about how the domain may use personal information it collects for internal purposes?

Q4   Does the Privacy Policy/Information Practice Statement say anything about whether the domain places cookies?

Q5   Does the Privacy Policy/Information Practice Statement make any special provisions for children?

Choice/ Consent

Q6   Does the Privacy Policy/ Information Practice Statement say that the domain provides consumers an opportunity to opt in or opt out of receiving future communications from the domain (other than those directly related to processing an order or responding to a consumer's question) (Choice)?

Q7   Does the Privacy Policy/Information Practice Statement say anything about whether the domain discloses personal information it collects to third parties?

Q8   Does the Privacy Policy/Information Practice Statement say whether the domain provides consumers an opportunity to opt in or opt out of the disclosure of personal identifying information to third parties

Access/ Participation

Q9   Does the Privacy Policy/Information Practice Statement say that the domain allows consumers to review at least *some* personal information about them?

Q10 Does the Privacy Policy/Information Practice Statement say that the domain allows consumers to have inaccuracies corrected in at least some personal information about them?

Q11 Does the Privacy Policy/Information Practice Statement say that it allows consumers to have at least some personal information about them deleted from the domain's records?

Security/ Integrity

Q12 Does the Privacy Policy/Information Practice Statement say that the domain takes steps to provide security, for personal information the domain collects, during transmission of the information from the consumer to the domain? Example: Secure Socket Layer Technology or SSL

Q13 Does the Privacy Policy/Information Practice Statement say that the domain takes steps to provide security, for personal information the domain has collected, after the domain has received the information (i.e., not during transmission, but after collection)?

Chapter 6
Reverse Engineering from an XML Document into an Extended DTD Graph

Herbert Shiu
City University of Hong Kong, Hong Kong

Joseph Fong
City University of Hong Kong, Hong Kong

ABSTRACT

Extensible Markup Language (XML) has become a standard for persistent storage and data interchange via the Internet due to its openness, self-descriptiveness and flexibility. This paper proposes a systematic approach to reverse engineer arbitrary XML documents to their conceptual schema – Extended DTD Graphs — which is a DTD Graph with data semantics. The proposed approach not only determines the structure of the XML document, but also derives candidate data semantics from the XML element instances by treating each XML element instance as a record in a table of a relational database. One application of the determined data semantics is to verify the linkages among elements. Implicit and explicit referential linkages are among XML elements modeled by the parent-children structure and ID/IDREF(S) respectively. As a result, an arbitrary XML document can be reverse engineered into its conceptual schema in an Extended DTD Graph format.

INTRODUCTION

As Extensible Markup Language (XML)(Bray, 2004) has become the standard document format, the chance that users have to deal with XML docu-ments with different structures is increasing. If the schema of the XML documents in Document Type Definition (DTD)(Bosak, 1998) is given or derived from the XML documents right away(Kay, 1999; Moh, 2000), it is easier to study the contents of the XML documents. However, the formats of

DOI: 10.4018/978-1-60960-521-6.ch006

these schemas are hard to read, not to mention rather poor user-friendliness.

XML has been the common format for storing and transferring data between software applications and even business parties, as most software applications can generate or handle XML documents. For example, a common scenario is that XML documents are generated and based on the data stored in a relational database — and there have been various approaches for doing so(Thiran, 2004; Fernandez, 2001). The sizes of XML documents that are generated based on the data stored in databases can be very large. Most probably, these documents are stored in a persistent storage for backup purposes, as XML is the ideal format that can be processed by any software applications in the future.

In order to handle the above scenario, it is possible to treat XML element instances in an XML document as individual entities, and the relationships from the different XML element types can be determined by reverse engineering them for their conceptual models, such as Extended DTD Graphs with data semantics. As such, users can have a better understanding of the contents of the XML document and further operations with the XML document become possible, such as storing and querying(Florescu 1999; Deutsch, 1999; Kanne, 2000).

This paper proposes several algorithms that analyze XML documents for their conceptual schema. Two main categories of XML documents exist — data-centric and narrative. As the contents of narrative XML documents, such as *DocBook*(Bob Stayton, 2008) documents, are mainly unstructured and their vocabulary is basically static, the necessity of handling them as structured contents and reverse engineering them into conceptual models is far less than that of handling data-centric ones. Therefore, this paper will concentrate on data centric XML documents.

Referential Integrity in XML documents

XML natively supports one referential integrity mechanism, which are ID/IDREF(S) types of attribute linkages. In every XML document, the value of an ID type attribute appears at most once and the value of the IDREF(S) attribute must refer to one ID type attribute value(s). An IDREF(S) type attribute can refer to any XML element in the same document, and each XML element can define at most one ID type attribute. Due to the nature of ID/IDREF(S) type attributes in XML documents, relationships among different XML element types can be realized and it is possible to use them to implement data semantics.

This paper will discuss the various data semantics and the possible ways to implement them. The algorithms presented in the paper are based on the observations of the common XML document structures.

1. Using the nested structure of an XML document (the relationship between a parent element and its child element(s)), in which the child elements implicitly refer to their parent element.
2. For an IDREF or IDREFS type attribute, the defining element is referred to the element(s) with an ID type attribute by the referred value. Such linkages are similar to the foreign keys in a relational database. The two associated element types are considered to be linked by an explicit linkage.
3. As an IDREFS type attribute can refer to more than one element, there is a one-to-many cardinality from the referring element type and the referred element type(s).

The schema of an XML document can restrict the order of the XML elements — and the order of the elements may be significant — which depends on the intentions of the original XML document

Table 1 Two equivalent XML documents that can represent the same data

DTD	XML Document
<!ELEMENT couples (husband*,wife*,couple*)> <!ELEMENT husband EMPTY> <!ELEMENT wife EMPTY> <!ATTLIST husband hid ID #REQUIRED name CDATA #REQUIRED> <!ATTLIST wife wid ID #REQUIRED name CDATA #REQUIRED> <!ATTLIST couple hid IDREF #REQUIRED wid IDREF #REQUIRED>	<?xml version="1.0"?> <couples> <husband hid="A123456" name="Peter"/> <husband hid="B234567" name="John"/> <wife wid="X123456" name="Amy"/> <wife wid="Y234567" name="Bonnie"/> <couple hid="A123456" wid="X123456"/> <couple hid="B234567" wid="Y234567"/> </couples>
<!ELEMENT couples (husband,wife)*> <!ELEMENT husband EMPTY> <!ELEMENT wife EMPTY> <!ATTLIST husband hid ID #REQUIRED name CDATA #REQUIRED> <!ATTLIST wife wid ID #REQUIRED name CDATA #REQUIRED>	<?xml version="1.0"?> <couples> <husband hid="A123456" name="Peter"/> <wife wid="X123456" name="Amy"/> <husband hid="B234567" name="John"/> <wife wid="Y234567" name="Bonnie"/> </couples>

designer. For example, two XML documents with their corresponding DTD's are shown in Table 1.

The two XML documents shown in table 1 are storing the same data, which are the data of two couples. For the former one, its couple elements use the two IDREF type attributes to denote the corresponding husband and wife elements. However, the use of ID/IDREF cannot ensure a particular husband or wife element must be referred by one couple element only. For the latter XML document, the DTD restricts that the husband and wife elements must exist as a pair. Furthermore, the use of ID type attributes hid and wid ensures any husband and wife element instance must exist in the document at most once.

Extended DTD Graph

As XML element instances are treated as individual entities, the relationships from the element types are therefore related not only to the structure of the XML document but also to the linkages from

the different types. As such, DTD cannot clearly indicate the relationships.

An Extended DTD Graph for XML is proposed to add data semantics into a DTD Graph so that the data semantics can be clearly identified, which is an excellent way of presenting the structure of an XML document. As such, in order to visualize the data semantics determined based on the XML document with its optional schema, it will provide the notations to be used for presenting the various data semantics. This paper uses the authors' notations of the Extended DTD graph for presenting the structure and the data semantics from the elements, as follows:

1. The vertexes as squares are drawn on the graph for elements, and vertexes as circles are drawn for occurrence operators (?, + and *) and selection operator (|).
2. Attributes and simple elements are omitted from the graph, as they specify a particular attribute of their defining and parent elements respectively.

Figure 1. A sample Extended DTD Graph

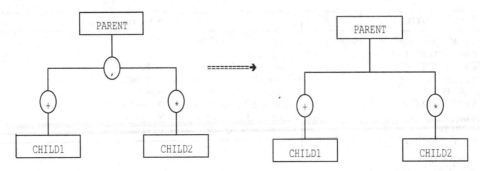

3. Data semantics, other than one-to-one and one-to-many cardinality relations, are presented in the graph as arrows pointing from the referring element to the referred element with suitable descriptions as legends.

Based on the above criteria, it is possible to consider the ELEMENT declarations only for constructing the Extended DTD graph. Three types of ELEMENT declarations can be identified as follows:

1. An ELEMENT declaration defines sub-elements only.
2. An ELEMENT declaration involves sub-elements and #PCDATA as its contents.
3. An ELEMENT declaration that defines #PCDATA as its contents only.

The above three types correspond to the following three examples:

```
<!ELEMENT PARENT (CHILD1+, CHILD2*)>
<!ELEMENT MIXED_ELEMENT (#PCDATA |
CHILD1 | CHILD2)*>
<!ELEMENT SIMPLE_ELEMENT (#PCDATA)>
```

For each ELEMENT declaration of the first type, the content model expression can be tokenized as individual elements and occurrence indicators and sequence separators (,), and represented as a tree structure with the element name

as the root node. For example, the first example above can be visualized as the following tree diagram. In Figure 1, the sequence "," is implied in the diagram.

DTD's mostly contain more than one ELEMENT declaration but each element type can only appear once. Therefore, to construct the complete DTD graph for a DTD, the tree structures of all ELEMENT declarations in a DTD are constructed first and they are eventually merged by replacing each sub-element node in a tree by the tree structure of that element. Such merging is repeated until there is only one tree structure or all sub-elements have been replaced with their corresponding tree structures.

Cardinality / Participation

Element types are visualized as rectangles in the graph and a cardinality relationship is presented as an arrow pointing from the referring element type to the referred element type, with double-line and single line for total participation and partial participation respectively. The cardinality types, including one-to-one (1/1), one-to-many (1/m), many-to-one (m/1) and many-to-many (m/m), are shown as legends of the arrows. If the cardinality relationship is implemented as explicit ID/IDREF(S) linkages, the name of the ID type attribute of the referring element is appended to the legend, such as 1/m (parent_id). To identify explicit linkages from implicit linkages, cardi-

Table 2. The arrows illustrating various cardinalities with participation types

Participation Cardinality	Partial	Total
One-to-one		
One-to-many		
Many-to-one		
Many-to-many		

nality relationships due to ID/IDREF(S) type attributes are shown as arrows with a curved line. Table 2 presents the eight possible combinations of arrows and legends.

N-ary Relationship

An *n-ary* relationship is implemented as a particular element type involved in more than two binary relationships. To represent such a relationship, a diamond-shaped vertex is used for such element types. Figure 2 presents a sample diagram with an *n-ary* relationship.

Aggregation Relationship

An aggregation relationship denotes that the involved element types must exist as a unity. In Figure 2, an aggregation exists as the defining characteristic of mandatory participation between parent and child elements. As such, a rectangle is to be drawn enclosing all involved element types.

RELATED WORK

In order to have a complete picture of the reasons behind the algorithms for determining various data semantics, this paper explains the existing approaches of constructing XML documents, especially those exported from relational databases.

The Determination of XML Schema

There is some existing work concerning the extraction of schema, such as DTD, from XML documents(Chidlovskii, 2001; Min, 2003). The outputs of these algorithms are the schemas that can validate the XML documents. However, the derived schemas provide no semantic interpretation other than the containment structures of the XML documents. The algorithms proposed in this paper concern the determination of data semantics from the XML element instances rather than simply XML schema among XML elements. Compared with the approach proposed by Goldman and Widom(Goldman, 1997) that directly manipulates semi-structured databases, such as an XML document, the algorithm proposed here provides the user with a clear picture of the data semantics from the XML element instances before further manipulating them.

Figure 2. A sample diagram with an n-ary relationship

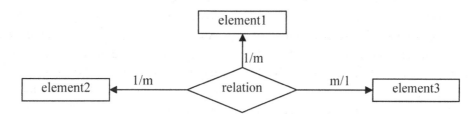

The Determination of Data Semantics from XML Documents

One approach exists that can reverse engineer data semantics from XML documents(Fong, 2004), but the algorithm maps some predefined templates of document structures to data semantics, and the algorithm can only be implemented with DOM(W3C, 2003), which needs to read the entire XML document to the memory — and that is inappropriate for huge XML documents. The methodology presented in this paper, however, determines basic candidate data semantics from arbitrary XML documents with SAX(Saxproject, 2004), which is applicable to XML documents of any size. Some of the determined data semantics may not be the intentions of the original writer and needs user supervision for verification.

The Implementation of Inheritance among XML Elements

Schema for Object-oriented XML (SOX)(W3C, 2005) introduced the idea of element and attribute inheritance, which enables an element to extend another element so that the derived element can have all attributes defined by the base element with its own new attributes.

Due to the limitations and low extensibility of DTD(Sahuguet, 2000), XML Schema Definition (XSD)(Sperberg, 2000) is becoming the popular replacement schema of DTD. Unlike DTD, XSD is an XML document itself and it can define more restrictive constraints and clear definitions of the XML documents to be validated. In other words, the set of capabilities for defining the structures and data types of XSD are the superset of that of DTD. As such, there has been research and software for converting DTD to XSD(Mello, 2001; W3C, 2000).

There are other alternative schemas, such as RELAX NG(Relaxng, 2003) and Schematron(Schematron, 2008) and Lee and Chu(Lee, 2000) evaluated six common XML schemas, including DTD and XSD. As they are not as popular as DTD and XSD, they are not discussed in this paper.

By constructing a graph by placing vertexes for elements — and the elements that are involved in a parent-child relation, which is defined by ELEMENT declaration in DTD, are connected with edges — it is possible to derive a graphical representation of the DTD that is commonly known as a DTD graph. Up to now, there is no formal standard for DTD graphs and various researchers are using their own conventions as in(Klettke, 2002; Shanmugasundaram, 2001; Lu, 2003; Böttcher, 2003), and the graph introduced in (Funderburk, 2002) is the first one that was denoted as a DTD graph.

There is a graphical representation of XSD(Fong, 2005) which derives an XML conceptual schema of an XML Tree Model from an XML schema of XSD. Its approach is different from this paper's approach by deriving an Extended DTD Graph from an XML document.

As the conventions of most graphs for presenting the structure of an XML document are applicable to different schema languages, the graph is also known as Semantic graph(An, 2005). Some researchers proposed other graphical representations of XML schemas, such as the use of UML(Booch, 1999).

The Application of Extended DTD Graph

Data Graph is a DTD in graph. (Zhao, 2007) described that DTD can be a good common data model when the majority of data sources are XML sources for the interoperability between relational databases and XML databases. Reserve engineering XML document into DTD graph is similar to data mining XML document into a data tree(Zhang, 2006). The former is a database schema while the later is an internal data in tree structure. (Trujillo, 2004) demonstrated that a DTD can be used to define the correct structure

Table 3. A comparison between the proposed and other existing approaches

	Proposed approach	Other approaches
Input	XML document with optional schema	XML document
Output	Conceptual schema with data semantics	Schema without data semantics
Completeness	All common data semantics can be determined	Schemas that can validate the XML document can be derived
User friendliness	Algorithms can be implemented with a user friendly GUI, such as the prototype.	Commercial products exist that provide a user friendly GUI.
Performance	Good	Not available as no mathematical proofs were provided.

and content of an XML document representing main conceptual Multidemension model for data warehouses.

Compared with the approach proposed by Goldman and Widom(Goldman, 1997) that directly manipulates semi-structured databases such as an XML document, the algorithm proposed in this paper enables the user to have a clear picture of the data semantics from the XML element instances before further manipulating them. Table 3 provides a comparison between the proposed algorithms and other existing approaches.

Reverse Engineering Methodology

There are basically two different definitions in a DTD, which are ELEMENT and ATTLIST. Each ATTLIST definition defines the attributes of a particular element, whereas ELEMENT defines its possible containments, and each ELEMENT definition can be represented in a tree structure with the element name as the root element with its child sub-elements as leaves, and there must be another ELEMENT definition for each of its child elements.

It is not mandatory to define the ELEMENT declaration prior to all its child elements, and it is actually uncertain which element is the root element of the corresponding XML documents. The root element of the XML document is defined by the DOCTYPE declaration before the root element start tag.

Implementations of various Data Semantics in XML

The following subsections provide all possible implementations of various data semantics, some of which are consistent with those proposed by other researchers(Lee, 2003; Lee, 2000).

Cardinalities

One-to-many cardinalities can be realized by both explicit and implicit referential linkages. By implicit referential linkages, a parent element can have child elements of the same type, such as,

```
<PURCHASE_ORDER>
    <PURCHASE_ORDER_LINE.../>
    <PURCHASE_ORDER_LINE.../>
</PURCHASE_ORDER>
```

The parent element PURCHASE_ORDER and the child elements PURCHASE_ORDER_LINE are implicitly in a one-to-many relationship. If the occurrences of child element PURCHASE_ORDER_LINE are at most one for all PURCHASE_ORDER elements, they are in a one-to-one relationship instead.

If the schema of the XML document is given, it can specify the ID/IDREF(S) type attributes. If an XML element defines an IDREF attribute and all such elements refer to the same element type, there is a one-to-many relationship between

Figure 3. A many-to-one cardinality implemented by an IDREF type attribute

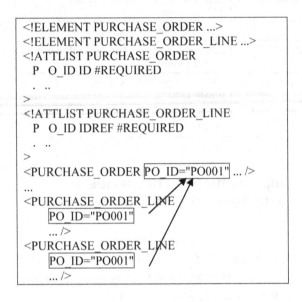

the referred and referring XML elements. For example, sample DTD and XML documents are shown in Figure 3.

For explicit referential linkages, to determine if the cardinality is one-to-one or one-to-many, it is necessary to scan the entire XML document. An XML element type may be involved in more than one one-to-many relationship. In other words, all elements of such XML element types define more than one linkage. For example, if an XML element type defines an IDREF(S) type attribute, all elements of such XML element type actually define two linkages, one implicit linkage by the nested structure and one explicit linkage by the IDREF(S) type attribute. If the two linkages are both one-to-many relationships, the two referred element types by such a referring element type can be considered to be in a many-to-many relationship. For example, the XML document in Figure 4 illustrates a many-to-many relationship.

Figure 4. A many-to-many cardinality implemented by an element type with two IDREF type attributes

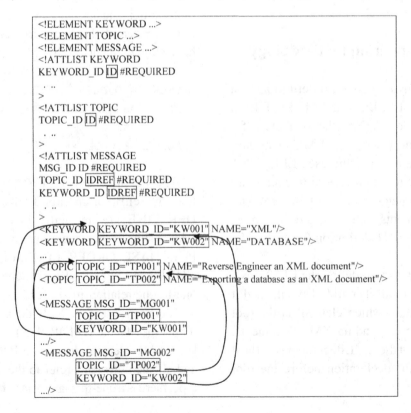

For an XML element type that defines two linkages and hence two one-to-many relationships, the two referred XML element types can be considered to be in a many-to-many relationship.

The linkages from the XML elements in an XML document are identified by the referring element name, linkage name and the referred element name. The algorithm shown in Box 1 is used to determine the following table 4 of the linkages.

Figure 5 illustrates the meanings of the four attributes.

There are eight XML elements in the document and there is only one implicit linkage from them. The values of the above four linkage attributes for such implicit linkage are shown in Table 5.

According to the combination of the values of the four attributes, it is possible to determine the cardinality data semantics for the involved elements. The rules are show in table 6.

The algorithm is composed of two passes of parsing of the same XML document. The first pass assigns a synthetic element identity to each XML element in the document and determines all ID type attribute values and their corresponding element types. For the second pass, the XML document is traversed again and the linkages of each XML element are investigated and their attributes are stored. Finally, the stored linkage attributes are consolidated to give the four linkage attributes mentioned above and in Table 4.

The algorithm shown in Figure 6 can determine whether the XML document is valid, in particular whether a non-existing ID value is referred by an IDREF(S) type attribute. If the XML document

Table 4. The attributes and their sources for determining data semantics

Attribute	Description	Value
MaxReferring	The maximum number of referred elements referred by a single referring element	Get from Referring Info with key *(RGE, RDE, L)*
MaxReferred	The maximum number of the referring elements that is referring to the same referred element with the same linkage type.	Get from Referred Info with key *(RGE, RDE, L)*
SumReferring	The number of referring elements that possess the linkage.	Get from ReferringInfo with key *(RGE, RDE, L)*
NumberElements	The number of referring elements in the document.	Get from ElementNameCount with key RGE

Figure 5. MaxReferring, MaxReferred, SumReferring & NumberElements example

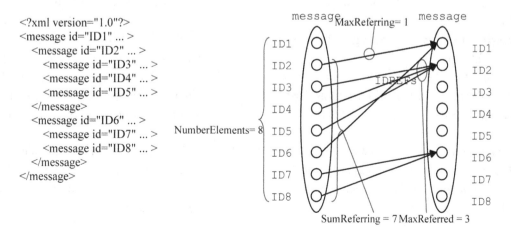

Table 5. Descriptions of variables in reverse engineering algorithms

Attribute Name	Value	Explanations
MaxReferring	1	All linkages are implicit and each child element has one implicit parent element only.
MaxReferred	3	The root message element with attribute id value ID1 is referred by two sub elements (with attribute id values ID2 and ID6). The message element with attribute id value ID2 is referred by three sub elements (with attribute id values ID3, ID4 and ID5). The message element with attribute id value ID6 is referred by two sub elements (with attribute id values ID7 and ID8). Therefore, the value of MND is 3.
SumReferring	7	Except the root message element with attribute id value ID1, all other message elements define such linkages. The value of NL is therefore 7.
NumberElements	8	There are eight message elements.

Table 6. Matrix for determining cardinality & participation based on the determined linkage attributes

		Participation	
		Total	**Partial**
Cardinality	One-to-one	MaxReferring= 1 MaxReferred = 1 SumReferring= NumberElements	MaxReferring = 1 MaxReferred= 1 SumReferring < NumberElements
	One-to-many	MaxReferring = 1 MaxReferred > 1 SumReferring = NumberElements	MaxReferring = 1 MaxReferred > 1 SumReferring < NumberElements
	Many-to-one	MaxReferring > 1 MaxReferred = 1 SumReferring = NumberElements	MaxReferring > 1 MaxReferred = 1 SumReferring < NumberElements
	Many-to-many	MaxReferring > 1 MaxReferred > 1 SumReferring = NumberElements	MaxReferring > 1 MaxReferred > 1 SumReferring < NumberElements

is valid, three tables can be obtained — *ReferringInfo*, *ReferredInfo* and *ElementNameCount*. The key for the former two tables is the composite key (RGE, RDE, L), that is, the referring element name, the referred element name and the linkage name, whereas the key for the *ElementNameCount* is simply the element name. With three such tables, it is possible to derive the linkage attributes as shown in Table 4.

The complete algorithm is presented in Box 1 and the following is a list of definitions for the variables to be used:

EID. The current element ID. While processing the XML document sequentially, the EID determines the ID to be assigned to individual element encountered.

E. The current element to be handled.

A. An attribute of the current element to be handled.

AV. The attribute value of attribute A.

L. A linkage of the current element. It can be an implicit linkage with its parent element or an explicit linkage with an IDREF(S) type attribute. For a non-root element without IDREF(S) attribute, the element has only one implicit linkage to its parent element. Otherwise, the element can have more than one linkage, one implicit linkage and at least one explicit linkages.

L_{value}. The Element ID of the linkage L for the current element E. For example, if L is an implicit linkage, L_{value} is the element ID of the parent element of E. Otherwise, L_{value} is

Figure 6. The determined data semantics

Type	Elements	Link name
many-to-many	element1 / element2	element3
one-to-many / Total	element1 / element3	idref1
one-to-many / Total	element2 / element3	idref2
one-to-many / Total	test / element1	- Implicit -
one-to-many / Total	test / element2	- Implicit -
one-to-many / Total	test / element3	- Implicit -

the attribute value of IDREF value and the value should be an ID type attribute of an element in the same document.

NG. The number of referring element of the same element name is referring to the same referred element with the same link.

RGE. The referring element of a link.

RDE. The referred element by a link.

The above operation can be represented by the following SQL,

```
SELECT
        RGE, RDE, L,
        ReferringInfo.MaxReferring,
        ReferredInfo.MaxReferred,
        ReferringInfo.SumReferring,
        ElementNameCount.NumberEle-
ments
FROM
        ReferringInfo
        INNER JOIN ReferredInfo
                ON ReferringInfo.RGE
= ReferredInfo.RGE
                AND ReferringInfo.
RDE = ReferredInfo.RDE
                AND ReferringInfo.L
= ReferredInfo.L
        INNER JOIN ElementNameCount
                ON ReferringInfo.RGE
= ElementNameCount.E
```

Once the four attributes of a linkage are determined, the data semantics can be determined by using the matrix shown in Table 6. According to the determined one-to-one and one-to-many relationships, it is then possible to consolidate the related ones into many-to-many and *n-ary* relationships.

As mentioned above, if an XML element type defines two linkages that are determined to be many-to-one cardinalities, the two referred XML element types are considered to be in a many-to-many relationship. Similarly, if an XML element type defines more than two linkages that are determined to be many-to-one cardinalities, the referred XML element types are considered to be in an *n-ary* relationship. Therefore, based on the one-to-many cardinalities determined by the previous algorithm, the many-to-many and *n-ary* relationships can be determined, and the algorithm is shown in Box 2.

The many-to-one relationship to be considered should be those implemented by explicit linkages; that is, those defined by ID/IDREF(S) linkages. Otherwise, an element type exhibits implicit a one-to-many relationship due to nested structure and defines a many-to-one relationship that will

Box 1.

Pass One:
Let $EID = 1$;
Repeat until all XML document elements are read
Let E be the current element to be processed
If $\exists$ record in $Table_{ElementNameCount}$ where $ElementName$ = element name of E
Get record ($ElementName$, $NumberElement$) from $Table_{ElementNameCount}$
Increment $NumberElement$ by 1;
Update ($ElementName$, $NumberElement$) into $Table_{ElementNameCount}$;
Else
Add ($ElementName$, 1) into $Set_{ElementNameCount}$;
End If
Add (EID, $ElementName$) into $Set_{ElementIDName}$;
If there exists ID type attribute A of element E with attribute value AV
Add (AV, $ElementName$) into $Set_{ElementIDName}$;
End If
Increment EID by 1;
Navigate to the next element E in the XML document

Pass Two:
Repeat until all XML document elements are read
Let RGE is the current element to be handled
For each linkage, L, of RGE
For each linkage value, L_{value} of linkage L of RGE
Get record (EID,$ElementName$) from $Table_{ElementIDName}$
where primary key value is L_{value}
If no such record exist in $Table_{ElementIDName}$
XML document is invalid
Else
Let $RDE = ElementName$ of the record obtained from $Table_{ElementIDName}$
End If

Get record (RGE, RDE, L, L_{value}, ND) from $Table_{RawReferredInfo}$
for primary key (RGE, RDE, L, L_{value});
If record exists
Increment ND of the record by 1;
Update the record to $Table_{RawReferredInfo}$;
Else
Add record (RGE, RDE, L, L_{value}, 1) to the $Table_{RawReferredInfo}$;
End If

For each referred element type, RDE
Let NG = number of RDE referred by this linkage, L;
Get record (RGE, RDE, L,$MaxReferring$, $SumReferring$)
from the $Table_{ReferringInfo}$ for primary key (RGE, RDE, L);
If record exists
If $NG > MaxReferring$ from the record
Update $MaxReferring$ of the record to be NG
End If
Increment $SumReferring$ of the record by 1;
Upda te the record to the $Table_{ReferringInfo}$;
Else
Add record (RGE, RDE, L, NG, 1) to the $Table_{ReferringInfo}$;
End If
End For
End For
End For
Navigator to the next element RGE in the XML document

Consolidate the records with same combination of (RGE, RDE, L) in table $RawReferredInfo$;
let $MaxReferred$ = maximum of the ND values of all records;
Add record (RGE, RDE, L, $MaxReferred$) to the table $ReferredInfo$;

Box 2. The algorithm for determining many-to-many and n-ary relationships

```
Get referring XML element types from one-to-many cardinalities;
For each referring XML element T_referring type
        Get referred XML element types, S_referred referred by T_referring via explicit linkages;
If the size of the set S_referred = 2
XML element types in S_referred = many-to-many relationship with T_referring;
Else
        If size of S_referred > 2
XML element types in S_referred = n-ary relationship with T_referring;
```

be considered to be a many-to-many relationship, but the two referred elements are actually not related at all.

Participation

Participation concerns whether all instances of a particular element type are involved in a relationship with the corresponding element type.

For implicit referential linkage by a parent-child relation, such as the following DTD ELEMENT declaration,

```
<!ELEMENT PARENT (CHILD*)>
```

and there are no other ELEMENT declarations that define CHILD as their child elements, all CHILD element instances must appear as the child element of a PARENT element, and hence the participation can be considered to be total, as all instances of CHILD must be involved in the one-to-many cardinality relation with PARENT. If no schema is provided, and if all instances of an element type always appear as the child elements of the same parent element type, the participation is also considered to be total.

For explicit referential linkage by ID/IDREF(S) attributes, if all instances of an element type use the same attribute with values referring instances of the same element type, the relationship is considered to be total participation. Otherwise, the relation is considered to be partial. The DTD of the XML document can only identify the ID/IDREF(S) type attributes but it cannot restrict the referring and

referred element types. As such, actually parsing the XML document is required to determine the type of participation.

Aggregation

An aggregation means that the creation of a whole part of an element depends on the existences of its component sub elements. An aggregation relation is signified by the scenario that elements of different types are considered to be a single entity and all constituting elements must exist altogether. An XML document by itself does not provide any facility to enforce such a constraint. At best, the schema can hint at the correlations of the existence of the elements in the corresponding XML document.

For implicit referential linkage by an aggregation relationship, such as the following DTD ELEMENT declaration,

```
<!ELEMENT AGGREGATION (COMPONENT_1,
COMPONENT_2,....COMPONENT_N)+>
```

For example, the following ELEMENT declaration can restrict the existence of the elements, enrollment, student and course.

```
<!ELEMENT enrollment (student,
course)+>
```

Besides, no student or course elements exist in the document that are not the sub-element of an enrollment element. For example, if there is another ELEMENT declaration in the same DTD, such as,

```
<!ELEMENT student_list (student*)>
```

student elements can exist in the document as the sub-elements of a student_list element. As such, the co-existence relationship of enrollment, student and course elements no longer holds.

Such a co-existence relationship specified in the schema can be extended to more than one nested level. For example, if the existence of a course element must be accompanied by a lecturer element and a tutor element, that is,

```
<!ELEMENT course (lecturer, tutor)+>
```

the elements, enrollment, student, course, lecturer and tutor, must exist as a whole. Then, all these elements are considered as an aggregation relationship. From another perspective, an aggregation relationship is actually composed of two one-to-one cardinality relations (course – lecturer and course – tutor) which are both total participation.

An exceptional case is that if the sub-elements are actually the attribute of the parent element, such as in example one, it is inappropriate to consider that the involved elements are in an aggregation relationship. As a result, user supervision is needed in the process.

Based on the DTD of the XML document, it is possible to determine the aggregation relationships from the elements. As the requirements of an aggregation relationship is the co-existence of the involved elements and the order of the sub-elements for a parent element is insignificant, the nested structure of the elements should first be simplified with the algorithm presented in Box 3 where T is an aggregation tree.

The determination of aggregation relationships is separated into two parts. The first part first discovers the pair of parent and child elements that must co-exist. Once the pairs are determined,

the second part of the algorithm treats each pair as a path from parent element to the child element in a sub-tree, and these sub-trees are merged to form a bigger tree. Eventually, the nodes in each tree must co-exist, and they are in aggregation relationship. The second part is straightforward except there is a tricky point that if a child element is found to be a non-root node of a particular sub-tree, it implies that such an element can have more than one parent element, and the aggregation relation that includes such element must start with the parent element.

For example, for a list of ELEMENT declaration in the DTD,

```
<!ELEMENT A (B, C)>
<!ELEMENT B (D)>
<!ELEMENT C (D)>
<!ELEMENT D (E, F)>
```

The determined pairs of raw aggregation relations are (A, B), (A, C), (B, D), (C, D), (D, E) and (D, F). While merging the raw aggregation relations,

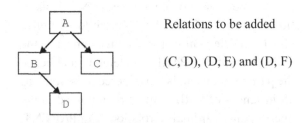

While adding the path (C, D) to the sub-tree, as D is not a root node, D should be removed from the sub-tree and it is considered to be an individual sub-tree with D as the single node.

Box 3. The algorithm for determining aggregation relationships

```
Let Set_temporary = empty;
For each ELEMENT declaration for element E_parent
  For each child element, element_child
  If element_child = mandatory and non-repeatable
  Add an aggregation relation (E_parent, E_child) to Set_temporary;
```
```
Let Set_aggregation and Set_root = empty;
For each relation R (E_parent, E_child) in Set_temporary
If (∃ tree, T, in Set_aggregation) ∧ (E_parent is a node in T) ∧ (E_child is not a node in T)
Add a path E_parent to E_child to T;
Else
        (∃ tree, T, in Set_aggregation) ∧ (E_child is a node of T) ∧ (E_parent is not a node)
If (E_child = root node) ∧ (E_child not in Set_root of T)
Add the path E_parent to E_child to T;
Else
Add E_child to Set_root
        Remove the sub-tree starting with E_child from T;
        If ∃ sub-tree starting with E_child in multiple nodes
            Add sub-tree to Set_aggregation;
```
```
Else
        ∃ tree T_i with a node for E_parent and T_j with E_child as root node;

Merge trees T_i and T_j with a path from node for E_parent in T_i to root of T_j
Else
        ¬∃ sub-tree in Set_aggregation with node for either E_parent and E_child;
Add a new tree with a path E_parent to E_child to Set_aggregation;
```

After the path (D, E) and (D, F) is added to the sub-tree with node D as the root node, two sub-trees are obtained,

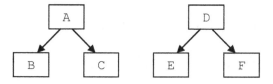

As such, the elements A, B and C, and the elements D, E and F, are considered as being two individual aggregation relationships.

Case Study and Prototype

To illustrate the applicability and correctness of the algorithms mentioned in this paper, a prototype was built that implements the algorithms proposed in this paper. For actually drawing the DTD graph, the algorithm proposed by (Shiren, 2001) is used to define the layout of the vertexes on the graph. With such a prototype, a sample XML document with DTD file as shown in Box 4 is provided to the prototype.

For this case study, both ID/IDREF type attributes are considered and the minimum number of common attributes is one. All elements with at least one attribute are sorted in ascending order of the lengths of their attribute lists. Therefore, the order of the elements to be processed is:

```
element1, element2, element3
```

According to the DTD of the XML document, only one ELEMENT declaration is used for constructing the Extended DTD Graph, as the contents of other element types are EMPTY.

```
<!ELEMENT test (element1*,element2*,e
lement3*)>
```

Therefore, only those explicit one-to-many relationships are to be added to the graph, and the graph will become the one shown in Figure

Box 4. test.xml and test.dtd

```
<?xml version="1.0"?>
<test>
 <element1 id="id1"/>
 <element1 id="id2"/>
 <element2 id="id3"/>
 <element2 id="id4"/>
 <element3 id="id5" idref1="id1" idref2="id3"/>
 <element3 id="id6" idref1="id2" idref2="id4"/>
 <element3 id="id7" idref1="id1" idref2="id4"/>
 <element3 id="id8" idref1="id2" idref2="id3"/>
</test>
```

```
<!ELEMENT test (element1*,element2*,element3*)>
<!ELEMENT element1 EMPTY>
<!ELEMENT element2 EMPTY>
<!ELEMENT element3 EMPTY>

<!ATTLIST element1
 id ID #REQUIRED>
<!ATTLIST element2
 id ID #REQUIRED>
<!ATTLIST element3
 id ID #REQUIRED
 idref1 IDREF #REQUIRED
 idref2 IDREF #REQUIRED>
```

6 and 7. The detailed derivation of the reverse engineering can be referred to (Shiu, 2006).

CONCLUSION

In order to make use of the XML document, software developers and end-users must have a thorough understanding of the contents in the XML document, especially those historical and huge XML documents. Sometimes the schemas of XML documents are missing and the XML documents cannot be opened to be inspected on the screen due to their huge size. Therefore, it is necessary to determine as much information as possible regarding the relationships from the elements in the document.

By reverse engineering the XML document with DTD, all explicit linkages can be determined and the resultant DTD Graph can be used to verify the correctness of ID/IDREF(S) linkages, as any incorrect IDREF(S) linkage will be indicated as an extra cardinality and shown in the Extended DTD graph. This paper provides algorithms to help the users to understand the relationships from the elements by reverse engineering data semantics from the XML document, including:

Figure 7. Extended DTD Graph based on the DTD and the determined cardinality References

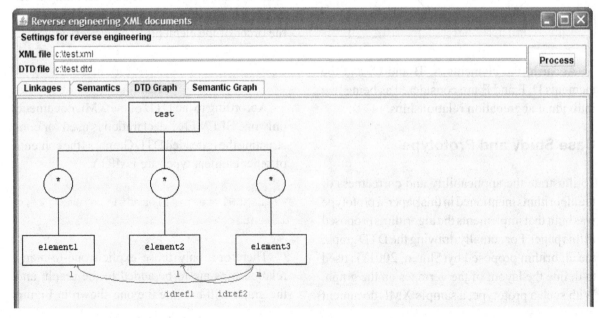

1. Cardinality relationships
2. Participation relationships
3. *n-ary* relationships
4. Aggregation relationships
5. Many-to-many relationships (a special case of cardinality relationships)

In summary, to visualize the determined data semantics, a new Extended DTD Graph is proposed. XML documents natively support one-to-one, one-to-many and participation, data semantics. With a corresponding schema, such as DTD, the ID and IDREFS attributes of the elements can be identified, and many-to-many, *n-ary* and aggregation relationships can also be determined.

ACKNOWLEDGMENT

This paper is funded by Strategic Research Grant 7002325 of City University of Hong Kong

REFERENCES

W3C(1998). Schema for Object-oriented XML, http://www.w3.org/TR/1998/NOTE-SOX-19980930/

W3C(2003). Document Object Model DOM. http://www.w3.org/DOM.

W3C(2004). Simple API for XML, SAX. http://www.saxproject.org/.

An, Y., Borgida, A., & Mylopoulos, J. (2005). Constructing Complex Semantic Mappings Between XML Data and Ontologies. *International Semantic Web Conference ISWC 2005, pp. 6-20.*

Booch, G., Christerson, M., Fuchs, M., & Koistinen, J. (1999). UML for XML schema mapping specification. http://xml.coverpages.org/fuchs-uml_xmlschema33.pdf

Bosak, J., Bray, T., Connolly, D., Maler, E., Nicol, G., Sperberg-McQueen, C. M., et al. (1998). Guide to the W3C XML Specification (XMLspec) DTD, Version 2.1, http://www.w3.org/XML/1998/06/xmlspec-report-v21.htm

Böttcher, S., & Steinmetz, R. (2003). A DTD Graph Based XPath Query Subsumption Test. *Xsym, 2003*, 85–99.

Bray, T., Paoli, J., Sperberg-McQueen, C. M., Maler, E., & Yergeau, F. (2004). Extensible Markup Language (XML) 1.0 (Third Edition), http://www.w3.org/TR/2004/REC-xml-20040204.

Chidlovskii, B. (2001). *Schema Extraction from XML Data: A Grammatical Inference Approach, KRDB'01 Workshop.* Knowledge Representation and Databases.

Deutsch, A., Fernandez, M., & Suciu, D. (1999). Storing Semi-structured Data with STORED, *SIGMOD Conference, Philadelphia, Pennsylvania.*

Fernandez, M., Morishima, A., & Suciu, D. (2001). Publishing Relational Data in XML: the SilkRoute Approach. *A Quarterly Bulletin of the Computer Society of the IEEE Technical Committee on Data Engineering, 24*(2), 12–19.

Florescu, D., & Kossmann, D. (1999). Storing and Querying XML Data Using an RDBMS. *A Quarterly Bulletin of the Computer Society of the IEEE Technical Committee on Data Engineering, 22*(3), 27–34.

Fong, J., & Cheung, S. K. (2005). Translating relational schema into XML schema definition with data semantic preservation and XSD graph, *Information and Software Technology, 47(7),pp.437-462.* Funderburk, JE., Kiernan, G., Shanmugasundaram, J., Shekita, E.,&Wei, C.(2002). XTABLES: Bridging relational technology and XML. *IBM Systems Journal, 41*(4), 2002.

Fong, J., & Wong, H. K. (2004). XTOPO, An XML-based Technology for Information Highway on the Internet. *Journal of Database Management, 15*(3), 18–44. doi:10.4018/jdm.2004070102

Goldman, R., & Widom, J. (1997). DataGuides: Enabling Query Formulation and Optimization in Kanne, CC.,(2000). Guido Moerkotte. Efficient storage of xml data. *Proc. of ICDE, California, USA, page 198.*

Kay, M. (1999) DTDGenerator – A tool to generate XML DTDs, http://users.breathe.com/mhkay/saxon/dtdgen.html

Klettke, M., Schneider, L., & Heuer, A. (2002). Metrics for XML document collections. *Akmal Chaudri and Rainer Unland, XMLDM Workshop, pages 162-176, Prague, Czech Republic.*

Koike, Y. (2001). A Conversion Tool from DTD to XML Schema. http://www.w3.org/2000/04/schema_hack/.

Lee, D. W., & Chu, W. W. (2000). Comparative Analysis of Six XML Schema Languages. *SIGMOD Record, 29*(3). doi:10.1145/362084.362140

Lee, D. W., & Chu, W. W. (2000). Constraints-Preserving Transformation from {XML} Document Type Definition to Relational Schema. *International Conference on Conceptual Modeling / the Entity Relationship Approach, pp 323-338.*

Lee, D. W., Mani, M., & Chu, W. W. (2003). *Schema Conversion Methods between XML and Relational Models.* Knowledge Transformation for the Semantic Web.

Lu, S., Sun, Y., Atay, M., & Fotouhi, F. (2003). A New Inlining Algorithm for Mapping XML DTDs to Relational Schemas. *Proc. Of the First International Workshop on XML Schema and Data Management, in conjunction with the 22nd ACM International Conference on Conceptual Modeling (ER2003).*

Mello, R., & Heuser, C. (2001). A Rule-Based Conversion of a {DTD} to a Conceptual Schema. *Lecture Notes in Computer Science, 2224,.* doi:10.1007/3-540-45581-7_12

Min, J. K., Ahn, J. Y., & Chung, C. W. (2003). Efficient extraction of schemas for XML documents. *Information Processing Letters, 85*(Issue 1),. doi:10.1016/S0020-0190(02)00345-9

Moh. C., Lim, e.,& Ng, W.,(2000). DTD-Miner: A tool for mining DTD from XML documents. *Proceedings of the second International Workshop on Advanced Issues of E-Commerce.*

Relaxng(2003). RELAX NG, http://www.relaxng.org/.

Sahuguet, A.,(2000). Everything You Ever Wanted to Know About DTDs, But Were Afraid to Ask. *WebDB-2000.*

Semistructured Databases. *Very Large Data Bases, Proceedings of the 23rd International Conference on Very Large Data Bases).*

Shanmugasundaram, J., Shekita, E., Kiernan, J., Krishnamurthy, R., Viglas, E., Naughton, J.,& Shematron(2008). Schematron, http://www.schematron.com/.

Shiren, Y., Xiujun, G., Zhongzhi, S.,&Bing, W.,(2001). Tree's Drawing Algorithm and Visualizing Method, *CAD/Graphics'2001.*

Shiu, H. (2006). Reverse Engineering Data Semantics from Arbitrary XML document, *Computer Science department, City University of Hong Kong, M.Phil dissertation, September 2006.*

Sperberg-MCQueen. C.,&Thompson,H.,(2000). W3C XML Schema,http://www.w3.org/XML/Schema.

Stayton, B. (2008). DocBook, http://www.docbook.org/

Tatarinov, I. (2001). A general technique for querying XML documents using a relational database system. *SIGMOD Record, 30*(3), 261–270.

Thiran, P. H., & Estiévenart, F. Hainaut. JL.,& Houben, GJ.,(2004). Exporting Databases in XML - A Conceptual and Generic Approach, *Proceedings of CAiSE Workshops (WISM'04)*.

Trujillo, J., & Luján-Mora, S. (2004). Applying UML and XML for Designing and Interchanging Information for Data Warehouses and OLAP Applications. *Journal of Database Management, 15*(Issue 1), 41–72. doi:10.4018/jdm.2004010102

Zhang, J., Liu, H., Ling, T., Bruckner, R., & Tija, A. (2006). A Framework for Efficient Association Rule Mining in XML Data. *Journal of Database Management, 17*(Issue 3), 19–40. doi:10.4018/jdm.2006070102

Zhao, L., & Siau, K. (2007). Information Mediation Using Metamodels: An Approach Using XML and Common Warehouse Metamodel. *Journal of Database Management, 18*(Issue 3), 69–82. doi:10.4018/jdm.2007070104

This work was previously published in Journal of Database Management (JDM) 20(2), edited by Keng Siau, pp. 38-57, copyright 2009 by IGI Publishing (an imprint of IGI Global).

120

Chapter 7
Scalable XML Filtering for Content Subscriptions

Ryan Choi[1]
KAIST, Korea

Raymond Wong
The University of New South Wales, Australia

ABSTRACT

Over the past few years, there have been an increasing number of Web applications that exchange various types of data on the Internet. In this article, we propose a technique for building efficient and scalable XML publish/subscribe applications. In particular, we look at the problem of processing streaming XML data efficiently against a large number of branch XPath queries. To improve the performance of XML data processing, the branch queries that have similar query characteristics are grouped, and common paths between the queries in the same group are identified. Then, these groups of queries are processed against an XML schema to validate query structures. After performing structural matching of queries, the queries are organized in a way that multiple queries can be evaluated simultaneously in the post-processing phase. In the post-processing phase, join operations are executed in a pipeline fashion, and intermediate join results are shared amongst the queries in the same group. The benefit of this approach is that, the total number of join operations performed in the post-processing phase is significantly reduced. In addition, we also present how to efficiently return all matching elements for each matching branch query. Experiments show that our proposal is efficient and scalable compared to previous works.

INTRODUCTION

With the development of the World Wide Web (WWW), a huge number of Web-based applica-

DOI: 10.4018/978-1-60960-521-6.ch007

tions have been developed over the past few years. Web 2.0 (O'Reilly, 2005) goes one step further than traditional web applications in a way that, they provide personalized services, as well as letting users create, publish, and share contents amongst other users who share similar interests.

Recent works include online finance (Nah, Siau, & Tian, 2005), education (Siau, Sheng, & Nah, 2006), government (Siau & Long, 2006), healthcare (Siau & Shen, 2006), and firewall (Benedikt, Jeffrey, & Ley-Wild, 2008) applications. Another important difference between Web 2.0 and traditional web applications is that, users of Web 2.0 applications *subscribe* to the contents that they are interested in, and the web contents are delivered directly to users. Furthermore, users with similar interests can share their subscriptions to quickly discover other related contents. This is quite different from traditional web applications, where users obtain contents of interest by visiting web sites, following links, etc.

As a motivating example of a Web 2.0 application, let us consider an online-based news feed application that delivers latest news articles to users. A unique characteristic of this application is that, it receives various types of streaming data from multiple data publishers, selects data of interest, and forwards the selected data to various groups of users who are interested in receiving such data. One problem associated with this application is that, since each data publisher is designed and implemented differently, the data format from one data publisher is usually incompatible with the formats from other peer data publishers. Having a unique format for each data publisher causes problems when the data are collected and processed by a single application. XML (Bray, Paoli, Sperberg-McQueen, Maler, & Yergeau, 2008) solves this problem by providing a way to represent any data from different publishers in a universal format, such that the data can be collected and processed by a single application. Moreover, while data are converted to XML, irregular data, which may have been represented by multiple data and metadata tables in relational database systems, can be intuitively and logically represented. Let us now assume that all data publishers use XML to represent their data.

While information searching and retrieval are well studied areas in research communities, the problems in this context are different from the traditional search problems in many ways. In this context, new data continuously arrive to our news feed application, and the application must select or *filter* the right data according to user subscriptions. In our application, we represent user subscriptions in XPath (Clark & DeRose, 1999) queries. Then, the "query results" in this context are a set of matching XPath queries for each streaming XML document. The use of XML and XPath to implement a filtering mechanism has a number of advantages over similar but non XML-based approaches. First, more expressive user subscriptions can be supported. Unlike keyword-based subscriptions, which simply report matching sets of keywords for each document, users can also utilize structural information implicitly integrated to XML documents to precisely specify the exact content that they wish to receive. For example, while it is logical to express an XPath subscription to find news articles in a financial section that talk about the impact of US mortgage crisis, such subscription is not trivial in keyword-based subscriptions. Second, there are more opportunities to optimize a filtering processor. For example, since subscriptions are written in XPath queries, it is possible to group similar queries and process groups of queries simultaneously. Third, the use of XML is perfect to model the increasing amount of semi-structured data on the Web.

There have been a number of research works on how to filter a stream of XML data according to user subscriptions. The application that implements such functionality is commonly known as an *XML publish/subscribe* system (or *XML pub/sub system* for short) in the literature. The main focus of these works is how to evaluate a large number of XPath queries efficiently against streaming XML data. To do so, these works proposed a number of ways to build, combine, and share XPath queries. However, some works are not suitable for our need as: (1) XFilter (Altinel & Franklin, 2000), LazyDFA (Green, Gupta, Miklau, Onizuka, & Suciu, 2004), Bloom Filter

(Gong, Yan, Qian, & Zhou, 2005), and AFilter (Candan, Hsiung, Chen, Tatemura, & Agrawal, 2006) cannot evaluate branch XPath queries; and (2) TwigStack (Bruno, Koudas, & Srivastava, 2002), FluX (Koch, Scherzinger, Schweikardt, & Stegmaier, 2004), XFPro (Huo et al., 2006), XSQ (Peng & Chawathe, 2003, 2005), SPEX (Bry et al., 2005; Olteanu, 2007), and Gou & Chirkova (2007) cannot process multiple XPath queries. Supporting branch XPath queries is important in Web service applications, as subscribers usually subscribe to the documents they are interested in by setting a few constraints that the documents should satisfy. To process a branch query, we split the query into a set of multiple linear queries, evaluate the linear queries against a streaming document, and report the branch query as matched if all of its linear queries are matched. This is similar to the approach proposed by YFilter (Diao, Fischer, Franklin, & To, 2002; Diao, Altinel, Franklin, Zhang, & Fischer, 2003) and Onizuka (2003). One characteristic of this approach is that, most of the processing time is spent in the post-processing phase where decomposed linear queries are combined and checked for validity. To reduce the processing time in the post-processing phase, it is necessary to: (1) identify and avoid any unsuccessful and duplicate processing of queries; and (2) branch queries must be evaluated as a group rather than individually by utilizing any commonalities between branch queries. Although many previous works (Chan, Felber, Garofalakis, & Rastogi, 2002b, 2002a; Diao et al., 2002, 2003; Gupta & Suciu, 2003; Onizuka, 2003; Rao & Moon, 2004; Kwon, Rao, Moon, & Lee, 2005) present some ways of combining states/stacks/nodes while parsing XML documents, they do not provide any approach that evaluates groups of queries without checking the status of each branch query individually. In addition, they only report matching query IDs per streaming document, and do not provide approaches for returning all matching elements for each matching query. In

this article, we propose a technique that addresses these problems.

First, to avoid unnecessary join operations, we only consider queries whose structures match the document structure against which the queries are evaluated. To identify such queries, we build a query index for a set of documents based on document structural information, and pre-process the queries against the query index prior to evaluating them against streaming XML documents. By doing so, we identify the queries whose structures match the document structures, and therefore, we only perform join operations for structurally matching queries in the post-processing phase. This method gives us two advantages over other methods that construct automata/trees from a set of queries without considering document structures. First, many join operations that lead to unsuccessful evaluation of queries are avoided. Second, the groups of queries whose twig patterns are equivalent but are written differently are identified. For example, while twig patterns of queries such as /a/b[c]/d and /a/b[d]/c are the same, they are written differently. By utilizing these information, unnecessary and duplicate processing of queries can be avoided.

Second, unlike YFilter, we do not evaluate branch queries individually. In addition, we reduce the processing time in the post-processing phase by reducing the total number of join operations that must be performed in order to evaluate the entire queries. This is based on the observation that there are many common paths between queries. For example, let us refer to the following two queries, q1:=/a[b]//c[d/e]/f[g] and q2:=/a[b]//c[d/e]/f[h] as the queries that have common paths, since both queries have the paths p1:=/a/b, p2:=/a//c/f, and p3:=/a//c/d/e in common. The total number of join operations needed to evaluate the entire queries are reduced when join operations are performed amongst a group of queries that have common paths. This is because some intermediate join results can be shared. For example, when the above queries are evaluated, we store the intermediate join results that are obtained when p1, p2, and p3 are joined while q1 is being evaluated, and reuse them when q2 is evaluated. In this example, compared to YFilter, the total number of join operations required to evaluate q1 and q2 is reduced from 8 to 5, since YFilter simply combines the decomposed queries without considering any common path. The effect of sharing intermediate join results becomes significant as the number of queries increases.

Finally, the query index used in our approach is closely modeled as Deterministic Finite Automaton (DFA), whereas YFilter is based on Nondeterministic Finite Automaton (NFA). Therefore, unlike YFilter, we can collect all information required to combine decomposed queries at near constant time without being influenced by the types of queries or documents. While NFA-based approaches guarantee space requirements, the performance of these approaches may vary, as the performance depends on the queries and streaming XML documents. Furthermore, it is accepted that DFA-based approaches are more efficient than NFA-based approaches in terms of processing costs required in runtime (He, Luo, & Choi, 2006). In addition, unlike the approaches by Onizuka (2003), Rao & Moon (2004), and Kwon et al. (2005), we do not distinguish queries that only differ by predicate orders, as we believe that there are more applications that require us to ignore such orders. For example, we interpret queries such as a/b[c][d] and a/b[d][c] the same.

This article is organized as follows. The second section presents related research works in the area of processing XPath queries against streaming XML documents. The third section presents the data structure and the SAX parser upon which our technique is built. The fourth section proposes our technique for processing branch XPath queries. The fifth section presents experiment results. The sixth section compares our technique with previous works in detail. Finally, we conclude this article in the last section.

RELATED WORK

We now describe related research works in the context of processing streaming XML messages. Felber, Chan, Garofalakis, and Rastogi (2003) provide an overview on scalable, Web-based XML data filtering services. Zhao and Siau (2007) provide system architecture for processing heterogeneous online information encoded in XML. Erickson and Siau (2008) discuss Web services, service-oriented architecture (SOA) and service-oriented computing (SOC), and Smolander and Rossi (2008) describe e-business architecture. Diao, Rizvi, and Franklin (2004) introduce an overall architecture of a scalable XML pub/sub system, and Chandramouli, Yang, Agarwal, Yu, and Zheng (2008) proposed an RDBS-based pub/sub architecture, which modifies the states of the database according to the events arrived from publishers.

XFilter (Altinel & Franklin, 2000) is one of the earliest XML pub/sub systems. In XFilter, each linear XPath query is decomposed to location steps, and these location steps are added to Query Index, which models the location steps as states in a finite state machine. Queries are evaluated by making state transitions when XML data arrive. To improve overall performance, it proposed a list balancing technique in which a pivot node is selected based on a selectivity of streaming nodes rather than the first location step. However, XFilter is limited in a way that, unlike our approach, it does not support branch XPath queries, and is designed towards handling small discrete XML documents. Nevertheless, XFilter proposed the concept of filtering XML documents according to a set of subscriptions written in XPath queries.

XTrie (Chan et al., 2002b, 2002a) is based on trie structures, and it supports branch XPath queries. It decomposes XPath twig patterns into longest substrings that only contain "/," and uses a trie to detect the occurrences of substring matches for each SAX event it receives. Moreover, decomposing queries into longest substrings also reduces the overall number of unnecessary query processing steps for non-matching documents. Compared to our approach, constructing a query index is similar, but in our approach, a query index is built based on the document structure rather than query structures. In addition, our approach identifies common paths between queries during index compilation phase. Lastly, our index provides faster element matching in runtime, as there are a smaller number of nodes to look up.

YFilter (Diao et al., 2002, 2003) is a successor of XFilter that supports branch XPath queries. It improves overall performance by sharing some paths between branch queries. Furthermore, it separates query matching process into structural and content matching parts. To achieve path sharing, an NFA of branch queries is built during index compilation phase. Similar to our approach, branch queries are decomposed into multiple linear queries, and in the post-processing phase, all matching linear queries are combined. In this approach, majority of query processing time is spent in the post-processing phase when all matching results are combined. Compared to our approach, YFilter evaluates branch queries individually in the post-processing phase, whereas we evaluate groups of queries that have different twig patterns. In addition, we share intermediate join results amongst the queries in the same group when the queries are combined. Since YFilter is NFA-based, its performance is affected by document and query structures. An advantage of an NFA-based approach is that, a set of queries that are vastly different in structures are generally better supported than a DFA-based approach. However, query and document structures in practice tend to be simple (Mignet, Barbosa, & Veltri, 2003). Thus, based on this observation, our approach is based on DFA, which is better suited in practice, and has a better runtime performance.

LazyDFA (Green, Miklau, Onizuka, & Suciu, 2003; Green et al., 2004) uses a DFA to evaluate a large number of linear XPath queries. Its experiments demonstrate that DFA-based approaches

take near constant processing time independent to the query size. One drawback of this approach is that, as pointed out in its experiments, the space requirement is not bounded. However, the size of LazyDFA is kept minimal by building a DFA at runtime lazily, which results in having small document structures for data-oriented documents. Its approach is efficient both in time and space for evaluating linear XPath queries for data-oriented documents. Our approach can also process linear XPath queries at near constant time.

XPush (Gupta & Suciu, 2003) extends LazyDFA to process branch XPath queries by using a deterministic pushdown automaton in a bottom up way. Although, in theory, it takes constant time to process each streaming element, it rarely achieves its theoretical performance due to a large memory requirement, especially when the queries with "*" are processed. In practice, the efficiency of this approach is about linear to the number of queries. In contrast, our approach expands queries with "*" according to a document schema, and evaluates the queries in the same way as queries without "*." Furthermore, our approach is not linear to the number of queries, as groups of structurally equivalent queries are evaluated rather than individually.

A study by Onizuka (2003) provides an improvement of LazyDFA. It reduces the number of states required to process complex XML documents by grouping linear queries into several clusters. In addition, it also supports branch queries by building an NFA that is shared by DFA states. Similar to other approaches, it decomposes branch queries, and evaluates each linear query using LazyDFA. As a result, its performance depends on the number of event invocations from its XPath processor, which also depends on the number of decomposed XPath queries. However, it shows how effective a DFA-based approach is compared to others. An approach by Uchiyama, Onizuka, & Honishi (2005) is built on top of LazyDFA. It proposed how workload of a Filtering Server can be redistributed amongst other Filtering Servers in order to prevent the overloading of a server.

Unlike previous approaches, Bloom Filter (Gong et al., 2005) improves the performance of filtering XML documents by sacrificing the accuracy of reporting matching queries (i.e., false positives are allowed). It uses Bloom filters (Bloom, 1970) to represent a group of linear queries, and provides a hash-based join approach to evaluate XPath queries. To improve query processing, queries with the same prefix are shared to reduce the overall number of candidate paths (i.e., Prefix Filters). However, it does not support branch queries, and by allowing inaccuracy, it is not suitable for certain applications.

XSQ (Peng & Chawathe, 2003, 2005) is different from many previous works in such a way that, it is designed to evaluate a query against a large streaming document in size (i.e., 100s of MB), and to return a set of matching elements for a given query. To achieve this, it builds an NFA for each branch query, and maintains its own buffer to store potential matching elements. Since it processes each NFA separately, and the states in NFA are not shared, it is not suitable for processing a large number of queries. Furthermore, the buffer management policy is not clear when a large number of elements, such as the entire document whose size is bigger than the physical amount of memory, are to be stored. Bar-Yossef, Fontoura, and Josifovski (2005) analyze the size of buffer required by a typical XML filtering processor. Grohe, Koch, and Schweikardt (2005) analyze memory requirements for automata-based approaches.

PRIX (Rao & Moon, 2004) and its successor FiST (Kwon et al., 2005) interpret both branch XPath queries and XML documents as twig patterns, and transform each branch query into a sequence of elements using a tree pre-order traversal and Prüfer Sequence, respectively. Then, they both match the sequence of streaming elements against the sequences of branch queries. Unlike other approaches, they do not decompose

branch queries into linear queries. Furthermore, they organize the sequences of queries into a hash-based index to improve the overall performance. However, the implicit order created by either the pre-order traversal or Prüfer Sequence imposes the implicit predicate order for branch queries. For example, a query a/b[c][d] is matched only if element b, c and d appear under a in that order. While there are applications that require to validate predicate order (e.g., English grammar checker), many online filtering applications need to ignore the order, as the order often does not contribute semantics in practice (e.g., requesting newspaper articles about "IBM" and "Apple" are the same as requesting newspaper articles about "Apple" and "IBM").

XPath-NFA (He et al., 2006) is a simplified version of YFilter that builds an NFA from XPath queries. However, it converts an NFA to DFAs through subset construction, and organizes automata in a way that, it utilizes CPU's L2 cache. It identifies the area where state transitions occur the most frequently in an automaton, and places these areas into an in-memory data structure, called hot buffer, for fast cache access. Hot buffers can also be configured to support incremental updates of XPath queries. This work provides a practical way of implementing XML filtering applications independent to underlying filtering algorithms. One possible future work is to adapt such technique to our approach to efficiently utilize today's high-end hardware.

Chan and Ni (2007) proposed an optimization technique in which queries are aggregated according to containment relationships between queries. However, their technique can only be applied to a query processor that processes queries individually. Hence, query processors that group queries such as YFilter and ours cannot benefit from this technique. Furthermore, the aggregation of queries requires much more preprocessing time, and there are cases where aggregated queries match, but individual queries do not match. In that case, separate processing steps are required to remove those non-matching queries. Zhou, Salehi, and Aberer (2009) proposed a distributed data dissemination architecture, which merges user subscriptions into a few representative queries that exploit common query results.

Unlike all the previous works, Huang, Chuang, Lu, and Lee (2006) and XFPro (Huo et al., 2006) optimize query processing by reducing the size of streaming documents. Huang et al. (2006) prefilter a streaming document by discarding the parts of the document that are not needed to evaluate a query. XFPro decomposes streaming document by using Hole-Filler (Fegaras, Levine, Bose, & Chaluvadi, 2002) approach. However, both approaches are designed to process a single query at a time.

There are a few stream-querying algorithms that utilize the multi-stack approach proposed by TwigStack (Bruno et al., 2002) to evaluate a query. AFilter (Candan et al., 2006) builds a reverse directed graph, prefix tree and suffix tree from linear XPath queries, and shares the query results amongst the queries that have the same prefix when the linear queries are evaluated. In addition, it reduces the number of graph traversals using the suffix tree when the queries with the same prefix are evaluated. It adapts the multi-stack approach to store/maintain nodes in a graph. However, AFilter cannot process branch queries. TwigM (Chen, Davidson, & Zheng, 2006) proposed a lazy stream-querying algorithm that evaluates an XPath query in polynomial time. It extends the multi-stack approach to compactly store candidate nodes from a recursive document. Gou & Chirkova (2007) proposed a state-of-the-art, stack-based algorithms, which do not store duplicate potential answer nodes. Since TwigM (Chen et al., 2006) and Gou and Chirkova (2007) are stream-querying algorithms, they are not suitable for building XML filtering applications. However, they presented how answer nodes can be efficiently computed against a large document in size.

While there are many works done in the context of evaluating XPath queries against streaming XML documents, there are only a few works that are related to evaluating queries with join operations. Many previous works (e.g., Chan et al. (2002a); Diao et al. (2003); Gupta & Suciu (2003); Onizuka (2003); Rao & Moon (2004); Uchiyama et al. (2005); Kwon et al. (2005)) present how a large number of XPath queries can be evaluated against a streaming XML document. While all these works return the set of matching XPath IDs for each document, they do not support queries with join operations. In addition, they do not return matching nodes for matching queries, and it is not clear how they can be extended to do so. Diao and Franklin (2003) extend YFilter, such that they can return matching elements for some matching queries. In their system, queries with conjunctive predicates of the form are supported. Hong et al. (2007) proposed a technique that processes queries with join operations. Their approach uses a customized query language to define queries with join operators. In the compilation phase, their system uses Query Templates to group queries in a way that, each group contains queries with similar join statements. In runtime, it uses a relational database to join elements. Their approach works with an existing XPath processor as an add-on module to support queries with join operators. However, their template-based approach only works for the queries that join two leaves of documents (i.e., queries that join non-leaves of documents are not supported). In addition, their approach is designed to process relatively small documents in size (i.e., documents with 3 levels deep with 16 leaves as shown in their experiments). This is because the number of Query Templates rapidly increases as the number of leaves per document increases. Due to the same reason, their approach does not scale well for the queries that join elements from multiple documents. Similar patterns are observed when the number of join operations per query increases. Chandramouli and Yang (2008) proposed a technique that supports a large number of select-join subscriptions for RDBS-based publish/subscribe systems.

There are some works that use XML algebra to efficiently process XPath and XQuery queries. Fegaras et al. (2002) transform an XQuery query into a set of XML algebra expressions to optimize the query according to a query plan. They then process XML documents that have been fragmented by its Hole-Filter approach. Both Raindrop (Su, Jian, & Rundensteiner, 2003; Su, Rundensteiner, & Mani, 2004, 2005) and R-Sox (S. Wang et al., 2006) also transform an XQuery query into XML algebra, but use NFAs to encode XPath path expressions. FluX (Koch et al., 2004) utilizes a document schema to optimize XQuery query processing. Li and Agrawal (2005) transform an XQuery query into a series of query execution steps in such a way that, the query can be evaluated against a streaming document. Su et al. (2005) model XML as an ordered tree, and utilize DTD to obtain the order in which the nodes in the XML tree occur, and using the order information, they proposed how unmatching nodes can be skipped. However, all these works (Fegaras et al., 2002; Su et al., 2003, 2004, 2005; S. Wang et al., 2006; Koch et al., 2004; Li & Agrawal, 2005) are designed to evaluate a single query at a time, and thus they are not suitable for building online applications that need to evaluate multiple queries simultaneously. Barta, Consens, and Mendelzon (2005) use document summaries to calculate heuristics and statistics, and optimize (nested) XPath query processing. Gottlob, Koch, and Pichler (2005) define and evaluate a subset of XPath queries called Core XPath. They also present how queries with aggregates and user-defined functions can be processed. However, the approaches in Barta et al. (2005) and Gottlob et al. (2005) are not suitable for processing streaming documents, as they need multiple passes of documents. In addition, they are designed to process a small set of queries against a large XML document. Nevertheless, all these works demonstrate how traditional query optimization techniques can be integrated to process (streaming) documents. Several optimization techniques can be integrated into our approach, and such work is left as part of our future work.

Unlike all the pub/sub algorithms or systems above, which are light-weight, in-memory-based, some systems, such as the ones by Seshadri (2003), Zeller (2003), Tian, Reinwald, Pirahesh, Mayr, and Myllymaki (2004), Fong and Wong (2004), Yin and Pedersen (2006), Grust, Rittinger, and Teubner (2007), and Chandramouli and Yang (2008) use relational databases to support XML document processing and filtering. Some works such as Boncz et al. (2006) and Grust et al. (2007) also apply query optimization techniques to evaluate XQuery and XPath queries efficiently. In all these relational database-based systems, XML subscriptions and documents are stored as sets of tuples, and join operations are performed to find matching subscriptions for each stored document. The advantage of this type of approach is that, the scalability of a system is not limited to the amount of physical memory that the system has, and since all subscriptions are stored in databases, the system is not volatile. Also some systems (e.g., Boncz et al. (2006); Grust et al. (2007)) support (almost) full features of XPath/XQuery including updates. However, the systems in this category do not meet our requirements, as they are substantially slower than other in-memory based approaches (e.g., Seshadri (2003); Zeller (2003); Tian et al. (2004); Fong and Wong (2004); Yin and Pedersen (2006); Grust et al. (2007)) and/or evaluate queries individually (e.g., Boncz et al. (2006); Grust et al. (2007)).

Other loosely related works include Barton et al. (2003) and Milo, Zur, and Verbin (2007). Barton et al. (2003) proposed how a single XPath query with both forward and backward axes can be rewritten and evaluated. Its techniques are applicable to all the works listed above. Milo et al. (2007) proposed how topic-based XML pub/sub systems can be optimized. It describes how different topics can be clustered to maximize the overall system performance. While all the works described above are about content-based pub/sub systems, techniques in Milo et al. (2007) may be integrated into these systems to extend/generalize content-based queries to identify/predict potential users who are likely interested in receiving certain events. Such extension is a possible future work.

In general, the problem of evaluating XPath queries efficiently can be solved by combining DFA-based approaches such as the one proposed by LazyDFA with the path sharing concepts such as the one proposed by YFilter. In addition, the runtime performance can be further improved by grouping queries that represent the same twig patterns, as it provides a way to eliminate duplicate processing of queries, and thus it reduces the total number of join operations to process. Unlike other previous works, our approach identifies queries that have the same twig patterns, and efficiently evaluates groups of branch queries by utilizing common paths found between queries in the same group. Furthermore, our approach can also return matching fragments of a document for each matching query efficiently. It is not clear how previous approaches can be extended to achieve this functionality.

PRELIMINARIES

We model XML data as a rooted, labeled, and unordered tree. All attributes and their values are treated as if they were leaf nodes that had child nodes. A *query tree* is a tree representation of a branch query, and a *node* of a query tree represents a location step of a query. A query tree contains two types of nodes: (1) *main* nodes, which are the nodes that represent the main path of a query; and (2) *predicate* nodes, which are the nodes that represent branch paths of a query. A node is a *leaf* node if it does not have any child node. A node is a *branch* node if it has at least one predicate node as a child. This section consists of two parts. The first part introduces a data structure called *structure*

index. The second part shows a modified SAX parser upon which our technique is built.

Structure index is a minimum document structure that represents a set of XML documents that share the same DTD. It contains a unique element and attribute names, and ignores: (1) document orders; and (2) both contents of elements and values of attributes. Figure 1(a) and 1(b) show an example of an XML document and its structure index, respectively. It is different from DTD in a way that, DTD provides the complete information about XML document structure, whereas a structure index simplifies DTD by removing recursive elements by expanding these elements up to the maximum depth of streaming documents. It is similar to DataGuides (Goldman & Widom, 1997) and ViST (H. Wang, Park, Fan, & Yu, 2003), but structure index is used to extract data structures in order to pre-process and expand queries, whereas both DataGuides and ViST are used to index data to improve query processing. Unlike the work by Shiu and Fong (2008), we do not focus on deriving a full DTD from an XML document. The size and complexity of structure index is small and simple in practice for data-oriented documents (Goldman & Widom, 1997), even though the DTDs from these documents allow us to have more complicated structures such as recursive elements. Mignet et al. (2003) also discovered that, 99% of a sample of 200,000 documents publicly available on the Web has less than 8 levels of nesting. Although a structure index is generated in the index compilation phase, each node in the structure index, denoted as an *index node*, is decorated with the information needed to evaluate branch queries while streaming documents are being processed.

We generate a structure index from a set of training documents, all of which represent various document structures of streaming documents. They can be sampled from publishers or generated randomly using a tool such as IBM XML Generator (Diaz & Lovell, 1999). We refer to the initial period of time during which a structure index is constructed as *update phase*. Furthermore,

Figure 1. Sample XML document, structure index, and modified SAX events

Structure Index

```
<a m="1">
  <b>
    <x>
      <x>1</x>
      <f>2</f>
      <x>3</x>
    </x>
    <y>4</y>
    <y>5</y>
  </b>
  <c>
    <y>6</y>
    <e>7</e>
    <e>8</e>
  </c>
  <d>9</d>
</a>
```

(a) An XML document

```
<a>
  <@m/>
  <b>
    <x>
      <x/>
      <f/>
    </x>
    <y/>
  </b>
  <c>
    <y/>
    <e/>
  </c>
  <d/>
</a>
```

(b) Structure index

```
startElem("a")
  startElem("@m")
  endElem("@m")
  startElem("b")
    startElem("x")
      startElem("x")
      endElem("x")
      startElem("f")
      endElem("f")
      startElem("x")
      endElem("x")
    endElem("x")
...
endElem("a")
```

(c) Modified SAX events

we refer to the stage where updates of structure index do not or hardly occur as *stable phase*. Lastly, index nodes in a structure index are labeled using the region-encoding scheme (Bruno et al., 2002).

SAX Parser and Element Processing

A SAX parser is modified as follows. Let us use the term *current element* to refer to the element that is currently being processed by a SAX parser. In addition, let us use the term *current index node* to refer to the index node in a structure index that is currently being examined and processed. startElem(*elem*) and endElem(*elem*) process attributes as if they were child elements of the current element. Figure 1(c) shows the (partial) events produced when a document shown in Figure 1(a) is parsed. Initially, the root of a structure index is set as the current index node. On startElem(*elem*) event, an index node whose name is the same as *elem* is searched amongst the children of the current index node. When such a child node is found, that child node becomes the current index node. The searching process takes $O(1)$, as the names of child nodes are hashed.

On endElem(*elem*) event, the parent of the current index node becomes the current index node if *elem* is the same as the name of the current index node and *elem* occurs at the same level as the current index node. Each time when startElem(*elem*) event is received, we assign an ID to *elem*, and store it in a table.

APPROACH

Having described a structure index and SAX parsers, we now propose a query processing technique. This section consists of five parts. The first part shows how matching instances of a branch query are identified using a structure index. The second part shows how matching instances are organized in a tree called filter tree. The third part shows how queries are processed while a streaming document is being parsed. The fourth part shows how branch queries are evaluated in the post-processing phase using filter trees. The last part shows how matching elements for each branch query can be returned.

Identifying Query Instances

We identify query instances of branch queries using a structure index as follows. First, we decompose each branch query into a group of linear queries by splitting the query at branch nodes. Figure 2 shows an example of how a query is decomposed into linear queries. After that, the linear queries are evaluated against a structure index. Figure 3 shows an example of a structure index after the decomposed queries shown in Fig-

ure 2(b) are evaluated against the structure index shown in Figure 1(b). In Figure 3, an attribute node representing @m is omitted for simplicity. In addition, to distinguish nodes with the same name, a suffix is added to each index node. A query is assigned to more than one index node if a decomposed query contains either // or *, or the structure index has more than one matching index node. Conversely, each index node can contain different decomposed queries. Second, for each matching index node v in the structure index, we obtain a group of index nodes that are along the path between the root of structure index and v. Let us define this group of index nodes as a *path instance*. Figure 4(a) shows the matching index nodes for the decomposed queries shown in Figure 2(b), and Figure 4(b) shows the path instances for the decomposed queries. Lastly, after collecting

Figure 2. Decomposing a branch query

```
Q1: a//*[.//x]//y
```

(a) A branch query

```
Q1-m: a//*//y
Q1-1: a//*//x
```

(b) Decomposed queries

Figure 3. Structure index with decomposed queries

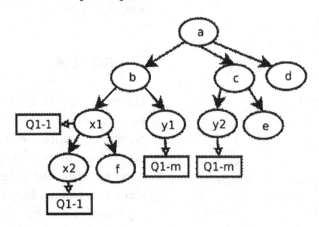

Figure 4. Obtaining path instances from matching leaf index nodes

```
Q1-m matches: y1, y2
Q1-1 matches: x1, x2
```

(a) Matching leaf index nodes

```
y1: /a/b/y1
y2: /a/c/y2
x1: /a/b/x1
x2: /a/b/x1/x2
```

(b) Path instances

all path instances for all decomposed queries from each branch query, we combine path instances using branch index nodes as "anchor" nodes to create a set of path instances that represent all possible matching instances of a branch query. Let us define one matching instance of a query as a *query instance*. Figure 5 shows all query instances of the query shown in Figure 2(a). Algorithm 1 outlines the above procedures (see Figure 6).

Building Filter Trees

A *filter tree* represents a collection of similar query instances that share one or more paths amongst query instances. It is built using a group of query instances in order to evaluate branch queries efficiently in the post-processing phase. By combining common join operations and sharing intermediate join results, we avoid duplicate processing of queries, and hence we reduce the total number of join operations required in the post-processing phase.

Prior to building filter trees, query instances are classified into groups, such that each group has query instances that have the same main leaf node. Figure 7 shows an example of query instances that are derived from three different branch queries. In this figure, all query instances have the same main leaf node, d. The grouping is achieved by first creating $((v),q'_i)$ pairs for each query instance, where (v) is a region encoding label of an index node in the structure index that matches main

leaf node; and q'_i is a query instance ID, and then inserting the pairs into a multi-hashtable. Table 1 shows an example of a multi-hashtable that contains $((v),q'_i)$ pairs of the query instances shown in Figure 5 and 6. The multi-hashtable contains groups of query instances, and each group represents the query instances that have the same main leaf node. Furthermore, grouping also implies that all query instances in the same group have the same main path, as the path between the root of structure index and the matching index node is the same for all query instances in the group.

Figure 8 shows an example of a filter tree that is created from the query instances shown in Figure 7. A filter tree is constructed as follows. For each query instance in a group found in the multi-hashtable, we first create $(l(v_b),l(v_l))$ pairs, where $l(v_b)$ and $l(v_l)$ are the name of each branch and leaf node of a query instance, respectively, and then group the pairs to represent the query instance. After that, all $(l(v_b),l(v_l))$ pairs are sorted. This is to reduce the total number of nodes in a filter tree. Table 2 shows all $(l(v_b),l(v_l))$ pairs cre-

Table 1. A multi-hashtable used to group similar query instances

Label	Query instances
(10,15,3)	Q1-1, Q1-3
(20,30,3)	Q1-2, Q1-4
(40,50,4)	Q2-1, Q3-1, Q4-1

Figure 5. The query instances of Q1 shown in Figure 2(a)

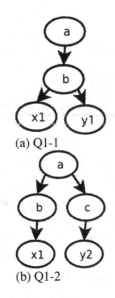

(a) Q1-1

(b) Q1-2

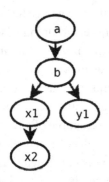

(c) Q1-3

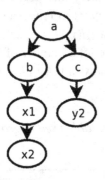

(d) Q1-4

ated from the query instances shown in Figure 7. In case where $(l(v_b),l(v_l))$ pair represents a main path, we set the name of a branch node as *null*. Let us use the term *current context node* to refer to a filter tree node that is currently being examined and processed. Initially, a filter tree contains only a root node, which represents the main leaf node, and the root node is set as the current context node. For each $(l(v_b),l(v_l))$ pair in a query instance, we add the pair as a child of the current context node, and this newly added child node becomes the current context node. If a child node that represents $(l(v_b),l(v_l))$ pair already exists, the existing child node is set as the current context node, and a new child node is not created. When the last $(l(v_b),l(v_l))$ pair is added to a filter tree, the original query ID that this $(l(v_b),l(v_l))$ pair represents is added to the matching filter tree node. Lastly, the above process is repeated for all query instances, and a filter tree is created for each group of query instances that share the same main leaf node. Algorithms 2 and 3 outline the above procedures (see Figure 9 and Figure 10).

While simple sorting of $(l(v_b),l(v_l))$ pairs reduces the total number of nodes in a filter tree, adaptively rearranging the order in which $(l(v_b),l(v_l))$ pairs are added can further reduce the number of nodes in a filter tree. For example, in Figure 8, adding (a,l), (b,f), and (c,h) pairs in this order results in creating additional (a,l), (b,f), and (c,h) nodes in the filter tree. However, creating new nodes can be minimized if the pairs are added in the sequence of (b,f), (c,h), and (a,l), as some of these nodes already exist in the tree. In this way, only (a,l) node is created.

Runtime Processing of Queries

We introduce additional operations and the data structures that we use when a streaming document is processed in runtime. In order to distinguish different elements with the same name, we assign each streaming element a unique ID. We also keep a global stack of elements from which

Figure 6. Algorithm 1

```
Algorithm 1: getQueryInstances(Q, SIRoot)

   input    : Q: branch queries to evaluate
              SIRoot: root of Structure Index
   output   : A group of query instances
 1 begin
 2     queryInstances ← {};
 3     foreach q ∈ Q do
 4         D ← splitBranchQuery(q);
 5         pathsSoFar ← {};
 6         foreach d ∈ D do
 7             {p₁, . . . , pₙ} ← applyDecomposedQuery(d, SIRoot);
 8             pathsSoFar.append({p₁, . . . , pₙ});
           /* combine paths to make query instances for q */
 9         {q'₁, . . . , q'ₘ} ← combinePaths(pathsSoFar);
10         queryInstances.add(q.getID(), {q'₁, . . . , q'ₘ});
11     return queryInstances;
12 end
```

a streaming element is pushed or popped when either startElem(*elem*) or endElem(*elem*) event is received, respectively. Furthermore, a table called *Visited Node Table (VNT)* is created for each index node in the structure index, and updated lazily in runtime. VNT contains sequences of element IDs. Each sequence in VNT represents the path taken to reach a streaming element from the root of the document. VNTs are later used when decomposed queries are combined in the post-processing phase. Lastly, we set the root of the structure index as the current index node. Since branch queries are evaluated in the post-processing phase, processing a streaming element is relatively simple. The procedures are described as follows.

On startElem(*elem*) event, an index node whose name is the same as *elem* is searched amongst the child nodes of the current index node, and that child node is set as the current index node. We then push the element ID that is currently being processed to the global stack. Lastly, we obtain the sequence of element IDs that are along the path between the root of the structure index and the current index node by scanning the global stack, and add this sequence of IDs to the VNT associated with the current index node. Figure 11

shows an example of a structure index, contents of the global stack, and VNTs after processing a couple of streaming elements.

On endElem(*elem*) event, the top element ID on the global stack is popped, and the parent of the current index node is set as the current index node. Algorithms 4 and 5 outline the above procedures (see Figure 12 and Figure 13).

Evaluating Queries

After parsing a streaming document, each filter tree is traversed, and the queries associated with a filter tree are evaluated using VNTs. Before a filter tree is traversed, we perform the following operations. We first check whether the VNT for the root of the filter tree is empty. If the VNT is empty, we skip to the next filter tree, as it implies that non of the queries associated with this filter tree can be matched. Otherwise, the root of the filter tree is set as the current filter tree node. Then, we create a stack called *filter tree stack* to keep track of the filter tree nodes that are along the path between the root of the filter tree and the filter tree node that is being processed. Each entry in the stack contains a storage area where

Figure 7. Query instances from three different queries that have the same main leaf node d

Figure 8. Filter tree

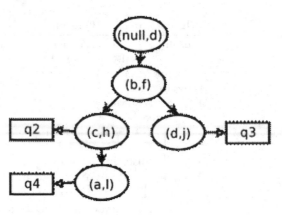

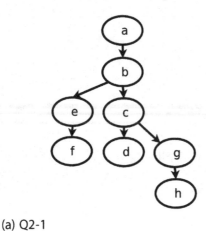

(a) Q2-1

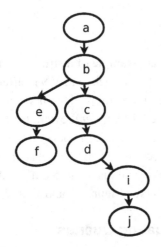

(b) Q3-1

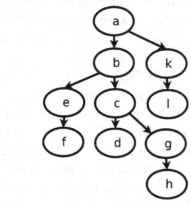

(c) Q4-1

intermediate join results are stored. Let us refer to such a storage area as a *buffer*. A buffer is used in order to reuse any intermediate join results when the queries in filter trees are evaluated. When a stack entry is pushed to an empty stack, the buffer in the stack entry is filled up with the entries found in the root's VNT. Figure 14 shows examples of VNTs and the contents of a filter tree stack when the filter tree shown in Figure 8 is traversed in pre-order traversal. In Figure 14, each stack entry has two components. The left box indicates the name of the filter tree node that this stack entry represents, and the right box displays the contents of the buffer.

A filter tree is traversed as follows. For each child node of the current filter tree node, we find its VNT using the name of a leaf index node. The name of a leaf index node $l(v_l)$ can be found from the name of the child filter tree node, which is in $(l(v_b), l(v_l))$ format. A VNT contains a group of all sequences of element IDs that have been visited during the document parsing. We join this VNT with the contents in the buffer found in a stack entry using a branch node v_b as a joining node. The new entries obtained from the join process are added to the filter tree stack along with the name of the filter tree node. For example, in Figure 14(c), the top stack entry (b,f) contains only (11,15,16,17) in its buffer after the top stack entry shown in Figure 14(b) is joined with f VNT

Table 2. Decomposing query instances

Name	Path	Branch	Leaf	$(l(v_b),l(v_l))$
Q2-m	/a/b/c/d	null	d	(null,d)
Q2-1	/a/b/e/f	b	f	(b,f)
Q2-2	/a/b/c/g/h	c	h	(c,h)
Q3-m	/a/b/c/d	null	d	(null,d)
Q3-1	/a/b/e/f	b	f	(b,f)
Q3-2	/a/b/c/d/i/j	d	j	(d,j)
Q4-m	/a/b/c/d	null	d	(null,d)
Q4-1	/a/k/l	a	l	(a,l)
Q4-2	/a/b/e/f	b	f	(b,f)
Q4-3	/a/b/c/g/h	c	h	(c,h)

Figure 9. Algorithm 2

```
Algorithm 2: buildFilterTrees(Q')
  input   : query instances
  output  : a collection of Filter Trees
begin
    multihashtable ← {};
    foreach q' ∈ Q do
        l ← q'.getMainLeafNode().getLabel();
        v ← q'.getID();
        multihashtable.add(l,v);
    filterTrees ← {};
    foreach k ∈ multihashtable.getKeys() do
        {q'_1,...,q'_n} ← multihashtable.get(k);
        filterTrees.add(buildFilterTree({q'_1,...,q'_n}));
    return filterTrees;
end
```

Figure 10. Algorithm 3

```
Algorithm 3: buildFilterTree({q'_1,...,q'_n})
  input   : a collection of query instances that share the same main leaf node
  output  : a Filter Tree
begin
    filterTree ← create a node that represents the main leaf node, and assign it
    as the root of Filter Tree;
    curNode ← filterTree.getRoot();
    foreach q ∈ {q'_1,...,q'_n} do
        /* generate (b,l) pairs from a query instance */
        {b_1,...,b_n} ← genPairs(q);
        /* (b,l) pairs are sorted such that minimum number of nodes
           are created in Filter Tree. */
        sort(filterTree, {b_1,...,b_n});
        foreach b ∈ {b_1,...,b_n} do
            curNode ← curNode.addChild(b);
        curNode.addQueryID(q.getID());
    return filterTree;
end
```

Figure 11. Structure index, contents of the global stack, and VNTs attached to index nodes in the structure index

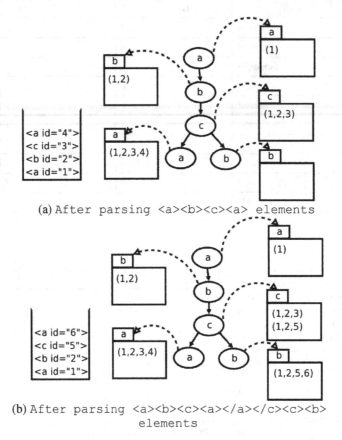

(a) After parsing <a><b><c><a> elements

(b) After parsing <a><b><c><a></a></c><c><b> elements

Figure 12. Algorithm 4

Algorithm 4: startElem(elem)

input	: the opening tag of the streaming element being processed
output	: returns nothing
requires	: curIndexNode: the Index Node that represents *elem*. Since Structure Index is globally defined, the Index Node can be accessed from anywhere.
	stack: a global stack that keeps track of streaming elements.

```
1 begin
2     curIndexNode ← curIndexNode.getChild(elem);
3     stack.push(curIndexNode.getID());
4     {v₁,...,vₙ} ← getNodesSoFar(stack);
5     curIndexNode.getVNT().add({v₁,...,vₙ});
6 end
```

shown in Figure 14(a). This is because the element with ID=15 is the only instance of the branch node v_b that is commonly found in both top stack entry and *f* VNT. Similarly, Figure 14(d) shows that the top stack entry (c,h) contains (11,15,16,17), because when *h* VNT is joined with the top stack entry shown in Figure 14(c), the element with ID=16 is the only instance of the branch node c

Figure 13. Algorithm 5

Algorithm 5: endElem(elem)
---
input   : the closing tag of the streaming element being processed
output   : returns nothing
requires : curIndexNode: the Index Node that represents *elem*. Since
             Structure Index is globally defined, the Index Node can be accessed
             from anywhere.
             stack: a global stack that keeps track of streaming elements.
1 **begin**
2   stack.pop();
3   curIndexNode ← curIndexNode.getParent();
4 **end**

Figure 14. Examples of VNTs and the contents of a filter tree stack when the filter tree shown in Figure 8 is traversed in pre-order traversal

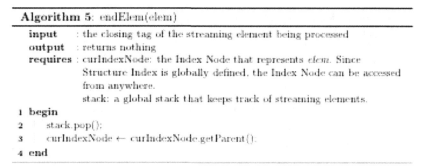

(a) Examples of VNTs

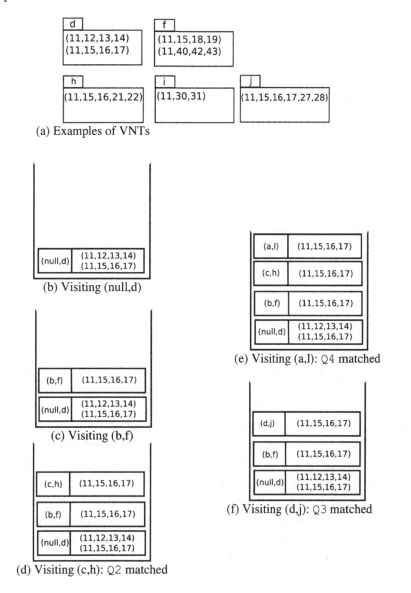

(b) Visiting (null,d)

(c) Visiting (b,f)

(d) Visiting (c,h): Q2 matched

(e) Visiting (a,l): Q4 matched

(f) Visiting (d,j): Q3 matched

Figure 15. Algorithm 6

```
Algorithm 6: evaluateQueries(filterTrees)

  input    : Filter Trees
  output   : matching query IDs
  requires : a collection of VNTs that are globally defined.
1 begin
2     matchingQueryIDs ← {};
3     foreach t ∈ filterTrees do
4         leafLabel ← t.getMainPath().getLeafLabel();
5         if VNTs.get(leafLabel) is not empty then
6             filter ← VNTs.get(leafLabel);
7             matchingQueryIDs ← matchingQueryIDs ∪
                 evaluateFilterTree(t.getRoot(), filter);

8     return matchingQueryIDs;
9 end
```

Figure 16. Algorithm 7

```
Algorithm 7: evaluateFilterTree(node, filter)

  input    : node: a Filter Tree node
             filter: a VNT associated with an Index Node
  output   : matching query IDs
  requires : a collection of VNTs that are globally defined.
1 begin
2     matchingQueryIDs ← {};
3     if filter exists and is not empty then
4         matchingQueryIDs.add(node.getQIDs());
5         foreach c ∈ node.getChildren() do
6             if !(c.isLeaf() ∧ c.allMatched()) then
7                 leafLabel ← c.getLeafNodeLabel();
8                 branchLabel ← c.getBranchNodeLabel();
9                 nextVNT ← VNTs.get(leafLabel);
10                if nextVNT exists and is not empty then
                      /* perform join operations */
11                    nFilter ← doFilter(filter, nextVNT, branchLabel);
12                    matchingQueryIDs ← matchingQueryIDs ∪
                          evaluateFilterTree(c, nFilter);

13    return matchingQueryIDs;
14 end
```

that is commonly found in both cases. Other examples are interpreted similarly. We then set the child of the current filter tree node as the current filter tree node, and repeat the above process for all nodes in the tree, unless the top stack entry's buffer becomes empty. In that case, we stop traversing the node, and we either go to the next child node or backtrack. While traversing the tree, we also report the queries associated with each index node as matched as long as the top stack entry's buffer does not become empty after performing join operations. For example, when we visit (c,h), (a,l), and (d,j) nodes shown in Figure 8, we report the queries Q2, Q4, and Q3 as matched, since the join operations shown in Figure 14(d), 14(e), and 14(f) do not return empty results, respectively. In addition, when we only report matching query IDs, we can further reduce the number of join operations by skipping leaf filter tree nodes that contain the queries that have already been reported as matched. Algorithms 6 and 7 outline the above procedures (see Figure 15 and Figure 16).

Returning Matching Elements

We have so far described how a set of matching query IDs for each streaming document can be reported. However, it is often necessary to return a set of all matching elements for each query registered to the system. For example, consider an XML news feed application that forwards news articles to subscribers. Using techniques from previous works (e.g., YFilter (Diao et al., 2002, 2003), PRIX (Rao & Moon, 2004), FiST (Kwon et al., 2005)), articles that match given subscriptions can be identified and forwarded to subscribers. However, the major limitation of previous works is that, entire news articles must be forwarded to subscribers, even though the subscribers are only interested in receiving only some parts of news articles. To overcome this problem, previous works process matching query IDs again at an application level to identify the matching parts of articles. In this section, we present how our system can be extended in such a way that, it can also return the complete sets of matching elements for each branch query registered to the system. The procedures are as follows.

First, both startElem(*elem*) and endElem(*elem*) events are extended such that, while a streaming document is being processed, a DOM representation of the document is created. It is easily achieved by interpreting the sequences of startElem(*elem*) and endElem(*elem*) events. Let us refer to such a document representation as a *document tree*. In addition, each sequence of element IDs stored in a VNT is also extended, such that it now contains a pointer that points to the matching node in the document tree.

Second, evaluteFilterTree() is extended, such that, instead of collecting all matching query IDs from each filter tree node using matchingQueryIDs, the top stack entry of the current filter tree stack is examined, and all sequences of element IDs are retrieved. After that, for each sequence of element IDs, a document tree node is retrieved by following the matching document node pointer.

Then, the set of matching query IDs obtained from the current filter tree node is added to this document tree node directly. At the end of processing all filter trees in this way, we produce a decorated document tree whose nodes contain groups of matching query IDs. Figure 17 shows an example of a document tree after the queries shown in Figure 7 (and along with others) have been evaluated. In Figure 17, matching query IDs for some nodes are omitted for simplicity. It is possible that non-leaf nodes contain matching query IDs. In this case, subtrees rooted at these non-leaf nodes are treated as matching elements. In addition, the same query IDs can be found in multiple document tree nodes, since queries may have more than one matching instance.

Finally, matching elements are returned in the following two ways: (1) the decorated document tree can be passed directly to an upper level application; or (2) this document tree can be traversed again to create mappings. One advantage of passing a document tree to an upper level application is that, given a node in a document tree, it is possible to immediately identify all matching query IDs for that node without performing further processing. This feature is useful for some applications such as news feed applications, as it quickly identifies the group of subscribers who are only interested in that specific part of the document. A side benefit of having a decorated document tree is that, a containment relationship between queries (i.e., Query $x \subseteq$ Query y for a document D) can be derived easily.

EXPERIMENTS

This section presents our experiment results in detail. All experiments were conducted on a Pentium 4 3.2 GHz machine with 1 GB ram running Ubuntu Linux with 2.6 kernel. Our approach was implemented in Java 1.5. The SAX parser we used was Xerces Java Parser 2.8.0 (The Apache XML Project, 2007). Our system was set to report

Figure 17. An example of a document tree decorated with matching query IDs

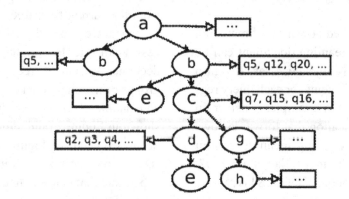

matching query IDs unless specified otherwise. We compared our system against YFilter (Diao et al., 2003), which is a state-of-the-art XML filtering engine. This section consists of two parts. The first part shows how we generated both documents and queries used in the experiments. The second part presents how our system performed on various datasets and queries.

Settings

Generating Documents. We used the NASA dataset obtained from UW Database Group (2002), and modified the dataset according to the experiment settings described by Kwon et al. (2005). In these settings, the dataset was split into smaller documents, and categorized into three datasets, each of which had ranges of [10 KB, 20 KB), [20 KB, 30 KB), and [30 KB, 60 KB), respectively. After that, we randomly selected the documents that we would use in the experiments from each dataset. Let us refer to each dataset as 10k, 20k, and 30k, respectively, in this section.

Generating XPath Queries. We generated queries for 10k dataset as follows. The same procedure was also repeated to generate queries for 20k and 30k datasets. First, all documents from 10k dataset were parsed, and the document structure for all 10k documents were generated. Second, a node from the document structure was

randomly chosen, and all nodes that were along the path between the root node and that chosen node were scanned. While scanning the nodes on the path, we selected nodes that would represent a path expression of a query. In our implementation, each node on the path had 80% probability of being selected to become a part of a path expression of a query. If a node was not selected, we replaced '/' of the next node on the path expression with '//.' Furthermore, amongst the selected nodes on the path expression, 10% of them were replaced with '*,' and 10% of '/'s were replaced with '//'s. After that, we randomly picked number of nodes on the path expression that would contain branch paths, and branch paths were generated similarly. Lastly, all duplicate queries were removed, and the second step was repeated until number of unique queries were generated.

In order to control the number of matching queries for a document, we obtained a set of queries that had at least one matching document. This was done by evaluating 10k dataset against the set of randomly generated queries. Similarly, we also obtained a set of queries that did not match any document. These two sets of queries were mixed to create sets of queries that had various number of matching queries. This approach gave us many advantages over previous ways of generating queries (e.g., YFilter (Diao et al., 2003)). By looking at the real document structure rather than entirely relying on a DTD/XML Schema of an XML document, we could generate queries that contained the elements that would actually occur. In addition, the depth of each query was no more than the maximum depth of matching documents, even though a document schema allowed documents to have infinite depths. More importantly, it allowed us to generate various sets of queries, each of which had a different number of matching queries for a given set of documents.

Results

Figure 18 shows the compilation time for building structure indexes for various number of queries in the index compilation phase. In addition, we also vary the number of branches per query. The compilation time increases as the number of queries increases. This is because the process of finding query instances is proportional to the number of queries to process. Similarly, the compilation time increases as the number of branches per query increases. This is because, as the number of branches increases, the number of decomposed queries increases, therefore the number of matching instances for decomposed queries also increases. While the compilation costs are higher than NFA-based approaches, compilation

only takes place once, and are compensated by the significant runtime improvement. For the following experiments, we use structure indexes that are created in this phase. In addition, all reported processing time represent runtime without initial index compilation time, and all queries were evaluated in the stable phase.

Figure 19 shows the processing time of our system (denoted as S-Index) and YFilter when various number of queries were evaluated against 10k, 20k, and 30k datasets. In this experiment, we used two sets of queries. In the first set, non of the queries match any document, and in the second set, all queries match at least one document. These two sets of queries are denoted as 0% and 100% matching in Figure 19, respectively. Moreover, similar patterns were observed when we varied the percentage of matching queries (i.e., 20%, 40%, etc). In addition, all queries used in the experiment had 2 branches. The processing time reported here are the average time taken to process documents from 10k, 20k, and 30k datasets, respectively.

Both Figure 19(a) and 19(b) show that, the rate of which our system increases in time as the number of queries increases is much slower than that of YFilter. It is explained as follows. First, unlike YFilter, which joins branch queries indi-

Figure 18. Compilation time for building structure indexes

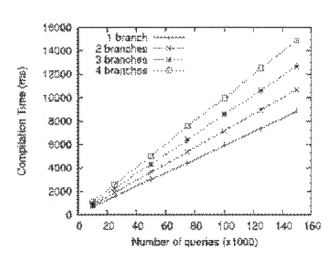

vidually, our system identifies groups of branch queries that are structurally equivalent, and processes each group only once in the post-processing phase. Therefore, the processing time is related to the number and the size of such groups that represent structurally different twig patterns. Second, by sharing intermediate join results using filter trees, we reduce the total number of join operations required when branch queries are evaluated. Since common branches found amongst queries are identified and organized in filter trees, we can reuse intermediate join results when decomposed queries are combined. As a result, we eliminate multiple processing of common branches. Therefore, the processing time is related to the number of common branches rather than the total number of decomposed queries. Third, we further reduce the total number of join operations by avoiding duplicate processing of queries. We do not repeatedly evaluate the queries that have already been identified as matched. Figure 19 also shows that both systems take more time to process larger documents. This is because, as the size of datasets increases, the number of matching elements increases, and therefore the number of elements that must be joined in the post-processing phase also increases. However, our system is much less sensitive to the size of datasets for the same reasons explained above. By reducing the number of join operations, our system scales better.

Figure 19. Evaluating various number of queries against 10k, 20k, and 30k datasets

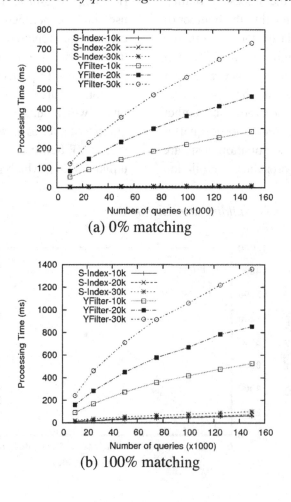

(a) 0% matching

(b) 100% matching

Furthermore, Figure 19 shows that both systems perform better when non of the queries match any document. This is because, as the number of matching queries decreases, the number of elements that must be joined also decreases. Our system is very efficient when there are a smaller number of matching queries, as our system implements two optimization techniques—short cut evaluations and skipping filter trees. In short cut evaluations, we immediately fail a branch of a filter tree in the following two cases: (1) when there is a node that has an empty VNT; or (2) when join operations that involve filter tree nodes return empty results. This approach works because a branch query is satisfied, only if all paths of the query are satisfied. In skipping filter trees, we skip evaluating the entire tree when the root of a filter tree has an empty VNT. The root of a filter tree has an empty VNT, only if the element for which the root represents cannot be found from a streaming document. Hence, all queries represented by that filter tree cannot be satisfied. By applying these optimizations, we increase the overall performance by executing a very small number of join operations when there are a smaller number of matching queries.

Figure 20 shows the processing time of the two systems when 150,000 queries that contain different percentage of matching queries were evaluated against 10k, 20k, and 30k datasets. In addition, all queries used in this experiment had 2 branches. The processing time of both systems increases as the percentage of matching queries increases, even though the number of queries does not change. The rate of which the processing time of our system increases is slower than that of YFilter, and our system is less sensitive to the size of datasets for all percentages of matching queries. Our system also shows that there is a steady increase in processing time when it processes queries whose percentage of matching are in between 0% and 60%. This is because, for the queries that have low percentage of matching, not all branches of filter trees are visited when the trees are traversed. As the number of matching queries increases, the number of nodes in filter trees that must be visited also increases. However, once the maximum number of nodes to visit has reached—which is the total number of nodes in all filter trees—the rate of which processing time increases drops. In this experiment, it happens when the percentage of matching is approximately 60%.

Figure 20. Evaluating 150,000 queries that contain different percentage of matching queries. All queries have 2 branches

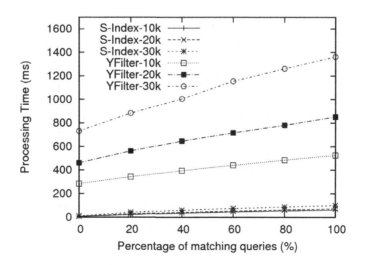

Figure 21 shows the processing time of the two systems when 150,000 queries that have 1–4 branches were evaluated against 10k, 20k, and 30k datasets. The two graphs show the performance when the percentage of matching queries are set to 0% and 100%, respectively. Both figures show similar patterns to the previous experiments for similar reasons. When the percentage of matching is set to 100%, the processing time of our system increases as the number of branches per query increases. This is because, as the number of branches increases, the depth of filter trees increases, which results in increasing the overall number of join operations to process in the post-processing phase.

Figure 22 shows the processing time when various number of queries that contain 1–4

branches were evaluated. In this experiment, we used 10k dataset, and the percentage of matching queries was set to 100%. The processing time of both systems increases as the number of queries increases. The slow rate of increase of our system compared to YFilter shows the effectiveness of using both structure index and filter trees together. Figure 22 also shows that there exists similar processing time increases for the queries that only differ by the number of branches.

Figure 23 shows the processing time when various number of queries with and without returning matching elements for each matching query were evaluated. In this experiment, the percentage of matching queries was set to 100%, the number of branches per query was set to 2, and 30k dataset was used. When we set our system

Figure 21. Evaluating 150,000 queries that have 1–4 branches against 10k, 20k, and 30k datasets

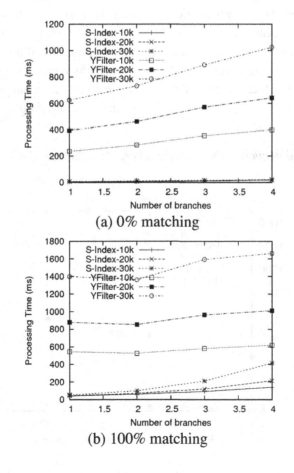

(a) 0% matching

(b) 100% matching

Figure 22. Evaluating various number of queries that have 1–4 branches

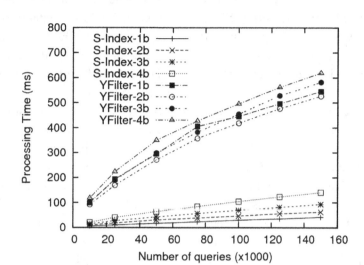

Figure 23. Evaluating various number of queries with and without returning matching elements

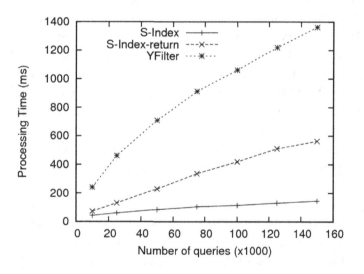

to return all matching elements, the processing time is increased compared to when we only report matching query IDs. This is related to how matching query IDs are collected in our implementation. When we add matching query IDs to matching nodes of a document tree, it is likely that the same query ID is added multiple times, as there exists multiple matching nodes. This is different from adding matching query IDs to a global list, as in this case, only one instance of a query ID is added to the list. Nevertheless, compared to YFilter, both our approaches require less processing time.

COMPARISON

Previous works on processing XML streaming data can be classified into the following categories: (1) approaches that process a large number of branch

XPath queries against many smaller documents; (2) approaches that only process linear XPath queries against many smaller documents; (3) approaches that process a single branch XPath/XQuery query against a large document; (4) approaches that process a single branch XPath query and return the complete set of matching elements; and (5) approaches that process a single XQuery on streaming XML data. Examples of previous works for each category include: (1) YFilter (Diao et al., 2002, 2003), XTrie (Chan et al., 2002b, 2002a), XPush (Gupta & Suciu, 2003), Onizuka (2003), Uchiyama et al. (2005), PRIX (Rao & Moon, 2004), and FiST (Kwon et al., 2005); (2) XFilter (Altinel & Franklin, 2000), LazyDFA (Green et al., 2004), Bloom Filter (Gong et al., 2005), and AFilter (Candan et al., 2006); (3) TwigStack (Bruno et al., 2002), FluX (Koch et al., 2004), XFPro (Huo et al., 2006), SPEX (Bry et al., 2005, Olteanu, 2007), and Gou & Chirkova (2007); (4) XSQ (Peng & Chawathe, 2003, 2005); and (5) Fegaras et al. (2002), Raindrop (Su et al., 2003), and R-Sox (S. Wang et al., 2006), respectively. Our work falls in the first category, but unlike others, we can also return matching elements for all matching queries. In this section, we compare our approach with the previous works that are in the same category as our work.

Unlike the approaches in other categories, processing a large number of branch XPath queries requires us to solve two important problems in order to increase the efficiency of query processing. These are: (1) the total number of processing steps must be minimized as well as the rate of must be increased, where n is the total number of processing steps taken to successfully evaluate queries; and N is the total number of processing steps attempted; and (2) any commonalities between queries must be identified and considered when queries are evaluated.

Many previous works presented partial solutions to the above issues. For example, to reduce the total number of processing steps, XTrie decomposes queries into longest substrings, and builds both a trie and a substring table. It also provides a method that detects redundant substrings. Onizuka creates shared NFAs, such that the states can be shared amongst similar queries. XPush reduces the total number of processing steps by maintaining a table that has information about various statuses of AFA (Alternating Finite Automata), and both PRIX and FiST maintain an index that has information about groups of queries that need to be processed for each streaming element. Some of the approaches also present optimization techniques—LazyXTrie for XTrie; Pruning, Early Notification and Training for XPush; and Avoiding Frequent Node Copying for FiST. However, they all suffer from one common problem. That is, they must iterate a group of (unrelated) queries associated with a node or NFA/DFA state for each streaming element, and check which queries have become satisfied. For example, XTrie needs to scan the substring table and its Trie for each streaming element, and checks for substring matches. When matching substrings are found, ancestor nodes of the current node in Trie must be recursively visited to update the status of potentially matching queries. Onizuka needs to process a group of related XPath queries for each streaming element, and recursively checks parent paths when child paths of a query are matched. FiST also needs to evaluate all queries individually whose keys are the same as the name of each streaming element in Sequence Index. As also noted by Chan et al. (2002a), traversing trees or checking states for matches for each streaming element is inefficient. This is because non-matching queries or queries with partial matches are also continuously evaluated until either the last streaming element is received or queries with partial matches become fully satisfied. For non-matching queries, the entire processes of evaluating nodes in a tree or NFA/DFA are wasted, and for queries with partial matches, the first n attempts of evaluating queries are wasted. To avoid this problem, our approach filters out structurally non-matching queries before we process queries, and when queries are evaluated in the post-processing phase, groups of unique twig patterns, each of which represents multiple queries, are processed only once, and if any failure of paths of the queries in a group are detected, the processing of the entire group of queries are aborted immediately. This approach is possible because when we process queries, we have the complete information about the positions of elements that are involved in queries.

While many previous works implemented some ways of sharing either nodes, stacks or DFA/NFA states during document parsing, they do not explore the commonalities between queries when queries are evaluated. For example, YFilter individually joins decomposed queries without sharing any common path between queries in its post-processing phase. Similarly, PRIX and FiST evaluate queries individually without sharing any common path between queries in its runtime. Furthermore, queries that have the same twig patterns but written differently are also processed multiple times. However, using filter trees, queries with the same twig patterns are processed only once. Moreover, the common paths between queries are identified, and the intermediate join results calculated during the post-processing phase are shared amongst similar queries. As a result, duplicate processing of common paths between queries are minimized, and hence, it reduces both total and unnecessary number of join operations.

In addition, the size of buffer we use is much smaller than that of many previous works. Furthermore, we do not temporarily buffer elements that may be used to evaluate queries in future. For example, XTrie needs to keep track of the subset of all child substrings when it evaluates queries that ignore branch orders. XPush also needs to keep track of a set of states from AFA. As a result, they both require a huge amount of memory. Our system, however, uses filter trees to organize branch queries into groups, and the nodes in filter trees are processed in a pipeline fashion in the post-processing phase.

Finally, our approach may be classified into combined approaches of Structural Summaries and Input Driven Techniques, according to the classification by Moro, Vagena, and Tsotras (2005). While the performance of the approaches based on Structural Summaries are reported as the fastest, the performance of the approaches based on Input Driven Techniques are reported rather poor in their experiments. This is because, in their experiments, query evaluation process is repeatedly executed every time when an end tag of a new streaming element arrives. Also the experiment is about how a system can process a single branch query against a large document—it is the third category according to our classification. Therefore, the studies and experiments by Moro et al. (2005) about Input Driven Techniques cannot be used to evaluate the performance of our work.

CONCLUSION

We have presented an efficient approach for evaluating a large number of branch XPath queries against streaming XML data using structure index and filter trees. Structure index is used to find all query instances of branch queries, and these query instances are classified into groups of equivalent twig patterns. Such process allows us to remove duplicate processing of queries. Furthermore, query instances that share one or more paths amongst them are also identified, and groups of filter trees are built based on the common paths between these query instances. Filter trees are then traversed to evaluate groups of queries in the post-processing phase. In addition, we also presented how to efficiently return all matching elements for each matching branch query. We have shown in our experiments that, by processing similar queries simultaneously and reusing intermediate join results, our approach can evaluate a large number of branch queries, and is more scalable and efficient than previous works.

There are several possibilities for future work. We are currently looking at extending our approach to process a large number of XQuery queries that contain both inter-document and value-based join operations, as well as returning matching elements for each matching query.

ACKNOWLEDGMENT

The first author of this research was partially supported by the National Research Foundation (NRF) of Korea and the World Class University (WCU) through the NRF of Korea both funded by the Korean government (MEST) (NRF Grant No: 2010–0000863; WCU Grant No: R31–2010–000–30007–0).

REFERENCES

Altinel, M., & Franklin, M. J. (2000, Sep). Efficient filtering of xml documents for selective dissemination of information. In *Proceedings of the 26th international conference on very large data bases* (pp. 53–64). San Francisco, CA: Morgan Kaufmann.

Bar-Yossef, Z., Fontoura, M., & Josifovski, V. (2005). Buffering in query evaluation over xml streams. In *Proceedings of the twenty-fourth acm sigmod-sigact-sigart symposium on principles of database systems* (pp. 216–227). New York, NY: ACM.

Barta, A., Consens, M. P., & Mendelzon, A. O. (2005, Aug–Sep). Benefits of path summaries in an xml query optimizer supporting multiple access methods. In *Proceedings of the 31st international conference on very large data bases* (pp. 133–144). Trondheim, Norway: ACM.

Barton, C., Charles, P., Goyal, D., Raghavachari, M., Fontoura, M., & Josifovski, V. (2003, Mar). Streaming xpath processing with forward and backward axes. In *Proceedings of the 19th international conference on data engineering* (pp. 455–466). Bangalore, India: IEEE Computer Society.

Benedikt, M., Jeffrey, A., & Ley-Wild, R. (2008, June). Stream firewalling of xml constraints. In *Proceedings of the acm sigmod international conference on management of data* (pp. 487–498). Vancouver, Canada: ACM.

Bloom, B. H. (1970). Space/time trade-offs in hash coding with allowable errors. *Communications of the ACM*, *13*(7), 422–426. doi:10.1145/362686.362692

Boncz, P. A., Grust, T., van Keulen, M., Manegold, S., Rittinger, J., & Teubner, J. (2006, Jun). Monetdb/xquery: a fast xquery processor powered by a relational engine. In *Proceedings of the acm sigmod international conference on management of data* (pp. 479–490). Chicago, IL: ACM.

Bray, T., Paoli, J., Sperberg-McQueen, C. M., Maler, E., & Yergeau, F. (2008, Nov). *Extensible markup language (xml) 1.0 (fifth edition)* (Tech. Rep.). W3C. (http://www.w3.org/TR/XML/)

Bruno, N., Koudas, N., & Srivastava, D. (2002, Jun). Holistic twig joins: optimal xml pattern matching. In *Proceedings of the acm sigmod international conference on management of data* (pp. 310–321). Madison, WI: ACM.

Bry, F., Coskun, F., Durmaz, S., Furche, T., Olteanu, D., & Spannagel, M. (2005, Apr). The xml stream query processor spex. In *Proceedings of the 21st international conference on data engineering* (pp. 1120–1121). Tokyo, Japan: IEEE Computer Society.

Candan, K. S., Hsiung, W.-P., Chen, S., Tatemura, J., & Agrawal, D. (2006, Sep). Afilter: Adaptable xml filtering with prefix-caching and suffix-clustering. In *Proceedings of the 32nd international conference on very large data bases* (pp. 559–570). Seoul, Korea: ACM.

Chan, C. Y., Felber, P., Garofalakis, M., & Rastogi, R. (2002a). Efficient filtering of xml documents with xpath expressions. *The VLDB Journal, 11*(4), 354–379. doi:10.1007/s00778-002-0077-6

Chan, C. Y., Felber, P., Garofalakis, M. N., & Rastogi, R. (2002b, Feb). Efficient filtering of xml documents with xpath expressions. In *Proceedings of the 18th international conference on data engineering* (pp. 235–244). San Jose, CA: IEEE Computer Society.

Chan, C. Y., & Ni, Y. (2007, Jun). Efficient xml data dissemination with piggybacking. In *Proceedings of the acm sigmod international conference on management of data* (pp. 737–748). Beijing, China: ACM.

Chandramouli, B., & Yang, J. (2008). End-to-end support for joins in large-scale publish/subscribe systems. *PVLDB, 1*(1), 434–450.

Chandramouli, B., Yang, J., Agarwal, P. K., Yu, A., & Zheng, Y. (2008, June). Prosem: scalable wide-area publish/subscribe. In *Proceedings of the acm sigmod international conference on management of data* (pp. 1315–1318). Vancouver, BC, Canada: ACM.

Chen, Y., Davidson, S. B., & Zheng, Y. (2006, Apr). An efficient xpath query processor for xml streams. In *Proceedings of the 22nd international conference on data engineering* (pp. 79). Atlanta, GA: IEEE Computer Society.

Clark, J., & DeRose, S. (1999, Nov). *Xml path language (xpath)* (Tech. Rep.). W3C. (http://www.w3.org/TR/xpath/)

Diao, Y., Altinel, M., Franklin, M. J., Zhang, H., & Fischer, P. (2003). Path sharing and predicate evaluation for high-performance xml filtering. *ACM Transactions on Database Systems, 28*(4), 467–516. doi:10.1145/958942.958947

Diao, Y., Fischer, P. M., Franklin, M. J., & To, R. (2002, Feb). Yfilter: Efficient and scalable filtering of xml documents. In *Proceedings of the 18th international conference on data engineering* (pp. 341–342). San Jose, CA: IEEE Computer Society.

Diao, Y., & Franklin, M. J. (2003, Sep). Query processing for high-volume xml message brokering. In *Proceedings of 29th international conference on very large data bases* (pp. 261–272). Berlin, Germany: Morgan Kaufmann.

Diao, Y., Rizvi, S., & Franklin, M. J. (2004, Aug–Sep). Towards an internet-scale xml dissemination service. In *Proceedings of the 30th international conference on very large data bases* (pp. 612–623). Toronto, Canada: Morgan Kaufmann.

Diaz, A. L., & Lovell, D. (1999, Sep). *IBM XML Generator.* (http://www.alphaworks.ibm.com/tech/xmlgenerator)

Erickson, J., & Siau, K. (2008). Web services, service-oriented computing, and service-oriented architecture: Separating hype from reality. *Journal of Database Management, 19*(3), 42–54. doi:10.4018/jdm.2008070103

Fegaras, L., Levine, D., Bose, S., & Chaluvadi, V. (2002, Nov). Query processing of streamed xml data. In *Proceedings of the 11th international conference on information and knowledge management* (pp. 126–133). McLean, VA: ACM.

Felber, P., Chan, C. Y., Garofalakis, M., & Rastogi, R. (2003). Scalable filtering of xml data for web services. *IEEE Internet Computing, 7*(1), 49–51. doi:10.1109/MIC.2003.1167339

Fong, J., & Wong, H. K. (2004). Xtopo: An xml-based topology for information highway on the internet. *Journal of Database Management, 15*(3), 18–44. doi:10.4018/jdm.2004070102

Goldman, R., & Widom, J. (1997, Aug). Dataguides: Enabling query formulation and optimization in semistructured databases. In *Proceedings of 23rd international conference on very large data bases* (pp. 436–445). Athens, Greece: Morgan Kaufmann.

Gong, X., Yan, Y., Qian, W., & Zhou, A. (2005, Apr). Bloom filter-based xml packets filtering for millions of path queries. In *Proceedings of the 21st international conference on data engineering* (pp. 890–901). Tokyo, Japan: IEEE Computer Society.

Gottlob, G., Koch, C., & Pichler, R. (2005). Efficient algorithms for processing xpath queries. *ACM Transactions on Database Systems, 30*(2), 444–491. doi:10.1145/1071610.1071614

Gou, G., & Chirkova, R. (2007, Jun). Efficient algorithms for evaluating xpath over streams. In *Proceedings of the acm sigmod international conference on management of data* (pp. 269–280). Beijing, China: ACM.

Green, T. J., Gupta, A., Miklau, G., Onizuka, M., & Suciu, D. (2004). Processing xml streams with deterministic automata and stream indexes. *ACM Transactions on Database Systems, 29*(4), 752–788. doi:10.1145/1042046.1042051

Green, T. J., Miklau, G., Onizuka, M., & Suciu, D. (2003, Jan). *Processing xml streams with deterministic automata. In 9th international conference of database theory* (pp. 173–189). Siena, Italy: Springer.

Grohe, M., Koch, C., & Schweikardt, N. (2005, Jul). Tight lower bounds for query processing on streaming and external memory data. In *Proceedings of 32nd international colloquium on automata, languages and programming* (pp. 1076–1088). Lisbon, Portugal: Springer.

Grust, T., Rittinger, J., & Teubner, J. (2007, Jun). Why off-the-shelf rdbmss are better at xpath than you might expect. In *Proceedings of the acm sigmod international conference on management of data* (pp. 949–958). Beijing, China: ACM.

Gupta, A. K., & Suciu, D. (2003, Jun). Stream processing of xpath queries with predicates. In *Proceedings of the acm sigmod international conference on management of data* (pp. 419–430). San Diego, CA: ACM.

He, B., Luo, Q., & Choi, B. (2006). Cache-conscious automata for xml filtering. *IEEE Transactions on Knowledge and Data Engineering, 18*(12), 1629–1644. doi:10.1109/TKDE.2006.184

Hong, M., Demers, A. J., Gehrke, J., Koch, C., Riedewald, M., & White, W. M. (2007, Jun). Massively multi-query join processing in publish/subscribe systems. In *Proceedings of the acm sigmod international conference on management of data* (pp. 761–772). Beijing, China: ACM.

Huang, C.-H., Chuang, T.-R., Lu, J. J., & Lee, H.-M. (2006, Sep). Xml evolution: A two-phase xml processing model using xml prefiltering techniques. In *Proceedings of the 32nd international conference on very large data bases* (pp. 1215–1218). Seoul, Korea: ACM.

Huo, H., Wang, G., Hui, X., Zhou, R., Ning, B., & Xiao, C. (2006, Apr). Efficient query processing for streamed xml fragments. In *Proceedings of the 11th international conference on database systems for advanced applications* (pp. 468–482). Singapore: Springer.

Koch, C., Scherzinger, S., Schweikardt, N., & Stegmaier, B. (2004, Aug). Schema-based scheduling of event processors and buffer minimization for queries on structured data streams. In *Proceedings of the thirtieth international conference on very large data bases* (pp. 228–239). Toronto, Canada: Morgan Kaufmann.

Kwon, J., Rao, P., Moon, B., & Lee, S. (2005, Aug–Sep). Fist: Scalable xml document filtering by sequencing twig patterns. In *Proceedings of the 31st international conference on very large data bases* (pp. 217–228). Trondheim, Norway: ACM.

Li, X., & Agrawal, G. (2005, Aug–Sep). Efficient evaluation of xquery over streaming data. In *Proceedings of the 31st international conference on very large data bases* (pp. 265–276). Trondheim, Norway: ACM.

Mignet, L., Barbosa, D., & Veltri, P. (2003, May). The xml web: a first study. In *Proceedings of the 12th international world wide web conference* (pp. 500–510). Budapest, Hungary: ACM.

Milo, T., Zur, T., & Verbin, E. (2007, Jun). Boosting topic-based publish-subscribe systems with dynamic clustering. In *Proceedings of the acm sigmod international conference on management of data* (pp. 749–760). Beijing, China: ACM.

Moro, M. M., Vagena, Z., & Tsotras, V. J. (2005, Aug–Sep). Tree-pattern queries on a lightweight xml processor. In *Proceedings of the 31st international conference on very large data bases* (pp. 205–216). Trondheim, Norway: ACM.

Nah, F. F.-H., Siau, K., & Tian, Y. (2005). Knowledge management mechanisms of financial service sites. *Communications of the ACM, 48*(6), 117–123. doi:10.1145/1064830.1064836

O'Reilly, T. (2005). *What is web 2.0.* O'Reilly Media. (http://oreilly.com/web2/archive/ what-is-web-20.html)

Olteanu, D. (2007). Spex: Streamed and progressive evaluation of xpath. *IEEE Transactions on Knowledge and Data Engineering, 19*(7), 934–949. doi:10.1109/TKDE.2007.1063

Onizuka, M. (2003, Nov). Light-weight xpath processing of xml stream with deterministic automata. In *Proceedings of the 12th international conference on information and knowledge management* (pp. 342–349). New Orleans, LA: ACM.

Peng, F., & Chawathe, S. S. (2003, Jun). Xpath queries on streaming data. In *Proceedings of the acm sigmod international conference on management of data* (pp. 431–442). San Diego, CA: ACM.

Peng, F., & Chawathe, S. S. (2005). Xsq: A streaming xpath engine. *ACM Transactions on Database Systems, 30*(2), 577–623. doi:10.1145/1071610.1071617

Rao, P., & Moon, B. (2004, Mar). Prix: Indexing and querying xml using prüfer sequences. In *Proceedings of the 20th international conference on data engineering* (pp. 288–300). Boston, MA: IEEE Computer Society.

Seshadri, P. (2003, Jun). Building notification services with microsoft sqlserver. In *Proceedings of the acm sigmod international conference on management of data* (pp. 635–636). San Diego, CA: ACM.

Shiu, H., & Fong, J. (2008). Reverse engineering from an xml document into an extended dtd graph. *Journal of Database Management, 19*(4), 62–80. doi:10.4018/jdm.2008100104

Siau, K., & Long, Y. (2006). Using social development lenses to understand e-government development. *Journal of Global Information Management, 14*(1), 47–62. doi:10.4018/jgim.2006010103

Siau, K., & Shen, Z. (2006). Mobile healthcare informatics. *Informatics for Health & Social Care, 31*(2), 89–99. doi:10.1080/14639230500095651

Siau, K., Sheng, H., & Nah, F. F.-H. (2006). Use of a classroom response system to enhance classroom interactivity. *IEEE Transactions on Education, 49*(3), 398–403. doi:10.1109/TE.2006.879802

Smolander, K., & Rossi, M. (2008). Conflicts, compromises and political decisions: Methodological challenges of enterprise-wide e-business architecture. *Journal of Database Management, 19*(1), 19–40. doi:10.4018/jdm.2008010102

Su, H., Jian, J., & Rundensteiner, E. A. (2003, Nov). Raindrop: a uniform and layered algebraic framework for xqueries on xml streams. In *Proceedings of the 12th international conference on information and knowledge management* (pp. 279–286). New Orleans, LA: ACM.

Su, H., Rundensteiner, E. A., & Mani, M. (2004, Aug–Sep). Semantic query optimization in an automata-algebra combined xquery engine over xml streams. In *Proceedings of the thirtieth international conference on very large data bases* (pp. 1293–1296). Toronto, Canada: Morgan Kaufmann.

Su, H., Rundensteiner, E. A., & Mani, M. (2005, Aug–Sep). Semantic query optimization for xquery over xml streams. In *Proceedings of the 31st international conference on very large data bases* (pp. 277–288). Trondheim, Norway: ACM.

The Apache XML Project. (2007). *Xerces2 Java Parser.* The Apache Software Foundation. (http://xerces.apache.org/xerces2-j/)

Tian, F., Reinwald, B., Pirahesh, H., Mayr, T., & Myllymaki, J. (2004, Jun). Implementing a scalable xml publish/subscribe system using a relational database system. In *Proceedings of the acm sigmod international conference on management of data* (pp. 479–490). Paris, France: ACM.

Uchiyama, H., Onizuka, M., & Honishi, T. (2005, Apr). Distributed xml stream filtering system with high scalability. In *Proceedings of the 21st international conference on data engineering* (pp. 968–977). Tokyo, Japan: IEEE Computer Society.

UW Database Group. (2002). *XML Data Repository.* UW CSE, University of Washington. (http://www.cs.washington.edu/ research/xmldatasets/)

Wang, H., Park, S., Fan, W., & Yu, P. S. (2003, Jun). Vist: A dynamic index method for querying xml data by tree structures. In *Proceedings of the acm sigmod international conference on management of data* (pp. 110–121). San Diego, CA: ACM.

Wang, S., Su, H., Li, M., Wei, M., Yang, S., & Ditto, D. (2006, Sep). R-sox: Runtime semantic query optimization over xml streams. In *Proceedings of the 32nd international conference on very large data bases* (pp. 1207–1210). Seoul, Korea: ACM.

Yin, X., & Pedersen, T. B. (2006). Evaluating xml-extened olap queries based on physical algebra. *Journal of Database Management, 17*(2), 85–116. doi:10.4018/jdm.2006040105

Zeller, H. (2003, Jun). Nonstop sql/mx publish/subscribe: Continuous data streams in transaction processing. In *Proceedings of the acm sigmod international conference on management of data* (pp. 636). San Diego, CA: ACM.

Zhao, L., & Siau, K. (2007). Information mediation using metamodels: An approach using xml and common warehouse metamodel. *Journal of Database Management, 18*(3), 69–82. doi:10.4018/jdm.2007070104

Zhou, Y., Salehi, A., & Aberer, K. (2009). Scalable delivery of stream query results. *PVLDB, 2*(1), 49–60.

ENDNOTE

[1] Part of work was done when the author was at The University of New South Wales, Australia.

Section 3

Chapter 8
Towards Autonomic Workload Management in DBMSs

Baoning Niu
Taiyuan University of Technology, China & Queen's University, Canada

Patrick Martin
Queen's University, Canada

Wendy Powley
Queen's University, Canada

ABSTRACT

Workload management is the discipline of effectively managing, controlling and monitoring work flow across computing systems. It is an increasingly important requirement of database management systems (DBMSs) in view of the trends towards server consolidation and more diverse workloads. Workload management is necessary so the DBMS can be business-objective oriented, can provide efficient differentiated service at fine granularity and can maintain high utilization of resources with low management costs. We see that workload management is shifting from offline planning to online adaptation. In this paper we discuss the objectives of workload management in autonomic DBMSs and provide a framework for examining how current workload management mechanisms match up with these objectives. We then use the framework to study several mechanisms from both DBMS products and research efforts. We also propose directions for future work in the area of workload management for autonomic DBMSs.

INTRODUCTION

Workload management involves the monitoring and control of work entering a system. Its goal is to ensure that sufficient resources are allocated to a workload so that a business can meet its management objectives (IBM Corporation, 2003a).

DOI: 10.4018/978-1-60960-521-6.ch008

Workload management is becoming increasingly important to businesses for several reasons. First, their workloads are becoming more diverse and complex. Second, the emerging trend of server consolidation has led to an environment with increased competition for shared resources between applications from potentially disjointed organizations, which results in a workload with diverse and dynamic resource demands and often competing performance objectives. Third, Web-based applications, especially Web services (Erickson & Siau, 2008), introduce a need for flexible and guaranteed application service levels because they tend to involve unpredictable workloads, with a high rate of overall growth in workload size (D. H. Brown Associate, Inc, 2004). Allocating DBMS resources to competing workloads to meet performance objectives is a challenge.

We believe that workload management stands to benefit greatly from the new paradigm of autonomic computing. The goal of autonomic computing is to simplify system complexity by governing all computations within a given system (Mainsah, 2002). Autonomic computing systems have four fundamental characteristics (Ganek & Corbi, 2003): self-configuring, self-healing, self-optimizing and self-protecting. Self-configuring means systems can automatically adapt to dynamically changing environments. New features, applications and servers can be dynamically added to the enterprise infrastructure with no disruption of services. Self-healing is the ability of systems to discover, diagnose and react to disruptions. Such a system needs to be able to predict problems and take necessary actions to prevent the failures from impacting the services. For a system to be self-optimizing, it should monitor itself and tune resources automatically to maximize resource utilization to meet users' performance requirements. Self-protecting means systems are able to anticipate, detect, identify, and protect themselves from attacks from anywhere.

The goal of this paper is to specifically examine the progress made towards providing autonomic workload management in DBMSs and, based on this examination, to identify directions for future research. Previous surveys of the autonomic computing area, such as those by Salehie and Tahvildari (2005) and Elnaffar, Powley, Benoit, and Martin (2003), tend to have a more general focus and use criteria focusing on the existence of facilities to support the general features of self-configuration, self-healing, self-optimization and self-protection.

We propose a framework, Autonomic Workload Management Framework (AWMF), for the examination of autonomic workload management and then analyze current products and research efforts with respect to it. The framework specifies a model of the key processes and functions in autonomic workload management as well as identifying criteria for evaluation.

The remainder of the paper is structured as follows. The following section discusses the objectives of workload management. We then outline our framework, AWMF, for autonomic workload management and examine workload management mechanisms taken from current DBMS products and research efforts and compare them using AWMF. A number of observations are derived from the comparison of the workload management mechanisms. We then validate AWMF using experiments with Query Scheduler, a prototype implementation of AWMF and finally summarize our survey and point out possible directions for future work.

MANAGEMENT OBJECTIVES

Workload management has evolved through three phases, from its infancy as a means for capacity planning (Lo & Douglas, 1986), to resource-oriented workload management, with the primary goal being resource utilization (D. H. Brown Associate, Inc, 2004; Castro, Tezulas, Yu, Berg, Kim, & Gfroerer, 2001), and finally to today's performance-oriented workload management, with a focus on business objectives (IBM Corporation, 2003a). The objectives of workload management have remained the same, namely cost sharing and meeting Service Level Objectives (SLOs) (Menascé, 2004; IBM Corporation, 2003a), but its style has changed from offline analysis to online adaptation.

Cost sharing consolidates multiple applications onto a single server to improve resource utilization and cut down costs. An SLO objectively defines the service level delivered to users in terms of system level metrics or business process level metrics. System level metrics include system availability, transaction response times and its distribution, transaction volumes and resource provisioning turnaround time. Business process level metrics include, for example, the time-frame for response and problem resolution (IBM Corporation, 2003a). Workload management is only interested in the system service levels, specifically the performance objectives and the importance of work requests for a business (D. H. Brown Associate, Inc, 2004). Usually one or more SLOs are associated with a group of work called a service class (Niu, Martin, Powley, Horman, & Bird, 2006). Meeting an SLO requires the system to dynamically allocate sufficient resources to the service class as the workload fluctuates, so that the service level objective is achieved.

As an example, we can consider a stock quote system that consists of three service classes: a subscribed class, which is the quote requests submitted by subscribed users, an unsubscribed class, which is the quote requests submitted by unsubscribed users, and an analysis class, which is the market analysis requests submitted by analysts. Subscribed users are more important than unsubscribed users because they directly produce revenue. Quote requests should be processed in real time, while market analysis requests can tolerate much longer delays than quote requests. The subscribed class is, therefore, assigned an SLO of 3 seconds per quote with highest importance, the unsubscribed class is assigned an SLO of 5 seconds per quote with medium importance, and the analysis class is assigned an SLO of 25 seconds per request with the lowest importance.

Both cost sharing and meeting SLOs pose challenges for workload management and they frequently conflict with each other. In the stock quote system example above, if there is no workload control then the analysis class would typically consume many resources and render the performance of quote requests unpredictable.

Satisfying SLOs, on the other hand, may require allocating resources exclusively to each application or service class, which is not compliant with the concept of resource sharing. Again, in the stock quote system, the subscribed class should have a certain amount of resources guaranteed in order to meet its SLO, since it is the most important class. The other classes cannot claim these resources even if they are not required by the subscribed class. Autonomic workload management attempts to resolve these conflicts with techniques such as adaptive processing and provisioning of resources.

EVALUATION FRAMEWORK: AWMF

In this section, we present our Autonomic Workload Management Framework (AWMF). We first present our model of autonomic workload management, then explain the criteria contained in AWMF to compare workload management mechanisms.

Model

We view a workload management system as consisting of two main processes. The *workload detection process* recognizes workload changes by monitoring, characterizing and predicting workloads presented to the system. The *workload control process* assigns resources to workload classes. There are three approaches to workload control. First, direct resource allocation allocates a certain amount of resources to a workload, a workload class or a single piece of work. Private memory for processes is usually allocated in this way. Second, admission control regulates resource allocation by controlling the contention level on resources. The more work requests that are admitted, the heavier the contention is on resources. Third, execution control directly manages the execution of specific queries or classes of queries by limiting their execution and so their access to system resources. As shown in Figure

1, four functional components are commonly involved in these two processes (Lo & Douglas, 1986; IBM Corporation, 2003a; Menascé, Ruan, & Gomaa, 2007): workload characterization, performance modeling, workload control and system monitoring.

Functional Components

Workload characterization is employed in order to understand and determine the resource usage and performance behavior for subsequent workload control. It predicts resource demands that are given as input to the performance models used in order to choose a resource allocation plan (Lo & Douglas, 1986).

Performance modeling predicts the performance of the target system through a model that describes the features of the target system (Menascé & Almeida, 1998). The inputs of a performance model are workload parameters (such as resource demand and arrival rate) generated by the workload characterization component. The outputs are system performance and resource utilization parameters. Performance models are usually developed offline (Lo & Douglas, 1986, Menascé & Almeida, 1998). In the autonomic era, systems are self-configurable, which calls for adaptive performance modeling techniques that can evolve performance models in response to changes in the system (Chen, Yin, & Zhang, 2005).

The workload control component finds and enforces an optimal workload control plan to meet the management objectives when fluctuation in the workload causes system performance to degrade. The control plan can consist of actions to perform resource allocation, admission control or execution control.

System monitoring, or feedback, tells how well the system is performing by continuously acquiring the execution information of the workload and the resource usage of the system. The feedback information can not only be used as an indicator for workload changes, and help the workload characterization component to characterize the workload, but it also assists in the evolution of performance models by tracking changes to systems (IBM Corporation, 2003a; Menascé, Ruan & Gomaa., 2007).

Criteria

AWMF uses three criteria to compare autonomic workload management mechanisms, namely

Figure 1. AWMF: Autonomic workload management framework

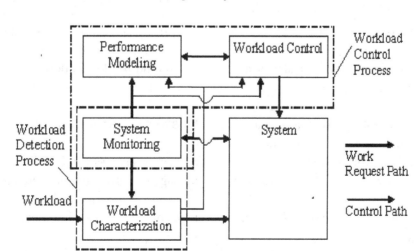

adaptability to workload changes, workload control methods, and system awareness.

Adaptability

Adaptability, which is the ability of a workload management system to adapt to workload perturbation and system reconfiguration in order to meet its management objectives, is central to autonomic computing. Adaptability is closely related to workload control methods because workload management systems need to map high level management objectives into low level resource allocation actions.

The adaptability of workload management systems depends on two issues: characterizing the changing workload and evolving the performance model. To be able to adapt to workload perturbations, the workload characterization component must be able to detect a perturbation in a timely manner, so that the workload management system can take necessary actions to avoid performance degradation. When the system configuration changes, the performance model may no longer be valid, therefore, the performance model should have the ability to evolve as the system configuration changes. We identify three levels of adaptability of workload management systems:

- **Assisted level:** Workload characterization tools are used to help administrators analyze the workload change and performance models are used to predict the effect of system reconfiguration. Any changes are performed by the administrator.
- **Reactive level:** Workload management systems detect the workload change through performance monitoring and reactively control the workload.
- **Proactive level:** Workload management systems are able to predict the workload change and proactively control the workload to meet the SLOs. This requires that the workload characterization component

is able to quantitatively track the workload change and the performance model component is able to evolve according to the changes in system configuration.

Workload Control Methods

Workload control methods deal with how resources can be allocated or regulated so that the management objectives can be achieved. We consider three workload control methods:

- **Resource allocation:** Resources are explicitly assigned to a work request or a group of work requests (Martin, Powley, Zheng, & Romanufa, 2005). This method has the most effective control over work requests without influencing other work requests. It requires that a workload management system directly control resources and is usually used at the operating system level.
- **Admission control:** This is the most widely used workload control method. It manages the resources allocated to a workload class by controlling the number of instances of a class executing at one time. Admission control has no effect on runaway work requests.
- **Execution control:** The executing requests are explicitly managed as a way of controlling the resources allocated to particular requests or workload requests. For example, the execution of a large query could be slowed down or paused in order to release some of its resources.

System Awareness

System awareness is the ability of the workload management system to acquire and to make use of health information about the system. Two types of health information need to be collected namely, performance information and resource usage information. The acquired data can be used to produce a report and/or feedback to other workload components. The feedback information is valuable for characterizing the workload, evolving the performance model, and making workload control decisions. We identify three levels of system awareness.

- **No system awareness:** There is no system monitoring component and the effect of workload control is unknown.
- **Report:** Health information is reported to the users for analysis and modeling. A well formed report should correlate performance goals to reports and reflect users' expectations by using the same terms as those used to express the performance goals.
- **Closed-feedback:** Health information is automatically used by the system to help characterize the workload, model the system, and make workload control decisions.

COMPARISON OF WORKLOAD MANAGEMENT MECHANISMS

In this section, we use the framework presented above to examine the degree to which a number

of workload management mechanisms achieve the goal of autonomic management. We discuss mechanisms currently used in commercial DBMSs and mechanisms proposed in the research literature. For ease of presentation, we group the mechanisms according to the main workload control method they employ, that is resource allocation, admission control and execution control. The discussion is then summarized in Table 1.

Resource Allocation

M & M

The M & M algorithm proposed by Brown, Mehta, Carey, and Livny (1994) is an early example of a workload management mechanism. The workload detection process characterizes the workload by partitioning it into classes where each class has an average response time goal. It monitors response times and provides feedback on whether or not each class is meeting its goal. The workload control process in M & M automatically determines new multiprogramming levels (MPLs) and memory allocations to achieve the set of per-class goals. The performance modeling consists of a set of heuristics to independently select appropriate MPLs and memory allocations for each class. M

Table 1. Summary of autonomic workload management mechanisms

Mechanisms	Adaptability	System Awareness	Workload Control Methods
M & M	Reactive	Closed-feedback	Resource allocation and Admission control (heuristics)
PAQRS	Reactive	Closed-feedback	Resource allocation and Admission control (heuristics)
ASM	Assisted	Report	Resource allocation and admission control (rules)
DB2 QP	Manual	Report	Admission control (thresholds)
EQMS	Reactive	Closed-feedback	Admission control (analytical model)
Query Scheduler	Reactive	Closed-feedback	Admission control (analytical model)
Utility Throttling	Reactive	Closed-feedback	Execution control (analytical model)
Query Throttling	Reactive	Closed-feedback	Execution control (analytical model)
BI Workload Management	Reactive	Closed-feedback	Execution control (fuzzy controller)

& M uses admission control to adjust the MPL for a class.

M & M takes a heuristic approach to adapt to workload changes by finding <MPL, memory> pairs to guide admission control and memory allocation for each class. It does not use any analytic performance model to predict performance, but uses heuristic rules developed to guide the resource allocation. Its adaptation is therefore at the reactive level.

M & M provides a closed-feedback level of system awareness. It monitors performance, calculates the observed average response time and compares it to the response time goal at well defined intervals (the number of query completions) for each workload class to determine whether its goals are being met. It assumes that the system is configured such that it is possible to satisfy the goals for all classes in steady state. This assumption simplifies the implementation by eliminating the need to monitor the health of the system.

PAQRS

In another early work, Pang, Carey, and Livny (1995) proposed an algorithm called Priority Adaptation Query Resource Scheduling (PAQRS) to minimize the number of missed deadlines for a multi-class query workload while at the same time ensuring that any deadline misses are scattered across the different classes according to an administratively-defined miss distribution. The workload detection process partitions the workload into classes. It constantly monitors the resource demand on memory, disk I/O and CPU. If the values indicate that a workload change is taking place then the workload control process is triggered to calculate a new MPL, reallocate memory, and adjust priorities. PAQRS therefore has a closed-feedback level of system awareness.

The workload control process uses heuristics to determine new resource allocations. The new MPL is calculated by applying two techniques: the miss ratio projection and the resource utilization

heuristic. The miss ratio projection uses a least squares fit to produce a quadratic equation based on the previous observations of the MPL and miss ratio. The current miss ratio is then projected to a new MPL based on the equation. The resource utilization heuristic tries to minimize the miss ratio by keeping the resource utilization within a health range. PAQRS uses resource allocation for memory and admission control to manage the MPL. It therefore has a reactive level of adaptability.

PAQRS uses two memory allocation strategies: a Max strategy and a MinMax strategy. The Max strategy allocates either the maximum memory a query needs or nothing. The MinMax strategy allocates memory in two passes. In the first pass, queries are allocated the minimum memory they need from the highest priority to lowest priority. If there is leftover memory, in the second pass, again from the highest priority to the lowest priority, the memory allocation for queries is adjusted from minimum to maximum, until no memory is left or no queries are left. It is possible that a query gets an amount of memory between its minimum and maximum.

PAQRS divides queries into two priority groups, a regular group and a reserve group, and assigns each query class a quota for the regular group. Queries in the regular group are assigned a priority based on their time deadlines, while queries in the reserve group are assigned a priority lower than those in the regular group. This ensures the queries in the regular group are admitted and get resources first. The miss ratio distribution is maintained by adjusting the regular group quota for each class.

ASM

Teradata Active System Management (ASM) (Brown, Richards, Zeehandelaar, & Galeazzi, 2002) is a goal-oriented workload management system capable of supporting complex workloads by adjusting resource allocation via rules for various types of workloads. It takes a preventive approach to workload changes.

ASM's workload detection process partitions queries into performance classes based on workload definitions. A workload definition is a tuple <classification rule, MPL, exception, service level goal>. Classification rules define the attributes that qualify a query to run under a workload definition. MPL defines how many queries can be running at one time under the definition. When the threshold is exceeded, new queries are placed on a delay queue. An exception specifies abnormal characteristics in a query's execution that force actions to be taken.

ASM monitors for the exceptions defined in the workload definition. It also logs query information and keeps track of the system demand from a workload-centric perspective. These logs can be accessed by workload analysis tools for workload definition, general workload understanding, and performance tuning. ASM therefore supports a report level of system awareness.

ASM's workload control process does not predict resource demand for each performance class. It instead maps a performance class to an allocation group with a fixed weight and these allocation groups compete for resources based on their weight. A performance class can have several periods and can be mapped to different allocation groups in different periods.

ASM uses both admission control and resource reallocation to control the workload in order to achieve its management objectives. It has an assisted level of adaptability. Admission control is based on rules set by the administrator to place restrictions on queries. These restrictions can be used to limit a query's access to certain data objects, limit a query's entry into the system based on its properties, or limit a query's entry based on current system conditions. Resource allocation is based on the relative weight of the allocation groups of the current queries. Relative weight for an allocation group is calculated as its weight divided by the sum of all the weights. The larger a group's relative weight, the higher its priority level.

Commercial DBMSs tend to adopt a similar approach as ASM, which maps performance classes (ie. the partitioned workload) into allocation groups that serve as resource allocation targets. For example, performance classes and allocation groups in ASM are similar to workload groups and resource pools in Microsoft SQL Server 2008 Resource Governor (Microsoft, 2009), and work classes and service class in DB2 Workload Manager (Chen et al., 2008).

Admission Control

DB2 Query Patroller

DB2 Query Patroller (DB2 QP) (IBM Corporation, 2003b) is the workload manager for IBM DB2. It dynamically controls the flow of queries against DB2 databases so that small queries and high-priority queries can run promptly, and system resources are used efficiently. The SQL Server Query Governor (Microsoft, 2007) and Oracle's Database Resource Manager (Oracle, 2001) perform a similar function.

DB2 QP's workload detection process classifies queries based on the total cost of queries, which is the resource demand estimated by the query optimizer. A query class is defined by specifying a cost range and a MPL threshold. The cost range is determined by studying the characteristics of the workload and is set by administrators. The MPL is the maximum number of queries of that class that can be concurrently executed. It is determined by considering the workload characteristics and system resources. The adaptability of DB2 QP is therefore at the manual level.

DB2 QP monitors the completion of queries in order to calculate a MPL for each query class and to make admission control decisions. It also acquires query execution information, including query identification and resource usage information, for the purposes of workload characterization and performance study. It generates reports that assist in identifying trends in database usage such as which objects are being accessed, which tables and indexes are frequently used, and which individuals or groups of users are the biggest contributors to the workload. DB2 QP's system awareness is therefore at the report level.

DB2 QP's workload control process uses a threshold-based decision process instead of a performance model. It employs three types of admission control to manage the workload. MPL-based admission control sets a MPL threshold for each query class. When the threshold is reached, new queries are put into the query queue and wait for scheduling until the MPL falls below the threshold. Priority-based admission control assigns a priority to queries based on the user submitting the query. When the MPL threshold for a query class is reached, new queries are inserted in the system wide query queue based on the admission priority. Cost-based admission control associates a cost threshold associated with each user and the system. When the cost of a query exceeds this threshold, the query is held until the system is not busy.

EQMS

Schroeder et al. (2006) propose an external scheduler called External Queue Management System (EQMS) to provide class-based QoS for transactional workloads. EQMS performs admission control based on MPL and decides the order in which transactions are dispatched to control the execution time and queuing time of the workload classes. With respect to achieving diverse QoS targets, EQMS maintains a low MPL, which allows the system to obtain a better estimate of a transaction's execution time within the DBMS, and hence maintains accurate estimates of the per-class mean execution times. This, in turn, gives users an upper bound on the queuing time for a transaction, which can be used to ensure that QoS targets are met.

EQMS classifies transactions into different classes based on their QoS specifications. Workload changes are detected by monitoring the performance of the workload classes. The dispatch order of transactions is adjusted to achieve the QoS targets. The system awareness of EQMS is at the closed-feedback level.

EQMS controls the workload by tuning the MPL parameter and scheduling the dispatch order of transactions. The main purpose of the MPL parameter is to control the execution time of transactions in the DBMS, which is calculated using a queuing model. The external queuing time of transactions is controlled by scheduling the dispatch order of transactions. The combined effect is QoS under control. The adaptability of EQMS is at the reactive level.

Query Scheduler

Query Scheduler (Niu et al., 2006; Niu et al., 2007) manages multiple classes of queries to meet their SLOs by allocating DBMS resources through admission control in the presence of workload fluctuation. A resource allocation plan is derived by maximizing an objective function that encapsulates the performance goals of all classes and their importance to the business. It uses DB2 QP to intercept queries, acquire query information and release queries to a DB2 database instance.

Query Scheduler's workload detection process classifies queries based on their SLOs, which encapsulate both performance goals and business importance. It monitors performance and detects if queries are not meeting their performance goals. The failure of queries with high business importance to meet their goals forces the workload control process to adapt the workload. Query Scheduler's system awareness is therefore at the closed-feedback level.

Query Scheduler's workload control process uses a cost-based approach. It periodically produces a new scheduling plan, which is a set of cost limits for the service classes, based on the incoming workload and system performance data collected over the previous interval. The cost limit for a service class represents the maximum allowable total cost of all concurrently executing queries belonging to that class. The cost limit indirectly controls the amount of resources allocated to a class. Query Scheduler is therefore at the reactive level with respect to adaptability.

Query Scheduler uses utility functions to capture how well a cost limit meets the goals of a service class. These utility functions are then combined to provide an objective function to be maximized in order to arrive at a scheduling plan. An analytical model is used to predict the system performance from the plan.

Execution Control

Utility Throttling

Online DBMS utilities such as database backup/restore, data reorganization and statistics collection, while an essential part of DBMS management, can severely degrade the performance of production applications. Parekh et al. (2004) examine the problem of managing the execution of DBMS utilities so that resulting performance degradation of production applications can be controlled. Their approach to solving the problem uses a self-imposed sleep to slow down, or *throttle*, the utility by a configurable amount.

The workload detection process characterizes the workload into two classes, namely utilities and production applications. It monitors the performance of the production applications and estimates the current performance degradation caused by the executing utilities. The degradation is determined by comparing the current performance with a baseline performance acquired while no utilities are running. Utility throttling exhibits a closed-feedback level of system awareness since the degradation is used to determine the amount of throttling required.

The workload control process provides a reactive level of adaptability. Its goal is to maintain the performance degradation at the level specified by the user. The performance model function, which uses a Proportional-Integral controller from linear control theory, calculates a throttling level for the next interval based on the error in the degradation in previous intervals. The workload control function translates the throttling level into a sleep fraction for the utilities and this new fraction now determines the sleep behaviour of the utilities.

Query Throttling

Managing long-running queries is one of the important issues of workload management in DBMSs. Long-running queries usually consume considerable system resources, which have a detrimental effect on the performance of the other workload classes competing for resources. Inspired by utility throttling, Powley et al. (2010) propose an execution control mechanism that throttles long-running queries to free up resources for competing workloads running concurrently in the system. Throttled queries continue to execute, albeit at a slower pace. Two controllers, a simple controller and a black-box model controller, are proposed to determine the amount of throttling necessary to allow other workload classes to meet their goals.

The workload is partitioned into two classes, namely, a long-running query class and an important class. There is a boundary denoted as ε for the performance goal the important class. The performance goal is considered to be achieved if the performance is within +/- ε of the goal. The system monitors the performance of the important class. If current performance falls outside the boundary, one of the controllers is called to determine the appropriate amount of throttling that should be applied. Therefore, Query Throttling exhibits a closed-feedback level of system awareness.

The simple controller is based on a diminishing step function to determine the amount of throttling. Throttling is initiated when the important class fails to meet its performance goals. Over time, the amount of throttling is increased when the goal is violated and decreased when the goal is exceeded. By using the diminishing step function, the amount of throttling decreases as the actual performance converges on the performance goal, which avoid thrashing.

The black-box model controller sees the system as a black-box. A linear difference equation is used to describe the relationship between the control inputs and the measured outputs: $y(k+1)=ay(k)+bu(k)$, where $y(k+1)$ is the predicted throughput in the $(k+1)$ time unit, $y(k)$ is the measured throughput in the k-th time unit and $u(k)$ is the amount of throttling for the target system in the k-th time unit, a and b are model parameters determined experimentally by using least-square regression.

The workload control process provides a reactive level of adaptability since the controllers are called when the performance goal of the important class is violated.

BI Workload Management

Krompass, Kuno, Dayal, and Kemper (2007) propose a workload management mechanism for Business Intelligence (BI) workloads on large data warehouses. BI workloads are challenging because BI queries can exhibit large variances in resource demands and response times, and they can have different SLOs. The approach combines execution control methods and admission control methods. Admission control is used to accommodate uncertainty in resource demands and SLOs. Execution control is used to deal with problem queries that consume too many resources for too long a time.

The workload detection process classifies the queries according to their SLOs, which are assumed to all be deadline-driven. The system monitoring function collects a number of detailed metrics of query execution for the execution control, including priority, number of cancellations, operator progress and resource contention. There is a closed-feedback level of system awareness since the information collected is used by the execution control component to manage running queries.

The workload control process involves both admission control and execution control. It provides a reactive level of adaptability. The admission control component regulates the submission of queries to the DBMS execution engine. It implements two basic scheduling algorithms, namely first-in-first-out and two queues. The execution control component is implemented with a fuzzy controller, which is a rule-based system based on fuzzy logic. The controller uses the metrics collected by the system monitor component and the inference engine to decide if an executing query should be reprioritized, killed or resubmitted once killed.

Observations

A summary of the discussion of the workload management mechanisms presented above is given in Table 1. In general, we see that all the workload management mechanisms use classification rules to partition the workload. The rules are based on the type of work, as in the case of Utility Throttling, resource demand or cost, as in the case of M & M and DB2 QP, or performance goals or SLOs, as in the case of PAQRS, ASM, EQMS, Query Scheduler, Query Throttling and BI Workload Management. Workload classification based on resource demand makes it easy to control resource allocation, while workload classification based on performance goals makes performance tracking easy. A two level classification based on both criteria is desirable for translating high level performance goals into low level resource allocation, which involves both performance tracking and resource allocation.

We first observe that while workload classification is the most frequently used method in the mechanisms studied, it has its limitations. Specifically, workload classification is relatively static and is only effective for workloads that have little or no change in the makeup of their classes. This is frequently not the case in practice and more dynamic partitioning methods, for example workload clustering, will likely be more effective since they can quickly adapt to changes in the workload. We also observe that SLOs, which encapsulate both the performance goals and the level of importance of a workload class, are likely to become more widely used in autonomic workload management mechanisms because they are able to capture the business importance of a class of work.

The mechanisms we studied use two approaches to detect workload changes: a workload characterization approach (PAQRS, DB2 QP, Query Scheduler, Utility Throttling, BI Workload Management) and a performance monitoring approach (M & M, ASM, EQMS, Query Throttling). A workload characterization approach tracks workload changes before performance is affected and makes proactive workload control possible. A performance monitoring approach, on the other hand, always takes control actions after the workload performance degrades.

DB2 QP and ASM provide monitoring reports for offline analysis. The remaining mechanisms use collected data in some form of a feedback loop to adjust workload control. M & M does not monitor resource usage and supposes that the DBMS always works in safe operation regions below a predetermined saturation point expressed by workload parameters such as MPL. PAQRS uses resource usage data for detecting workload changes. All other systems use performance data for detecting workload changes.

We observe that monitoring is a double-edged sword in autonomic workload management. While continuous monitoring is vital to the timely provision of the information needed to make management decisions, it also has a negative impact on the performance of the applications the management decisions are intended to help. New light-weight and intelligent monitoring techniques, such as those proposed by Chaudhuri, Konig, and Narasayya (2004) and Daniel and Pozzi (2008), are therefore needed in DBMSs to support autonomic management.

The approaches to solving performance problems used in the mechanisms are a performance model approach (EQMS, Query Scheduler, Utility Throttling, Query Throttling), a heuristic or rule-based approach (M & M, PAQRS, BI Workload Management), and threshold control (DB2 QP, ASM). A performance model approach is the best approach to adapt to workload changes because it can capture system characteristics at a finer granularity than the other approaches. The heuristic and threshold approaches solve performance problems at a much coarser granularity than the performance model approach. We observe that, as autonomic workload management advances, there is a trend towards the use of performance modeling techniques in workload control. Accuracy of performance models is vital, which will lead to the need for evolvable performance models that can automatically adapt to changes in system configurations and system environments.

We observed that execution control is a new trend for workload management in DBMSs. More and more systems use execution control to control workload to meet SLOs. Current work focuses on controlling long-running queries. Execution control methods include throttle (Utility Throttling, Query Throttling), cancel (BI Workload Management), and, suspend and resume (Chandramouli, Bond, Babu, & Yang, 2007). We noticed that autonomic workload management in DBMSs is facing two challenges in providing accurate workload control. One is the calibration of resource demand. All the approaches, more or less, take workload control actions based on the resource demand of workload. Due to the complexity of resource usage in DBMSs, improving the estimation accuracy of resource demand is hard, and needs to be addressed in order to make accurate control decisions. The other is the development of sophisticated performance models which describe multiple resources of DBMSs, and therefore, allow fine granular control over multiple resources. The complexity of performance models increases dramatically with the increase of number of resources. A tradeoff of complexity with accuracy should be carefully balanced.

AWMF VALIDATION

Query Scheduler, which was introduced above, is a prototype implementation of our AWMF. We describe Query Scheduler in more detail and discuss the results of experiments we conducted with it to validate the AWMF.

The Structure of Query Scheduler

The structure of Query Scheduler is shown in Figure 2. It is built on top of DB2 QP and makes use of its interfaces to intercept queries, acquire query information, and release queries. When a query comes into DB2, DB2 QP intercepts the query by blocking the agent responsible for the query, and passes the query information, including query identification information, query cost and query execution information, to the Monitor. The Classifier assigns the query to a service class and puts it into the appropriate queue for execution. The Scheduling Planner receives SLOs and the query execution information from the Monitor and consults the Performance Solver in order to come up with a scheduling plan for the current workload mix. A scheduling plan consists of a set of class cost limits, which is the maximum allowable total cost of all concurrently executing queries of a service class. The Dispatcher schedules queries in the class queues according to the scheduling plan given by the Scheduling Planner and informs DB2 QP to release queries for execution. Details of the implementation of Query Scheduler are available elsewhere (Niu et al., 2006; Niu et al., 2007).

Figure 2. Query Scheduler

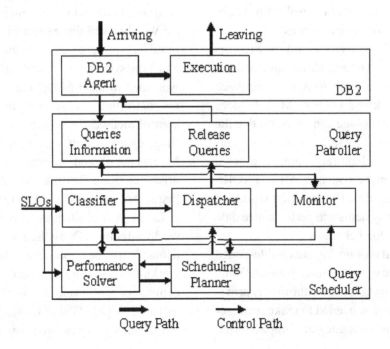

Experimental Results

We describe three experiments to show that Query Scheduler can manage multiple service classes of database workload towards their performance goals while taking their business importance into account. The results of these experiments validate our AWMF.

The computer system used as the database server is an IBM xSeries® 240 machine with dual 1 GHZ CPUs, four PCI/ISA controllers, and 17 Seagate ST 318436LC SCSI disks. We use IBM DB2 UDB Version 8.2 and Query Patroller as supporting components.

The workload used in the experiments consists of two classes of TPC-H queries submitted by interactive clients with zero think time, each class having a performance goal. Class 0 is deemed more important than Class 1. The database consists of 500MB of data. Workload intensity is controlled by the number of clients for each class (see Figure 3). Each test ran for 12 hours and consists of 6 2-hour periods. TPC-H queries have widely varying response times so a velocity-type goal is most appropriate (Niu et al., 2006). Motivated by the need to see a clear division between waiting and execution when performing admission control, we use the metric *Query_Velocity*, which we define as: *Query_Velocity = Execution_time / Response_Time.*

The wait time for admission is dependent upon the policy governing admission control. In order to make a meaningful comparison between different admission control policies, it is necessary to ensure that the expected execution time for a query is stable when the system is busy. We do this by setting a constant total cost limit for concurrently executing queries. Under this condition a higher *Query_Velocity,* indicates better performance.

The first experiment has no class control exerted over the workload and serves as our baseline measure to observe how the performance changes with the changes of workload. The result is shown in Figure 4. The second experiment uses DB2 QP to control the workload. A higher priority is set for Class 0 than for Class 1. This experiment is designed to show how current workload managers control workload. The result is shown in Figure 5. The third experiment uses Query Scheduler

Figure 3. Workload

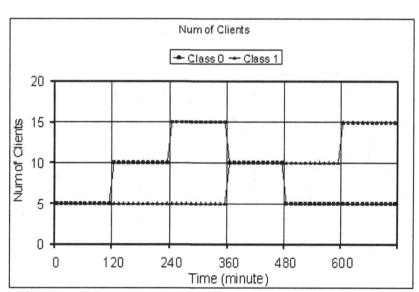

Figure 4. No class control

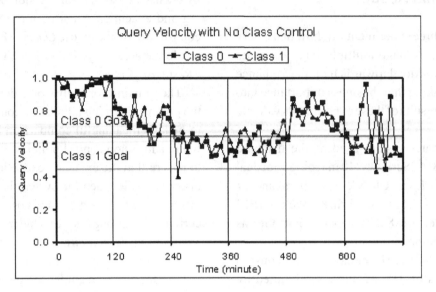

to control the workload. The performance goals for Class 0 and Class 1 are set as 0.65 and 0.45 respectively. The result is shown in Figure 6. The dynamic adjustment of the cost limits to achieve the performance in Figure 6 is shown in Figure 7.

The results of our experiments show that both DB2 QP and Query Scheduler can provide differentiated services, while the no-class-control case cannot. DB2 QP provides differentiated services by assigning static priorities to service classes. As shown in Figure 5, Class 0 with the higher priority always performs better than Class 1, even when it is exceeding its performance goal and Class 1 is in violation of its goal in periods 2, 4 and 6. As shown in Figure 6 for Query Scheduler, Class 0 can better meet its performance goal

Figure 5. DB2 QP control

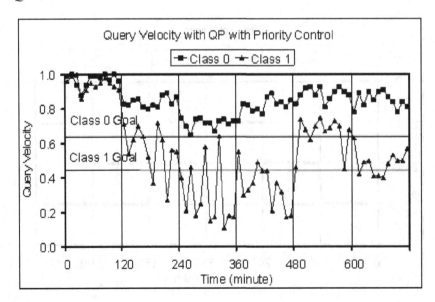

Figure 6. Query Scheduler control

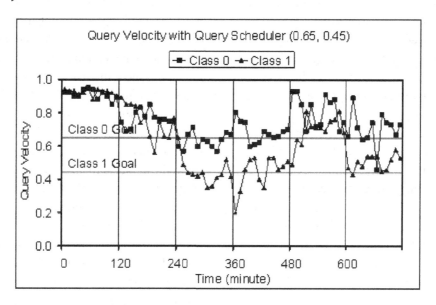

than Class 1 because Class 0 is more important than Class 1. Although Query Scheduler always gives preference to the important class, Class 0, it never allocates too many resources to Class 0 to prevent Class 1 from meeting its performance goal if possible as shown in the periods 2, 4 and 6 in Figures 6. When the workload is too heavy to meet both performance goals in periods 3 and 4, DB2 QP cannot meet the performance goals for Class 1, while Query Scheduler is able to keep both classes converging on their performance goals. From Figure 7, we observe that Query Scheduler adjusts the class cost limits according to the work-load changes. A higher class cost

Figure 7. Adjustment of class cost limit of Query Scheduler

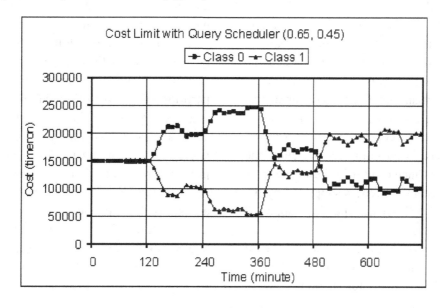

limit means more resources are allocated to the class. The amount of resources allocated to a class is based on its need to meet its performance goal, as shown in periods 2, 5 and 6 in Figures 7. In the case of DB2 QP, Class 0 always has the privilege to possess more resources even when it exceeds its performance goal.

To conclude, Query Scheduler, as a prototype implementation of AWMF, is effective. It is able to respond to the workload changes using admission control to give preference to important service classes, or to the service classes whose performance goals are violated. This validates the feasibility and effectiveness of AWMF.

SUMMARY

Workload management is an established research discipline that has evolved significantly over the years. With the emergence of autonomic computing, the transformation from traditional workload management to autonomic workload management is taking place. In this paper, we provide an overview of the development of workload management leading to the realization of autonomic workload management.

A general framework for the comparison autonomic workload management mechanisms is proposed. It involves a model of autonomic workload management and a set of criteria with which to compare mechanisms. The model consists of two processes, namely workload detection and workload control, and four functional components, namely workload characterization, performance modeling, workload control and system monitoring. The criteria for comparison include the workload control method used by the mechanism, the level of system awareness supported by the mechanism and the level of adaptability supported by the mechanism.

Using the framework, we discuss a number of workload management mechanisms for DBMSs and analyze their support for autonomic workload management. We see that, as expected, the mechanisms from the research literature in general provide a stronger level of support for autonomic workload management than the mechanisms currently available in DBMS products. The mechanisms from the DBMS products (DB2 QP, ASM) still rely on the administrator to make decisions and guide their actions, which is reflected by the lower levels of system awareness and adaptability in these mechanisms. They also only employ simple performance models based on heuristics or thresholds. The mechanisms from the research literature, on the other hand, all provide some level of automation in the workload management. They all provide a closed-feedback level of system awareness and a reactive level of adaptability. A number of these mechanisms (Query Scheduler, Utility Throttling, BI Workload Management) employ analytical models for their performance models.

We believe that, while autonomic workload management is a promising approach to improving the effectiveness of DBMSs, our study shows that there is still much interesting work to be done before it can be achieved. One area of research is the integration of the workload control methods. We see from our study that the three workload control methods, namely resource allocation, admission control and execution control, all have situations in which they are useful. A unified framework in which the three methods can be used in a complimentary fashion is required.

A second area of future research is workload partitioning. As we observed above, workload classification, which is used now, is relatively static and not suited for dynamically changing workloads. Clustering is a more promising approach for workload management and online clustering incorporating system feedback will be an important technique.

A third area of future research is suitable performance models for autonomic workload management. These models will be grounded in the areas of queuing network models and control theory.

Some specific issues for further study include the use of tracking techniques, such as Kalman filters, to improve the quality of the workload parameters feeding the models and evolving performance models to automatically accommodate changes in the system and its environment.

A final area of future research is DBMS monitoring. As we noted above, continuous monitoring is vital to autonomic workload management but it has a negative impact on the performance of system's applications. The monitoring facilities currently available in DBMSs are not suitable. New techniques must be developed that are lightweight, selective and adaptable.

ACKNOWLEDGMENT

This research is supported by the IBM Centre for Advanced Studies (CAS), Toronto, the Natural Sciences and Engineering Research Council of Canada, the Centre for Communication and Information Technology, a division of Ontario Centres of Excellence Inc, Shanxi Scholarship Council of China, and Shanxi Natural Science Foundation of China.

REFERENCES

Brown, D. P., Richards, A., Zeehandelaar, R., & Galeazzi, D. (2002). "Teradata Active System Management". Retrieved February 15, 2008. [Online]. Available: http://www.teradata.com/t/page/ 145613/index.html.

Brown, K. P., Mehta, M., Carey, M. J., & Livny, M. (1994). Towards automated performance tuning for complex workloads. *Proceedings of the 20th Very Large Data Base Conference,* Santiago, Chile, 72-84.

Brown Associate, D. H. Inc. (2004). HP raises the bar for UNIX workload management. Retrieved February 15, 2008. [Online]. Available: http://whitepapers.silicon.com/ 0,39024759,60104905p- 39000654q,00.htm.

Castro, S., Tezulas, N., Yu, B., Berg, J., Kim, H., & Gfroerer, D. (2001). *AIX 5L Workload Manager*.

Chandramouli, B., Bond, C. N., Babu, S., & Yang, J. (2007). Query suspend and resume. *Proceedings of the ACM SIGMOD International Conference on Management of Data*, Beijing, China, 557-568.

Chaudhuri, S., Konig, A., & Narasayya, V. (2004). SQLCM: A continuous monitoring framework for relational database engines. *Proceedings of the 20th International Conference on Data Engineering*, Toronto, Canada, 473-485.

Chen, J., Yin, X., & Zhang, S. (2005). Online Discovery of Quantitative Model for Web Service Management. *Advances in Natural Computation, LNCS 3611*, Springer Berlin, 539-542.

Chen, W. J., Comeau, B., Ichikawa, T., Kumar, S. S., Miskimen, M., & Morgan, H. T. (2008). *DB2 Workload Manager for Linux, Unix, and Windows*. IBM RedBooks.

Corporation, I. B. M. (2003a). *MVS Planning: Workload Management*, (7th ed.).

Corporation, I. B. M. (2003b). *DB2 Query Patroller Guide: Installation*. Administration, and Usage.

Daniel, F., & Pozzi, G. (2008). An Open ECA Server for Active Applications. *Journal of Database Management*, *19*(4), 1–20. doi:10.4018/jdm.2008100101

Elnaffar, S., Powley, W., Benoit, D., & Martin, P. (2003). Today's DBMSs: How autonomic are they? *Proceedings of Dexa Workshops - First International Workshop on Autonomic Computing Systems*, Prague, 651-655.

Erickson, J., & Siau, K. (2008). Web Services, Service-Oriented Computing, and Service-Oriented Architecture: Separating Hype from Reality. *Journal of Database Management, 19*(3), 42–54. doi:10.4018/jdm.2008070103

Ganek, A. G., & Corbi, T. A. (2003). The Dawning of the Autonomic Computing Era. *IBM Systems Journal, 42*(1), 5–18. doi:10.1147/sj.421.0005

Krompass, S., Kuno, H., Dayal, U., & Kemper, A. (2007). Dynamic workload management for very large data warehouses – Juggling feathers and bowling balls. *Proceedings of 33rd International Conference on Very Large Databases (VLDB 2007)*, Vienna Austria, 1105-1115.

Lo, T., & Douglas, M. (1986). The evolution of workload management in data processing industry: A survey. *Proceedings of 1986 Fall Joint Computer Conference*, Dallas, TX, USA, 768-777.

Mainsah, E. (2002). Autonomic computing: the next era of computing. *Electronics & Communication Engineering Journal, 14*(1), 2–3. doi:10.1049/ecej:20020105

Martin, P., Powley, W., Zheng, M., & Romanufa, K. (2005). Experimental Study of a Self-Tuning Algorithm for DBMS Buffer Pools. *Journal of Database Management, 16*(2), 1–20. doi:10.4018/jdm.2005040101

Menascé, D. A. (2004). Performance and availability of internet data centers. *IEEE Internet Computing, 8*(3), 94–96. doi:10.1109/MIC.2004.1297280

Menascé, D. A., & Almeida, V. A. F. (1998). *Capacity Planning for Web Performance: Metrics, Models, and Methods*. Upper Saddle River, NJ: Prentice Hall.

Menascé, D. A., Ruan, H., & Gomaa, H. (2007). QoS management in service-oriented architectures. *Performance Evaluation, 64*(7-8), 646–663. doi:10.1016/j.peva.2006.10.001

Microsoft. (2007). Query Governor cost limit option. Retrieved February 15, 2008. [Online]. Available: http://msdn2.microsoft.com/ en-us/ library/ ms190419.aspx.

Microsoft. (2009). Managing SQL Server Workloads with Resource Governor. Retrieved December 12, 2009. [Online]. Available: http://msdn. microsoft.com/ en-us/library/ bb933866.aspx

Niu, B., Martin, P., Powley, W., Bird, P., & Horman, R. (2007). Adapting mixed workloads to meet SLOs in autonomic DBMSs. *Proceedings of 2007 IEEE 23rd International Conference on Data Engineering Workshops (2nd International Workshop on Self-Managing Database Systems)*, Istanbul, Turkey, 478-484.

Niu, B., Martin, P., Powley, W., Horman, R., & Bird, P. (2006). Workload adaptation in autonomic DBMSs. *Proceedings of CASCON 2006*, Toronto.

Oracle. (2001). Oracle Database Resource Manager. [Online]. Available: http://www.oracle.com/ technology/products/ manageability/database/ pdf/9i_Resource_Mgr_TWP.pdf

Pang, H., Carey, M. J., & Livny, M. (1995). Multiclass query scheduling in real-time database systems. *IEEE Transactions on Knowledge and Data Engineering, 7*(4), 533–551. doi:10.1109/69.404028

Parekh, S., Rose, K., Hellerstein, J., Lightstone, S., Huras, M., & Chang, V. (2004). Managing the performance impact of administrative utilities. In *Self Managing Distributed Systems* (pp. 130–142). Heidelberg: Springer Berlin.

Powley, W., Martin, P., Zhang, M., Bird, P., & McDonald, K. (2010). Autonomic workload execution control using throttling. *Proceedings of 2010 IEEE 26th International Conference on Data Engineering Workshops (5th International Workshop on Self-Managing Database Systems)*, Long Beach, CA, USA.

Salehie, M., & Tahvildari, L. (2005). Autonomic computing: Emerging trends and open problems. *Proceedings of Workshop on Design and Evolution of Autonomic Application Software (DEAS 2005)*, St. Louis Missouri, 82-88.

Schroeder, B., Harchol-Balter, M., Iyengar, A., Nahum, E., & Wierman, A. (2006). How to Determine a Good Multi-Programming Level for External Scheduling. *Proceedings of the 22nd International Conference on Data Engineering*, Atlanta, GA, USA.

Chapter 9

XTEngine:
A Twin Search Engine for XML

Kamal Taha
The University of Texas at Arlington, USA

ABSTRACT

There has been extensive research in XML Keyword-based and Loosely Structured querying. Some frameworks work well for certain types of XML data models while fail in others. The reason is that the proposed techniques overlook the context of elements when building relationships between the elements. The context of a data element is determined by its parent, because a data element is generally a characteristic of its parent. Overlooking the contexts of elements may result in relationships between the elements that are semantically disconnected, which lead to erroneous results. We present in this chapter a context-driven search engine called XTEngine for answering XML Keyword-based and Loosely Structured queries. XTEngine treats each set of elements consisting of a parent and its children data elements as one unified entity, and then uses context-driven search techniques for determining the relationships between the different unified entities. We evaluated XTEngine experimentally and compared it with three other search engines. The results showed marked improvement.

INTRODUCTION

Extensive research has been done in keyword querying using relational data (Agrawal & Chaudhuri & Das, 2002; Aditya & Bhalotia & Sudarshan, 2002; Hristidis & Papakonstantinou,

DOI: 10.4018/978-1-60960-521-6.ch009

2002). Research in XML querying has significant boost with the emergence of World Wide Web, online businesses, and the concept of ubiquitous computing. Some of these works model XML data as a rooted tree (Liu & Chen, 2007; Xu & Papakonstantinou, 2005; Li & Yu & Jagadish, 2004; Cohen & Mamou & Sagiv, 2003). Others, model it as a graph (Cohen & Kanza, 2005; Balmin &

Hristidis & Papakonstantinon, 2003; Balmin & Hristidis & Papakonstantinon, 2004; Botev & Shao & Guo, 2003). Most of these works target either: (1) naïve users (such as business' customers) by proposing Keyword-based search engines, or (2) sophisticated users, by proposing fully structured search engines.

Business' customers are most likely not aware of the exact structure of the underlying data. On the other hand, business' employees are likely to be aware of some labels (or attributes) of elements containing data, but they are unlikely to be fully aware of the underlying data structure. Thus, business' customers need a pure Keyword-based search engine, while business' employees need a Loosely Structured search engine for answering their queries. A Loosely Structured query combines keywords and element names. We propose in this chapter: (1) an XML Keyword-based search engine called XTEngine-K for answering business' customers, and (2) an XML Loosely Structured search engine called XTEngine-L for answering business' employees. Consider that the user wants to know the data D, which is contained in an element labeled E. If the user knows *only* the keywords k_1, k_2,..., k_n, which are relevant to D, he/she can submit a Keyword-based query to XTEngine-K in the form: Q ("k_1", "k_2",..., "k_n"). If, however, the user knows the label E and the labels $l_{k_1}, l_{k_2}, ..., l_{k_n}$ (which are the labels of the elements containing the keywords k_1, k_2,.., k_n respectively), but this user is unaware of the structure of the data, he/she can submit a Loosely Structured query to XTEngine-L in the form: Q $(l_{k_1}$ = "k_1", ..., l_{k_n} = "k_n", E?). XTEngine is built on top of XQuery search engine (Katz, 2005).

A few works (Cohen & Mamou & Sagiv, 2003; Li & Yu & Jagadish, 2004) have proposed XML search engines that answer both Keyword-based and Loosely Structured queries. Other works (Liu & Chen, 2007; Xu & Papakonstantinou, 2005) have proposed XML search engines that answer only Keyword-based queries. Computing the

Lowest Common Ancestor (LCA) of elements containing keywords is the common denominator among these engines. Despite their success, they suffer *recall* and *precision* limitations. As we will show in the coming sections, the reason for these limitations stems from the fact that these engines employ mechanisms for building relationships between data elements based solely on their labels and proximity to one another, while overlooking the *contexts* of these elements. In our work, the context of a data element is determined by its parent, because a data element is generally a characteristic of its parent element. If for example a data element is labeled "title", we cannot determine whether it refers to a book title or a job title without referring to its parent. Consider as another example that an XML document containing two elements labeled "name", one of them refers to the name of a student, while the other refers to the student's school name. Building a relationship between these two "name" elements without consideration of their parents may lead to the incorrect conclusion that the two elements belong to the same type. Building relationships between data elements while overlooking their contexts may lead to relationships that are semantically disconnected. Consequently, the results generated by non context-driven systems are susceptible to errors, especially if the XML document contains more than one element having the same label but representing different types of information or having different labels but representing the same type. XTEngine-L and XTEngine-K avoid the pitfalls cited above of non context-driven search engines by employing novel context-driven search techniques. These techniques consider each set of elements in an XML tree consisting of a parent and children data elements as one *unified entity*.

Example 1: Consider that an XML tree containing interior elements labeled book, job, student, and school. Consider that *each* of elements book and job has a *child data element* labeled title, and *each* of elements student and school has a *child data element* labeled name. XTEngine-L and

XTEngine-K will consider *each* of the following sets (which consists of a parent and its child(ren) data element(s)) as one *unified entity*: {book, title}, {job, title}, {student, name}, and {school, name}. Therefore, XTEngine-L and XTEngine-K will be able to determine that the two elements labeled title are not semantically identical, since they refer to two different types of entities; likewise, the two elements labeled name refer to two different types of entities.

The frameworks of XTEngine-L and XTEngine-K determine the relationships between data elements based on the *semantic relationships* between the unified entities containing them. Let e_i be a unified entity containing a data element labeled n_x, and let e_j be a unified entity containing a data element labeled n_y. If e_i and e_j are semantically related, data elements n_x and n_y are also related, and vice versa. We propose in this chapter novel *context-driven* search techniques for establishing the semantic relationships between different unified entities. We make the following contributions in this chapter:

- We propose novel mechanisms that determine each set of semantically related unified entities.
- We propose context-driven mechanisms for determining the data elements that contain the answers for Keyword queries and Loosely Structured queries.
- We experimentally evaluate the quality and efficiency of XTEngine and compares it with three non context-driven search systems: XSeek (Liu & Chen, 2007), Schema-Free XQuery (Li et al., 2004), and XSEarch (Cohen et al. 2003).

BACKGROUND

Keyword querying in relational databases has been studied extensively (Agrawal et al., 2002; Aditya et al., 2002; Hristidis et al., 2002). These studies model the database as a graph in which tuples are regarded as the graph's nodes and the relationships between the tuples are regarded as the graph's edges. Then a keyword query is answered by returning a subgraph that satisfies the search keywords. A number of studies (Cohen & Kanza, 2005; Balmin et al., 2003; Balmin et al., 2004; Botev et al., 2003) propose modeling XML documents as graphs, and keyword queries are answered by processing the graphs based on given schemas.

The studies (Liu & Chen, 2007; Xu & Papakonstantinou, 2005; Li et al., 2004; Cohen et al. 2003) are the most related to the work in this chapter, since they propose semantic search techniques for establishing relationships between nodes in XML documents modeled as trees. Despite their success, however, they suffer recall and precision limitations as a result of overlooking nodes' contexts. We take (Liu & Chen, 2007; Xu & Papakonstantinou, 2005; Li et al., 2004; Cohen et al. 2003) as sample of non-context driven search engines and overview below the techniques employed by each of them.

Schema-Free XQuery (Li et al., 2004): The system uses an algorithm called MLCAS for computing the Meaningful Lowest Common Ancestor (MLCA) of nodes containing keywords. Nodes a and b are considered *meaningfully related* and their Lowest Common Ancestor (LCA) node c is considered the MLCA of a and b, iff c is *not* an ancestor of some node d, which is a LCA of node b and another node that has the same label as a. Consider for example nodes 2, 10, and 19 in Figure 1. Node 19 (area) and node 2 (name) are not related, because their LCA (node 1) is an ancestor of node 9, which is the LCA of nodes 19 and 10, and node 10 has the same label as node 2. Therefore, node 19 is related to node 10 and not to node 2. Algorithm MLCAS uses a stack, with the head of each stack node being a descendant of the stack node below it. The basic idea is to perform one single merge pass over the nodes, in the order of their traversal in the XML tree using Depth First Search, and conceptually merge them into rooted trees containing MLCAs. Within each such tree, the root is a MLCA, and the leaf level contains nodes from different ML-CAs sharing the same root. The time complexity of the algorithm is $O(h\sum_{i=1}^{m} n_i + \prod_{i=1}^{m} n_i)$ where h is the height of the XML tree, m is the number of input nodes, and n_i is the number of nodes having the same label as node i. The system adopts the Loosely Structured query's form of (Chamberlin et al. 2007), but *only* the descendant operator (//) is used to indicate that the terms in the query are descendants of the root element. So, the format of a Loosely Structured query is as follows:

```
for $d in doc("XML document
name")
    where $d//node's label =
"keyword"
    return $d//node's label
```

XKSearch (Xu & Papakonstantinou, 2005): The system uses an algorithm called the Stack Algorithm to compute the Smallest Lowest Common Ancestor (SLCA) of nodes containing keywords. The algorithm is based on stack sort-merge approach. It computes the longest common prefix of each node and the node denoted by the top entry of the stack. It then pops the top entries containing Dewey components that are not part of the common prefix. If a popped entry contains all keywords, it is considered a SLCA. The SLCA is a root of a subtree, where the nodes of the subtree contain all query's keywords and they have no descendant node(s) that also contain all keywords. Consider for example Figure 1 and the query *Q*("XML", "Julie Smith"). Consider that node 13 contains the value "XML" instead of "XQuery". Since the keyword "XML" is contained in both nodes 5 and 13, the answer subtree will be the one rooted at node 9, which contains nodes 10 and 13, and not the one rooted at node 4, which contains nodes 5 and 10. Nodes in XKSearch are labeled with Dewey numbers. The Dewey numbers of nodes containing keywords are stored in the stack after being merged together. XKSearch builds relationships between nodes containing keywords based solely on their labels and proximity to one another, while overlooking their contexts.

XSeek (Liu & Chen, 2007): XSeek uses the approach of XKSearch for identifying search predicates by determining SLCA (which XSeek calls it *VLCA nodes*). The contribution of XSeek

Figure 1. A graduate school's authors and coauthors bibliography XML tree

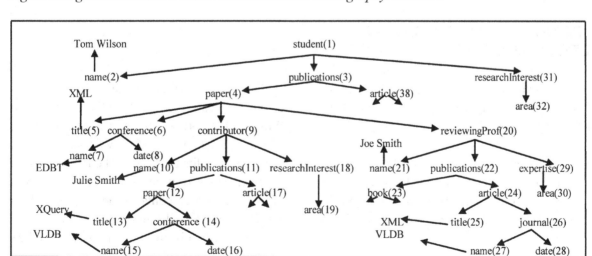

is the inference of *desirable* result nodes. Each desirable node is a data node that either: (1) matches one of the query's result nodes: if the label of node n_1 matches keyword k_1 and there does not exist a descendant node n_2 of n_1 whose label matches another keyword k_2, n_1 is considered a result node, or (2) matches a predicate: a keyword that does not satisfy the condition in (1) is considered a predicate.

XSEarch (Cohen et al. 2003): XSEarch uses an algorithm called ComputeInterconnectionIndex, which employs dynamic programming to compute the relationships between all pairs of nodes in an XML tree. If the *relationship tree* of nodes a and b (the set of nodes in the path from a to b) contains two or more nodes with the same label, then nodes a and b are *unrelated;* otherwise, they are related. Consider for example Figure 1 and the relationship between nodes 2 and 32. The two nodes are related, since their relationship tree (which contains nodes 2, 1, 31, 32) does not contain more than one node having the same label. On the other hand, node 2 is unrelated to node 13, because their relationship tree (which contains nodes 2, 1, 3, 4, 9, 11, 12, 13) includes two nodes (nodes 4 and 12), whose labels are the same. A Loosely Structured query has the form $Q(l{:}k_1,\ldots,l_m{:}k_m,\ldots,l_z{:},\ldots l_n{:})$, where each $l{:}k$ pair denotes *label-keyword* and "$l_z{:}, \ldots l_n{:}$" are the answer return elements.

LIMITATION OF NON CONTEXT-DRIVEN XML SEARCH SYSTEMS

Non context-driven search engines may return a faulty answer for a query that meets one of the following criteria:

- The search term element or the return element of the Loosely Structured query has the same label as one of the nodes in the XML tree that have the *same label and type*.

- The query is submitted against an XML document, whose XML tree contains: (1) a set S of nodes having ancestor-descendant relationships and containing all the query's keywords, and (2) a node $\notin S$ containing one of the query's keywords.
- The query is submitted against an XML document, whose XML tree contains nodes having different labels but the same type.
- The query is submitted against an XML document, whose XML tree contains nodes having the same label but different types.
- The Loosely Structured query's search term and return elements have the same label.

Let us take (Xu & Papakonstantinou, 2005; Li et al., 2004; Cohen et al. 2003) as sample of non context driven XML search systems. We demonstrate below the pitfalls and limitations of these systems that caused by overlooking nodes' contexts. These pitfalls are demonstrated by running query samples against the data shown in Figures 1, 2, and 3.

Schema-Free XQuery (Li et al., 2004): The following queries demonstrate the problems of the techniques employed by the system:

- Consider Figure 1 and the query:

```
for    $d in doc("doc name")
where $d// name = "Tom Wilson"
return $d//name
```

The query asks for the names of the coauthors of the publication that was authored by "Tom Wilson". The correct answer is nodes 10 and 21. However, Schema-Free XQuery would return null as the answer for the query. The reason it does not return node 10 is because node 1 is the LCA of nodes 2 (which contains the keyword "Tom Wilson") and node 10 and it is also an ancestor of node 4, which is the LCA of nodes 10 and 21 and the label of node 21 is the same as the label

Figure 2. Fragments of XML documents

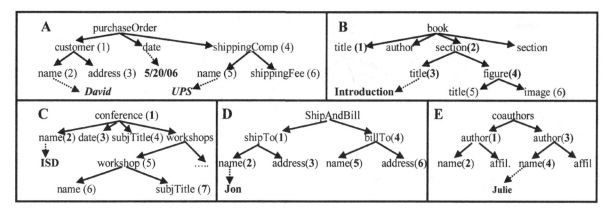

of node 2. Therefore, Schema-Free XQuery would consider node 10 is related to node 21 and not to node 2 and that node 4 is the MLCA of nodes 10 and 21. In the same token, Schema-Free XQuery would not return node 21, because it considers it related to node 10 and not to node 2.

- Consider Figure 2-B and the query:

```
for    $d in doc("doc name")
where $d// title = "Introduction"
return $d// image
```

The query asks for the image presented in the section titled "Introduction". The correct answer is node 6. However, Schema-Free XQuery would return null. The reason is that the LCA of node 3 (which contains the keyword) and node 6 is node 2, and node 2 is an ancestor of node 4, which is the LCA of nodes 6 and 5, and node 5 has the same label as node 3. Therefore, Schema-Free XQuery would consider node 6 is related to node 5 and not to node 3.

- Consider if we prune node 30 (area) from Figure 1 and we have the following query:

```
for    $d in doc("doc name")
where $d// title = "Joe Smith"
```

```
return $d// area
```

The query asks for the area of expertise of "Joe Smith" (node 21). The correct answer is null. But, Schema-Free XQuery will return node 19, because the LCA of nodes 21 and 19 is *not* a descendant of a LCA of node 21 and another node labeled "area".

- Consider Figure 2-C and the query:

```
for    $d in doc("doc name")
where $d// name = "ISD"
return $d// subjTitle
```

The query asks for the subject title of the ISD conference. The correct answer is node 4. Instead of returning node 4 only, Schema-Free XQuery would return also node 7.

- Consider Figure 3 and the following query:

```
for    $d in doc("doc name")
where $d// title = "XML and the
Web"
return $d//name
```

The query asks for the author of the publication titled "XML and the Web" (node 10). The correct answer is node 13, but Schema-Free XQuery

Figure 3. XML tree representing customer publication order

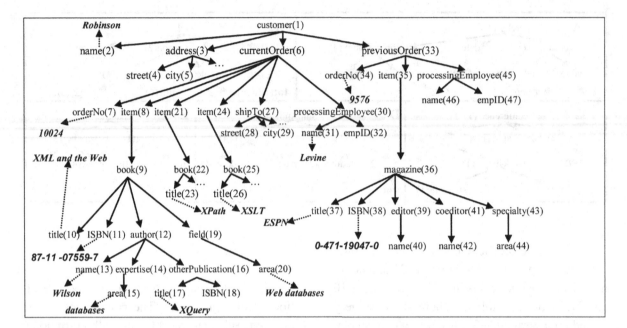

would return null. The reason is that the LCA of nodes 10 and 13 is node 9, and node 9 is an ancestor of node 12, which is the LCA of nodes 13 and 17 (which shares node 10 the label). Therefore, Schema-Free XQuery considers node 13 is related to node 17 and not to node 10.

- Consider Figure 3 and the following query:

```
for    $d in doc("doc name")
where $d// orderNo = "10024"
return $d// title
```

The query asks for the title of the publication that was ordered in order number is "10024". Instead of returning node 10 only, Schema-Free XQuery would return also node 17, which is irrelevant.

- Consider Figure 3 and the following query:

```
for    $d in doc("doc name")
where $d// ISBN "87-11-07559-7"
return $d// ISBN
```

The query asks for the ISBN of the publication that had been ordered by a customer, who also ordered a publication with ISBN "87-11-07559-7". Instead of returning node 38, Schema-Free XQuery would return node 18, because the LCA of nodes 38 and 11 is node 1, and node 1 is an ancestor of node 9, which is the LCA of nodes 11 and 18, and the label of node 18 is the same as the label of node 38. Thus, Schema-Free XQuery considers node 18 is related to node 11, while node 38 is not.

XSEarch (Cohen et al. 2003): The following sample of queries demonstrates the problems of the techniques employed by XSearch:

- Consider Figure 1 and the query *Q*(name:"Tom Wilson", area:). The query asks for the research interest area of "Tom Wilson". The correct answer is node 32. Instead of returning node 32 only, XSearch would return also nodes 19 and 30, because the relationship tree of nodes 2 and 19 and the relationship tree of nodes 2 and 30 do not contain two or more nodes with the same label.

- Consider Figure 2-E and the query Q(name: "Julie", name:). The query asks for the other coauthor of the publication that was coauthored by Julie. The correct answer is node 2. But, XSearch would return null, since the relationship tree of nodes 4 and 2 contains two nodes having the same label (nodes 1 and 3, which have the same label "author").

- Consider Figure 2-A and the query: Q(date: "5/20/06", name:). The query could be interpreted either as "what is the customer's name, who placed an order on 5/20/06" or as "what is the name of the shipping company that delivered an order placed on 5/20/06". The correct answer is node 2 "David". XSearch would return both nodes 2 and 5 as a *one unified answer* even though the two nodes refer to two entities with different types.

- Consider Figure 2-D and the query: Q(name: "Jon", address:). The query asks for the shipping address of Jon. The correct answer is node 3. XSearch would return both node 3 "address" and node 6 "address", because the relationship tree of nodes 2 and 3 and the relationship tree of nodes 2 and 6 do not contain two nodes with the same label.

- Consider Figure 3 and the query Q(orderNo: "10024", title:). The query asks for the title of the publication that was ordered in order number "10024". Instead of returning node 10 only, XSEarch would return also nodes 37 and 17, because the relationship tree of nodes 37 and 7 and the relationship tree of nodes 17 and 7 do not contain two or more nodes having the same label. If XSEarch employs an ontological concepts, it would have discovered that the first relationship tree contains nodes 33 (previousOrder) and 6 (currentOrder) which belong to the same type, and the second relationship tree contains nodes 9 (book) and 16 (otherPublica-

tion) which also belong to the same type (publication).

- On the flip side, consider Figure 3 and the query: Q(ISBN: "87-11-07559-7", ISBN:). The query asks for the ISBN of the publication that had been ordered by the same customer, who ordered a publication with ISBN "87-11-07559-7". Instead of returning node 38, XSEarch would return node 18, because the relationship tree of nodes 38 and 11 contains more than one node having the same label (nodes 35 and 8). And, the relationship tree of nodes 18 and 11 does not contain more than one node having the same label.

XKSearch (Xu & Papakonstantinou, 2005): The following Keyword-based query demonstrates the problems of the Stack Algorithm of XKSearch. Consider Figure 1 and the query: Q("Smith", "XML", "VLDB"). The query asks for information about an author, whose last name is "Smith" and who authored a publication titled "XML", which appeared in a "VLDB" conference proceedings or journal. As can be seen from Figure 1, there are two candidate answer subtrees. The first is rooted at node 4 and contains the three keywords in nodes 5, 10, and 15. The second is rooted at node 20 and contains the three keywords in nodes 21, 25, and 27. The first one is an incorrect answer, because the publication titled "XML" (node 5) and authored by "Julie Smith" was published in an "EDBT" conference proceedings (node 7) and not in a "VLDB". Rather, the author's publication titled "XQuery" (node 13) is the one that was published in "VLDB" proceedings. The second answer subtree is a correct answer, because "Joe Smith" (node 21) authored a publication titled "XML" (node 25), which appeared in a "VLDB" journal (node 27). We show below how the Stack Algorithm of XKSearch answers the query by returning both the incorrect and correct answer subtrees as a result of not employing context-driven search techniques.

After labeling the nodes of the XML tree in Figure 1 with Dewey numbers, the keyword lists would be as follows. Keyword "XML" list = [0.1.0.0, 0.1.0.3.1.1.0], which corresponds to nodes 5 and 25. Keyword "Smith" list =[0.1.0.2.0, 0.1.0.3.0], which corresponds to nodes 10 and 21. Keyword "VLDB" list = [0.1.0.2.1.0.1.0, 0.1.0.3.1.1.1.0], which corresponds to nodes 15 and 27. The third and fourth states of the Stack Algorithm of XKSearch are shown in Figures 4-a and 4-b, where "T" means that the node represented by the entry contains the corresponding keyword and "F" is the negation of that. The key problem of XKSearch, which would lead it to return the faulty answer is caused by the stack in Figure 4-b, as follows. When popping the top entry in the previous stack state (the third state), XKSearch passes the keyword information of the popped entry to the parent entry. In the sixth stack state, XKSearch will return the correct answer subtree. Then, when all of the keyword lists are exhausted, line 19 of the Stack Algorithm of XKSearch will find that all the fields of array keywords at entry 0.1.0 contain "T" (see Figure 4-b); therefore, it will consider node 0.1.0 (node 4) a SLCA and return it as the root of an answer subtree. As can be seen the semantic of the answer is incorrect, because "Julie Smith" (node 10) authored a paper titled "XML" but it did not appear in a "VLDB" conference proceedings; rather, her publication "XQuery" is the one appeared in a "VLDB" conference proceedings. XKSearch could have returned only the correct answer if it employs a context-driven search technique.

CONCEPTS USED IN XTENGINE FRAMEWORK

We model XML documents as rooted and labeled trees. A tree t is a tuple: $t = (n, e, r, \lambda t)$ where n is the set of nodes, $e \subseteq n \times n$ is the set of edges, r is the root node of t, and $\lambda t: n \rightarrow \Sigma$ is a node labeling function where Σ is an alphabet of node labels. A node in a tree represents an element in an XML document. We use the terms "data node" and "leaf node" interchangeably, where a data node/leaf node is a node of a tree data structure that has no child node and it always has a value. Nodes are numbered for easy reference.

The framework partitions XML trees to subtrees, where each consists of a parent and its children data nodes. Each subtree is treated as a unified entity, called a *Canonical Tree*. A Canonical Tree is a metaphor of real-world entities. Two real-world entities may have different names but belong to the same type, or they may have the same name but refer to two different types. To overcome that labeling ambiguity, we observe that if we cluster Canonical Trees based on the ontological concepts of the parent nodes components of the Canonical Trees, we will identify a number of *clusters*. That is, each cluster contains Canonical Trees whose parent nodes components belong to the same ontological concept. Consider for example Figure 1. Using this clustering scheme, we will be able to determine that the two Canonical Trees whose parent nodes components are nodes 4 "paper" and 24 "article" fall under the same cluster, since both "paper" and "article" belong to the same ontological concept of "publication". We will also be able to determine that the two data nodes labeled "name" (nodes 2 and 7) are not semantically identical (they refer to two different types of entities), since they belong to

Figure 4. Stack states of XKSearch: (a) the third state. (b) the fourth state

	S	X	V
0	F	F	T
1	F	F	F
0	F	F	F
1	F	F	F
2	T	F	F
0	F	T	F
1	F	F	F
0	F	F	F

	S	X	V
0	T	F	F
3	F	F	F
0	T	T	T
1	F	F	F
0	F	F	F

(a)   (b)

Canonical Trees falling under different clusters: the ontological concepts of "student" and "conference" are "person" and "publication proceedings" respectively. We use the term Ontology Label to refer to the ontological concept of a parent node. We now formalize the Ontology Label and Canonical Tree concepts in Definitions 1 and 2.

Definition 1 - Ontology Label (OL) and Ontology Label Abbreviation (OLA): Let m "is-a" m' denote that class m is a subclass of class m' in an Object-Oriented ontology. For example, a student "is a" person. m' is the most general superclass (root node) of m in a defined ontology hierarchy. If m is an interior node's label, m' is called the Ontology Label of m, and is expressed as $OL(m)=m'$. Figure 5 shows an example of ontology hierarchy. For example, since student is a subclass of person (see Figure 5-b), the Ontology Label of node student(1) in Figure 1 is expressed as OL(student) = person. m' is a cluster set that contains entities sharing the same domain, properties, and cognitive characteristics (e.g., the cluster person contains the entities of student, author, etc.). The framework of XTEngine applies the above clustering concept to all parent nodes in an XML tree, and the label of each of these clusters is an

Ontology Label (OL). Table 1 shows the Ontology Labels and clusters of parent nodes in the XML tree in Figure 1. The table is an alternative representation of the information in Figure 5. We abbreviate each OL to a *letter* called an Ontology Label Abbreviation (OLA). Table 1 shows the OLAs of the OLs in the table.

Definition 2 - Canonical Tree (CT): Canonical Tree T is a pair, $T=(OL(n'), N)$, where $OL(n')$ is the Ontology Label of an interior node n' and N is a finite set of data nodes and/or attributes. Let (n',n) denote that there is an edge from node n' to node n in the XML tree. $N=\{n|$ n is a data node, and (n',n), or n is an attribute of $n'\}$. In Figure 1 for example, the parent node student(1) and its child data node name(2) constitute a Canonical Tree. The parent node component student(1) is represented in the Canonical Tree by its Ontology Label "person" (see the root Canonical Tree T_1 in Figure 6). The Ontology Label of a Canonical Tree is the Ontology Label of the parent node component of the Canonical Tree. For example, the Ontology Label of Canonical Tree T_1 in Figure 6 is the Ontology Label of the parent node component student(1), which is "person". A Canonical Tree is represented by a

Figure 5. Example of ontology hierarchy

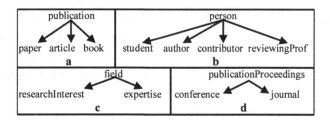

Table 1. OLs and OLAs of the parent nodes in Figure 1

parent nodes (with their IDs)	OL	OLA
paper (4,12), article (17,24), book(23)	publication	b
student (1), contributor (9), reviewingProf(20)	person	P
researchInterest (18,31), expertise (29)	field	f
conference (6), journal (26)	publication-Proceedings	s

Figure 6. CTG depicting the relationships between the CTs constructed from the XML tree presented in Figure 1

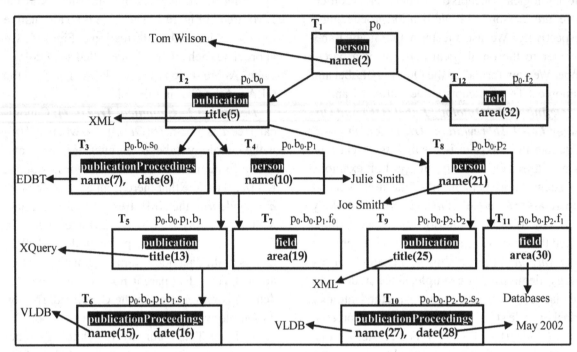

rectangle, and is labeled with a numeric ID. For example, in Figure 6 the label of the root Canonical Tree is T_1. We use the abbreviation "CT" throughout the dissertation to denote "Canonical Tree".

A *Canonical Trees Graph (CTG)* is a hierarchical representation depicting the relationships between CTs. Figure 6 shows a CTG depicting the relationships between the CTs constructed from the XML tree in Figure 1. Let n and n' be two interior nodes in an XML tree. They are the parent nodes components of CTs T and T' respectively. CTs T and T' have parent-child relationship in the CTG if there does not exist in the XML tree any node n'' on the path from n to n' where n'' has children data nodes or attributes. In Figure 1 for example, since node paper(4) is a descendant of node student(1) and since there is no interior node in the path from student(1) to paper(4) that has children data nodes or attributes, the CT whose parent node component is node 4 (CT T_2 in Figure

6) is a child of the CT whose parent node component is node 1 (CT T_1 in Figure 6). We now formalize the CTG concept.

Definition 3 - Canonical Trees Graph (CTG):
A *CTG* is a pair of sets, $CTG = (T_S, E)$, where T_S is a finite set of CTs and E, the set of edges, is a binary relation on T_S, so that $E \subseteq T_S \times T_S$. $T_S = \{T_i \mid T_i \text{ is a CT, and } 1 \leq i \leq |T_S|\}$. The CTG is constructed as follows: If the two interior nodes n, n' in the XML tree both have children data nodes and/or attributes, and if either (1) (n,n') is an edge in the XML tree, or (2) n is an ancestor of n', and there does not exist any node n'' on the path from n to n' where n'' has children data nodes or attributes, then (T_1, T_2) will be an edge in the CTG, where $T_1 = (OL(n), N_1)$ and $T_2 = (OL(n'), N_2)$: N_1 and N_2 are the sets of children data nodes/attributes of n and n' respectively.

Definition 4 - Dewey ID: Each CT is labeled with a Dewey number-like label called a Dewey ID. A Dewey ID of CT T_i is a sequence of components, each having the form OLA_x where OLA is an Ontology Label Abbreviation (recall Definition 1 and table 1) and x denotes a subscript digit. Each OLA represents the Ontology Label of an ancestor CT T_j of a CT T_i and the digit x represents the number of CTs preceding T_j in the graph using Depth First Search, whose Ontology Labels are the same as the Otology Label of T_j. When the sequence of components OLA_x in the Dewey ID of CT T_i are read from left to right, they reveal the chain of ancestors of T_i and their Ontology Labels, starting from the root CT; the last component reveals the Ontology Label of T_i itself. Consider for example CT T_4 in Figure 6. Its Dewey ID $p_0.b_0.p_1$ reveals that the Dewey ID of the root CT is p_0 and its Ontology Label is "person". It also reveals that the Dewey ID of the parent of T_4 is $p_0.b_0$ and its Ontology Label is "publication". The last component p_1 reveals the Ontology Label of T_4, which is "person", and the subscript 1 attached to p indicates that there is one CT preceding T_4 in the graph using Depth First Search, whose Ontology Label is "person".

Definition 5 - Semantically Related CTs: CTs T and T' are semantically related iff the paths from T and T' to their Lowest Common Ancestor (not including T and T') do not contain more than one CT with the same Ontology Label. The Lowest Common Ancestor of T and T' is the only CT that contains the same OL in the two paths to T and T'.

Notation 1- Keyword Context (KC): KC is a CT containing a keyword of a query. That is, one of the data nodes of the KC holds a value matching one of the query's keywords. Consider Figure 6 and the query Q("XML"). CTs T_2 and T_9 are the KCs for the query.

Notation 2- OL_T and OL_{KC}: OL_T denotes the Ontology Label of CT T. For example, OL_{T_1} is "person". OL_{KC} denotes the Ontology Label of the KC.

Notation 3- Intended Answer Node (IAN): IAN is a data node in the XML tree containing the data that the user is looking for. Consider, for example, Figure 1 and the query Q("Julie Smith", "VLDB"). As the semantics of the query implies, the user wants to know information about the publication(s) authored by "Julie Smith" (node 10) and appeared in "VLDB" conference proceedings (node 15). This information is contained in nodes 13 and 16. Therefore, each of these two nodes is called an IAN.

XTENGINE CONTEXT-DRIVEN SOLUTION

XTEngine-L and XTEngine-K avoid the problems of non context-driven search systems by employing novel mechanisms that account for the contexts of nodes. We implemented these mechanisms in XTEngine-L and XTEngine-K prototype systems. XTEngine-L answers Loosely Structured queries, whereas XTEngine-K answers Keyword-based queries. The basic idea is as follows. Each CT represents a real-world entity. A Canonical Trees Graph (e.g., Figures 6 and 7) depicts the hierarchical relationships between the entities represented by the CTs. A relationship between two CTs could be described as either *immediate* or *extended*. We call each CT that *can* contain an IAN for a KC an Immediate Relative of the KC. Consider, for example, Figures 1 and 6 and the Keyword-based query Q("XQuery"). XQuery is a title of a paper and is contained in node 13. It is intuitive that data nodes 10, 15, and/or 16 be IANs, but it is not intuitive that data node 2 be an IAN since "Tom Wilson" (node 2) did not author that paper. Since "XQuery" is contained in CT T_5, we can determine that the CTs containing nodes 10, 15, and 16 are Immediate Relatives of T_5, while the CT containing node 2 is not an Immediate Relative of T_5. We use the notation "$T \in IR_{KC}$" to denote that CT T is an Immediate Relative of the KC. Let CT T be a *KC*. The Immediate Relatives of T is a set IR_T, $IR_T = \{T'|T'$ *is a CT that can contain an IAN for a query whose keyword(s) is contained in CT T*$\}$

XTEngine-L Mechanisms for Answering Loosely Structured Queries

If the keyword k of a Loosely Structured query is contained in a CT T, the IAN should be contained in either T itself or in IR_T. If the keywords k_1 and k_2 of a Loosely Structured query are contained in CTs T_1 and T_2 respectively, the IAN should be contained in T_1, T_2, and/or the intersection $IR_{T1} \cap IR_{T2}$, etc.

XTEngine-K Mechanisms for Answering Keyword-Based Queries

XTEngine-K answers a Keyword-based query by returning a subtree rooted at a CT called the *Lowest Meaningful Common Ancestor (LMCA)*. The leaves of the subtree are the CTs containing the keywords (the KCs). The set of CTs located in a path from the *LMCA* to a Keyword Context KC_i are called *Related Ancestor Canonical Trees of* KC_i (denoted by $RACT_{KC_i}$). The concept of RACT is formalized in Definition 6.

Definition 6 - Related Ancestor Canonical Trees (RACT): Let $A^T_{KC_i}$ denote CT T is an ancestor of Keyword Context KC_i. If $A^T_{KC_i}$ and $T \in IR_{KC_i}$, then T is a Related Ancestor Canonical Tree (RACT) of KC_i. That is, if a CT T is both an ancestor and an Immediate Relative of KC_i, then it is a RACT of KC_i (denoted by $RACT_{KC_i}$).

The LMCA is located in the intersection of the RACTs of the KCs. That is, if a query has n KCs, then the LMCA $= \bigcap_{i=1 \to n} RACT_{KC_i}$.

Figure 7. CTG of the XML tree presented in Figure 3

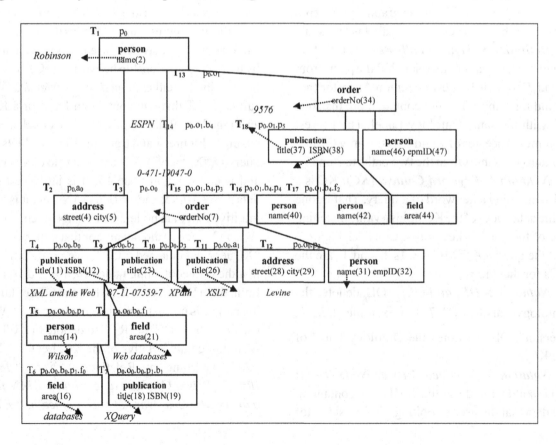

Query Processing Strategy

Each of XTEngine-L and XTEngine-K has two processing phases. We call the first phase pre-query processing phase and the second phase post-query processing phase.

XTEngine-L pre-query processing phase: In this phase, an XML schema is input to the system for the creation of the following: (1) the Ontology Labels for the interior nodes in the schema, (2) a CTG based on the schema, and (3) the IR_T for *each* CT T in the CTG. Since computing IR_i online is expensive, XTEngine-L *pre-computes* (offline) for each CT T in the CTG its IR_T and saves this information in a hash table called IR_TBL for future references.

XTEngine-K pre-query processing phase: In this phase, an XML schema is input to the system for the creation of the following: (1) the Ontology Labels for the interior nodes in the schema, (2) a CTG based on the schema, and (3) the $RACT_T$ for *each* CT T in the CTG. XTEngine-K *pre-computes* (offline) for each CT T in the CTG its RACT and saves this information in a hash table called RACT_TBL for future references.

XTEngine-L post-query processing phase: This phase starts when a Loosely Structured query is submitted to XTEngine-L. The engine first locates the CTs containing the query's keywords (the KCs). It then determines the Immediate Relatives of each KC by accessing the hash table IR_TBL. Finally, the engine locates the IAN*s* as follows. Let the query's KCs be contained in a set called *S*. Each IAN will be located in a CT T, where $T \in \bigcap_{KC_i \in S} IR_{KC_i}$ (T is located in the intersection of the Immediate Relatives of the KCs).

XTEngine-K post-query processing phase: This phase starts when a Keyword-based query is submitted to XTEngine-K. The engine first locates the CTs containing the query's keywords (the KCs). It then determines for each KC, its $RACT_{KC}$ by accessing the hash table RACT_TBL. The engine then locates the LMCA in the intersection $\bigcap_{i=1 \to n} RACT_{KC_i}$, where *n* is the number of KCs of the query. Finally, the engine constructs the answer subtree rooted at the LMCA.

Because there are many abbreviation of concepts in the paper, we summarize them in Table 2 for easy reference.

XTENGINE CONTEXT-DRIVEN TECHNIQUES

A CT can contain an IAN, if it has *strong* association with the KC. Thus, IR_{KC} is a set of CTs that have strong associations with the KC. The IR_{KC} concept enables the search to be focused on a specific part of the XML document, which enhances the accuracy of results and efficiency of the search.

Semi-structured data encompass most of the modeling features of the Object Oriented (OO) model (Li & Bressan & Dobbie & Wadhwa, 2001), and static aspects from the OO modeling semantics can be found in XML data modeling (Widjaya et

Table 2. Abbreviations of concepts (Abb denotes abbreviation)

Abb	Concept	Abb	Concept
IAN	Intended Answer Node	KC	Keyword Context
CT	Canonical Tree	LCA	Lowest Common Ancestor
RACT	Related Ancestor Canonical Trees	OL_{KC}	Ontology Label of the KC
IR_{KC}	Immediate Relatives of KC	OL_T	Ontology Label of CT T
CTG	Canonical Trees Graph	OLA	OL Abbreviation

al., 2003; Conrad et al., 2000). Therefore, many researchers took advantage of the richness of OO conceptual modeling to model XML data and describe its complex interrelationships (Conrad et al., 2000; Pardede et al., 2004; Widjaya et al., 2003; Widjaya et al., 2002; Xiaou, 2001). The concept of *existence dependency* was first proposed for Entity-Relationship modeling (Elmasri & Navathe, 2007), and has been adapted for use in OO conceptual modeling (Widjaya et al., 2003). Existence dependency has some correspondences with the IR_{KC} concept. An object x is existence-dependent on an object y if the existence of x is dependent on the existence of y (Widjaya et al., 2003. Following this definition, we can see the closeness between the existence dependency and IR_{KC} concepts: both denote that an object has a strong association with another object (in our case the KC). All CTs that are existence-dependent on the KC belong to IR_{KC}, but not necessarily all CTs belonging to the IR_{KC} are existence-dependent on the KC. In this section we propose three rules for the determination of IR_{KC}. The first rule will be validated through the existence dependency concept. The three rules will be verified heuristically. A formal strategy of deriving IR_{KC} will be given later in the section.

The first rule we propose is as follows. If CT T $\in IR_{KC}$, then $OL_T \neq OL_{KC}$. We are going to validate this rule by checking whether it conforms to the structural characteristics of existence dependency. Snoeck et al. (1998) argue that the existence dependency relation is a partial ordering of *object types*. The authors transform an OO schema into a graph consisting of the object types found in the schema and their relations. The object types in the graph are related only through associations that express existence dependency. Notice the resemblance between the concept of this graph and the concept of the CTG, where both are type-oriented (an Ontology Label can be viewed as a type of a CT). The authors demonstrated through the graph that an object type is never existence-dependent on

itself. That is, if the two objects O_i and O_j belong to the same type, O_i cannot be dependent on O_j and vice versa. This finding is in agreement with our proposed rule if we view a CT as an object and its Ontology Label as the object's type. Thus, if a CT T has the same Ontology Label as the KC, T can never be existence-dependent on the KC; therefore, it can never be its Immediate Relative.

After validating the first rule, we now verify it heuristically: verify that CT T may contain an IAN for a KC (which means $T \in IR_{KC}$) if $OL_T \neq OL_{KC}$. Let T_i and T_j be two distinct CTs having the same Ontology Label. Therefore, the two CTs share common entity characteristics, and some of their data nodes are likely to have the same labels. Let n_1, n_2, n_3, n_4, n_5, and n_6 be data nodes, where n_1, n_2, $n_3 \in T_i$ and n_4, n_5, $n_6 \in T_j$. Let n_1 and n_4 have the same label l_1, n_2 and n_5 have the same label l_2, n_3 has the label l_3, and n_6 has the label l_4. Let $d_{m'}^{m}$ denote the distance between data nodes m and m' in the XML tree. Now consider the query $Q(l_1 = "k_i", l_2?)$. The keyword "k_i" is contained in data node $n_1 \in T_i$ (the KC is T_i) and l_2 is the label of the IAN. Intuitively the IAN is $n_2 \in T_i$ and not $n_5 \in T_j$, because $d_{n_2}^{n_1} < d_{n_5}^{n_1}$. If the label of the IAN in the same query is l_3 (instead of l_2), then obviously the IAN is $n_3 \in T_i$. However, if the label of the IAN in the same query is l_4, then the query is meaningless and unintuitive. Now consider the query $Q(l_3 = "k_i", l_1?)$. Intuitively the IAN is n_1 and not n_4 due to the proximity factor. If the label of the IAN in the same query is l_2 (instead of l_1), intuitively the IAN is n_2 and not n_5. Thus, we can conclude that in order for the query to be meaningful and intuitive, the IAN cannot be contained in CT T_j if the keyword is contained in CT T_i. In other words, an IAN of a query cannot be contained in a CT whose Ontology Label is the same as the Ontology Label of the KC, unless this CT is the KC itself. If the IAN is contained in a CT T, then either $OL_T \neq OL_{KC}$ or T is the KC.

The following is the second rule we propose for determining IR_{KC}. If CT T is an Immediate Relative of a KC, then $OL_T \neq OL_{T'}$ where T' is a CT located between T and the KC in the CTG. We can verify this rule as follows. Let: (1) CT T' $\in IR_{KC}$, (2) T' be a descendant of the KC and (3) CT T be a descendant of T'. In order for T to be an Immediate Relative of the KC, intuitively T has to be an Immediate Relative of T', because T' relates (connects) T with the KC. If T and T' have the same OL, then $T \notin IR_{T'}$ (according to the first rule). Therefore, in order for T to be an Immediate Relative of the KC, $OL_T \neq OL_{T'}$.

The following is the third rule we propose for determining IR_{KC}. If CT $T' \notin IR_{KC}$ and CT T is related to the KC through T' then $T \notin IR_{KC}$. We can validate this rule as follows. A KC has a domain of influence. This domain covers CTs, whose *degree of relativity* to the *KC* is strong. Actually these CTs are the Immediate Relatives of the *KC*. If CT $T' \notin IR_{KC}$, then the degree of relativity between T' and the KC is weak. Intuitively the degree of relativity between any other CT T and the KC is even weaker if T is related to the KC through T', due to the proximity factor.

Based on the above, we now present Definition 7 to formalize the Immediate Relatives concept.

Definition 7, Immediate Relatives of a KC (IR_{KC}): The Immediate Relatives of a KC is a set IR_{KC}, IR_{KC}={ $T|T$ is a CT, where $OL_T \neq OL_{KC}$ and $OL_T \neq OL_{T'}$, where T' is a CT located between T and the KC in the CTG}.

We can determine IR_{KC} by pruning from the CTG all CTs $\notin IR_{KC}$, and the remaining ones would be IR_{KC}. We present below three properties that regulate the pruning process. The properties are inferred from Definition 7.

Property 1: *When computing IR_{KC}, we prune from the CTG any CT whose Ontology Label is the same as the Ontology Label of the KC.*

Property 2: *When computing IR_{KC}, we prune CT T' from the CTG if: (1) there is another CT*

T" located between T' and the KC, and (2) the Ontology Label of T" is the same as the Ontology Label of T'.

Property 3: *When computing IR_{KC}, we prune from the CTG any CT that is related (connected) to the KC through a CT T, $T \notin IR_{KC}$.*

We present examples below based on Figures 3 and 7 to show how IR_{KC} is determined using the three properties described above.

Example 2: Let us determine $IR_{T_{14}}$: By applying property 2, CT T_3 is pruned from the CTG, because it is located in the path T_{14} T_{13} T_1 T_3 and its Ontology Label is the same as the Ontology Label of T_{13}, which is closer to T_{14}. By applying property 3, CTs T_4, T_5, T_6, T_7, T_8, T_9, T_{10}, T_{11}, and T_{12} are pruned, because they are related to T_{14} through the pruned T_3. The remaining CTs in the CTG are $IR_{T_{14}}$ (see Figure 8).

Example 3: Let us determine IR_{T_3}. By applying property 1, T_{13} is pruned, because its Ontology Label is the same as the Ontology Label of T_3. By applying property 3, T_{14}, T_{15}, T_{16}, T_{17}, and T_{18} are pruned because they are related to T_3 through the pruned T_{13}. By applying property 2, T_7 is pruned, because it is located in the path T_3 T_4 T_5 T_7 and its Ontology Label is the same as that of T_4, which is closer to T_3. The remaining CTs in the CTG are IR_{T_3} (see Figure 9).

Example 4: Let us determine IR_{T_1}. By applying property 1, T_5, T_{12}, T_{15}, T_{16}, and T_{18} are pruned, because their Ontology Labels are the same as the Ontology Label of T_1. By applying property 3, T_6 and T_7 are pruned because they are related to T_1 through the pruned T_5. The remaining CTs in the CTG are IR_{T_1} (see Figure 10).

Example 5: Figures 11, 12, 13, 14, and 15 show IR_{T_6}, IR_{T_8}, IR_{T_4}, $IR_{T_{13}}$, and IR_{T_5} respectively.

Figure 8. IR_{T_1}

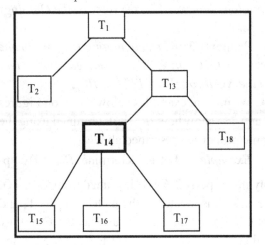

Figure 10. IR_{T_1}

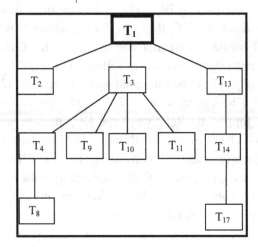

Figure 9. IR_{T_6}

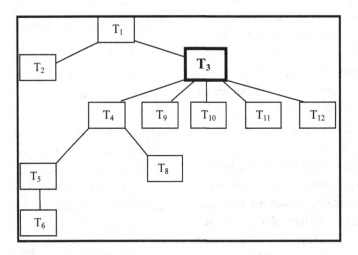

ANSWERING A LOOSELY STRUCTURED QUERY USING XTENGINE-L

The naïve approach for computing IR_{KC} is to apply properties 1, 2, and 3 to *each* CT in the CTG. The time complexity of this approach for computing the Immediate Relatives of all CTs in the graph is $O(|T|^2)$. XTEngine-L employs an alternative and efficient algorithm called ComputeIR (see Figure 16), which takes advantage of property 3 as follows. To compute IR_{KC}, instead of examin-

ing each CT in the graph to determine if it satisfies one of the three properties, the Algorithm examines *only* the CTs that are *adjacent* to any CT T' $\in IR_{KC}$. That is, if the algorithm determines that a CT $T' \in IR_{KC}$, it will then examine the CTs that are adjacent to T'. However, if the algorithm determines that $T' \notin IR_{KC}$, it will not examine any CT T'' that is connected to the KC through T', because T'' is known to be not an Immediate Relative of the KC (according to property 3). The Algorithm works as follows. Set S_{KC}^T (line 8) contains the Ontology Label of each CT located

Figure 11. IR$_{T_6}$

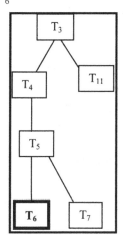

Figure 12. IR$_{T_8}$

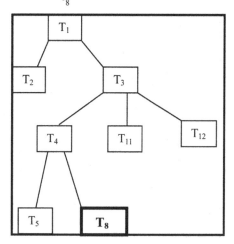

Figure 13. IR$_{T_4}$

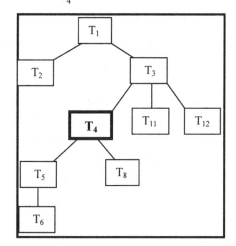

Figure 14. IR$_{T_{13}}$

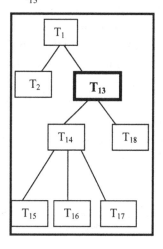

between CT T and the KC. In line 6, if the Ontology Label of T' is not the same as the Ontology Label of the KC (which means that T' is not satisfying property 1) and if this Ontology Label does not match one of the Ontology Labels in set S_{KC}^T (which means that T' is not satisfying property 2), then: (1) $T' \in IR_{KC}$ and it is inserted in set IR_{KC} (line 7), (2) the Ontology Label of T' is inserted in set $S_{KC}^{T'}$ (line 8), and (3) the CTs adjacent to CT T' are recursively examined (line 9). Otherwise, $T' \notin IR_{KC}$ and all CTs connected to the KC through T' will be ignored. The Algorithm's time complexity is $O\left(\sum_{i=1}^{|T|}\left|IR_{T_i}\right|\right)$.

The key difference between a Keyword-based query and a Loosely Structured query lies in their search terms. The search term of the former is a keyword "k", and *each* node containing k is considered when computing the answer. The search term of the later is a label-keyword *pair* (l = "k"), and *only* nodes whose labels is l and containing the keyword k are considered when computing

Figure 15. IR_{T_5}

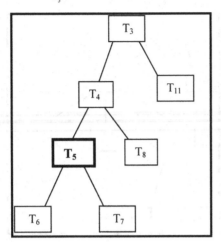

Figure 16. Algorithm ComputeIR

```
ComputeIR (KC) {
1. T ← KC
2. S_{KC}^{KC} ← null
3. IR_{KC} ← null
4. ExamineCT (T) {
5.   for each CT T' ∈ Adj [T] {   /* T' is adjacent to T */
6.     if ( OL_{T'} ≠ OL_{KC}  &  OL_{T'} ∉ S_{KC}^T )
7.       then { IR_{KC} = IR_{KC} ∪ T'   /* T' is IR of KC */
8.             S_{KC}^{T'} ← S_{KC}^T ∪ OL_{T'}
9.             ExamineCT (T')
        }/*end if */
     }/*end for*/
   }/*end of the algorithm*/
```

the answer. Thus, Loosely Structured querying restricts the search. XTEngine-L employs three techniques for answering Loosely Structured queries. It employs the first technique if a query's search term(s) is contained in one CT. It employs the second technique if a query's search terms are contained in more than one CT. It employs the third technique if a query's search term element and requested return element have the same label. We describe these techniques in the following subsections.

A Query whose Search Term(s) is Contained in One CT

If the keyword(s) of the query is contained in one CT, the IAN should be contained in the Immediate Relatives of that CT. The following examples show how a Loosely Structured query, whose search term(s) is contained in one CT is answered, using properties 1, 2, and 3. The examples are based on Figures 3 and 7.

Example 6: Consider the query: Q (ISBN="0-471-19047-0", name?). The keyword "0-471-19047-0" is the ISBN (node 38) of the magazine that was ordered by customer "Robinson" (node 2) prior to his current book order. Therefore, the answer for the query should be the "name" nodes

involving the magazine order *only*. That is, the answer should not include the "name" nodes 13 and 31. Since the keyword "0-471-19047-0" is contained in CT T_{14}, the IAN "name" should be contained in a CT $\in IR_{T_{14}}$ (recall Figure 8). Thus, the answer for the query is nodes $2 \in T_1$, $40 \in T_{15}$, $42 \in T_{16}$, and $46 \in T_{18}$.

Example 7: Consider Figures 3 and 7 and the query: Q (name = "Robinson", title?). The query asks for the titles of publications ordered by customer "Robinson". Since the keyword "Robinson" is contained in T_1, the IAN "title" should be contained in CTs $\in IR_{T_1}$ (recall Figure 10). The IANs are nodes $10 \in T_4$, $23 \in T_9$, $26 \in T_{10}$, and $37 \in T_{14}$. Thus, the answer is "XML and the Web", "XPath", "XSLT", and "ESPN".

Example 8: Consider the following two queries: Q_1 (area = "databases", title?) and Q_2 (area = "web databases", title?). Q_1 asks for the titles of the publications that were authored by an author, whose area of expertise is "databases". Since the keyword "databases" is contained in CT T_6, the IAN title should be contained in a CT $\in IR_{T_6}$ (recall Figure 11). Thus, the IAN title is node 10 $\in T_4$ and node 17 $\in T_7$. Query Q_2 on the other hand asks for the title of the publication, whose field area is "web databases" (node 20). Since the keyword "web databases" is contained in T_8, the answer should be contained in a CT$\in IR_{T_8}$ (see Figure 12). Thus, the IAN is node 10 $\in T_4$.

Example 9:*Q* (title = "XML and the Web", orderNo?). Since the keyword "XML and the Web" is contained in T_4, the answer should be contained in a CT $\in IR_{T_4}$ (recall Figure 13). The IAN orderNo is node 7$\in T_3$.

A Query whose Search Terms are Contained in More Than One CT

Definition 8: Canonical Relationship Tree: The Canonical Relationship Tree of CTs *T* and *T'*(denoted by $R_{T,T'}$) is the set of CTs in the CTG located in the path from CT *T* to CT *T'* including CTs *T* and *T'*. For example, the Canonical Relationship Tree of CTs T_1 and T_{17} in Figure 7 is the set $\{T_1, T_{13}, T_{14}, T_{17}\}$.

Definition 9: Collective Keyword Contexts (CKC): Let *S* be the set of CTs containing the search terms of a query (the KCs). Let the subset $\{T, T'\} \subseteq S$, and that this subset contains at least *one occurrence of each keyword*. The CTs in set $R_{T,T'}$ collectively constitute the KC of the query and called Collective Keyword Contexts (CKC), if either: (1) the CTs in set $R_{T,T'}$ have *distinct* Ontology Labels, or (2) only *T* and *T'* have the *same* Ontology label, which is *different* than the Ontology Labels of the other CTs in $R_{T,T'}$. If set *S* contains *n* subsets satisfying the conditions specified above, there will be *n* CKCs. The following is the reason behind considering the CTs in set $R_{T,T'}$ that do not contain keywords as part of the KCs of the query. Consider that CT T_b is located in the Canonical Relationship Tree of CTs T_a and T_c (R_{T_a,T_c}). CT T_b is related to both T_a and T_c and it semantically *relates* and connects T_a with T_c. Thus, without T_b, the relationship between T_a and T_c is semantically disconnected.

Example 10: Consider Figures 3 and 7 and the query: *Q*((name = "Wilson", orderNo = "10024", title?). Consider that node 46 contains

the keyword "Wilson". Thus, nodes 46 and 13 are *both* now containing this keyword. The keyword "Wilson" is contained in CTs T_5 and T_{18}, while the keyword "10024" is contained in CT T_3. Each of the subsets $\{T_3, T_5\}$ and $\{T_3, T_{18}\}$ contains one occurrence of each keyword. $R_{T_3,T_5} = \{T_3, T_4, T_5\}$ and $R_{T_3,T_{18}} = \{T_3, T_1, T_{13}, T_{18}\}$. Set $R_{T_3,T_{18}}$ contains CTs T_1 and T_{18}, whose Ontology Labels are the same; therefore, this set is not a valid CKC. Since the CTs in set R_{T_3,T_5} have distinct Ontology Labels, they constitute *collectively* the CKC of the query.

Locating an IAN

Each IAN is contained in a CT *T*, $T \in \bigcap_{T_j \in CKC_i} IR_{T_j}$, where CKC_i is one of the query's CKCs. That is, each IAN is contained in a CT located in the intersection of the Immediate Relatives of the CTs composing one of the query's CKCs. Example 11 illustrates that.

Example 11: Consider again the query presented in Example 10. The query asks for the title of one of the books that was ordered in order number "10024" and authored by "Wilson". As described in Example 10, the CKC = $\{T_3, T_4, T_5\}$. Recall Figures 9 and 13 for IR_{T_3} and IR_{T_4} respectively. The intersection of $IR_{T_3} \cap IR_{T_4} \cap IR_{T_5} = \{T_3, T_4, T_5, T_6, T_8, T_{11}\}$. The IAN title is node 10 $\in T_4$.

Counting Number of Answers

XTEngine-L employs a function called count to count the number of result items in the answer of a query. The form of a query containing function count is as follows: $Q \ (l_{k_1} = "k_1", \ldots, l_{k_n} = "k_n",$ count(E?)), where k_i denotes a keyword, l_{k_i} denotes the label of the data node containing k_i, and *E* denotes one of the requested return nodes. The answer of a query with this form consists of: (1)

the data item contained in each IAN labeled E, and (2) the *number* of these data items.

Theorem 1: Let E be a requested return node of a query. In each document record, the number of result items contained in the IANs E equals the number of CKCs in the record.

Proof: Let CKC_i be one of a query's CKCs. Let intersect be a set, where $intersect = \bigcap_{T_j \in CKC_i} IR_{T_j}$. In each document record, one instance of the IANs E should be contained in a CT $\in$ intersect. According to properties 1 and 2, the CTs contained in each IR_{T_j} should have *distinct* Ontology Labels. Therefore, if CTs $T, T' \in$ intersect, then T and T' have *different* Ontology Labels, since they are both contained in *each* IR_{T_j}. That is, the CTs contained in set intersect have distinct Ontology Labels. Let each of CTs T and T' be containing a data node labeled E. Since T and T' have different Ontology Labels, an instance of the IANs E should be either node E contained in T or node E contained in T', *but not both*. To illustrate this, consider that T represents a student (OL_T = "person"), T' represents the student's school ($OL_{T'}$ = "institution"), and the requested return node is "name"; the IAN *cannot be both* the "name" of the student and the "name" of the student's school. Thus, set intersect in each document record contains *only one* instance of IANs E. Accordingly, if there are n CKCs for the query in a document record, there will be n instances of the IANs E in the record. Thus, in each document record, the number of result items contained in the IANs E equals the number of CKCs in the record.

Based on Theorem 1, function count counts the number of CKCs of a query in each document record as the number of result items in the record. We now present Example 12 to illustrate function count.

Example 12: Consider Figures 3 and 7 and the query: Q(orderNo = "10024", count(title?)). The query asks for the title of books ordered in order number "10024", and also asks for the number of these books. The answer is as follows:

Returning the titles books: Since the keyword "10024" is contained in CT T_3, the IANs "title" should be contained in IR_{T_3} (recall Figure 9). The IANs are nodes $10 \in T_4$, $23 \in T_9$, and $26 \in T_{10}$. Thus, the answer is "XML and the Web", "XPath", and "XSLT".

Returning the number of books: Since the keyword "10024" is contained in CT T_3 and each of CTs T_4, T_7, T_9, T_{10}, and T_{14} contains a data node labeled *title*, there are 5 Canonical Relationship Trees: R_{T_3, T_4}, R_{T_3, T_7}, R_{T_3, T_9}, $R_{T_3, T_{10}}$, and $R_{T_3, T_{14}}$. The CTs contained in $R_{T_3, T_{14}}$ *do not* constitute a CKC (because CTs T_3 and T_{13} have the same Ontology Label), and also the CTs contained in R_{T_3, T_7} *do not* constitute a CKC (because CTs T_4 and T_7 have the same Ontology Label). The CTs contained in each of the remaining 3 Canonical Relationship Trees constitute a CKC. Thus, there are 3 CKCs. Therefore, function count will return 3 as the number of books ordered in order number "10024".

A Query whose Search Term Element and Requested Return Element Have the Same Label

In this type of queries, the search term element and the requested return element have the same label. Consider for example Figure 3 and the query "what *other* books have a customer bought who has bought a book titled *XML and the Web*". This query can be expressed as follows: Q(**title** = "XML and the Web", **title**?"). In this query, "**title**" is the label of both, the search term element and the requested return element. When searching for the CTs containing the IANs of this query, we *only* search for ones whose Ontology Labels is "publication". So, when answering this type of queries, we search only for CTs, whose Ontology Labels are the same as the Ontology Label of the CT containing the search term element. CTs whose Ontology Labels are the same behave as *rivals*: they either *cooperatively* have done something to a CT T', or something has been done to them *collectively* by T'. We call CT T' a *pivoting entity* (denoted by T_{piv}). In Figure 7 for example, CTs T_4, T_9, T_{10}, and T_{14} were *collectively* ordered by the pivoting entity CT T_1 (the publications contained in CTs T_4, T_9, T_{10}, and T_{14}, were ordered by the customer contained in CT T_1). On the other hand, CTs T_{15} and T_{16} *cooperatively* edited the pivoting entity CT T_{14} (the editors contained in CTs T_{15} and T_{16} edited the publication contained in CT T_{14}).

In this type of query, the IAN(s) is located as follows. Starting from the CT T_i in the CTG that contains the search term element we search ascending and descending T_i for the closest CT T_j in the graph, whose Immediate Relatives include T_i ($T_i \in IR_{T_j}$) and also includes at least one other CT, whose Ontology Label is the same as the Ontology Label of T_i. CT T_j is the pivoting entity (T_{piv}), and one or more of its Immediate Relatives must contain the IAN(s). That is, the IAN(s) must be contained in a CT $T \in IR_{T_{piv}}$.

Example 12 and 13 illustrate that.

Example 12: Consider Figures 3 and 7 and the query: Q(title = "XML and the Web", title?). The query engine will interpret this query in two different ways (two different queries) as follows: query Q_1 (what are the *other* title of publications, which have been bought by customers who have bought a book titled *XML and the Web*), and query Q_2 (what are the title of the *other* publications have an author published who has authored a publication titled *XML and the Web*). So, the query engine will return two *separate* answers for the user to select from, as follows. The keyword "XML and the Web" is contained in CT T_4. The closest CT(s) to T_4, whose Immediate Relatives include T_4 and also include another CT, whose Ontology Label is the same as the Ontology Label of T_4, are CTs T_1 and T_5. So, there are two pivoting entities, T_1 and T_5. IR_{T_1} contains the answer of Q_1, while IR_{T_5} contains the answer of Q_2, as follows:

- **The answer of Q_1, whose pivoting entity is T_1:** The IANs "title" should be contained in CTs $\in IR_{T_1}$ (recall Figure 10). Thus, the IANs are nodes 23 $\in T_9$, 26 $\in T_{10}$, and 37 $\in T_{14}$. Therefore, the answer is: "XPath", "XSLT", and "ESPN".
- **The answer of Q_2, whose pivoting entity is T_5:** The IANs "title" should be contained in CTs $\in IR_{T_5}$ (recall Figure 15). Thus, the IAN is node 17 $\in T_7$. Therefore, the answer is: "XQuery".

Example 13: Consider Figures 3 and 7 and the query: Q(orderNo = "10024", orderNo?). The query is interpreted as "what are the *other* orders numbers of items that have been ordered by a customer, who has ordered an item in order number 10024". The keyword "10024" is contained in CT T_3. The closest CT to T_3, whose Immediate Relatives include T_3 and also include another CT, whose Ontology Label is the same as the Ontology Label of T_3 (which is order), is CT T_1. So, the pivoting entity is T_1. The IAN(s) should be contained in CT(s) $\in IR_{T_1}$ (recall Figure 10). The IAN is node 34 $\in T_{13}$. Therefore, the answer is: "9576".

ANSWERING A KEYWORD QUERY USING XTENGINE-K

XTEngine-K answers a Keyword-based query by returning a subtree rooted at a CT called the *Lowest Meaningful Common Ancestor (LMCA)*. The leaves of the subtree are the CTs containing the query's keywords (the KCs). The set of CTs located in a path from the *LMCA* to a Keyword Context KC_i are called *Related Ancestor Canonical Trees of KC_i* (denoted by $RACT_{KC_i}$) – recall Definition 6.

XTEngine-K uses an efficient algorithm for computing RACTs, called ComputeRACT (see Figure 17-a). The input to the algorithm is the Dewey ID (recall Definition 4) of a KC. A *Dewey ID component* is an OLA_x. The Algorithm pushes the components of the Dewey ID into a stack called *stack*. If OLA_i, OLA_j, ..., and OLA_k are the Dewey ID components in the stack from the *bottom entry* to the *stack entry*, then: (1) the *bottom entry* represents the KC, whose Dewey ID is $OLA_i.OLA_j.....OLA_k$ and (2) the stack entry represents the root CT in the CTG, whose Dewey ID is OLA_i. For example, in the stack shown in Figure 18-a, the *bottom entry* represents the KC, which is CT $p_0.o_0.b_0.p_1.b_1$ (see CT T_7 in Figure 7), the *stack entry* represents CT p_0 (see CT T_1 in Figure 7), and the *middle entry* represents CT $p_0.o_0.b_0$ (see CT T_4 in Figure 7). That is, each entry in the stack above the *bottom entry* represents an ancestor CT of the KC. Algorithm ComputeRACT pops off the stack each entry representing a CT that is *not* an Immediate Relative of the KC, so that the remaining entries would represent CTs that are RACT of the KC ($RACT_{KC}$). The Algorithm works as follows. Line 5 uses function OLAin (see Figure 17-b) and checks properties 1 and 2 as follows. Let OLA_x be a component contained in entry *stack[j]* and let OLA_y be a component contained in entry *stack[i]*. If the subcomponent OLA of OLA_x is the same as the subcomponent OLA of OLA_y, then either property 1 or property 2 is satisfied (this indicates that the CT represented by entry stack[i] is not an Immediate Relative of the KC). Therefore, line 7 pops off the stack all

Figure 17. (a) Algorithm ComputeRAC. (b) Function OLAin

```
ComputeRACT(Dewey ID of a KC) {
1.  Push the components composing the Dewey ID of the
    KC into a stack called stack.
2.  while (stack.size > 0 )
    {
3.    for (stack.size ≥ i > 0)
      {
4.      for (i > j ≥ 0)
        {
5.        if (OLAin (stack[j]) = OLAin (stack[i])   /* Check properties 1 and 2 */
          {
6.          while (stack.size ≥ i)
7.          stack.pop() /*Pop entries starting from stack[i]*/
8.          Exit from both, the inner and outer for
          } /* end if */
        } /* end for */
      } /* end for */
    { /* end while */
9.  while (stack.size > 0)
    {
10.   comp ← stack.pop()
11.   Output comp.
    } /* end while */
  } /* end the Algorithm
```

(a)

```
OLAin( stack[i] ) {
1. Extract from the component OLAx (which is contained in
   stack[i]) the subcomponent OLA by stripping the subscript x.
2. Return the subcomponent OLA.  }
```

(b)

entries located above *stack[i]* (to satisfy property 3) and also pops entry *stack[i]*. When the *for* in line 3 finishes iterations, each component remains in stack *stack* represents the *right-most* component in the Dewey ID of one of the CTs $\in RACT_{KC}$, and line 11 outputs it. The time complexity of the Algorithm for computing the RACT of *each* CT in the CTG is $O(h|KC|)$, where h is the maximum depth of the CTG and $|KC|$ is the number KCs. We now present examples 14 and 15 to illustrate Algorithm ComputeRAC.

Example 14: Consider Figure 7. Let us compute the RACT of CT T_7 ($RACT_{T_7}$) using Algorithm ComputeRAC. The Dewey ID of CT T_7 is $p_0.o_0.b_0.p_1.b_1$. Figure 18-a shows stack *stack* after the components of Dewey ID T_7 are pushed into the stack. The remaining states of the stack (which are shown in Figures 18-b and 18-c) are created by the Algorithm as shown in Figure 17:

- **Line 3 of the Algorithm, where i = *stack.size* = 4:** When j = 3 (line 4), OLAin(*stack[3]*)= o and OLAin(*stack[4]*) = p (line 5); therefore, the *if* condition will evaluate to *false*. When j = 2, OLAin(*stack[2]*)= b and OLAin(*stack[4]*) = p; therefore, the *if* condition will evaluate to *false*. When j = 1, OLAin(*stack[1]*)= p and OLAin(*stack[4]*) = p; therefore, the *if* condition will evaluate to *true*. Thus, according to property 2, the CT represented by *stack[4]* (which is CT T_1 in Figure 7)

is *not* an Immediate Relative of the KC (which is CT T_7). Then, *stack[4]* (line 7) is popped off the stack, and the new stack state becomes as shown in Figure 18-b.

- **Line 3 of the Algorithm, where i = *stack.size* = 3:** *for* in line 4 will iterate 3 times (j = 2, 1, 0), and the *if* condition will evaluate to *false* in each of the 3 iterations.

- **Line 3 of the Algorithm, where i = 2:** When j = 1, OLAin(*stack[1]*)= p and OLAin(*stack[2]*) = b (line 5); therefore, the *if* condition will evaluate to *false*. When j = 0, OLAin(*stack[0]*)= b and OLAin(*stack[2]*) = b (line 5); therefore, the *if* condition will evaluate to *true*. Thus, according to property 1, the CT represented by *stack[2]* (which is CT T_4 in Figure 7) is *not* an Immediate Relative of the KC. And, according to property 3, the CT represented by *stack[3]* (which is CT T_3 in Figure 7) is also *not* an Immediate Relative of the KC. *stack[3]* and *stack[2]* are popped off the stack, and the new stack state becomes as shown in Figure 18-c (line 7).

- **Line 3 of the Algorithm, where i = *stack.size* = 1:** *for* in line 4 will iterate one time (j = 0), and the *if* condition will evaluate to *false*. Line 10 will pop the component $\mathbf{p_1}$ off the stack. The CT, whose Dewey ID's *right-most* component is $\mathbf{p_1} \in RACT_{T_7}$. Thus, CT $p_0.o_0.b_0.\mathbf{p_1}$ (CT T_5) is a RACT of

Figure 18. (a), (b), and (c) stack states. (d) $\in$

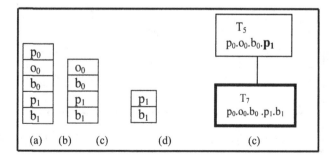

the KC (CT T_7.). Figure 18-d depicts $RACT_{T_7}$ graphically.

Example 15: Figures 19-a, 18-b, and 18-c show $C \& ftcontains(x, "k") \rightarrow x \prec y$, $\prec$, and $RACT_{T_{14}}$ respectively. We constructed algorithm ComputeAnsSubTreIe (see Figure 20), for computing answer subtrees. The algorithm works as follows. The inputs to the Algorithm are the RACTs of the query's KCs that were output by Algorithm ComputeRAC (recall Figure 17-a). Line 1 determines the *LMCA* by locating it in the intersection of the n input RACTs. Line 2 stores the LMCA and the n KCs in a set called *AnsT*, which will eventually contain all the CTs composing the answer subtree. For *each* an input $\prec$, lines 3-5 check *each* CT $T_j \cup \prec$ to determine whether its hierarchical level in the CTG is lower than the hierarchical level of the LMCA, using function level, which returns the hierarchical level of an input CT. If it is lower, line 6 adds CT T_j to set *AnsT*. Note that function level considers the hierarchical levels in the CTG increase in the direction bottom-top. Finally, set *AnsT* will contain all the CTs composing the answer subtree, and line 7 will output it. We now present Example 16 to show how the Algorithm constructs an answer subtree.

Example 16: Consider Figures 3 and 7. Let us construct the answer subtree for the Keyword-based query Q ("XML and the Web", "ESPN"), using algorithm ComputeAnsSubTree. Since the keyword "XML and the Web" is contained in CT T_4 and the keyword "ESPN" is contained in CT T_{14}, the inputs to the algorithm are $\prec$ and $RACT_{T_{14}}$ (recall Figure 19-a for $\in$ and Figure 19-c for $RACT_{T_{14}}$). Line 1 of the Algorithm will determine that the LMCA is CT T_1. In line 2, set $AnsT = \{T_1, T_4, T_{14}\}$. The Algorithm will proceed as follows.

Line 3, where $i = 1$: line 4 will iterate over CTs T_1 and T_3, which $\theta(V+E) \prec$, and line 5 will

Figure 20. Algorithm ComputeAnsSubTree

$\boldsymbol{ComputeAnsSubTree}\ (RACT_{KC_1}, ..., RACT_{KC_n})\ \{$

1. $LMCA \leftarrow \bigcap_{i=1 \rightarrow n} RACT_{KC_i}$
2. $AnsT \leftarrow LMCA \cup KC_1 \cup ... \cup KC_n$
3. **for** $i = 1 \rightarrow n$ {
4.   **for** each CT $T_j \in RACT_{KC_i}$ {
5.   **if** (level(T_j) < level($LMCA$)
6. $AnsT = AnsT \cup T_j$
    { /* end for */
  { /* end for */
7. Output *AnsT*
}

Figure 19. (a) $\cup$. (b) $\neq$. (c) $RACT_{T_{14}}$

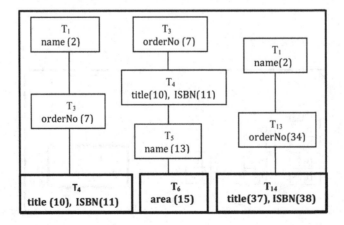

determine that only CT T_3 satisfies the *if* condition. Line 6 will add CT T_3 to set *AnsT*.

Line 3, where $i = 2$: line 4 will iterate over CTs T_1 and T_{13}, which $\theta(V+E)\ RA\ CT_{T_{14}}$, and line 5 will determine that only CT T_{13} satisfies the *if* condition. Line 6 will add CT T_{13} to set *AnsT*.

At the end, set *AnsT* will contain $\{T_1, T_4, T_{14}, T_3, T_{13}\}$. Figure 21 shows the Canonical Trees composing the answer subtree, and Figure 22 shows the actual answer subtree returned to the user.

SYSTEM IMPLEMENTATION AND ARCHITECTURE

Figures 23 and 24 show the system architecture of XTEngine-L and XTEngine-K respectively. The two engines employ the same initial processing steps, which *create the Ontology Labels* and *build a CTG* for an input XML schema. They differ in the remaining processing steps.

Figure 21. The CTs composing the answer subtree for the query in Example 16

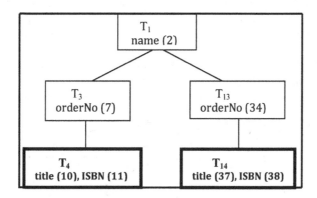

Figure 22. The actual answer subtree returned to the user for the query in Example 16

```
                            <customer>
    <name> Robinson </name>
    <currentOrder>
      <orderNo> 10024 </orderNo>
                                    <item>
                                      <book>
        <title> XML and the Web </title>
        <ISBN> 87-11-07559-7</ISBN>
        </book>
      </item>
    </currentOrder>
    <previousOrder>
      <orderNo> 9576 </orderNo>
                                    <item>
                                      <magazine>
        <title> ESPN </title>
        <ISBN> 0-471-19047-0 </ISBN>
        </magazine>
      </item>
    </previousOrder>
    </customer>
```

Initial Processing Steps

XTEngine-L and XTEngine-K use module *OntologyBuilder* to create Ontology Labels and use module *GraphBuilder* to create CTGs (see Figures 23 and 24).

Creating Ontology Labels: The XML schema describing the structure of the XML document is input to module *OntologyBuilder* (see Figures 23 and 24), which creates a list of Ontology Labels corresponding to the interior nodes in the XML schema. There are many ontology editor tools available that can be used for determining the Ontology Labels of nodes. These tools are listed in (Denny, 2002). The *OntologyBuilder* uses

Protégé ontology editor (Knublauch & Musen & Rector, 2002), which allows a system administrator to build taxonomies of concepts and relations and to add constraints onto domains of relations. We *imported* to Protégé ontologies available in electronic form (ontologies done by others). Many ontologies are already available in electronic form and can be imported into an ontology development environment. The formalism in which an ontology is expressed often does not matter, since many knowledge-representation systems can import and export ontologies. We imported the ontologies using namespaces co-ordination. The ontologies being imported have their namespaces and namespaces prefix set up. To import ontolo-

Figure 23. XTEngine-L System architecture

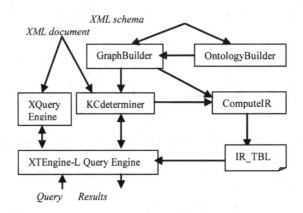

Figure 24. XTEngine-K System architecture

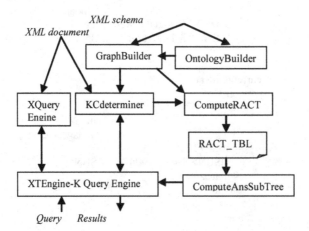

gies in Protégé, we first located the ontologies and determined their *URL*. By ticking the import tickbox, the ontologies will be found at the location specified by the namespace *URI* (*URL*).

If module *OntologyBuilder* could not determine the Ontology Label of an interior node, it processes the node's label as follows:

1. It tokenizes the label by parsing it into a set of tokens using delimiters. The module tokenizes the label to determine if it is composed of lexemes, because in heterogeneous environments, node's label could be a combination of lexemes (Nayak, 2008). In Figure 3 for example, the label processingEmployee will be tokenized into {processing, employee}, the label otherPublication will be tokenized into {other, publication}, and the label currentOrder will be tokenized into {current, order}. If the label contains extraneous punctuations, module *OntologyBuilder* eliminates them after tokenizing the label: for example, label Driver_License will be tokenized into {driver, license}.

2. The *OntologyBuilder* then checks to determine if there is an ontology in the system for the *suffix* token name that was determined in step 1. In the examples stated in step 1, the module will check if there are ontologies in the system for the *suffix* token names: employee (of label processingEmployee), publication (of label otherPublication), order (of label currentOrder), and license (of label Driver_License).

3. If the module could not find in step 2 an ontology for the suffix token name, it will alert the system administrator that *taxonomy of a concept* is missing, so that the system administrator creates and adds it to the systems. The creation of new ontologies is usually simple, since we only need to create two ontology hierarchies (classes and subclasses) as opposed to semantic web, where

many levels of ontology hierarchies may be needed.

Finally, for each Ontology Label OL_i, module *OntologyBuilder* stores in a table called OL_TBL all tag names whose Ontology Label is OL_i (the format of the table is similar to table 1).

Constructing CTGs: Module *GraphBuilder* creates a CTG for the input XML schema, using Algorithm BuildCTreesGraph (see Figure 25-a). The inputs to Algorithm are: (1) table OL_TBL, which was output by module *OntologyBuilder* and contains the list of Ontology Labels corresponding to the interior nodes in the input XML schema, and (2) the list of nodes adjacent to each node in the XML tree: for example, the adjacency list of node 6 in Figure 3 consists of nodes 1, 7, 8, 21, 24, 27, and 30. The Algorithm works as follows. Lines 1-12 construct the individual CTs, and lines 13-19 construct the CTG by connecting the CTs by edges.

Constructing CTs by Algorithm BuildCTrees-Graph: Line 5 iterates over the nodes that are adjacent to each interior node n in the XML tree. If n' is a *leaf data node* (line 6), it will be contained in set T_z, which represents CT T_z (lines 8 and 12). In line 9, function setParentComp sets node n as the *parent node component* of CT T_z, as follows. Function setParentComp (see Figure 25-b) stores in variable π, for each CT T_z its parent node component n (in Figure 7 for example, $\pi[T_3] \leftarrow 6$, since node 6 is the parent node component of CT T_3). Eventually, each set T_z will contain all the leaf children data nodes n' of node n, where n is the parent node component of CT T_z (in Figure 7 for example, set $T_2 \rightarrow \{4, 5\}$). Each parent node component of a CT is stored in a set called Parent-Comps (line 10); when *for* in line 2 finishes iterations, the set will contain the parent node components of all the CTs.

Constructing the CTG by Algorithm Build-CTreesGraph: If function getCT (lines 15 and 16) is input a node n, it will return the ID of the CT, whose parent node component is n. Consider

Figure 25. (a) Algorithm BuildCTreesGraph. (b) Function setParentComp. (c) Function setCTparent. (d) Function setOL

```
BuildCTreesGraph {
1.  z = 0
2.  for each node  n  ∈ OL_TBL
    {
3.     flag = 0
4.     z = z + 1
5.     for each node  n' ∈ adj [ n ]
       {
6.       if (isLeafNode ( n' ) = true)
         {
7.         then if (flag = 0)
             {
8.           then {T_Z = T_Z ∪ n'
9.             setParentComp ( n ,T_Z)
10.            ParentComps = ParentComps ∪ n
11.              flag = 1
             }
12.          else T_Z = T_Z ∪ n'
         }/*end if*/
       }/*end if*/
     }/*end for*/
   }/*end for*/
13.  for each node m ∈ ParentComps {
14.    m' ← Closest ancestor node to m in set ParentComps
15.      T_x ← getCT ( m' )
16.      T_y ← getCT (m)
17.      setCTparent (T_y, T_x)
18.      O_m ← getOL (m)
19.      setOL (O_m , T_y)
     }/*end for */
   } /*end of the algorithm */
```
(a)

```
setParentComp ( n ,T_Z) {
  π[T_z] ← n  }
```
(b)

```
setCTparent (T_y, T_x) {
  λ[T_y] ← T_x  }
```
(c)

```
setOL (O_m , T_y) {  σ[T_y] ← O_m  }
```
(d)

for example Figures 3 and 7. If function getCT is input node 6, it will return T_3, since node 6 is the parent node component of CT T_3. Lines 13-19 process *each* node *m* contained in set ParentComps as follows:

- Line 14 finds the *closest ancestor* interior node *m'* to *m* contained in set ParentComps.

- Lines 15 and 16 use function getCT to determine the IDs of the CTs, whose parent node components are *m'* and *m*.

- Function setCTparent in line 17, connects the two CTs (whose IDs were determined in lines 15 and 16) by an edge (setting parent-child relationship), as follows: Function setCTparent (see Figure 25-c), stores in variable λ, for each CT T_y its parent CT T_x (in Figure 7 for example, $\lambda[T_3]$ $\leftarrow T_1$).

- When function getOL in line 18 is input a node *m*, it returns the Ontology Label of *m* by accessing table OL_TBL.

- Line 19 uses function setOL to assign an Ontology Label for CT T_y similar to the Ontology Label of node *m* as follows. Function setOL (see Figure 25-d) stores in variable σ the Ontology Label O_m of each CT T_y (in Figure 7 for example, $\sigma[T_3] \leftarrow$ order).

The time complexity of Algorithm BuildC-TreesGraph is $O(|V|+|E|)$, where $|V|$ is the number of nodes and $|E|$ is the number of edges in the XML tree. Note that, the CTG and the Ontology Labels of a given schema S_i are *computed only one time* and then cached. That is, they are not computed every time a user submits a query against this schema. Instead, the query engines will access these saved resources every time a query is submitted against the XML document generated from schema S_i. As a result, when considering the computation overhead of constructing a CTG and its Ontology Labels in the search performance, the average query execution time deceases as the number of submitted queries increases.

The Remaining Processing Steps of XTEngine-L

The modules that process the remaining steps of XTEngine-L are shown in Figure 23. Module *ComputeIR* uses algorithm *ComputeIR* (recall Figure 16) to compute for each CT *T* in the CTG its IR$_T$ and saves this information in a hash table called *IR_TBL* for future references. After XTEngine-L receives a Loosely Structured query, it extracts the query's keywords and accesses the *KCdeterminer* to locate the KCs. Using the input XML document, the CTG, and the query's set of keywords the *KCdeterminer* locates the KCs.

The engine then accesses table *IR_TBL* to locate the CTs containing the IANs. Then, XTEngine-L accesses *XQuery Engine* (Katz, 2005) to extract the data contained in each IAN.

The Remaining Processing Steps of XTEngine-K

The modules that process the remaining steps of XTEngine-K are shown in Figure 24. Module *ComputeRACT* uses algorithm *ComputeRACT* (see Figure 17-a) to compute for each CT *T* in the CTG its $RACT_T$ and saves this information in a hash table called *RACT_TBL* for future references. After XTEngine-K receives a Keyword query, it accesses the *KCdeterminer* to locate the KCs. Using the input XML document, the CTG, and the query's set of keywords the *KCdeterminer* locates the KCs. The engine then accesses table *RACT_TBL* to determine for each KC its $RACT_{KC}$. The engine then accesses module *ComputeAnsSubTree*, which uses Algorithm ComputeAnsSubTree (see Figure 20) to determine the LMCA and construct the answer subtree. Then, XTEngine-K accesses *XQuery Engine* (Katz, 2005) to extract the data contained in the nodes of the answer subtree.

EXTRACTING DATA USING OO TECHNIQUES

After the answer data nodes for a query have been determined, the data contained in these nodes can be extracted using either an XQuery search engine or Object Oriented (OO) techniques. This section describes how the system can extract the data OO techniques. Due to the nature and construct resemblance of an object in OO programming and a CT entity, OO programming could be used as an efficient mechanism for extracting and caching the data contained in CTs. If we incorporate *behavior (methods)* to a CT entity, this entity will have all the characteristics of an object in OO programming. Every CT object is associated with a class.

Constructing Classes

We convert XML data to object model. Towards this, we used castor (Dion, 2001) API in the implementation of XTEngine. Castor API contains methods to parse and convert "unmarshal" the stream of XML data to an object model and methods to convert back "marshal" an object model to XML data. Castor enables one to deal with the data defined in an XML document through the object model. When the XML schema describing an XML document is input to castor, castor *creates* classes, where each one represents one of the interior elements, and its name is the element's label. If an interior element n_2 is a child of an interior element n_1, the class representing the interior element n_1 will have a method that returns a reference to the object of the class representing element n_2. In the implementation of XTEngine,

we modified these classes slightly as follows. Let n be the label of an interior element, which is contained in a CT, whose label is L. We change the name of the class representing n from "n" to "L". Each method that returns a reference to the object representing a child element will also be changed so that it returns instead the reference to the CT object containing that element. Consider for example the interior node paper(4) in Figure 1. Castor will create a class named Paper to represent this node. After the class is created, we change its name from "paper" to "T_2", where T_2 is the label of the CT containing node paper (4) (recall Figure 6). A fragment of the modified class written in Java is shown in Figure 27-A. Initially, this class contained methods that return references to the children nodes of paper(4), such as method getReviewingProf, which returns a reference to the object representing the child node reviewing-

Figure 26. Fragments of supertype classes: A) Class Publication. B) Class Person. C) Class ProceedingsSponsor

```
public class Publication{
    ..........................
    public void getData(){ title = getTitle(); }
    String getTitle() {return title;}
    ...............................
}
                    A
public class Person {
    ...............................
    void getData() {name = getName(); }
    String getName() {return name;}
    ...............................
}
                    B
public class ProceedingsSponsor{
    ..........................
    public void getData() {
                name = getName();
                date =getDate();
                }
    String getName() {return name;}
    String getDate() {return date;}
    ...............................
}
                    C
```

Figure 27. Fragments of subtype classes: A) Class T_2, which represent CT T_2. B) Class T_8, which represents CT T_8. C) Class T_9, which represents CT T_9. D) Class T_10, which represents T_{10}

```
public class T_2 extends Publication {
    ...................
    T_8  getT_8 () {return T8; }
    ...........................
}
                    A
public class T_8 extends Person{
    ...............................
    T_9  getT_9 () {return T9; }
    T_11  getT_11 () {return T11; }
    ............
}
                    B
public class T_9 extends Publication {
    ......................
    T_10  getT_10 () {return T10; }
    ...............................
}
                    C
public class T_10 extends ProceedingsSponsor {
    ...........................................
}
                    D
```

Prof(20). In the modified class, these methods are changed to return references to the CTs, whose parent nodes components are the original children nodes. For instance, in class T_2 (Figure 27-A) we changed method getReviewingProf to method getT_8() to returns a reference to the object representing CT T_8, whose parent node component is node reviewingProf(20). Figures 27-A, B, C, and D show fragments of classes T_2, T_9, T_8, and T_10 written in Java. A CT class is a subclass that inherits the data structure and methods defined in its superclass, whose name is the Ontology Label of the CT. For example, subclass T_2 (Figure 27-A) inherits the data structure and methods defined in its superclass, class Publication (Figure 26-A). A superclass contains getter and setter methods for extracting and storing the data contained in its subclasses. For example, if we have determined that the answer returned node for a query is node 5, which is contained in CT T_2, we can extract its data using method getData().

After the XML document is converted to an object model using castor, it is then converted back (marshaled) to an XML data *using the modified classes*. Each record in the new XML document is assigned an ID.

Justification of Using OO Techniques

1. In client-server architecture, OO techniques could be used to cache in the server the data contained in Frequently Used KCs and their Immediate Relatives, which improves significantly the search performance. That is, if a CT T is a Frequently Used KC, we cache in the server the data contained in it as well as the data contained in each CT $T' \in IR_T$. In the implementation of XTEngine we used some of the mechanisms we proposed in our previous work XPCache (Taha & Elmasri, 2007) for determining Frequently Used KCs. Figure 28 shows a fragment of class FUKC (written in Java), which caches

the Frequently Used CTs of the Canonical Trees Graph in Figure 6. Array FUKCarray in the class holds objects, where each one contains the ID of a Frequently Used KC and the ID of the record containing this KC. That is, for each object $O \in$ FUKCarray, O.KC contains the ID of a Frequently Used KC and O.bibID contains the ID of the record containing the KC. Function unmarshal() converts the XML document to an object model. The fragment of class FUKC in Figure 28 shows how the data contained in CT T_{10} and its Immediate Relatives is cached (assuming CT T_{10} is a Frequently Used KC). This data is stored in an object called KC_10. For example, in the line "KC_10 = doc.getT_2().getT_8().getData()" CT T_2 object returns a reference to its child CT T_8 object and method getData() gets the data contained in node 21 (recall Figures 1 and 6), which is then stored in object KC_10. Function CacheObj() caches this object and assigns it two IDs for identification purpose, the ID of the KC (e.g., T_{10}) and the ID of the record containing it (bibID).

2. One powerful feature of using OO techniques after converting an XML document to an object model is the efficiency and ease of using data presentation code. Data presentation processing tasks are handed off to the client. The data presentation codes are generated in real time on the client. Thus, you can hand off large data sorting tasks to the client. You can create, in real time, client-specific background processing code to execute on the client machine and to perform operations on client-requested data. This is done as follows. We create inline presentation code fragments and store them in external files in the server. These codes deal with the data through the getter and setter methods of the superclasses. These codes are ID tags and can be bound to an HTML tag to enable conditional activation of the code. One way

of doing that is the use of data island, which is an XML feature supported by IE and Netscape navigator, which allows you to pull in XML code fragments from external files.

EXPERIMENTAL RESULTS

We implemented XTEngine and all its techniques described in this chapter using Java. The experiments were carried out on an AMD Athlon XP 1800+ processor, with a CPU of 1.53 GHz and 736 MB of RAM, running the Windows XP operating system.

We examined and compared the recall, precision, and search performance of XTEngine with XSeek (Liu & Chen, 2007), Schema-Free XQuery (Xu & Papakonstantinou, 2005), and XSEarch (Cohen & Mamou & Sagiv, 2003). The implementation of Schema-Free XQuery has been released as part of the TIMBER project

Figure 28. Fragment of class FUKC, which caches Frequently Used KCs and their Immediate Relatives

```
public class FUKC {
.............
FUKC doc = unmarshal (newFileReader ("bib.xml");
 for (int x=1; x<= FUKCarray.length; x++)
  {
  Object obj = FUKCarray[x];
  switch (obj.KC)  {
   .........................
   case T_10: {
   KC_10 = doc.getT_2().getT_8().getT_9().getT_10().getData();
   KC_10 = doc.getT_2().getT_8().getData();
   KC_10 = doc.getT_2().getT_8().getT_9().getData();
   KC_10 = doc.getT_2().getT_8().getT_11().getData();

   CacheObj (KC_10, obj.bibID) ;
   break;
   }
   .....................
  }
  ..............
 }
 ................
}
```

(Jagadish & Patel, 2006). So, we used TIMBER for the evaluation of Schema-Free XQuery. As for XSEarch and XSeek, we implemented their entire proposed systems from scratch. To fully evaluate the system, we used test data from five different sources, as follows:

- **Source 1:** The test-suite of the 2004 edition of the INEX XML retrieval evaluation initiative (Tombros & Malik & Larsen, 2005).
- **Source 2:** XML Query Use Cases-W3C (Chamberlin & Fankhauser & Florescu & Robie, 2007). Each use case is accompanied by DTDs, sample data, and a number of queries. We selected 15 use cases accompanied by 38 queries.
- **Source 3:** XMark Benchmark (Schmidt & Waas & Kersten & Florescu & Manolescu & Carey & Busse, 2002). XMark provides 100 MB XML document accompanied by 20 queries.
- **Source 4:** We collected 20 Heterogeneous data models from the web and then constructed challenging test queries based on the data. Note that, the queries of this source and their results have not been assessed by an independent party.
- **Source 5:** We created an XML document and queries based on the XML tree shown in Figure 1.

Recall and Precision Evaluation

To evaluate the quality of results returned by XTEngine, we measured its recall and precision and compared it with XSEarch, Schema-Free XQuery, and XSeek.

Evaluating recall and precision using test data from source 1: In this evaluation, we used the INEX test data. Some of the documents in the INEX test collection are scientific articles (marked up in XML) from publications of the IEEE Computer Society covering a range of topics in the field of computer science. There are two types of queries included in the INEX test collection, *Content-and-structure (CAS)* queries and *Content-only (CO)* queries. All topics contain the same three fields as traditional IR topics: title, description, and narrative. The title is the actual query submitted to the retrieval system. The description and narrative describe the information need in natural language. The described information need is used to judge the relevancy of the answers retrieved by a system. The difference between the CO and CAS topics lies in the topic title. In the case of the CO topics, the title describes the information need as a small list of keywords. In the case of CAS topics, the title describes the information need using descendant axis (//), the Boolean *and/or*, and *about* statement (it is the IR counterpart of *contains* function in XPath). CAS queries are Loosely Structured queries while CO queries are Keyword queries. We used the CAS and CO topics for measuring the recall and precision of the four systems: XTEngine, XSEarch, Schema-Free XQuery, and XSeek. In each topic, we compared the results returned by each of the four systems against the expected results stated in the description and narrative fields of the topic. Figures 29 and 30 show the results.

Evaluating recall and precision using test data from sources 2, 3, 4, and 5: In this evaluation, we used test data from XML Query Use Cases, XMark, test data collected from the Web, and the XML document in Figure 1. For each of the test data, we generated XML documents of different sizes, using ToXgene (Barbosa & Mendelzon & Keenleyside & Lyons, 2002). The sizes of the documents ranged from 100 to 300 MB. Each of the test data is accompanied by schema-aware queries. Only XML Query Use Cases provides answers for the queries (expected results). To compute the answers for the schema-aware queries accompanied with the rest of the test data we ran these queries using XQuery (Katz, 2005) and recorded the results. These results of these queries represent the correct answers, which would be compared with the results returned by each of the four systems. We converted each of the schema-aware queries into an equivalent Keyword-based and Loosely Structured query accepted by XTEngine, XSeek, Schema-Free XQuery, and XSEarch. We simply extracted the keywords from the search terms of each schema-aware query and plugged them in the query forms of the four systems. The following are the query

Figure 29. Avg Recall using INEX

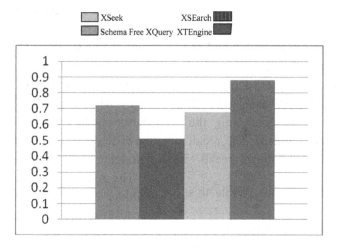

Figure 30. Avg Precision using INEX

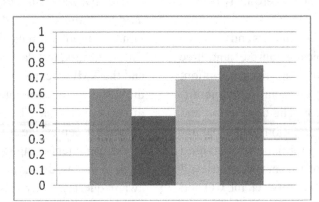

forms of XSeek, Schema-Free XQuery, and XSEarch.

- **Schema-Free XQuery:** The Keyword-based form is $mlcas(k_1, ..., k_n)$, and the answer is the Meaningful Lowest Common Ancestor (MLCA) of nodes containing the keywords. The Loosely Structured form contains FLOWR statements (for, where, and return) but *only* descendant axis (//) are used.
- **XSEarch:** The Keyword-based form is $Q(:k_1, ..., :k_n)$, and the Loosely Structured query form is $Q(l_1:k_1, ..., l_n:k_n, l_1:, ...l_j:)$, where each *l-k* pair denotes label-keyword and *l:* denotes the label of a return element.
- **XSeek:**$Q(k_1, ..., k_n)$. The answer is a set of Smallest Lowest Common Ancestor (SLCA) of nodes containing the keywords.

Let Q_s denote a schema-aware query and Q_k denote the same query after being converted to Keyword-based. Let y denote the set of result records of query Q_S. Let x denote the set of result records of query Q_k (records containing the query's keywords are not included). The recall and precision are measured as follows: recall = $\frac{|x \cap y|}{|y|}$, and precision = $=\frac{|x \cap y|}{|y|}$. While this recall measure is a good indicative of the actual

recall of a system, the precision measure may not reflect the actual precision of the system, because the number of result records of query Q_k is usually more than the number of result records of query Q_s. This precision measure, however, can accurately *compare* the precision of different Keyword-based systems: it may not reflect the actual precisions of the four systems, but it ranks their precisions accurately. Figures 31 and 32 show the results

As can be seen from Figures 29-32 that XTEngine outperforms the other three systems, the recall of Schema-Free XQuery outperforms those of XSEarch and XSeek, and XSEarch performs poorly. The recall and precision performance of XTEngine is attributed to its context-driven search techniques inferred from the three properties presented previously, and to the fact that the other three systems build relationships between data nodes based solely on their labels and proximity to one another, while overlooking the contexts of the nodes. We observed that the recall and precision of the other 3 systems drop significantly when an XML document contains more than one node having the same label but representing different types, or having different labels but belonging to the same type.

The reason that the recall of Schema-Free XQuery outperforms XSEarch and XSeek is because the technique it uses for building relation-

Figure 31. Average Recall using test data from sources 2, 3, 4, and 5

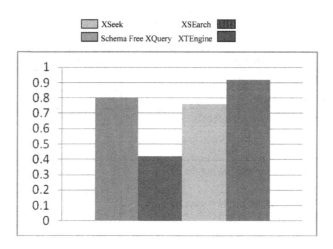

Figure 32. Average Precision using test data from sources 2, 3, 4, and 5

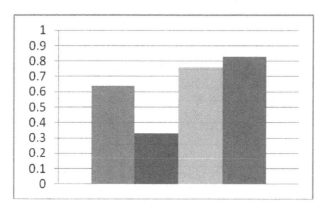

ships between nodes is based on the hierarchical relationships (ascendant-descendant relationships) between the nodes, which alleviates node labeling conflicts.

Behavior of the Four Systems under Different Data Models/Queries Criteria

Based on the results of the different experiments, we constructed Table 3 to summarize the criteria of data models and queries that caused each of the four systems to achieve good or bad results. The sign "-" denotes that the system achieves bad recall or precision, while the sign "+" denotes

the system achieves good recall or precision. *R* denotes Recall and *P* denotes Precision. *XS* refers to XSEarch, *SF* refers to Schema Free XQuery, *XK* refers to XSeek, and XT refers to XTEngine.

Search Performance Evaluation

To evaluate the search performance of XTEngine, we compared its execution times with XSeek, XSEarch, and Schema-Free XQuery. We measured the average query execution time of each of the four systems using queries with variable number of keywords and then using documents of variable sizes.

Table 3. Behavior of the four systems under different criteria of data models and query types

Criteria of a data model/query	XS		SF		XK		XT	
	R	P	R	P	R	P	R	P
All nodes in a data model have distinct labels and types	+	+	+	+	+	+	+	+
Two or more nodes have the same label but different types	+	-	+	-	+	-	+	+
Two or more nodes have the same label and type	-	+	-	+	+	+	+	+
Two or more nodes in a data model have different labels but belong to the same type	-	-	+	+	-	-	+	+
Query type B	-	+	-	+	+	-	+	+
The label of a node matches the query's return element but the node doesn't satisfy the query's search term	-	-	-	-	-	-	+	+
The data model contains a parent node n_i that has a child interior node n_j, and both n_i and n_j have the same Ontology Label and each of them has a child/children data node	+	+	-	+	-	+	-	-

Figure 33. Avg query execution times using XMark

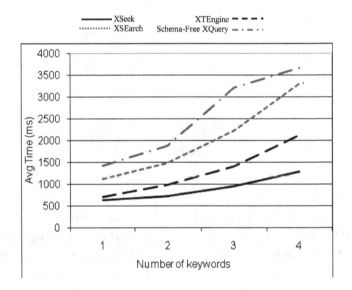

Evaluating the execution times under different number of keywords: We used 100 MB documents of XMark and XQuery Use Cases and computed the average query execution time of the four systems using queries containing 1, 2, 3, and 4 keywords. For each (different) number of keywords, we ran 20 random queries (using random-selection software). Figures 33 and 34 show the results, where the average query execution time for each number of keywords is shown.

Evaluating the execution times using different document sizes: To evaluate the execution time of XTEngine under different document sizes, we ran queries using different document sizes (150, 200, 250, and 300 MB) of XMark and XQuery Use Cases. For each of the four document sizes, we ran 60 random queries (using random-

Figure 34. Avg query execution times using XML Query Use Cases

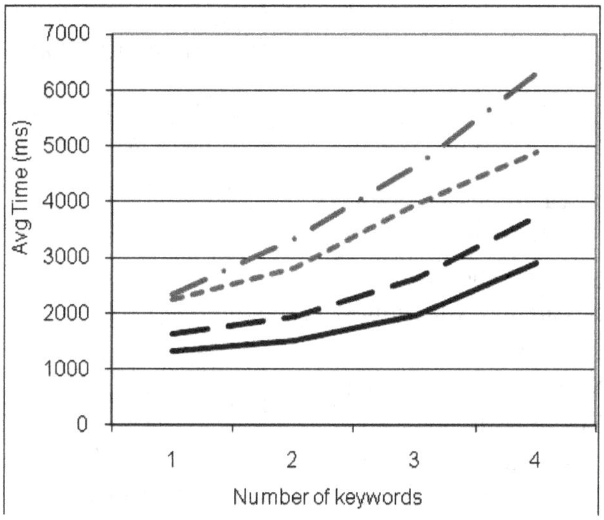

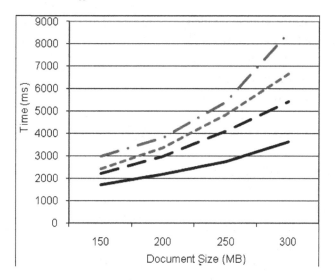

Figure 35. Execution times under different document sizes

selection software) and computed the average execution time. We repeated the same process using XSeek, XSEarch, and Schema-Free XQuery. Figure 35 shows the results.

As can be seen from Figures 33-35, the running times of XTEngine are less than those of XSEarch and Schema-Free XQuery. This is attributed to the efficiency of the pre-computation of IRs and RACTs. And, the reason for the expensive running times of XSEarch and Schema-Free XQuery stems from the fact that they build a relationship between *each* two nodes containing keywords, and *then* filter results according to search terms. Recall that the time complexity of Schema-Free XQuery is $O\left(h\sum_{i=1}^{m} n_i + \prod_{i=1}^{m} n_i \right)$, which indicates that the running time can be very expensive in large XML trees, where many elements may share the same label and/or if the query contains many search terms and return elements.

CONCLUSION

Non-context-driven XML search engines build relationships among data nodes based solely on their labels and proximity to one another while overlooking their contexts (parents), which may cause these engines to return faulty answers. Using three works, XSEarch, XSeek, and Schema-Free XQuery as sample of non context-driven search systems, we demonstrated how such systems are likely to return wrong and/or redundant answers. The reason is that the label of a node by itself is not sufficient to convey the semantics of the node.

In this chapter, we have introduced XTEngine, an XML context-driven search engine, which answers Keyword-based and Loosely Structured queries. XTEngine accounts for nodes' contexts by considering each set consisting of a parent and its children data nodes in the XML tree as one entity (CT). The framework considers the contexts of nodes by fragmenting XML trees to CTs, where a CT is the simplest meaningful entity, and it consists of a parent node and its children leaf data nodes. We proposed mechanisms for determining semantic relationships between different CTs. We also proposed novel Object Oriented techniques for extracting data from answer nodes. We experimentally evaluated the quality and efficiency of XTEngine and compared it with XSEarch, XSeek, and Schema- Free XQuery. The results showed that the recall, precision, and search performance of XTEngine outperform those of the other three systems.

REFERENCES

Aditya, B., Bhalotia, G., & Sudarshan, S. (2002). *BANKS: Browsing and Keyword Searching in Relational Databases*, In Proc. VLDB'02.

Agrawal, S., Chaudhuri, S., & Das, G. (2002). *DBXplorer: a System for Keyword-based Search Over Relational Databases*, In Proc. ICDE'02.

Balmin, A., Hristidis, V., & Papakonstantinon, Y. (2003). *Keyword Proximity Search on XML Graphs,* In Proc. ICDE'03.

Balmin, A., Hristidis, V., & Papakonstantinon, Y. (2004). *ObjectRank: Authority-Based Keyword Search in Databases,* In Proc. VLDB'04.

Balmin, A., Hristidis, V., Papakonstantinon, Y., & Koudas, N. (2003). *A System for Keyword Proximity Search on XML Databases,* In Proc. VLDB'03.

Barbosa, D., Mendelzon, A., Keenleyside, J., & Lyons, K. (2002). *ToXgene: a template-based data generator for XML*, In Proc. WebDB'02. Downloaded: http://www.cs.toronto.edu/ tox/ toxgene/ downloads.html

Botev, C., Shao, F., & Guo, L. (2003*). XRANK: Ranked Keyword Search over XML Documents*, In Proc. GMOD'03.

Chamberlin, D., & Fankhauser, P., & Florescu, D., & Robie, J. (2007). XML Query Use Cases. *W3C Working Draft 2007.*

Cohen, S., & Kanza, Y. (2005). *Interconnection Semantics for Keyword Search in XML*, In Proc. CIKM'05.

Cohen, S., Mamou, J., & Sagiv, Y. (2003). *XSEarch: A Semantic Search Engine for XML*, In Proc. VLDB'03.

Conrad, R., Scheffner, D., Freytag, C. "XML Conceptual Modeling Using UML", *Proc. ER2000.*

Denny, M. (2002). Ontology Building: A Survey of Editing Tools. *O'Reilly XML.COM.* Retrieved from: http://www.xml.com/ 2002/11/06/ Ontology_Editor_Survey.html

Dion, A. (2001). XML Data Binding with Castor. *O'Reilly ON Java.com*. Retrieved from: http://www.onjava.com/ pub/a/onjava/2001/10/24/xmldatabind.html

Elmasri, R., & Navathe, S. (2007). *Fundamentals of Database Systems*. Addison-Wesley Computing.

Hristidis, V., & Papakonstantinou, Y. (2002). *DISCOVER: Keyword search in Relational Databases*, In Proc. VLDB'02.

Jagadish, H. V., & Patel, J. M. (2006). TIMBER. *University of Michigan*. Retrieved from: http://www.eecs.umich.edu/ db/timber/

Katz, H. (2005). XQEngine version 0.69. *Fatdog Software*. Retrieved from: http://www.fatdog.com/. Engine downloaded from: http://sourceforge.net/ projects/xqengine

Knublauch, H., Musen, M., & Rector, A. (2002). *Editing Description Logic Ontologies with the Protégé OWL Plugin. Technical discussion for logicians*. CA: Stanford University.

Li, G., Bressan, S., Dobbie, G., Wadhwa, B. "XOO7: Applying O7 Benchmark to XML Query Processing Tools", *CIKM'01*.

Li, Y., Yu, C., & Jagadish, H. (2004). *Schema-Free XQuery*, In Proc. VLDB'04.

Liu, Z., Chen, Y., "Identifying Meaningful Return Information for XML Keyword Search", *SIGMOD'07*.

Nayak, R. (2008). Fast and effective clustering of XML data using structural information. *Knowledge and Information Systems*, *14*(2), 197–215. doi:10.1007/s10115-007-0080-8

Pardede, E., Rahayu, J., & Taniar, D. "On Using Collection for Aggregation and Association Relationships in XML Object-Relational Storage", *Proc. ACM SAC'04*.

Schmidt, A. R., Waas, F., Kersten, M. L., Florescu, D., Manolescu, I., Carey, M. J., & Busse, R. (2002). The XML Benchmark Project. *Technical Report INS-R0103, CWI*. Retrieved from: http://www.xml-benchmark.org/.

Snoeck, M. (1998). Dedene, G. "Existence Dependency: The key to semantic integrity between structural and behavioral aspects of object types. *IEEE Transactions on Software Engineering*, *24*(24), 233–251. doi:10.1109/32.677182

Taha, K., & Elmasri, R. (2007), *XPCache: An Efficient Query Processor for Client-Server Architecture*, In Proc. SWOD'07.

Tombros, A., Malik, S., & Larsen, B. (2005). *Report on the INEX 2004 Interactive Track*. ACM SIGIR Forum, Vol. 39 No. 1.

Widjaya, N., Rahayu, W. Association Relationship Transformation of XML Schemas to Object-Relational Databases, *iiWAS'02*.

Widjaya, N., Taniar, D., & Rahayu, W. (2003). Aggregation Transformation of XML Schema to Object-Relational Databases. *Innovative Internet Community Systems, LNCS, 2877*, 251–262. doi:10.1007/978-3-540-39884-4_21

Xiaou, R., Dillon, T., Feng, L. "*Modeling and Transformation of Object-Oriented Conceptual Models into XML Schema*", *DEXA'01*.

Xu, X., & Papakonstantinou, Y. (2005). *Efficient Keyword Search for Smallest LCAs in XML Databases*, In Proc. SIGMOD'05.

Chapter 10
Towards Structured Flexibility in Information Systems Development:
Devising a Method for Method Configuration

Fredrik Karlsson
Örebro University, Sweden

Pär J. Ågerfalk
Uppsala University, Sweden & University of Limerick, Ireland

ABSTRACT

Method configuration is a specific type of Method Engineering (ME) that takes an existing organization-wide Information Systems Development Method (ISDM) as its point of departure. Existing assembly-based ME approaches are not well suited to this task. As an alternative, this paper suggests a metamethod approach to tailoring organization-wide ISDMs. We refer to this approach as the Method for Method Configuration (MMC). MMC takes into account the need to combine structure, which is one reason for choosing an organization-wide ISDM in the first place, with flexibility, which is essential for making the chosen ISDM fit actual projects. The metamethod is built using a three-layered reuse model comprising method components, configuration packages, and configuration templates. These concepts are combined efficiently to produce a situational method and thereby to facilitate the work of method engineers.

DOI: 10.4018/978-1-60960-521-6.ch010

INTRODUCTION

Ineffective development practice is a perennial problem for many Information Systems (IS) development organizations (Brancheau, Janz, & Wetherbe, 1996; Riemenschneider, Hardgrave, & Davis, 2002; Roberts, Gibson, Fields, & Rainer, 1998). In response to this problem, many IS Development Methods (ISDMs) have been developed (Fitzgerald, Russo, & Stolterman, 2002; Roberts et al., 1998). There is clearly a need for structured and standardized ways of working in IS development. At the same time, there is a need for flexible work practices (Bajec, Vavpotič, & Krisper, 2006; Fitzgerald et al., 2002; Riemenschneider et al., 2002; Xiping & Osterweil, 1998).

A standardized way of working makes projects effective and predictable and increases the likelihood of meeting deadlines, staying within budget constraints, and achieving a desired quality (Fitzgerald et al., 2002). Standardization of IS development practice occurs at three different levels. At the individual level, project members choose ISDMs and specific techniques for use in specific tasks to improve their personal and collaborative practice. At the project level, a wider agreement can be made concerning the use of a particular ISDM. Finally, at the organizational level, a specific ISDM can be chosen as the organization-wide 'standard' method to be used in all projects. The expected benefits from implementing a standard ISDM across an organization include effective communication and reduced training costs due to a common modeling language, lowered maintenance costs, and the utilization of industry standards and existing tools. The search for organization-wide ISDMs has resulted in 'off-the-shelf' ISDMs such as the Unified Process. Such ISDMs are often fully comprehensive, aimed at covering every aspect of IS development, and bundled with training, support and various development tools from a specific vendor.

However, practical experience reveals that all projects are unique and require unique methodological support (van Slooten & Hodes, 1996). Some have also criticized organization-wide ISDMs, suggesting that they are too inflexible and hard to comprehend (Beck, 2000). The various parts of an ISDM are developed and included in the ISDM to minimize risks and to maximize the probability of success (Ropponen & Lyytinen, 2000). Because ISDMs aim to cover many different aspects of software practice, they will contain parts and address risks that are not of interest to every project. Hence, organization-wide ISDMs must be tailored to suit the particular development context (Fitzgerald, Russo, & O'Kane, 2003; Fitzgerald et al., 2002). To this end, different approaches have been suggested, ranging from formalized ones (Fitzgerald et al., 2003; Harmsen, 1997; Rolland, Prakash, & Benjamen, 1999; van Slooten & Hodes, 1996) to informal guidelines (Cameron, 2002; Cockburn, 2000). A rigorous approach to creating and tailoring ISDMs is that of Method(ology) Engineering (ME; Brinkkemper, 1996; Kumar & Wellke, 1992). ME concerns methods for developing ISDMs, also known as 'metamethods.' Traditionally, metamethods support the selection and integration of ISDM parts that together form consistent 'situational methods.' This approach to situational ME is therefore assembly-based, whereby new methods are constructed for each new project. Such an approach does not take advantage of any existing organization-wide method.

In this paper, we explore a different approach, called 'method configuration' and defined as the planned and systematic adaptation of a specific method via the use of 'reusable assets.' Here, a reusable asset is a pretailored part of an ISDM that fits a specific aspect of a development context. Method configuration is therefore a form of ME that explicitly utilizes an existing organization-wide ISDM. Furthermore, it promotes modularization to facilitate the exclusion, addition, and replacement of reusable ISDM parts. Specifically, we elaborate on the design and use of a Method for Method Configuration (MMC).

The paper is organized as follows. The next section presents an overview of related research, followed by the research approach adopted. The following two sections are devoted to MMC. The first of these covers MMC's core concepts, namely method components, configuration packages, and configuration templates. The second reports on empirical experiences from a number of action case studies of the use of MMC and provides an in-context perspective of the metamethod. A concluding discussion summarizes the paper and points out implications for practice and research.

RELATED RESEARCH

Various approaches to ISDM and process tailoring can be found in the literature, primarily within the research areas of Software Process Improvement (SPI) and ME. One difference between the two is that SPI tends to focus on the performance of actual software processes and empirical metrics, while ME emphasizes coherent and cohesive method representations as a basis for tailoring situational ISDMs (Ågerfalk & Ralyté, 2006). Because our focus in this paper is on the design of a metamethod to support the tailoring of ISDMs, rather than on assessing existing software processes, we will concentrate on ME in the following discussion.

Reusable Assets and Situational ISDMs

Published overviews of ME research have focused on the categorization of existing research (Odell, 1996) and on combining existing approaches into a generic model for situational ME (Ralyté, Deneckère, & Rolland, 2003). The latter presents existing strategies using map models (Rolland et al., 1999), allowing nondeterministic ordering of a method engineer's intentions along with possible strategies for achieving them. Much attention has

been given to reuse strategies in combination with a modular construction of ISDMs (Ågerfalk et al., 2007), in which situational ISDMs are generated from predefined building blocks, such as 'method fragments' (Harmsen, 1997), 'method chunks' (Rolland & Prakash, 1996), 'method components' (Goldkuhl, Lind, & Seigerroth, 1998), and 'process components' (Henderson-Sellers, 2002). In these approaches, much effort has been devoted to decomposing existing ISDMs into modules, which are then assembled into situational methods. As stated above, this assembly-based approach to situational ISDMs does not take advantage of any existing organization-wide ISDM, which is fundamental to our suggested method configuration approach.

There are, however, approaches with a scope similar to that of MMC. Examples include the selection of 'paths' in the Information Engineering Method (Hares, 1992), the use of 'roadmaps' in the Rational Unified Process (RUP), and the Work Product Description (WPD) approach (Cameron, 2002). It is unclear, however, how paths and roadmaps can be generalized into reusable assets rather than merely being pretailored versions of specific ISDMs. An interesting feature of the WPD approach is its use of method rationale, which expresses the purpose of work products and is used in the selection of work product descriptions based on project characteristics. However, it is not clear how actually to use these characteristics in the tailoring process. Another approach, referred to as the Process Configuration Approach (PCA) (Bajec et al., 2006), addresses issues similar to MMC but is based on two assumptions that our research has shown to be unjustified in practice. First, it is based on a view of 'method parts' that is at too low a level, thereby tending towards the traditional method fragment idea. Second, PCA takes activities as the starting point and then relates these to 'deliverables.' As discussed below and in other method tailoring research (Cameron, 2002), a more useful starting point is the deliverable (or 'artifact'), and the method part concept should embrace this starting point. This is explicitly addressed by the MMC method component concept, which, as opposed to method chunks and method fragments, provides a fixed level of abstraction for delimiting method parts, namely the deliverable. Our empirical findings also indicate that a fixed level of abstraction is more intuitive and easier to use than are hierarchically structured concepts.

The generic model for situational ME (Ralyté et al., 2003) mentioned above also covers method configuration to some extent. In this model, it is possible to combine a method-based strategy with an extension-based strategy, offering the possibility of extending an existing ISDM using the concept of method chunks. However, extension is only one possibility when making an existing ISDM situational. For example, a central aspect of method configuration is deciding what to *exclude* from the ISDM. In many situations, it is actually not a question of extension or restriction but rather of a combination of the two. Clearly, replacement can be treated as a combination of cancellation and addition (Ralyté et al., 2003), which removes the need for its own operator. However, the focus of the extension-based strategy has been on the addition operator alone.

Method Rationale

MMC draws significantly on the idea of 'method rationale,' which is the systematic treatment of the arguments for and reasons behind a particular ISDM (Rossi, Ramesh, Lyytinen, & Tolvanen, 2004; Ågerfalk & Wistrand, 2003). Method rationale is a powerful concept (Stolterman, 1991) but has not yet received due consideration in the ME field (Ågerfalk & Fitzgerald, 2006). A related concept, namely 'intention,' has been suggested for the contextual retrieval of method chunks when working with, for example, the assembly strategy (Mirbel & Ralyté, 2006; Rolland & Prakash, 1996). However, the notion of intention seems to focus more on the activity as such, rather than on the underlying goals that can be achieved via the use

of a specific method chunk. While the intention of a method chunk is typically expressed in terms of the action that immediately satisfies the goal, method rationale aims to direct method engineers' attention to the underlying assumptions of those actions and promote a critical attitude towards the actions prescribed by an ISDM. A broader view of intention has been suggested as a foundation for model-based method integration (Nilsson, 1999). However, method integration again sets the focus on the extension of ISDMs and is therefore not central to method configuration.

In considering method rationale, it is possible to distinguish between public and private rationality (Stolterman & Russo, 1997). Public rationality concerns the objective (or intersubjective) understanding of actions and results prescribed by an ISDM. This aspect of method rationale therefore relates to the way the ISDM is described and communicated in, for example, method handbooks. Private rationality, on the other hand, is personal and cannot be externalized in every aspect. It is expressed in a person's skills and professional ethical and esthetic judgments (Stolterman & Russo, 1997) and relates to the way the ISDM is enacted in actual development practice. To make ISDMs useful, the method creator has not only to influence public rationality but must also take into account the fundamental thinking of the method user, namely the private rationality of the developer applying the ISDM. Otherwise, method users do not find the ISDM meaningful and useful in their software practice (cf. Riemenschneider et al., 2002). Such perceived lack of support can be understood as a lack of 'rationality resonance' (Stolterman, 1991). Rationality resonance appears when the private rationality and the public rationality overlap. This can be achieved by: (1) making the underlying ISDM rationale explicit and easy to comprehend, and (2) creating methods with many options. The latter often occurs with organization-wide ISDMs. However, choosing the parts of an ISDM to use is not a trivial task, which is where method configuration comes into play. Method configuration aims to increase the possibility of achieving rationality resonance.

The basic idea of MMC is to add a filter function between the organization-wide ISDM's rationale and that of the situational method. The experience of competent developers, together with the ISDM's rationale, the characteristics of typical projects, and the project at hand, is then used to 'filter out' unnecessary parts of the ISDM. It is important to note that this should not be interpreted as disrespect for competent developers' method tailoring in action. Rather, it is a way of facilitating tailoring by reducing the number of choices that have to be made.

Structured Flexibility

MMC embraces the need for both structure and flexibility in IS practice. Another approach to flexibility in software development is that suggested by proponents of 'agile' methods, such as eXtreme Programming (Beck, 2000) and Scrum (Schwaber & Beedle, 2002). The reason for focusing on plan-based approaches in this research is based on our action research sentiment, namely that the organizations we worked with used these approaches and believed in their value. Interestingly, claims have been put forth that even a heavyweight ISDM such as RUP can indeed be used in an agile manner (Ambler, 2002; Evans, 2003; Hirsch, 2002). It is no surprise that the only requirement is proper configuration. In addition, agile methods are no exception to the need for method configuration. They must also be tailored, as for any other ISDM (Henderson-Sellers & Serour, 2005; Fitzgerald, Hartnett, & Conboy, 2006).

Research Approach

MMC is the result of an action research project carried out between the early spring of 2000 and the late autumn of 2004. The research was a collaborative project involving researchers from Örebro University, University of Limerick, University College of Borås, and three Swedish software development organizations. These were Volvo IT (a multinational software and technology consultancy organization with headquarters in Gothenburg), Posten IT (the information technology division of Posten AB), and Precio (a middle-sized software consultancy company).

The research method used can be characterized as multigrounded (Lind & Goldkuhl, 2006) action research. Being similar to grounded action research (Baskerville & Pries-Heje, 1999), it draws on the well-established qualitative research method known as Grounded Theory, particularly as it has evolved in the tradition of Strauss and Corbin (1998). In a multigrounded approach, both evolving and existing theory play important parts in data collection and analysis (cf. Klein & Myers, 1999). The idea is to ground theory not only in empirical data but also internally and in other existing knowledge of a theoretical character. This gives rise to the three grounding processes that were applied in this research, namely 'internal grounding,' 'external grounding,' and 'empirical grounding.'

Internal grounding means reconstructing and articulating a priori knowledge and defining the concepts used and their interrelationships. The important contribution of this process is a consistent conceptual model of MMC, free from ambiguities and with concepts that are anchored in explicit values and goals. External grounding is concerned with relationships between the developed knowledge and other knowledge of a theoretical character. In our case, this meant ensuring that MMC builds on existing ME wisdom in a constructive way and that it does not contradict relevant previous studies. Empirical grounding emphasizes the importance of applying developed knowledge in practice to validate the concepts and their relationships. In our case, this involved designing parts of MMC in collaboration with qualified practitioners, as well as gaining experience from using MMC in real projects when specifying situational ISDMs. Knowledge was also generated via the classification of empirical phenomena, which resulted in refinement of MMC, thereby triggering further internal and external grounding.

Our Multigrounded Action Research (MGAR) approach can be understood in terms of the traditional 'canonical' action research method, which has cycles of diagnosing, action planning, action taking, evaluating, and specifying learning (Baskerville & Wood-Harper, 1998). The project comprised two such action research cycles, as illustrated in Table 1. Within these two cycles, seven 'action cases' (Braa & Vidgen, 1999) were performed. An action case involves competent practitioners in collaborative design and evaluation efforts. Problems are discussed and design decisions taken by researchers and practitioners together, which implies continuous feedback and interaction between them (Mathiassen, 2002).

The selection of action cases was motivated by finding a mixture of different organization-wide ISDMs and organizations. The choice of organizations was based on two premises: they had to use different, preferably well-known, organization-wide ISDMs, and they had to agree to commit resources to support the envisaged collaboration. The sizes of organizations in this study ranged from quite small to very large, and the ISDMs used in these organizations were RUP and the Microsoft Solution Framework (MSF) (see Table 2). Each action case served specific objectives of the final research product and was related to the action cycle phases shown in Table 1.

THE METHOD FOR METHOD CONFIGURATION (MMC)

Method configuration according to MMC is organized around three core concepts: the 'method component,' the 'configuration package,' and the 'configuration template.' Together, these function as reusable assets that support method configura-

tion in organizations working with organization-wide ISDMs.

A method component is the smallest meaningful and coherent part of an ISDM, and the organization-wide ISDM has to be represented as a set of such components in order to use MMC. Method components are used as modularization blocks that may be excluded from or added to the organization-wide ISDM, or be replaced by method components from complementary ISDMs. For example, an ISDM might include a method component concerned with software packaging and which involves copying the software on distributable medium, printing handbooks, and designing a cardboard box with a sales cover. In projects where the final product is delivered using the Internet, such a component might be considered superfluous and could be excluded.

Configuration packages and configuration templates are used to represent situational versions of an ISDM. The main difference between these two concepts is the degree to which they represent a situational method. Briefly, a configuration package can be described as a prefabricated method configuration designed to fit one single specific development 'characteristic.' Using the example in the previous paragraph, we would be working with an Internet delivery characteristic. In such a case, the characteristic should affect method components relevant to product distribution. Information about how such method components are selected with respect to this characteristic is described in the configuration package. This selection of components can, if required, include components from complementary ISDMs.

Real-life development situations clearly comprise a combination of several characteristics. For example, a single project might involve diverse characteristics such as unstable requirements, a low level of management support, a new technical platform, and Internet delivery. The configuration template then describes this more complex configuration and is a preconfiguration of the complete organization-wide ISDM for a typical

Table 1. Summary of the Multigrounded Action Research project

MGAR Cycle 1 (Spring 2000 to Spring 2002)
Research collaborators • Volvo IT • ESI
Phase 1—Diagnosing (Action case 1) Difficulties related to tailoring an organization-wide method (RUP) for a specific project were explored at Volvo IT via a series of workshops with a systems development project requiring a situational ISDM. Problems with the current way of tailoring the organization-wide ISDM were documented. Based on principles from the situational ME literature, a vision of how to improve method configuration was formulated. *Data sources* • Logs from three workshop sessions • Organization-wide ISDM (RUP) • Situational method • Project deliverables *Data analysis* To separate real problems from symptoms, problem analysis (Goldkuhl & Röstlinger, 1993) was performed. Conceptual models of the organization-wide ISDM were created to facilitate understanding of the phenomena (using the Unified Modeling Language (UML) and other well-known techniques).
Phase 2—Action planning (Action case 2) A set of design principles for improved method configuration was developed in a series of workshops. These were anchored in the formulated vision, prioritized problems, and principles from the situational ME literature. The proposed design principles were: • The principle of modularization • The principle of method rationale for selecting method parts • The principle of a multilayered reuse model *Data sources* • Logs from two planning sessions • Vision document
Phase 3—Action taking (Action cases 2 & 3) Based on the design principles, a prototype of MMC was developed. In a series of workshops, a conceptual structure and a classification schema were produced, along with a number of instructions for the 'method engineer' role. The four main concepts were: the method fragment (based on established situational ME principles (Harmsen, 1997)), the base method (the organization-wide ISDM), the configuration package, and the configuration template. The latter two concepts were introduced to facilitate modular reuse of method configurations. Volvo IT provided a set of existing projects as input for the design sessions, and emerging concepts were tried against those projects' requirements. A summary of the work to date was presented at an international workshop (Karlsson, Ågerfalk, & Hjalmarsson, 2001). When MMC had stabilized sufficiently, it was used in a small-scale project at ESI (about 350 man-hours over three calendar months), which enabled active participation throughout the project. The chosen base method was RUP. *Data sources* • Logs from 12 design sessions • Preliminary version of MMC
Phase 4—Evaluation (Action case 3) The first full-scale evaluation of MMC was based on the active participation in the ESI project, in which the first author was the project manager and method engineer. *Data sources* • Situational ISDM and defined reusable assets (configuration templates) • Project artifacts • Project results • Project log book *Data analysis* The data sources were analyzed, focusing on encountered problems and achieved design goals. Documented problems were traced to possible causes. For example, some of these causes could be traced back to the situational method and MMC, the systems developer's knowledge of the base method, or a combination of these. The developed software was evaluated via interviews with end users and change requests tracking (Karlsson, 2005).
Phase 5—Specifying learning From the data analysis in Phase 4, the lessons learned were outlined, including practical advice on use of the proposed metamethod and change requests. A summary of the work to date was published in an international journal (Karlsson & Ågerfalk, 2004).
MGAR Cycle 2 (Autumn 2002 to Autumn 2004)

continued on following page

Table 1. Continued

MGAR Cycle 1 (Spring 2000 to Spring 2002)
Research collaborators • Posten IT • Precio The planning of MGAR Cycle 2 was presented at an international conference (Ågerfalk et al., 2003).
Phase 6—Diagnosing The diagnosing phase was based on the specified lessons learnt and change requests from the first MGAR cycle. These lessons were ana-lyzed from two different perspectives: design flaws in the MMC prototype, and the need for a Computer-Aided ME (CAME) tool based on MMC. (Note that the tool aspect is beyond the scope of this paper and is only mentioned here for completeness.) *Data sources* • Lessons learnt from MGAR Cycle 1 *Data analysis* To separate real problems from symptoms, problem analysis (Goldkuhl & Röstlinger, 1993) was performed.

Phase 7—Action planning (Action cases 4 & 5)
Based on lessons from the first MGAR cycle, the set of design principles was refined to:
• The principle of modularization:
  • Self-contained modules
  • Internally consistent and coherent modules
  • Support for information hiding
  • Implementable via a CAME tool
• The principle of method rationale for selecting method parts:
  • Support analysis of potential to achieve rationality resonance
  • Support 'method-in-action' (Fitzgerald et al., 2002) decisions
• The principle of a multilayered reuse model

Phase 8—Action taking (Action cases 4–7) MMC was redesigned using the refined principles. A new modularization concept was introduced, based on a modification of an existing ME concept, namely the 'method component.' This concept was integrated with the concepts of configuration package and configuration template. Following this redesign, the classification schema was also changed. The method rationale and method component concepts were presented at international conferences (Wistrand & Karlsson, 2004; Ågerfalk & Wistrand, 2003) and in an international journal (Karlsson & Wistrand, 2006). *Data sources* • Logs from four design sessions • MMC The redesigned MMC was used in projects at Posten IT and Precio. In these projects, RUP and MSF were used as base methods. In total, MMC was used in four different project settings.
Phase 9—Evaluation (Action cases 4–7) Evaluation of MMC (Phase 8) was performed during its use at Posten IT and Precio. Throughout these projects, group interviews were performed with project members. *Data sources* • Six configuration workshops • Situational method and defined reusable assets • Project artifacts • Four group interviews *Data analysis* The data sources were analyzed, focusing on encountered problems and achieved design goals.
Phase 10—Specifying learning From the data analysis in Phase 9, lessons learned and change requests were outlined. The first category contained practical advice on how to use MMC. The second category contained identified design flaws that have had subsequent design implications.

project situation in the organization. A configura-tion template is constructed from a selection of configuration packages (each one representing a characteristic) and can be viewed as an aggregate of configuration packages. Hence, a configuration template reflects a recurring development pattern within an organization.

The remainder of this section is structured around the three core concepts introduced above. The focus will be on the configuration package

Table 2. Action cases in chronological order

Action case	Business	ISDM	Case role
1. Volvo IT—pre case	Large	RUP	Method configuration diagnosis
2. Volvo IT	Large	RUP	MMC design, configuration application
3. ESI	Small	RUP	MMC validation, configuration application
4. Posten IT	Large	RUP	MMC redesign & validation, configuration application
5. Posten IT	Large	RUP	MMC redesign & validation, reconstruction of configuration
6. Precio	Medium	MSF	MMC validation, creating configuration
7. Precio	Medium	MSF	MMC validation, reconstruction of configuration

and template concept and how they are used together with method components. For an extensive presentation of the method component concept, see Karlsson and Wistrand (2006) and Wistrand and Karlsson (2004). The Unified Modeling Language (UML) class diagram in Figure 1 provides an overview of the main MMC concepts and their associations. The selection of concepts is based on those MMC parts that should be understood during empirical method configuration activities.

We provide definitions of these concepts in Table 3 and elaborate on each of them in the following sections.

The Method Component Concept

To achieve a systematic yet straightforward way of working with method configuration, a modularization concept that implements information hiding is required. Such a concept makes it possible to

Figure 1. Main concepts of MMC

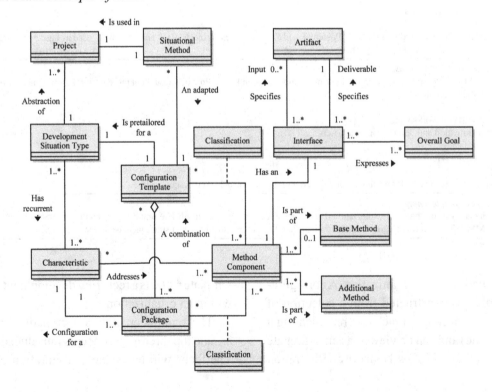

Table 3. Definitions of the main MMC concepts

Concept	Definition
Additional Method	Any complementary method that is not the base method.
Artifact	A final or intermediate work product that is produced and used by actors during a systems development project.
Base Method	The method chosen as the starting point for the configuration work.
Characteristic	A delimited part of a development situation type, focusing on a certain problem or aspect that the method configuration aims to solve or handle.
Classification	The planned use of the method component.
Configuration Package	A configuration of the base method suitable for a characteristic's value.
Configuration Template	A combined configuration, based on configuration packages, for a set of recurrent characteristics.
Development Situation Type	An abstraction of one or more previous or future systems development projects with common characteristics.
Interface	A reference to a selection of method elements and rationale that is relevant to the present task.
Method Component	A self-contained part of an ISDM that expresses the transformation of one or more artifacts into a defined target artifact and the rationale for such a transformation.
Overall Goal	A verifiable state of the world towards which effort is directed. Constitutes an important part of the method rationale.
Project	A complex undertaking with a defined objective, performed during a delimited period, made up of interrelated actions performed by assigned actors and having budgeted resources.
Situational Method	A configuration template fine-tuned and adapted to a specific project.

define the smallest coherent ISDM part that can be suppressed, added, or replaced. A 'method component' is a self-contained part of an ISDM that expresses the transformation of one or more artifacts into a defined target artifact and the rationale for such a transformation.

The Method Component Content

A method component has two parts, namely its content and the rationale that expresses why the content is designed as it is and what it can achieve. The content of a method component is an aggregate of 'method elements.' A method element is a part of an ISDM that manifests a method component's target state or facilitates the transformation from one defined state to another.

The method element concept can be specialized into five categories. First, there are three interrelated parts frequently mentioned in the literature, namely 'prescribed action,' 'concept,' and 'notation.' Prescribed actions, together with sequence restrictions, guide the performance of activities and tell project members what actions to take in specific situations. In performing these actions, the concepts direct developers' attention towards specific phenomena in the problem domain. Hence, concepts are used to express an understanding of the problem domain and of the ISDM itself. The results of the prescribed actions are documented using a specific notation, which gives the concepts a concrete representation. An example is the use of a line to show an association between two classes in a UML class diagram.

Based on empirical observations from MGAR Cycle 1, these three categories are complemented by the 'artifact' and 'actor role' as the two remaining subtypes of the method element concept. Project members tended to discuss ISDMs from an artifact perspective during method configuration and software development projects. This is also in line with previous research emphasizing the importance of "keeping the focus on what is being produced" (Cameron, 2002, p. 72). Artifacts are deliverables from the transformation process as well as inputs to this process. Our use of the term 'input' should not be interpreted in terms of a precondition. ISDMs are here viewed as heuristic procedures ('heurithms') and consequently *specified* inputs are considered as *recommended* inputs. However, a method component must have at least one input. Otherwise, the method component will have no meaningful support in the method. An exception is method components initiating new activities later integrated with the results from other method components. The selection of actor roles is determined by the prescribed actions that must be part of the transformation process. Actor roles are involved either as drivers of the prescribed actions in the method component or as participants. Empirical observations from MGAR Cycle 1 show that actor roles are important when mapping the situational ISDM to the actual work organization.

The method rationale part of the method component has two parts, namely 'goals' and 'values,' which represent the reasons behind method elements. A goal is a verifiable state of the world toward which effort is directed. Each goal is anchored in the method creator's values (Goldkuhl et al., 1998; Ågerfalk & Fitzgerald, 2006). Taken together, goals and values are important parts of an ISDM's perspective (Goldkuhl et al., 1998) or 'philosophy' (Fitzgerald et al., 2002). In MMC, method rationale is considered more important than the deliverable as such. The method rationale makes it is possible to address the goals that are essential to reach the specific project objectives. Prescribed actions and artifacts are only the means to achieve something, and method rationale can therefore prevent developers losing sight of that ultimate result and can help them find alternative ways forward.

However, when defining method components, we restrict the modeling of method rationale to include only goals. This design decision is prag-

matic, being based on our empirical finding that method engineers and developers tend to reason about the purpose of certain method components and often omit any discussion of values. In addition, it is important to note that we are not searching for objective goal statements but rather for pragmatic and situated statements that describe method component usage and its effects.

The Method Component Interface

The second aim of the method component concept is to hide unnecessary details during method configuration, providing a kind of encapsulation. For this, we draw on the traditional usage of the component concept in software engineering (McIlroy, 1968; Stevens & Pooley, 2006). How a task is executed is not interesting from an external view of the component. A user of a component is primarily interested in its results and the required inputs needed to achieve them. This reduction of complexity is achieved via the 'method component interface,' which refers to a selection of method elements and rationale relevant to the present task.

The interface creates an external view of method components, and its content depends on the present task (Karlsson & Wistrand, 2006). Empirical observations from MGAR Cycle 1 show that the method component's overall goals and artifacts are central during method configuration. Therefore, they are part of the interface during method configuration. An artifact is, as discussed above, designated as an input and/or a deliverable (output). This is necessary in order to deal with the three fundamental actions that can be performed on an artifact: create, update, or delete. In cases where an artifact is created only by a method component, it is classified as a deliverable. If the artifact can be updated by the same method component, it is also classified as an input. Furthermore, we stipulate that a component can have one or more input artifacts, but has only one deliverable. Finally, the interface also expresses the overall goals of the method component representing the method rationale. These goals are used during method configuration and when discussing the possibility of achieving rationality resonance in a project with certain characteristics.

The Configuration Package Concept

Method configuration has its starting point in a specific organization-wide ISDM. Consequently, this ISDM plays a particular role in method configuration. The term 'base method,' as opposed to 'additional method,' is used to distinguish this 'base' ISDM. The base method is the ISDM chosen as the starting point for configuration, and an additional method is any complementary method that is not the base method.

The base method is the ISDM chosen by an organization to support software practice in that specific organization. Consequently, the selected ISDM exists in and is tailored for the context of the organization's software projects. These projects are unique in some sense but are still similar in that they are affected by experiences from previous and contemporary projects, institutionalized norms, and their final products (Karlsson & Ågerfalk, 2004). Hence, the 'development situation type' is assessed by examining previous and future projects via the elicitation of project team members' experience. A development situation type is an abstraction of one or more previous or future systems development projects with common characteristics.

Development situation types are distinguished by variations in 'characteristics.' One characteristic difference might be the power that the development team can exercise on the user group. For example, building e-commerce systems differs from building time-report systems for in-house use in this respect. In the former situation, developers must act cautiously, because the cost to users of switching to another e-commerce site is low, literally just one click away. However, with a time-reporting system, there might not be

any other options for the users and the decision to use the system can be enforced. We define a characteristic as a delimited part of a development situation type that focuses on a certain problem or aspect that the method configuration aims to solve or handle.

Method configuration decides which method components in a base method are to be performed, and to what extent. This refers to the focus that a characteristic has on the rationale of a method, which is expressed through the method components' interfaces. A characteristic is viewed as a question about one aspect of the development situation type. The question can have one or more possible answers, which form the characteristic's 'dimension.' One possible answer is termed a 'configuration package' in MMC. Each characteristic addresses one or more method components and their reason for existence, as illustrated in Figure 1. Each configuration package has a 'scope,' namely the method components that are of interest for classification based on the characteristic. The scope is specified to reduce the number of classification operations that have to be performed when creating a configuration package.

A configuration package, therefore, is a classification of method components in terms of the relevance of their overall goals to a specific answer along a characteristic's dimension. An example of a characteristic is "Business processes already well understood?" which could address method components concerned with business modeling. Two possible answers are "We have good knowledge about existing business processes" and "We have no knowledge about existing business processes." In this case, the dimension comprises two answers, or configuration packages. Thus, component-based method configuration links to the idea of larger reusable blocks of method modules, where the blocks are configuration packages. A configuration package is a configuration of the base method suited to one characteristic value.

Table 4 shows the classification schema on which the classification of method components is based, which has two dimensions. The vertical dimension quantifies the 'attention' that method users should devote to a particular method component, namely 'None,' 'Insignificant,' 'Normal' or 'Significant.' If, at this stage, the method user or the method engineer finds a method component to be unimportant, it can immediately be classified as 'Omit.' For example, the user-interface prototype component in RUP does not add any value in a development situation concerned with an embedded system that has no user interface. Consequently, the method user should not give any attention ('None') to such a method component, and it should be classified as 'Omit.' In a different situation, such as when developing an information system for end user self-service, the method users might need to pay 'Significant' attention to the user interface prototyping component to make the self-service aspect work.

The three aspects of the horizontal dimension, namely 'Satisfactory,' 'Unsatisfactory,' and 'Missing,' cut across the vertical dimension. This dimension is referred to as the potential for achieving 'rationality resonance,' based on the content of the base method and the method users' intentions. Aligning with the work of Stolterman (1991), we define rationality resonance as the overlap between private rationality and public rationality. For example, if the method users agree with the overall goals of the user-interface prototype component in RUP, then we have a 'Satisfactory' potential for achieving rationality resonance. In the case of the user self-service system, we might end up with an 'Emphasize as is' classification.

Each of the columns of Table 4 can be associated with one of the three fundamental method configuration scenarios (Wistrand & Karlsson, 2004) that have to be supported, namely 'selection,' 'replacement,' and 'addition.' Satisfactory potential to achieve rationality resonance maps to the selection of method components. This selection is based on articulated goals, which means that the expressed rationale is believed to be in line with the project members' intentions (i.e., rationality resonance). We must therefore consider to what extent it is important to achieve the prescribed goals. If it is important to achieve these goals, then significant attention should be paid to the method component, and the recommended classification is 'Emphasize as is.' Unsatisfactory potential for achieving rationality resonance is associated with replacing existing method components with external method components that are more relevant. Finally, there is the situation where the potential for achieving rationality resonance is missing. This could be when method components that support this aspect of the development situation type are not to be found in the base method. The classification is then some variant of 'Add,' depending on the attention the method component is to receive.

All method components outside the configuration package's scope are classified as 'Not applicable' and must be covered by other configuration packages to be made situational. For example, if the scope of the current configuration package is database design, then components that have to do with user interaction are out of scope and consequently 'Not applicable.'

Table 4. Classification schema for method components

Attention given to method component	Potential to achieve rationality resonance		
	Satisfactory	*Unsatisfactory*	*Missing*
None	Omit	–	–
Insignificant	Perform informal	Replace informal	Add informal
Normal	Perform as is	Replace as is	Add as is
Significant	Emphasize as is	Replace emphasized	Add emphasized

The Configuration Template Concept

The configuration package concept is used, together with characteristics, to simplify analysis of the base method, through a narrow scope that reduces complexity. However, software projects are not simple, and neither are situational methods. Consequently, configurations must reflect a more complicated picture, containing combinations of characteristics. The 'configuration template' concept is used for this purpose, where a configuration template is a combined method configuration, based on one or more configuration packages, for a set of recurrent project characteristics.

Configuration templates make it possible to tailor the base method more efficiently, because the concept allows for the reuse of combined configuration packages that target development situation types common within the organization. Configuration templates are, in general, derivable from configuration packages, provided the candidate configuration packages are not changed and do not overlap. However, this is not an efficient use of resources because configuration packages have a number of possible combinations, which increases with the number of configuration packages being considered, and only a limited selection and combination of configuration packages will be of interest, based on the characteristics of previous and future projects.

It is not possible to automate fully the task of combining configuration packages (Karlsson & Wistrand, 2004), and the intersections between configuration packages have to be managed. Situations occur where configuration packages overlap. For example, two different configuration packages can address the same method component with contradictory classifications. It is natural for conflicting classifications to occur when combining configuration packages because they represent an analysis based on demarcated perspectives (one problem or aspect at a time). However, when these characteristics are combined, a decision has to be made regarding a method component's clas-

sification, and the decision cannot be represented within any single configuration package. Instead, this decision is represented in the configuration template.

The classification of method components in a configuration template follows the classification schema presented in Table 4. When it comes to conflicting classifications, the recommendation is divided into two parts:

(1) Which characteristic and configuration package most essentially reflects the development situation type?
(2) Which configuration package requires the most method support? For example, when comparing the two classification alternatives 'Omit' and 'Perform as is,' we can conclude that the latter would require more method support.

The situational method is based on a selected configuration template and is the ISDM delivered for the project team to use. This method is then turned into 'method-in-action' when enacted by the project team members. There is, therefore, a difference between the tailored version of the base method and the method-in-action (Ågerfalk & Fitzgerald, 2006). Experiences from the latter should be fed back to the configuration process, to improve the configuration templates and/or configuration packages. This feedback is typically given by the method users to the method engineer continuously throughout the project, at the ends of the iterations for example, or during project closeout.

EPISODES OF USE

As described above, the development of MMC was conducted in collaboration with industrial partners to generate and validate the metamethod via practical use. This section contains a selection of significant parts of MGAR Cycle 2 (see Table

1) for illustrative purposes. They show, as part of the empirical grounding, that the design principles of MMC and the MMC itself are useable in real projects. The empirical grounding is used (1) to gather practical experience of the usefulness of MMC, resulting in lessons learned, and (2) to identify design flaws that are fed back into the design process as design implications. As with every development project, the resulting artifacts pass through different stages of maturity. In this research, they have ranged from the smaller parts of MMC to versions that are more complete. In order to distinguish a specific action case study from the presented part thereof, we term the latter an 'episode.'

Posten IT

The empirical work at Posten IT included two action cases (Action cases 4 and 5 in Table 1). One project had the aim of adapting an existing IS to new regulations, and the other was in the electronic government area. From a research point of view, the first case was a reconstruction project, with the research aim being to test possibilities for reconstructing reusable patterns, based on how a project had been working. In the second case, a configuration team was to deliver reusable patterns for an upcoming project.

Both projects shared some features, which we exemplify with a configuration package concerning requirements engineering and method maturity. At the time, Posten IT was introducing RUP as their base method, resulting in varying levels of knowledge about this particular ISDM. Furthermore, there had been little previous use of ISDMs. The method engineers at Posten IT stated that the organization had "low method maturity." Therefore, configuring the base method was "a necessity." Both projects came to share a similar way of addressing requirements engineering. This meant that the configuration package presented in Table 5, "Basic requirements engineering," was reused for the second of these two projects.

Table 5. Configuration package: "Basic requirements engineering."

Method component	Method component's rationale	CP: Basic requirements engineering
1. Requirements Management Plan	To specify the information to be collected and the control mechanisms to be used for measuring, reporting, and controlling changes to the product requirements	Omit
2. Glossary	To provide a consistent set of definitions to help avoid misunderstandings	Omit
3. Requirements Attributes	To provide a repository of the requirements text	Omit
4. Supplementary Specifications	To capture system requirements that are not readily captured as functional requirements	Perform as is
5. Stakeholder Requests	To capture all requests made in the project and how they were addressed	Omit
6. Vision	To capture the 'essence' of the envisaged solution in the form of high-level requirements and design constraints	Perform as is
7. Use-Case Model	To capture the system's intended functions	Perform as is
8. Storyboard	To explore, clarify, and capture the behavioral interaction envisioned by the user	Omit
9. Use Case	To define a sequence of actions that a system performs to yield an observable result of value to a particular actor	Perform as is
10. Software Requirements Specification	To capture the software requirements for the complete system	Omit
11. Use-Case Package	To structure the Use-Case model by dividing it into smaller parts	Omit
12. Software Requirement	To specify the capability needed by the user to solve a problem	Omit

The configuration package in Table 5 was associated with the characteristic 'Type of requirements situation.' The method engineers regarded it as essential to improve the way requirements engineering was performed, because "a clear picture of the requirements is often missing." However, they also took into consideration the fact that the current experience of ISDMs was rather limited. Consequently, they created a configuration package for "Basic requirements engineering," rather than more specialized types of requirements engineering. The term 'Basic' implies that we aimed to reach what the method engineers considered "a minimum level" of structure for working with requirements.

The left column of Table 5 shows the configuration package's method components (the scope), the middle column shows the method components' rationale, and the right column shows the classifications made in the configuration package. The rationale expressed in Table 5 is based on the rationale for each of the method components' deliverables, according to how it is expressed in RUP. This configuration package contains 'Omit' and 'Perform as is' classifications. The three top rows of Table 5 explain the line of reasoning behind these 'Omit' classifications, namely that they are not essential to basic requirements engineering according to the method engineers who participated in this workshop. For example, the Requirements Management Plan was considered "too advanced" by one of the method engineers, with regard to the project members' knowledge of the base method. The Glossary component was suppressed because "we do not want a focus on concepts," as one method engineer expressed it. Evidently, these classifications can all be traced back to project members' 'method maturity.' The fourth component, the Supplementary Specifications, was classified as 'Perform as is.' As expressed in the middle column, this component is used for capturing nonfunctional requirements. In these projects, the method engineers stated that each project has "to consider nonfunctional

requirements" and therefore has a need for this component.

Precio

The empirical work at Precio had similarities with the studies conducted at Posten IT, although Precio used MSF as their base method rather than RUP. Two action cases were carried out with Precio (Action cases 6 and 7 in Table 1). One was a reconstruction case and the other involved method configuration in preparation for an upcoming project. The reconstruction case concerned a booking system, with two companies sharing a new IS. The second project concerned the extension of an existing IS to include a Report module. The selection of cases was based on the current project portfolio and aimed to find two projects that had similarities. The idea was to find reusable parts during reconstruction and configuration work and aim to share the configuration packages between the two projects. Both projects were rather small, involving a handful of project members and extending over a period of approximately six months. Both project managers were of the opinion that the small project team enabled an informal communication structure to be adopted. A project member of the Report module team expressed this as "we are such a small team that I only have to turn around and ask my colleague."

The two projects came to share the same characteristic base but not all configuration packages. One of the characteristics was 'Type of project team' and the configuration package 'Small project team.' This configuration package addressed method components such as the Project Structure, the Communication Plan, and the Master Project Plan. For this part of the development situation type, informal communication played a central role. The rationale of the Communication Plan was considered superfluous in the light of the extensive informal communication and was therefore omitted. On the other hand, the Master Project Plan was necessary for communication with various stakeholders outside the project team and was therefore classified 'Perform as is.'

When it came to requirements engineering, the two projects differed in their configuration packages. The Booking system project expressed it as "No, problems are not likely to occur" during requirements engineering, while the Report module project represented the situation as "Yes, problems can occur." This latter configuration package is presented in Table 6. The main idea behind this configuration package was to make the requirements visible. This meant that the Prototype component became more important. Via the use of prototypes, it is possible to express features and their design. Hence, there is potential to make the requirements more tangible. This was expressed by one project member as "It [the Prototype] creates reactions. You cannot design it like that, it must look like …." Therefore, there was potential to achieve rationality resonance with this component, and the Report module project team argued that significant attention should be devoted to this component. The component is classified as 'Emphasize as is' in Table 6. To some extent, this emphasis on the Prototype component meant that the attention devoted to other requirement components decreased. For example, the Usage Scenarios component was omitted from the configuration package. The Report module team concluded that "these artifacts overlap," which is another way of indicating that they contribute to the same goal.

LESSONS LEARNED FROM THESE EPISODES

The two episodes discussed above showed that MMC was valuable when working with method configuration. The project team members who were part of the configuration work in the workshops found value in the basic idea of reuse, as expressed by MMC. As the project members for the Report module project stated, "Method configuration in general is valuable. You discuss the project and consider each part." Furthermore, they stated that using MMC "was well invested time" and that its design reduced the time needed to discuss details about projects and their implications for the base method. As the project manager of the booking system expressed it, "…reuse of configurations is essential. You often lack time and need to decide on the fly." A method engineer at Posten IT stated that MMC "reduces the dependency on specific persons during method tailoring."

Table 6. Configuration package: "Yes, problems can occur."

Method component	Method component's rationale	CP: Yes, problems can occur
1. Current State Infrastructure	To describe all legacy systems in place	Omit
2. Vision/Scope	To achieve team and customer agreement on the desired solution and overall project direction	Perform as is
3. Prototype	To express the features needed and their design	Emphasize as is
4. Business Requirements	To provide a bottom-line context for the solution	Omit
5. Functional Specification	To provide the essence/summary of a contract between the customer and the team	Omit
6. Usage Scenarios	To express why the solution is needed and what it must do	Omit
7. Feature Proposal	To focus the most important characteristics of the solution	Omit
8. User Requirements	To define the nonfunctional aspects of the user's interaction with the solution	Perform as is

This empirical grounding showed that the artifact focus of a method component together with method rationale is a useful starting point for method engineers and project team members when discussing method configuration. According to one of the method engineers at Posten IT, "it makes the use of method goal-focused," and, as a systems developer at the same company stated, "it is important to focus on what to deliver [the artifact]." The project manager of the Booking system project said that "it is easy to translate to the use of deliverables" and a team member of the Report module project described method components as "easy to grasp." This emphasizes how the method component and its deliverable can contribute to the next step in the development process.

An example of this is that both project teams at Precio suppressed the use of the Communication Plan component. Based on the method components' rationale, they considered this method component superfluous, given the size of their project teams. The method component's conceptual design made it possible to suppress the artifact as such and also the prescribed actions that are associated with creating and modifying it. In addition, the concepts and notation used in this artifact were suppressed as well. An advantage of this was that none of the latter method elements had to be explicitly discussed during these workshops. The information-hiding concept was considered natural to use, and a member of the Report module team found a "natural translation to object-oriented development."

Another example is that the project members of the Report module project chose to prioritize the use of the Prototype component. (A note of caution is appropriate here: suppressing method components based on method rationale does assume that the method engineer is a competent method user.) The project team members chose to suppress method components based on their knowledge that the Prototype component implements the required rationality better than, for example, the Usage Scenarios component. As discussed above, the Report module project team referred to 'overlap' between artifacts.

Compared to building configuration packages based on the method fragment concept (as for the MGAR Cycle 1 (Karlsson & Ågerfalk, 2004)), we have less data to trace. This is due to the integration of the product and process model. Furthermore, viewing method components as networked, instead of using the layer idea of method fragments, also reduces complexity. Consequently, it is easier to balance precision and cost during configuration work than it was when using the first version of MMC.

Furthermore, the possibility of structuring configuration work around a few initial ideas about characteristics is an advantage. During the second project at Precio, the characteristics from the first project were used as inputs, which provided a focus for the discussions. The downside of this approach can be that the search for new characteristics is given less attention. To some extent, these projects also illustrate that we tend to work with just a few characteristics, which implies that we tend to have rather large configuration packages. The choice of working with few characteristics was deliberate, aiming to reduce the choices necessary to create a project profile and select a configuration template. The smaller the configuration packages created, the less chance we have of creating a conceptual layer between method components and configuration templates.

In the action cases, it was observed that practitioners tended to focus on the goals of method components in preference to values. The use of values tends to become more abstract and distracts from what it is possible to achieve. Furthermore, it is another way to reduce the number of details that must be handled during method configuration work. If, however, conflicting goals emerge, the values base can potentially be useful as a source of advice.

DESIGN IMPLICATIONS OF THESE EPISODES

The team members of the Report module project suggested design improvements for the method component interface. They expressed a need for more "precise goals" to illustrate how a component's deliverable could be used subsequently. At that time, the conceptual framework only allowed the interface to contain one goal. This limitation meant that it was impossible to express multiple purposes for a method component. The participating developers stressed that the resulting artifact of a method component is sometimes "used for different purposes." The method component must therefore facilitate the expression of multiple purposes. The current design therefore limited potential discussions of method components. This design restriction had forced the rewriting of goals found in the base method into one comprehensive goal for each component, which then became ambiguous. As a result, the conceptual design of the method component was changed to include the possibility of expressing multiple purposes in the method component's interface.

On several occasions during the configuration workshops, the project members from both Precio cases expressed a need for an informal classification of method components, saying, "We conduct a risk analysis, but do not formally document the results." During these workshops, the prescribed actions were considered essential, unlike the deliverable, a classification that the classification schema did not allow at that time. However, after these workshops, we introduced the possibility of giving a method component 'Insignificant' attention (see Table 4), and of classifying the use as 'Informal.' This means that the prescribed actions are performed but the results are not formally documented.

CONCLUDING DISCUSSION

This paper has addressed the adaptation and tailoring of 'off the shelf' ISDMs. Such methods are provided by specific vendors and are often adopted as organization-wide ISDMs with the aim of covering every aspect of software/IS development. While beneficial in many ways, this also brings problems, such as the need to tailor the methods to the software/IS development project at hand. Therefore, structured support for the flexible tailoring of organization-wide ISDMs is needed, support that in many ways has been insufficient to date. In response, this paper describes an approach called 'method configuration,' which is formalized in MMC. MMC takes into account the need to combine structure, which is one reason for choosing an organization-wide ISDM in the first place, with flexibility, which is essential for making the chosen ISDM fit actual projects.

The metamethod presented rests on three major design principles, namely modularization, method rationale, and reuse. These principles were generated during empirical and internal grounding and were validated during external theoretical and empirical grounding. Hence, the empirical grounding has had both a generating and validating role. Table 7 shows the collaborations that led to the development and testing of the three design principles and how they are related to MMC concepts and to the three grounding processes.

The external theoretical grounding mainly involved ME research. During empirical grounding, we identified two principles that contribute significant value to the development process, namely the use of method rationale for selecting method parts and the principle of information hiding. The latter is a subprinciple of the modularization design principle. The empirical grounding shows that these two principles bring a new dimension to method configuration, especially when combined. Together, the three major design principles have resulted in a three-layered reuse

Table 7. The three major design principles and MMC concepts related to the grounding processes

		Grounding processes		
Design principle	**Instantiation**	**Internal**	**External theoretical**	**Empirical**
Modularization	Method component	Posten IT	ME research	Posten IT and Precio
Method Rationale	Selection schema	Volvo IT, Posten IT	ME research	Volvo IT, ESI, Posten IT, Precio
Reuse	Configuration Package and Configuration Template	Volvo IT, Posten IT	ME research	Volvo IT, ESI, Posten IT, Precio

model built around method components, configuration packages, and configuration templates.

MMC reduces the number of details to keep track of during configuration work, and this eased the burden of method engineers in the organizations studied. A subset of relevant details is made available via the method component interface. We have found that hiding details of the method component construct contributed to a focus on the possibility of achieving rationality resonance between the method components and the project members.

The three-layered reuse model of MMC proved useful in the organizations studied, where the three major MMC concepts were not used to the same degree. The selection of configuration templates is the most frequently used concept when a repository has been built. Configuration templates are selected and fine-tuned to become situational methods for specific projects. Consequently, the organizations did not have to perform a complete method assembly or method configuration for each new project.

The actual configuration is based on the classification schema that is provided with MMC. It is based on two dimensions, namely the potential to achieve rationality resonance and the method users' attention. The first dimension builds on the integrated design of method rationale for the selection of method components in that the content of the base method is matched with the method users' intentions regarding how to implement a specific part of the project. The second dimension, the method users' attention, addresses the importance

of the method users having to reach the method component's goals. Together, these two dimensions offer a balance between the intentions of the project members in the organizations studied and the needs of the projects. Furthermore, the attention dimension provides support for method-in-action, the final tailoring that project members perform during method use. The method users can use the attention classification as a recommendation about the effort to be put into implementing a specific method component.

IMPLICATIONS FOR PRACTICE

As discussed above, previous research has clearly indicated that ISDMs must be adapted and tailored to the specific context in which they are used. To date, MMC has been shown to provide a useful and structured approach to achieving the required flexibility. This work, therefore, lays a sound foundation for achieving structured flexibility in IS development.

The practical relevance of this work has been ensured through choosing the MGAR approach. The implications for practice exist at two levels. First, a concrete metamethod (MMC) has been devised and explained in this paper. MMC has proven useful in the studied cases, and it should be possible to adapt it to suit other organizations and base methods. Although the empirical validation reported in this paper is limited to RUP and MSF and to particular organizational settings, there is nothing to suggest that the approach would not also work in other contexts. In fact, such transferability was one of the design goals of MMC from the outset. Second, this research proves that it is possible to devise a metamethod to support structured flexibility in IS development. This is important because, even if a particular organization chooses not to adopt MMC, the very fact that MMC has proved useful should encourage any similar endeavor.

IMPLICATIONS FOR RESEARCH

This research provides an elaborated and empirically validated conceptual framework for method configuration and its implementation as the MMC metamethod. As discussed above, method configuration is a specific type of ME, for which one organization-wide ISDM is the point of departure. This type of situational ME brings its own problems of striking a balance between structure and flexibility. Hence, this research advances the field of ME via elaboration of this important subfield.

MMC is anchored in the general underlying principles of ISDMs, but, as pointed out above, the metamethod has only been empirically validated for RUP and MSF. Therefore, additional tests to determine the effectiveness of MMC in practice are needed. To facilitate such tests, computerized tool support for MMC should be developed. Although MMC can potentially ease the burden of method engineers, it still relies on manual work, which may limit its adoption by practitioners.

The method component concept evolves from an existing concept, now redesigned for method configuration purposes. This evolution includes the introduction of two distinctive ideas, namely the operationalization of the interface concept and the idea of method components as nonhierarchic (as opposed to method fragments and method chunks). The artifact focus that has emerged in this research indicates the importance of having a fixed level of abstraction for a modularization concept to aid collaboration with method engineers and developers. Together with information hiding, it increases the focus on method rationale rather than details and encourages the participation of developers during method configuration work.

However, the method component concept can be elaborated further. The concept has a generic interface, and its content can change depending on the situation. In this paper, we have presented a relevant selection of method configurations, resulting from collaboration with project team members. However, it is possible to identify other situations where the content might be different. Examples include updating the base method, use of method components during systems development, and education on specific method components. It is also worth noticing that the goals expressed by a method component interface serve a purpose similar to that of 'intentions' in method tailoring based on method chunks (Rolland, Souveyet, & Moreno, 2006), namely to identify and represent the purpose of the component. Importantly, however, the notion of method rationale emphasizes the formulation of these goals at a higher level than that used in the method chunks literature. The difference in emphasis may be attributed to the fixed level of abstraction promoted by MMC. It may also be a result of differing theoretical perspectives, where the MMC construct is based on Weber's (1978) notion of practical rationality rather than the strict means–end rationality inherent in the method chunk concept of intention (cf. Ågerfalk & Fitzgerald, 2006). An interesting venue for further research, clearly, would be to investigate more thoroughly the extent to which the two approaches are complementary.

Another important part of the method rationale aspect of this research is the elaborated support for decisions about whether to perform, wholly or partially, the method components in a base method. The classification schema provided with MMC supports profound method configuration decisions, which will facilitate future methods in action.

The use of the adopted research method is in itself an important contribution and suggests that other ME studies could fruitfully use a similar approach (cf. Karlsson & Ågerfalk, 2007). Specifically, this will be used in our future MMC research, aiming to investigate more thoroughly both the applicability of the metamethod to other contexts and the configuration of MMC itself for different ME situations.

ACKNOWLEDGMENT

This work has been financially supported by the Swedish Knowledge Foundation and the Science Foundation Ireland Investigator Programme, Lero – The Irish Software Engineering Research Centre. The authors are grateful to Anders Hjalmarsson, University College of Borås, who participated in the research at Volvo IT and contributed considerably to the initial development of MMC.

REFERENCES

Ågerfalk, P. J., Brinkkemper, S., Gonzalez-Perez, C., Henderson-Sellers, B., Karlsson, F., Kelly, S., et al. (2007). Modularization Constructs in Method Engineering: Towards Common Ground? In J. Ralyté, S. Brinkkemper, & B. Henderson-Sellers (Eds.), *Proceedings of IFIP WG8.1 Working Conference on Situational Method Engineering: Fundamentals and Experiences* (pp. 359–368). Springer.

Ågerfalk, P. J., & Fitzgerald, B. (2006). Exploring the Concept of Method Rationale: A Conceptual Tool for Method Tailoring. In Siau, K. (Ed.), *Advanced Topics in Database Research* (*Vol. 5*). Hershey, PA: Idea Group.

Ågerfalk, P. J., & Ralyté, J. (2006). Situational Requirements Engineering Processes: Reflecting on Method Engineering and Requirements Practice. *Software Process Improvement and Practice*, *11*(5), 447–450. doi:10.1002/spip.289

Ågerfalk, P. J., & Wistrand, K. (2003, 23–26 April 2003). *Systems Development Method Rationale: A Conceptual Framework for Analysis*. Paper presented at the 5th International Conference on Enterprise Information Systems (ICEIS 2003), Angers, France.

Ågerfalk, P. J., Wistrand, K., Karlsson, F., Börjesson, G., Elmberg, M., & Möller, K. (2003). *Flexible Processes and Method Configuration: Outline of a Joint Industry-Academia Research Project*. Paper presented at the 5th International Conference on Enterprise Information Systems (ICEIS 2003), Angers, France.

Ambler, S. W. (2002). *Agile Modelling: Effective Practices for eXtreme Programming and the Unified Process*. New York, NY: John Wiley & Sons, Inc.

Bajec, M., Vavpotič, D., & Krisper, M. (2006). Practice-driven approach for creating project-specific software development methods. *Information and Software Technology*, *49*(4), 345–365. doi:10.1016/j.infsof.2006.05.007

Baskerville, R., & Pries-Heje, J. (1999). Grounded action research: a method for understanding IT in practice. *Accounting. Management & Information Technologies*, *9*, 1–23. doi:10.1016/S0959-8022(98)00017-4

Baskerville, R., & Wood-Harper, A. T. (1998). Diversity in information systems action research methods. *European Journal of Information Systems*, *7*(2), 90–107. doi:10.1057/palgrave.ejis.3000298

Beck, K. (2000). *Extreme Programming explained: embrace change*. Reading, MA: Addison-Wesley.

Braa, K., & Vidgen, R. (1999). Interpretation, intervention, and reduction in the organizational laboratory: a framework for in-context information system research. *Accounting. Management and Information Technologies, 9*(1), 25–47. doi:10.1016/S0959-8022(98)00018-6

Brancheau, J. C., Janz, B. D., & Wetherbe, J. C. (1996). Key Issues in information systems management: 1994-95 SIM Delphi results. *Management Information Systems Quarterly, 20*(2), 225–242. doi:10.2307/249479

Brinkkemper, S. (1996). Method engineering: engineering of information systems development methods and tools. *Information and Software Technology, 38*(4), 275–280. doi:10.1016/0950-5849(95)01059-9

Cameron, J. (2002). Configurable Development Processes. *Communications of the ACM, 45*(3), 72–77. doi:10.1145/504729.504731

Cockburn, A. (2000). Selecting a Project's Methodolohy. *IEEE Software*, 64–71. doi:10.1109/52.854070

Evans, G. (2003, September). Agile RUP for Non-Object-Oriented Projects. *The Rational Edge*.

Fitzgerald, B., Hartnett, G., & Conboy, K. (2006). Customising Agile Methods to Software Practices at Intel Shannon. *European Journal of Information Systems, 15*(2), 197–210. doi:10.1057/palgrave.ejis.3000605

Fitzgerald, B., Russo, N. L., & O'Kane, T. (2003). Software Development Method Tailoring at Motorola. *Communications of the ACM, 46*(4), 65–70. doi:10.1145/641205.641206

Fitzgerald, B., Russo, N. L., & Stolterman, E. (2002). *Information Systems Development - Methods in Action*. London: McGraw-Hill.

Goldkuhl, G., Lind, M., & Seigerroth, U. (1998). Method integration: The need for a learning perspective. *IEE Proceedings. Software, 145*(4), 113–118. doi:10.1049/ip-sen:19982197

Goldkuhl, G., & Röstlinger, A. (1993). Joint elicitation of problems: An important aspect of change analysis. In Avison, D. E., Kendall, J. E., & DeGross, J. I. (Eds.), *Human, Organizational, and Social Dimensions of Information Systems Development* (pp. 107–125). North-Holland.

Hares, J. S. (1992). *Information engineering for the advanced practitioner*. Chichester, UK: Wiley.

Harmsen, A. F. (1997). *Situational Method Engineering*. Utrecht, The Netherlands: Moret Ernst & Young Management Consultants.

Henderson-Sellers, B. (2002). Process Metamodelling and Process Construction: Examples Using the OPEN Process Framework (OPF). *Annals of Software Engineering, 14*(1-4), 341–362. doi:10.1023/A:1020570027891

Henderson-Sellers, B., & Serour, M. K. (2005). Creating a Dual-Agility Method: The Value of Method Engineering. *Journal of Database Management, 16*(4), 1–24. doi:10.4018/jdm.2005100101

Hirsch, M. (2002). Making RUP agile. In *OOPSLA 2002 Practitioners Reports*. Seattle, Washington.

Karlsson, F. (2005). Method Configuration - A Systems Development Project Revisited. In A. G. Nilsson, R. Gustas, W. Wojtkowski, W. G. Wojtkowski, S. Wrycza, & J. Zupancic (Eds.), *The Fourteenth International Conference on Information Systems Development (ISD 2005)*. Karlstad, Sweden: Springer.

Karlsson, F., & Ågerfalk, P. J. (2004). Method Configuration: Adapting to Situational Characteristics while Creating Reusable Assets. *Information and Software Technology, 46*(9), 619–633. doi:10.1016/j.infsof.2003.12.004

Karlsson, F., & Ågerfalk, P. J. (2007). Multi-Grounded Action Research in Method Engineering: The MMC Case. In J. Ralyté, S. Brinkkemper, & B. Henderson-Sellers (Eds.), *Proceedings of IFIP WG8.1 Working Conference on Situational Method Engineering: Fundamentals and Experiences* (pp. 19–32): Springer.

Karlsson, F., Ågerfalk, P. J., & Hjalmarsson, A. (2001, 4–5 June). *Process Configuration with Development Tracks and Generic Project Types*. Paper presented at the 6th CAiSE/IFIP8.1 International Workshop on Evaluation of Modelling Methods in Systems Analysis and Design (EMMSAD'01), Interlaken, Switzerland.

Karlsson, F., & Wistrand, K. (2004, 7-8 June). *MC Sandbox: Tool Support for Method Configuration*. Paper presented at the Ninth CAiSE/IFIP8.1/ EUNO International Workshop on Evaluation of Modeling Methods in Systems Analysis and Design (EMMSAD'04), Riga, Latvia.

Karlsson, F., & Wistrand, K. (2006). Combining method engineering with activity theory: theoretical grounding of the method component concept. *European Journal of Information Systems, 15*, 82–90. doi:10.1057/palgrave.ejis.3000596

Klein, H. K., & Myers, M. D. (1999). A Set of Principles for Conducting and Evaluating Interpretive Field Studies in Information Systems. *Management Information Systems Quarterly, 1*, 67–94. doi:10.2307/249410

Kumar, K., & Wellke, R. J. (1992). Methodology Engineering: A proposal for situation specific methodology construction. In Cotterman, W. W., & Senn, J. A. (Eds.), *Challenges and Strategies for Research in Systems Development* (pp. 257–269). Washington, DC: John Wiley & Sons.

Lind, M., & Goldkuhl, G. (2006). How to develop a Multi-Grounded Theory: The Evolution of a Business Process Theory. *Australian Journal of Information Systems, 13*(2), 69–85.

Mathiassen, L. (2002). Collaborative Practice Research. *Information Technology & People, 15*(4), 321–345. doi:10.1108/09593840210453115

McIlroy, M. D. (1968). *Mass Produced Software Components.* Paper presented at the North Atlantic Treaty Organisation (NATO) Conference on Software Engineering, Garmisch-Partenkirchen, Germany.

Mirbel, I., & Ralyté, J. (2006). Situational method engineering: combining assembly-based and roadmap-driven approaches. *Requirements Engineering, 11*(1), 58–78. doi:10.1007/s00766-005-0019-0

Nilsson, A. G. (1999). The Business Developer's Toolbox: Chains and Alliances between Established Methods. In Nilsson, A. G., Tolis, C., & Nellborn, C. (Eds.), *Perspectives on Business Modelling: Understanding and Changing Organisations* (pp. 217–241). Heidelberg: Springer Verlag.

Odell, J. J. (1996). A primer to method engineering. In S. Brinkkemper, K. Lyytinen & R. J. Welke (Eds.), *Method Engineering: Principles of method construction and tool support (IFIP TC8, WG8.7/8.2 Working conference on method engineering)*. Atlanta, USA.

Ralyté, J., Deneckère, R., & Rolland, C. (2003). Towards a Generic Model for Situational Method Engineering. In M. M. Johann Eder (Ed.), *Advanced Information Systems Engineering, 15th International Conference, CAiSE 2003 2681*, 95-110. Berlin: Springer.

Riemenschneider, C. K., Hardgrave, B. C., & Davis, F. D. (2002). Explaining Software Developer Acceptance of Methodologies: A Comparison of Five Theoretical Models. *IEEE Transactions on Software Engineering, 28*(12), 1135–1145. doi:10.1109/TSE.2002.1158287

Roberts, T. L. Jr, Gibson, M. L., Fields, K. T., & Rainer, R. K. Jr. (1998). Factors that Impact Implementing a System Development Methodology. *IEEE Transactions on Software Engineering, 24*(8), 640–649. doi:10.1109/32.707699

Roland, C., Souveyet, C., & Moreno, M. (2006). An Approach for Defining Ways-of-Working. *Information Systems, 20,* 337–359. doi:10.1016/0306-4379(95)00018-Y

Rolland, C., & Prakash, N. (1996, 26–28 August). 1996). A Proposal For Context-Specific Method Engineering. In S. Brinkkemper, K. Lyytinen, & R. Welke (Eds.), Method Engineering: Principles of method construction and tool support (pp. 191–208). Chapman & Hall.

Rolland, C., Prakash, N., & Benjamen, A. (1999). A Multi-Model View of Process Modelling. *Requirements Engineering, 4*(4), 169–187. doi:10.1007/s007660050018

Ropponen, J., & Lyytinen, K. (2000). Components of Software Development Risk: How to Address Them? A Project Manager Survey. *IEEE Transactions on Software Engineering, 26*(2), 98–112. doi:10.1109/32.841112

Rossi, M., Ramesh, B., Lyytinen, K., & Tolvanen, J.-P. (2004). Managing Evolutionary Method Engineering by Method Rationale. *Journal of the Association for Information Systems, 5*(9), 356–391.

Schwaber, K., & Beedle, M. (2002). *Agile Software Development with Scrum.* Upper Saddle River, NJ: Prentice-Hall.

Stevens, P., & Pooley, R. (2006). *Using UML: Software Engineering with Objects and Components.* Essex, England: Addison Wesley.

Stolterman, E. (1991). *Designarbetets dolda rationalitet: en studie av metodik och praktik inom systemutveckling.* Doctoral Dissertation in Swedish, Umeå University, Umeå, Sweden.

Stolterman, E., & Russo, N. L. (1997). *The Paradox of Information Systems Methods: Public and Private Rationality.* Paper presented at the The British Computer Society 5th Annual Conference on Methodologies, Lancaster, England.

Strauss, A. L., & Corbin, J. M. (1998). *Basics of qualitative research: techniques and procedures for developing grounded theory* (2nd ed. ed.). Thousand Oaks, CA: SAGE.

van Slooten, K., & Hodes, B. (1996). Characterizing IS development projects. In Brinkkemper, S., Lyytinen, K., & Welke, R. (Eds.), *Method Engineering: Principles of method construction and tool support* (pp. 29–44). Chapman & Hall.

Weber, M. (1978). *Economy and society.* Berkeley, CA: University of California Press.

Wistrand, K., & Karlsson, F. (2004). Method Components - Rationale Revealed. In A. Persson & J. Stirna (Eds.), *The 16th International Conference on Advanced Information Systems Engineering (CAiSE 2004), 3084,* 189-201. Berlin: Springer.

Xiping, S., & Osterweil, L. J. (1998). Engineering Software Design Processes to Guide Process Execution. *IEEE Transactions on Software Engineering, 24*(9), 759–775. doi:10.1109/32.713330

This work was previously published in Journal of Database Management (JDM) 20(3), edited by Keng Siau, pp. 51-75, copyright 2009 by IGI Publishing (an imprint of IGI Global).

Chapter 11
On Efficient Evaluation of XML Queries

Sherif Sakr
University of New South Wales, Australia

ABSTRACT

Recently, the use of XML continues to grow in popularity, large repositories of XML documents are going to emerge, and users are likely to pose increasingly more complex queries on these data sets. In 2001 XQuery is decided by the World Wide Web Consortium (W3C) as the standard XML query language. In this article, we describe the design and implementation of an efficient and scalable purely relational XQuery processor which translates expressions of the XQuery language into their equivalent SQL evaluation scripts. The experiments of this article demonstrated the efficiency and scalability of our purely relational approach in comparison to the native XML/XQuery functionality supported by conventional RDBMSs and has shown that our purely relational approach for implementing XQuery processor deserves to be pursued further.

INTRODUCTION

The eXtensible Markup Language (XML) (Bray, Paoli, Sperberg-McQueen, Maler, & Yergeau, 2006) has been introduced by the end of the 1990's in order to create a standard data-format for the World Wide Web which can be easily handled by computers as well as by humans. In recent years,

XML has found practical application in numerous domains including data interchange, streaming data and data storage. The semi structured nature of XML allows data to be represented in a considerably more flexible nature than in the traditional relational paradigm. However, the tree-based data model underlying XML poses many challenges especially with regard to the problem of performing efficient query evaluations.

DOI: 10.4018/978-1-60960-521-6.ch011

As XML continues to grow in popularity, large repositories of XML documents are going to emerge, and users are likely to pose increasingly more complex queries on these data sets. Consequently, there is a great demand for efficient XML data management systems for managing complex queries over large volumes of the XML data. In 2001 XQuery is decided by the World Wide Web Consortium (W3C) as the standard XML query language (Boag et al., 2006).

XQuery is based on a hierarchical and ordered document model which supports a wide variety of constructs and use cases. The language addresses a wide range of requirements, thus incorporating a rich set of features.

The work of this article was developed within the Pathfinder project (Pathfinder, 2003). The aim of the Pathfinder project is to implement XQuery as a query language that can be used to query XML data stored on relational database systems. The architecture of Pathfinder is designed in a front-end/back-end fashion. Pathfinder receives an XQuery expression, which is parsed, normalized, and translated into XQuery Core. The Core expression is then simplified, type checked optimized, and translated into an intermediate algebraic plan. Initially, Pathfinder used the MonetDB main memory RDBMS as its target back-end. In this development branch (Boncz et al., 2006), the Pathfinder intermediate algebraic plan is translated into MIL (Monet Interpreter Language) code (Boncz & Kersten, 1999) which is then executed by the kernel of MonetDB. The MIL code generated by the Pathfinder compiler relies on some extensions added to the MonetDB back-end such as the staircase join algorithm (Grust, Keulen, & Teubner, 2003) which is designed as an efficient algorithm to evaluate XPath expressions. Although the approach of Pathfinder/MonetDB XQuery processor has been shown to be highly efficient and scalable, it is very tightly bound to the Monet DBMS and thus cannot be used with any other relational back end. Another disadvantage of using MonetDB is that it requires huge main memory sizes to store large XML documents. The limitation of this approach was the main motivation behind our purely relational approach for implementing XQuery processor described in this article.

In this article, we describe the design and implementation of an efficient and scalable purely relational XQuery processor which translates expressions of the XQuery language into their equivalent SQL evaluation scripts. The proposed XQuery processor is enhanced with an accurate algebraic-based cost model (Sakr, 2007) which facilitates the processor's ability to generate enhanced cardinality aware SQL translation scripts. Figure 1 illustrates the different alternative back-ends for the Pathfinder XQuery compiler. In particular, the main contribution of the work of this article is that it describes the design and implementation of an efficient and scalable purely relational XQuery processor. The proposed relational XQuery processor stores source XML documents in a relational repository using a tree aware relational encoding scheme and translates the XQuery expressions into SQL evaluation

Figure 1. Alternative back-ends for the Pathfinder XQuery compiler

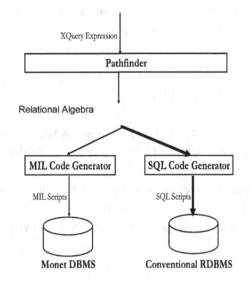

scripts. The main features of the proposed XQuery processor are:

- It supports an almost complete dialect of the XQuery language.
- It can reside on any relational database system and exploits its well known matured query optimization techniques as well as its efficient and scalable query processing techniques.
- It can target any RDBMS which supports the standard SQL:1999 language interface with no need for the relational database back-end to support the SQL/XML standard or to provide an XML column type of any kind.
- The relational database kernel remains untainted as there is no need for additional query processing operators or special structural join algorithms to be injected.
- It exhibits good performance characteristics when run against high-volume XML data as well as complex XQuery expressions.

The rest of this article is organized as follows. In Section 2, we give an overview of the XPath accelerator relational encoding scheme for the XML documents as the basis of our proposed XQuery processor. In Section 3, we give an overview of the loop-lifting compilation technique which translates XQuery expressions into their equivalent intermediate relational algebraic plans. Section 4 describes the design and the implementation of the cardinality-aware and purely relational XQuery engine which translates the intermediate Pathfinder algebraic plans into their equivalent SQL evaluation scripts that can be efficiently executed over any conventional RDBMS. In Section 5, we present a performance study of the Pathfinder as a purely relational XQuery engine. Section 6 reviews the related work before we conclude in Section 7.

XML Relational Encoding

Having an appropriate XML storage scheme is a crucial part for any relational implementation of an XQuery processor. Several research efforts have proposed different relational storage schemes for storing XML documents (O'Neil et al., 2004), (Li & Moon, 2001), (Amagasa, Yoshikawa, & Uemura, 2003), (Florescu & Kossmann, 1999). In (Yoshikawa, Amagasa, Shimura, & Uemura, 2001), Yoshikawa has classified the different XML relational storage schemes into two main classes:

1. **Structure-mapping storage:** a class of storage schemes which defines a relational schema that reflects the semantics of the XML document and makes use of its DTD or XML Schema information.
2. **Model-mapping storage:** a class of storage schemes which define a fixed relational schema that works for storing XML documents independent of the presence or absence of the XML document schema information.

One of the main focuses of this article is to present a scalable and efficient implementation of a purely relational XQuery processor. Therefore, having a proper relational storage for the XML documents is a crucial first step. The work detailed in this article is a part of the Pathfinder project which makes use of the XPath Accelerator designed by Torsten Grust (Grust, 2002) as a basis of its own encoding scheme.

XPath Accelerator

XPath Accelerator is an efficient, scalable and Model-mapping storage scheme which maps the information of the XML node hierarchy to a relational table and preserves the structural relationship between the XML nodes. Given an XML tree T, its representation on persistent relational storage using (pre/size/level) encoding is obtained by a single sequential document read using a normal SAX parser. During the parsing process, the pre-order rank *pre(v)* is assigned for each node v. In a preorder traversal of a tree, each node is visited and assigned its pre-order rank before its children. Hence, the preorder traversal of a document's tree representation is equivalent to its textual representation order, the document parser can assign the pre-order rank for each node when its *startElement* event is triggered. In addition to the pre-order rank *pre(v)*, each node descriptor also needs to include the following components:

- *Size(v):* is the number of nodes in the sub-tree bellow the node v.
- *Level(v):* represents the number of inter-mediate levels between the root node and a node v. This component is mainly used to distinguish between the children and de-scendant nodes for a node v.
- *Parent(v):* stores the pre-order rank for each node's parent.
- *Kind(v):* stores the kind of the encoded document node. An encoded document node kind can be document, element, at-tribute, text, name space, or processing in-struction node.
- *Name(v):* stores the tag name for the ele-ment nodes.

- *Value(v):* stores the atomic values for nodes with the kind of *text* or *attribute* and stores null for the nodes of the other types.
- *Fragment(v):* a unique document number is assigned for all nodes related to the same XML document or fragment. The main us-age of this component is to distinguish be-tween the nodes from multiple documents or fragments.

The *(pre/size/level)* encoding naturally maps the encoded space of the XML node descriptors into a tabular relational representation. Figure 2 (c) represents an example of the relational rep-resentation of an XML document using the *(pre/size/level)* encoding. The *(pre/size/level)* encoding has a main important advantage as the element sub-tree copying necessary for representing the element construction expression is very easy and straightforward as we will show in Section 3.1.

XPath-to-SQL Translation

Based on the XPath Accelerator storage scheme, the evaluation conditions of the 12 XPath axes could be defined as depicted in Table 1.

Figure 2. Pre/Size/Level encoding

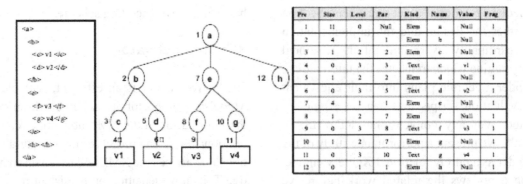

Pre	Size	Level	Par	Kind	Name	Value	Frag
1	11	0	Null	Elem	a	Null	1
2	4	1	1	Elem	b	Null	1
3	1	2	2	Elem	c	Null	1
4	0	3	3	Text	c	v1	1
5	1	2	2	Elem	d	Null	1
6	0	3	5	Text	d	v2	1
7	4	1	1	Elem	e	Null	1
8	1	2	7	Elem	f	Null	1
9	0	3	8	Text	f	v3	1
10	1	2	7	Elem	g	Null	1
11	0	3	10	Text	g	v4	1
12	0	1	1	Elem	h	Null	1

(a) Sample XML Document.

(b) The tree representation of the XML Document annotated with the pre-order rank for each document node.

(c) The relational representaion for the pre/size/level encoding for the XML document.

Sample interpretations of the XPath axes evaluation conditions represented in Table 1 are given as follows:

- Given two XML nodes x and y in an XML tree T, y is a child of x if and only if *(parent(y)= pre(x)) $\wedge$ (kind(y)!= att)*.
- Given two XML nodes x and y in an XML tree T, y is a descendant of x if and only if *(pre(y)>pre(x)) $\wedge$ (pre(y)$\leq$ pre(x)+size(x)) $\wedge$ (kind(y)!= att)*.
- Given two XML nodes x and y in an XML tree T, y is a following-sibling of x if and only if *(pre(y)>pre(x)) $\wedge$ (parent(y)= parent(x)) $\wedge$ (kind(y)!= att)*.

Translating the XPath expressions into SQL Queries is a straightforward process by using the available knowledge of the encoded XML document trees in the XPath Accelerator document table and the defined XPath axes conditions. An XPath expression with a series of location steps represented as S1/S2/.../Sn is converted into a series of pipelined compositional n region queries where the node sequence output by axis step Si is the context node sequence for the subsequent step S_{i+1}. Figure 3 shows an example for the evaluation of the XPath expression v/preceding/ancestor. In the shown example, the referenced document table represents the relational table representation of the (pre/size/level) encoding of the target XML document (an example of this document table was presented in Figure 2 (c)). The referenced context table represents the sequence of the input XML context nodes. The evaluation condition of the preceding axis is represented in line 4 and the evaluation conditions of the ancestor axis are represented in lines 5 and 6 of the SQL Query. Since the XPath semantics (Draper et al., 2006) requires that the result of an XPath expression to be duplicate-free and represented in the document order, we had to use the SQL constructs of DISTINCT and ORDERBY in the result SQL evaluation query.

XQuery Algebraic Compilation

Relational algebra has been a main component in relational database systems, and has played an important role in their success for gaining widespread usage. A corresponding XML algebra would have the same importance and substantial role for XML query processing. In our context, having an adequate algebraic compilation for

Table 1. XPath axes evaluation conditions

XPath Axis	Axis Conditions
self	pre(x)=pre(y)$\wedge$ kind(y) != att
attribute	parent(y)=pre(x)$\wedge$ kind(y) = att
parent	parent(x)=pre(y)$\wedge$ kind(y) != att
child	parent(y)=pre(x) $\wedge$ kind(y) != att
descendant	pre(y) > pre(x) $\wedge$ pre(y) $\leq$ pre(x)+size(x) $\wedge$ kind(y) != att
descendant-or-self	pre(y) $\geq$ pre(x)$\wedge$ pre(y) $\leq$ pre(x)+size(x) $\wedge$ kind(y) != att
ancestor	pre(y) < pre(x)$\wedge$ pre(x) $\leq$ pre(y)+size(y) $\wedge$ kind(y) != att
ancestor-or-self	pre(y) $\leq$ pre(x) $\wedge$ pre(x) $\leq$ pre(y)+size(y) $\wedge$ kind(y) != att
following	pre(y) > pre(x)+size(x) $\wedge$ kind(y) != att
following-sibling	pre(y) > pre(x) $\wedge$ parent(y)=parent(x)$\wedge$ kind(y)!=att
preceding	pre(y) + size(y) < pre(x) $\wedge$ kind(y) != att
preceding-sibling	pre(y) < pre(x)$\wedge$ parent(y) = parent(x) $\wedge$ kind(y) != att

Figure 3. An example for the SQL evaluation for an XPath expression based on the XPath accelerator encoding scheme

```
1    SELECT DISTINCT doc3.*
2    FROM context AS ctx, document AS doc1, document AS doc2, document AS doc3
3    WHERE ctx.pre=doc1.pre
4    AND doc2.pre + doc2.size < doc1.pre
5    AND doc3.pre < doc2.pre AND doc2.pre <= doc3.pre + doc3.size
6    AND doc3.kind <>'Att'
7    ORDER BY doc3.pre
```

XQuery expressions provides us with the solid infrastructure for predicating the cardinality of the main XQuery expressions and its sub-expressions in a very convenient and accurate way. Many proposals for an algebra for XML query processing have been introduced (Brantner, Helmer, Kanne, & Moerkotte, 2005), (Chen, Jagadish, Lakshmanan, & Paparizos, 2003), (Sartiani & Albano, 2002), (Jagadish, Lakshmanan, Srivastava, & Thompson, 2001), (Paparizos, Al-Khalifa, Jagadish, Niermann, & Wu, 2002), (H.Zhang & F.W.Tompa, 2003). According to (Re, Simeon, & Fernandez, 2006) existing algebras for XQuery fall into two classes:

Tuple-based algebra: this class of algebra tries to facilitate the use of relational optimization techniques as well as the whole relational query processing framework (theory, compilation, optimization, execution).

Tree-based algebra: this class of algebra provides more natural support for novel XML-specific optimizations and manipulates XML data modelled as forests of labelled ordered trees.

The Pathfinder project has a special module for compiling XQuery expressions into its own dialect of tuple-based algebra producing equivalent relational query plans. The Pathfinder algebra is quite primitive such that it can efficiently fit within the capabilities of SQL-based systems. Pathfinder compiles the XQuery core dialect listed in Table 2 into relational query plans using the set of algebraic operators listed in Figure 4.

PATHFINDER ALGEBRAIC OPERATORS

The Pathfinder algebraic operators are designed to receive one or more inputs and produce one or more outputs. These inputs and outputs are in the form of sets of tuples. Most of the operators perform quite simple and standard relational operations which allow the query optimizer to employ the usual relational algebraic optimization techniques such as the pushdown of the selection operator. In this section, we will first provide a detailed description for the operators and then in Section 4.2, we define their associated SQL translation templates. Figure 5 illustrates the behaviour for some of the Pathfinder algebraic operators.

Projection/Attribute Renaming: The project operator ($\pi_{a1:b1,\dots,an:bn}$) receives a relational table R and a list of projection attributes (a_1, a_2,..., a_n). The operator returns the tuples of the relation R with a schema filtered to the list of the projected attributes. An optional attribute renaming operation could be done during the projection operation by changing the attribute names of the schema from (a_1, a_2,..., a_n) to (b_1, b_2,..., b_n) according to the specification of each renaming pair(a_1: b_1). Due to the design of the Pathfinder compilation

Table 2. Pathfinder supported XQuery dialect

atomic literals	document order (e1 <<e2)
sequences(e1,e2)	node identity (e1 is e2)
variables	arithmetics (+,-,*,...)
let $v:=e1 return e2	comparisons (=,<,>,...)
for $v [at$p] in e1 return e2	Boolean connectives (and,or)
if (e1) then e2 else e3	user-defined functions
e1 order by e2,...,en	fn:doc(.), fn:root(.), fn:data(.)
unordered {e}	fn:id(.), fn:idref(.)
element {e1},{e2}	fn:distinct-values(.)
attribute {e1},{e2}	op:union(.), op:intersect(.),op:difference(.)
text {e}	fn:count(.), fn:sum(.), fn:max(.),...
XPath Location Steps	fn:position (.), fn:last(.)
typeswitch (e1) case[$v as]t return e2	

Figure 4. Pathfinder algebraic operators

$\pi_{a_1:b_1,...,a_n:b_n}$	Projection	$\#_a$	Unsorted Row Numbering
$@_{a:v}$	Attachment	$\varrho_{a:(o_1,...,o_n)/P}$	Sorted Row Numbering
σ_a	Selection	$\uplus$	Disjoint Union
$\backslash$	Difference	$Agg_{v:a/p}$	Aggregation, $Agg \in (count, max, min, ...)$
$\times$	Cartesian Product	$\textcircled{a}_{a:(b,c)}$	Arithmetic, $\circ \in (+, -, *, \backslash, mod, div)$
$\bowtie_{a=b}$	Equi-Join	$\boxed{\circ}_{a:(b,c)}$	Comparison, $\circ \in (<, \leq, =, !=, >, \geqslant)$
δ	Duplicate Elimination	$\sqcap_{Item:(a,n)}$	XPath Location Step Evaluator
$\neg_{nitem:item}$	Negation	$\Delta_{nvalue:item}$	Document Access
A **B**	Tables	$(\varepsilon/\tau)_{e_1,e_2}$	Element / Text Construction

rules, the project operator has a specific property that it does not need to perform any duplicates removal operation.

Attachment: The attachment operator ($@_{a:v}$) receives a relational table R and a list of attaching attributes ($a_1: v_1, a_2: v_2,..., a_n: v_n$). It appends one or more new attributes a_i to the tuples of the input relation R. The values for the new attributes are assigned the value v_i.

Selection: The selection operator (σ_a) receives a relational table R and a Boolean selection attribute a. It returns a new relation where the tuples of R which have the value of the attribute a equal to *false* are missing. The Boolean selection at-

tributes (a) are usually produced using the comparison operator ($\boxed{\circ}$).

Disjoint Union: The union operator ($\uplus$) is a common relational operator. It receives two input relations R and S. It ensures that the input relations are union compatible and returns one relation containing the tuples of the two input relations. In Pathfinder algebraic plans, the two input relations of the union operator are guaranteed to be always disjoint due to the design of the Pathfinder compilation rules.

Difference: The difference operator (\) receives two relations R and S and returns all tuples

Figure 5. Illustrating Examples for the behavior of some Pathfinder algebraic operators

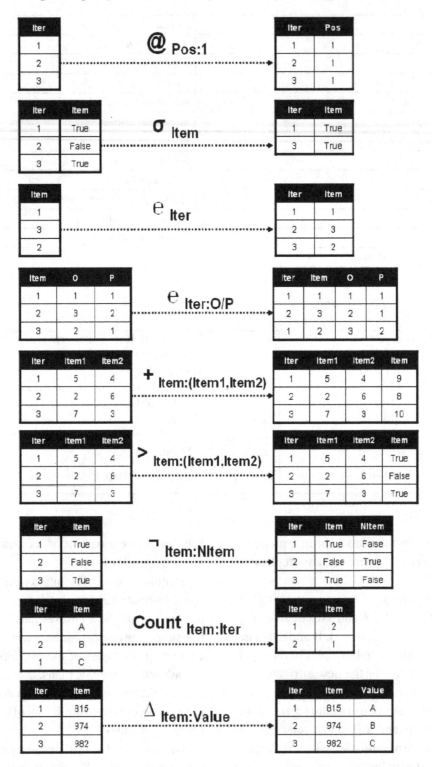

of the first input relation R that have no matching tuples in the second relation *S*.

Cartesian Product: The Cartesian product operator (×) receives two input relations *R* and *S*. It returns one relation which combines each tuple of the first relation R with all the tuples of the second relation *S*. The output relation has a schema which concatenates the schemes of the two input relations.

Equi-Join: The equi-Join operator ($\bowtie_{(a=b)}$) is a well-known standard relational operator. It receives two input relations *R* and *S* as well as a predicate *P* (In Pathfinder algebraic plans, the predicate *P* is always an equality predicate of the form $a = b$). It evaluates the predicate *P* over each pair of tuples $(t1, t2) \in (R \times S)$, returning only the pairs satisfying *P*. The primary usage of the Equi-Join operator in Pathfinder's algebraic plan is the representation of the iteration concept for the FLWOR expression as it will be shown in Section 3.2

Duplicate Elimination: The duplicate elimination operator (δ) is used to remove the duplicate tuples in the required places inside the relational plan. This operator is a specific operator that is unique to the Pathfinder algebra and thus there is no equivalent operator in the conventional relational algebra.

Unsorted Row Numbering: The unsorted row numbering operator (#*a*) and the sorted row numbering operator ($Q_{a:(o1,...,on)/p}$) are two of the most important Pathfinder's algebraic operators. Together, they are responsible of preserving the order concept defined by the XQuery/XPath specifications (Fernandez, Malhotra, Marsh, Nagy, & Walsh, 2006). The unsorted row numbering operator (#*a*) receives an input relation R and returns the same relation extended with a new consecutive numbering attribute (*a*) from 1 to *n* where *n* is the cardinality of the input relation *R*.

Sorted Row Numbering: The sorted row numbering operator ($Q_{a:(o1,...,on)/p}$) receives an input relation *R*, an ordering attribute list (*o1,..., on*) and an optional partitioning attribute *p*. It returns the

same relation extended with a new consecutive numbering attribute (*a*). The numbering attribute (*a*) respects the tuple sorting of relation R defined by the order specification (*o1,..., on*) and restarts the numbering from 1 for each partition defined by the optional partitioning attribute (*p*).

Arithmetic: The arithmetic operator ($\odot_{a:(b,c)}$) represents the standard arithmetic operations (+, −, *, \, mod, div). It receives a relational table *R* and a pair of argument attributes *(b, c)*. The output relation is the input relation extended with one more attribute (*a*) representing the result of applying the arithmetic operation (∘) over the two argument attributes *(b, c)*.

Comparison: The comparison operator ($\boxdot_{a:(b,c)}$) represents the standard comparison operations (<, ≤, =, !=, >, ≥). It receives a relational table *R* and a pair of comparison attributes *(b,c)*. The output relation is the input relation extended with one more attribute (*a*) that represents the result of applying the comparison operation (∘) over the two comparing attributes *(b, c)*.

Negation: The negation operator ($\neg_{a:b}$) receives a relational table R and a Boolean attribute(*b*). The output relation is the input relation extended with one more attribute (*a*) representing the negations of the Boolean values of the attribute (*b*).

Aggregation: The aggregation operator ($Agg_{v:a/p}$) represents the standard aggregation operations (Count, Sum, Min, Max, Average). The Pathfinder aggregate operator appears in Pathfinder algebraic plans in one of the following two possible versions:

1. The first version, receives a relation *R* and an aggregate attribute (*a*). It returns a single value which is computed by applying the aggregate function *Agg* on the values of the aggregate attribute (*a*) for the input tuples.

2. The second version, receives a relation *R*, an argument attribute *(a)* and an grouping attribute (*p*). In this version, the aggregate operator returns a binary relation (*p,a*) which

is computed by applying the aggregate function *Agg* on the values of the aggregate attribute a for the input tuples grouped by the values of the attribute *p*. Usually, the grouping attribute of an input relation *R* represents its iterating attribute *iter.*

Tables: The tables operator $\boxed{}$ is normally used in Pathfinder algebraic plan for the representation of literals. It receives no input, is represented as a relational table storing the values of the literals and is usually preceded with an attachment (@) operator.

Document Access: The document access operator ($\Delta_{nvalue:item}$) receives three inputs:

1. A context relation (*ctx*).
2. A node identification attribute (*item*).
3. An encoded XPath accelerator relation for the associated live nodes fragment (Γ) (usually represented by the encoded XPath accelerator document table or transient nodes for XML document fragments constructed at the runtime using the construction operators(ϵ/τ)).

The document access operator applies a join operation between the context relation and the live nodes fragment relation (ctx$\bowtie_{(item=pre)}\Gamma$)and returns the input relation *ctx* extended with one more node values attribute (*nvalue*). The values of the new attribute are computed by retrieving the (value) attribute from the relation representing the input live nodes fragment (Γ) for the tuples with the pre-order values contained in the node identification attribute (*item*) of the input relation (*ctx*).

XPath Location Step Evaluator: The XPath location step evaluator operator ($\boxed{}_{item:(\alpha,n)}$) is another very important and special Pathfinder algebraic operator. This operator is responsible for evaluating XPath expressions. In the general case, the operator is independent of the relational document encoding used for storing the

XML documents and the technique used for evaluating the XPath expressions. Hence, in our context, it is based on our use of the XPath accelerator encoding scheme and the mechanism of evaluating XPath expression described in Section 2.2. The XPath Evaluator operator ($\boxed{}$) receives three inputs:

1. A context relation (ctx) which stores the node identifiers of the input context nodes.
2. An encoded XPath accelerator relation for the associated live nodes fragment (Γ).
3. The evaluated XPath step (ctx/α:: n), where α represents the XPath location step's axis and n represents the location step's node test (n). The XPath Evaluator operator applies the evaluation conditions of the XPath step (α, n) over the input context nodes (ctx) using the information of the live nodes fragment (Γ) and returns the result as a sequence of tuples representing the node identifiers of the resulting nodes. The resulting nodes from applying the XPath Evaluator operator are: duplicate free, preserving the document order, and maintaining both of the iteration and fragment information of the input context nodes relation (ctx).

Element/Text Construction: The XQuery language provides the capability of creating transient nodes and document fragments during the runtime execution of the XQuery expressions. The element / text Construction operator (ϵ/τ(e1,e2)) is responsible for implementing such functionality in the Pathfinder algebra. The implementation of the element construction operator is a bit more complex and is thus not as straightforward as the rest of the operators. It receives three inputs:

1. An encoded XPath accelerator relation for the associated live nodes fragment (Γin) (Figure 6 (a)).

2. An element names relation (T) that stores the tag names of the newly constructed node (one tuple per iteration) (Figure 6 (b)).
3. A context relation (ctx) that stores the node identifiers of the input context nodes (Figure 6 (c)).

The Element Construction operator (ε) processes its input relations and returns two output relations as follows:

1. An output live nodes relation (Γout) (Figure 6 (d)). This relation extends the input live nodes relation (Γin)with the tuples representing the newly created transient nodes. The new tuples of the transient nodes are created as follows:
   - For each tuple in the element names relation (T), we insert a new tuple into the output live nodes relation (Γout) representing the root node of the new subtree.
   - For each tuple with node identifier in the context relation (ctx), we insert a new tuple into the output live nodes relation (Γout)and copy the tuples from the input live nodes relation(Γin) representing its associated subtree.
   - Each iteration in the element names relation (T) with no context nodes in the context relation (ctx) will be represented with only a single tuple for the root node with the size of 0 for an empty subtree.
   - The pre-order values of the new tuples (transient nodes) are generated in a consecutive manner starting from the maximum pre-order value of the input live nodes relation (Γin)+ 1.
   - Each group of a new root node and its associated copied subtree for the same iteration is represented as a new fragment.

2. An output context relation (Figure 6 (e)). This relation stores the pre-order values of the newly constructed transient root nodes and is used as an input context relation for the immediate parent operator in the relational plan.

Figure 6 shows an example describing the behavior of the element construction operator. In principal, the text construction operator ($\tau(e1,e2)$) is responsible of converting the string values resulting from the valuation of XQuery expression *e2* into text nodes with tag names specified by the XQuery expression e1. Hence, the behavior of the text construction is very similar to the element construction operator with the following two differences:

i. In the input context relation (*ctx*), the item column stores the strings evaluating the expression e2and which will be converted to text nodes instead of storing the node identifiers of the nodes to be constructed in the case of the element construction operator.

ii. For each tuple with string value in the context relation (*ctx*), we only insert a new tuple into the output live nodes relation (*Γout*) with no need for subtrees copying (in element construction we need).

Figure 7 shows an example describing the behavior of the text construction operator.

Compiling XQuery into Relational Algebra

Pathfinder compiles the XQuery core dialect listed in Table 2 into relational query plans using the algebraic operators described in Section 3.1. In this section, we give an overview of the Pathfinder loop-lifting technique, which is considered to be the heart of this compilation process. For a detailed and complete description of this technique and

Figure 6. An illustrating example for the behavior of the element construction operator

(a) Input live nodes fragment

Pre	Size	Par	Level	Kind	Name	Value	Frag
1	11	Null	0	Elem	a	Null	1
2	4	1	1	Elem	b	Null	1
3	1	2	2	Elem	c	Null	1
4	0	3	3	Text	c	v1	1
5	1	2	2	Elem	d	Null	1
6	0	5	3	Text	d	v2	1
7	4	1	1	Elem	e	Null	1
8	1	7	2	Elem	f	Null	1
9	0	8	3	Text	f	v3	1
10	1	7	2	Elem	g	Null	1
11	0	10	3	Text	g	v4	1
12	0	1	1	Elem	h	Null	1

(b) Elem names

Iter	Item
1	New1
2	New2
3	New3

(c) Input context nodes

Iter	Item
1	2
3	7

ε

(e) Output context nodes

Iter	Item
1	13
2	19
3	20

(d) Output live nodes fragment

Pre	Size	Par	Level	Kind	Name	Value	Frag
1	11	Null	0	Elem	a	Null	1
2	4	1	1	Elem	b	Null	1
3	1	2	2	Elem	c	Null	1
4	0	3	3	Text	c	v1	1
5	1	2	2	Elem	d	Null	1
6	0	5	3	Text	d	v2	1
7	4	1	1	Elem	e	Null	1
8	1	7	2	Elem	f	Null	1
9	0	8	3	Text	f	v3	1
10	1	7	2	Elem	g	Null	1
11	0	10	3	Text	g	v4	1
12	0	1	1	Elem	h	Null	1
13	5	Null	0	Elem	New1	Null	2
14	4	13	1	Elem	b	Null	2
15	1	14	2	Elem	c	Null	2
16	0	15	3	Text	c	v1	2
17	1	14	2	Elem	d	Null	2
18	0	17	3	Text	d	v2	2
19	0	Null	0	Elem	New2	Null	3
20	5	Null	0	Elem	New3	Null	4
21	4	20	1	Elem	e	Null	4
22	1	21	2	Elem	f	Null	4
23	0	22	3	Text	f	v3	4
24	1	21	2	Elem	g	Null	4
25	0	24	3	Text	g	v4	4

(f) Original tree.

g) Newly constructed tree fragments

its translation rules we refer to (Teubner, 2006), (Grust, Sakr, & Teubner, 2004), (Grust, 2005). In a nutshell, loop-lifting is the key technique used to compile XQuery iterations into efficient bulk style application of algebraic operators. The principal idea behind the compilation scheme is that every XQuery expression occurs in the scope of iteration. The iterations of each scope are en-

Figure 7. An illustrating example for the behavior of the text construction operator

(a) Input live nodes fragment

Pre	Size	Par	Level	Kind	Name	Value	Frag
1	11	Null	0	Elem	a	Null	1
2	4	1	1	Elem	b	Null	1
3	1	2	2	Elem	c	Null	1
4	0	3	3	Text	c	v1	1
5	1	2	2	Elem	d	Null	1
6	0	5	3	Text	d	v2	1
7	4	1	1	Elem	e	Null	1
8	1	7	2	Elem	f	Null	1
9	0	8	3	Text	f	v3	1
10	1	7	2	Elem	g	Null	1
11	0	10	3	Text	g	v4	1
12	0	1	1	Elem	h	Null	1

(b) Elem names

Iter	Item
1	New1
2	New2
3	New3

(c) Input context nodes

Iter	Item
1	John
3	Smith

(e) Output context nodes

Iter	Item
1	13
2	15
3	16

(d) Output live nodes fragment

Pre	Size	Par	Level	Kind	Name	Value	Frag
1	11	Null	0	Elem	a	Null	1
2	4	1	1	Elem	b	Null	1
3	1	2	2	Elem	c	Null	1
4	0	3	3	Text	c	v1	1
5	1	2	2	Elem	d	Null	1
6	0	5	3	Text	d	v2	1
7	4	1	1	Elem	e	Null	1
8	1	7	2	Elem	f	Null	1
9	0	8	3	Text	f	v3	1
10	1	7	2	Elem	g	Null	1
11	0	10	3	Text	g	v4	1
12	0	1	1	Elem	h	Null	1
13	5	Null	0	Elem	New1	Null	2
14	4	13	0	Elem	New1	John	2
15	0	Null	0	Elem	New2	Null	3
16	5	Null	0	Elem	New3	Null	4
17	4	20	1	Elem	New3	Smith	4

(f) Original tree.

g) Newly constructed tree fragments

coded by a column iter in the associated relational representation. In order to clarify the loop-lifting idea, we will show some examples of Pathfinder loop-lifted translations for some XQuery expressions into their associated Pathfinder algebraic relational representation.

Sequences The XQuery language is designed to operate over ordered, finite sequences of items as its principal data type. The evaluation of any XQuery expression yields an ordered sequence of $n \geq 0$ items. These items can be either atomic values (integers, strings,..., etc) or XML tree nodes. An XQuery item sequence $(x_1,..., x_n)$ is encoded with the following relational table:

pos	item
1	x_1
⋮	⋮
n	x_n

iter	pos	item
1	1	x_1
2	1	x_2
⋮	⋮	⋮
n	1	x_n

The column *pos* is used to preserve the order information between the items inside the target sequence. The *item* column is a polymorphic column. In the case of atomic items, it stores the values of the encoded atomic items (1,"A",...) and in the other case of XML tree nodes, it stores the pre-order ranks of the encoded nodes. The RDBMS supports the representation of such polymorphic columns using the *Variant* data type. The empty sequence () is encoded with an empty table with the same schema (*pos, item*).

FLWOR Expressions. The FLWOR expression is one of the main features provided by the XQuery language. It is used for representing iterations and for the binding of variables to intermediate results. It is also used for computing joins between two or more sequences and for restructuring data. A loop of *n* iterations is represented by a relation **loop** with a single column *iter* of *n* values (1,2,...,n).

pos
1
⋮
n

Based on the relational representation for the sequence (x_1,..., x_n) we presented in the previous section, we can now represent the compilation of variables bound in the iterations of FLWOR expression using the following XQuery for-loop example:

for $v in $(x_1,...,x_n)$ return *e*.

This example expression binds each x_i item to variable $v and evaluates the loop body *e* for each iteration. The relational encoding of the variable $v has the following form:

This translation encodes all bindings of $v in a single relation. In general, each tuple of the encoding relation *(i, p, x)* indicates that for the *i*-th iteration, the item at position *p* stores the value *x*.

Path Steps. The compilation of path steps is represented in Pathfinder algebraic plans using the XPath evaluator operator (⃞). It takes a context relation (*iter, item*) as input, where the *item* column stores the *node identifiers* of the input context nodes. It uses the relation of the current live nodes *Γ(pre, size, level, kind, name, value, frag)* to evaluate the path step (*α, n*)and returns a new relation with the same schema (*iter, item*). In the output relation, the *item* column stores the node identifiers of the resulting nodes. Figure 8 illustrates an example for the loop-lifted compilation of the path step where Figure 8(a) represents the input context nodes, Figure 8(b) represents the sample source XML document and Figure 8(c) represents the output context nodes from applying the path step *child::c* over input context nodes and the sample source XML document.

Arithmetic and Comparison Expressions. Given the relational representation *R1 (iter1, item1)* and *R2 (iter2, item2)* of two XQuery expression e_1 and e_2, the design of the loop-lifting compilation of the arithmetic and comparison expressions requires that the schema of the relational representation (R_i)of each argument expression (e_i) must have a single node identifier column (*item_i*) for each iteration (*iter_i*) with no order preserving column (*pos*). The arithmetic expression e1⊙e2 is evaluated by joining *R1* and *R2* over their iterations attribute *iter*, for each tuple of the result we apply the arithmetic operator (∘) over the two arguments columns *item1* and *item2*, and store the result in a new column res. The al-

Figure 8. An illustrating example for the loop-lifted compilation of the path steps

a) Input context nodes.　　b) XML document.　　c) Output context nodes.

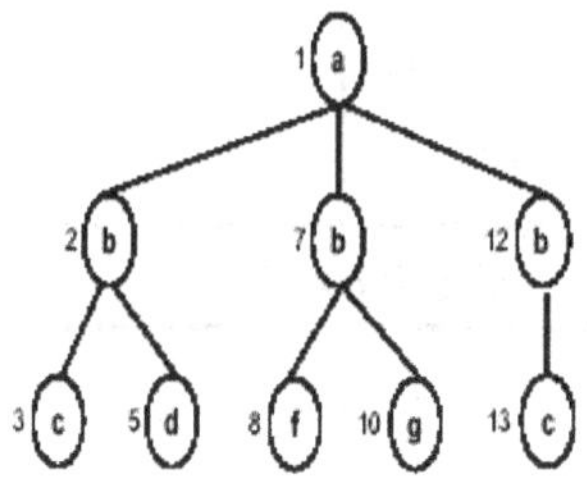

gebraic representation of the arithmetic expression (e1⊙e2) is defined as follows:

$$e1 \circ e2 \Rightarrow \pi_{iter1:iter,res}(\odot_{res:(item1,item2)}(R1 \bowtie_{(iter1=iter2)} R2))$$

where *R1* and *R2* are consequentially representing the relational representation of the two expressions *e1* and *e2*.

Similarly, the comparison expression e1 ⊡ e2 is evaluated by joining *R1* and *R2* over their iterations attribute *iter*, for each tuple of the result we apply the comparison operator (∘) over the two argument attributes *item1* and *item2*, and store the result in a new attribute *res*. The comparison operators are normally followed by a selection operator to filter the tuples satisfying the comparison condition. The algebraic representation of the comparison expression (e1 ⊡ e2) is defined as follows:

$$e1 \circ e2 \Rightarrow \sigma_{res}(\pi_{iter1:iter,res}(\boxed{\odot}_{res:(item1,item2)}(R1 \bowtie_{(iter1=iter2)} R2)))$$

CARDINALITY AWARE XQUERY-TO-SQL TRANSLATION

XQuery-to-SQL Framework

Figure 9 represents the framework of Pathfinder as a relational XQuery engine. The query engine translates its input of XQuery expressions into SQL evaluation scripts through the following steps:

1. The source XML documents that are processed by the engine have to be mapped (shredded) into the XPath Accelerator relational scheme using the (*pre/size/level*) encoding introduced in Section 2.1.

2. Based on the list of Pathfinder algebraic operator and the *loop-lifting* compilation technique introduced in Section 3, the Pathfinder algebraic translation module translates the input XQuery expression into its equivalent relational algebraic plan.

3. The SQL generator module receives the algebraic plans produced in step two as well as the SQL translation templates (Section 4.2) to generate the equivalent SQL script for evaluating the results of the input XQuery expression.

4. The SQL script generated in step three is using a standard SQL: 1999 code which can be executed on any conventional RDBMS such as IBM DB2, Microsoft SQL server and Oracle.

5. An XML serialization module receives the relational tuples resulting from the evaluation process of the SQL script using the conventional RDBMS and serializes them into an equivalent output of the XML model. We refer to (Grust, Keulen, & Teubner, 2004) for a detailed description of this serialization algorithm.

Figure 9. The framework of Pathfinder relational XQuery engine

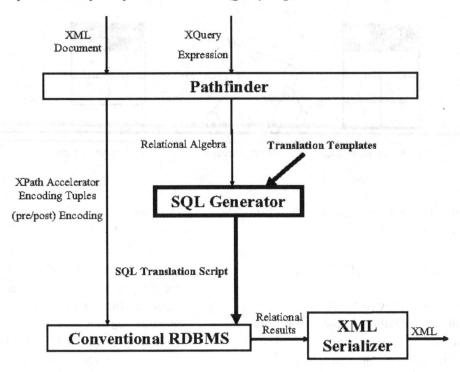

Translation Templates

For each of the Pathfinder algebraic operators described in Section 3.1, we define a corresponding SQL translation template. During the SQL translations, the parameters for the algebraic operator are properly transformed from one operator to another according to the DAG plan. Figures 10 and 11 illustrate the inference rules for translating Pathfinder algebraic operators into SQL code. Remarks about the inference rules of SQL translation is given as follows:

A sample interpretation of the inference rule Trans-1 representing the translation of Pathfinder algebraic project operator(π) is: Given the information that the relational object (*Table-View*) q represents the SQL evaluation of the expression e, the translation of the Pathfinder algebraic project operator ($\pi_{a1,a2:b2,...,an}(e)$) is defined using the following SQL code:

```
CREATE VIEW op_i
AS SELECT a_1, a_2 AS b_2,..., a_n
FROM q;
```

where i represents the operator number of the translated project operator in the associated algebraic plan.

In the inference rule Trans-5 for translating the difference operator (\), the notation $q1.Schema:$ *(f1, f2)* means that the schema of the relational object q consists of the columns *(f1, f2)*.

In the inference rule Trans-14 for translating the table operator $\overset{(c}{\underset{v}{\square}}.)$, the referenced relational table *OneRowTable* represents a standard data dictionary table for any RDBMS that consists exactly of one column and one record.

In the inference rule Trans-18 for translating the XPath location step evaluator operator (978-1-60960-521-6.ch011.f42$_{item:(\alpha,n)}$(e)), the referenced function *XPathEvaluationConditions(d2,α,n)*

Figure 10. Inference rules of SQL translation (1)

$$\frac{SQL(e) : q}{\left(\begin{array}{l} SQL(\pi_{a_1, a_2:b_2, \ldots, a_n}(e)) \Rightarrow \\ \text{CREATE VIEW op}i \text{ AS} \\ \text{SELECT } a_1, a_2 \text{ AS } b_2, \ldots, a_n \\ \text{FROM } q; \end{array}\right)} \text{(TRANS-1)} \qquad \frac{SQL(e) : q}{\left(\begin{array}{l} SQL(@_{a:v}(e)) \Rightarrow \\ \text{CREATE VIEW op}i \text{ AS} \\ \text{SELECT } v \text{ AS } a, q.* \\ \text{FROM } q; \end{array}\right)} \text{(TRANS-2)}$$

$$\frac{SQL(e) : q}{\left(\begin{array}{l} SQL(\sigma_a(e)) \Rightarrow \\ \text{CREATE VIEW op}i \text{ AS} \\ \text{SELECT *} \\ \text{FROM } q \\ \text{WHERE } a = \text{'true'}; \end{array}\right)} \text{(TRANS-3)} \qquad \frac{SQL(e_1) : q_1 \qquad SQL(e_2) : q_2}{\left(\begin{array}{l} SQL(e_1 \cup e_2) \Rightarrow \\ \text{CREATE VIEW op}i \text{ AS} \\ \text{SELECT *} \\ \text{FROM } q_1 \\ \text{UNION ALL} \\ \text{SELECT *} \\ \text{FROM } q_2; \end{array}\right)} \text{(TRANS-4)}$$

$$\frac{SQL(e_1) : q_1 \qquad SQL(e_2) : q_2 \qquad q1.Schema : (f1, f2) \qquad q2.Schema = q1.Schema}{\left(\begin{array}{l} SQL(e_1 \setminus e_2) \Rightarrow \\ \text{CREATE VIEW op}i \text{ AS} \\ \text{SELECT *} \\ \text{FROM } q_1 \\ \text{EXCEPT} \\ \text{SELECT f1,f2} \\ \text{FROM } q_2; \end{array}\right)} \text{(TRANS-5)}$$

$$\frac{SQL(e_1) : q_1 \qquad SQL(e_2) : q_2}{\left(\begin{array}{l} SQL(e_1 \times e_2) \Rightarrow \\ \text{CREATE VIEW op}i \text{ AS} \\ \text{SELECT *} \\ \text{FROM } q_1, q_2; \end{array}\right)} \text{(TRANS-6)} \qquad \frac{SQL(e_1) : q_1 \qquad SQL(e_2) : q_2}{\left(\begin{array}{l} SQL(e_1 \bowtie_{a=b} e_2) \Rightarrow \\ \text{CREATE VIEW op}i \text{ AS} \\ \text{SELECT *} \\ \text{FROM } q_1, q_2 \\ \text{WHERE } q_1.a = q_2.b; \end{array}\right)} \text{(TRANS-7)}$$

$$\frac{SQL(e) : q}{\left(\begin{array}{l} SQL(\delta(e)) \Rightarrow \\ \text{CREATE VIEW op}i \text{ AS} \\ \text{SELECT DISTINCT *} \\ \text{FROM } q; \end{array}\right)} \text{(TRANS-8)} \qquad \frac{SQL(e) : q}{\left(\begin{array}{l} SQL(\#_a(e)) \Rightarrow \\ \text{CREATE VIEW op}i \text{ AS} \\ \text{SELECT ROW\_NUMBER() OVER () AS } a, q.* \\ \text{FROM } q; \end{array}\right)} \text{(TRANS-9)}$$

$$\frac{SQL(e) : q}{\left(\begin{array}{l} SQL(\varrho_{a:(o_1, \ldots, o_n/p)}(e)) \Rightarrow \\ \text{CREATE VIEW op}i \text{ AS} \\ \text{SELECT ROW\_NUMBER() OVER (PARTITION BY p ORDER BY } o_1, .., o_n) \text{ AS } a, q.* \\ \text{FROM } q; \end{array}\right)} \text{(TRANS-10)}$$

$$\frac{SQL(e) : q \qquad \circ \in (+, -, *, \setminus, mod, div)}{\left(\begin{array}{l} SQL(\circledcirc_{a:(b,c)}(e)) \Rightarrow \\ \text{CREATE VIEW op}i \text{ AS} \\ \text{SELECT } q.*, q.b \circ q.c \text{ AS } a \\ \text{FROM } q; \end{array}\right)} \text{(TRANS-11)} \qquad \frac{SQL(e) : q \qquad \theta \in (<, \leq, =, ! =, >, \geqslant)}{\left(\begin{array}{l} SQL(\boxtimes_{a:(b,c)}(e)) \Rightarrow \\ \text{CREATE VIEW op}i \text{ AS} \\ \text{SELECT } q.*, \text{'True' AS } a \\ \text{FROM } q \\ \text{WHERE } b \theta c \\ \text{UNION ALL} \\ \text{SELECT } q.*, \text{'False' AS } a \\ \text{FROM } q \\ \text{WHERE NOT}(b \theta c); \end{array}\right)} \text{(TRANS-12)}$$

Figure 11. Inference rules of SQL translation (2)

$$\frac{SQL(e):q}{\left(\begin{array}{l} SQL(\neg_{a:b}(e)) \Rightarrow \\ \text{CREATE VIEW op}i\text{ AS} \\ \text{SELECT } q.*, \text{ 'True' AS a} \\ \text{FROM } q \\ \text{WHERE b = 'False'} \\ \text{UNION ALL} \\ \text{SELECT } q.*, \text{ 'False' AS a} \\ \text{FROM } q \\ \text{WHERE b = 'True';} \end{array}\right)} \text{(TRANS-13)}$$

$$\frac{}{\left(\begin{array}{l} SQL\!\left(\begin{smallmatrix}c\\v\end{smallmatrix}\right) \Rightarrow \\ \text{CREATE VIEW op}i\text{ AS} \\ \text{SELECT v AS c} \\ \text{FROM OneRowTable;} \end{array}\right)} \text{(TRANS-14)}$$

$$\frac{SQL(e):q \qquad Agg \in (count, max, min, sum, avg)}{\left(\begin{array}{l} SQL(Agg_{v:a}(e)) \Rightarrow \\ \text{CREATE VIEW op}i\text{ AS} \\ \text{SELECT Agg(a) AS v} \\ \text{FROM } q; \end{array}\right)} \text{(TRANS-15)}$$

$$\frac{SQL(e):q \qquad Agg \in (count, max, min, sum, avg)}{\left(\begin{array}{l} SQL(Agg_{v:a/p}(e)) \Rightarrow \\ \text{CREATE VIEW op}i\text{ AS} \\ \text{SELECT p, Agg(a) AS v} \\ \text{FROM } q \\ \text{GROUP BY p;} \end{array}\right)} \text{(TRANS-16)}$$

$$\frac{\begin{array}{c} SQL(e):q \qquad SQL(\Gamma): OpLiveNodes \\ OpLiveNodes.Schema : (pre, size, parent, kind, level, name, value, frag) \end{array}}{\left(\begin{array}{l} SQL(\Delta_{v:i}(e)) \Rightarrow \\ \text{CREATE VIEW op}i\text{ AS} \\ \text{SELECT } q.*, \text{ OpLiveNodes.value AS v} \\ \text{FROM } q \\ \text{WHERE } q.i = \text{OpLiveNodes.pre;} \end{array}\right)} \text{(TRANS-17)}$$

$$\frac{\begin{array}{c} SQL(e):q \qquad SQL(\Gamma): OpLiveNodes \\ OpLiveNodes.Schema : (pre, size, parent, kind, level, name, value, frag) \end{array}}{\left(\begin{array}{l} SQL(\exists_{item:(\alpha,n)}(e)) \Rightarrow \\ \text{CREATE VIEW op}i\text{ AS} \\ \text{SELECT DISTINCT } q.\text{iter, } d2.\text{pre AS item} \\ \text{FROM } q, \text{ OpLiveNodes AS } d1, \text{ OpLiveNodes AS } d2 \\ \text{WHERE } q.\text{item} = d1.\text{pre} \\ \text{AND XPathEvaluationConditions}(d2,\alpha,n) \\ \text{ORDER BY } d2.\text{pre;} \end{array}\right)} \text{(TRANS-18)}$$

represents the evaluation conditions of the different XPath location steps which was described earlier in Section 2.2.

Due to the complexity of the element/Text construction operators (ε/τ), we do not use the inference rule notation for representing its translation. A detailed explanation of the translation steps of these operators will be presented as follows:

Element Construction Translation

Input Parameters:

1. The live nodes fragment: *OpLiveNodes*.

2. The relation of the element names: *OpElementNames*.

3. The input context relation: *OpContext*.

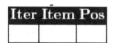

Step 1: Creating the output live nodes fragments (see Algorithm 1).

i.   The lines 2 and 3 generate the new pre-order ranks for the newly constructed nodes.
ii. The line 7 generates the new identifier for the newly created transient XML document fragments.
iii. The lines from 8 to 17 create the new root nodes for the constructed sub-tree (one root node per iteration).
iv. The lines from 21 to 27 copies the required sub-trees from the input live node fragment.

v.   The lines 28 and 29 specify the maximum pre-order rank and maximum fragment identifier of the input live node fragment. The (maximum pre-order rank + 1) is used as the starting pre-order rank in step (i) while the (maximum fragment identifier + 1) is used as the starting fragment number in step (ii).

Step 2: Creating the output context nodes (see Algorithm 2).

The SQL script for creating the output context nodes is similar to the SQL script for creating the output live nodes fragment with minimal changes. It deals only with constructing the pre-order ranks of the newly constructed *root* nodes as a subset from the information maintained by the step of creating the output live nodes fragments.

i.   The lines 2 and 3 generate the new pre-order ranks for the newly constructed nodes.
ii. The lines from 4 to 9 create the new *root* nodes for the constructed sub-tree (one root node per iteration).
iii. The lines from 13 to 17 copy the required sub-trees from the input live node fragment.
iv. Line 18 specifies the maximum pre-order rank of the input live node fragment. The (maximum pre-order rank + 1) is used as the starting pre-order rank for generation step (i).
v.   Line 19 filters the tuples to be stored in the output context relation. The stored tuples are only the tuples representing the newly constructed *root* nodes.

Figure 6 illustrated an example describing the behavior of the element construction operator.

Text Construction Translation As we discussed in Section 3.1, the behavior of the text construction operator is very similar to the behavior of the element construction operator with minimal changes. The input parameters of the text construction operator are the same as the input parameters of the element construction operator

Algorithm 1.

```
1     CREATE VIEW OpOutputLiveNodes AS
2     SELECT MaxPre.pre +
3           ROW_NUMBER() OVER (ORDER BY iter,pos,
4                                 ElementConstruction.pre) AS pre,
5         ElementConstruction.size, ElementConstruction.level,
6         ElementConstruction.kind, ElementConstruction.name,
7         ElementConstruction.value,
8         MaxPre.frag + DENSE_RANK() OVER (ORDER BY iter) AS frag
9     FROM (SELECT  OPElementNames.iter, 0 AS pos, -2 AS pre,
10               COALESCE(SUM(size + 1), 0) AS size,
11               0 AS level, 'Elem' AS kind,
12               OpElementNames.item AS name,
13               NULL AS value
14          FROM OpContext INNER JOIN OpLiveNodes
15              ON OpContext.item = OpLiveNodes.pre
16          RIGHT OUTER JOIN OpElementNames
17              ON OpElementNames.iter = OpContext.iter
18     GROUP BY OpElementNames.iter,OpElementNames.item
19
20     UNION ALL
21
22     SELECT OpContext.iter, OpContext.pos,
23           d2.pre AS pre, d2.size, d2.level - d1.level + 1 AS level,
24           d2.kind, d2.name, d2.value AS value
25     FROM OpContext, OpLiveNodes AS d1, OpLiveNodes AS d2
26     WHERE d1.pre = OpContext.item
27         AND d2.pre >= d1.pre
28         AND d2.pre <= d1.pre + d1.size)  AS ElementConstruction,
29     (SELECT MAX(pre) AS pre,Max(frag) AS frag
30     FROM OpLiveNodes ) AS MaxPre;
```

with only one difference. In the element construction operator, the *item* column of the input context relation *OpContext* stores the *node identifiers* of the newly constructed nodes while in the case of the text construction operator, this *item* column stores the strings of the newly constructed text nodes. The SQL translation template of the text construction operator is defined in Box 1.

As we discussed in Section 3.1, the element construction operator require sub-trees copying for the input context nodes from the input live node fragments relation *OpLiveNodes* while the text construction operator does not involve any

sub-tree copying for the newly constructed text nodes. Figure 7 illustrated an example describing the behavior of the text construction operator.

Translation Approaches

The SQL code generator uses three different approaches for generating the evaluation SQL scripts (Grust, Mayr, Rittinger, Sakr, & Teubner, 2007):

1. **View-Based Approach:** In this approach, each operator of the associated relational algebraic plan is compiled into an SQL:1999

Algorithm 2.

```
1    CREATE VIEW OpOutputContext AS
2    SELECT ElementConstruction.Iter,
3          MaxPre.pre + ROW_NUMBER() OVER (ORDER BY iter,pos,
4                                          ElementConstruction.pre) AS Item
5    FROM (SELECT  OPElementNames.iter, 0 AS pos, -2 AS pre
6          FROM OpContext INNER JOIN OpLiveNodes
7                ON OpContext.item = OpLiveNodes.pre
8          RIGHT OUTER JOIN OpElementNames
9                ON OpElementNames.iter = OpContext.iter
10   GROUP BY OpElementNames.iter
11
12   UNION ALL
13
14   SELECT OpContext.iter, OpContext.pos, d2.pre AS pre
15   FROM OpContext, OpLiveNodes AS d1, OpLiveNodes AS d2
16   WHERE d1.pre = OpContext.item
17         AND d2.pre >= d1.pre
18         AND d2.pre <= d1.pre + d1.size)  AS ElementConstruction,
19   (SELECT MAX(pre) AS pre FROM OpLiveNodes ) AS MaxPre
20   WHERE ElementConstruction.Level = 0;
```

view definition using the SQL translation templates defined in the previous Subsection 4.2. The view definition that represents the SQL translation of an algebraic operator is represented in the following form:

```
Create View OP(i) AS...;
```

where *i* represents the operator number in the associated algebraic plan. The generated SQL scripts using any of the three different approaches always end up with an additional single query to retrieve the results of the evaluation script. This additional evaluation step is represented as follows:

```
SELECT * FROM OP1;
```

where OP1 is a relational object *(View-Table)* which stores the result of the final *(root)* operator of the algebraic plan. The structure of the general form of the generated *view-based* translation scripts can be illustrated as follows:

```
CREATE VIEW OP(n) AS…;
CREATE VIEW OP(n-1) AS…;
…
…
CREATE VIEW OP1 AS …;
SELECT * From OP1;
```

where n represents the number of algebraic operators in the associated algebraic plan. Although the performance comparisons between the three different approaches (Section 5.1) shows that the *view-based* translation scripts usually performs the best for most of the XMark queries, this approach suffers from two disadvantages. These disadvantages are:

a.   The resulting query plans for the final query statement:

```
SELECT * FROM OP1;
```

for some scripts are more complex and nested such that the query optimizer of some conventional

Box 1.

```
Step 1: Creating the output live nodes fragments.
CREATE VIEW OpOutputLiveNodes AS
Select MaxPre.pre +
                ROW_NUMBER() OVER (ORDER BY iter,pos,pre) AS pre,
        TextConstruction.size, TextConstruction.level,
        TextConstruction.kind, TextConstruction.name,
        TextConstruction.value,
        MaxPre.frag + DENSE_RANK() Over (ORDER BY iter) AS frag
From (SELECT OPElementNames.iter, 0 AS pos, 0 AS pre,
                        1 AS size, 0 AS level, 'Elem' AS kind,
                        OpElementNames.item AS name, null AS value
                FROM OpContext
                RIGHT OUTER JOIN OpElementNames
                ON OpElementNames.iter = OpContext.iter
UNION ALL
SELECT OpContext.iter, OpContext.pos,
                1 AS pre, 0 AS size, 1 AS level, 'Text' as kind,
                OpElementNames.item as name, OpContext.item AS value
FROM OpContext, OpElementNames
WHERE OpContext.iter = OpElementNames.iter) AS TextConstruction,
(SELECT MAX(pre) AS pre,Max(frag) AS frag FROM OpLiveNodes) AS MaxPre;
Step 2: Creating the output context nodes.
CREATE VIEW OpOutputContext AS
SELECT Text Construciton.Iter,
        MaxPre.pre + ROW_NUMBER() OVER (ORDER BY iter,pos,pre) AS Item
FROM (SELECT OPElementNames.iter, 0 AS pos, 0 AS pre
        FROM OpContext
        RIGHT OUTER JOIN OpElementNames
        ON OpElementNames.iter = OpContext.iter
UNION ALL
SELECT OpContext.iter, OpContext.pos, 1 AS pre
FROM OpContext) AS TextConstruction,
(SELECT MAX(pre) AS pre FROM OpLiveNodes) AS MaxPre
WHERE TextConstruction.Level = 0;
```

RDBMS are unable to process them. In this case, the SQL code generator must break the nesting of the view definitions by materializing the results of an intermediate relation using a temporary table object. For example, by running the *view-based* SQL translation script for the XMark query Q8 using Microsoft SQL Server 2005, the system gives the message that "itisnotpossibletoexecutetherequiredstatementbecausethelevelofnestingistoodeep".

Box 2.

```
For $x in //person, $yin//department return
<ParentItem>
<ChildItem1>{$x/@id}</ChildItem1>
<ChildItem2>{$y/@id}</ChildItem2>
</ParentItem>
```

Box 3.

```
CREATE TABLE OP(i)....;
INSERT INTO TABLE OP(i)
...
[View Definition Of The View-Based Translation]
...;
```

b. The XQuery language provides the facility of constructing *nested (hierarchical)* element structures as a result of an XQuery expression. An example of using this facility is the expression in Box 2.

The process of evaluating the generated SQL scripts for such expressions using the *view-based* approach is relatively inefficient. The main reason behind this inefficiency is that the resulting transient nodes created during the runtime evaluation of the first element construction step has no index information. This constraint of the absence of the index information makes the evaluation of the second element construction step very expensive and inefficient especially if the size of the intermediate fragments is big.

2. **Table-Based Approach:** In this approach, each operator of the associated relational algebraic plan is compiled into a temporary relational table object using the same predefined SQL translation templates with minimal modifications. In general, the *CREATE VIEW* statement of each translation template is replaced with a *CREATE TABLE* statement. The content of each temporary table is specified using the corresponding *view definition* of each operator. The general form of the Table-Based version of the SQL translation template can be illustrated in Box 3.

where i represents the operator number in the associated algebraic plan. For the sake of addressing the performance issues, the table-based translation needs to instantiate some CREATE *INDEX* statements for the intermediate created temporary table. These *CREATE INDEX* statements are added to the table-based version of the translation templates for some of the algebraic operators such as the join operator ($\bowtie$), document access operator (Δ) and element construction operator (ε). For example, in the table-based translation template of the join operator we firstly index the join attributes before applying the join operation itself to accelerate its evaluation time (Rule 1). Examples of these Table-Based modified templates are illustrated in Figure 12. As illustrated in the Rule 1, the SQL code generator's decision to utilize the *UNIQUE* feature of each created index influenced by the inferred key properties of the algebraic operator (Grust, 2005). Consequently, The structure of the general form of the gener-

Figure 12. Examples of the inference rules of table-based SQL translation

$$\frac{SQL(e_1):q_1 \qquad SQL(e_2):q_2 \qquad a \in e_1.key \qquad b \notin e_2.key}{\left(\begin{array}{l} SQL(e_1 \bowtie_{a=b} e_2) \Rightarrow \\ \text{CREATE UNIQUE INDEX q1a ON q1 (a);} \\ \text{CREATE INDEX q2b ON q2 (b);} \\ \text{CREATE TABLE op}i([\text{Attributes of OpInput1}],[\text{Attributes of OpInput1}]); \\ \text{INSERT INTO op}i \\ \dots \\ \text{(View Definition Of The View-Based Translation)} \\ \dots; \end{array}\right)} \quad (1)$$

$$\frac{SQL(e):q}{\left(\begin{array}{l} SQL(\varrho_{a:(o_1,\dots,o_n/p)}(e)) \Rightarrow \\ \text{CREATE INDEX qSort ON q } (o_1,\dots,o_n); \\ \text{CREATE INDEX qPartition ON q (p);} \\ \text{CREATE TABLE op}i(a \text{ int},[\text{OpInput Attributes}]); \\ \text{INSERT INTO op}i \\ \dots \\ \text{(View Definition Of The View-Based Translation)} \\ \dots; \end{array}\right)} \quad (2)$$

$$\frac{SQL(e):q \qquad SQL(\Gamma):OpLiveNodes}{OpLiveNodes.Schema:(pre,size,parent,kind,level,name,value,frag)} \\ \frac{}{\left(\begin{array}{l} SQL(\Delta_{v:i}(e)) \Rightarrow \\ \text{CREATE INDEX qItem ON q(i);} \\ \text{CREATE TABLE op}i([\text{OpInput Attributes}], v \text{ int}); \\ \text{INSERT INTO op}i \\ \dots \\ \text{(View Definition Of The View-Based Translation)} \\ \dots; \end{array}\right)} \quad (3)$$

ated table-based translation scripts can be illustrated in Box 4.

where n represents the number of algebraic operators in the associated algebraic plan. Using the table-based translation approach has two different sides to it. On the one hand, it solves the two mentioned problems of the view-based approach and executes the evaluation scripts of the queries with nested element construction in a more efficient way. And on the other hand, the performance comparisons between the three different approaches (Section 5.1) shows that the execution time of the table-based translation scripts is mostly longer than the execution time of the view-

based translation scripts for the set of XMark queries when no nested element construction expressions are used.

3. **Hybrid-Based Approach:** The *hybrid* approach attempts to combine the advantages of the two other approaches in an elegant way. The *hybrid-based* translation follows in standard the *view-based* translation for translating the algebraic operator of the associated plan (therefore, it has the high performance advantages associated with this approach) and follows the table-based translation in situations where the view-

Box 4.

```
CREATE TABLE OP(n)….;
INSERT INTO TABLE OP(n)….;
CREATE TABLE OP(n-1)….;
INSERT INTO TABLE OP(n-1)….;
…
CREATE INDEX IOP(n-i) on TABLE OP(n-i)([Indexing Attributes]);
…
CREATE TABLE OP1….;
INSERT INTO TABLE OP1….;
SELECT * FROM OP1;
```

Box 5.

```
CREATE VIEW OP(n) AS …;
CREATE VIEW OP(n-1) AS …;
…
CREATE TABLE OP(n-i)….;
INSERT INTO Table OP(n-i)….;
CREATE INDEX IOP(n-i) on Table OP(n-i)([Indexing Attributes]);
…
CREATE VIEW OP1 AS …;
SELECT * FROM OP1;
```

based approach suffers from the already mentioned performance problems (either in the case where the view definitions will lead to a too nested or complex query plan or in the case where the occurrences of nested element constructions steps are detected in the translated algebraic plans).

The structure of the general form of the generated hybrid-based translation scripts can be illustrated in Box 5.

where n represents the number of algebraic operators in the associated algebraic plan.

Clearly, there is a trade-off between the number of materialization points and the query processing time. In our context, we are using the available cardinality information during the SQL translation process (Sakr, 2007) to select the materialization

points in a more intelligent and efficient way. We are applying a *conditional* intermediate results materialization mechanism where the estimated size of the intermediate results is passed to the SQL code generator which uses these estimates to evaluate the relative benefits from materializing these intermediate results and picks some of them for materialization with the goal of minimizing the total query costs. The main *rule of thumb* of this mechanism is: if the estimated size of the intermediate result is expected to be large, then we decide to materialize them in the following two situations:

- Before applying any binary or ternary algebraic operators (join operator ($\bowtie$), difference operator (\), document access operator (Δ), XPath evaluator operator ($\unicode{x2321}$), element / text construction operators (ε/τ)).

- In the case when the estimated large intermediate results are used by more than one operator, a decision to materialize is to be made.

Actually, the size of *large* intermediate results is a *vague* concept. As such an intermediate result is defined as being large by a system parameter which can be specified by the system administrator according to the available main memory size. To illustrate our mechanism let us consider the two XMark queries (Schmidt et al., 2002) Q8 and Q20. Although both of them use nested element construction, the hybrid translation approach for Q20 does not decide to materialize any of the input intermediate results at any element construction step because in each of them only one new element need to be constructed independent of the size of the source XML document. However, the hybrid translation approach for Q8 - in case of processing large documents - decides to materialize the input intermediate results before applying the element construction steps because the size of the input relations is estimated to be large. The experiments of Section 5.1 support the idea of our mechanism. In these experiments, materializing the intermediate results for the XMark query Q8 before applying the nested element construction steps was efficient because the size of these intermediate results was relatively *large* while for Q20 materializing the intermediate results was inefficient because for this query the size of the intermediate results for the element construction operations are consisting of only one tuple. In this case, materializing these *small* intermediate results yield to extra non-required overhead costs.

Translation Patterns

As discussed, the direct translation of relational algebraic plans into its equivalent SQL scripts is achieved by traversing the associated DAG in a bottom up fashion and then translating each algebraic operator into its equivalent SQL evaluation step using the defined SQL translation templates. Therefore, the direct translation approach leads to a number of SQL evaluation steps that is equal to the number of the algebraic operators in the associated algebraic plan. Consequently, the SQL scripts resulting from this direct translation approach tends to be cumbersome, lengthy and suffers from performance degradation. The performance degradation is a result of the consequence execution of huge number of detailed evaluation steps especially in the case of the table-based translation approach where extra non-required intermediate tables are created and extra intermediate tuples are inserted.

To avoid these limitations, the SQL code generator uses a *Pattern-Based Translation Approach* for merging and rewriting the translation of a group of operators (Pattern) into a single SQL evaluation step. The *Pattern-Based Translation Approach* used by the SQL code generator is very similar to the tree matching approach for code generation described in (Aho, Ganapathi, & Tjiang, 1989). The use of this Pattern-Based Translation Approach yields a more efficient, amenable and compact SQL script. The number of intermediate evaluation steps for the generated scripts using the Pattern-Based Translation Approach is approximately equal to 1/3 of the number of the evaluation steps for scripts generated using the direct translation approach. The experiments detailed in Section 5.3 will present a comparison between the two approaches in terms of the number of evaluation steps and the execution time of the resulting SQL scripts. Practically, the SQL code generator stores a library of algebraic patterns that varies from simple patterns consisting of two operators (for example: Project(π)/Select(σ) - Project(π)/Union($\cup$) - Attach(@)/Project(π),...,etc) to complex patterns merging 6 or 7 algebraic operators. During the translation process, the code generator detects the occurrences of its defined patterns and uses them for generating more elegant and efficient SQL scripts. Algorithm 3 illustrates the pattern-based algorithm for translating the relational algebraic plans into equivalent SQL scripts. Remarks about the translation algorithm are given as follows:

- The lines from 11 to 23 are representing a pre-processing step for detecting the occurrences of the stored translation patterns in the processed algebraic plan.

- The function call *G.setTranslatePropertyForAllNodesEqualToTrue*() in line number 11 initiates the translate property of all operators in the processed algebraic plan to the Boolean value *True*. The value of the translate property for each operator will be used in line number 27 to decide if the SQL translation of this operator will be added to the resulting translation script or if it will be combined with the translation of other operators in a pattern translation.

- The function call *G.setPatternPropertyForAllNodesEqualToFalse*() in line number 12 initiates the *pattern* property of all operators in the processed algebraic plan to the Boolean value *False*. The value of the pattern property of each operator will be used in line number 28 to decide the translation template of this operator if it is pattern-based or direct based (in case of the *translate* property of this operator is equal to true).

- The function *getNextTranslationPattern*() in line number 13 is used for retrieving the stored patterns from the SQL code generator library of patterns one by one and in a deterministic order according to their size and generality to avoid the problem of overlapping patterns. For example the pattern ($@\backslash\pi\backslash 1$) will be retrieved before the pattern ($\pi\backslash 1$).

- The function call *detectPatternInstance*(G, p) detects the occurrences of the stored patterns in the processed algebraic plan and returns a list of the detected instances. The

function *detectPatternInstance* operates only over the nodes where the *translate* property is equal to *True* and the *pattern* property is equal to *False*. If the *translate* property is equal to *False* or the pattern property is equal to *True*, then it means that this operator is detected inside the occurrence of previously retrieved pattern which avoids the problem of *overlapping patterns*. Each operator in the detected instance of the pattern in the processed plan must have only a single parent operator otherwise the existence of the pattern is ignored from the returning instances.

- For each operator in the sub-tree of detected pattern, the *False* value is assigned to the translate property. For the root operator of the pattern, the *True* value is assigned to the pattern property and the pattern name is stored in the *patternKind* property.

- The lines from 25 to 35 are performing the SQL translation process by traversing the operators of the processed algebraic plan in a *postorder* fashion. In the translation process, the operators with the translate property equal to *False* are ignored and for the operators with the translate property equal to *True*, the adequate translation templates are chosen based on the information of the pattern and the *patternKind* properties.

To illustrate, we will represent an example for the Translation Patterns idea used by the SQL code generator and in Section 4.5, we will present an example of translating the relational algebraic plans into equivalent SQL evaluation scripts.

Combined XPath Steps. Figure 13 illustrates an example of the *Combined XPath Steps* translation pattern. The annotation numbers within the symbol ○ represents the operator identifier numbers in the algebraic plan. In this pattern, a sequence of XPath Evaluator algebraic operators (⌐) appears in the algebraic plan in a consecutive manner where the output of one operator is used as

Algorithm 3.

```
1      PatternBasedSQLTranslation (AlgebraicPlan G)
2      {
3      BEGIN
4          TranslationScript t;
5          Pattern p;
6          InstanceArray instances;
7          int counter;
8          Node v;
9          Node n;
10
11         G.setTranslatePropertyForAllNodesEqualToTrue();
12         G.setPatternPropertyForAllNodesEqualToFalse();
13         p=getNextTranslationPattern()
14         DO WHILE (p != null)
15             instances=detectPatternInstance(G,p);
16             FOR counter = 1 to instances.count
17                 FOR EACH v IN instances(i).subTree
18                     v.translate = False;
19                 NEXT
20                 instances(i).root.pattern= True;
21                 instances(i).root.patternKind = p.name;
22             NEXT
23         LOOP
24
25         n = G.getNextPostorderNode();
26         DO WHILE (n != null)
27             IF (n.translate == True) THEN
28                 if (n.pattern == True) THEN
29                     t.add(translatePattern(n));
30                 ELSE
31                     t.add(translateOperator(n));
32                 END IF
33             END IF
34             n = G.getNextPostorderNode();
35         LOOP
36         RETURN t;
37     END
38     }
```

an input for the following operator. Applying the direct translation approach over the example of combined XPath steps pattern illustrated in Figure 13 will evaluate each operator in a separate step as seen in Algorithm 4.

The lines from 1 to 10 represents the evaluation of the XPath Evaluator operator (⤶)⑨ in the algebraic plan with the path step (*child::site*). The lines from 12 to 21 represent the evaluation of the XPath Evaluator operator (⤶)⑧ in the alge-

Figure 13. An example of a translation pattern of combined XPath steps

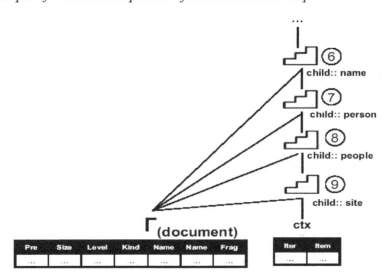

braic plan with the path step (*child::people*). The lines from 23 to 32 represents the evaluation of the XPath Evaluator operator (⏎)⑦ in the algebraic plan with the path step (*child::person*). The lines from 34 to 43 represent the evaluation of the XPath Evaluator operator (⏎)⑥ in the algebraic plan with the path step (*child::name*).

The pattern translation will combine the evaluation of the four XPath Evaluator algebraic operators in a single step as seen in Algorithm 5.

The lines from 8 to 10 represent the evaluation conditions of the path step (*child::site*)⑨. The lines from 11 to 13 represent the evaluation conditions of the path step (*child::people*)⑧. The lines from 14 to 16 represent the evaluation conditions of the path step (*child::person*)⑦. The lines from 17 to 19 represent the evaluation conditions of the path step (*child::name*)⑥.

Comparing the resulting two scripts of the direct translation and pattern translation reveals the improved efficiency provided by the pattern translation in terms of the reduction in the number of evaluation steps. The pattern translation combines the evaluation steps of the operators ⑨,⑧,⑦,⑥ in a single step while the direct translation uses four separate evaluation steps. From a performance perspective, the pattern translation approach generates SQL scripts that are clearly more efficient than those generated by direct translation especially in the context of the *table based* translation approach because it avoids the creation of additional structures and tuples insertion in a larger number of the intermediate results.

Translation Examples

In this section, we represent an example for translating the Pathfinder intermediate algebraic plans into SQL scripts.

This example is based on the *"auction.xml"* XML document from the XMark Becnhmark project (Schmidt et al., 2002). In the SQL script, we refer to the document table as an equivalent for the *XPath accelerator* relational encoding for the XML document *"auction.xml"*. Figure 14 illustrates the Pathfinder relational algebraic plan for the XQuery query Q1 (Algorithm 6). The SQL translation of the illustrated algebraic plan using the *View* Based approach is defined in Appendix A.

The SQL translation script of the algebraic plans seems to be very lengthy. However, using the relational database infrastructure such as the

Algorithm 4.

```
1    CREATE UNIQUE INDEX CtxItem ON Ctx(item);
2    CREATE TABLE OP9 (iter int,item int);
3    INSERT INTO OP9
4        SELECT DISTINCT ctx.iter,d2.Pre
5        FROM ctx, document AS d1,document AS d2
6        WHERE ctx.item=d1.pre
7        AND d2.pre > d1.pre AND d2.pre <= d1.pre + d1.size
8        AND d2.level=d1.level +1 AND d2.kind ='Elem'
9        AND d2.name='site'
10       ORDER BY d2.pre;
11
12   CREATE UNIQUE INDEX OP9Item ON OP9(item);
13   CREATE TABLE OP8 (iter int,item int);
14   INSERT INTO OP8
15       SELECT DISTINCT ctx.iter,d2.Pre
16       FROM OP9, document AS d1,document AS d2
17       WHERE ctx.item=d1.pre
18       AND d2.pre > d1.pre AND d2.pre <= d1.pre + d1.size
19       AND d2.level=d1.level +1 AND d2.kind ='Elem'
20       AND d2.name='people'
21       ORDER BY d2.pre;
22
23   CREATE UNIQUE INDEX OP8Item on OP8(item);
24   CREATE TABLE OP7 (iter int,item int);
25   INSERT INTO OP7
26       SELECT DISTINCT ctx.iter,d2.Pre
27       FROM OP8, document AS d1,document AS d2
28       WHERE ctx.item=d1.pre
29       AND d2.pre > d1.pre AND d2.pre <= d1.pre + d1.size
30       AND d2.level=d1.level +1 AND d2.kind ='Elem'
31       AND d2.name='person'
32       ORDER BY d2.pre;
33
34   CREATE UNIQUE INDEX OP7Item on OP7(item);
35   CREATE TABLE OP6 (iter int,item int);
36   INSERT INTO OP6
37       SELECT DISTINCT ctx.iter,d2.Pre
38       FROM OP7, document AS d1,document AS d2
39       WHERE ctx.item=d1.pre
40       AND d2.pre > d1.pre AND d2.pre <= d1.pre + d1.size
41       AND d2.level=d1.level +1 AND d2.kind ='Elem'
42       AND d2.name='person'
43       ORDER BY d2.pre;
```

Algorithm 5.

```
1       CREATE UNIQUE INDEX CtxItem on Ctx(item);
2       CREATE TABLE OP6 (iter int, item int);
3       INSERT INTO OP6
4           SELECT DISTINCT ctx.iter,d5.Pre
5           FROM ctx, document AS d1,document AS d2,document AS d3,
6                   document AS d4,document AS d5
7           WHERE ctx.item=d1.pre
8           AND d2.pre > d1.pre AND d2.pre <= d1.pre + d1.size
9           AND d2.level=d1.level +1 AND d2.kind ='Elem'
10          AND d2.name='site'
11          AND d3.pre > d2.pre AND d3.pre <= d2.pre + d2.size
12          AND d3.level=d2.level +1 AND d3.kind ='Elem'
13          AND d3.name='people'
14          AND d4.pre > d3.pre AND d4.pre <= d3.pre + d3.size
15          AND d4.level=d3.level +1 AND d4.kind ='Elem'
16          AND d4.name='person'
17          AND d5.pre > d4.pre AND d5.pre <= d4.pre + d4.size
18          AND d5.level=d4.level +1 AND d5.kind ='Elem'
19          AND d5.name='name'
20          ORDER BY d5.pre;
```

query optimization techniques and the indexing mechanisms yields to very efficient execution times. The experiments of Section 5 will give the evidences which are supporting our claim.

XPath Optimization in A Relational XQuery Engine

Partitioned B-tree Indexes Path expressions are the basic building block for the XQuery language. They are used inside the XQuery expression for retrieving the target data from the XML tree. Optimizing the evaluation of path expression is therefore a crucial step in order to optimize the evaluation of XQuery expressions. In Section 2.2, we described the SQL evaluation of XPath expression using the *XPath accelerator* encoding scheme. As discussed, the evaluation of XPath expression with a series of location steps $S_1/S_2/.../S_n$ is translated into a series of compositional n

region queries where the node sequence output by axis step S_i is the context node sequence for the subsequent step S_{i+1}. Consequently, the evaluation of XPath expressions requires multiple self-joins (n) for the relational encoding of the target XML document and the number of these self-join operations is equal to the number of the location steps in the path expression. Generally, the relational encoding schemes for storing the XML documents lack of the understanding of the tree nature of the underlying XML data. To avoid this limitation, several join algorithms have been proposed for efficient processing of the XPath axes over the relational storage schemes (Al-Khalifa et al., 2002), (Bruno, Koudas, & Srivastava, 2002), (Chien, Vagena, Zhang, Tsotras, & Zaniolo, 2002), (Jiang, Wang, Lu, & Yu, 2003). In our context, Grust have proposed in (Grust et al., 2003) the staircase join algorithm based on *XPath accelerator* storage scheme. This algorithm was designed to speed up

Figure 14. The Pathfinder algebraic plan for XQuery Q1

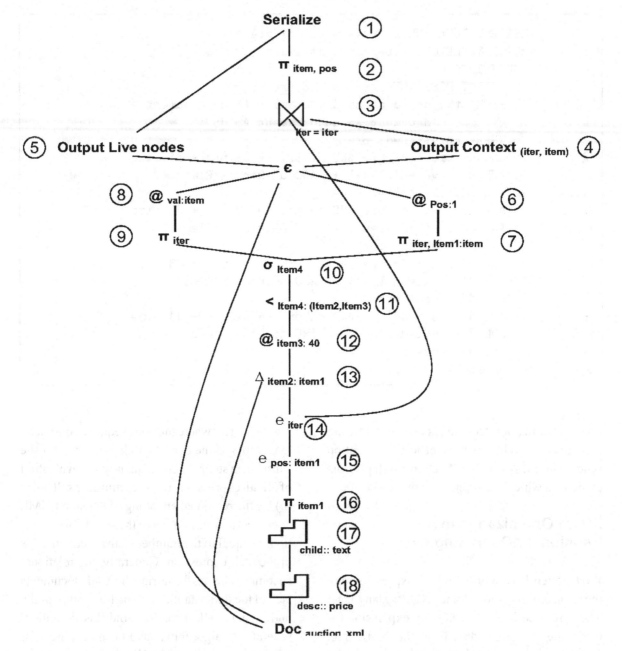

Algorithm 6.

```
                        ─── Q1 ───
   for $x in doc("auction.xml")//price/text()
       where $x < 40
       return <item> {$x} </item>
```

the SQL-based evaluation of XPath expressions by incorporating the specific knowledge about the XML tree and the (*pre/size/level*) encoding. Although the work of (Mayer, Grust, Keulen, & Teubner, 2004) has shown the possibility of incorporating the staircase join into the open source conventional RDBMS *PostgreSQL*. We are, however, not able to exploit such optimized join algorithm in our approach because it requires modifications to the internals of the underlying RDBMS kernel which is not easily applicable in commercial RDBMS systems (e.g, IBM DB2, Microsoft SQL Server, Oracle, etc).

Relational database indexes have proven to be a very efficient technique for enhancing the performance of evaluating the SQL expressions over the stored relational tables. The R-trees indexing data structure proved its efficiency for indexing multi-dimensional information and in (Grust, 2002), Grust has shown the effectiveness of using R-tree indexing for supporting the processing of the evaluation condition (*range conditions*) of the XPath axes using the *XPath accelerator* encoding scheme. However, we are not able to depend on this indexing technique in our approach because the R-tree indexing technique is not commonly supported by many of the RDBMS systems where B-tree indexing is the still the most common used technique.

Since we represent our work as a *purely* relational implementation of XQuery, we decided to use the B-tree indexing as this is commonly available database technique for accelerating the processing of the XPath evaluation conditions. Specifically, we use a slight variant of the B-tree indexing structure called *partitioned B-tree*. The idea of the partitioned B-trees is represented by Graefe in (Graefe, 2003) where he recommended using of low-selectivity leading columns to maintain the partitions within the associated B-tree. In (Grust, Rittinger, & Teubner, 2007), Grust has demonstrated the possibility of achieving comparable XPath performance by exploiting existing database functionality and purely relational

means. One of these demonstrated techniques is *partitioned B-trees* indexes. Examples for our used *partitioned B-trees* indexes are given as follows:

- Supporting the processing of the evaluation condition of the *descendant, descendant-or-self, ancestor and ancestor-or-self* XPath axes can be achieved in terms of (*kind,pre*) and (*kind,name,pre*) indexes.
- Supporting the processing of the evaluation condition of the *child* and *parent* XPath axes can be achieved in terms of (*kind,level,pre*) and (*kind,name,level,pre*) indexes.
- Supporting the processing of the evaluation condition of the *attribute, following-sibling* and *preceding-sibling* XPath axes can be achieved in terms of *(kind,parent,pre)* and *(kind,name,parent,pre)* indexes.

The experiments detailed in Section 5.4 aims to prove the effectiveness of our proposed indexes for the evaluation of the XPath and consequently XQuery expressions.

Guide Node SQL Scripts Materialized views are other well-known physical structures that can significantly accelerate the performance of the evaluation of SQL queries. There has been a lot of work done in the general problem of rewriting SQL queries using materialized views (Agrawal, Chaudhuri, & Narasayya, 2000) and on the specific area of rewriting XML queries using materialized XPath views (Xu & Meral, 2005), (Balmin, zcan, Beyer, Cochrane, & Pirahesh, 2004), (Barta, Consens, & Mendelzon, 2004).

In our context, during the shredding process of the source XML document we build a summarized tree structure, *Statistical Guide*, of the source XML document (Sakr, 2007). The *Statistical Guide* represents an implementation for the *Data Guide* summary tree structure presented in (Goldman & Widom, 1997) and is very similar to the *path tree* summary structure presented by Aboulnaga in (Aboulnaga, Alameldeen, &

Algorithm 7.

```
─────────────────────── S1 ───────────────────────
for $x in doc("auction.xml")/site/open_auctions/open_auction
return $x
```

Naughton, 2001). Every node in the *Statistical Guide* is a *Guide Node* which is representing a *correspondent* group of nodes in the source XML document which are sharing the same rooted path starting from the root node. Each *Guide Node* with its associated pre-order rank represents a form of *PathID* for their correspondent nodes in the source XML documents (Sakr, 2007). To make use of this point, we extended our encoding relation (*document table*) of the source XML document with an additional attribute to store the *PathID* information for each *correspondent* node. Additionally, we build a *partitioned B-tree* index over the (*pathid, pre*) attributes to form the basis of a materialized view which establishes the link between each original XML node and its correspondent *Guide Node*.

During the compilations process, we are able to infer the *Guide Node* property of the XPath evaluator operators in the algebraic plan (Sakr, 2007).

Our mechanism is based on the observation that we can rewrite the SQL translation of the rooted XPath expressions in the algebraic plan using the *Guide Node* information of the last path step in the rooted sequence. To illustrate let us consider Algorithm 7.

Figure 15 illustrates the algebraic plan of the XQuery expressions S1. The conventional SQL translation of the combined XPath steps translation pattern of the operators ⑦,⑥,⑤,④ is shown in Algorithm 8.

Where line number 3 represents the evaluation conditions of the operator ⑦, lines 5 and 6 represent the evaluation conditions of the operator ⑥, lines 8 and 9 represent the evaluation conditions of the operator ⑤, lines 11 and 12 represent the evaluation conditions of the operator ④. Using the Guide Node information of the Pathfinder algebraic operators, we can discard the operators ⑦,⑥,⑤ and use the Guide Node property of the

Algorithm 8.

```
1    SELECT d4.pre as item
2    FROM document AS d1,document AS d2,document AS d3,document AS d4
3    WHERE d1.kind = 'Doc' and d1.name='auction.xml'
4
5    AND d2. pre >= d1.pre AND d2.pre <=d1.pre + d1.size
6    AND d2.level=d1.level+1 AND d2.name='site' AND d2.kind='Elem'
7
8    AND d3. pre >= d2.pre AND d3.pre <=d2.pre + d2.size
9    AND d3.level=d2.level+1 AND d3.name='open_auctions' AND d3.kind='Elem'
10
11   AND d4. pre >= d3.pre AND d4.pre <=d3.pre + d3.size
12   AND d4.level=d3.level+1 AND d4.name='open_auction' AND d4.kind='Elem';
```

Figure 15. Pathfinder algebraic plan of the XQuery expression S1.

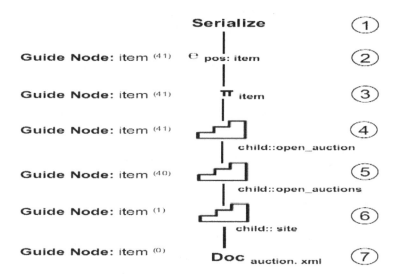

algebraic operator ④ to rewrite the SQL translation of the same combined XPath steps translation pattern as follows:

```
SELECT pre AS item
FROM document
WHERE path_Id = 41;
```

This rewriting mechanism using the *PathID* materialized view has shown to be very efficient especially in the case of rewriting long rooted XPath expressions with high evaluation costs for the conventional mechanisms as well as in the case of processing large XML documents.

In addition, rewriting the SQL evaluation of XPath expression using the *guide node* information could be considered as a form of *schema aware optimization*. Using the information of the *statistical guide* and the *guide node* annotation mechanism we could avoid the evaluation of XPath expressions which yield to an empty sequences of context nodes (Barta, Consens, & Mendelzon, 2005).

Applying the path steps of such path expression over the *statistical guide* will yield to an algebraic operator with an empty set of *guide*

node annotations. Such instances of the algebraic operators could be translated into a very cheap *SELECT* statement from an *empty* table instead of using the relatively expensive conventional SQL translation.

Selectivity Influences

The DBMS query optimizers are responsible for determining the most efficient evaluation strategy for every given SQL query. For any given SQL query, there are a large number of alternative execution plans. These alternative execution plans may differ significantly in their use of system resources or response time and usually this difference can be in orders of magnitude difference in performance between the best and worst plans which makes selecting the right plan a very important task (Reddy & Haritsa, 2005).

Optimizing the evaluation of SQL queries depends crucially on the ability to obtain effective compile-time estimates for the selectivity of the referenced "WHERE" conditions over the underlying stored relational tuples and attribute values. Sometimes query optimizers are not able to select the most optimal execution plan for the

Figure 16. Selectivity value effect on the query response time.

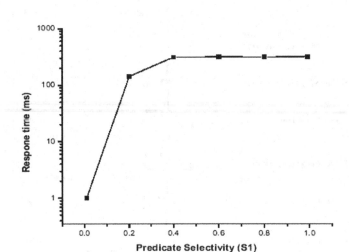

input queries because of the unavailability or the inaccuracy of the required statistical information. SQL is a declarative query language which enables the user to define "WHICH" data need to be accessed but not "HOW" this access should be done. To solve this problem, modern RDBMS such as IBM DB2 and Oracle give the users the ability to give hints to influence the query optimizers by providing additional *selectivity* information for the individual predicates of the given SQL queries. In this context, *selectivity* values are ranging between the values 0 and 1 for each individual predicate. A lower *selectivity* value (close to 0) will inform the query optimizer that the associated predicate will return fewer result rows while a higher *selectivity* value (close to 1) will inform the query optimizer that the associated predicate will return a larger number of result rows. In the case of the correctness of this additional selectivity information hinted to the query optimizers, it will help the query optimizers to make the right decisions in several situations such as: selecting the right order of the join operations and selecting the most suitable indexes. On the other side, hinting the query optimizer with incorrect selectivity information will lead the query optimizer to

incorrect decisions and consequently to inefficient execution plans. Figure 16 illustrates the effect of assigning different selectivity values for a specific predicate ($S1$) on the response time of the SQL query shown in Algorithm 9.

In our implementation, we used the available cardinality information from the XQuery estimation module to provide the query optimizers with selectivity values hints of the used predicates during the SQL translation process. Remarks about the computation of these selectivity values are given as follows:

- The SQL translation templates for the algebraic operators described in Section 4.2 implement the predicates using the "SQL WHERE" conditions in the translation templates of the following Pathfinder algebraic operators: the selection operator (σ), the join operator ($\bowtie$), the comparison operators ($\circledcirc$), the document access operator (Δ) and the XPath evaluator operator($\bowtie$).

- The translation templates of the selection operator(σ) and the comparison operators($\circledcirc$) use a single predicate which are represented using a single "WHERE" condi-

Algorithm 9.

```
SELECT d3.pre
FROM document as d1,document as d2,document as d3
WHERE d1.kind = 'Doc' SELECTIVITY S1
AND d2.pre >= d1.pre
AND d2.pre <= d1.pre + d1.size
AND d2.level=d1.level + 1
AND d2.name ='site';
```

tions in each of them. For these two operators, the selectivity of the associated "WHERE" condition is computed by dividing the estimated cardinality of the resulting relation by the estimated cardinality of the input relation.

- The translation templates of the join operator ($\bowtie$) and the document access operator(Δ) are also using a single predicate. The only difference here is these operators are *binary* operators which are receiving two input relations while the selection operator (σ) and the comparison operators ($\boxdot$) are *unary* operators which are receiving a single relation. Hence, for these two operators, the selectivity of the associated "WHERE" condition is computed by dividing the estimated cardinality of the resulting relation by the resulting value from multiplying estimated cardinalities of the two input relations.

- The translation template of XPath evaluator operator ($\boxdot$) is using multiple predicates represented with the multiple conjunctive "WHERE" conditions for the different evaluation conditions of the different path steps which are previously described in Section 2.2. Although, the XQuery estimation module is able to estimate the cardinality of the resulting relation from applying the associated path step over the input context relation, this infor-

mation is not useful in this context because the query optimizers accept to receive hints for the selectivity information of each individual predicate separately and not for a group of predicates. In this case, the selectivity of each predicate is computed using the information of the *Statistical Guide* and the associated guide node information.

Experiments

In this section, we present a performance study of the Pathfinder as a purely relational XQuery engine. In our experiments we are using the data generated by the XMark benchmark (Schmidt et al., 2002). We generated XML documents using the XMark benchmark for three scaling factors, 0.009 (1 Mb), 0.09 (10 Mb), and 0.9 (100 Mb). The experiments of this article are performed on Linux based server with two 3,2 GHZ Intel Xeon processors, 8 GB main memory storage and 280 GB SCSI secondary storage. We verified the correctness of the execution strategies by comparing the output of the SQL translation scripts of each query over different XQuery engines using a text comparison tool. In principle, our experiments have the following goals:

- To compare the difference in performance characteristics between the different SQL

Algorithm 10.

```
let $auction := doc("auction.xml") return
for $p in $auction/site/people/person
let $a :=
    for $t in $auction/site/closed_auctions/closed_auction
      where $t/buyer/@person = $p/@id
      return $t
return <item person="{$p/name/text()}">{count($a)}</item>
```

translation approaches (*view-based, table-based, hybrid*).

- To test the quality of our XQuery-to-SQL translation approaches with regards to leveraging the RDBMS technology by measuring their performance efficiency and scalability.

- To test the effectiveness of the various optimization techniques used by our approach (pattern translation, partitioned B-tree indexing).

- To demonstrate the efficiency of our *purely relational* approach for implementing XQuery processor in comparison to the native XML/XQuery functionality supported by DB2 version 9.

All reported numbers are the average of five executions with the highest and the lowest values removed. In our five readings for each query, we noticed that the first reading is always expensively inconsistent with the other readings. This is because the relational database uses buffer pools as a caching mechanism, the initial period when the database spends its time loading pages into the buffer pools is known as the *warm up* period. During this period the response time of the database declines with respect to the normal response time. For efficient testing for the important and most time consuming feature of XQuery, *nested element constructions*, we have made slight changes to the XMark queries. We replaced the

attribute construction expressions into *element construction* expressions of a *child* element. For example the original version of XMark query Q8 is defined in Algorithm 10 while our modified version is defined in Algorithm 11.

The same modification has been applied for Q3, Q9, Q11, Q12, Q13 and Q19.

View-Based vs. Table-Based vs. Hybrid

In Section 4.3, we described three approaches (*view-based, table-based, hybrid*) for translating the intermediate Pathfinder algebraic plan into SQL scripts. Figure 17 illustrates a comparison between the execution times of the SQL translation scripts of the 20 XMark queries using the three different approaches. This experiment has used an instance of XMark document which has the size of 100 MB and contains around 3 million nodes. Remarks about the results of this figure are given as follows:

- The *view-based* approach has demonstrated its effectiveness over the table-based approach for the queries which are not using nested element construction expressions (Q1, Q4, Q5, Q6, Q7, Q14, Q15, Q16, Q17, Q18)while the table-based approach has demonstrated its effectiveness for the queries which are using nested element construction expression (Q3, Q8, Q9,

Algorithm 11.

```
let $auction := doc("auction.xml") return
for $p in $auction/site/people/person
let $a :=
    for $t in $auction/site/closed_auctions/closed_auction
     where $t/buyer/@person = $p/@id
     return $t
return <item>
            <person>{$p/name/text()}</person>
            <count>{count($a)}</count>
        </item>
```

Figure 17. Comparison between view -table -hybrid SQL translation approaches. Execution times for the 20 XMark queries ran against 100 MB XMark document instance hosted by DB2

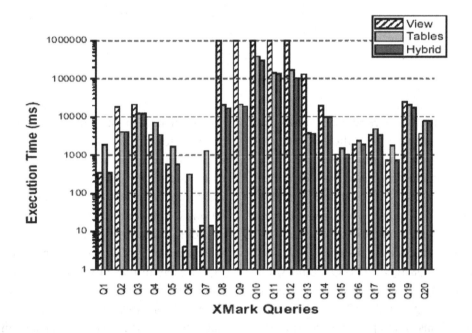

Q10, Q11, Q12, Q13, Q19). As discussed in Section 4.3, the main reason behind this is that by evaluating the upper element construction step, the view-based approach suffers from the limitation of missing the indexing information for the resulting transient nodes created during the runtime evaluation of the child element construction step.

- The *hybrid* approach uses the *view-based* approach as the standard approach and the table-based approach when nested element construction expressions are used (see Section 4.3). The results of Figure 17 have shown that the *hybrid* approach is the most efficient in all of the 20 XMark queries except for Q20. In Q20, although nested element construction expressions are used,

Figure 18. Pathfinder scalability. Execution times for three XMark document instances with sizes 1 MB, 10 MB and 100 MB

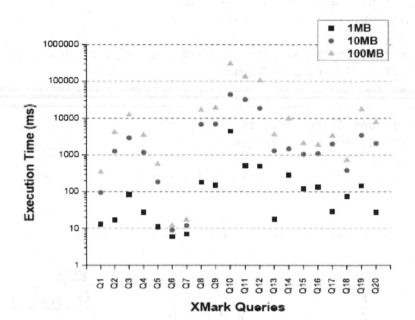

materializing the intermediate results of these expressions is not efficient because each intermediate result consists of only one tuple which do not have any side effect on the nested element construction evaluation step. Hence, the hybrid approach in this case suffers from the extra overhead of inefficient materialization steps.

- The queries Q8, Q9, Q10, Q11 and Q12 have the longest execution times. For queries Q8, Q9, Q11 and Q12, this is due to XQuery joins that produce substantial intermediate XML results which hurts the evaluation of the nested element construction steps. For Q10 the reason is different as several required nested element construction evaluation steps are executed in addition to the deeper nesting level of the element construction steps. The *view-based* translation scripts for these queries could not complete the evaluation process within the time frame of three hours.

One of the main advantages of using a relational database to store and process XML documents is to exploit their well-know *scalability* feature. To assess the scalability of our approach, Figure 18 illustrates the execution times for the SQL translations scripts for the 20 XMark queries over the encoding relations of three XMark documents with sizes of 1 MB, 10 MB and 100 MB. The SQL scripts of these experiments are generated using the *hybrid* approach. The figure shows that the execution times of our system scales in a near linear fashion with respect to the document size..

Direct Translation vs. Pattern Translation

In Section 4.4, we presented our Pattern-Based translation approach which combines and rewrites the translation of a group of algebraic operators (Pattern) of the processed Pathfinder algebraic plan into a single SQL evaluation step. Using the pattern-based translation approach has a sig-

Figure 19. Direct translation vs. pattern translation

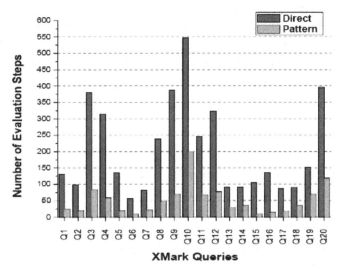

Comparison between the direct translation and the pattern translation approaches in terms of the number of the evaluation steps.

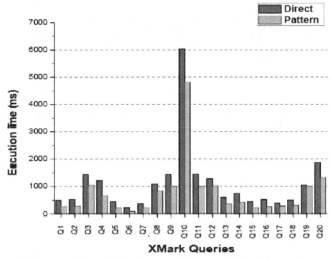

Comparison between the direct translation and the pattern translation approaches in terms of execution times. The execution times are for the 20 XMark queries ran against 1 MB XMark document instance hosted by DB2.

nificant effect on the generated SQL evaluation scripts in terms of reducing the number of the evaluation steps and consequently accelerating the execution time. Figure 19(a) illustrates the comparison between direct translation and the pattern translation approaches in terms of the number of the evaluation steps for the XMark queries. On average, the number of the evaluation steps by using the pattern-based translation approach is

equal to 1/4 the number of the evaluation steps of the direct approach. Figure 19(b) illustrates the comparison between the two approaches in terms of their execution times for the SQL translation scripts for the XMark queries against the relational encoding of XMark document with size of 1 MB (25000 nodes) hosted by DB2. On average, the execution time of the SQL scripts using the pattern-based translation approach is equal to 70%

of the execution time of the execution time of the SQL scripts using the direct approach. The SQL scripts of this experiment are generated using the table-based approach where the pattern translation approach is more effective in terms of execution time because of its avoidance of extra creation for intermediate results.

Indexes Effectiveness

The performance of queries evaluation in relational database systems is very sensitive to the defined indexes structures over the data of the source tables. Using relational indexes can accelerate the performance of queries evaluation in several ways (Valentin, Zuliani, Zilio, Lohman, & Skelley, 2000). For example, by applying predicates, it can limit the data that must be accessed to only those rows that satisfy those predicates. In addition, query evaluations can be achieved using *index-only access* and save the necessity to access the data pages by providing all the columns needed for the query evaluation. In Section 4.6, we presented our mechanism of using the *partitioned B-tree* indexing mechanism for accelerating the SQL

evaluation of XPath expressions and consequently accelerating the evaluation of XQuery expressions. Leveraging our *purely* relational approach for storing and querying the XML documents, we are able to use ready made tools provided by the RDBMSs to propose the candidate indexes that are effective for accelerating our queries work loads. However, similar approaches and tools are still not available by the native XML support of these systems. In this experiment, we used the *db2advis* tool provided by the DB2 engine to recommend the suitable index structure for our query workload. Using this tool significantly improves the quality of our designed indexes and speeds up the evaluation of our queries by reducing the number of the calls to the database engine. Figure 20 illustrates the substantial effect of using the *Partitioned B-tree* indexing mechanism and the index structures proposed by db2advis on the execution time of the SQL translation scripts of XMark queries. We have compared between the execution times of the SQL translation scripts of XMark queries *with* and *without* the indexes information. The experiments of this section uses an XMark document instance with a size of 10

Figure 20. The effect of using partitioned B-tree indexes on the execution times of the SQL translation of scripts of XMark queries

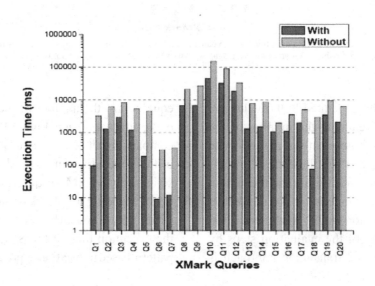

MB and use the hybrid approach for generating the SQL translation scripts for XMark Queries. On average, the execution time of the SQL translation scripts *with* the index information is equal to 1/3 of the execution time *without* index information.

DB2 Native XML vs. DB2 XQuery/SQL

Figure 21 illustrates a comparison between the execution times of our *purely* relational implementation of an XQuery processor and the native XML/XQuery functionality supported by DB2 pureXML. The execution times of these experiments are collected by running the XMark queries against an XML document instances with a size of 100 MB. The result of this experiment confirms the efficiency advantage of our *purely* relational approach over DB2 pureXML with respect to the evaluation of all XMark queries. DB2 pureXML could not complete the evaluation of queries Q8, Q9, Q10, Q11 and Q12 within the time frame of two hours. Excluding the uncompleted queries by DB2 pureXML, the execution time of our *purely* relational approach is on average equal to 15%

of the execution time of DB2 pureXML. This experiment indicates that our *purely* relational approach for implementing XQuery processor deserves to be pursued further.

Related Work

The design and implementations of different XQuery processors have been presented in the literature of recent years (Boncz et al., 2005), (Fernandez, Simeon, hoi, Marian, & Sur, 2003), (Fiebig et al., 2003), (X-Hive.), (Paparizos et al., 2003), (Beyer et al., 2005). In principle, these proposed XQuery engines can be classified into three main classes: Native XML/XQuery Processors, Streaming XQuery Processors and Relational XQuery Processors (Grust et al., 2009).

Native XML/XQuery Processors

The implementations of this approach make use of storage models, indexing and querying mechanisms that have been designed specifically for XML data.

Figure 21. Pathfinder vs. DB2

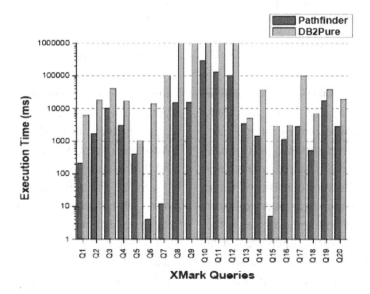

TIMBER (Paparizos et al., 2003) is a native XML database which is able to store and query XML documents. In TIMBER, XML data is stored directly in its natural tree structure. It uses the tree-based query algebra (TAX) (Jagadish et al., 2001) which considers collections of ordered labelled trees as the basic unit of manipulation that means each operator on this algebra would take one or more sets of trees as input and produce a set of trees as output. The evaluation of XQuery expressions are achieved through the following steps:

a. The XQuery expressions are parsed into an algebraic operator tree by the query parser.

b. The query optimizer reorganizes this tree and based on a set of rules it performs the required mapping from logical to physical operators (Paparizos et al., 2002).

c. The resulting query plan tree is evaluated by the query evaluator and pipelined one operator at a time. The query execution in TIMBER heavily depends on structural joins. Hence, the authors have developed efficient structural join algorithms (Al-Khalifa et al., 2002) as well as structural join order algorithms (Wu, Patel, & Jagadish, 2003a) to achieve acceptable performance results. Additionally, query optimization in TIMBER involve estimating costs of all promising sets of evaluation plans (Wu, Patel, & Jagadish, 2003b) before selecting the best one.

Natix (Fiebig et al., 2003) is another native XML database which clusters subtrees of XML documents into physical records of limited size. The XML data tree is partitioned into small subtrees and each subtree is stored into a data page. The Natix architecture consists of three main components: Storage Layer, Service Layer and Binding Layer. The bottommost layer is the storage layer which manages all persistent data structures. On top of it, the service layer provides all DBMS functionality required in addition to simple storage and retrieval. The binding layer consists of the modules that map application data and requests from other APIs to the Natix engine and vice versa. The two components responsible for query processing in Natix are the Query Compiler and the Query Execution Engine. The query compiler in Natix follows the following steps:

1. The parser module generates an abstract syntax tree for the input query.

2. The NSFT module performs Normalization, Semantic analysis, Factorization of common sub-expressions and Translation into an internal representation. This internal representation is a mixture of Natix algebra (Brantner et al., 2005) and a calculus representation.

3. Some query rewriting rules are applied such as queries unnesting.

4. The plan generator module replaces the calculus representation of query blocks with algebraic expressions.

5. The code generator module generates the code for the query evaluation plan.

The query execution engine consists of an iterator-based implementation of algebraic operators which process ordered sequences of tuples. Tuple attributes either hold base type values such as strings, numbers and tree node references, or ordered sequences.

DB2/System RX in (Nicola & Linden, 2005), Nicola and Linden have described the native XML support and XQuery implementation in IBM DB2. In this work, DB2 introduces the new XML data type which can be used like any other SQL type. A column of type XML can hold one well-formed XML document for every row of the table while the NULL value is used to indicate the absence of an XML document. Relational and XML data are stored differently, while the relational columns are stored in traditional row structures, the XML data is stored in hierarchical structures. An XML column can hold schema-less documents as well as documents for many different or evolving XML schemas. Schema validation is optional on a per-document basis i.e. the association between schemas and documents is per document and not per column, which provides maximum flexibility. Every node contains pointers to its parent and children to support efficient navigational queries. Thus, path expressions are evaluated directly over the native format on buffered pages without copying or transforming the data. Additionally, the store also supports direct access to a node, which avoids the top-down traversal through every node from the root to the target node. DB2 support three classes of XML indexes:

1. Structural Indexes which map distinct node names, paths, or tag-based path expressions to all matching node instances.
2. Value Indexes which allow quick retrieval of nodes based upon the nodes data value.
3. Full-text Indexes which map tokens to the nodes that contain the token.

DB2 supports interfaces for both SQL/XML (Eisenberg & Melton, 2002), (Eisenberg & Melton, 2004) and XQuery (Boag et al., 2006) as the primary languages for querying XML data in an integrated and unified query model. Different parsers are used to read SQL/XML and XQuery queries, after which a single compiler is used for both languages where no translation from XQuery to SQL is done. The queries compilation is done using the following three steps:

1. The query statement is compiled into an internal query graph model (QGM) (Pirahesh, Hellerstein, & Hasan, 1992), which is a semantic network used to represent the data ow in a query.
2. Rewrite transformations are applied to normalize, simplify, and optimize the data ow.
3. The optimizer uses this graph to generate a physical plan, which is translated into executable code by the process of code generation.

The optimizer scans a QGM graph and produces alternative execution plans. The optimizer utilizes data statistics to build a cardinality model, which is then used to estimate costs for the execution plans. However, intermediate plans can be pruned based on costs and plan properties such as the order of input data after which the cheapest cost is chosen for execution. In fact, the DB2 XQuery implementation does not implement static typing and does not normalize the XPath expression into explicit FLWOR blocks, where iteration between steps and within predicates is expressed explicitly.

(Balmin et al., 2008) have described the DB2 approach for Grouping and Optimizing the evaluation of XPath Expressions. In particular, they proposed an approach for adopting a combination of heuristic-based rewrite transformations in order to decide which XPath expressions should be grouped for concurrent evaluation, and cost-based optimization to globally order the groups within the query execution plan, and locally order the branches within individual groups. (Elghandour et al., 2008) presented an XML Index advising tool for DB2 that automatically recommends the best set of XML indexes and index patterns for a given database and query workload. One of the key features of this Index Advisor is that it is tightly coupled with the query optimizer. In order to enumerate the candidate index patterns for a query, and to evaluate the benefit to a query of having a particular index configuration. This tight coupling with the query optimizer helps to leverage the index selection and cost estimation capabilities, and provides an easy way for ensuring that the recommended indexes will be actually used by the optimizer in its generated query execution plans. (Lillis & Pitoura, 2008) have presented an approach for building a cooperative caching scheme for XML documents that allows sharing cache content among a number of peers. To facilitate sharing, a distributed prefix-based index is built based on the queries whose results are cached. In the loosely-coupled sharing approach, each peer stores in its local cache results of its own queries and just publishes the associated queries to the index. In the tightly-coupled approach, each peer is assigned a specific part of the query space and stores in its local cache the results of the corresponding queries.

Streaming XQuery Processors

The implementations of this approach receive the XML data in the form of continuous streams of tokens and apply on-the-fly the query processing functionalities over them.

BEA/XQRL in (Florescu et al., 2003) Florescu et al. have described the design and the implementation of the BEA/XQRL streaming XQuery processor. The processor is a central component of the 8.1 release of BEAs WebLogic Integration (WLI) product (BEA WebLogic Integration) and was designed to provide very high performance for message processing applications. In BEA/XQRL, XML data is represented as a stream of tokens which minimizes the memory requirements of the engine and allows the lazy evaluation of queries. At runtime, each runtime operator consumes its input a token at a time and input data that is not required is simply discarded. The query engine is implemented entirely as a library, so it is can be embedded in any application that might need to manipulate XML data. The XQuery compiler is composed of three managers: the Expression Manager, the Context Manager and the Operation Manager. In addition, there are three functional components: the Query Parser, the Query Optimizer and the Code Generator. The expression manager holds the internal representation for all kinds of XQuery expressions and implements various functionalities required for query optimization like variable and substitution management, type derivation, semantic properties derivation, copying, sub-expression cut and paste, etc. The operation manager holds all the information about the _rst-order functions and operators available to the query engine such as the operator names and signatures, semantic properties, pointers to the class implementing each operator and to the Java code for type derivation of polymorphic operators. The context manager holds the context information passed through all query processing phases in the form of a variety of environmental properties. The task of the parser component is to translate the input XQuery string into the corresponding internal representation. Subsequently, the task of the optimizer component is to translate the expression generated by the parser into an equivalent expression that is cheaper to evaluate. The task of the code generator component is to translate the internal representation into an executable plan represented as a tree of token iterators. Finally, the Runtime System interprets the query execution plan using a library of iterators containing implementations for all functions and operators of XQuery. Unfortunately, the BEA/ XQRL XQuery process can not process larger XML documents. Additionally, it does not handle aggregate functions as well as its query optimizer only makes use of heuristics instead of using a cost-based model.

FluXQuery in (Koch, Scherzinger, Schweikardt, & Stegmaier, 2004a), Koch et al. have presented the FluXQuery streaming XQuery processor that is based on an internal query language called FluX. FluX extends the main structures of XQuery by introducing a construct for event-based query processing. It firstly translates the input XQuery expressions into its internal query language (Koch, Scherzinger, Schweikardt, & Stegmaier, 2004b). The buffer size is then optimized by analysing the schema constraints derived from the DTD information as well as the query syntax. The optimized FluX queries are then transformed into physical query plans which are translated into executable JAVA code or interpreted and executed using the Streamed Query Evaluator. Although, the FluXQuery XQuery processor is designed with a strong emphasis on buffer-conscious query processing on structured data streams, it suffers from the same limitations of the BEA/XQRL processor.

Relational XQuery Processors

The implementations of this approach make use of the relational indexing and querying mechanisms for querying the source XML data. Large body of research work has been done on the domain of relational XPath evaluation. However it is surprising that very few approaches have tried to leverage the relational systems in the XQuery domain. To date and to the best of our knowledge, the work of this article is the first instance of a purely relational implementation of an XQuery processor that can reside in any conventional RDBMS and exhibits the efficiency, scalability and the well-know maturity of the relational infrastructure.

In (Manolescu, Florescu, & Kossmann, 2001), Manolescu et al. have presented the first attempt for translating XQuery expression into SQL queries. The approach of this work is implemented in the Agora data integration system (Manolescu, Florescu, Kossmann, Xhumari, & Olteanu, 2000). In Agora, relational and XML data are defined as a view over the global schema (Levy, 1999). Agora employs XML as the user interface format. When queries posed to the system, all data flows inside the query processor consists of relational tuples and the results are formatted as XML making the underlying relational engine transparent to the user. In Agora, the source XML documents are stored using edge-based relation schema similar to the one presented in (Florescu & Kossmann, 1999) as a fully normalized version of the hierarchical structure of an XML documents. Unfortunately, this approach only supports the translation of a very limited subset of the XQuery language. Additionally, the use of edge-based encoding does not capture any information on the document order. This means that the results of the translation are limited to nested loops as an attempt to preserve the document order.

In (DeHaan, Toman, Consens, & Ozsu, 2003), DeHaan et al. have presented an approach for translating XQuery expressions into a single equivalent SQL query statement using a dynamic interval encoding scheme for the source XML documents. In principle, the used dynamic interval encoding in this work is very similar to the XPath accelerator mapping scheme (Grust, 2002) we are using in our work. In this work, the authors have proposed a compositional translation of a subset of the XQuery language into SQL that supports arbitrary combinations and nesting of basic functions and FLWOR expressions without the need of using a general purpose programming language. The translation of XQuery expressions to relational queries is done by translating the XQuery expressions into a basic set of operations on XML forests and then using a set of SQL templates for fragments of queries that are composed to produce the final query. In fact, the work of (DeHaan et al., 2003) is similar to our approach described in this article. However, our approach supports a larger subset of the XQuery language. Additionally, DeHaan's work suffers from a major limitation in terms of the complexity and the execution cost of the generated SQL statements. In order to solve this problem the authors have proposed some modification to the relational engine to achieve an acceptable performance while our proposed approach are purely relational and does not require any changes to the underlying DBMS.

The Pathfinder/MonetDB XQuery processor (Boncz et al., 2006), as its name implies, consists of two main parts: the Pathfinder XQuery Compiler and MonetDB, a relational main memory database system (Boncz, 2002). MonetDB is a main memory database system which is mainly focusing on exploiting CPU caches for query optimization. The Pathfinder/MonetDB XQuery processor encodes the source XML documents using the XPath Accelerator relational mapping scheme (Grust, 2002). Since MonetDB only supports the use of Binary Association Tables (BATs) for storing the relational data, every relation in MonetDB is vertically fragmented into BATs. Each BAT consists of two columns, a head, often containing a unique identifier and a tail for storing attribute data. Hence, to get a full table view of a relation, its BAT fragments have to be joined together. The choice of using a data storage model with binary tables only was with the aim to minimize main memory access. The Pathfinder XQuery compiler translates XQuery expression into an algebra which is very similar to the convention relational algebra (Grust & Teubner, 2004). The intermediate algebraic plans are translated into scripts of the Monet Interpreter Language (MIL) (Boncz & Kersten, 1999) which is then passed to and -can be only-processed by the MonetDB's MIL interpreter (Rittinger, 2005). Although the approach of Pathfinder/MonetDB XQuery processor has been shown to be one of the fastest XQuery processors, it is very tightly coupling to the Monet DBMS and it requires huge main memory sizes to store large XML documents. (Grust et al., 2010) presented an algebraic plan rewriting procedure that derives isolated and optimized join graphs that can be expressed as a single *SELECT-DISTINCT-FROM-WHERE-ORDER BY* block and lets the relational database query optimizer face a problem known inside out despite the source language not being SQL. In particular, the join graph isolation process emits a bundle of self-joins over the tabular XML document encoding connected by conjunctive equality and range predicates.

CONCLUSION

This article presented Pathfinder as a purely relational implementation of an XQuery processor. In Pathfinder, firstly the source XML documents are encoded using the XPath accelerator relational encoding scheme. Secondly, using the *loop-lifting* technique, XQuery expressions are translated into intermediate algebraic plans. Thirdly, Pathfinder algebraic plans are then optimized and annotated with their own special properties for the algebraic operators. Finally, SQL code generator uses a certain group of well defined SQL translation templates and utilizes the cardinality information

inferred by relational cost model to translate the intermediate algebraic plans into their equivalent enhanced *cardinality aware* SQL scripts and to influence the RDBMS query optimizers for a better selection for the SQL execution plans. The experiments of this article demonstrated the efficiency and scalability of our *purely relational* approach in comparison to the native XML/XQuery functionality supported by conventional RDBMSs and has shown that our *purely relational* approach for implementing XQuery processor deserves to be pursued further.

REFERENCES

Aboulnaga, A., Alameldeen, A. R., & Naughton, J. F. (2001, September). Estimating the Selectivity of XML Path Expressions for Internet Scale Applications. In Proceedings of the 27th international conference on very large data bases (VLDB)(p. 591-600). Roma, Italy.

Agrawal, S., Chaudhuri, S., & Narasayya, V. R. (2000, September). Automated Selection of Materialized Views and Indexes in SQL Databases. In Proceedings of the 26th international conference on very large data bases (VLDB)(p. 496-505). Cairo, Egypt.

Aho, A. V., Ganapathi, M., & Tjiang, S. W. K. (1989). Code Generation Using Tree Matching and Dynamic Programming. *ACM Trans. Program. Lang. Syst.*, *11*(4), 491–516. doi:10.1145/69558.75700

Al-Khalifa, S., Jagadish, H. V., Patel, J. M., Wu, Y., Koudas, N., & Srivastava, D. (2002, March). Structural Joins: A Primitive for Efficient XML Query Pattern Matching. In Proceedings of the 18th international conference on data engineering (ICDE). San Jose, Canada.

Amagasa, T., Yoshikawa, M., & Uemura, S. (2003, March). QRS: A Robust Numbering Scheme for XML Documents. In Proceedings of the 19th international conference on data engineering (ICDE) (p. 705-707). Bangalore, India.

Balmin, A., Ozcan, F., Beyer, K. S., Cochrane, R., & Pirahesh, H. (2004, September). A Framework for Using Materialized XPath Views in XML Query Processing. In Proceedings of the 30th international conference on very large data bases (VLDB)(p. 60-71). Toronto, Canada.

Balmin, A., Ozcan, F., Singh, A., & Ting, E. (2008, June). Grouping and Optimization of XPath Expressions in DB2 pureXML. In Proceedings of the ACM SIGMOD International Conference on Management of Data (p. 1065-1074). Vancouver, Canada.

Barta, A., Consens, M. P., & Mendelzon, A. O. (2004, June). XML Query Optimization Using Path Indexes. In Proceedings of the 1st international workshop on XQuery implementation, experience and perspectives (XIME-P), in cooperation with ACM SIGMOD. Maison de la Chimie, Paris, France.

Barta, A., Consens, M. P., & Mendelzon, A. O. (2005, September). Benefits of Path Summaries in an XML Query Optimizer Supporting Multiple Access Methods. In Proceedings of the 31st international conference on very large data bases (VLDB)(p. 133-144). Trondheim, Norway.

BEA WebLogic Integration. http://www.bea.com

Beyer, K. S., Cochrane, R., Josifovski, V., Kleewein, J., Lapis, G., Lohman, G. M., et al. (2005, June). System RX: One Part Relational, One Part XML. In Proceedings of the ACM SIGMOD international conference on management of data (p. 347-358). Baltimore, Maryland, USA.

Boag, S., Chamberlin, D., Fernandez, M. F., Florescu, D., Robie, J., & Sim'eon, J. (2006, November). XQuery 1.0: An XML Query Language. World Wide Web Consortium Proposed Recommendation. (http://www.w3.org/TR/xquery)

Boncz, P. A. (2002). Monet: A Next-Generation DBMS Kernel For Query-Intensive Applications. Ph.D. Thesis, Universiteit van Amsterdam, Amsterdam, The Netherlands.

Boncz, P. A., Grust, T., van Keulen, M., Manegold, S., Rittinger, J., & Teubner, J. (2005, September). Path_nder: XQuery - The Relational Way. In Proceedings of the 31st international conference on very large data bases (p. 1322-1325). Trondheim, Norway.

Boncz, P. A., Grust, T., van Keulen, M., Manegold, S., Rittinger, J., & Teubner, J. (2006, June). MonetDB/XQuery: A Fast XQuery Processor Powered by a Relational Engine. In Proceedings of the ACM SIGMOD international conference on management of data (p. 479-490). Chicago, Illinois, USA.

Boncz, P. A., & Kersten, M. L. (1999, October). MIL Primitives for Querying a Fragmented World. *The VLDB Journal, 8*(2), 101–119. doi:10.1007/s007780050076

Brantner, M., Helmer, S., Kanne, C.-C., & Moerkotte, G. (2005, April). Full-fledged Algebraic XPath Processing in Natix. In Proceedings of the 21st international conference on data engineering (ICDE) (p. 705-716). Tokyo, Japan.

Bray, T., Paoli, J., Sperberg-McQueen, C. M., Maler, E., & Yergeau, F. (2006, August). World Wide Web Consortium, Extensible Markup Language (XML) 1.0 (Fourth Edition). (http://www.w3.org/TR/xml)

Bruno, N., Koudas, N., & Srivastava, D. (2002, June). Holistic twig joins: optimal XML pattern matching. In Proceedings of the ACM SIGMOD international conference on management of data (p. 310-321). Madison, Wisconsin.

Chen, Z., Jagadish, H. V., Lakshmanan, L. V. S., & Paparizos, S. (2003, September). From Tree Patterns to Generalized Tree Patterns: On Efficient Evaluation of XQuery. In Proceedings of the 29th international conference on very large data bases (VLDB)(p. 237-248). Berlin, Germany.

Chien, S.-Y., Vagena, Z., Zhang, D., Tsotras, V. J., & Zaniolo, C. (2002, September). Efficient Structural Joins on Indexed XML Documents. In Proceedings of the 28th international conference on very large data bases (VLDB).

DeHaan, D., Toman, D., Consens, M. P., & Ozsu, M. T. (2003, June). A Comprehensive XQuery to SQL Translation using Dynamic Interval Encoding. In Proceedings of the ACM AIGMOD international conference on management of data (p. 623-634). San Diego, California, USA.

Draper, D., Fankhauser, P., Fernandez, M. F., Malhotra, A., Rose, K., Rys, M., et al. (2006, November). XQuery 1.0 and XPath 2.0 Formal Semantics. World Wide Web Consortium Proposed Recommendation. (http://www.w3.org/TR /xquery-semantics/)

Eisenberg, A., & Melton, J. (2002). SQL/XML is making good progress. *SIGMOD Record, 31*(2), 101–108. doi:10.1145/565117.565141

Eisenberg, A., & Melton, J. (2004). Advancements in SQL/XML. *SIGMOD Record, 33*(3), 79–86. doi:10.1145/1031570.1031588

Elghandour, I., Aboulnaga, A., Zilio, D., Chiang, F., Balmin, A., Beyer, K., & Zuzarte, C. (2008, June). An XML Index Advisor for DB2. In Proceedings of the ACM SIGMOD International Conference on Management of Data (p. 1267-1270). Vancouver, Canada.

Fernandez, M. F., Malhotra, A., Marsh, J., Nagy, M., & Walsh, N. (2006, November). XQuery 1.0 and XPath 2.0 Data Model (XDM). World Wide Web Consortium Proposed Recommendation. (http://www.w3.org/TR /xpath-datamodel)

Fiebig, T., Helmer, S., Kanne, C.-C., Moerkotte, G., Neumann, J., & Schiele, R. (2003). A Technology Overview. In *Revised papers from the node 2002 web and database-related workshops on web, web-services, and database systems*. London, UK: Natix.

Florescu, D., Hillery, C., Kossmann, D., Lucas, P., Riccardi, F., Westmann, T., et al. (2003, September). The BEA/XQRL Streaming XQuery Processor. In Proceedings of the 30th international conference on very large data bases (VLDB)(p. 997-1008). Berlin, Germany.

Florescu, D., & Kossmann, D. (1999). Storing and Querying XML Data using an RDMBS. *IEEE Data Eng. Bull., 22*(3), 27–34.

Goldman, R., & Widom, J. (1997, August). DataGuides: Enabling Query Formulation and Optimization in Semistructured Databases. In Proceedings of the 23rd international conference on very large data bases (VLDB). Athens, Greece.

Graefe, G. (2003). Sorting And Indexing With Partitioned B-Trees. In Proceedings of the 1st international conference on data systems research (CIDR).

Grust, T. (2002, June). Accelerating XPath location steps. In Proceedings of the 2002 acm sigmod international conference on management of data (p. 109-120). Madison, Wisconsin.

Grust, T. (2005, June). Purely Relational FLWORs. In Proceedings of the 2nd international workshop on XQuery implementation, experience and perspectives (XIME-P), in cooperation with acm sigmod. Baltimore, Maryland, USA.

Grust, T., Jagadish, H. V., Özcan, F., & Yu, C. (2009). XQuery Processors. Encyclopedia of Database Systems 2009 (p. 3671-3676).

Grust, T., Mayr, M., & Rittinger, J. (2010, March). Let SQL drive the XQuery workhorse (XQuery join graph isolation). In Proceedings of the 13th International Conference on Extending Database Technology. Lausanne, Switzerland.

Grust, T., Mayr, M., Rittinger, J., Sakr, S., & Teubner, J. (2007, June). A SQL:1999 Code Generator for the Pathfinder XQuery Compiler. In Proceedings of the ACM SIGMOD international conference on management of data. Beijing, China.

Grust, T., Rittinger, J., & Teubner, J. (2007, June). Why Off-The-Shelf RDBMSs are Better at XPath Than You Might Expect. In Proceedings of the 26th acm sigmod international conference on management of data. Beijing, China.

Grust, T., Sakr, S., & Teubner, J. (2004, September). XQuery on SQL Hosts. In Proceedings of the 30th international conference on very large data bases (VLDB)(p. 252-263). Toronto, Canada.

Grust, T., & Teubner, J. (2004, June). Relational Algebra: Mother Tongue XQuery: Fluent. In Proceedings of the 1st twente data management workshop (tdm) (p. 7-14). Enschede, The Netherland.

Grust, T., van Keulen, M., & Teubner, J. (2003, September). Staircase Join: Teach a Relational DBMS to Watch its (Axis) Steps. In Proceedings of the 29th international conference on very large data bases (VLDB)(p. 524-525). Berlin, Germany.

Grust, T., van Keulen, M., & Teubner, J. (2004). Accelerating XPath evaluation in any RDBMS. *ACM Transactions on Database Systems, 29*, 91–131. doi:10.1145/974750.974754

Jagadish, H. V., Lakshmanan, L. V. S., Srivastava, D., & Thompson, K. (2001, September). TAX: A Tree Algebra for XML. In Proceedings of the 8th international workshop of database programming languages (DBPL). Frascati, Italy.

Jiang, H., Wang, W., Lu, H., & Yu, J. X. (2003, September). Holistic Twig Joins on Indexed XML Documents. In Proceedings of the 29th international conference on very large data bases (VLDB) (p. 273-284). Berlin, Germany.

Koch, C., Scherzinger, S., Schweikardt, N., & Stegmaier, B. (2004a, September). FluXQuery: An Optimizing XQuery Processor for Streaming XML Data. In Proceedings of the 30th international conference on very large data bases (VLDB)(p. 1309-1312). Toronto, Canada.

Koch, C., Scherzinger, S., Schweikardt, N., & Stegmaier, B. (2004b). Schema-based Scheduling of Event Processors and Buffer Minimization for Queries on Structured Data Streams. In Proceedings of the 30th international conference on very large data bases (VLDB)(p. 228-239).

Levy, A. Y. (1999, June). Logic-Based Techniques in Data Integration. In Workshop on logic-based artificial intelligence. College Park, Maryland.

Li, Q., & Moon, B. (2001, September). Indexing and Querying XML Data for Regular Path Expressions. In Proceedings of the 27th international conference on very large data bases (VLDB)(p. 361-370). Roma, Italy.

Lillis, K., & Pitoura, E. (2008, June). Cooperative XPath Caching. In Proceedings of the ACM SIGMOD International Conference on Management of Data (p. 327-338). Vancouver, Canada.

Manolescu, I., Florescu, D., & Kossmann, D. (2001). Answering XML Queries on Heterogeneous Data Sources. In Proceedings of the 27th international conference on very large data bases (VLDB)(p. 241-250). San Francisco, CA, USA.

Manolescu, I., Florescu, D., Kossmann, D., Xhumari, F., & Olteanu, D. (2000). Agora: Living with xml and relational. In Proceedings of the 26th international conference on very large data bases (VLDB)(p. 623-626).

Mayer, S., Grust, T., van Keulen, M., & Teubner, J. (2004). An Injection of Tree Awareness: Adding Staircase Join to PostgreSQL. In Proceedings of the 30th international conference on very large data bases(VLDB).

O'Neil, P. E., O'Neil, E. J., Pal, S., Cseri, I., Schaller, G., & Westbury, N. (2004, June). OR-DPATHs: Insert-Friendly XML Node Labels. In Proceedings of the acm sigmod international conference on management of data. Paris, France.

Paparizos, S., Al-Khalifa, S., Jagadish, H., Niermann, A., & Wu, Y. (2002). *A Physical Algebra for XML (Tech. Rep.)*. University of Michigan.

Pathfinder. (2003). (http://pathfinder-xquery.org/)

Pirahesh, H., Hellerstein, J. M., & Hasan, W. (1992). Extensible/Rule Based Query Rewrite Optimization in Starburst. In Sigmod conference (p. 39- 48).

Re, C., Simeon, J., & Fernandez, M. F. (2006, April). A Complete and Efficient Algebraic Compiler for XQuery. In Proceedings of the 22nd international conference on data engineering (ICDE) (p. 14). Atlanta, GA, USA.

Reddy, N., & Haritsa, J. R. (2005). Analyzing Plan Diagrams of Database Query Optimizers. In Proceedings of the 31st international conference on very large data bases (VLDB)(p. 1228-1240).

Rittinger, J. (2005). Pathfinder/MonetDB: A Relational Runtime for XQuery. Master thesis, Konstanz University.

Sakr, S. (2007). Cardinality-Aware and Purely Relational Implementation of an XQuery Processor. Phd thesis, University of Konstanz. (http://www.ub.uni-konstanz.de/ kops/volltexte/2007/3259/)

Sartiani, C., & Albano, A. (2002, July). Yet Another Query Algebra For XML Data. In Proceedings of the international database engineering & applications symposium (IDEAS) (p. 106-115). Edmonton, Canada.

Schmidt, A., Waas, F., Kersten, M. L., Carey, M. J., Manolescu, I., & Busse, R. (2002, September). XMark: A Benchmark for XML Data Management. In Proceedings of the 28th international conference on very large data bases (VLDB) (p. 974-985). Hong Kong, China.

Teubner, J. (2006). Pathfinder: XQuery Compilation Techniques for Relational Database Targets. PHD doctoral dissertation, Technical University of Munich.

Valentin, G., Zuliani, M., Zilio, D. C., Lohman, G. M., & Skelley, A. (2000). DB2 Advisor: An Optimizer Smart Enough to Recommend Its Own Indexes. In Proceedings of the 22nd international conference on data engineering (ICDE).

Wu, Y., Patel, J. M., & Jagadish, H. V. (2003a). Structural Join Order Selection for XML Query Optimization. In Proceedings of the 19th international conference on data engineering (ICDE) (p. 443-454).

Wu, Y., Patel, J. M., & Jagadish, H. V. (2003b). Using histograms to estimate answer sizes for XML queries. *Information Systems, 28*(1-2), 33–59. doi:10.1016/S0306-4379(02)00048-0

X-Hive. http://www.x-hive.com/ xquery

Xu, W., & Meral, Z. (2005, September). Rewriting XPath queries using materialized views. In Proceedings of the 31st international conference on very large data bases (VLDB)(p. 121-132). Trondheim, Norway.

Yoshikawa, M., Amagasa, T., Shimura, T., & Uemura, S. (2001). XRel: a path-based approach to storage and retrieval of XML documents using relational databases. ACM Trans. *InternetTechn., 1*(1), 110–141.

Zhang, H., & Tompa, F. W. (2003, September). XQuery Rewriting at the Algebraic Level. Trends in XML Technology for the Global Information Infrastructure, a special issue of Journal of Computer Systems. *Science, and Engineering, 18*, 241–262.

APPENDIX A

```
-- Step 1 (Path Expression)
CREATE VIEW OP16 AS
        SELECT d3.pre AS item1
        FROM document AS d1,document AS d2,document AS d3
        WHERE d1.kind ='Doc'
        AND d2.pre > d1.pre AND d2.pre <=d1.pre + d1.size
        AND d2.name ='price'
        AND d3.pre > d2.pre AND d3.pre <=d2.pre + d2.size
        AND d3.level = d2.level+1 AND d3.kind ='Text';


-- Step 2 (Row Numbering)
CREATE VIEW OP14 AS
        SELECT ROW_NUMBER() OVER () AS iter,
                ROW_NUMBER() OVER(ORDER BY item1) AS pos, item1
        FROM OP16;


-- Step 3 (Document Access + Attachment)
CREAT VIEW OP12 AS
        SELECT OP14.iter, OP14.pos, OP14.item1,
                d.value AS item2, 40 AS item3
        FROM OP14, document AS d
        WHERE OP14.item1 = d.pre;


-- Step 4 (Comparison Operation)
CREAT VIEW OP10 AS
        SELECT iter, item1
        FROM OP12
        WHERE item2 < item 3;


-- Step 5 (Attachment + Projection)
CREAT VIEW OP8 AS
        SELECT iter, 'item' AS item
        FROM OP10;


-- Step 6 (Attachment + Projection)
CREAT VIEW OP6 AS
        SELECT iter, item1 AS item, 1 AS pos
        FROM OP10;


-- Step 7 (Element Construction)
CREATE VIEW OP5 AS
        SELECT MaxValues.Mpre +
```

```
                ROW_NUMBER() OVER (ORDER BY iter,pos,pre) AS pre,
                ElementConstruction.size, ElementConstruction.level,
                ElementConstruction.kind, ElementConstruction.name,
                ElementConstruction.value,
                MaxValues.frag + DENSE_RANK() OVER (ORDER BY iter_ AS frag
        FROM (SELECT OP8.iter, 0 AS pos, -2 AS pre,
                    COALESCE(SUM(size +1), 0) AS size,
                    0 AS level, 'Elem' AS kind,
                    OP8.item AS name,
                    null AS value
            FROM OP6 INNER JOIN document
                    ON OP6.item = document.pre
            RIGHT OUTER JOIN OP8
                    ON OP8.iter = OP6.iter
        GROUP BY OP8.iter, OP8.item
        UNION ALL
        SELECT OP6.iter, OP6.pos,
                d2.pre AS pre, d2.size, d2.level - d1. Level + 1 AS level
                d2.kind, d2.name, d2.value AS value
        FROM OP6, document AS d1, document AS d2
        WHERE d1.pre = OP6.item
        AND d2.pre >= d1.pre
        AND d2.pre <= d1.pre + d1.size) AS ElementConstruction,
        (SELECT MAX(pre) AS Mpre,MAX(frag) AS frag
        FROM Document) AS MaxValues;


CREATE VEIW OP6 AS
        SELECT ElementConstruction.Iter,
                MaxValues.Mpre + ROW_NUMBER()
                                    OVER (ORDER BY iter,pos,pre) AS Item
        FROM (SELECT OP8.iter, 0 AS pos, -2 AS pre, 0 as level
            FROM OP6 INNER JOIN document
                        ON OP6.item = document.pre
            RIGHT OUTER JOIN OP8
                        ON OP8.iter = OP6.iter
            GROUP BY OP8.iter
        UNION ALL
            SELECT OP6.iter, OP6.pos, d2.pre AS pre,
                        d2.level - d1.level + 1 AS level
            FROM OP6, document AS d1, document AS d2
            WHERE d1.pre = OP6.item
                AND d2.pre >= d1.pre
                AND d2.pre <= d1.pre +d1.size) AS ElementConstruction,
        (SELECT MAX(pre) AS Mpre FROM document) AS MaxValues
```

```
        WHERE ElementConstruction.Level = 0;

-- Step 8 (Project + Join)
CREATE VIEW OP1 AS
        SELECT OP4.item, OP14.pos
        FROM OP4, OP14
        WHERE OP4.iter = OP14.iter;
SELECT * from Op1;
```

Section 4

Chapter 12
Cost Modeling and Range Estimation for Top–k Retrieval in Relational Databases

Anteneh Ayanso
Brock University, Canada

Paulo Goes
University of Arizona, USA

Kumar Mehta
George Mason University, USA

ABSTRACT

Relational databases have increasingly become the basis for a wide range of applications that require efficient methods for exploratory search and retrieval. Top-k retrieval addresses this need and involves finding a limited number of records whose attribute values are the closest to those specified in a query. One of the approaches in the recent literature is query-mapping which deals with converting top-k queries into equivalent range queries that relational database management systems (RDBMSs) normally support. This approach combines the advantages of simplicity as well as practicality by avoiding the need for modifications to the query engine, or specialized data structures and indexing techniques to handle top-k queries separately. This paper reviews existing query-mapping techniques in the literature and presents a range query estimation method based on cost modeling. Experiments on real world and synthetic data sets show that the cost-based range estimation method performs at least as well as prior methods and avoids the need to calibrate workloads on specific database contents.

INTRODUCTION

In many relational database applications, end-users are more interested in conveniently exploring the data around some attribute values of interest. However, relational queries establish rigid qualification to deal only with data that exactly match selection conditions (Motro, 1988). Due to the exactness in nature of the query model in the RDBMS, users face the challenge of routinely

DOI: 10.4018/978-1-60960-521-6.ch012

specifying value ranges of attributes in search of approximate matches, particularly in the event of empty answers or too many answers (Huh and Lee, 2001; Shin, Huh, Park, and Lee, 2008). Top-k querying enhances the information retrieval (IR) capability of RDBMSs and provides mechanisms for effective retrieval of data that are more appealing to end-user (Ilyas et al., 2006).

Supporting top-k querying in existing RDBMSs, however, is a challenging task and the topic has received significant attention from the database community in recent years (Ilyas, Beskales, and Soliman, 2008). Much of the existing research has focused on techniques that involve high-performance indexing which requires significant changes in the relational query engines. Our technique presented here is motivated by the mechanism of mapping a top-k query into an equivalent range query that is normally supported by RDBMS (Bruno, Chaudhuri, and Gravano, 2002; Chaudhuri and Gravano, 1999; Donjerkovic and Ramakrishnan, 1999). In this approach, top-k querying is defined as a method of specifying relational queries by target values of attributes in order to obtain a desired number of "best matches" based on some ranking (distance) functions. In contrast to using new query operators or specialized index structures to support top-k queries, the query-mapping approach relies on summary statistics that are available in database systems in the form of histograms. Using these statistics, the approach deals with techniques for estimating approximate range queries for efficient top-k retrieval.

Given the enormous installed base of relational database systems in various application domains, developing top-k retrieval methods that work within the operational constraints is crucial. The query-mapping approach not only has operational advantages, but also provides effective mechanisms for range query estimation (Ayanso, Goes, and Mehta, 2007; Bruno et al., 2002; Chaudhuri and Gravano, 1999). Nevertheless, prior techniques for query-mapping are either simple heuristics that lead to significant performance variation by database setting (for example, Chaudhuri and Gravano, 1999) or workload-adaptive that requires learning of the data using a set of queries with pre-specified data characteristics (for example, Bruno et al., 2002; Chen and Ling, 2002).

This paper presents a cost-based query-mapping methodology that allows evaluation of cost tradeoff at the level of an individual query. The query-level method is an improvement over the workload-adaptive method which may lead to inefficient performance for queries that deviate in characteristics or distribution from pre-specified workloads. Our cost-based range estimation methodology accounts for cost and performance factors for each query and shows relatively consistent performance under different experimental settings.

The remainder of this paper is organized as follows. The following section reviews the literature on top-k querying with an emphasis on the query-mapping approach. The subsequent section presents the cost-based range estimation procedure and its model components and assumptions. This will be followed by the discussion of the experimental setting used to assess the performance efficiency of the cost-based strategy and the results obtained. The final sections discuss limitations and future research directions, and provide concluding remarks.

RELATED LITERATURE

The Web has proved to be an ideal example for the performance impact of top-k querying. As a result, document and multi-media retrieval has been the focus of most research in the IR field (Baeza-Yates and Ribeiro-Neto, 1999; Bertino, Rabbiti, and Gibbs, 1988; Bustos, Keim, Saupe, Schreck, and Vranić, 2005; Chan, 2006; Chaudhuri, Gravano, and Marian, 2004; Fagin, 1998; Kwok and Zhao, 2006; Salton and McGill, 1983). Although RDBMSs primarily support exact matches to queries, the ability to explore data around specific values of interest is highly desirable, particularly in conditions where there is no prior knowledge about the distribution of the data. In the absence of efficient methods for ad-hoc search and retrieval, the naïve approach requires an exhaustive search in the database. This is obviously not a viable approach for many applications which warrant more efficient exploratory search and retrieval capabilities. Consequently, several top-k processing techniques have been proposed in the database literature recently (Ilyas et al., 2008).

The early research on top-k querying focused on extending the relational query model. For example, Motro (1988) introduced the idea of query relaxation and approximate matches by proposing vague query capabilities for the relational query model. Carey and Kossmann (1997, 1998) suggested specialized sorting (indexing) techniques by adding a STOP AFTER clause to the traditional SQL's SELECT statement. However, such specialized indexes and data structures (see also Berchtold, Keim, Kriegel, and Seidl, 2000; Lomet and Salzberg, 1990; Nene and Nayar, 1997; Orlandic and Yu, 2005; Tao, Xiao, and Pei, 2007) are not supported by RDBMSs, thus requiring at least one full sequential scan of the database.

Recent top-k processing techniques in the literature vary primarily at the level of support in the RDBMS, depending on whether they can be incorporated at the core of query engines or outside query engines at an application layer (Ilyas et at., 2008). For example, the techniques that work at the core of query engines propose specialized rank-aware query operators or introduce new query algebra for query optimization (Chang and Hwang, 2002; Ilyas, Aref, and Elmagarmid, 2002, 2003; Ilyas et al., 2006; Li, Chang, and Ilyas, 2006; Li, Chang, Ilyas, and Song, 2005). Other techniques work at an application level but suggest specialized indexes (for example, Chang et al., 2000; Tsaparas, Palpanas, Kotidis, Koudas, and Srivastava, 2003) or materialized views (for example, Das, Gunopulos, Koudas, and

Tsirogiannis, 2006; Hristidis, Koudas, and Papakonstantinou, 2001) to improve query response time during execution. In a middleware setting, we find rank-aggregation algorithms that define the database as multiple lists and incorporate efficient ways to produce a global rank from multiple input rankings (for example, Fagin, 1999; Fagin, Lotem, and Naor, 2001; Güntzer, Balke, and Kießling, 2000; Nepal and Ramakrishna, 1999). Marian, Bruno, and Gravano (2004) proposed a sequential algorithm for processing top-k queries in a setting where the relation attributes might not be available other than through external web-accessible sources with a variety of access interfaces. Their algorithm maximizes source-access parallelism to minimize query response time, while satisfying source-access constraints.

Closely related to the approach presented here are techniques that belong to the query-mapping stream (Ayanso et al., 2007; Bruno et al., 2002; Chaudhuri and Gravano, 1999; Chen and Ling, 2002; Donjerkovic and Ramakrishnan, 1999). These techniques work at an application level and provide a mechanism to formulate a top-k query into a conventional range query. To do so, the techniques rely on summary statistics (histograms) maintained in RDBMSs or sample tuples obtained during query execution. These techniques have shown that database profiles can be used to estimate approximate range queries in order to avoid the requirement of a full sequential scan of the database. The cost-based range estimation method presented here further incorporates the trade-off in query processing costs and avoids the need for training workloads for range query formulation (Ayanso, Goes, and Mehta, 2009).

Using Summary Statistics for Range Estimation

Major commercial database systems keep statistics in the form of histograms to summarize attribute values and their frequency of occurrence in the database (Ramakrishnan and Gehrke, 2003). The purpose of histograms is to create a partition of a data set into buckets of uniform tuple distribution so that query execution plans are estimated with good accuracy (Mannino, Chu, and Sager, 1998). Range query formulation involves identifying appropriate search bounds using a distance function and the histogram maintained in RDBMSs about the value distribution of the data. Thus, the main components that form the basis for the query-mapping approach include histograms and distance functions for measuring the "closeness" of database tuples to query conditions. Distance functions based on *l*-norms (e.g., *Summation, Euclidean*, and *Maximum* distances) are commonly used in database research to measure similarity and rank order relevant tuples. Although the *l*-norm distance functions are not unique to the top-k query problem, they share properties that are suitable to the query-mapping approach. The most significant property of the *l*-norm distance functions in top-k research is the *monotonicity* property described in prior query-mapping techniques (Bruno et al., 2002; Chaudhuri and Gravano, 1999). According to this property, if a tuple is closer along each attribute to the values of a query than any other tuple, then the distance from this tuple to the query point cannot be greater than any other tuple.

Therefore, the query-mapping approach assumes the existence of a given number of tuples between lower and upper bounds of a search distance obtained from histograms. The distance to the lower bound will not give the required number of results (i.e., *k*), where as the distance to the upper bound is guaranteed to give at least *k* results. If an arbitrary cut-off distance is used to construct a range query, there will be two possible database tasks in order to meet the requirement of the top-k request. One possibility is that the range used may lead to fewer than *k* results, leading to a re-processing effort to obtain the remaining results. Or, the range used may provide results far in excess of the required number, requiring additional operation to rank order the results. Moving

from the lower bound to the upper bound of the search decreases the likelihood of re-executing the query, while increasing the potential for retrieving excess results. The goal in query-mapping methods is, therefore, to determine the appropriate range that retrieves the required *k* results. For example, Chaudhuri and Gravano (1999) proposed two basic strategies, *Restart* and *No-Restart*. The *Restart* strategy is based on the most optimistic search distance that is likely to retrieve the desired *k* results. On the other hand, the *No-Restart* strategy is based on the most pessimistic search distance that guarantees the *k* tuples. The *Restart* strategy assumes that all tuples in a given histogram bucket are as close to the query point as possible and uses the closest possible distance from the query point to each histogram bucket. In contrast, the *No-Restart* strategy assumes that all tuples in a histogram bucket are as far from the query point as possible and uses the furthest possible distance for each histogram bucket. In both strategies, the range is estimated by including the histogram buckets in ascending order of their respective distances so that the region that contains all possible tuples below this distance includes at least *k* tuples.

Based on the above framework, two other heuristics (*Inter1* and *Inter2*) were also proposed by Chaudhuri and Gravano (1999). The *Inter1* and *Inter2* strategies represent the *1/3* and *2/3* positions or cut-off points between the restart and no-restart points, respectively. Compared to the *Restart* strategy, the *Inter1* and *Inter2* strategies are less likely to lead to a restart. However, unlike the *No-restart* strategy, these strategies do not guarantee all the required *k* results. Further, the parametric workload-adaptive strategy proposed by Bruno et al. (2002) considers the above four strategies as special cases of a generalized strategy with parameter α (i.e., $d(\alpha) = d_1 + \alpha(d_2 - d_1)$, $0 \le \alpha \le 1$). Using a workload of queries for each *k* value of interest, the method first calibrates parameter α such that the search distance $d(\alpha^*)$

minimizes the average number of tuples retrieved from the database. The parameter $\alpha *$ is then used to determine the cut-off distance for query sets having similar spatial distributions with the training workload. Chen and Ling (2002) proposed a similar parametric strategy using random samples of the database as a source of summary statistics in place of histograms.

COST-BASED RANGE ESTIMATION

The cost-based range estimation method incorporates the tradeoff between the cost of dealing with excess tuples and the cost of re-executing (restarting) a query when an estimated range fails to meet the desired number of tuples. The objective is to determine a cost-optimal range by minimizing the sum of the expected costs of re-processing and the expected costs of handling results in excess of the required number.

The basic objective in query optimization is the minimization of the database system's processing efforts. These involve cost components such as secondary storage access costs, CPU (computation) costs, and communication costs (Jarke and Koch, 1984; Mannino et al., 1998). Mathematical representation of costs for database operations requires specific assumptions in a particular setting. Our problem environment is characterized by a centralized database with simple selection queries over a single relation. In such environments, the secondary storage access costs dominate the cost of typical database operations (Jarke and Koch, 1984; Ramakrishnan and Gehrke, 2003). Accordingly, our cost-based approach accounts for disk I/O costs in terms of the number of page I/Os for evaluating query execution costs. Moreover, optimizing query execution depends on the type of file organization used in the database system and the available access paths to records. Physical ordering of files and availability of indexes can significantly influence the data retrieval efficiency of the RDBMS. As the I/O costs are assessed by

the efficiency of the access path utilized, different scenarios can be considered to show the degree of variation of these costs (Ramakrishnan and Gehrke, 2003). The conventional strategy is through B+ tree index, the efficiency of which depends on whether or not the index is clustered or unclustered. If the index is clustered, the chance of obtaining qualifying tuples in the same page is higher, which reduces the page I/O costs. On the other hand, if the index is unclustered, the access path could lead to one page I/O for each qualifying tuple. In this case, each index entry may possibly point to a qualifying tuple on a different page. In the worst-case scenario, the use of unclustered index could lead to number of page I/Os that could correspond to the number of qualifying tuples, which represents the more realistic scenario. Accordingly, our cost-based range estimation assumes the cost of accessing and retrieving records using unclustered B+ tree index.

Furthermore, in order to meet the objective of top-k querying, the results obtained from an estimated range query need to be sorted before the required results are presented to the user. Ayanso et al. (2007) proposed a cost framework that assumes *in-memory* sorting of query results. However, this cost framework is limited when query results do not necessarily fit in main memory. Most commercial database systems (e.g., IBM DB2, Informix, MS SQL Server, Oracle, Sybase ASE) use external sorting when the data to be sorted does not necessarily fit in main memory (Graefe, 2006; Ramakrishnan and Gehrke, 2003). Therefore, our cost-based range estimation assumes the DBMS supports external sorting. External sorting is handled by breaking a file into smaller sub files, sorting the sub files and then merging them using a minimal amount of memory. This process involves using repeated passes over the data. In each pass, the pages in the file are read, processed, and written out, resulting in 2 disk I/Os per page and per pass. The number of passes is approximated by $\left\lceil \log_{B-1} \left\lceil N / B \right\rceil \right\rceil + 1$, where B is the number of buffer pages used and N is the number of pages in the file. The total cost is represented by $2N(\lceil \log_{B-1} \lceil N / B \rceil \rceil + 1)$ I/Os (Ramakrishnan and Gehrke, 2003).

In developing the cost-based range estimation procedure, we follow the mechanism used by Bruno et al. (2002) for the initial step of our method which deals with obtaining lower and upper search bounds from histogram buckets. This involves computing the furthest distance from a query point to each histogram bucket and ranking the buckets in ascending order of the respective distances. The key to this step is the *monotonicity* property of the *l*-norm distance functions which simplifies the task of locating data points in histogram buckets that are the furthest from the query point. This provides us with the required search interval and the number of tuples available within this interval. For consistency with the literature, this search interval is defined using the same terminology - *restart* and *no-restart* points. The mathematical descriptions of the procedure for finding the cost-optimal cut-off distance are summarized in the appendix. For the derivation of the cost expressions, we refer the reader to Ayanso et al. (2009).

EXPERIMENTAL SETTING

Data Sets

Our experiments are based on real world and synthetic data sets which were also used in previous top-k research (Bruno et al., 2002). The real data sets are fragments of US Census Bureau data, containing about 210K records (Blake and Merz, 1998). The data set *Census2D* has the attributes "*income*" and "*age*", and *Census3D* has an additional attribute, "*number of weeks worked per year*". The synthetic data sets are *Array2D* and *Array3D* data sets with 500K records each. The array data sets are generated over the data domain

of [0, 10000]. Each dimension has 60 distinct values which are generated independently. After the value sets of each dimension are generated, attribute values from the different dimensions are joined to form records. Given the cardinality of the data sets, frequencies are generated from a *Zipfian* distribution with a skew factor of 1 and randomly assigned to each record (Zipf, 1949).

Query Sets

For each data set, an experimental set of 100 queries is generated by randomly selecting attribute values from the data records. Results are reported for each efficiency metric based on the average performance on the experimental queries.

Distance Functions

As illustrated in previous research (Bruno et al., 2002; Chaudhuri and Gravano, 1999), the *l*-norm distance functions yield different shapes in defining the boundary of the top-k set in a multi-dimensional space (for example, a circle around $q(k)$ for the *Euclidean* distance). Due to this variation, the mapping of the estimated distance into a range query may lead to the retrieval of tuples outside of the top-k region. The only exception to the *l*-norm distance functions that defines a top-k region that matches the region defined by the corresponding range query is the *max* distance function. This is because the *max* distance function defines the boundary of the top-k set in a box around $q(k)$. In order to take advantage of this as well as allow comparison with existing histogram-based strategy, we use the *max* distance function for our experiments.

Histogram Type and Size

In a recent study (Ayanso et al., 2007), we discuss the structural differences of the three most commonly used histogram types and their impacts on top-k retrieval. These include *Equi-Count*

Figure 1. Selection of Histogram Sizes

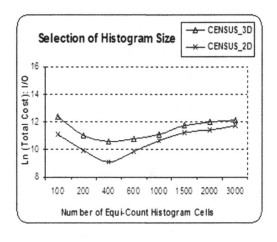

(a.) Census Data Sets

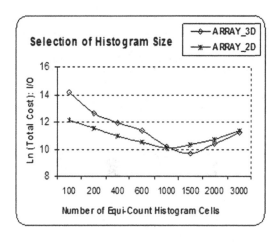

(b) Array Data Sets

histogram (Muralikrishna and DeWitt, 1988; Piatetsky-Shapiro and Connell, 1984), *Equi-Width* histogram (Ramakrishnan & Gehrke, 2003), and *MHist* histogram (Poosala and Ioannidis, 1997; Poosala, Ioannidis, Haas, and Shekita, 1996). In determining the specific settings for our experiments, we provide a reasonable ground for comparative performance assessment with existing methods. Previous histogram-based methods show relatively better performance using the *Equi-Count* histogram. Hence, while the proposed method is not limited to a particular histogram type, we use the *Equi-Count* histogram for reporting the results of our experiments and comparing performance with extant techniques.

Furthermore, the histogram size for each data set was set by initially analyzing the total cost performance of the cost-based strategy over a wide range of histogram sizes. The use of total cost provides better information for assessing the effect of histogram size on the overall efficiency of the method and selecting appropriate histogram size. The total cost performance was examined on both the real and synthetic multi-dimensional data sets over equi-count histogram cells, ranging from 100 cells to 3000 cells. Figure 1 shows the

average total cost of the experimental query set. We used a default setting of $k=100$ and the *max* distance function. To minimize the scale differences across the different data sets, we plotted the natural log of the average total cost.

The average total cost indicates a trend of optimality for each data set, where it initially declines, and then increases as the number of histogram cells increases. The census data sets attain this level at the histogram size of about 400 histogram cells. We use this histogram size for the census data sets throughout the experiments. On the other hand, the array data sets have relatively higher frequency variability due to the skew factor, thus requiring larger number of histogram cells to attain this level. For the Array2D, the total cost is lower at about 1000 histogram cells. For the Array3D, this level is attained at about 1500. For consistency, however, we use 1500 histogram cells for the array data sets throughout the experiments.

Efficiency Metrics

In order to show the performance efficiency of the cost-based range estimation method, we report the

Figure 2. Average Excess Ratio

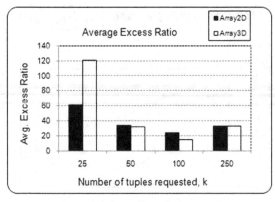

(a.) Array Data Sets

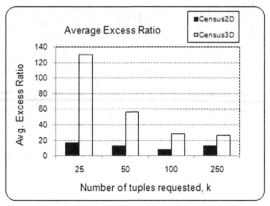

(b) Census Data Sets

number of excess results retrieved as well as the frequency of restarts encountered using efficiency metrics *Average Excess Ratio* and *Percentage of Restarts*, respectively.

The excess ratio measures the ratio of total tuples retrieved to the size of k. We report the average ratio for all queries in the experimental set. This metric can be related to another metric, *Percentage of Database Retrieved*, which was used in previous research to measure the number of tuples retrieved as a percentage of the database size. We use the excess ratio in this research as it provides a more relevant measure of result size that can be directly contrasted to the size of k. The *Percentage of Restarts* has been used in prior research and represents the percentage of queries that failed to retrieve all the required tuples in the first execution.

In addition, the major difference between the cost-based strategy and prior query-mapping strategies is on the "optimality" of the range used to formulate the corresponding range query. As a result, we use the *Average Total Cost* as the main basis for the overall performance evaluation and for comparison with existing method.

EXPERIMENTAL RESULTS

The experimental results are presented in two parts: 1) performance analysis of the cost-based strategy, and 2) performance comparison with the dynamic workload-based strategy.

Performance Analysis of the Cost-Based Range Estimation

Figure 2 and Figure 3 show the performance of the cost-based method in terms of the *Average Excess Ratio* and *Percentage of Restarts*, respectively.

In terms of the average excess ratio, the worst performance is observed for smaller k values (see Figure 2 for k=25 for all data sets). With the exception of the Census3D data set, the average excess ratio dropped as k increased from 25 to 100, and then slightly increased for k= 250. The Census2D had lower excess ratio than Census3D for all k values. This pattern, however, was not seen for the array data sets (see Figure 2(a) for k=50 and k=100).

The percentage of restarts is below 30% across all data sets and k values used in the experiment (see Figure 3). In fact, with the exception of k=25, the percentage of restarts in all cases is below 15%. The Array2D data set had very few restarts for

Figure 3. Percentage of Restarts

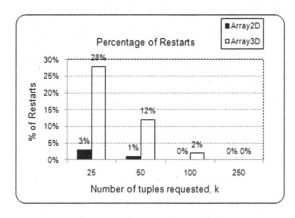

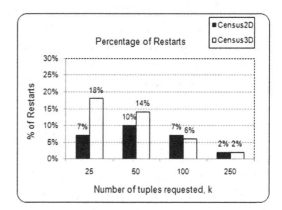

(a.) Array Data Sets

(b) Census Data Sets

Figure 4. Average Total Cost (I/Os) (log scale)

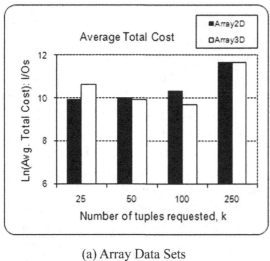

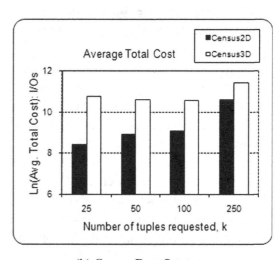

(a) Array Data Sets

(b) Census Data Sets

smaller k sizes and the restarts dropped to zero for higher k sizes. Overall, the percentage of restarts tends to drop for higher k values. In addition, the restarts were higher for the three dimensional data sets, Array3D and Census3D.

The overall performance of the cost-based method can be examined from the average total cost in Figure 4.

In order to show how the tradeoff between the costs of restarts and excess results can be effectively evaluated by the total cost, it is important to see some specific results. For example, for

k=100, the Census3D had lower percentage of restarts than Census2D. However, its total cost was higher due to its significantly higher average excess ratio. Note also that for k=100, Array3D had higher percentage of restarts than Array2D, but its total cost is lower due to its significantly lower average excess ratio.

Figure 4 also shows that the average total cost increased as k increased for the data sets Array2D and Census2D (see Figure 4(a) for Array2D and Figure 4(b) for Census2D). This pattern, however, was not seen for Array3D and Census3D data sets. This could be mainly due to the deteriorating quality of the histograms as the dimensionality increases. As the value of k gets smaller, estimating range using coarser histograms can lead to a significant number of excess tuples or a restart, and subsequently, a higher total cost.

Performance Comparison with the Dynamic Workload-Based Strategy

This section presents the performance comparison of our cost-based strategy with the dynamic workload based strategy proposed by Bruno et al. (2002). For convenience, we refer to the dynamic workload based strategy as DWBS and our strategy as QLOCS (Query-Level Optimal Cost Strategy) in the rest of this section. Our choice of the DWBS as the benchmark method is due to its substantially improved performance over the specialized sorting (indexing) methods proposed by Carey and Kossmann (1997, 1998), as well as the histogram-based heuristics proposed by Chaudhuri and Gravano (1999).

Both DWBS and QLOCS provide a query-mapping solution based on histograms and distance functions. However, there is a fundamental difference in the range estimation procedure between the two methods. The performance objective of DWBS is to optimize average performance for a given workload. Thus, the cut-off distance is determined by minimizing the average number of tuples retrieved for a training workload, which

contains queries with similar spatial distribution with the experimental queries. On the other hand, QLOCS provides a cost-optimal cut-off distance for a single top-k query based on the restart-excess cost tradeoff. Therefore, performance comparison solely on the average results will be clearly biased towards DWBS and this may hide other performance factors such as robustness or variability across queries. To avoid this bias, we also report the performance variability in terms of the *coefficient of variation* for the queries in the experimental set (i.e., *Coefficient of variation = St. Deviation/Average*).

We implement the DWBS so that the settings are kept identical for both strategies. Since DWBS requires a second set of queries or training load, we generated similarly another set of 100 queries for the calibration of the cut-off parameter α^*. For each k value, the cutoff parameter α^* for DWBS is estimated for the queries in the calibration set. This parameter is then used to determine the range for the queries in the validation set. We report the performance comparison using the *Average Excess Ratio, Percentage of Restarts* and the *Average Total Cost* metrics. The total cost formulation is applied to DWBS based on the excess results and the percentage of restarts obtained from the experiments. The experimental results reported in this section represent a default setting for $k = 100$ tuples.

Figure 5 shows the comparison of the average excess ratio and the coefficient of variation, and Figure 6 shows the percentage of restarts for the queries in the validation set. Though the average excess ratio does not show one method consistently outperforming the other, the *coefficient of variation* clearly shows that QLOCS has lower performance variability across the data sets (see Figure 5). In addition, the restart percentages for QLOCS are generally lower for almost all the data sets, particularly in the comparison for the Census2D data set (see Figure 6).

Figure 7 shows the performance comparison in terms of the average total costs for the two

Figure 5. Comparison of Average Excess Ratio and Variability

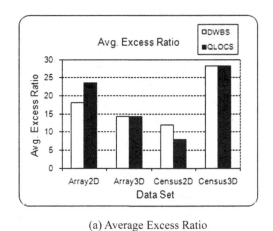

(a) Average Excess Ratio   (b) Excess Ratio Variability

Figure 6. Percentage of Restarts

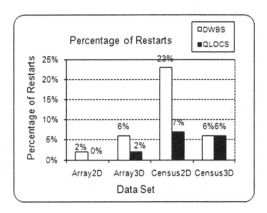

Figure 7. Comparison of Average Total Cost and Variability

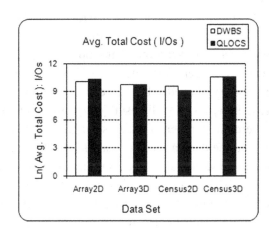
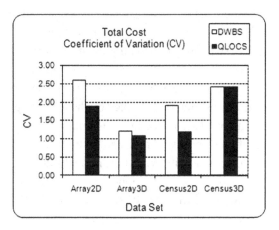

methods. The comparisons reveal a more comprehensive picture of the overall performance. Overall, the cost-based method performs better, especially by keeping the efficiency variability across queries lower and providing robust performance.

Note also that while the average total cost of QLOCS for Array2D is slightly higher than that of DWBS, the comparison of the cost variability across the queries clearly shows the opposite. This is because the DWBS provides aggregate performance without considering the performance variability across different queries. In reality queries are random and they are often executed as they are posed to the system. This requires the DWBS to keep the cut-off parameter up-to-date for any spur-of-the-moment query. In this respect, the relative performance of QLOCS has important practical implication in justifying the optimization of database operations at a query level.

LIMITATIONS AND FUTURE RESEARCH DIRECTIONS

There are several limitations and challenges that can be addressed in future research. Because of the broad scope of the problem, future research can be carried out in many angles. These include limitations related to the histogram environment, the distance functions, or the type of data to deal with (e.g., numerical versus categorical data). One common limitation of the query-mapping techniques is the lack of scalability in providing database profiles as the basis for accurate range query estimation. For example, the use of histograms as the basis for range query estimation is limited by the following major factors. One major factor is related to data distribution where histograms are assumed to have uniform tuple density within individual buckets. Although the cost-based approach provides an analytical framework for estimating cost tradeoffs in query processing, the range query estimation can be affected by the degree to which histogram

buckets conform to uniform tuple density (Ayanso et al., 2007). The actual distribution of tuples in the database and the quality of histograms in partitioning the underlying data may affect the assumptions as well as the performance of the cost-based range estimation method. For example, the *income* attribute in the census data has natural clusters of values which make it difficult to obtain uniform distribution of tuples in any given partition of the data. Another challenge is related to dimensionality and the lack of scalability in maintaining multi-dimensional histograms. This imposes a constraint on extending histogram-based methods into more complex database settings in terms of type of queries, number of attributes, number of data sources, among others. The underlying premise in histogram-based methods is that most customer-centric applications involve search attributes limited to only a few dimensions. However, as top-k querying becomes more pervasive in several application domains, the scalability of the methods becomes critical. Addressing these limitations requires new approaches that are not only efficient but also scalable to various application settings. Therefore, future work in query-mapping should aim at overcoming these limitations through mechanisms that can generate database profiles with more accurate data representation.

Future research can also consider extending the cost-based range estimation method to a distributed database environment. In an environment where databases are distributed over n different sites, a straightforward extension of the single database approach is to send the same top-k query to all databases. Each site then returns k results from its database that need to be merged at a common site to identify the overall best matches. In situations where the number of databases is large, accessing all the databases can be avoided if there is a database selection mechanism that identifies the subset of databases which can adequately answer the query. Further improvement can be obtained if an effective mechanism for merging results is also integrated with a database selection mechanism.

The key challenge in the distributed database setting is to minimize the total number of database accesses and at the same time maximize the number of close matches retrieved from selected databases (Yu, Sharma, Meng, and Qin, 2001). The use of histograms to represent individual databases has similar limitations described earlier. Therefore, another future research direction is to address the top-k retrieval issues in a distributed database setting by augmenting effective mechanisms for database selection as well as merging results from multiple data sources.

CONCLUSION

Top-k retrieval in RDBMSs is an active area of research. The problem warrants study from different perspectives. For many customer-centric applications, top-k retrieval aims to address the needs of the user as well as the performance requirements of database systems supporting different user applications. Efficient techniques will have profound significance given the enormous installed base of RDBMSs in various application domains.

Top-k queries are becoming increasingly important with the continued increase in the number of applications that require exploratory searches. The key advantage of the query-mapping approach is that it can be operationalized at an application layer outside of core query engines. Therefore, the practical appeal of the query-mapping approach provides significant opportunity if the underlying technical limitations are overcome through continuous research. The cost-based range estimation method presented here significantly extends existing query-mapping techniques. It extends the histogram-based approach for estimating range query by undertaking cost optimization at a query level. Explicit consideration for conflicting efficiency objectives (i.e., excess and restarts) and the formulation of the relevant cost components allow the method to optimally tradeoff performance on

one for the other. The experimental results from real world and synthetic multi-dimensional data sets clearly show that the cost-based method is able to tradeoff the two conflicting efficiency objectives and provide robust performance across the data sets and other experimental settings. Under identical settings, the cost-based range estimation method shows relatively better overall performance over the workload-based technique, particularly in terms of the performance variability.

REFERENCES

Ayanso, A., Goes, P. B., & Mehta, K. (2007). A practical approach for efficiently answering top-k relational queries. *Decision Support Systems*, *44*(1), 326–349. doi:10.1016/j.dss.2007.04.005

Ayanso, A., Goes, P. B., & Mehta, K. (2009). A cost-based range estimation for mapping top-k selection queries over relational databases. *Journal of Database Management*, *20*(4), 1–25. doi:10.4018/jdm.2009062501

Baeza-Yates, R., & Ribeiro-Neto, B. (1999). *Modern Information Retrieval*. New York: ACM Press.

Berchtold, S., Keim, D. A., Kriegel, H.-P., & Seidl, T. (2000). Indexing the solution space: a new technique for nearest neighbor search in high-dimensional space. *IEEE Transactions on Knowledge and Data Engineering*, *12*(1), 45–57. doi:10.1109/69.842249

Bertino, E., Rabbiti, F., & Gibbs, S. (1988). Query processing in a multimedia document system. *ACM Transactions on Information Systems*, *6*(1), 1–41. doi:10.1145/42279.42281

Blake, C., & Merz, C. (1998). UCI Repository of Machine-Learning Databases. [Online]. Available: http://archive.ics.uci.edu/ml/

Bruno, N., Chaudhuri, S., & Gravano, L. (2002). Top-k selection queries over relational databases: mapping strategies and performance evaluation. *ACM Transactions on Database Systems*, 27(2), 153–187. doi:10.1145/568518.568519

Bustos, B., Keim, D. A., Saupe, D., Schreck, T., & Vranić, D. V. (2005). Feature-based similarity search in 3D object databases. *ACM Computing Surveys*, 37(4), 345–387. doi:10.1145/1118890.1118893

Carey, M. J., & Kossmann, D. (1997). On saying 'Enough Already!' in SQL. *Proc. ACM SIGMOD Int'l Conf. Management of Data (SIGMOD'97)*.

Carey, M.J., & Kossmann, D. (1998). Reducing the breaking distance of an SQL query engine. *Proc. 24th Int'l Conf. Very Large Data Bases (VLDB'98)*.

Chan, S. W. K. (2006). Beyond keyword and cue-phrase matching: a sentence-based abstraction technique for information extraction. *Decision Support Systems*, 42(2), 759–777. doi:10.1016/j.dss.2004.11.017

Chang, K. C., & Hwang, S. (2002). Minimal probing: supporting expensive predicates for top-k queries. *Proc. ACM SIGMOD Int'l Conf. Management of Data (SIGMOD'02)*, 346–357.

Chang, Y., Bergman, I. D., Castelli, V., Li, C., Lo, M., & Smith, J. R. (2000). The onion technique: indexing for linear optimization queries. *Proc. ACM SIGMOD Int'l Conf. Management of Data (SIGMOD'00)*, 391–402.

Chaudhuri, S., & Gravano, L. (1999). Evaluating top-*k* selection queries. *Proc. 25th Int'l Conf. Very Large Data Bases (VLDB'99)*, 397-410.

Chaudhuri, S., Gravano, L., & Marian, A. (2004). Optimizing top-*k* selection queries over multimedia repositories. *IEEE Transactions on Knowledge and Data Engineering*, 16(8), 992–1009. doi:10.1109/TKDE.2004.30

Chen, C.-M., & Ling, Y. (2002). A sampling-based estimator for top-*k* selection query. *Proc. 18th Int'l Conf. Data Engineering (ICDE'02)*, 617-627.

Das, G., Gunopulos, D., Koudas, N., & Tsirogiannis, D. (2006). Answering top-k queries using views. *Proc. 32nd Int'l Conf. Very Large Data Bases (VLDB'06)*, 451–462.

Donjerkovic, D., & Ramakrishnan, R. (1999). Probabilistic optimization of top N queries. *Proc. 25th Int'l Conf. Very Large Data Bases (VLDB'99)*, 411- 422.

Fagin, R. (1998). Fuzzy queries in multimedia database systems. *Proc. 17th ACM Symp. Principles of Database Systems (PODS'98)*, 1-10.

Fagin, R. (1999). Combining fuzzy information from multiple systems. *Journal of Computer and System Sciences*, 58(1), 83–99. doi:10.1006/jcss.1998.1600

Fagin, R., Lotem, A., & Naor, M. (2001). Optimal aggregation algorithms for middleware. *Proc. 20th ACM Symp. Principles of Database Systems (PODS'01)*, 102-113.

Graefe, G. (2006). Implementing sorting in database systems. *ACM Computing Surveys*, 38(3), 10. doi:10.1145/1132960.1132964

Güntzer, U., Balke, W.-T., & Kießling, W. (2000). Optimizing multi-feature queries for image databases. *Proc. 26th Int'l Conf. Very Large Data Bases (VLDB'00)*, 419-428.

Hristidis, V., Koudas, N., & Papakonstantinou, Y. (2001). PREFER: A system for the efficient execution of multi-parametric ranked queries. *Proc. ACM SIGMOD Int'l Conf. Management of Data (SIGMOD'01)*. 259–270.

Huh, S.-Y., & Lee, J.-W. (2001). Providing approximate answers using a knowledge abstraction database. *Journal of Database Management*, 12(2), 14–24. doi:10.4018/jdm.2001040102

Ilyas, I. F., Aref, W. G., & Elmagarmid, A. K. (2002). Joining ranked inputs in practice. *Proc. 28th Int'l Conf. Very Large Data Bases (VLDB'02)*, 950–961.

Ilyas, I. F., Aref, W. G., & Elmagarmid, A. K. (2003). Supporting top-*k* join queries in relational databases. *Proc. 29th Int'l Conf. Very Large Data Bases (VLDB'03)*, 754-765.

Ilyas, I. F., Aref, W. G., Elmagarmid, A. K., Elmongui, H. G., Shah, R., & Vitter, J. S. (2006). adaptive rank-aware query optimization in relational databases. *ACM Transactions on Database Systems*, *31*(4), 1257–1304. doi:10.1145/1189769.1189772

Ilyas, I. F., Beskales, G., & Soliman, M. A. (2008). A survey of top-k query processing techniques in relational database systems. *ACM Computing Surveys*, *40*(4), 11. doi:10.1145/1391729.1391730

Jarke, M., & Koch, J. (1984). Query optimization in database systems. *ACM Computing Surveys*, *16*(2), 111–152. doi:10.1145/356924.356928

Kwok, S. H., & Zhao, J. L. (2006). Content-based object organization for efficient image retrieval in image databases. *Decision Support Systems*, *42*(3), 1901–1916. doi:10.1016/j.dss.2006.04.013

Li, C., Chang, K. C., & Ilyas, I. F. (2006). Supporting ad-hoc ranking aggregates. *Proc. ACM SIGMOD Int'l Conf. Management of Data (SIGMOD'06)*, 61-72.

Li, C., Chang, K. C.-C., Ilyas, I. F., & Song, S. (2005). RankSQL: Query algebra and optimization for relational topk queries. *Proc. ACM SIGMOD Int'l Conf. Management of Data (SIGMOD'05)*, 131-142.

Lomet, D. B., & Salzberg, B. (1990). The hB-tree: a multi-attribute indexing method with good guaranteed performance. *ACM Transactions on Database Systems*, *15*(4), 625–658. doi:10.1145/99935.99949

Mannino, M. V., Chu, P., & Sager, T. (1998). Statistical profile estimation in database systems. *ACM Computing Surveys*, *29*(2), 191–221.

Marian, A., Bruno, N., & Gravano, L. (2004). Evaluating top-*k* queries over web-accessible databases. *ACM Transactions on Database Systems*, *29*(2), 319–362. doi:10.1145/1005566.1005569

Motro, A. (1988). VAGUE: A user interface to relational databases that permits vague queries. *ACM Transactions on Office Information Systems*, *6*(3), 187–214. doi:10.1145/45945.48027

Muralikrishna, M., & DeWitt, D. J. (1988). Equi-depth histograms for estimating selectivity factors for multi-dimensional queries. *Proc. ACM SIGMOD Int'l Conf. Management of Data (SIGMOD'88)*, 28-36.

Nene, S. A., & Nayar, S. K. (1997). A simple algorithm for nearest neighbor search in high dimensions. *IEEE Transactions on Pattern Analysis and Machine Intelligence*, *19*(9), 989–1003. doi:10.1109/34.615448

Nepal, S., & Ramakrishna, M. V. (1999). Query processing issues in image (multimedia) databases. *Proc. 15th Int'l Conf. Data Engineering (ICDE'99)*, 22-29.

Orlandic, R., & Yu, B. (2004). Scalable QSF-trees: retrieving regional objects in high- dimensional spaces. *Journal of Database Management*, *15*(3), 45–59. doi:10.4018/jdm.2004070103

Piatetsky-Shapiro, G., & Connell, C. (1984). Accurate estimation of the number of tuples satisfying a condition. *Proc. ACM SIGMOD Int'l Conf. Management of Data (SIGMOD'84)*, 256-276.

Poosala, V., & Ioannidis, Y. E. (1997). Selectivity estimation without the attribute value independence assumption. *Proc. 23rd Int'l Conf. Very Large Data Bases (VLDB'97)*, 486- 495.

Poosala, V., Ioannidis, Y. E., Haas, P. J., & Shekita, E. J. (1996). Improved histograms for selectivity estimation of range predicates. *Proc. ACM SIG-MOD Int'l Conf. Management of Data (SIGMOD' 96)*, 294-305.

Press, W. H., Teukolsky, S. A., Vetterling, W. T., & Flannery, B. P. (1992). *Numerical Recipes in C. The Art of Scientific Computing*. Cambridge University Press.

Ramakrishnan, R., & Gehrke, J. (2003). *Database Management Systems* (3rd ed.). McGraw-Hill.

Salton, G., & McGill, M. J. (1983). *Introduction to Modern Information Retrieval*. McGraw-Hill.

Shin, M. K., Huh, S. Y., Park, D., & Lee, W. (2008). Relaxing queries with hierarchical quantified data abstraction. *Journal of Database Management*, *19*(4), 47–61. doi:10.4018/jdm.2008100103

Tao, Y., Xiao, X., & Pei, J. (2007). Efficient skyline and top-k retrieval in subspaces. *IEEE Transactions on Knowledge and Data Engineering*, *19*(8), 1072–1088. doi:10.1109/TKDE.2007.1051

Tsaparas, P., Palpanas, T., Kotidis, Y., Koudas, N., & Srivastava, D. (2003). Ranked join indices. *Proc. 19th Int'l Conf. Data Engineering (ICDE'03)*, 277-288.

Yu, C., Sharma, P., Meng, W., & Qin, Y. (2001). Database selection for processing k nearest neighbors queries in distributed environments. *1st ACM/IEEE-CS Joint Conf. on DL*, 215-222.

Zipf, G. K. (1949). *Human Behavior and the Principle of Least Effort*. Addison-Wesley.

APPENDIX

COST-BASED RANGE ESTIMATION: MODEL FORMULATION

Table 1. List of Symbols and Notation

Symbol	Description
$q(k)$	The top-k query requesting the k best tuples
Q	The corresponding range query
d_1	The restart distance range
d_2	The no-restart distance range
$[d_1, d_2]$	The distance interval within which the optimal distance is determined
k_1	The total number of qualifying tuples at the restart distance d_1
k_2	The number of tuples to be retrieved from the distance interval $[d_1, d_2]$; Note: $k_2 = k - k_1$
N	The total number of qualifying tuples within the distance interval $[d_1, d_2]$
d^*	The cost-optimal distance for obtaining the k_2 tuples
B	The number of buffer pages used

The optimal distance that provides the k tuples is bounded by the *restart* and *no-restart* distances or the interval $[d_1, d_2]$. Depending on whether the k tuples can be obtained from one bucket or more, there will be two possible scenarios for obtaining this interval. For a top-k query $q(k)$ that falls in a given bucket, the distance to the furthest point of the bucket is guaranteed to retrieve all the tuples inside this bucket. If the number of tuples within this distance is more than k, this distance represents the guaranteed or no-restart distance d_2, and the restart distance d_1 is zero. On the other hand, if the number of tuples within the first distance is less than k, the next bucket point in the rank is used. In this case, the distance to the first point is d_1, which guarantees k_1 tuples (i.e., $k_1 < k$) and the distance to the next point is d_2, which has additional N tuples (i.e., $k_1 + N \geq k$). Thus, the distance interval $[d_1, d_2]$ is used to determine the optimal cut-off point for the remaining tuples, k_2 (i.e., $k_2 = k - k_1$). This case generalizes the first case because k_2 equals k when there are no tuples at distance d_1 (i.e., $k_1 = 0$). Thus, throughout our model we represent the number of tuples to be retrieved from the distance interval $[d_1, d_2]$ by k_2 and the total number of qualifying tuples in the interval by N.

Given the search interval $[d_1, d_2]$, the optimal cut-off distance d^* is determined based on the cost tradeoff between the expected cost of a restart operation and the expected cost of handling excess tuples. In a typical database, the actual distribution of tuples is not known in advance, thus requiring a mechanism to handle this uncertainty. By normalizing the interval $[d_1, d_2]$ into a continuous interval $[0, 1]$, we use the function $f(t)$ to describe the probability density function for the distribution of tuples over this interval. The probability of a randomly chosen tuple being within distance d in the interval is given by

$$p = \int_0^d f(t)dt \qquad (1)$$

We assume that the likelihood of a tuple being included within d is independent of other tuples in the interval. Thus, the function in (1) represents the success probability p of a Bernoulli trial, and the probability of retrieving j tuples within the distance d, where the interval contains N tuples, follows the Binomial distribution. Given a binomial random variable X, the probability of obtaining exactly j tuples is given by

$$P(X = j) = \binom{N}{j} p^j (1-p)^{N-j}, \text{ where } j = 0, 1, ...N. \tag{2}$$

Considering the uniform tuple density assumption in histogram construction, we use the uniform probability density function in (1). Hence, the success probability p at any distance d can be represented by the distance point d itself and the probability in (2) can be re-written as

$$P(X = j) = \binom{N}{j} d^j (1-d)^{N-j}, \text{ where } d \in [0, 1], \text{ and } j = 0, 1, ...N. \tag{3}$$

In order to estimate cost, we account for the number of qualifying tuples at any given cut-off distance. Depending on the number of tuples to be retrieved, there are three cases to consider.

Case-1: $j < k_2$;
Case-2: $j > k_2$;
Case-3: $j = k_2$;

Under *Case-1*, a restart operation is required as the number of tuples obtained will be fewer than the desired number at distance d in the interval. Let the probability of obtaining fewer than k_2 tuples or the probability of a restart at d be *P(restart)*. Using the probability distribution in (3), *P(restart)* is expressed as

$$P(restart) = P(j < k_2) = \sum_{j=0}^{k_2-1} \binom{N}{j} d^j (1-d)^{N-j} \tag{4}$$

If a restart occurs, the range query Q will be constructed using the no-restart distance d_2. As in previous query-mapping techniques, we consider only one restart, which guarantees at least k tuples during the re-execution. Thus, we estimate the expected cost of a restart by determining the probability of obtaining fewer than k_2 tuples and the corresponding page I/O costs of re-executing the range query Q using the no-restart distance d_2. This includes the costs of retrieving as well as sorting all qualifying tuples at the no-restart range.

Definition 1.*The cost of a restart is the expected cost of re-executing the query using the no-restart range, if the original range query fails to retrieve the desired number of tuples.*

We estimate the expected I/O costs on the basis of unclustered B+ tree index for accessing qualifying tuples and the complexity order of the external merge-sort algorithm for sorting and returning the top-k set. In the worst-case scenario, the I/O costs of accessing the tuples correspond to the number of qualifying tuples at the no-restart range. The number of tuples available at the no-restart range is known from the histogram information. Let the total number of qualifying tuples at the no-restart distance range be T_{NR}. This includes the tuples at the restart distance d_1 and the additional N tuples from the search interval (i.e., $T_{NR} = k_1 + N$). In addition, the cost of sorting the tuples based on the complexity order of the external sorting algorithm (omitting the rounding notation $\lceil \ \rceil$ for ease of presentation only) is given by:

$$2T_{NR}(\log_{B-1}(\tfrac{T_{NR}}{B})+1),$$

where B is the number of buffer pages used, and $T_{NR} > B > 1$. (5)

Thus, the expected cost of a restart operation at distance d is given by:

$$ERC(d, j, k_2) = P(restart)(T_{NR} + 2T_{NR}(\log_{B-1}(\tfrac{T_{NR}}{B})+1)),$$

where $T_{NR} = k_1 + N$; and $T_{NR} > B > 1$. (6)

Under *Case-2*, the expected cost of handling excess tuples is formulated based on the costs of accessing and sorting tuples in excess of the desired number. Let the total number of tuples that are retrieved at distance d be T_S. This includes the k_1 tuples at the restart distance d_1 and the j tuples from the search interval (i.e., $T_S = k_1 + j$). If $j > k_2$, the total number of tuples retrieved, T_S exceeds the desired number k (note: $k = k_1 + k_2$).

Definition 2.*The cost of handling excess tuples is the expected cost of accessing and sorting results in excess of the desired number k.*

Thus, the expected cost of handling excess tuples is given by:

$$EEC(d, j, k_2) = \sum_{j=k_2+1}^{N} P(j)\left(\begin{bmatrix} T_S + 2T_S(\log_{B-1}(\tfrac{T_S}{B})+1) \end{bmatrix} \\ -\begin{bmatrix} k + 2k(\log_{B-1}(\tfrac{k}{B})+1) \end{bmatrix}\right),$$

where $T_S = k_1 + j$; $k = k_1 + k_2$; and $T_S > k > B > 1$ (7)

Finally, *Case-3* represents the ideal condition, where the total number of tuples retrieved at distance d equals the desired number. If $j = k_2$, then $T_S = k$ and there will be neither a restart nor excess tuples.

Thus, the expected total tradeoff cost for all the three cases can be expressed as

$$ETC(d, j, k_2) = \begin{cases} P(restart)(T_{NR} + 2T_{NR}(\log_{B-1}(\tfrac{T_{NR}}{B})+1)) & \text{if } j < k_2 \\ \sum_{j=k_2+1}^{N} P(j)\left(\begin{bmatrix} T_S + 2T_S(\log_{B-1}(\tfrac{T_S}{B})+1) \end{bmatrix} \\ -\begin{bmatrix} k + 2k(\log_{B-1}(\tfrac{k}{B})+1) \end{bmatrix}\right) & \text{if } j > k_2 \\ 0 & \text{if } j = k_2 \end{cases}$$

where $T_{NR} = k_1 + N$; $T_S = k_1 + j$; $k = k_1 + k_2$; and $T_{NR} \geq T_S > k > B > 1$ (8)

Therefore, $ETC(d, j, k_2) = ERC(d, j, k_2) + EEC(d, j, k_2)$ and the optimal distance d^* can be evaluated by setting the conditions $ETC'(d^*, j, k_2) = 0$ and $ETC''(d^*, j, k_2) > 0$.

Due to the absence of a closed form solution, the optimal distance is determined using numerical root-finding methods. Two closely related root-finding methods were used, the *successive approximation* method and the *secant* method (Press, Teukolsky, Vetterling & Flannery, 1992). The *secant* method is considered a more reliable alternative to the successive approximation method. We experimented this for several combinations of values for both root-finding methods and found the *secant* method consistently reliable and converging reasonably fast. The other advantage of the *secant* method is that it does not require the second derivative of the total cost function in the model. Thus, the iterations in the *secant* method are relatively in-expensive iterations.

The following example illustrates the *restart-excess* cost tradeoff and the optimal distance obtained using the cost-based method.

Example: *Consider a relation and a top-k query q(20) for k=20. Based on histogram statistics that summarize this relation, suppose there are a total of N=100 tuples available within the search interval [d₁, d₂]. For simplicity, assume that this search interval and the available tuples in this interval are related to a single histogram bucket (i.e., d₁=0 and k₁=0). Thus, the goal is to estimate the range that will retrieve the required 20 tuples from this interval (i.e., k₂=k=20). Based on these statistics, Figure 8 illustrates the expected restart-excess cost tradeoff that determines the optimal distance within the normalized distance interval [0,1].*

As Figure 8 shows, the expected cost of a restart decreases as the distance increases over the interval. On the other hand, the expected excess cost increases as the distance increases over the interval. However, both the restart and excess cost curves have positive values over the distance interval $[0,1]$. The cost-optimal distance obtained using the *secant* method is $d^* = 0.2876$. This cost-optimal distance is used to formulate the corresponding range query.

Figure 8. Illustration of the restart-excess cost-tradeoff

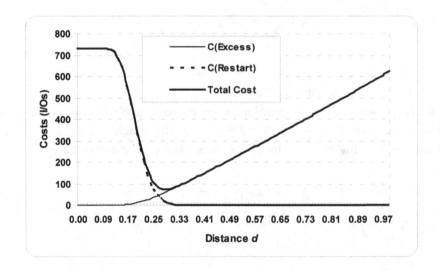

Figure 9. Sensitivity of the Total Trade-off Cost to the Buffer Size B

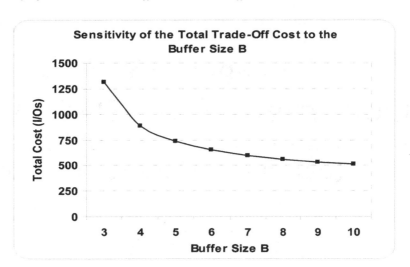

For the above example, we also examined the effect of the buffer size B on the estimation of total tradeoff cost. The total tradeoff cost remains stable as the buffer size increases (see Figure 9).

The above sensitivity analysis indicates that increasing the buffer size almost equally impacts both the restart and excess cost components, thus not significantly affecting the optimal distance in the cost tradeoff. Based on this observation, we set the buffer size at 5 buffer pages throughout our experiments.

Chapter 13

Document SQL (DSQL):
A Conservative Extension to SQL as an Ad-hoc Querying Frontend for XQuery

Arijit Sengupta
Wright State University, USA

V. Ramesh
Indiana University, USA

ABSTRACT

This chapter presents DSQL, a conservative extension of SQL, as an ad-hoc query language for XML. The development of DSQL follows the theoretical foundations of first order logic, and uses common query semantics already accepted for SQL. DSQL represents a core subset of XQuery that lends well to query optimization techniques; while at the same time allows easy integration into current databases and applications that use SQL. The intent of DSQL is not to replace XQuery, the current W3C recommended XML query language, but to serve as an ad-hoc querying frontend to XQuery. Further, the authors present proofs for important query language properties such as complexity and closure. An empirical study comparing DSQL and XQuery for the purpose of ad-hoc querying demonstrates that users perform better with DSQL for both flat and tree structures, in terms of both accuracy and efficiency.

INTRODUCTION

XQuery, the query language for XML, originally proposed as early as 2001 (Don Chamberlin, Clark, et al., 2001), was ratified as a candidate W3C recommendation late 2005, and became an official W3C recommendation in January 2007 (Boag et al., 2007). With the increase in the popularity of XML as the next generation of documentation representation language for the hyped Web 2.0

(O'Reilly, 2005), the need for a standard way of retrieving information from XML documents was considered a critical issue, which resulted in the design and eventual recommendation of XQuery. XQuery came from a marriage of two directions of querying: (i) pattern-based languages based on the tree structure of XML documents such as XPath (Clark & DeRose, 1999) and XQL (Robie, Lapp, & Schach, 1998), and (ii) a more logic-oriented approach with conditions and output specifications such as XML-QL (Deutsch, Fernandez, Florescu, Levy, & Suciu, 1998). Interestingly, however,

DOI: 10.4018/978-1-60960-521-6.ch013

both of these approaches used a syntactic convention significantly different from the predominant database query language SQL (Structured Query Language). Although there are some attempts towards including XML querying support in SQL, including SQLX (or SQL/XML), an effort by the International Standards Organization - SQL-03 (ANSI/ISO, 2003) from the International Standards Organization (ISO) to incorporate XML support directly into SQL, a common decision among XML query language designers was to create a completely new language for the purpose of querying XML data. One motivation for such a decision may have been the idea that the query language itself would use XML syntax. XQuery is defined as a "full programming language, and supports user-defined functions, with support for arbitrary levels of recursion and arbitrarily large memory usage" (Boag et al., 2007). This is a direction away from previous query language research, which tended to ensure the complexity of SQL stayed within reasonable complexity bounds. The problem is that having a full programming language may not be suitable for ad-hoc querying, which will explain why after 7 years of the development of XQuery, it is still not close to the level of popularity as an ad-hoc query language for XML.

Typically, a declarative (as opposed to a procedural) language is one that can specify an expression by declaring the structure and conditions of the intended result, instead of explicitly providing the steps necessary to obtain those results. For example, an SQL query need only specify the output attributes, the input relations, and properties of the output. The advantage of a declarative language is that the query engine can decide what steps to take to generate the output, by considering all query optimization possibilities. Some characteristics of XML schema make it possible to write queries using a declarative language. Although XML documents have a complex hierarchical structure, the strong presence of meta-data in XML documents makes it

fairly intuitive to write declarative queries based purely on logical combinations of the properties of the intended results. Declarative query languages where the primary focus is on the properties of the result, rather than the process of extracting the result itself, are very suitable for structured data, because they allow the possibility of letting the system optimize the queries instead of relying on the users' capabilities for writing an efficient query. We present a declarative query language, Document SQL (DSQL) that has the same look and feel as SQL and was designed by updating the semantics of SQL operations in the structured document domain. At the same time, DSQL was designed such that all queries written in it have equivalent counterparts in XQuery. Thus, by using such a language, users can take advantage of their existing SQL knowledge when writing ad-hoc queries without losing the expressive power of XQuery. In addition to describing the syntax and semantics of the language we also present the results of an experiment that investigates whether a language like DSQL make it possible for users to write more accurate and efficient queries than XQuery.

The rest of the paper is organized as follows. We start by reviewing some current research in this area. We then illustrate a data model for representing XML documents. We then develop the DSQL query language, and provide a comparison between DSQL and XQuery. Next, we describe a study comparing DSQL with XQuery, discuss the findings of this study and finally, provide some concluding remarks.

LITERATURE REVIEW

Query languages for documents and other hierarchical structures have been a topic of research ever since XML became a force in document representation. W3C (http://www.w3.org) initiated a working group for XML Query, for the purpose of designing query languages for document databases, and proposed a set of requirements (D. Chamberlin, Fankhauser, Marchiori, & Robie, 2003) for a query language for XML. A number of query languages came out of this stream of research, including XQL (Robie et al., 1998), XML-QL (Deutsch et al., 1998), Quilt (Don Chamberlin, Robie, & Florescu, 2001). All of these efforts were incorporated by the XQuery Working group into the query language XQuery (Boag et al., 2007). Several other query languages have been designed prior to XQuery with the intent of performing structured queries on complex data. We discuss some of the relevant languages in this section.

The research on programming languages, and on query languages in particular, has had two major variations: (i) procedural and (ii) declarative. Programming languages are designed to be fully Turing complete (capable of expressing all computable expressions), and are required to be able to perform all computable operations. However, traditionally query languages are not designed to be fully Turing-complete, and intentionally restricted to ensure optimizability and safety. Although some early research (e.g., Welty & Stemple, 1981) shows that a procedural query language such as TABLET provides better user performance than SQL, the database community has still accepted SQL, a declarative language, as the premier query language for relational databases. The primary reason behind this approach is the fact that users do not need to understand the structure of the data and the semantics of the language for writing queries; they only need to understand the logical relationships between components of the query result. The same effect is seen in the design of the Object Query Language (OQL)(Cluet, 1998) for object-oriented databases. It is somewhat surprising, however, to notice the shift in momentum towards more procedural languages in the query language development for XML. We present some background literature by presenting the W3C recommendation XQuery and its immediate predecessor Quilt as an example

of a procedural language, and a semistructured database query language Lorel (Abiteboul, Quass, McHugh, Widom, & Wiener, 1997) as an example of a non-procedural language, and then follow up with other such efforts in both procedural and non-procedural domains.

XQuery and Quilt

XQuery is an extension of an earlier query language *Quilt* (Don Chamberlin, Robie, et al., 2001), with features from many other languages as well. Originally designed to be a functional query language to specify queries in a simple human-readable form, Quilt has a fairly procedural structure that includes iterations (FOR), variable assignment (LET), conditionals (IF-ELSE) and functions (FUNCTION). Quilt was proposed mainly as a query language syntax capable of expressing queries as specified in the W3C query requirements, with no appreciable theoretical background. The proposal of XQuery was followed by an XML Query algebra, currently also known as the XPath/XQuery Formal Semantics (Draper et al., 2007), as a theoretical backend of XQuery. Unfortunately neither the language itself nor the algebra is used to prove the complexity or safety of this language. Although the language is able to express many different types of queries, the overall expressive power of the language is unexplored. However, because of the unrestricted nature of the functions and recursion supported in the language, Quilt (and hence XQuery) is Turing-complete.

Examples of XQuery queries are shown in Table 8 in Appendix B.

Lorel: the Lore Language

Abiteboul, et al (1997) proposed Lorel, which is a query language in Lore (Lightweight Object Repository), a system developed at Stanford for storing semistructured data. Lore is developed on top of an object-oriented database, and the language has many features of the Object-Oriented language OQL (see e.g., Cattell et al., 1997; Cluet, 1998). The language has an SQL like syntax and uses OQL path expressions to traverse structures. The language Lorel also has advanced path expression structures (referred to as "General Path Expressions"), which allow regular expressions on paths, path variables, and variable substitutions.

One of the issues with a declarative query language with complex data is the need for comparison between objects, sets and atomic data. Lorel uses a concept called "coercion" that forces the comparison between incompatible types by an implicit conversion instead of returning an error. Although this performs "intuitive" comparisons between objects, it affects the semantics of the language; especially since coercion affects the basic equivalence properties of equality (equality is no longer symmetric or transitive). Moreover, coercion of inequality is non-trivial.

Other Languages

Literature shows quite a few other languages that have been proposed and implemented as part of the research on document query languages. One prominent query language is UnQL (Buneman, Fernandez, & Suciu, 2000), a language similar to Lorel that is based on semistructured data and is capable of highly expressive structure traversal and creation operations. Other languages have also been proposed that are capable of querying XML. W3C's own XPath (Clark & DeRose, 1999) is capable of querying a single XML document using path traversal-like constructs. Robie, et al (1998) developed XQL building on an existing stylesheet language XSL (Deach, 1998) which can provide querying functionality using functional syntax. Literature also shows languages like XREL (Yoshikawa, Amagasa, Shimura, & Uemura, 2001) that provide interesting implementation-based methodologies for querying indexed version of document structures. Complex pattern-based languages have also been proposed, such as EquiX

(Cohen et al., 2002), which allows users to build a structured pattern via a user-interface that can be used to retrieve matching structures from the documents. Graphical languages such as XML-GL (Ceri et al., 1999) have also been proposed as alternatives to textual languages, as well as graphical frontends for complex query processing tasks. In addition, languages such as XML Stylesheet Language – XSL (Deach, 1998) As mentioned earlier, SQL-03, the latest SQL standard, includes support for building XML structures and comparing XML strings via pre-defined functions (ANSI/ISO, 2003), such efforts have not become commonplace, and have been overshadowed by the developments in XQuery. A succinct comparison between some of the languages mentioned above can be found in (Bonifati & Ceri, 2000).

Summary

The query languages described here are capable of expressing queries on complex structured data. However, whether or not these languages have the potential for worldwide acceptance and durability like SQL is highly questionable. None of the languages described here have the rigid theoretical basis like SQL, which can be used to prove the safety, complexity and other properties of the language. W3C is currently in the process of defining an XML Query algebra, which is equivalent to XQuery, although the algebra is still plagued with intractable complexity and expressive power. Furthermore, none of the languages proposed are compatible to SQL. Although Lorel is very close in syntax to SQL, many of the quirks of the language make Lorel queries quite distant from the semantics of SQL. The use of a highly procedural language such as XQuery for ad-hoc query formulation against XML documents is also somewhat intriguing, since a procedural language is extremely difficult to optimize.

If we take a look back at SQL, we realize that SQL has been a standard for over twenty years, and multiple research projects have compared

SQL with other (procedural) query languages and shown results both in favor and against SQL (Welty, 1990). Given its success in the "test of time", however, it seems logical that a declarative language like SQL cannot be ignored even for XML query processing. The success of SQL can be attributed to three factors: (i) its acceptance in the standards bodies and in the industry, (ii) its theoretical strength and foundation, and (iii) its relative ease of use. It should not be ignored that SQL is based on years of research and acceptance on formal logic, which yielded the Relational Calculus and Algebra. In our view, a lasting query language should be based on strong theoretical foundation. In this paper we present a language which provides a conservative extension to SQL, capable of performing a complete set of queries that can be easily implemented and understood, and demonstrate how such a language does make a difference in users' cognition and use.

DOCUMENT DATA MODEL

W3C has published two data models for XML: (i) a data model as the basis for XQuery and XPath (Fernandez, Malhotra, Marsh, Nagy, & Walsh, 2007), and (ii) an object-model DOM (Document Object Model) a low-level model for internal representation of XML (Le Hors et al., 2004). While the XPath/XQuery data model is adequate for formally explaining the semantics of XQuery, it is not very well-suited for the presentation for general theoretical concepts that we intend to cover in this article. Hence, we present a more conceptual model for documents, where, instead of treating documents as sequences of nodes with identifiers and ordered children, we use a more structural approach. In this section, we define the notion of a document data model, in which the concepts of documents and databases are defined as follows:

- *Document.* Intuitively, a document is a valid or well-formed tagged text. Defined more rigidly, a document is an instance of a DTD (Document Type Definition) or XML schema. The type of a document is determined by the DTD/schema that it conforms to (however, in the absence of a DTD/schema for well-formed documents, the type can be implied from the document structure). A DTD (or schema) can be modeled as a grammar represented by a quintuple $d = (\tau, G, A, C, P)$ where $\tau \in$ **doc** is a document type; $G \subset$ **gi** is a set of generic identifiers; $A \subset$ **att** is a set of attributes; and $C \subset$ **dom** is a set of constants. (Here **doc, dom, gi, att** represent universal sets of documents, string data domains, element names or generic identifiers, and attribute names respectively). P is a set of production rules describing the structure of conforming document instances. A document instance **d** belongs to the schema d iff $d \mapsto \mathbf{d}$. Analogous to the relational database model, the DTD serves as the schema for the managed data, and documents conforming to the DTD serve as instances of the schema.
- *Document Relation.* A document relation R is a finite unordered set of document instances **d** of a given type d.
- *Database.* A database, in this setting, is a finite set of document relations.

The document model presented here is a simplified version of the more formal Heterogeneous Nested Relations (HNR) model (Sengupta & Mohan, 2003) where each document is treated as a tuple in a heterogeneous nested relation (document relation). The heterogeneity in HNR comes from the fact that all elements of a relation may not be of the same type (because of the presence of "OR" types in XML. For example, consider the line in a DTD (Box 1).

Box 1.

```
<!ELEMENT article (journalarticle | conferencearticle) >
```

Figure 1. A simple poem database schema

```
<!DOCTYPE POEM [
<!ELEMENT poem - - (head, body)>
<!ELEMENT head - - (period, poet, title)>
<!ELEMENT body - - (stanza)+>
<!ELEMENT stanza - - (line)+>
<!ELEMENT (period | poet | title | line) - O (PCDATA)>
]>
```

The type *article* can now contain either *journalartiel*s or *conferencearticle*s, and hence is a heterogeneous type. All the formalisms presented here apply to both HNR as well as this simplified document model. Henceforth we will refer to this document model synonymously with the HNR model.

In the rest of this section, we are going to describe an algebra called Document Algebra (DA) over the document instances defined above, providing a set of operations for expressing queries on documents. Since the language is based on the concept of path expressions necessary for traversing the document structures, we first introduce the notion of simple path expressions that we use in the algebra. To demonstrate the capabilities of the language, we are going to use a simple structure of a poem as a running example. The structure is shown in Figure 1.

Simple Path Expression

Path expressions are well-accepted mechanisms for structural traversal in complex objects such as XML documents. Although the language we are presenting does include the core XPath language, we present a simpler notion of path expressions here to simplify the formalisms in this paper. We define the concept of simple path expressions or SPE's (relative to the document type $d = (\tau, G, A, C, P)$), as follows:

- *Null path.* ε, the null path, is an SPE. The null path essentially denotes the current node in the path and is in the language as a base case.

- *Basic path.* Every $x \in G$ is an SPE, and is termed "basic path." So, in the DTD in Figure 1, poem is a basic path, representing all poem tags, and title is a basic path representing all titles.

- *Listed path*: A listed path P is a fully expanded SPE of the form $A_1.A_2. \cdots .A_n$, where $n \geq 1$, and for every i, $A_i \in G$, and A_{i+1} is a direct child of A_i for $1 \leq i \leq n-1$. For example, poem.head. title is a listed path, identifying titles of the poems.

- *Abbreviated path.* An abbreviated path P of the form $P_1..P_2.. \cdots ..P_k$ is an SPE, where $k \geq 1$, and for every i, P_i is a basic or listed path. This notion is similar to the partial path specification in (Van den Bussche & Vossen, 1993) and the ".." operator in (Christophides, Abiteboul, Cluet, & Scholl, 1994). For example, poem..title represents any title as a descendant of the poem tag.

- *Indexed path.* A path expression of the form $P(iexp)$ is an indexed path where P is a basic, listed, or abbreviated path, and $iexp$ is of one of the following forms:
- Constant: $iexp \in N, iexp > 0$.
- Range: $iexp$ is of the form n_1 TO n_2. where $n_1, n_2 \in N$ and $n_1 \leq n_2$.

For example, poem..stanza[1] denotes the first stanza of a poem.

Semantics of SPEs: As mentioned above, path expressions are always defined in the context of a Document relation R. A path expression P applied to a set of documents is a function from a set of documents to another set of documents rooted at $last(P)$, such that the documents in the new set are rooted at elements that are reachable from the roots of the original documents by following the path P. Here, $last(P)$ refers to the last element (or generic identifier) in P.

Document Algebra (DA)

Given the above document model, we can now describe a formal language that captures operations on the data model. We call this language the "Heterogeneous Nested Relational Algebra" (HNRA) or simply, "Document Algebra" (DA). Every DA expression E^τ represents a set of documents of a particular type τ. We define DA expressions inductively by first defining the basic document expression and then defining the operations *path selection* ($\circ$), cross product ($\times$), selection (σ), union ($\cup$), intersection ($\cap$), set difference ($-$), nest (ν) and unnest (μ). Other useful operations such as *join* ($\bowtie$), projection (π), generalized product ($\prod$) and root addition (ρ), can be constructed from these primitive operations.

- **Document:** Any document relation name R is a valid DA expression, the type of the expression given by the type of R. In the poetry example, the expression poem is a DA expression representing all poems in the document relation poem.

- **Union** ($\cup$): Union in the context of HNRA is the normal set union operation without the restriction that both operands of the union be of the same type (we would also refer to this operation as "generalized union" or "heterogeneous union"). Given two DA expressions $E_1^{\tau_1}$ and $E_2^{\tau_2}$, the result of the union $E_1^{\tau_1} \cup_R E_2^{\tau_2}$ is a set of documents of a new type R which is created by adding a union type R, τ_1 and τ_2 in an option group. For example, the expression poem..title $\cup_{\text{alltext}}$ poem..line creates a new structure with type alltext, which contains titles or lines. The union operation will then create a set of alltext tags combining all titles and lines from the poem.

- **Path selection** ($\circ$): Given a DA expression E^τ and a SPE P, $E^\tau \circ P$ ($\circ$ representing either path operator ".." or ".." as discussed earlier) is a DA expression that returns the set of documents rooted at $last(P)$ obtained by traversing the path P from each of the documents in E^τ. For example, poem..period represents all periods in the poem relation.

- **Intersection** ($\cap$): The intersection operation in DA is the standard set intersection $E_1^\tau \cap E_2^\tau$, representing documents that are in both E_1^τ and in E_2^τ. For example, poem..title $\cap$ poem..line retrieves lines that are also titles in poems.

- **Set difference** ($-$): The set difference operation in DA is the standard set difference operation $E_1^\tau - E_2^\tau$, containing the set of documents in E_1^τ not in E_2^τ. For example, poem..title − poem..line retrieves titles that do not appear as lines in poems.

- **Cross product** ($\times$): Given two DA expressions $E_1^{\tau_1}$ and $E_2^{\tau_2}$, the expression $E_1^{\tau_1} \times_R E_2^{\tau_2}$ is a DA expression, and it represents a set of documents with a new type R, the members of which contain two subcomponents: one from the set $E_1^{\tau_1}$ and the other from $E_2^{\tau_2}$. Every member in the resulting set is of type R, and each member of the set $E_1^{\tau_1}$ is paired with each member of the set $E_2^{\tau_2}$ under an instance of R. For example, poem..poet $\times_{\text{combo}}$ poem..title pairs up all poets in the database with all poem titles under a new type combo.

- **Selection** (σ): The selection operation $\sigma_\gamma E^\tau$ extracts a subset of documents from the input set E^τ that satisfy a selection condition γ. γ can be of one of two forms: (i) $P\theta c$ where P is a path expression, θ is in $\{\ni, \not\ni\}$ and $c \in \mathbf{dom}$, and (ii) $P_1 \theta P_2$ where P_1 and P_2 are path expressions and $\theta \in \{=, \neq, \subseteq,, \cap \cap\}$. See below for several examples of selection.

- **Nest** (ν): The nest operation groups together document tuples that have the same value in the nesting elements. So, $E = \nu_X^R(E_1^\tau)$, where E creates a new structure with X extracted from τ and every τ with the same value of X has a $\tau - X$ structure grouped together with one instance of X. For example, $\nu_{\text{head.period}}^{\text{periodgroup}}(poem.head)$ creates a new structure poetgroup by extracting the period from each head nesting all headings with the same value of period together.

- **Unnest** (μ): The unnest operation creates multiple document tuples by taking every item from the nested set and combining the nesting element with every item of the set.

So, $E = \mu_X^R(E_1^\tau)$, where E has a new structure, with values of X repeated for every set it is associated with in τ. For example, $\mu_{\text{poem..title}}^{\text{strange}}(poem..line)$ creates a new structure called strange which has the title of each poem repeated along with every line of the poem.

Examples

To demonstrate the operators, here are a few example DA queries based on the DTD in Figure 1.

Find all poems that contain the word "love" in the poem title.

$$\sigma_{poem..title \ni \text{``love''}} Poem$$

Extract titles and authors of all poems in the database.

$$\pi_{poem..title, poem..poet}^{AT} Poem$$

Find the poems that do not have the word "love" in the title.

$$Poem - \sigma_{poem..title \ni \text{``love''}} Poem$$

Find the pairs of names for poets who have at least one common poem title.

$$\pi_{P_1..poet, P_2..poet} \left(\sigma_{P_1..poet \cap P_2..poet} \left(\rho_{P_1} Poem \bowtie_{P_1..title \cap P_2..title}^R \rho_{P_2} Poem \right) \right)$$

Find the periods of literature during which all poems written had the word "love" in their titles. We solve this query using stages.

$$Periods = Poem \circ poem..period$$
$$PT = \pi^P T_{poem..period, poem..title} Poem$$
$$Result = Periods - \left(PT - \sigma_{PT.title \ni \text{``love''}} PT \right) \circ PT.period$$

We have proved many interesting properties of DA, as demonstrated in Appendix A.

DOCUMENT SQL (DSQL)

Although a formal query language is highly desirable for demonstrating the properties of the query language, a more user-friendly language is essential for the query language to be usable in real-world. Here we present DSQL (Document SQL), a query language derived from and equivalent to the Document Algebra. One of the most important criteria in the design of DSQL was to ensure that it was as close to SQL as possible. Later in this section we will present a syntactic equivalence property that will demonstrate the consequence of this design.

DSQL is structured after SQL. Although its operations are based on DA, the syntax of DSQL is essentially the same as the syntax of SQL, with a few small differences to accommodate path expressions and dynamic structure creation, both of which are essential in a query language for XML databases. In this section, we will describe the DSQL language, and demonstrate the properties of this language.

DSQL has the same basic structure as SQL, with recognizable SELECT, FROM and WHERE clauses for retrieval, and GROUP BY, HAVING and ORDER BY clauses for grouping and ordering of the results. The GROUP BY clause in DSQL, unlike that of SQL is actually an integral part of the querying method, since GROUP BY turns out to be an elegant way of restructuring the results. Here we briefly mention each of the query clauses of the language.

Every DSQL query has the following basic syntax (Box 2).

As in SQL, only the SELECT and the FROM clauses are required. The other clauses are optional. Also, multiple SELECT queries can be combined using the standard set operations (Union,

Box 2.

```
SELECT output_structure
FROM input_specification
WHERE conditions
grouping_specs
ordering_specs
```

Intersect, Minus). The following sections describe in detail the above constructs of DSQL.

The Select Clause

The SELECT clause in DSQL has the same major structure of SQL, with the main difference that the SELECT clause can create complex structures, and can traverse paths in the items to retrieve. To keep the language simple and close to SQL, generation of attributes has not been included in the base language. In fact, the formal specification of the language uses a form of XML known as ENF (Element Normal Form). An early definition of ENF was provided by (Layman, 1999), that ensures that any XML document with attributes can be re-written without the use of attributes and vice versa. Given these observations, we have the following output structure of the SELECT clause (Box 3) in Backus-Naur Form (BNF). The complete BNF of DSQL is included in Appendix B.

The above BNF allows select clauses such as (Box 4).

The only omitted part of the actual BNF for the SELECT clause involves the use of aggregate functions. As is evident from the BNF and the examples above, this extension of the SELECT clause allows the creation of structures with arbitrary levels of nesting. Notice that any grouping is not inherent in this specification and is, instead, the task of the grouping_specs.

Box 3.

```
output_structure::= ['ALL' | 'DISTINCT'] output
         output::= scalar_exp_list | '*'
 scalar_exp_list::= scalar_exp [',' scalar_exp]*
     scalar_exp::= name<scalar_exp_list> | atom | col
            col::= path_exp
```

Box 4.

```
SELECT *
SELECT output<*>
SELECT result<B.title, B.author>
SELECT booklist<B.author, books<B.title, B.year>>
```

Box 5.

```
input_specification::= db_list
           db_list::= db [,db]*
                db::= path_exp [alias]
          path_exp::= SPE
```

Box 6.

```
FROM books.xml B
FROM books.xml B, authors.xml A
FROM http://www.mycompany.com/docs/invoices.xml V, V..items I
```

The From Clause

The BNF for the FROM clause is as follows (Box 5).

In the above BNF, SPE represents the notion of Simple Path Expressions discussed earlier. The above specification of FROM clause allows the following types of expressions in the FROM clause (Box 6).

The Where Clause

WHERE conditions in DSQL are similar to those in SQL. The main difference in semantics is due to paths, *i.e.*, all expressions in DSQL are path expressions, so operators are often set operators. For example, consider the following query (Box 7).

The WHERE expression evaluates to true if the path expression yields a singleton set containing an atom identical to `Extending SQL`. Set membership operations such as in and contains are also available in DSQL.

Grouping and Ordering Clauses

SQL has several ways of specifying post query formatting and layout generation. The following

Box 7.

```
SELECT result<B.title>
FROM bibdb..book B
WHERE B.title = `Extending SQL'
```

Table 1. Semantics of GROUP BY

	Before grouping	After grouping by A
Query	SELECT result<A,B,C>	SELECT result<A,B,C>... GROUP BY A
Structure	result::= A, B, C	result::= A, (B,C)*
Data	<result> <A>a1</A><B>b1</B><C>c1</C> </result> <result> <A>a1</A><B>b2</B><C>c2</C> </result> <result> <A>a1</A><B>b3</B><C>c3</C> </result> <result> <A>a2</A><B>b4</B><C>c4</C> </result>	<result> <A>a1</A> <B>b1</B><C>c1</C> <B>b2</B><C>c2</C> <B>b3</B><C>c3</C> </result> <result> <A>a2</A> <B>b4</B><C>c4</C> </result>

are the grouping and ordering specifications in DSQL:

- ORDER BY (sorting): DSQL has the same semantics for ORDER BY as SQL. The expressions in the SELECT clause can be ordered by expressions in the ORDER BY clause, regardless of whether or not the ordering expressions appear in the SELECT clause, as long as the expressions are logically related, i.e., a possible ordering is possible using the ordering expression.
- Aggregate functions: DSQL supports the same five basic aggregate functions as SQL (sum, count, min, max, avg).
- GROUP BY: In DSQL, GROUP BY is a restructuring operation but unlike SQL, the aggregate function is optional. The semantics of the restructuring operation is explained using the production that defines the created structure, as shown in Table 1.

There are a few consequences of this type of grouping:

- *Grouping without aggregate functions* Grouping tasks can be performed with or without aggregate functions. In the case no aggregate functions are specified, grouping is essentially a restructuring operation. In the case aggregate functions are specified, the aggregate functions are performed for each set in the structures produced by the grouping.
- *Group by null* An interesting effect of the grouping semantics is the possibility of grouping without any grouping clause which would cause the following restructuring operation: result::= A, B, C transformed to result::= (A, B, C)*

The above is essentially a standard set formation operation caused by nesting on the full relation.

Box 8.

```
SELECT Books<B.Author, Years<B.year, B.title>>
FROM Bib B
GROUP Books by B.Author
GROUP Years by B.Year
```

- *Multiple group-by clauses* A complex structure could be grouped many times. In such cases, the structure to be grouped needs to be specified. For example (Box 8).

Examples of some queries on the poetry database using DSQL are shown in Table 8 in Appendix B.

Equivalence Between DSQL and DA

Here we provide a sketch of the proof that DSQL and DA are equivalent languages. This result is highly significant, since queries expressed in DSQL can be easily converted into DA and executed and optimized procedurally, although queries can be expressed using the simple declarative language. The complete proof requires the use of the Document Calculus (DC), which is beyond the scope of this paper. We present a partial proof here.

Theorem T.1 DSQL and DA are equivalent.

The above statement can be re-stated as: Any DA Expression E can be expressed as an equivalent DSQL query Q, and vice versa.

The proof follows in two parts:

Part 1 (DA-DSQL Translation)

For every DA expression E, there exists a DSQL query Q such that $E \equiv Q$

The proof is by structural induction on E.

- **Base case.** The base case is for $E_0 = D$, D being a document relation. The equivalent DSQL query S_0 is simply (Box 9.)

Box 9.

```
SELECT * FROM D.
```

Box 10.

```
SELECT * FROM E1..P
```

- **Induction hypothesis** Assume that for some DA expression E_i there is an equivalent DSQL Query Q_i.

- **Inductive step** We now need to show by induction that for any DA expression E, there is an equivalent DSQL query Q. We are going to use the strong induction method for this proof, by assuming that every E_i that is structurally less complex than E, there exists an equivalent Q_i. The proof follows by taking the case for each of the algebraic operations:

  ○ **Path selection** $E = E_1 \circ P$. The equivalent DSQL query is (Box 10).

  ○ **Union** ($\cup$) Given two DA expressions $E_1^{\tau_1}$ and $E_2^{\tau_2}$, the result of the union is $E = E_1^{\tau_1} \cup_R E_2^{\tau_2}$, which has the following DSQL equivalent(Box 11).

  ○ **Intersection** ($\cap$) The intersection operation is $E = E_1^{\tau} \cap E_2^{\tau}$, which has the following DSQL equivalent(Box 12).

327

Box 11.

```
SELECT R<T1> FROM E1 UNION SELECT R<T2> FROM E2
```

Box 12.

```
SELECT R<T> FROM E1 INTERSECT SELECT R<T> FROM E2
```

Box 13.

```
SELECT R<T> FROM E1 MINUS SELECT R<T> FROM E2
```

Box 14.

```
SELECT R<T1,T2> FROM E1, E2
```

Box 15.

```
(a)  SELECT * FROM E WHERE E..P = c
(b)  SELECT * FROM E WHERE E..P1 = E..P2
```

- **Set difference** ($-$) The set difference operation $E = E_1^\tau - E_2^\tau$, has the following DSQL equivalent (Box 13).
- **Cross product** ($\times$) The cross product expression $E = E_1^{\tau_1} \times_R E_2^{\tau_2}$ has the following DSQL equivalent (Box 14).
- **Selection** (σ) As before, the selection operation $E = \sigma_\gamma E^\tau$ is translated based on two forms of γ: (i) $P\theta c$ and (ii) $P_1\theta P_2$. The DSQL equivalents for the two cases are as follows (Box 15).
  Notice, however, that θ is assumed to be equality in this case. A $\ni$ would be translated using the contains operator.
- **Nest** (ν) The nest operation is represented as $E = \nu_X^R(E_1^\tau)$. In order for

this operation to be valid, however, X needs to be part of τ. Say Y is the rest of τ, i.e., $Y = \tau - X$. Then E has the following DSQL equivalent (Box 16).
- **Unnest** (μ) The unnest operation is represented as $E = \mu_X^R(E_1^\tau)$. Again, in order for this operation to be valid, τ should have the form $\tau = <Y,<X>>$. Then E will have the following DSQL equivalent (Box 17).

Part 2. DSQL-DA Translation

For every DSQL query Q, there exists a DA expression E such that $Q \equiv E$

Proof. Since DSQL does not have an inductively defined structure, a rigorous proof of this property is not possible. The intuition of this result,

Box 16.

```
SELECT R<X,Y> FROM E1 GROUP R BY X
```

Box 17.

```
SELECT R<P.X, P.Y> FROM E1.T P
```

Box 18.

```
SELECT R<D1..P1, D2..P2>
FROM D1, D2
WHERE D1..P3 = D2..P4
GROUP R BY D1..P1
```

however, follows from the fact that the forward translation shown above covers all of the structural forms of DSQL, which indicates that every structural form of DSQL queries can be converted to an equivalent DA expression. This conversion can be shown by construction as follows:

Consider a DSQL query over two documents D_1 and D_2. We can construct a query containing all the core DSQL constructs described above (Box 18).

We can now construct a DA expression for the above DSQL query as follows, creating temporary symbols which are subsequently removed.

$$E_1 = \pi^R_{X.D_1..P_1,X.D_2..P2}\sigma_{R.D_1..P3=R.D_2..P4}(D_1 \times^R D_2)$$

$$E = \nu_{R.D_1..P1}E_1$$

Such algebra expressions can be generated for any DSQL query. If a query involves subquery, the same method can be used to create (potentially parameterized) DA expressions for each subquery.

Given the results of parts 1 and 2, we can now say that for every DA expression, there is a DSQL query, and vice versa. Hence DA and DSQL are equivalent.

DSQL VS. XQUERY

As mentioned earlier, the acceptance of XQuery as a query language recommendation by W3C has virtually stopped any further research in the domain of query languages for XML. We do recognize the necessity of the existence of a widely accepted language, but there are many valid shortcomings of XQuery that need to be addressed. We have earlier pointed out that XQuery is a highly expressive language. In fact, XQuery is Turing-complete (Kepser, 2003) and easily an unsafe (capable of generating infinite output) language. Turing completeness (Turing, 1936) relates to the expressive power of a language, and a Turing-complete language is capable of expressing all computable expressions (including those that may take exponential or infinite time). In addition, the XQuery specification clearly states "Arbitrary recursion is possible, as is arbitrarily large memory usage, and implementations may place limits on CPU and memory usage, as well as restricting access to system-defined functions." In database literature, languages that have no bounds on the space used by queries are referred to as unsafe languages, and Document Algebra is exhibits Logspace space complexity just like relational algebra. Given that XQuery is such a powerful language, having only XQuery available to the users for the means for writing ad-hoc queries could involve a fair amount of risk to database implementers and administrators. In Table 2 we show a summary of comparison of the fundamental properties of the two languages.

We argue that even with the popularity of XQuery, there is a benefit to having DSQL serve as a potential ad-hoc query writing front-end to XQuery. In other words, DSQL can be used to formulate queries that can be internally translated to XQuery (or executed directly) by a query ex-

Table 2. Comparison of DSQL against XQuery. Note that Turing completeness indicates all computable (including infinite computations) are possible.

Property	XQuery	DSQL
Language type	full programming language	declarative query language
Function support	yes	no
Recursion support	yes	no
Turing completeness	yes	no
Safety	none	Logspace safe
Complexity	Unbounded	PTIME bound
Conservativity	no	yes

ecution engine, which will immediate prevent users from accidentally using any of the unsafe features of XQuery. In order to facilitate this, we need to show that every query expressed by DSQL has an equivalent query in XQuery that will generate the same result. In addition, the equivalent XQuery expression can be generated only from the DSQL query. In this section, we present a sketch of a proof for this property.

Theorem T.2 DSQL is a subset of XQuery, i.e., any DSQL expression has a corresponding equivalent XQuery expression.

Proof: The proof of this theorem is based on the Theorem T.1, where we showed that DSQL and DA are semantically equivalent. Based on this, we can now restate the theorem as: for any DA expression E, there is an equivalent XQuery expression X.

The proof is now by induction on the structure of DA expressions.

- **Base case.** The base case is for $E_0 = D$ where D is a document relation. This case is trivial, since the equivalent XQuery query S_0 is simply(Box 19).

- **Induction hypothesis** Assume that for some DA expression E_i there is an equivalent XQuery Q_i.

- **Inductive step** The induction step for this theorem is similar to the induction step in

Box 19.

```
{FOR $d IN D RETURN {$d}}.
```

Box 20.

```
{FOR $d IN E1//P RETURN {$d}}
```

Theorem T.1. We now need to show by induction that for any DA expression E, there is an equivalent XQuery Q. We are going to use the strong induction method for this proof, by assuming that every E_i that is structurally less complex than E, there exists an equivalent Q_i. The proof follows by taking the case for each of the algebraic operations:

- **Path selection** $E = E_1 \circ P$. The equivalent XQuery is (Box 20).

  ○ **Union** ($\cup$) Given two DA expressions $E_1^{\tau_1}$ and $E_2^{\tau_2}$, the result of the union is $E = E_1^{\tau_1} \cup_R E_2^{\tau_2}$, which has the following XQuery equivalent(Box 21).

  ○ **Intersection** ($\cap$) The intersection operation is $E = E_1^\tau \cap E_2^\tau$, which has the following XQuery equivalent (Box 22).

Box 21.

```
<R> FOR e1 IN E1 RETURN e1
union
FOR e2 IN E2 RETURN e2 </R>
```

Box 22.

```
{FOR $e1 IN E1 RETURN {$e1}
 INTERSECT
 FOR $e2 IN E2 RETURN {$e2}}
```

Box 23.

```
{FOR $e1 IN E1 RETURN {$e1}
 EXCEPT
 FOR $e2 IN E2 RETURN {$e2}}
```

Box 24.

```
FOR e1 IN E1
FOR e2 IN E2
RETURN <R> e1 e2 </R>
```

- ○ **Set difference (−)** The set difference operation $E = E_1^\tau - E_2^\tau$, has the following XQuery equivalent(Box 23).
- ○ **Cross product (×)** The cross product expression $E = E_1^{\tau_1} \times_R E_2^{\tau_2}$ has the following XQuery equivalent(Box 24).
- ○ **Selection (σ)** The selection operation $E = \sigma_\gamma E^\tau$ is translated based on two forms of γ: (a) $P\theta c$ and (b) $P_1\theta P_2$. The XQuery equivalents for the two cases are as follows(Box 25).
- ○ **Nest (ν)** The nest operation is represented as $E = \nu_X^R(E_1^\tau)$. As before, assume $Y = \tau - X$. Then E has the following XQuery equivalent(Box 26).
- ○ **Unnest (μ)** The unnest operation is represented as $E = \mu_X^R(E_1^\tau)$. Again, in order for this operation to be valid, τ should have the form $\tau = <Y, <X>>$. Then E will have the following XQuery equivalent(Box 27).

Thus we have shown that for every DA expression, there is an equivalent XQuery. Hence DA $\subseteq$ XQuery, and using Theorem T.1, we have DSQL $\subseteq$ XQuery.

In addition, it is fairly easy to show that DSQL $\subset$ XQuery (*i.e.*, DSQL is a proper subset of XQuery), noting the fact that XQuery has features such as functions and recursive calls to functions, which do not have any equivalents in DSQL. Hence DSQL $\subset$ XQuery.

Limitations of DSQL

Since DSQL is a proper subset of XQuery, there are operations in XQuery for which there is no DSQL query. The types of queries that cannot be performed using DSQL can be categorized under the following:

- *No support for built-in ad-hoc functions*: DSQL does not have built-in implementations of some of the functions in XQuery, such as +bags-are-equal+, etc. Some of these functions can be implemented as views or macros.
- *No support for branching and looping*: DSQL does not provide users with a means for structuring queries with comparison statements like *if* or looping structures like *for* or *while*. Comparisons can be performed using a union operation, and looping is always implicit in DSQL queries - comparisons are always performed on all elements of the current set.

Box 25.

```
(a)   { FOR $e in E WHERE $e//P = c RETURN {$e}}
(b)   { FOR $e in E WHERE $e//P1 = $e//P2 RETURN {$e}}
```

Box 26.

```
<R> FOR y in distinct (E1/Y)RETURN y
    FOR x in E1[Y=y]/X return x   </R>
```

Box 27.

```
FOR e1 in E1 LET y = e1/Y
RETURN
FOR x IN e1/X RETURN <R> y x </R>
```

- *No support for user-defined functions and recursion*: DSQL does not have a way of creating user-defined functions and function calls. Providing functions, calls and comparison immediately increases the complexity of the language to full Turing completeness, and makes queries prone to unsafe computation such as infinite recursion.
- *Limited path expression support*: DSQL only supports a simple form of path expressions (SPE) discussed earlier, and does not have all the advanced XPath features. Many of XPath's capabilities can be performed using the SELECT and WHERE clauses in DSQL. Full XPath 2 features once again involve Turing complete operations and are intentionally left out.
- *No metadata querying capabilities*: XQuery allows queries on metadata, where searches and comparisons can be performed on the names of the elements. This is not part of DSQL. Reflexive query languages have been studied in the context of relational databases by several articles

such as Wyss & Van Gucht (2001) and could be applied to DSQL as future work.
- *No intrinsic support for namespaces*: DSQL does not provide direct support for namespaces; however, namespace queries can be performed by treating namespace-prefixed elements as standard elements. In XQuery namespace features are available with a set of ad-hoc functions, and we did not find it necessary to increase the complexity of DSQL by adding such features.

In summary, although in theory, DSQL is less powerful and restricted compared to XQuery, the features that DSQL omits are scarcely used for ad-hoc querying, and the limitations makes DSQL a clean and stable language, in which queries look concise and are guaranteed to terminate and not require excessive computing resources to execute. In addition, having such a language as a frontend to XQuery would ensure that users have the option of using a familiar environment to write queries and still use the advanced functionality of structured documents.

EXPERIMENT

In the previous sections we demonstrated that DSQL represents a viable (declarative) alternative to the procedural XQuery language, especially for ad hoc queries. We conducted an empirical study to determine if users will be more accurate and efficient when writing queries using DSQL than XQuery.

Research Questions

The primary question of interest in our study was to understand the circumstances under which it would be more appropriate to use the two languages outlined above. Since XML can be used to represent both flat and tree-like structures, we investigated the use of the two query languages on these two types of XML structures. Such an investigation allows us to examine the "fit" between the characteristics of the representation and the characteristics of the language. Flat structures are akin to relational database schema whereas tree structures are more hierarchical in nature possibly containing several levels of nesting. Thus, the theory of cognitive fit (Vessey & Galletta, 1991) would suggest that in the case of a flat XML schema an SQL like language would perform better than its procedural counterpart since users will be able to use the same cognitive processes that allow them to write successful queries against relational schema. At the same time, when confronted with a hierarchical structure the procedural constructs in XQuery should prove of benefit since the nature of the representation requires the use of cognitive processes that are similar to that used in writing procedural programs. Given this background we pose the following research questions:

RQ1: Will users be more accurate and efficient when writing queries for **flat XML** schema using DSQL rather than XQuery?

RQ2: Will users be more accurate and efficient when writing queries for **tree XML** schema using DSQL rather than XQuery?

Experimental Design and Tasks

We used a controlled laboratory experiment to answer these research questions. The experimental task required subjects to formulate queries in one of the two languages described above. Subjects were assigned to either the DSQL or XQuery condition.

We adapted two "use cases" from the W3C Use Case document (Chamberlain, Fankhauser, Florescu, Marchiori, & Robie, 2002), since these use cases were created to serve as exemplars of the types of queries that should be supported by an XML query language. Specifically, we used the use case "R" and "Tree" for our purposes. The use case "R" contains a schema that is a representation of a (multi-table) relational database. While the original use case "R" presents data in tabular format, to avoid any confounds caused by presentation format, we chose to present our data to users in the form a textual XML schema. The use case "Tree" contains a schema for a book wherein it is possible to use elements in a nested fashion, e.g., a section in a book can contain other sections. As with the previous use case, the data was presented in the form of a textual XML schema. We then created a total of 10 queries (5 for each schema) with differing degrees of complexity (for each schema). To counter any order effects related to the type of schema, half the subjects (at random) in each condition (DSQL or XQuery) first wrote queries related to the "R" use case while the other half wrote the "Tree" case. The questions used in the study are shown in Table 4.

Subjects

Subjects were students from a senior level MIS class on Object-Oriented Design and Programming at a major Midwestern state university. They had prior exposure in their curriculum to both database and programming concepts. In particular, they had been exposed to SQL in one course and the C programming language in another. Given their background we believe that these students represented an appropriate surrogate for our target population, moderately knowledgeable users, i.e., those that are likely to write ad hoc queries on XML schema.

Table 4. Questions given to participants to solve

No	Schema	Type	Question
1	Flat	Simple	List the item number and description of all bicycles with a reserved price of over $25, ordered by item number.
2	Flat	Simple	List each person who has an item up for auction, find the total reserved price of all of his/her items.
3	Flat	Complex	Find cases where a user with a rating worse (alphabetically, greater) than "C" is offering an item with a reserve price of more than 1000.
4	Flat	Complex	For all bicycles, list the item number, description, and highest bid (if any), ordered by item number.
5	Flat	Complex	List item numbers and descriptions of items that have no bids.
6	Tree	Simple	List books published by Addison-Wesley after 1991, including their year and titles, sorted by the year.
7	Tree	Simple	Find the section titles that contain the word "database", regardless of the level of nesting.
8	Tree	Simple	Display each publisher in the database, along with the number of distinct books from the publisher.
9	Tree	Complex	Display the titles of the top-level sections of the book titled "Foundations of DB" along with a count of all figures anywhere in that section, regardless of where they are listed.
10	Tree	Complex	For each book published before 1995, display the book's title and publisher. For each book published after 1995, display only the book's title.

Experimental Procedure

Students were randomly assigned to the DSQL or XQuery condition. Students participating in the experiment received extra course credit. However, we still found that a few participating students, for whatever reasons, did not write any usable queries. In the end, useful data was collected from 46 students. Of these, 21 students were in the DSQL condition and 25 students were in the XQuery condition.

Students in each group received instruction (through a 35 minute lecture) on how to write queries using DSQL or XQuery. An example scenario (same one for both conditions) different from the ones used in the experimental materials was used for training purposes. The queries presented in the training materials incorporated examples of all the constructs, e.g., GROUP BY, ORDER BY etc., that students would need while performing their assigned task. After the training period was complete students were given the use case descriptions (on paper). Students were allowed to keep the training materials as reference while writing their queries. The use case context was assigned to the students in random order, i.e., they were presented with the 5 queries relating to one of the two use cases (in random order) followed by the 5 queries relating to the other. The order of queries within a use case was however kept constant (progressing from easy to difficult). All of the student queries were entered directly into a PC. Each query was presented to the students through a web based interface. Students were then instructed to enter their query in a text box and to press the submit button when satisfied with their answer. The system recorded the time it took to a student to answer each query.

Assessment of Performance

The performance variables of interest in our study were accuracy and efficiency. Efficiency was measured using the time taken to write each query. To measure accuracy, we adapted the procedure and coding scheme from De, et al. (2001). For each query we identified errors in the following categories: range selection (RS), attribute selection (AS), condition specification (CS), and query display (QD) specification. In addition, we also evaluated the time taken to write

Table 5. Categories of Query Errors, Adapted from (De, Sinha, & Vessey, 2001)

Range Selection Errors (RS)
1. Inappropriate object in the FROM clause
2. Improper dereferencing within FROM clause objects
3. Object in WHERE clause not specified in the FROM clause
Attribute Selection Errors (AS)
1. Omission of attributes in SELECT clause
2. Redundant attributes in SELECT clause
Condition Specification Errors(CS)
1. Missing Condition
2. Wrong Condition
3. Improper path expression in condition specification
4. Incorrect subquery comparison
5. Improper group by and having clauses
Query Display Errors (QD)
1. Incorrect sequence and/or nesting of elements in the SELECT clause
2. Missing or incorrect tag specification in the SELECT clause
3. Aggregation on improper attributes in the SELECT clause

each query (TIME). Table 5 gives a description of each of these errors.

RESULTS

Because the data for range selection violated some of the assumptions necessary for the use of parametric tests, we evaluated that item alone using both one-way ANOVA and the conservative, non-parametric Mann-Whitney test (Mann & Whitney, 1947). Since the overall findings remain unchanged, in the section below we report our one-way ANOVA findings for all categories. Below, we report on the result of the comparison between DSQL and XQuery for the queries written against the flat and tree schema individually.

For queries written against the flat schema, a oneway ANOVA revealed that there were significant differences in errors between the DSQL and XQuery conditions for Range Selection $(F(1,44) = 61.11, p < .001)$, Condition Specification $(F(1,44) = .034, p < .05)$, and Query Display $(F(1,44) = 46.31, p < .001)$. There was also a significant difference in time taken to write the queries, $F(1,44) = 10.315, p < .01$. However, no significant differences were observed for attribute specification.

For queries against the tree schema, a oneway ANOVA revealed that there were significant differences in errors between the DSQL and XQuery conditions for Range Selection $(F(1,44) = 57.96, p < .001)$, and Query Display $(F(1,44) = 32.97, p < .001)$. There was also a significant difference in time taken to write the queries, $F(1,44) = 9.79, p < .01$. However, no significant differences were observed for attribute specification or condition specification.

Table 6 and Table 7 presents the means, standard deviations and statistical comparisons for the dependent variables for queries written against flat and tree schema, respectively. Perusal of the tables indicates a results pattern that indicates that DSQL users were more accurate and efficient when writing queries against both flat and tree schema types.

The above results provide clearly demonstrate that using a declarative language like DSQL can provide a significant advantage in performance in terms of accuracy and efficiency over XQuery for writing ad hoc queries on XML schema.

CONCLUSION

In this paper, we have presented DSQL, a query language for processing XML queries. The pri-

Table 6. Comparison between DSQL and XQuery for Flat Schema Notes: $* p < .05; ** p < .01;$ $*** p < .001;$ NS indicates non-significant differences

		Mean	Std. Deviation
RS	DSQL	.27	.256
	XQuery	1.58	.735
	Difference	***	
AS	DSQL	.419	.3572
	XQuery	.408	.3581
	Difference	NS	
CS	DSQL	1.505	.5162
	XQuery	1.176	.5011
	Difference	*	
QD	DSQL	.200	.2449
	XQuery	1.216	.6453
	Difference	***	
Time (seconds)	DSQL	299.42	144.061
	XQuery	450.063	169.538
	Difference	**	

Table 7. Comparison between DSQL and XQuery for Tree Schema Notes: $* p < .05; ** p < .01;$ $*** p < .001;$ NS indicates non-significant differences

		Mean	Std. Deviation
RS	DSQL	.181	.227
	XQuery	.848	.342
	Difference	***	
AS	DSQL	.514	.355
	XQuery	.456	.380
	Difference	NS	
CS	DSQL	.952	.404
	XQuery	.936	.403
	Difference	NS	
QD	DSQL	.210	.248
	XQuery	1.096	.668
	Difference	***	
Time (seconds)	DSQL	147.16	64.01
	XQuery	201.22	53.20
	Difference	**	

mary contribution of DSQL is the theoretical basis, and the experience of building a language capable of expressing queries on XML data using well-known and well-understood techniques. DSQL is based on a conservative extension property, which distinguishes it from other SQL-like languages (such as, Abiteboul et al., 1997; Buneman et al., 2000). For flat-to-flat transformations, DSQL has the same semantic and syntactic structure as SQL, enabling DSQL to be easily incorporable into current database systems. The safety and complexity properties of DSQL that we have proved ensure that any query written in DSQL can be guaranteed to be processed using low system resources. Such properties make DSQL highly suitable as a front-end to XQuery for user-centered ad-hoc querying. Although DSQL and XQuery are both designed to query XML document structures, they have completely different flavors. While XQuery is primarily procedural, DSQL is declara-

tive, and is based on the familiar language SQL. Moreover, DSQL's independence of a specific markup structure (such as XML) enables it to be used with any structured document format, such as HTML, SGML, and even files that use proprietary tagging mechanisms, as long as a parser for such tagging is available.

Through a controlled laboratory experiment, we demonstrated that DSQL clearly surpasses XQuery in terms of user cognition leading to better user efficiency and accuracy, both for flat and structured content. Although the current industry push makes it almost certain that XQuery will become the "standard" XML query language, our paper clearly demonstrates that DSQL is a viable and necessary front-end to systems implementing XQuery, especially for ad-hoc querying, and should prove to be a valuable tool for XML query processing. Database researchers recognize the importance of XQuery, and the power and flexibility it brings to querying XML data. However, the authors of this article strongly believe that a theoretically stable language with demonstrable properties have to exist that is accessible to end-users in order for XML to survive as a universal data format, and not disappear into non-existence like the object-oriented and object-relational databases. DSQL may not be **the** solution, yet it shows directions where a 25 year old language can take a modern query language, keeping all the modernism while at the same time delivering the usability and simplicity that we are used to.

REFERENCES

Abiteboul, S., & Beeri, C. (1995). The Power of Languages for the Manipulation of Complex Values. *The VLDB Journal*, *4*(4), 727–794. doi:10.1007/BF01354881

Abiteboul, S., Quass, D., McHugh, J., Widom, J., & Wiener, J. (1997). The Lorel Query language for Semistructured Data. *International Journal on Digital Libraries*, *1*, 68–88.

ANSI/ISO. (2003). *ANSI TC NCITS H2 ISO/IEC JTC 1/SC 32/WG 3 Database (ISO-ANSI Working Draft) Information Technology - Database Languages - SQL - Part 14: XML-Related Specifications*. SQL/XML.

Boag, S., Chamberlin, D., Fernandez, M., Florescu, D., Robie, J., & Simeon, J. (2007). XQuery 1.0: An XML Query Language. Retrieved March 2010, from http://www.w3.org/TR/xquery/

Bonifati, A., & Ceri, S. (2000). Comparative analysis of five XML query languages. *SIGMOD Record*, *29*(1), 68–79. doi:10.1145/344788.344822

Buneman, P., Fernandez, M. F., & Suciu, D. (2000). UnQL: a query language and algebra for semistructured data based on structural recursion. *VLDB Journal: Very Large Data Bases*, *9*(1), 76–110. doi:10.1007/s007780050084

Cattell, R. G. G., Barry, D., Bartels, D., Berler, M., Eastman, J., Gamerman, S., et al. (1997). The Object Database Standard: ODMG 2.0.

Ceri, S., Comai, S., Damiani, E., Fraternali, P., Paraboschi, S., & Tanca, L. (1999). *XML-GL: a Graphical Language for Querying and Restructuring WWW Data*. Paper presented at the 8th Int. World Wide Web Conference, WWW8.

Chamberlain, D., Fankhauser, P., Florescu, D., Marchiori, M., & Robie, J. (2002). XML Query Use Cases

Chamberlin, D., Clark, J., Florescu, D., Robie, J., Simeon, J., & Stefanescu, M. (2001). XQuery 1.0: An XML Query Language.

Chamberlin, D., Fankhauser, P., Marchiori, M., & Robie, J. (2003). XML Query (XQuery) Requirements - W3C Working Draft 12 November 2003.

Chamberlin, D., Robie, J., & Florescu, D. (2001). Quilt: an XML Query Language for Heterogeneous Data Sources. *The World Wide Web and Databases, Third International Workshop WebDB 2000, Dallas, Texas, USA, May 18-19, 2000, Selected Papers* (Vol. 1997, pp. 1-25): Springer.

Christophides, V., Abiteboul, S., Cluet, S., & Scholl, M. (1994). From Structured Documents to Novel Query Facilities. *SIGMOD Record*, *23*(2), 313–324. doi:10.1145/191843.191901

Clark, J., & DeRose, S. (1999). XML Path Language XPath Version 1.0. Retrieved from http://www.w3.org/TR/xpath

Cluet, S. (1998). Designing OQL: Allowing Objects To Be Queried. *Information Systems*, *23*(5), 279–305. doi:10.1016/S0306-4379(98)00013-1

Cohen, S., Kanza, Y., Kogan, Y., Sagiv, Y., Nutt, W., & Serebrenik, A. (2002). EquiX---a search and query language for XML. *Journal of the American Society for Information Science and Technology*, *53*(6), 454–466. doi:10.1002/asi.10058

De, P., Sinha, A., & Vessey, I. (2001). An Empirical Investigation of Factors Influencing Object-Oriented Database Querying. *Information Technology Management*, 2(1), 71–93. doi:10.1023/A:1009934820999

Deach, S. (Artist). (1998). *Extensible Style Language (XSL) Specification*.

Deutsch, A., Fernandez, M., Florescu, D., Levy, A., & Suciu, D. (1998). XML-QL: A query language for XML.

Draper, D., Fankhauser, P., Fernandez, M., Malhotra, A., Rose, K., Rys, M., et al. (2007). XQuery 1.0 and XPath 2.0 Formal Semantics. Retrieved from http://www.w3.org/TR/xquery-semantics/

Fernandez, M., Malhotra, A., Marsh, J., Nagy, M., & Walsh, N. (2007). XQuery 1.0 and XPath 2.0 Data Model (XDM). Retrieved from http://www.w3.org/TR/xpath-datamodel/

Kepser, S. (2003). *A Simple Proof for the Turing-Completeness of XSLT and XQuery*. Paper presented at the Proceedings: ACM SIGACT-SIGMOD-SIGART Symposium on Principles of Database Systems.

Lc Hors, A., Le Hegaret, P., Wood, L., Nicol, G., Robie, J., Champion, M., et al. (2004). Document Object Model (DOM) Level 3 Core Specification. Retrieved from http://www.w3.org/TR/2004/REC-DOM-Level-3-Core-20040407/

Mann, H. B., & Whitney, D. R. (1947). On a test of whether one of two random variables is stochastically larger than the other. *Annals of Mathematical Statistics*, 18, 50–60. doi:10.1214/aoms/1177730491

O'Reilly, T. (2005). What is Web 2.0 - Design Patterns and Business Models for the Next Generation of Software.

Robie, J., Lapp, J., & Schach, D. (1998). *XML Query Language*. XQL.

Sengupta, A., & Mohan, S. (2003, March). *Formal and conceptual models for XML structures - the past, present and future*.

Turing, A. (1936). On Computable Numbers, with an Application to the Entscheidungsproblem. *Proceedings of the London Mathematical Society*, 42, 230–265. doi:10.1112/plms/s2-42.1.230

Van den Bussche, J., & Vossen, G. (1993). *An Extension of Path Expressions to Simplify Navigation in Object-Oriented Queries*. Paper presented at the Proceedings of the third international conference on Deductive and Object-Oriented Databases (DOOD).

Vessey, I., & Galletta, D. (1991). Cognitive Fit: An Imperical Study of Information Acquisition. *Information Systems Research*, 2, 63–84. doi:10.1287/isre.2.1.63

Welty, C. (1990). Human Factors Studies of Database Query Languages: SQL as a metric. *Journal of Database Administration*, 1(1), 2–10.

Welty, C., & Stemple, D. W. (1981). Human Factors Comparison of a Procedural and a Nonprocedural Query Language. *ACM Transactions on Database Systems*, 6(4), 626–649. doi:10.1145/319628.319656

Wyss, C. M., & Van Gucht, D. (2001). *A Relational Algebra for Data/Metadata Integration in a Federated Database System*. Paper presented at the Proceedings of the 2001 ACM CIKM International Conference on Information and Knowledge Management.

Yoshikawa, M., Amagasa, T., Shimura, T., & Uemura, S. (2001). XRel: A Path-Based Approach to Storage and Retrieval of XML Documents Using Relational Databases. *ACM Transactions on Internet Technology*, 1(1), 110–141. doi:10.1145/383034.383038

APPENDIX

Properties of DA

The DA operators form an analog of operations from the Nested Relational Algebra (NRA) (see, e.g., Abiteboul & Beeri, 1995) and adapts them to the document database domain. These operators combine to form a language that exhibits a number of highly desirable properties of a query language.

These properties are as follows:

Closure: The closure property ensures that the inputs and outputs of queries are of the same type, so that queries can be composed, and stored as views for subsequent execution. Formally, if D is a set of well-formed XML documents, then E_D, a DA expression over D is also well-formed.

Proof sketch. The closure property can be proved by structural induction on the algebra expressions, noticing that the queries always generate well-formed XML documents by creating a root when a set of items are returned. This property can be extended from "well-formedness" to "validity" by noticing that every query that creates a new structure, the structure is known in advance, and is independent of the result, and hence the information on the new structure can be added to the output schema.

Safety: Safety ensures that none of the queries written in this language can result in an infinitely large output set. The size of the output of every query can be approximately computed, a property that will be highly useful for query optimization purposes.

Proof. The proof is by structural induction on the DA operations. We use a total induction technique to build this proof, and show that for any $n \geq 0$, a DA expression E_n^τ containing n DA operators, will return a finite number of documents.

Base case. The base case is provided by the expression $E_0 = D$. The proof follows from the assumption, since there are only a finite number of documents corresponding to D.

Induction Hypothesis. For some $k > 0$, every DA expression E_i^τ with type τ and i operators ($0 \leq i \leq k$) will only return a finite number of documents as the result.

Induction step. We denote the number of documents returned by a DA expression E_k^τ by $|E_k^\tau|$, and consider all possible cases for building E_{k+1} using only the primitive algebraic operators:

- $E_{k+1} = E_k^\tau \circ P$. By the induction hypothesis, $|E_k^\tau|$ is finite. Since each of the documents in E^τ is of finite size, the operation $\circ$ only returns nodes in the document structure, in the worst case, $|E_{k+1}| = |E_k^\tau| \times m$, where m is the maximum number of nodes among the documents returned by E_k^τ.

- $E_{k+1} = E1_p^{\tau_1} \cup_R E2_q^{\tau_2}, k = p + q$. By the induction hypothesis, $|E1_p^{\tau_1}|$ and $|E2_q^{\tau_2}|$ are finite, since p and q are both less than k. Since the operation is essentially a union operation, we have in the worst case $|E_{k+1}| = |E1_p^{\tau_1}| + |E2_q^{\tau_2}|$, which is finite.

- $E_{k+1} = E1_p^\tau \cap E2_q^\tau, k = p + q$. By the induction hypothesis, $|E1_p^\tau|$ and $|E2_q^\tau|$ are finite. So in the worst case, $|E_{k+1}| = max(|E1_p^\tau|, |E2_q^\tau|)$, a finite number.

- $E_{k+1} = E1_p^\tau - E2_q^\tau, k = p + q$. Since this is a regular set difference operation, in the worst case, $|E_{k+1}| = |E1_p^\tau|$, which is finite by the induction hypothesis.

- $E_{k+1} = E1_p^{T_1} \times_R E2_q^{T_2}, k = p + q$. By the induction hypothesis, $\mid E1_p^{T_1} \mid$ and $\mid E2_q^{T_2} \mid$ are finite. Hence, $\mid E_{k+1} \mid = \mid E1_p^{T_1} \mid \times \mid E2_q^{T_2} \mid$, a finite number.

- $E_{k+1} = \sigma_\gamma E_k^\tau$. By the induction hypothesis, $\mid E_k^\tau \mid$ is finite. Since the selection operation returns a subset of the input, we have $\mid E_{k+1} \mid \leq \mid E_k^\tau \mid$, and hence, is finite, regardless of the structure of γ.

- $E_{k+1} = \nu_X^R(E1_k^\tau)$. By the induction hypothesis, $\mid E1_k^\tau \mid$ is finite. Noticing that the Nest operation does not create any new documents, and simply restructures the existing structure, the result of the nest is also finite.

- $E_{k+1} = \mu_X^R(E1_k^\tau)$. Again, by induction hypothesis, $\mid E1_k^\tau \mid$ is finite. Since [EQUATION] is a path expression and hence returns a finite number of nodes, say, $\mid X \mid$ - the worst case size of E_{k+1} is $\mid X \mid \times \mid E1_k^\tau) \mid$, and hence is finite as well.

In the above, we show that for every way of constructing a DA expression, if the constituent expressions are finite, the resulting size of the expression is finite. Hence, by structural induction, DA is safe.

Expressive power: Document algebra is within PTIME. Any query written in the language will have a time complexity of sub-polynomial time in the size of the input. However, since it has no mechanism for looping, it cannot solve all PTIME queries such as transitive closure queries, unless the transitive closure is built in the XML structure.

Formally, Given a DA expression E on database D with size $m \times n$ (as above), there is an algorithm A^E that can evaluate E in $O(f(m, n))$ time, where f is a polynomial function with parameters m and n.

Proof. We prove this by strong induction on the number of operators of E, as follows:

Induction hypothesis. Given an algebraic expression E with k operators ($k > 0$), there is an algorithm A^E that can evaluate E using at most $f(m, n)$ operations, where f is a polynomial function. The possible operations here are (i) traversal based on node label (**gi**) and (ii) comparison of the leaf with a query value. Both operations are considered atomic and are assumed to take constant time.

Base case. The base case is trivial. Here $E = D$ (number of operators = 0), and D can be evaluated in constant time.

Induction. We consider all the possible algebraic operators discussed above and describe algorithms that can evaluate the expression. (Note that the algorithms here are essentially brute-force algorithms, and no claim on efficiency is being made at this time.)

- $E_n = E \circ P$. Consider the following algorithm:
  - Let the number of trees in E be n_E.
  - For each GI in the path expression P, perform a breadth-first search on each of the n_E trees to select trees rooted at that particular gi, append any new matched node to a temporary list of trees, and after all the original trees have been considered, replace original list by the created temporary list. Continue this for every GI in P.

If the number of GIs in the path is p, then the maximum number of traversal operations is given by:

$$\underbrace{m \times n_E + m \times (m \times n_E) + \dots}_{k\text{times}} = m \times f'(m,n) \times (1 + m + m^2 + \dots + m^{k-1}) = f_{poly}(m,n)$$

where $n_E = f'(m,n)$ is a polynomial in m, n by the induction hypothesis.

- $E_n = E_1^{\tau_1} \cup_R E_2^{\tau_2}$. This is trivial. By the induction hypothesis, we have E_1 and E_2 can be computed in polynomial operations. Assume that E_1 and E_2 return n_{E_1} and n_{E_2} trees respectively and that the maximum number of nodes in these trees is m. A simple algorithm to compute the union will start with one set, and for every element of the second set, check if the element is already in the result, including it if not. This step requires comparison of two trees, and since exact matches are only considered, the number of string comparison operations required is the minimum of the nodes in the two trees (m in the worst case). The number of operations is $O(n_{E_1} \times n_{E_2} \times m)$, a polynomial from induction hypothesis. Note that this is not necessarily the most efficient way of performing this operation, but it is sufficient to show that the operation has a polynomial complexity.

- $E_n = E_1^{\tau} - E_2^{\tau}$. Computation of this operation is also trivial and similar to the above, with the number of operations being $O(n_{E_1} \times n_{E_2} \times m)$, which is a polynomial (since by the induction hypothesis n_{E_n} and n_{E_2} are polynomials on the size of the input).

- $E_n = E_1^{\tau} \cap E_2^{\tau}$. Computation of intersection is also trivial and has the same complexity as the above.

- $E_n = E_1^{\tau_1} \times_R E_2^{\tau_2}$. Once again, this operation can be computed by two bounded loops, one each for the two operands. Thus, the number of operations is $O(n_{E_1} \times n_{E_2} \times m)$, which is a polynomial (since by the induction hypothesis n_{E_n} and n_{E_2} are polynomials on the size of the input).

- $E_n = \sigma_\gamma E^{\tau}$. We need to consider the following two cases, based on the form of γ:

  (a) $\gamma = P\theta c$. Suppose the expression E^{τ} has n_E results. Consider the following algorithm:

   - For each of the trees $e^{\tau} \in E^{\tau}$, compute $e^{\tau} \circ P$ using the method described above.
   - Compute the set membership of c on each of the results in the previous step.
   - Select the e^{τ} which returns non-zero members.

Once again, the number of traversal operations in the first step is polynomial from before. Since c is a constant, the number of comparisons in the second as well as the third step is linear. Hence the total time is also polynomial.

  (b) $\gamma = P_1\theta P_2$. This is essentially the same as the previous method, the only difference being that, in the first step, both the operands need to be evaluated, while in the second step, the operation is a set intersection instead of membership. The combination is still a polynomial operation.

Hence, the proof follows by induction.

Conservativity: Document algebra is a conservative extension of relational algebra. This means that any query written in RA with flat relational inputs and outputs is equivalent to a DA query that produces the same output with the same given input.

The proof of this theorem uses HNR (Heterogeneous nested Relations), a more rigorous formal language as a basis.

Equivalence: DA belongs to a set of mutually equivalent languages. DA is equivalent to DC (Document Calculus, a declarative first-order calculus language) which is equivalent to the proposed DSQL language. This implies that any DSQL query can be translated to the algebra for execution and query optimization purposes.

The equivalence of DA and DC can be proved in the same manner as the equivalence of relational algebra and calculus.

B. DSQL BNF and Examples

The complete BNF for DSL is given below in Table 8. (terminals shown in bold, constants in plain font and non-terminals in italics).

Table 8.

query-exp	::=	*query-term* | *query-exp* UNION [ALL] *query-term*
query-term	::=	*query-spec* | (*query-exp*)
query-spec	::=	SELECT [ALL| DISTINCT] *output qry-body*
output	::=	*target* | **outputname**(*target*) | *dtd-exp*
target	::=	*scalar-exp-list* | *
scalar-exp-list	::=	*scalar-exp* [, *scalar-exp*]*
dtd-exp	::=	DTD ***filename***
qry-body	::=	*from-clause* [*where-clause*] [*group-by-clause* [*having-clause*]]*
from-clause	::=	FROM *db-list*
db-list	::=	*db* [,*db*]*
db	::=	*rooted-path* [**alias**]
where-clause	::=	WHERE *search-cond*
group-by-clause	::=	GROUP BY *col-list*
col-list	::=	NULL | *col* [, *col*]*
col	::=	*complete-path*
having-clause	::=	HAVING *search-cond*
search-cond	::=	*bool-term* | *search-cond* OR *bool-term*
bool-term	::=	*bool-factor* | *bool-term* AND *bool-factor*
bool-factor	::=	[NOT] *bool-primary*
bool-primary	::=	*predicate* | (*search-cond*)
predicate	::=	*comp-pred* | *between-pred* | *like-pred* | *testnull*
		| *in-pred* | *univqnt* | *existqnt*
comp-pred	::=	*scalar-exp ops* { *scalar-exp* | *subquery* }
ops	::=	= | ≠ | > | < | ≥ | ≤

between-pred	::=	*scalar-exp* [NOT] BETWEEN *scalar-exp* AND *scalar-exp*
like-pred	::=	*col* [NOT] LIKE [**atom** | *prox-exp*]
prox-exp	::=	**atom** [NOT] *prox-ops***atom**
prox-ops	::=	NEAR | FBY
testnull	::=	*col* IS [NOT] NULL
in-pred	::=	*scalar-exp* [NOT] IN { *subquery* | **atom** [, **atom**]* }
univqnt	::=	*scalar-exp* *ops* [ALL | ANY | SOME] *subquery*
existqnt	::=	[NOT] EXISTS *subquery*
subquery	::=	(*query-spec*)
scalar-exp	::=	**atom** | *col* | *function*
function	::=	COUNT(*) | *distfunc* | *allfunc* | *attfunc*
distfunc	::=	{ AVG | MAX | MIN | SUM | COUNT }
allfunc	::=	{ AVG | MAX | MIN | SUM | COUNT } ([ALL] *scalar-exp*)
attfunc	::=	ATTVAL (*col, attrib*)
		| { AVG | MAX | MIN | SUM | COUNT } (ATTVAL (*col, attrib*))
path-exp	::=	*path-list* [.. *path-list*]*
path-list	::=	**gi** [. **gi**]*
rooted-path	::=	**root** {. |.. } *path-exp*
complete-path	::=	**root** {. |.. } *path-exp* {. |.. } **leaf**

Table 9. Examples of DSQL queries in the Poetry database.

Query Type	Query	DSQL Solution	XQuery Solution
Selection	Find poems written by Keats with the word "love" in the first line.	SELECT P.* FROM Poetry Poem P WHERE P.poet lastname='Keats' AND P..fline like '%love%'	\<Results> { FOR $p in Poetry.xml//Poem WHERE $P/poet//lastname='Keats' AND $P//fline '%love%' RETURN $P } \</Results>
Join	Find the poet pairs who have at least one poem with the same title.	SELECT pair\<P1.poet, P2.poet> FROM Poetry.Poem P1, Poetry.Poem P2 WHERE P1.poet lastname < P2.poet lastname AND P1.title = P2.title	\<Results> {FOR $P1 in Poetry.xml//Poem $P2 in Poetry.xml//Poem WHERE $P1/poet//lastname < $P2.poet..lastname AND $P1/title = $P2/title RETURN \<pair> { $P1.poet } { $P2.poet } \</pair>} \</Results>

Query Type	Query	DSQL Solution	XQuery Solution
Restructuring	Display titles of all poems written under each historical period in the database.	SELECT agegroup<P.histage, poems<P..title>> FROM Poetry.Poem P GROUP by P.histage	<Results> {FOR $A in distinctvalues(Poetry.xml//histage) RETURN <agegroup> <age>$A</age> <poems> {FOR $P in Poems.xml//Poem WHERE $P/histage = $A RETURN $P//title} </poems> </agegroup> }</Results>
Aggregation	For poets who have written more than 10 poems, display their names and the number poems written by them.	SELECT P.poet, count(distinct P.title) FROM Poetry.Poem P GROUP BY P.poet HAVING count(distinct P.title)>10	<Results> {FOR $A IN Poems.xml//Poet FOR $P IN Poems.xml//Poem[Poet=$A] RETURN {IF (count(distinct $P) > 10) THEN <poet>{$A}</poet></poet> <poemcount>{count(distinct $P)) </poemcount> } }</Results>
Set membership/ Quantification	Find poems written by Keats that have no stanza with the word "mortal".	SELECT P.* FROM Poetry.Poem P WHERE P.poet lastname = 'Keats' AND not exists (SELECT * FROM Poetry.Poem P1 WHERE P1=P AND P.stanza like '%mortal%')	<Results> {FOR $P IN Poems.xml//Poem LET $S = $P//Stanza[contains(text(),'mortal')] WHERE $P/POET//lastname = 'Keats' RETURN IF (fn:exists($S)) THEN {} ELSE {$P} } </Results>

Chapter 14
Range–Sum Queries over High Dimensional Data Cubes Using a Dynamic Grid File

Feng Yu
Southern Illinois University, USA

Cheng Luo
Coppin State University, USA

Xiaoguang Yu
Southern Illinois University, USA

Wen-Chi Hou
Southern Illinois University, USA

Chih-Fang Wang
Southern Illinois University, USA

Michael Wainer
Southern Illinois University, USA

ABSTRACT

In this chapter, the authors propose to use the grid file to store multi-dimensional data cubes and answer range-sum queries. The grid file is enhanced with a dynamic splitting mechanism to accommodate insertions of data. It overcomes the drawback of the traditional grid file in storing uneven data while enjoying its advantages of simplicity and efficiency. The space requirement grows linearly with the dimension of the data cube, compared with the exponential growth of conventional methods that store pre-computed aggregate values for range-sum queries. The update cost is O(1), much faster than the pre-computed data cube approaches, which generally have exponential update cost. The grid file structure can also respond to range queries quickly. They compare it with an approach that uses the R*-tree structure to store the data cube. The experimental results show that the proposed method performs favorably in file size, update speed, construction time, and query response time for both evenly and unevenly distributed data.

DOI: 10.4018/978-1-60960-521-6.ch014

INTRODUCTION

A data warehouse is a large collection of integrated data, built to assist knowledge workers, such as executives, managers, analysts, etc., to make better and faster decisions. It is often required that data be summarized at various levels of detail and on various attributes to allow knowledge workers to analyze the data through a variety of views in on-line analytical processing (OLAP). Typical OLAP applications include product performance and profitability, effectiveness of sales programs or marketing campaigns, sales forecasting, capacity planning, etc. Data warehousing and OLAP have increasingly become a focus of the database industry.

OLAP systems generally support a multidimensional data model, which is also known as the data cube (Gray, 1997). Construction of a data cube is based on the set of selected attributes of the database. Certain attributes are chosen to be the measure attributes, i.e., attributes whose values are of interest, while some others are selected as dimension or functional attributes (Geffner, 1999). The values of the measure attributes are often aggregated according to the dimension attributes for analysis. The size of a data cube can be huge when the number of combinations of dimension attribute values is large.

The storage of data cubes is essential to OLAP. Much research (Agarwal, 1996; Beyer, 1999; Han, 2001; Morfonios, 2006; Xin, 2003; Zhao, 1997) has focused on the materialization of data cubes, that is, to pre-compute and store all possible combinations of multi-dimensional aggregates for fast multi-dimensional analysis. Some notable cube materialization algorithms proposed include ROLAP-based multi-dimensional aggregate computation (Agarwal, 1996, Morfonios, 2006), multi-way array aggregation (Beyer, 1999), BUC (Han, 2001), H-cubing (Xin, 2003), Star-cubing (Zhao, 1997), Minimal cubing (Li, 2004), etc. Since materializing data cubes are generally computationally intensive and space

consuming, much effort has been devoted to reducing the computation and storage space of data cubes. These efforts include partial materialization of data cubes (Harinarayan, 1996), iceberg cube computation (Han, 2001; Xin, 2003; Zhao, 1997), computation of condensed, dwarf, and quotient cubes (Lakshmanan, 2002; Lakshmanan, 2003; Sismanis, 2002; Beyer, 1999; Wang, 2002), and computation of approximate cubes (Barbara, 1997; Cuzzocrea, 2006; Shanmugasundaram, 1999). While these pre-computed data cubes can be used to answer queries quickly, tremendous overhead is incurred in maintaining these pre-computed aggregate values as updates can propagate to a large number of relevant cells.

A range-sum query is used to compute the sum of the values of data cube cells that fall in the ranges specified by the query. It is very useful in finding trends and discovering relationships between attributes in the databases. Ho et al. (1997) proposed to compute prefix sums of data cube cells for range-sum queries. Although this method can respond to queries quickly, an update in the worst case can propagate to the entire prefix-sum cube. Therefore, it may not be suitable for data cubes that undergo frequent changes. Some efforts have been made to reduce the update propagations of prefix-sum cubes. Geffner et al. (1999) computed the relative prefix-sums to limit cascading updates to sub-cubes. More recently, they proposed (Geffner, 2000) to decompose the prefix-sum cubes recursively to control the cascading of updates. Although these measures can reduce the cost of updates to a certain degree, the cost can still increase exponentially with the number of dimensions of the data cubes. Chan et al. (1999) proposed a class of hierarchically organized prefix-sum cubes to reduce the update cost. However, the cost of update still increases exponentially with the number of dimensions. Gao et al. (2005) discussed efficient processing of range-sum queries over hierarchical cubes using parallel computing systems. In general, update propagation is a common problem for all pre-computed data cube approaches even though some improvements have been made. Note that all these approaches also require at least as much space as the original data cubes to store the prefix-sum cubes.

Instead of materializing pre-computed data cubes for range-sum queries, Hu et al. (2002) chose to store data cube cells in a slightly modified version of the R*-tree (Beckmann, 1990), called the DCA-tree. Updates to the data cube are accomplished by updating the corresponding points in the R*-tree.

Similar to Hu's approach (Hu, 2002) we attempt to design a spatial data structure to facilitate data cube storage and range-sum query processing. We propose a dynamic grid file structure as a natural fit to the structure of data cubes. The data cube space is partitioned into grid cells and each grid cell, which contains a number of data cube cells, is stored in a separate disk block. The proposed structure adapts itself to insertions of new data by splitting the grid cells dynamically. It minimizes the drawback of traditional grid files for uneven data while enjoying its advantages of simplicity and efficiency. The dynamic grid file facilitates range-sum query processing by identifying the grid cells that intersect with the queries quickly.

It is observed that given a fixed number of nonzero data cube cells, the space requirement for a grid file grows linearly with the dimensions of the data cubes, compared with the exponential growth of the prefix sum approaches (Chan, 1999; Geffner, 1999; Geffner, 2000; Ho, 1997). The update cost is O(1), compared with the exponentially increased update cost for the prefix sum approaches. The grid file can also respond to range-sum queries quickly. For example, it takes around 1 second (elapsed) time to process a range-sum query over a 24-dimensional data cube, which should be very acceptable for OLAP. The proposed file structure is very efficient even for high-dimensional data cube applications.

Our approach is similar to Hu's (Hu, 2002) as we also use a spatial data structure to store the

data cube. We conducted extensive experiments to compare our grid file with Hu's DCA-tree (or the R*-tree) in terms of file size, construction time, update speed, query response time, etc. The experimental results show that the new dynamic grid file performs much better than Hu's in all these measures.

The rest of the article is organized as follows. Section 2 introduces related work. Section 3 presents the dynamic grid file structure and range-sum query evaluation algorithm. Section 4 reports the performance evaluation. Section 5 concludes this article.

RELATED WORK

There has been considerable research on data cubes, including computing data cubes (Agarwal, 1996; Gupta, 1997; Harinarayan, 1996; Johnson, 1997; Shukla, 1996), pre-computing subsets of a data cube (Gupta, 1997; Harinarayan, 1996), estimating the size of multidimensional aggregates (Johnson, 1997), and indexing pre-computed summaries (Shukla, 1996). In this article, we shall focus on those methods that process range-sum queries over data cubes.

The range-sum query is a useful tool for analysis. It sums up the measure attribute values of data cube cells that fall in the ranges specified by the query. The range-sum query can be very useful in finding trends and discovering relationships among attributes in databases. With the growing interest in database analysis, particularly in OLAP, efficient range-sum query processing is becoming an increasingly important issue in database research.

Prefix-sum cube (PC) (Ho, 1997) pre-computes the prefix sums of data cube cells so that range-sum queries can be answered quickly. The value of a cell $P(x_1, x_2, ..., x_D)$ in the prefix sum cube is the sum of the values of data cube cells $C(y_1, y_2, ..., y_D)$, where D is the dimension of the data cube, and $y_i \leq x_i$, i = 1, ..., D. The prefix-sum cube requires the same amount of storage space as the data cube itself. A range-sum query that specifies range constraints on q of the D dimensions can be answered in 2^q accesses, each for a corner cell of the q-dimensional hyper-rectangle defined by the q ranges of the query. While this approach may respond to queries fast, its update cost can be prohibitive since a modification to a data cube cell can propagate to a large number of cells in a PC. It has been shown that the update cost of this prefix sum method is $O(n^D)$, where D is the dimension of the data cube and n is the size of each dimension. In the worst case, it could require rebuilding the entire prefix-sum cube. It is not suitable for situations where data undergo constant changes.

Several attempts have been made to reduce the cost of updates in prefix-sum cubes, however, at the price of increased range query complexity. Geffner, et al. (1999) presented the relative prefix-sum cube approach (RPC). It partitions a data cube into a number of disjoint sub-cubes of equal size and calculates local prefix-sums for each sub-cube. It limits the cascading updates to individual prefix-sum sub-cubes, thereby reducing the update cost. The update cost is reduced to $O(m^D)$ in RPC, where m is the number of partitions on each dimension of the sub-cubes. Since a query may cover an area that crosses sub-cube boundaries, RPC pre-computes an additional overlay cube to convey information across the sub-cube boundaries. It has been shown that a range-sum query can be answered in no more than $(D+2) 2^q$ accesses, where D is the dimension of the data cube.

Chan et al. (Chan, 1999) decomposed the data cube space hierarchically. Prefix sums are calculated for cells based on their locations in the hierarchical structure. A data cube cell update can affect only the cells in the corresponding sub-cube at the same level. It has a worst case update cost of $O(n^D)$, where D is the dimension of the data

cube and n is the size of each dimension, and a best case of $O(m^D)$, where m is the size of each dimension of the sub-cube. A range-sum query is converted into a set of local range-sum queries and local prefix range-sum queries. A range sum query has a time complexity of $O(s^2 2^q)$, where s is the number of sub-cubes at each level.

Hu et al. (2002) proposed the DCA-tree, which is a variant of the R*-tree. Nonzero cells of a data cube are treated as points and stored in the DCA-tree in the same way as in the R*-tree. Each minimum bounding rectangle/region (MBR) is associated with the aggregate value of the cells in it. It uses the R*-tree to reduce overlaps among bounding rectangles when splitting. The DCA-tree reduces the update cost to $O(logN_u)$, where N_u is the number of changed cells.

A DYNAMIC GRID FILE FOR RANGE-SUM QUERIES

The majority of research work on fast processing of range-sum queries over data cubes (Chan, 1999; Geffner, 1999; Geffner, 2000; Ho, 1997) has chosen to store pre-computed aggregate values. While these approaches may be able to answer queries quickly, they are accompanied by serious drawbacks in terms of storage usage and update complexity of the pre-computed aggregate values. In general, the storage space and update complexity of these methods increase exponentially with the dimensionality of the data cubes, rendering these approaches infeasible for high-dimensional data cube applications. For example, consider a data cube of only 6 dimensions with each dimension having 100 values. The data cube would comprise at least 10^{12} data cube cells, which may already exceed the capacity of many modern disks.

The DCA-tree uses an R*-tree to store the data cube. It stores only the nonzero cells of the data cube. An update to the data cube is accomplished by an update to the corresponding R*-tree, and a

Figure 1. A Dynamic Grid File

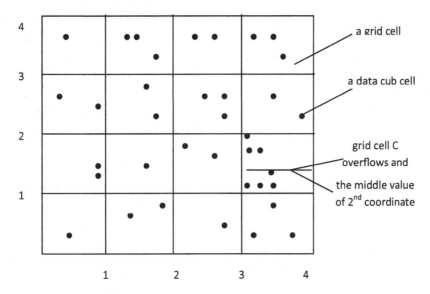

range-sum query over the data cube is achieved by a spatial search in the R*-tree.

In this article, we propose to use the grid file for high-dimensional data cube storage and range-sum querying.

3.1 The Dynamic Grid File Structure

The data cube is partitioned into hyper-rectangles, called data cube cells, and each cell is associated with a set of measure attribute values. The grid file (Nievergelt, 1984) is a natural fit to the storage of data cubes as it conforms to the structure of the data cubes nicely. The grid file structure we propose here has two parts: a grid file and a grid file directory. The former stores the nonzero data cube cells while the latter is an index into the grid file for fast accesses to the desired cells.

3.1.1 The Grid File

Let us first discuss the grid file. Assume each dimension is divided into $p_i \geq 1$, $1 \leq i \leq D$, partitions, where D is the number of dimensions of the data cube. The entire data cube space is

thus partitioned into $G = \prod_{i=1}^{D} p_i$ multi-dimensional grid cells, of which each encloses a fixed number of data cube cells. Each grid cell $(j_1, j_2, ..., j_D)$, $1 \leq j_i \leq p_i$, $i = 1, 2, ... D$, is intended to be stored in a disk page (block) in the grid file. Figure 1 shows a 2-dimensional data cube space that is divided into $4^2 (= 16)$ equal sized grid cells.

Nonzero data cube cells are represented by their coordinates as points. The values of a data cube cell become the values of the corresponding point. Points that fall in the same grid cell are intended to be stored, if possible, on the same disk page in the grid file. The grid cell $(j_1, j_2, ...j_D)$ is stored as the bth page ($1 \leq b \leq \prod_{i=1}^{D} p_i$) of the grid file based on the following formula

$$b = (j_1 - 1)p_2 p_3 \cdots p_D + (j_2 - 1)p_3 p_4 \cdots p_D + \cdots + (j_{D-1} - 1)p_D + j_D$$

(1)

Initial Grid File Structure

Let us discuss how to determine the number of grid cells $G = \prod_{i=1}^{D} p_i$ into which the data cube space is to be partitioned. Let M be the number of measure attributes and D the number of the dimensional attributes. Let N be the initial number of nonzero data cube cells, which can be an estimate. Assume the storage space for each dimensional or measure attribute value is V bytes. Then, the estimated data set size S can be computed by the following formula,

$$S = N(D + M) V. \qquad (2)$$

Extra space can be reserved by replacing S with a greater value for later insertions of data points.

Let page_size be the size of a page on the disk, e.g., 8K bytes. S/page_size is the size of the dataset in pages. The number of grid cells G ought to satisfy the following relationship:

$$G = \prod_{i=1}^{D} p_i \geq S / page\_size, \qquad (3)$$

where $p_i (\geq 1)$ is the number of partitions in the ith dimension. If one wishes not to partition a dimension, say i, then p_i is set to 1. Hereafter, we shall call the set of dimensions, whose $p_i > 1$, the partition dimensions.

The selection of partition dimensions can have a great impact on the search. If a dimension is partitioned, the portions that satisfy the range constraints on that dimension can be easily identified and the search can be effectively confined. Heuristics, such as selecting the most frequently referenced or important dimensions can be very useful as many queries can benefit from such partitions.

Handling Overflow

When overflows happen in a grid cell, the cell is split into two subcells. The subcells can split themselves repeatedly as necessary. The splitting is performed along a selected dimension, here called a split dimension. Note that a split dimension is used to distribute overflow points in a (sub)cell

while a partition dimension is used to confine search area of a query. Many heuristics, such as random selection, selecting the most spread dimension, etc., can be used in selecting the split dimension. However, unless the data exhibit extreme peculiarity in a (sub)cell, the difference among these splitting methods should be small. Therefore, for simplicity, we choose the split dimension in a round-robin fashion as it does not require memorizing the split dimension.

To distribute points in an overflow grid cell evenly to two sub-grid cells, the cell splits at the middle of the range of the points' values on the selected dimension. For example, in Figure 1, the grid cell C overflows. The points in C are (3.1, 1.9), (3.2, 1.75), (3.25, 1.4), (3.3, 1.09), (3.19, 1.11), (3.5, 1.12), and (3.6, 1.71). Assume the split dimension is the 2nd dimension. The set of the 2nd dimension values are {1.9,1.75,1.4,1.09, 1.11,1.12,1.71} and the middle of the range is computed as (minimum + maximum)/2, which is (1.9+1.09) / 2 = 1.49. Thus, the cell C splits into two at 1.49 along the 2nd dimension as shown in the figure. The points (3.3, 1.09), (3.19, 1.11), (3.5, 1.12), and (3.25, 1.4) go to one sub-cell while (3.2, 1.75), (3.6, 1.71), and (3.1, 1.9) go to the other sub-cell. This scheme requires storing minimum and maximum values of the points on each dimension in a cell. Although we could have chosen the median or mean of the values to split, the middle range value is probably the simplest to compute as it does not need to examine the points in the cell. In addition, the minimum and maximum information on each dimension can be used for another purpose (discussed in Section 3.2).

3.1.2 The Grid Directory

A grid directory is stored to facilitate query processing. Each entry in the directory corresponds to a grid cell in the file. It records the sum of the values of the points in the grid cell and the minimum and maximum coordinate values along each dimension of these points (as just mentioned ear-

Figure 2. The Grid Directory

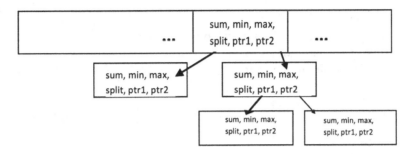

lier), and a pointer to the disk page that physically stores the points of the grid cell. The minimums and maximums indeed represent the minimum bounding rectangle/region (MBR) of the points in the grid cell. This information is not only used in splitting cells, but also used in determining more precisely whether the points in a cell intersect with the query window or not.

In Figure 2, we show the structure of the directory. Initially, each entry in the directory has a sum, a min and a max for each dimension, a split (value), and two pointers, ptr1 and ptr2, where ptr1 points to the disk page storing the grid cell (while ptr2 is not used initially). When a grid cell overflows and splits into two subcells, the directory entry spawns two subentries, one for each subcell. The split value and pointers to these two subentries are registered in the split, ptr1, and ptr2 of the original entry, respectively. The grid file can grow like a binary tree if overflows happen repeatedly in a (sub)cell, as shown in Figure 2. Note that only the ptr1 field of the leaf nodes of the binary tree points to a disk page in the grid file; other pointers in the non-leaf nodes point to nodes of the binary trees.

Each entry or subentry requires a small amount of space: 4 bytes for the sum, 4 bytes for the min and max on each dimension, and 4 bytes for each of the split, ptr1, and ptr2. That is, totally 16+8D bytes for each entry in the directory. The entire directory structure, including the spawned entries, is generally small. Therefore, in this research we load it into memory at initiation (before any que-

rying and updates are posted). It can be observed that given an arbitrary data cube cell, by searching the in-memory directory, the physical disk page storing the data cube cell can be directly located in one disk access.

3.1.3 Update of the Grid File

As mentioned above, given a data cube cell, one can directly locate the page storing it through the grid directory. For an insertion, the page is first fetched into memory (in 1 disk access). If there is enough space left in the page, the point is added to it and the page is written back to the disk (in 1 disk access). If the page overflows, it is split into two. The level of the directory entry in the tree corresponding to the data cube cell determines the dimension to split (as it is selected in a round robin fashion), and the minimum (min) and maximum (max) coordinate values of the points in the cell on the selected dimension are used to split the points. The directory (sub)entry spawns two (sub) entries with each one pointing to a split page on disk. At the end, the two pages are written back to the disk (2 disk accesses) and the sum fields of the entries and their ancestors are updated accordingly to reflect the insertion. All in all, no more than three disk accesses are needed for an insertion. Figure 3 summarizes the operations.

As new points are added to the file, the average amount of unused space in a page decreases and the chance of splits increases. As splits increase, more and more space becomes available and the

Figure 3. Insertion Operation

```
Insertion(point)
{ fetch the page containing the point into memory;
  if the page has enough space
    add the point to the page;
  else
  { split the page into two;
    spawn two new directory entries, each pointing to a split page;
    compute the sum values for the two new entries;
  }
  write the page(s) to disk;
  update the sum fields of ancestor entries;
}
```

rate of splits decreases. This cycle repeats as points are added to the file. We shall empirically study this phenomenon in Section 4.

To delete a point, the page containing the point is first brought into memory as in the insertion operation. The point is then removed and the page is written back to the disk. Only two disk accesses are required. If a page becomes empty after deletions, it is released by adding it to an "unused page" list. The "unused pages" on the list can be reused later when a page splits requiring an additional page. The sum fields of the corresponding entry and its ancestors in the directory are updated accordingly.

Update is performed in a similar way by first fetching the page into memory, updating the value, and then writing it back to the disk (in two disk accesses). The sum fields of the entry and its ancestors are modified accordingly.

3.2 Range-Sum Queries

When performing a range-sum query, the grid cells that intersect with the query window need to be identified. If a grid cell is completely contained in the query window, we can directly use the stored sum value for that grid cell in the grid directory. Otherwise, we have to access the grid cells on disk.

For instance, the cells 10 and 11 in Figure 4 are fully contained in the window. Therefore, we can simply retrieve their sums from respective directory entries without physically accessing the disk blocks. If the cells are not fully contained in the range-sum window, like the cells 5, 6, 7, 8, 9, 12, 13, 14, 15, 16, they may have to be retrieved from the disk to check if there are any points in the cells falling in the window.

Recall that we have also stored the MBRs in the directory, i.e., the minimum and maximum coordinate values on each dimension of the data cube cells. One can further eliminate the need to access those grid cells, such as 12, 13, and 15, that do not intercept with the query window using the MBRs. As a result, only grid cells 5, 6, 7, 8, 9, 14, and 16 need to be retrieved from the disk. The detailed range-sum query algorithm is presented in Figure 5.

3.3 Comparisons

Let us make some general comparisons between the prefix-sum methods (Chan, 1999; Geffner, 1999; Geffner, 2000; Ho, 1997) and the spatial data structure methods, including the DCA-tree

Figure 4. Range-sum query

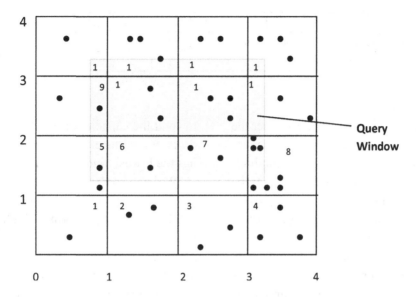

Figure 5. Algorithm for the Range-Sum Query

```
Range-Sum Query (Qwindow)
{  cell: a record with fields: sum, MBR, split, ptr1, ptr2.
   range-sum = 0;
   For each cell intersecting with Qwindow
      if ( cell.MBR ⊂ Qwindow )  range-sum += cell.sum;
      else if (cell.MBR ∩ Qwindow) ≠ φ {
         read the page into memory,
            for each point p
               if (p ∈ Qwindow) add its value to range-sum;
      }
}
```

(Hu, 2002) and our dynamic grid file. Let n be the size of each dimension and D the dimension of the data cube. The prefix-sum approaches need a space at least as large as the size of the data cube (n^D), while the spatial methods need only to store the nonzero cells of the data cube, which is no greater than the number of tuples in the data set. Since the space requirements of prefix-sum methods grow exponentially with the dimension, prefix-sum methods generally are not suitable for high dimensional data cube applications. On the other hand, spatial approaches have no such limitation.

The prefix-sum cube (PC) (Ho, 1997) has the fastest range-sum query processing time among the prefix-sum methods with 2^q accesses, where q ($\leq$ D) is the number of dimensions on which the query poses range constraints. Recall that RPC (Geffner, 1999) requires (D+1) 2^q accesses while Chan's hierarchical cubes HC (Chan, 1999) need $s^2 2^q$ accesses. As for the spatial methods, they need to search the area specified by the q ranges.

Table 1. Features of the Dynamic Grid File

D - dimensionality	4	8	12	16	20	24	28	32	36	40
d - # of dimensions to be partitioned	4	6	9	10	10	10	10	11	11	11
p - # of partitions in the selected dimensions	4	3	2	2	2	2	2	2	2	2

In general, the larger the q value, the smaller the area specified. When q is small, e.g., 3 or 4 dimensions, PC can be faster than the spatial methods because 2^q is small and the search area may be large for the spatial methods. When q is large, e.g., $q > 8$, 2^q becomes large while the search area becomes much smaller. Consequently, PC can be slower than the spatial methods. In fact, PC may not even be feasible for such medium dimensional cubes due to its huge storage requirements.

As for update, the prefix-sum methods are generally more complex and time consuming than the spatial methods. Even for the update efficient prefix-sum methods, such as RPC (Geffner, 1999; Geffner, 2000) and HC (Chan, 1999), they still need $O(m^D)$ accesses, where m ($\leq n$) is the size of the dimension of the sub-cube. In high dimensional cases, the update cost can be substantial. Recall that the grid file needs only 2 to 3 disk accesses, regardless of dimension.

As a short summary, the prefix-sum methods are generally suitable for only low-dimensional and static applications, while the spatial methods are suitable for a much wider range of dimensions, including medium and high dimensions, and for both dynamic and static applications.

PERFORMANCE EVALUATION

In this section, we report the experimental results of the dynamic grid file and the DCA-tree under a wide range of dimensions, from 4 to 40. The prefix-sum methods are excluded from the comparisons as they are not suitable for the medium and high dimensional experiments we performed. In fact, all theses methods would require too much space,

beyond the capacity of many, if not all, modern disks, for all the experiments except the one that has the lowest dimensions, i.e., 4.

We have implemented the dynamic grid file in C++ and compiled it with GNU C/C++ Complier V3.2.3. The test platform is Redhat Linux 3.2.3 running on a Dell Precision 360 workstation with a 3.3 GHZ CPU and 1GB RAM. Each dimension attribute is assumed to have a domain of [0, 99]. Both uniformly and nonuniformly distributed datasets are generated. Each dataset has 100,000 points (or 100,000 nonzero data cube cells). In the nonuniformly distributed datasets, points are distributed among 10 clusters as it is claimed that real-life data are often clustered (Dobra, 2002; Vitter, 1999). The centers of the clusters are randomly picked and the points are normally distributed around the centers with a standard deviation of 10% of the range along each dimension. The physical page size is set to 8,192 bytes to match the default logical disk block size of the operating system. We measure the number of disk accesses, as well as the CPU time, to compare the performance.

To divide the data cube space into grid cells, we determine the number of dimensions d to be partitioned and the number of partitions p in each selected dimension following Eq. (3) of Section 3. In order to partition as many dimensions as possible, we have chosen to partition each selected dimension into two, the smallest number of partitions (except for no partition). In Table 1, we list the d and p values for our dynamic grid files with 100,000 points in 4 to 40 dimensions.

In the following subsections, we present the experimental results on construction time, file

Figure 6. Construction Time

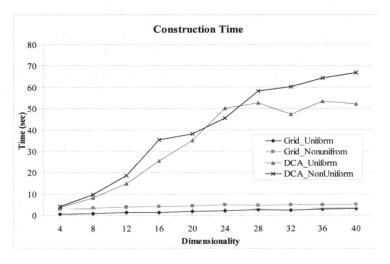

Figure 7. File Size

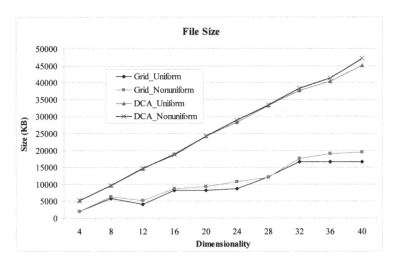

size, CPU time, and number of disk accesses for both uniform and nonuniform datasets.

4.1 Construction Time and File Size

As stated earlier, the dynamic grid file is simple and easy to build and maintain. These advantages demonstrate themselves in the experiments, as shown in Figure 6 and Figure 7. Due to the complex nature of the DCA-tree, its construction time and file size are substantially higher than those of the dynamic grid file. The DCA-tree's construction time increases faster with the increase in dimension because the overlaps of MBRs exacerbate in higher dimensional spaces. Building a DCA-tree could take 10 times longer than building a dynamic grid file when the dimension is greater than 24 in the experiments, as shown in Figure 6.

The DCA-tree generally stores many pointers and rectangles in the data file. In addition, it also stores supporting files, such as the data-path directory and dir-path directory. Consequently, the

DCA-tree used 1.72 to 3.21 times more space than the dynamic grid file as shown in Figure 7.

The construction time and file size for the nonuniform datasets are slightly higher than those for the uniform ones. The increases in construction time and file size in the dynamic grid file are due to the additional pages allocated for the overflow grid cells. Both approaches seem to handle non-uniform distributions very well.

4.2. Insertion

After the file is loaded with the initial 100,000 points, an additional 5,000 points are inserted into the file to measure the cost of insertion. Here, we measure the number of disk accesses to the data file (Figure 8) and CPU time (Figure 9) for inserting a point. Note that all of the disk accesses here refer to accesses to data files, not including accesses to indices or directories, as they are generally small and can be loaded entirely into memory. Later, we will show (in Figure 10) how the file grows due to splitting when there are a large number of points inserted.

As discussed earlier, it takes one read to get the desired grid cell into memory and one or two writes (if a page splits) to store the page(s) back to the dynamic grid file. Since page splits do not

Figure 8. Disk Accesses for an Insertion

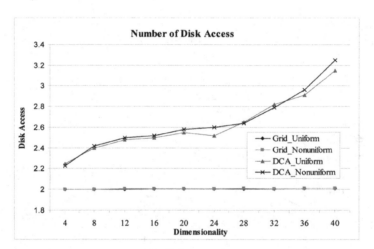

Figure 9. CPU Time for an Insertion

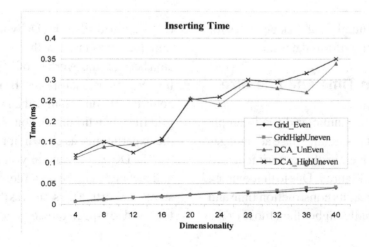

occur very often in the experiments, the average number of disk accesses for inserting a point into the dynamic grid file is just slightly above 2, as shown in Figure 8. Since the MBRs of a DCA-tree overlap significantly, it may take more than one read to find a desired point and thus requires more disk accesses than the dynamic grid file. As the dimension increases, overlaps become more severe and more disk accesses are incurred, compared with the almost constant cost of the grid file.

Figure 9 shows the average CPU time for an insertion. The computation involved in an insertion to the dynamic grid file is simple and straightforward. The slight increase in CPU time in higher dimensions is due to the greater number of coordinate values needing to be checked. As mentioned above, the DCA-tree may need to examine more than one page due to the overlaps among MBRs. As a result, DCA-tree takes more time to insert a point than the grid file. As the dimension increases, overlaps become more severe and the cost of insertion increases more quickly in the DCA-tree.

In Figure 10, we show how the file grows through splitting by continuously inserting points into a 4-dimensional data cube. As points are inserted into the dynamic grid file, the amount of unused space in each page decreases, which increases the chance of splitting. Splitting increases the size of the file and leaves more room in the pages for new points. When space becomes abundant, the rate of splitting moderates. This cycle repeats. This phenomenon is more evident in the uniform data case than the nonuniform data case as pages tend to get full around the same time in the former case.

The DCA-tree does not reserve pages at the beginning. It grows by splitting. The entire splitting process is rather smooth and thus results in an almost linear increase in the file size. The file size is generally greater than ours as it stores additional information in the data file.

We have also measured the space utilization, that is, the average percentage of space being occupied by the data. In general, the dynamic grid file has space utilization ranging from 72% to 88% for the uniform data sets and 65% to 83% for the nonuniform data sets. These figures are obtained when the number of points grows from 200,000 to 500,000. As for the DCA-tree, the space utilization ranges from 74% to 82%. There is little difference in space utilization between uniform and nonuniform distributions for the DCA-tree.

Figure 10. File Growth

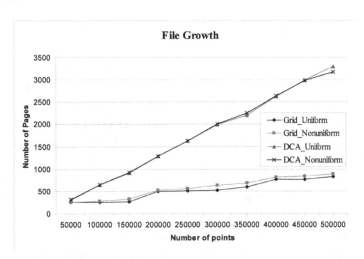

Figure 11. CPU Time for Range-Sum Queries

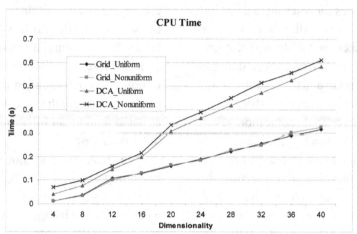

(a) Query Range: Two Constraints, 10% Range

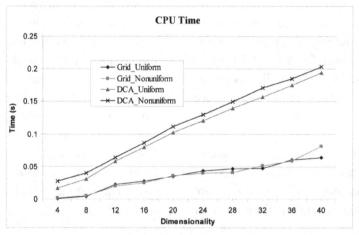

(b) Query Range: Four Constraints, 10% Range

4.3 Range Queries

4.3.1 CPU Time

In the experiments, we generated queries with two or four range constraints to see how the complexity of queries can affect the performance. All of the two or four range constraints are assumed to be defined over the partition dimensions. Each range constraint covers 10% of the range of the respective dimension. Figure 11 shows the CPU time consumed by the dynamic grid file and the DCA-tree for up to 40 dimensions. It is observed that the DCA-tree took more CPU time than our dynamic grid file for both the uniform and nonuniform datasets. This is mainly due to the larger number of MBRs needing to be examined in the DCA-tree. The CPU time of the DCA-tree increases faster than that of the dynamic grid file as the dimension increases. This is because the number of MBRs intersecting with the query window in the DCA-tree increases faster than that for the dynamic grid file as the dimension increases.

The nonuniformity of the data distributions seems to have a greater impact on the DCA-tree than the dynamic grid file. This is because as more

Figure 12. Disk Accesses for Rang-Sum Queries

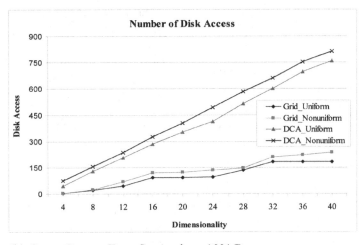

(a) Query Range: Two Constraints, 10% Range

(b) Query Range: Four Constraints, 10% Range

and more data points fall within close vicinity, more overlaps among MBRs occur and thus more time is needed to process queries in the DCA-tree. As for the dynamic grid file, the effect of data distributions is minimal. It shows that our method of splitting cells into nonoverlapping sub-cells is highly effective and our approach performs very well for both distributions.

Figure 11(a) and Figure 11(b) show the execution time of queries with two and four range constraints, respectively. The number of cells satisfying queries with two constraints (less re-

strictive) is greater than those with four constraints (more restrictive). As a result, the time spent in the former (Figure 11 (a)) is greater than that the latter (Figure 11(b)).

4.2.2 Number of Disk Accesses

Figure 12 shows the number of disk accesses of the two approaches. Once again, the dynamic grid file performs much better than the DCA-tree. Similar to the CPU time, the disk access count of the dynamic grid file increases slower than that of the DCA-tree.

Greater numbers of disk accesses are needed for queries over nonuniform datasets for both approaches. The increase in the DCA-tree is due to the increased overlaps among MBRs. The slight increase in the grid file is due to the increased splits of the grid cells caused by the concentration of data points.

As explained above, as the number of constraints increases, the query becomes more selective, and the number of cells satisfying the query decreases. As a result, more disk accesses are required for the two-constraint queries than for the four-constraint ones.

CONCLUSION

In this article, we propose the dynamic grid file for multi-dimensional data cube storage and range-sum query processing. While the conventional prefix sum data cubes can be used to answer range-sum queries quickly for low dimensional data cubes, they require tremendous amounts of space to store and considerable computations to update. The proposed enhancement to the traditional grid file has a natural appeal to the data cube storage as it conforms to the grid structure of the data cubes. It adapts itself to insertions of new data by splitting the grid cells as needed. It minimizes the drawback of the traditional grid files for uneven data while enjoying its advantages of simplicity and efficiency. The space requirement grows linearly with the dimension of the data cubes, compared with the exponential growth for the conventional prefix-sum data cubes. The experimental results show that the dynamic grid file outperforms the R*-tree based DCA-tree in all ranges of dimensions tested for both uniformly and nonuniformly distributed datasets. The proposed file structure can also answer range-sum queries quickly. We believe the dynamic grid

file presents a promising solution to medium to high-dimensional OLAP applications.

REFERENCES

Agarwal, S. Agrawal, R., Deshpande, P., Gupta, A., Naughton, J., Ramakrishnan, R., & Sarawagi, S. (1996). On the Computation of Multidimensional Aggregates. *VLDB Conference* (pp. 506-521).

Barbara, D., & Sullivan, M. (1997). Quasi-cubes: Exploiting Approximation in Multidimensional Databases. *SIGMOD Record, 26,* 12–17.

Beckmann, N., Kriegel, H., Schneider, R., & Seeger, B. (1990). The R*-Tree: an Efficient and Robust Access Method for Points and Rectangles. *ACM SIGMOD Conference* (pp. 322-331).

Beyer, K., & Ramakrishnan, R. (1999). Bottom-up Computation of Sparse and Iceberg Cubes. *ACM SIGMOD Conference* (pp. 359-370).

Chan, C., & Ioannidis, Y. (1999). Hierarchical Cubes for Range-sum Queries. *VLDB Conference* (pp. 675-686).

Cuzzocrea, A. (2006). Improving Range-sum Query Evaluation on Data cubes via Polynomial Approximation. *Data & Knowledge Engineering, 56*(2), 85–121. doi:10.1016/j.datak.2005.03.011

Dobra, A., Garofalakis, M., Gehrke, J., & Rastogi, R. (2002). Processing Complex Aggregate Queries over Data Stream. *ACM SIGMOD Conference* (pp. 61-72).

Gao, H., & Li, J. (2005). Parallel Data Cube Storage Structure for Range Sum Queries and Dynamic Updates. *Journal of Computer Science and Technology, 20*(3), 345–356. doi:10.1007/s11390-005-0345-1

Geffner, S., & Agrawal, D. El., & Abbadi, A. (2000). The Dynamic Data Cubes. *International Conference on Extending Database Technology* (pp. 237-253).

Geffner, S., Agrawal, D., El Abbadi, A., & Smith, T. (1999). Relative Prefix Sums: an Efficient Approach for Quering Dynamic OLAP Data Cubes. *ICDE Conference* (pp. 328-335).

Gray, J., Chaudhuri, S., Bosworth, A., Layman, A., Reichart, D., & Venkatrao, M. (1997). Data Cube: A Relational Aggregation Operator Generalizing Group-By, Cross-Tab, and Sub-Totals. *Data Mining and Knowledge Discovery, 1,* 29–54. doi:10.1023/A:1009726021843

Gupta, H., Harinarayan, V., Rajaraman, A., & Ullman, J. (1997). Index Selection for OLAP. *ICDE Conference* (pp. 208-219).

Han, J., Pei, J., Dong, G., & Wang, K. (2001). Efficient Computation of Iceberg Cubes with Complex Measures. *ACM SIGMOD Conference* (pp. 1-12).

Harinarayan, V., Rajaraman, A., & Ullman, J. (1996). Implementing Data Cubes Efficiently. ACM *SIGMOD Conference* (pp. 205-216).

Ho, C., Agrawal, R., Megiddo, N., & Srikant, R. (1997). Range Queries in OLAP Data Cubes. *ACM SIGMOD Conference* (pp. 73-88).

Hu, K., Dong, Y., & Xu, L. (2002). DCA-Tree: A High Performance Structure for Incremental Update Cube on MDDW. *International Conference on Machine Learning and Cybernetics 2002, 4,* 2069-2072.

Johnson, T., & Shasha, D. (1997). Hierarchically split cube forests for decision support: descriotion and tuned design, 1996. *Bullettin of Technical Committee on Data Engineering, 20*(1).

Lakshmanan, L., Pei, J., & Han, J. (2002). Quotient cube: How to summarize the semantics of a data cube. *VLDB conference* (pp. 766-777).

Lakshmanan, L., Pei, J., & Zhao, Y. (2003). Qc-trees: An efficient summary structure for semantic olap. *ACM SIGMOD Conference* (pp. 64-75).

Li, X., Han, J., & Gonzalez, H. (2004). High-Dimensional OLAP: A Minimal Cubing Approach. *VLDB Conference* (pp. 528-539).

Morfonios, K., & Ioannidis, Y. (2006). Cure for Cubes: Cubing Using a ROLAP Engine. *VLDB Conference* (pp. 379-390).

Nievergelt, J., Hinterberger, H., & Sevcik, K. (1984). The Grid File: An Adaptable Symmetric Multikey File Structure. *ACM Transactions on Database Systems, 9*(1), 38–71. doi:10.1145/348.318586

Shanmugasundaram, J., Fayyad, U., & Bradley, P. (1999). Compressed Data Cubes for OLAP Aggregate Query Approximation on Continuous Dimensions. *Knowledge Discovery and Data Mining Conference* (pp. 223-232).

Shukla, A., Deshpanda, P., Naughton, J., & Ramasamy, K. (1996). Storage Estimation for Multidimensional Aggregates in the Presence of Hierarchies. *VLDB Conference* (pp. 522-531).

Sismanis, Y., Roussopoulos, N., Deligianannakis, A., & Kotidis, Y. (2002). Dwarf: Shrinking the Petacube. *ACM SIGMOD Conference* (pp. 464–475).

Vitter, J., & Wang, M. (1999). "Approximate Computation of Multidimensional Aggregates of Sparse Data Using Wavelets". *ACM SIGMOD Conference* (pp. 193- 204).

Wang, W., Lu, H., Feng, J., & Yu, J. (2002). Condensed cube: An Effective Approach to Reducing Data Cube Size. *ICDE Conference* (pp. 155-165).

Xin, D., Han, J., Li, X., & Wah, W. B. (2003). Starcubing: Computing iceberg cubes by top-down and bottom-up integration. *VLDB Conference* (pp. 476-487).

Zhao, Y., Deshpande, P., & Naughton, J. (1997). An Array-based Algorithm for Simultaneous Multidimensional Aggregates. *ACM SIGMOD Conference* (pp. 159-170).

Compilation of References

Abiteboul, S.,. Beeri, C. (1995). The Power of Languages for the Manipulation of Complex Values. *The VLDB Journal, 4*(4), 727–794. doi:10.1007/BF01354881

Abiteboul, S., Quass, D., McHugh, J., Widom, J.,. Wiener, J. (1997). The Lorel Query language for Semistructured Data. *International Journal on Digital Libraries, 1*, 68–88.

Aboulnaga, A., Alameldeen, A. R.,. Naughton, J. F. (2001, September). Estimating the Selectivity of XML Path Expressions for Internet Scale Applications. In Proceedings of the 27th international conference on very large data bases (VLDB)(p. 591-600). Roma, Italy.

Aditya, B., Bhalotia, G.,. Sudarshan, S. (2002). *BANKS: Browsing and Keyword Searching in Relational Databases*, In Proc. VLDB'02.

Agarwal, R., De, P.,. Sinha, A.P., A.P. (2003). Object Oriented Modeling with UML:. Study of Developer Perceptions. *Communications of the ACM, 46*(9), 248–256. doi:10.1145/903893.903944

Agarwal, S. Agrawal, R., Deshpande, P., Gupta, A., Naughton, J., Ramakrishnan, R.,. Sarawagi, S. (1996). On the Computation of Multidimensional Aggregates. *VLDB Conference* (pp. 506-521).

Ågerfalk, P. J.,. Ralyté, J. (2006). Situational Requirements Engineering Processes: Reflecting on Method Engineering and Requirements Practice. *Software Process Improvement and Practice, 11*(5), 447–450. doi:10.1002/spip.289

Ågerfalk, P. J.,. Fitzgerald, B. (2006). Exploring the Concept of Method Rationale:. Conceptual Tool for Method Tailoring. In Siau, K. (Ed.), *Advanced Topics in Database Research* (*Vol. 5*). Hershey, PA: Idea Group.

Ågerfalk, P. J.,. Wistrand, K. (2003, 23–26 April 2003). *Systems Development Method Rationale:. Conceptual Framework for Analysis.* Paper presented at the 5th International Conference on Enterprise Information Systems (ICEIS 2003), Angers, France.

Ågerfalk, P. J., Brinkkemper, S., Gonzalez-Perez, C., Henderson-Sellers, B., Karlsson, F., Kelly, S., et al. (2007). Modularization Constructs in Method Engineering: Towards Common Ground? In J. Ralyté, S. Brinkkemper,. B. Henderson-Sellers (Eds.), *Proceedings of IFIP WG8.1 Working Conference on Situational Method Engineering: Fundamentals and Experiences* (pp. 359–368). Springer.

Ågerfalk, P. J., Wistrand, K., Karlsson, F., Börjesson, G., Elmberg, M.,. Möller, K. (2003). *Flexible Processes and Method Configuration: Outline of. Joint Industry-Academia Research Project.* Paper presented at the 5th International Conference on Enterprise Information Systems (ICEIS 2003), Angers, France.

Agrawal, S., Chaudhuri, S.,. Das, G. (2002). *DBXplorer:. System for Keyword-based Search Over Relational Databases*, In Proc. ICDE'02.

Agrawal, S., Chaudhuri, S.,. Narasayya, V. R. (2000, September). Automated Selection of Materialized Views and Indexes in SQL Databases. In Proceedings of the 26th international conference on very large data bases (VLDB) (p. 496-505). Cairo, Egypt.

Aho, A. V., Ganapathi, M.,. Tjiang, S. W. K. (1989). Code Generation Using Tree Matching and Dynamic Programming. *ACM Trans. Program. Lang. Syst., 11*(4), 491–516. doi:10.1145/69558.75700

Alatovic, T. (2001). *Capabilities aware, planner, optimizer, executioner for Context Interchange project.* Unpublished master's thesis, Massachusetts Institute of Technology, Cambridge, MA, USA.

Albert, T. C., Goes, P. B.,. Gupta, A. (2004). GIST:. model for design and management of content and interactivity of customer-centric web sites. *Management Information Systems Quarterly, 2*(28), 161–182.

Al-Khalifa, S., Jagadish, H. V., Patel, J. M., Wu, Y., Koudas, N.,. Srivastava, D. (2002, March). Structural Joins:. Primitive for Efficient XML Query Pattern Matching. In Proceedings of the 18th international conference on data engineering (ICDE). San Jose, Canada.

Altinel, M.,. Franklin, M. J. (2000, Sep). Efficient filtering of xml documents for selective dissemination of information. In *Proceedings of the 26th international conference on very large data bases* (pp. 53–64). San Francisco, CA: Morgan Kaufmann.

Amagasa, T., Yoshikawa, M.,. Uemura, S. (2003, March). QRS:. Robust Numbering Scheme for XML Documents. In Proceedings of the 19th international conference on data engineering (ICDE) (p. 705-707). Bangalore, India.

Ambler, S. W. (2002). *Agile Modelling: Effective Practices for eXtreme Programming and the Unified Process.* New York, NY: John Wiley. Sons, Inc.

An, Y., Borgida, A.,. Mylopoulos, J. (2005). Constructing Complex Semantic Mappings Between XML Data and Ontologies. *International Semantic Web Conference ISWC 2005, pp. 6-20.*

Angeles, P. (1981). *Dictionary of philosophy.* New York: Harper Perennial.

Angioni, M., Carboni, D., Pinna, S., Sanna, R., Serra, N.,. Soro, A. (2006). Integrating XP project management in development environments. *Journal of Systems Architecture, 52*(11), 619–626. doi:10.1016/j.sysarc.2006.06.006

Angst, C. M.,. Agarwal, R. (2009). Adoption Of Electronic Health Records In The Presence Of Privacy Concerns: The Elaboration Likelihood Model And Individual Persuasion. *Management Information Systems Quarterly, 33*(2), 339–370.

ANSI/ISO. (2003). *ANSI TC NCITS H2 ISO/IEC JTC 1/ SC 32/WG. Database (ISO-ANSI Working Draft) Information Technology. Database Languages. SQL. Part 14: XML-Related Specifications.* SQL/XML.

Ayanso, A., Goes, P. B.,. Mehta, K. (2007).. practical approach for efficiently answering top-. relational queries. *Decision Support Systems, 44*(1), 326–349. doi:10.1016/j.dss.2007.04.005

Ayanso, A., Goes, P. B.,. Mehta, K. (2009).. cost-based range estimation for mapping top-k selection queries over relational databases. *Journal of Database Management, 20*(4), 1–25. doi:10.4018/jdm.2009062501

Baddeley, A. D. (1992). Working Memory. *Science, 255,* 556–559. doi:10.1126/science.1736359

Baeza-Yates, R.,. Ribeiro-Neto, B. (1999). *Modern Information Retrieval.* New York: ACM Press.

Bajec, M., Vavpotič, D.,. Krisper, M. (2006). Practice-driven approach for creating project-specific software development methods. *Information and Software Technology, 49*(4), 345–365. doi:10.1016/j.infsof.2006.05.007

Balmin, A., Hristidis, V.,. Papakonstantinon, Y. (2003). *Keyword Proximity Search on XML Graphs,* In Proc. ICDE'03.

Balmin, A., Hristidis, V.,. Papakonstantinon, Y. (2004). *ObjectRank: Authority-Based Keyword Search in Databases,* In Proc. VLDB'04.

Balmin, A., Hristidis, V., Papakonstantinon, Y.,. Koudas, N. (2003).. *System for Keyword Proximity Search on XML Databases,* In Proc. VLDB'03.

Balmin, A., Ozcan, F., Beyer, K. S., Cochrane, R.,. Pirahesh, H. (2004, September).. Framework for Using Materialized XPath Views in XML Query Processing. In Proceedings of the 30th international conference on very large data bases (VLDB)(p. 60-71). Toronto, Canada.

Balmin, A., Ozcan, F., Singh, A.,. Ting, E. (2008, June). Grouping and Optimization of XPath Expressions in DB2 pureXML. In Proceedings of the ACM SIGMOD International Conference on Management of Data (p. 1065-1074). Vancouver, Canada.

Barbara, D.,. Sullivan, M. (1997). Quasi-cubes: Exploiting Approximation in Multidimensional Databases. *SIGMOD Record, 26*, 12–17.

Barbosa, D., Mendelzon, A., Keenleyside, J.,. Lyons, K. (2002). *ToXgene:. template-based data generator for XML*, In Proc. WebDB'02. Downloaded: http://www.cs.toronto.edu/ tox/toxgene/ downloads.html

Barta, A., Consens, M. P.,. Mendelzon, A. O. (2005, Aug–Sep). Benefits of path summaries in an xml query optimizer supporting multiple access methods. In *Proceedings of the 31st international conference on very large data bases* (pp. 133–144). Trondheim, Norway: ACM.

Barta, A., Consens, M. P.,. Mendelzon, A. O. (2004, June). XML Query Optimization Using Path Indexes. In Proceedings of the 1st international workshop on XQuery implementation, experience and perspectives (XIME-P), in cooperation with ACM SIGMOD. Maison de la Chimie, Paris, France.

Barta, A., Consens, M. P.,. Mendelzon, A. O. (2005, September). Benefits of Path Summaries in an XML Query Optimizer Supporting Multiple Access Methods. In Proceedings of the 31st international conference on very large data bases (VLDB)(p. 133-144). Trondheim, Norway.

Barton, C., Charles, P., Goyal, D., Raghavachari, M., Fontoura, M.,. Josifovski, V. (2003, Mar). Streaming xpath processing with forward and backward axes. In *Proceedings of the 19th international conference on data engineering* (pp. 455–466). Bangalore, India: IEEE Computer Society.

Bar-Yossef, Z., Fontoura, M.,. Josifovski, V. (2005). Buffering in query evaluation over xml streams. In *Proceedings of the twenty-fourth acm sigmod-sigact-sigart symposium on principles of database systems* (pp. 216–227). New York, NY: ACM.

Baskerville, R.,. Pries-Heje, J. (1999). Grounded action research:. method for understanding IT in practice. *Accounting. Management. Information Technologies, 9*, 1–23. doi:10.1016/S0959-8022(98)00017-4

Baskerville, R.,. Wood-Harper, A. T. (1998). Diversity in information systems action research methods. *European Journal of Information Systems, 7*(2), 90–107. doi:10.1057/palgrave.ejis.3000298

Batra, D. (2008). Unified Modeling Language (UML) Topics: The Past, the Problems, and the Prospects. Guest Editorial Preface. *Journal of Database Management, 19*(1), i–vii.

Batra, D. (2009). Devising Information Systems Modeling Techniques Using the Cognitive Load Theory. Guest Editorial Preface. *Journal of Database Management, 20*(1), i–vi.

Bechky, B. A. (2003). Sharing Meaning Across Occupational Communities: The Transformation of Understanding on. Production Floor. *Organization Science, 14*(3), 312–330. doi:10.1287/orsc.14.3.312.15162

Bechky, B. A. (2006). Talking About Machines, Thick Description, and Knowledge Work. *Organization Studies, 27*(12), 1757–1768. doi:10.1177/0170840606071894

Beck, K. (2000). *Extreme Programming explained: embrace change*. Reading, MA: Addison-Wesley.

Beck, K.,. Cunningham, W. (1989).. Laboratory for Teaching Object Oriented Thinking. *Proceedings of the 1989 ACM OOPSLA Conference on Object-Oriented Programming*, (pp. 1-6).

Beckmann, N., Kriegel, H., Schneider, R.,. Seeger, B. (1990). The R*-Tree: an Efficient and Robust Access Method for Points and Rectangles. *ACM SIGMOD Conference* (pp. 322-331).

Benedikt, M., Jeffrey, A.,. Ley-Wild, R. (2008, June). Stream firewalling of xml constraints. In *Proceedings of the acm sigmod international conference on management of data* (pp. 487–498). Vancouver, Canada: ACM.

Berchtold, S., Keim, D. A., Kriegel, H.-P.,. Seidl, T. (2000). Indexing the solution space:. new technique for nearest neighbor search in high-dimensional space. *IEEE Transactions on Knowledge and Data Engineering, 12*(1), 45–57. doi:10.1109/69.842249

Berendt, B., Günther, O.,. Spiekermann, S. (2005). Privacy in e-commerce: stated preferences vs. actual behavior. *Communications of the ACM*, (48): 4.

Bertino, E., Rabbiti, F.,. Gibbs, S. (1988). Query processing in. multimedia document system. *ACM Transactions on Information Systems, 6*(1), 1–41. doi:10.1145/42279.42281

Beyer, K. S., Cochrane, R., Josifovski, V., Kleewein, J., Lapis, G., Lohman, G. M., et al. (2005, June). System RX: One Part Relational, One Part XML. In Proceedings of the ACM SIGMOD international conference on management of data (p. 347-358). Baltimore, Maryland, USA.

Beyer, K.,. Ramakrishnan, R. (1999). Bottom-up Computation of Sparse and Iceberg Cubes. *ACM SIGMOD Conference* (pp. 359-370).

Bhattacherjee, A. (2002). Individual trust in online firms: scale development and initial test. *Journal of Management Information Systems*, 19(1), 211–241.

Blaha, M.,. Rumbaugh, J. (2005). *Object-Oriented Modeling and Design with UML* (2nd ed.). Pearson Prentice Hall.

Blake, C.,. Merz, C. (1998). UCI Repository of Machine-Learning Databases. [Online]. Available: http://archive.ics.uci.edu/ml/

Bloom, B. H. (1970). Space/time trade-offs in hash coding with allowable errors. *Communications of the ACM*, 13(7), 422–426. doi:10.1145/362686.362692

Boag, S., Chamberlin, D., Fernandez, M., Florescu, D., Robie, J.,. Simeon, J. (2007). XQuery 1.0: An XML Query Language. Retrieved March 2010, from http://www.w3.org/TR/xquery/

Bodart, F., Patel, A., Sim, M.,. Weber, R. (2001). Should Optional Properties Be Used in Conceptual Modelling?. Theory and Three Empirical Tests. *Information Systems Research*, 12(4), 384–405. doi:10.1287/isre.12.4.384.9702

Boland, R. (1985). Phenomenology:. preferred approach to research in information systems. In Mumford, E., Hirschheim, R., Fitzgerald, G.,. Wood-Harper, T. (Eds.), *Research methods in information systems*. Elsevier.

Bolloju, N.,. Leung, F. S. (2006). Assisting the Novice Analyst in Developing Quality Conceptual Models with UML. *Communications of the ACM*, 49(7), 108–112. doi:10.1145/1139922.1139926

Boncz, P. A.,. Kersten, M. L. (1999, October). MIL Primitives for Querying. Fragmented World. *The VLDB Journal*, 8(2), 101–119. doi:10.1007/s007780050076

Boncz, P. A. (2002). Monet:. Next-Generation DBMS Kernel For Query-Intensive Applications. Ph.D. Thesis, Universiteit van Amsterdam, Amsterdam, The Netherlands.

Boncz, P. A., Grust, T., van Keulen, M., Manegold, S., Rittinger, J.,. Teubner, J. (2006, Jun). Monetdb/xquery:. fast xquery processor powered by. relational engine. In *Proceedings of the acm sigmod international conference on management of data* (pp. 479–490). Chicago, IL: ACM.

Boncz, P. A., Grust, T., van Keulen, M., Manegold, S., Rittinger, J.,. Teubner, J. (2005, September). Path_nder: XQuery. The Relational Way. In Proceedings of the 31st international conference on very large data bases (p. 1322-1325). Trondheim, Norway.

Boncz, P. A., Grust, T., van Keulen, M., Manegold, S., Rittinger, J.,. Teubner, J. (2006, June). MonetDB/XQuery:. Fast XQuery Processor Powered by. Relational Engine. In Proceedings of the ACM SIGMOD international conference on management of data (p. 479-490). Chicago, Illinois, USA.

Bonifati, A.,. Ceri, S. (2000). Comparative analysis of five XML query languages. *SIGMOD Record*, 29(1), 68–79. doi:10.1145/344788.344822

Booch, G. (1986). Object-Oriented Development. *IEEE Transactions on Software Engineering*, 12(2), 211–221.

Booch, G. (1994). *Object oriented analysis and design with applications*. Redwood City, CA: Benjamin/Cummings.

Booch, G., Christerson, M., Fuchs, M.,. Koistinen, J. (1999). UML for XML schema mapping specification. http://xml.coverpages.org/fuchs-uml_xmlschema33.pdf

Bosak, J., Bray, T., Connolly, D., Maler, E., Nicol, G., Sperberg-McQueen, C. M., et al. (1998). Guide to the W3C XML Specification (XMLspec) DTD, Version 2.1, http://www.w3.org/XML/1998/06/xmlspec-report-v21.htm

Botev, C., Shao, F.,. Guo, L. (2003*). XRANK: Ranked Keyword Search over XML Documents*, In Proc. GMOD'03.

Böttcher, S.,. Steinmetz, R. (2003).. DTD Graph Based XPath Query Subsumption Test. *Xsym, 2003*, 85–99.

Braa, K.,. Vidgen, R. (1999). Interpretation, intervention, and reduction in the organizational laboratory:. framework for in-context information system research. *Accounting. Management and Information Technologies*, *9*(1), 25–47. doi:10.1016/S0959-8022(98)00018-6

Brancheau, J. C., Janz, B. D.,. Wetherbe, J. C. (1996). Key issues in information systems management: 1994-95 SIM Delphi results. *Management Information Systems Quarterly*, *20*(2), 225–242. doi:10.2307/249479

Brantner, M., Helmer, S., Kanne, C.-C.,. Moerkotte, G. (2005, April). Full-fledged Algebraic XPath Processing in Natix. In Proceedings of the 21st international conference on data engineering (ICDE) (p. 705-716). Tokyo, Japan.

Braumandl, R., Keidl, M., Kemper, A., Kossmann, D., Kreutz, A., Seltzsam, S.,. Stocker, K. (2001). ObjectGlobe: Ubiquitous query processing on the Internet. *The VLDB Journal*, *10*(1), 48–71.

Bray, T., Paoli, J., Sperberg-McQueen, C. M., Maler, E.,. Yergeau, F. (2008, Nov). *Extensible markup language (xml) 1.0 (fifth edition)* (Tech. Rep.). W3C. (http://www.w3.org/TR/XML/)

Brewer, J.,. Lorenz, L. (2003). Using UML and Agile Development Methodologies to Teach Object-Oriented Analysis and Design Tools and Techniques. *Proceedings of the 4th Conference on Information Technology Education*, (pp. 54-57).

Brinkkemper, S. (1996). Method engineering: engineering of information systems development methods and tools. *Information and Software Technology*, *38*(4), 275–280. doi:10.1016/0950-5849(95)01059-9

Brown Associate, D. H. Inc. (2004). HP raises the bar for UNIX workload management. Retrieved February 15, 2008. [Online]. Available: http://whitepapers.silicon.com/ 0,39024759,60104905p- 39000654q,00.htm.

Brown, D. P., Richards, A., Zeehandelaar, R.,. Galeazzi, D. (2002). "Teradata Active System Management". Retrieved February 15, 2008. [Online]. Available: http://www.teradata.com/t/page/ 145613/index.html.

Brown, K. P., Mehta, M., Carey, M. J.,. Livny, M. (1994). Towards automated performance tuning for complex workloads. *Proceedings of the 20th Very Large Data Base Conference,* Santiago, Chile, 72-84.

Bruno, N., Chaudhuri, S.,. Gravano, L. (2002). Top-k selection queries over relational databases: mapping strategies and performance evaluation. *ACM Transactions on Database Systems*, *27*(2), 153–187. doi:10.1145/568518.568519

Bruno, N., Koudas, N.,. Srivastava, D. (2002, June). Holistic twig joins: optimal XML pattern matching. In Proceedings of the ACM SIGMOD international conference on management of data (p. 310-321). Madison, Wisconsin.

Bry, F., Coskun, F., Durmaz, S., Furche, T., Olteanu, D.,. Spannagel, M. (2005, Apr). The xml stream query processor spex. In *Proceedings of the 21st international conference on data engineering* (pp. 1120–1121). Tokyo, Japan: IEEE Computer Society.

Buneman, P., Fernandez, M. F.,. Suciu, D. (2000). UnQL:. query language and algebra for semistructured data based on structural recursion. *VLDB Journal: Very Large Data Bases*, *9*(1), 76–110. doi:10.1007/s007780050084

Bunge, M. A. (1977). *Ontology i: The furniture of the world* (*Vol. 3*). Dordrecht, Holland: D. Reidel Publishing Company.

Bunge, M. A. (1979). *Ontology ii:. world of systems* (Vol. 4). Dordrecht, Hallond: D. Reidel Publishing Company.

Burton, P.,. Bruhn, R. (2004). Using UML to Facilitate the Teaching of Object-Oriented Systems Analysis and Design. *Journal of Computing Sciences in Colleges*, *19*(3), 278–290.

Burton-Jones, A.,. Meso, P. (2006). Conceptualizing Systems for Understanding: An Empirical Test of Decomposition Principles in Object-Oriented Analysis. *Information Systems Research*, *17*(1), 38–60. doi:10.1287/isre.1050.0079

Bustos, B., Keim, D. A., Saupe, D., Schreck, T.,. Vranić, D. V. (2005). Feature-based similarity search in 3D object databases. *ACM Computing Surveys*, *37*(4), 345–387. doi:10.1145/1118890.1118893

Cameron, J. (2002). Configurable Development Processes. *Communications of the ACM*, *45*(3), 72–77. doi:10.1145/504729.504731

Candan, K. S., Hsiung, W.-P., Chen, S., Tatemura, J.,. Agrawal, D. (2006, Sep). Afilter: Adaptable xml filtering with prefix-caching and suffix-clustering. In *Proceedings of the 32nd international conference on very large data bases* (pp. 559–570). Seoul, Korea: ACM.

Carey, M. J.,. Kossmann, D. (1997). On saying 'Enough Already!' in SQL. *Proc. ACM SIGMOD Int'l Conf. Management of Data (SIGMOD'97)*.

Carey, M. J.,. Kossmann, D. (1998). Reducing the breaking distance of an SQL query engine. *Proc. 24th Int'l Conf. Very Large Data Bases (VLDB'98)*.

Castañeda, J. A.,. Montoro, F. J. (2007). The effect of internet general privacy concern on customer behavior. *Electronic Commerce Research*, *7*(2), 117–141. doi:10.1007/s10660-007-9000-y

Castro, S., Tezulas, N., Yu, B., Berg, J., Kim, H.,. Gfroerer, D. (2001). *AIX 5L Workload Manager*.

Cattell, R. G. G., Barry, D., Bartels, D., Berler, M., Eastman, J., Gamerman, S., et al. (1997). The Object Database Standard: ODMG 2.0.

Ceri, S., Comai, S., Damiani, E., Fraternali, P., Paraboschi, S.,. Tanca, L. (1999). *XML-GL: Graphical Language for Querying and Restructuring WWW Data*. Paper presented at the 8th Int. World Wide Web Conference, WWW8.

Chalmers, M. (2004). Hermeneutics, information, and representation. *European Journal of Information Systems*, *13*, 210–220. doi:10.1057/palgrave.ejis.3000504

Chamberlain, D., Fankhauser, P., Florescu, D., Marchiori, M.,. Robie, J. (2002). XML Query Use Cases

Chamberlin, D.,. Fankhauser, P.,. Florescu, D.,. Robie, J. (2007). XML Query Use Cases. *W3C Working Draft 2007*.

Chamberlin, D., Clark, J., Florescu, D., Robie, J., Simeon, J.,. Stefanescu, M. (2001). XQuery 1.0: An XML Query Language.

Chamberlin, D., Fankhauser, P., Marchiori, M.,. Robie, J. (2003). XML Query (XQuery) Requirements. W3C Working Draft 12 November 2003.

Chamberlin, D., Robie, J.,. Florescu, D. (2001). Quilt: an XML Query Language for Heterogeneous Data Sources. *The World Wide Web and Databases, Third International Workshop WebDB 2000, Dallas, Texas, USA, May 18-19, 2000, Selected Papers* (Vol. 1997, pp. 1-25): Springer.

Chan, C. Y., Felber, P., Garofalakis, M.,. Rastogi, R. (2002a). Efficient filtering of xml documents with xpath expressions. *The VLDB Journal*, *11*(4), 354–379. doi:10.1007/s00778-002-0077-6

Chan, S. W. K. (2006). Beyond keyword and cue-phrase matching:. sentence-based abstraction technique for information extraction. *Decision Support Systems*, *42*(2), 759–777. doi:10.1016/j.dss.2004.11.017

Chan, C. Y.,. Ni, Y. (2007, Jun). Efficient xml data dissemination with piggybacking. In *Proceedings of the acm sigmod international conference on management of data* (pp. 737–748). Beijing, China: ACM.

Chan, C.,. Ioannidis, Y. (1999). Hierarchical Cubes for Range-sum Queries. *VLDB Conference* (pp. 675-686).

Chan, Y., Culnan, M., Laden, G., Levin, T.,. Smith, J. (2004). Panel: information privacy management: proactive versus reactive approaches. *Proceedings of the Twenty-Fifth Annual International Conference on Information Systems*, Washington, D.C., 12-15.

Chandramouli, B.,. Yang, J. (2008). End-to-end support for joins in large-scale publish/subscribe systems. *PVLDB*, *1*(1), 434–450.

Chandramouli, B., Bond, C. N., Babu, S.,. Yang, J. (2007). Query suspend and resume. *Proceedings of the ACM SIGMOD International Conference on Management of Data*, Beijing, China, 557-568.

Chandramouli, B., Yang, J., Agarwal, P. K., Yu, A.,. Zheng, Y. (2008, June). Prosem: scalable wide-area publish/subscribe. In *Proceedings of the acm sigmod international conference on management of data* (pp. 1315–1318). Vancouver, BC, Canada: ACM.

Chang, K. C.,. Hwang, S. (2002). Minimal probing: supporting expensive predicates for top-k queries. *Proc. ACM SIGMOD Int'l Conf. Management of Data (SIGMOD'02)*, 346–357.

Chang, Y., Bergman, I. D., Castelli, V., Li, C., Lo, M.,. Smith, J. R. (2000). The onion technique: indexing for linear optimization queries. *Proc. ACM SIGMOD Int'l Conf. Management of Data (SIGMOD'00)*, 391–402.

Charette, R. (2005) Why Software Fails. *IEEE Spectrum Online*. http://www.spectrum.ieee.org/ sep05/1685 Accessed September 11, 2007.

Chatterjee, D., Pacini, C.,. Sambamurthy, V. (2002). The shareholder-wealth and trading-volume effects of information-technology infrastructure investments. *Journal of Management Information Systems*, 2(19), 7–42.

Chatterjee, D., Richardson, V. J.,. Zmud, R. W. (2001). Examining the shareholder wealth effects of announcements of newly created CIO positions. *Management Information Systems Quarterly*, 1(25), 43–70. doi:10.2307/3250958

Chaudhuri, S., Gravano, L.,. Marian, A. (2004). Optimizing top-*k* selection queries over multimedia repositories. *IEEE Transactions on Knowledge and Data Engineering*, 16(8), 992–1009. doi:10.1109/TKDE.2004.30

Chaudhuri, S.,. Gravano, L. (1999). Evaluating top-*k* selection queries. *Proc. 25th Int'l Conf. Very Large Data Bases (VLDB'99)*, 397–410.

Chaudhuri, S., Konig, A.,. Narasayya, V. (2004). SQLCM:. continuous monitoring framework for relational database engines. *Proceedings of the 20th International Conference on Data Engineering*, Toronto, Canada, 473-485.

Chawathe, S. S., Garcia-Molina, H., Hammer, J., Ireland, K., Papakonstantinou, Y., Ullman, J. D.,. Widom, J. (1994). The TSIMMIS project: Integration of heterogeneous information sources. *Proceedings of the 16th Meeting of the Information Processing Society of Japan*, 7–18.

Chellappa, R. K.,. Sin, R. G. (2005). Personalization versus privacy: an empirical examination of the online consumer's dilemma. *Information Technology Management*, 6(2-3), 181–202. doi:10.1007/s10799-005-5879-y

Chen, W. J., Comeau, B., Ichikawa, T., Kumar, S. S., Miskimen, M.,. Morgan, H. T. (2008). *DB2 Workload Manager for Linux, Unix, and Windows*. IBM RedBooks.

Chen, C.-M.,. Ling, Y. (2002).. sampling-based estimator for top-*k* selection query. *Proc. 18th Int'l Conf. Data Engineering (ICDE'02)*, 617-627.

Chen, J., Yin, X.,. Zhang, S. (2005). Online Discovery of Quantitative Model for Web Service Management. *Advances in Natural Computation, LNCS 3611*, Springer Berlin, 539-542.

Chen, Y., Davidson, S. B.,. Zheng, Y. (2006, Apr). An efficient xpath query processor for xml streams. In *Proceedings of the 22nd international conference on data engineering* (pp. 79). Atlanta, GA: IEEE Computer Society.

Chen, Z., Jagadish, H. V., Lakshmanan, L. V. S.,. Paparizos, S. (2003, September). From Tree Patterns to Generalized Tree Patterns: On Efficient Evaluation of XQuery. In Proceedings of the 29th international conference on very large data bases (VLDB)(p. 237-248). Berlin, Germany.

Chidlovskii, B. (2001). *Schema Extraction from XML Data:. Grammatical Inference Approach, KRDB'01 Workshop*. Knowledge Representation and Databases.

Chien, S.-Y., Vagena, Z., Zhang, D., Tsotras, V. J.,. Zaniolo, C. (2002, September). Efficient Structural Joins on Indexed XML Documents. In Proceedings of the 28th international conference on very large data bases (VLDB).

Christophides, V., Abiteboul, S., Cluet, S.,. Scholl, M. (1994). From Structured Documents to Novel Query Facilities. *SIGMOD Record*, 23(2), 313–324. doi:10.1145/191843.191901

Cilia, M., Haupt, M., Mezini, M.,. Buchmann, A. (2003). *The convergence of aop and active databases: Towards reactive middleware.* Paper presented at the International Conference on Generative Programming and Component Engineering GPCE.

Clark, J.,. DeRose, S. (1999, Nov). *Xml path language (xpath)* (Tech. Rep.). W3C. (http://www.w3.org/TR/xpath/)

Clark, J.,. DeRose, S. (1999). XML Path Language XPath Version 1.0. Retrieved from http://www.w3.org/TR/xpath

Cluet, S. (1998). Designing OQL: Allowing Objects To Be Queried. *Information Systems*, 23(5), 279–305. doi:10.1016/S0306-4379(98)00013-1

Coad, P.,. Yourdon, E. (1990). *Object-oriented analysis*. Englewood Cliffs, NJ: Yourdon Press.

Coad, P.,. Yourdon, E. (1991). *Object-oriented design*. Englewood Cliffs, New Jersey: Prentice-Hall, Inc.

Cockburn, A. (2000). Selecting. Project's Methodolohy. *IEEE Software*, 64–71. doi:10.1109/52.854070

Cockroft, S.,. Rowles, S. (2003). *Ontological evaluation of health models: Some early findings.* Paper presented at the 7th Pacific Asia Conference on Information Systems PACIS, Adelaide, Australia.

Cohen, S., Kanza, Y., Kogan, Y., Sagiv, Y., Nutt, W.,. Serebrenik, A. (2002). EquiX---a search and query language for XML. *Journal of the American Society for Information Science and Technology, 53*(6), 454–466. doi:10.1002/asi.10058

Cohen, S.,. Kanza, Y. (2005). *Interconnection Semantics for Keyword Search in XML*, In Proc. CIKM'05.

Cohen, S., Mamou, J.,. Sagiv, Y. (2003). *XSEarch:. Semantic Search Engine for XML*, In Proc. VLDB'03.

Conrad, R., Scheffner, D., Freytag, C. "XML Conceptual Modeling Using UML", *Proc. ER2000.*

Cranor, L. F., Guduru, P.,. Arjula, M. (2006). User interfaces for privacy agents. [TOCHI]. *ACM Transactions on Computer-Human Interaction, 13*(2). doi:10.1145/1165734.1165735

Culnan, M. J. (2000). Protecting privacy online: is self-regulation working? *Journal of Public Policy. Marketing, 1*(19), 20–26. doi:10.1509/jppm.19.1.20.16944

Culnan, M. J.,. Armstrong, P. K. (1999). Information privacy concerns, procedural fairness, and impersonal trust: an empirical investigation. *Organization Science, 1*(10), 104–116. doi:10.1287/orsc.10.1.104

Culnan, M. J.,. Bies, R. J. (2003). Consumer privacy: balancing economic and justice considerations. *The Journal of Social Issues, 2*(59), 323–342. doi:10.1111/1540-4560.00067

Culnan, M. J.,. Williams, C. C. (2009). How Ethics Can Enhance Organizational Privacy Lessons from the Choicepoint and Tjx Data Breaches. *Management Information Systems Quarterly, 33*(4), 673–687.

Culnan, M.J. (1995). Consumer awareness of name removal procedures: implications for direct marketing. *Journal of Direct Marketing*, (9), 10-15.

Cuzzocrea, A. (2006). Improving Range-sum Query Evaluation on Data cubes via Polynomial Approximation. *Data. Knowledge Engineering, 56*(2), 85–121. doi:10.1016/j.datak.2005.03.011

Daniel, F.,. Pozzi, G. (2008). An Open ECA Server for Active Applications. *Journal of Database Management, 19*(4), 1–20. doi:10.4018/jdm.2008100101

Das, G., Gunopulos, D., Koudas, N.,. Tsirogiannis, D. (2006). Answering top-k queries using views. *Proc. 32nd Int'l Conf. Very Large Data Bases (VLDB'06)*, 451–462.

DB2 Information Center. (2006, March 14). Retrieved January, 31, 2007 from http://publib.boulder.ibm.com/ infocenter/db2luw/v8//index.jsp.

DB2 Information Integrator Wrapper Developer's Guide. (2004, September 8). Retrieved January, 31, 2007 from http://publibfp.boulder.ibm.com/epubs/pdf/c1891740.pdf

De, P., Sinha, A.,. Vessey, I. (2001). An Empirical Investigation of Factors Influencing Object-Oriented Database Querying. *Information Technology Management, 2*(1), 71–93. doi:10.1023/A:1009934820999

Deach, S. (Artist). (1998). *Extensible Style Language (XSL) Specification.*

DeHaan, D., Toman, D., Consens, M. P.,. Ozsu, M. T. (2003, June).. Comprehensive XQuery to SQL Translation using Dynamic Interval Encoding. In Proceedings of the ACM AIGMOD international conference on management of data (p. 623-634). San Diego, California, USA.

Dennis, A.,. Wixom, B. (2000). *System Analysis and Design: An Applied Approach.* New York: John Wiley and Sons.

Denny, M. (2002). Ontology Building:. Survey of Editing Tools. *O'Reilly XML.COM.* Retrieved from: http://www.xml.com/ 2002/11/06/ Ontology_Editor_Survey.html

Deutsch, A., Fernandez, M.,. Suciu, D. (1999). Storing Semi-structured Data with STORED, *SIGMOD Conference, Philadelphia, Pennsylvania.*

Deutsch, A., Fernandez, M., Florescu, D., Levy, A.,. Suciu, D. (1998). XML-QL:. query language for XML.

Devaraj, S., Fan, M.,. Kohli, R. (2002). Antecedents of b2c channel satisfaction and preference: validating e-commerce metrics. *Information Systems Research, 3*(13), 316–333. doi:10.1287/isre.13.3.316.77

Dewan, R. M., Freimer, M. L.,. Zhang, H. (2002). Management of valuation of advertisement-supported web sites. *Journal of Management Information Systems, 3*(19), 87–98.

Diao, Y., Altinel, M., Franklin, M. J., Zhang, H.,. Fischer, P. (2003). Path sharing and predicate evaluation for high-performance xml filtering. *ACM Transactions on Database Systems, 28*(4), 467–516. doi:10.1145/958942.958947

Diao, Y.,. Franklin, M. J. (2003, Sep). Query processing for high-volume xml message brokering. In *Proceedings of 29th international conference on very large data bases* (pp. 261–272). Berlin, Germany: Morgan Kaufmann.

Diao, Y., Fischer, P. M., Franklin, M. J.,. To, R. (2002, Feb). Yfilter: Efficient and scalable filtering of xml documents. In *Proceedings of the 18th international conference on data engineering* (pp. 341–342). San Jose, CA: IEEE Computer Society.

Diao, Y., Rizvi, S.,. Franklin, M. J. (2004, Aug–Sep). Towards an internet-scale xml dissemination service. In *Proceedings of the 30th international conference on very large data bases* (pp. 612–623). Toronto, Canada: Morgan Kaufmann.

Diaz, A. L.,. Lovell, D. (1999, Sep). *IBM XML Generator.* (http://www.alphaworks.ibm.com/ tech/xmlgenerator)

Diney, T.,. Hart, P. (2006). An extended privacy calculus model for e-commerce transactions. *Information Systems Research, 17*(1), 2006.

Dion, A. (2001). XML Data Binding with Castor. *O'Reilly ON Java.com*. Retrieved from: http://www.onjava.com/pub/a/onjava/2001/10/24/ xmldatabind.html

Dobing, B.,. Parsons, J. (2000). Understanding the role of use cases in UML:. review and research agenda. *Journal of Database Management, 11*(4), 28–36. doi:10.4018/jdm.2000100103

Dobing, B.,. Parsons, J. (2008). Dimensions of UML Diagram Use:. Survey of Practitioners. *Journal of Database Management, 19*(1), 1–18. doi:10.4018/jdm.2008010101

Dobing, B.,. Parsons, J. (2006). How UML is Used. *Communications of the ACM, 49*(5), 109–113. doi:10.1145/1125944.1125949

Dobra, A., Garofalakis, M., Gehrke, J.,. Rastogi, R. (2002). Processing Complex Aggregate Queries over Data Stream. *ACM SIGMOD Conference* (pp. 61-72).

Donjerkovic, D.,. Ramakrishnan, R. (1999). Probabilistic optimization of top. queries. *Proc. 25th Int'l Conf. Very Large Data Bases (VLDB'99),* 411- 422.

Dori, D. (2002). Why Significant UML Change is Unlikely. *Communications of the ACM, 45*(11), 82–85. doi:10.1145/581571.581599

Dos Santos, B. L., Peffers, K.,. Mauer, D. C. (1993). The impact of information technology investment announcements on the market value of the firm. *Information Systems Research, 1*(4), 1–23. doi:10.1287/isre.4.1.1

Douglass, B. (1998). UML for Systems Engineering. *Computer Design's. Electronic Systems Technology. Design, 37*(11), 44–49.

Draper, D., Fankhauser, P., Fernandez, M., Malhotra, A., Rose, K., Rys, M., et al. (2007). XQuery 1.0 and XPath 2.0 Formal Semantics. Retrieved from http://www.w3.org/TR/xquery-semantics/

Dussart, A., Aubert, B. A.,. Patry, M. (2004). An evaluation of inter-organizational workflow modeling formalisms. *Journal of Database Management, 15*(2), 74–104. doi:10.4018/jdm.2004040104

Eisenberg, A.,. Melton, J. (2002). SQL/XML is making good progress. *SIGMOD Record, 31*(2), 101–108. doi:10.1145/565117.565141

Eisenberg, A.,. Melton, J. (2004). Advancements in SQL/XML. *SIGMOD Record, 33*(3), 79–86. doi:10.1145/1031570.1031588

Elghandour, I., Aboulnaga, A., Zilio, D., Chiang, F., Balmin, A., Beyer, K.,. Zuzarte, C. (2008, June). An XML Index Advisor for DB2. In Proceedings of the ACM SIGMOD International Conference on Management of Data (p. 1267-1270). Vancouver, Canada.

Elmasri, R.,. Navathe, S. (2007). *Fundamentals of Database Systems*. Addison-Wesley Computing.

Elnaffar, S., Powley, W., Benoit, D.,. Martin, P. (2003). Today's DBMSs: How autonomic are they? *Proceedings of Dexa Workshops. First International Workshop on Autonomic Computing Systems*, Prague, 651-655.

Erickson, J.,. Siau, K. (2008). Web services, service-oriented computing, and service-oriented architecture: Separating hype from reality. *Journal of Database Management, 19*(3), 42–54. doi:10.4018/jdm.2008070103

Evans, G. (2003, September). Agile RUP for Non-Object-Oriented Projects. *The Rational Edge.*

Evermann, J.,. Wand, Y. (2005). Ontology-Based Object-Oriented Business Modelling: Fundamental Concepts. *Requirements Engineering Journal, 10*(2), 146–160. doi:10.1007/s00766-004-0208-2

Evermann, J.,. Wand, Y. (2006). Ontological modelling rules for UML: An empirical assessment. *Journal of Computer Information Systems, 47*(1).

Evermann, J. (2005). Thinking Ontologically. Conceptual versus Design Models in UML. In: Rosemann, M. and Green, P. (eds.) *Ontologies and Business Analysis.* Idea Group Publishing, 82-104.

Evermann, J. (2005). *The association construct in conceptual modeling. an analysis using the bunge ontological model.* Paper presented at the 17th International Conference on Advanced Information Systems Engineering, Porto, Portugal.

Fagin, R. (1999). Combining fuzzy information from multiple systems. *Journal of Computer and System Sciences, 58*(1), 83–99. doi:10.1006/jcss.1998.1600

Fagin, R. (1998). Fuzzy queries in multimedia database systems. *Proc. 17th ACM Symp. Principles of Database Systems (PODS'98),* 1-10.

Fagin, R., Lotem, A.,. Naor, M. (2001). Optimal aggregation algorithms for middleware. *Proc. 20th ACM Symp. Principles of Database Systems (PODS'01),* 102-113.

Federal Trade Commission. (2000, May). *Self-regulation and privacy online:. report to congress.* [Online]. Available: http://www.ftc.gov/privacy.

Fedorowicz, J.,. Villeneuve, A. (1999). Surveying Object Technology Usage and Benefits:. Test of Conventional Wisdom. *Information. Management, 35*(6), 331–345. doi:10.1016/S0378-7206(98)00098-6

Fegaras, L., Levine, D., Bose, S.,. Chaluvadi, V. (2002, Nov). Query processing of streamed xml data. In *Proceedings of the 11th international conference on information and knowledge management* (pp. 126–133). McLean, VA: ACM.

Felber, P., Chan, C. Y., Garofalakis, M.,. Rastogi, R. (2003). Scalable filtering of xml data for web services. *IEEE Internet Computing, 7*(1), 49–51. doi:10.1109/MIC.2003.1167339

Fernandez, M., Morishima, A.,. Suciu, D. (2001). Publishing Relational Data in XML:the SilkRoute Approach.. *Quarterly Bulletin of the Computer Society of the IEEE Technical Committee on Data Engineering, 24*(2), 12–19.

Fernandez, M. F., Malhotra, A., Marsh, J., Nagy, M.,. Walsh, N. (2006, November). XQuery 1.0 and XPath 2.0 Data Model (XDM). World Wide Web Consortium Proposed Recommendation. (http://www.w3.org/TR / xpath-datamodel)

Fernandez, M., Malhotra, A., Marsh, J., Nagy, M.,. Walsh, N. (2007). XQuery 1.0 and XPath 2.0 Data Model (XDM). Retrieved from http://www.w3.org/TR/xpath-datamodel/

Fiebig, T., Helmer, S., Kanne, C.-C., Moerkotte, G., Neumann, J.,. Schiele, R. (2003).. Technology Overview. In *Revised papers from the node 2002 web and database-related workshops on web, web-services, and database systems.* London, UK: Natix.

Firat, A., Madnick, S., Yahaya, N., Kuan, C.,. Bressan, S. (2005). Information aggregation using the Caméléon# web wrapper. *Lecture Notes in Computer Science, 3590*(1), 76–86.

Firat, A., Madnick, S.,. Siegel, M. (2000). The Caméléon web wrapper engine. *In Proceedings of the VLDB2000 Workshop on Technologies for E-Services,* 1-9.

Fitzgerald, B., Hartnett, G.,. Conboy, K. (2006). Customising Agile Methods to Software Practices at Intel Shannon. *European Journal of Information Systems, 15*(2), 197–210. doi:10.1057/palgrave.ejis.3000605

Fitzgerald, B., Russo, N. L.,. O'Kane, T. (2003). Software Development Method Tailoring at Motorola. *Communications of the ACM, 46*(4), 65–70. doi:10.1145/641205.641206

Fitzgerald, B., Russo, N. L.,. Stolterman, E. (2002). *Information Systems Development. Methods in Action*. London: McGraw-Hill.

Florescu, D., Levy, A.,. Mendelzon, A. (1998). Database techniques for the World-Wide Web:. Survey. *SIGMOD Record, 27*(3), 59–74.

Florescu, D.,. Kossmann, D. (1999). Storing and Querying XML Data Using an RDBMS.. *Quarterly Bulletin of the Computer Society of the IEEE Technical Committee on Data Engineering, 22*(3), 27–34.

Florescu, D., Hillery, C., Kossmann, D., Lucas, P., Riccardi, F., Westmann, T., et al. (2003, September). The BEA/ XQRL Streaming XQuery Processor. In Proceedings of the 30th international conference on very large data bases (VLDB)(p. 997-1008). Berlin, Germany.

Fong, J.,. Cheung, S. K. (2005). Translating relational schema into XML schema definition with data semantic preservation and XSD graph, *Information and Software Technology, 47(7),pp.437-462*. Funderburk, JE., Kiernan, G., Shanmugasundaram, J., Shekita, E.,&Wei, C.(2002). XTABLES: Bridging relational technology and XML. *IBM Systems Journal, 41*(4), 2002.

Fong, J.,. Wong, H. K. (2004). XTOPO, An XML-based Technology for Information Highway on the Internet. *Journal of Database Management, 15*(3), 18–44. doi:10.4018/ jdm.2004070102

Fowler, M. (1997). *Analysis Patterns: Reusable Object Models*. Addison-Wesley Pearson Education.

Fowler, M. (2004). *UML Distilled Third Edition:. Brief Guide to the Standard Object Modeling Language*. Addison-Wesley Pearson Education.

France, R., Kim, D.-K., Ghosh, S.,. Song, E. (2004).. UML-based Pattern Specification Technique. *IEEE Transactions on Software Engineering, 30*(3), 193–206. doi:10.1109/TSE.2004.1271174

Fynn, K. (1997).. *planner/optimizer/executioner for context mediated queries*. Unpublished master's thesis, Massachusetts Institute of Technology, Cambridge, MA, USA.

Gadamer, H.-G. (1976). *Philosophical hermeneutics*. University of California Press.

Ganek, A. G.,. Corbi, T. A. (2003). The Dawning of the Autonomic Computing Era. *IBM Systems Journal, 42*(1), 5–18. doi:10.1147/sj.421.0005

Gao, H.,. Li, J. (2005). Parallel Data Cube Storage Structure for Range Sum Queries and Dynamic Updates. *Journal of Computer Science and Technology, 20*(3), 345–356. doi:10.1007/s11390-005-0345-1

Geer, D. (2003). Federated Approach Expands Database-Access Technology. *Computer, 36*(5), 18–20. doi:10.1109/ MC.2003.1198230

Gefen, D., Karahanna, E.,. Straub, D. W. (2003). Trust and tam in online shopping: an integrated model. *Management Information Systems Quarterly, 1*(27), 51–90.

Geffner, S.,. Agrawal, D. El., &Abbadi, A. (2000). The Dynamic Data Cubes. *International Conference on Extending Database Technology* (pp. 237-253).

Geffner, S., Agrawal, D., El Abbadi, A.,. Smith, T. (1999). Relative Prefix Sums: an Efficient Approach for Querying Dynamic OLAP Data Cubes. *ICDE Conference* (pp. 328-335).

Gemino, A.,. Wand, Y. (2003). Evaluating Modeling Techniques Based on Models of Learning. *Communications of the ACM, 46*(10), 79–84. doi:10.1145/944217.944243

Gemino, A.,. Wand, Y. (2004). Dimensions in Experimental Evaluation of Conceptual Modeling Techniques. *Requirements Engineering Journal, 9*(4), 248–260. doi:10.1007/s00766-004-0204-6

Gemino, A.,. Wand, Y. (2005). Simplicity versus Clarity: An Empirical Comparison of Mandatory and Optional Properties in Conceptual Modeling. *Data. Knowledge Engineering, 55*, 301–326. doi:10.1016/j.datak.2004.12.009

Gemino, A. (1999). *Empirical comparisons of systems analysis modeling techniques*. Unpublished PhD Thesis, The University of British Columbia, Vancouver, BC.

George, J. F., Batra, D., Valacich, J. S.,. Hoffer, J. A. (2006). *Object-Oriented Systems Analysis and Design* (2nd ed.). Prentice Hall.

Goldkuhl, G., Lind, M.,. Seigerroth, U. (1998). Method integration: The need for. learning perspective. *IEE Proceedings. Software, 145*(4), 113–118. doi:10.1049/ip-sen:19982197

Goldkuhl, G.,. Röstlinger, A. (1993). Joint elicitation of problems: An important aspect of change analysis. In Avison, D. E., Kendall, J. E.,. DeGross, J. I. (Eds.), *Human, Organizational, and Social Dimensions of Information Systems Development* (pp. 107–125). North-Holland.

Goldman, R.,. Widom, J. (1997). DataGuides: Enabling Query Formulation and Optimization in Kanne, CC.,(2000). Guido Moerkotte. Efficient storage of xml data. *Proc. of ICDE, California, USA, page 198.*

Gong, X., Yan, Y., Qian, W.,. Zhou, A. (2005, Apr). Bloom filter-based xml packets filtering for millions of path queries. In *Proceedings of the 21st international conference on data engineering* (pp. 890–901). Tokyo, Japan: IEEE Computer Society.

Gottlob, G., Koch, C.,. Pichler, R. (2005). Efficient algorithms for processing xpath queries. *ACM Transactions on Database Systems, 30*(2), 444–491. doi:10.1145/1071610.1071614

Gou, G.,. Chirkova, R. (2007, Jun). Efficient algorithms for evaluating xpath over streams. In *Proceedings of the acm sigmod international conference on management of data* (pp. 269–280). Beijing, China: ACM.

Graefe, G. (2006). Implementing sorting in database systems. *ACM Computing Surveys, 38*(3), 10. doi:10.1145/1132960.1132964

Graefe, G. (2003). Sorting And Indexing With Partitioned B-Trees. In Proceedings of the 1st international conference on data systems research (CIDR).

Gray, J., Chaudhuri, S., Bosworth, A., Layman, A., Reichart, D.,. Venkatrao, M. (1997). Data Cube:. Relational Aggregation Operator Generalizing Group-By, Cross-Tab, and Sub-Totals. *Data Mining and Knowledge Discovery, 1*, 29–54. doi:10.1023/A:1009726021843

Green, P.,. Rosemann, M. (2000). Ontological analysis of integrated process modelling. *Information Systems, 25*(2). doi:10.1016/S0306-4379(00)00010-7

Green, T. J., Gupta, A., Miklau, G., Onizuka, M.,. Suciu, D. (2004). Processing xml streams with deterministic automata and stream indexes. *ACM Transactions on Database Systems, 29*(4), 752–788. doi:10.1145/1042046.1042051

Green, T. J., Miklau, G., Onizuka, M.,. Suciu, D. (2003, Jan). *Processing xml streams with deterministic automata.* In *9th international conference of database theory* (pp. 173–189). Siena, Italy: Springer.

Greenaway, K. E.,. Chan, Y. E. (2005). Theoretical explanations for firms' information privacy behaviors. *Journal of the Association for Information Systems,* (6): 6.

Grohe, M., Koch, C.,. Schwelkardt, N. (2005, Jul). Tight lower bounds for query processing on streaming and external memory data. In *Proceedings of 32nd international colloquium on automata, languages and programming* (pp. 1076–1088). Lisbon, Portugal: Springer.

Gruninger, M.,. Lee, J. (2002). Ontology applications and design. *Commmunications of the ACM, 45*(2).

Grust, T., van Keulen, M.,. Teubner, J. (2004). Accelerating XPath evaluation in any RDBMS. *ACM Transactions on Database Systems, 29*, 91–131. doi:10.1145/974750.974754

Grust, T. (2002, June). Accelerating XPath location steps. In Proceedings of the 2002 acm sigmod international conference on management of data (p. 109-120). Madison, Wisconsin.

Grust, T. (2005, June). Purely Relational FLWORs. In Proceedings of the 2nd international workshop on XQuery implementation, experience and perspectives (XIME-P), in cooperation with acm sigmod. Baltimore, Maryland, USA.

Grust, T.,. Teubner, J. (2004, June). Relational Algebra: Mother Tongue XQuery: Fluent. In Proceedings of the 1st twente data management workshop (tdm) (p. 7-14). Enschede, The Netherland.

Grust, T., Jagadish, H. V., Özcan, F.,. Yu, C. (2009). XQuery Processors. Encyclopedia of Database Systems 2009 (p. 3671-3676).

Grust, T., Mayr, M.,. Rittinger, J. (2010, March). Let SQL drive the XQuery workhorse (XQuery join graph isolation). In Proceedings of the 13th International Conference on Extending Database Technology. Lausanne, Switzerland.

Grust, T., Mayr, M., Rittinger, J., Sakr, S.,. Teubner, J. (2007, June).. SQL:1999 Code Generator for the Pathfinder XQuery Compiler. In Proceedings of the ACM SIGMOD international conference on management of data. Beijing, China.

Grust, T., Rittinger, J.,. Teubner, J. (2007, Jun). Why off-the-shelf rdbmss are better at xpath than you might expect. In *Proceedings of the acm sigmod international conference on management of data* (pp. 949–958). Beijing, China: ACM.

Grust, T., Sakr, S.,. Teubner, J. (2004, September). XQuery on SQL Hosts. In Proceedings of the 30th international conference on very large data bases (VLDB) (p. 252-263). Toronto, Canada.

Grust, T., van Keulen, M.,. Teubner, J. (2003, September). Staircase Join: Teach. Relational DBMS to Watch its (Axis) Steps. In Proceedings of the 29th international conference on very large data bases (VLDB) (p. 524-525). Berlin, Germany.

Guarino, N.,. Welty, C. (2002). Evaluating ontological decisions with ontoclean. *Communications of the ACM*, *45*(2), 61–65. doi:10.1145/503124.503150

Güntzer, U., Balke, W.-T.,. Kießling, W. (2000). Optimizing multi-feature queries for image databases. *Proc.26thInt'l Conf. Very Large Data Bases (VLDB'00)*, 419-428.

Gupta, A., Jukic, B., Stahl, D. O.,. Whinston, A. B. (2000). Extracting consumers' private information for implementing incentive-compatible internet traffic pricing. *Journal of Management Information Systems*, *1*(17), 9–29.

Gupta, A. K.,. Suciu, D. (2003, Jun). Stream processing of xpath queries with predicates. In *Proceedings of the acm sigmod international conference on management of data* (pp. 419–430). San Diego, CA: ACM.

Gupta, H., Harinarayan, V., Rajaraman, A.,. Ullman, J. (1997). Index Selection for OLAP. *ICDE Conference* (pp. 208-219).

Haas, L. M., Lin, E. T.,. Roth, M. A. (2002). Data integration through database federation. *IBM Systems Journal*, *41*(4), 578–596.

Haas, L. M., Kossmann, D., Wimmers, E. L.,. Yang, J. (1997). Optimizing Queries Across Diverse Data Sources. In *Proceedings of the 23rd international Conference on Very Large Data Bases*. M. Jarke, M. J. Carey, K. R. Dittrich, F. H. Lochovsky, P. Loucopoulos, and M. A. Jeusfeld, Eds. Very Large Data Bases. Morgan Kaufmann Publishers, San Francisco, CA, 276-285.

Hadar, I.,. Soffer, P. (2006). Variations in conceptual modeling: Classification and ontological analysis. *Journal of the AIS*, *7*(8).

Halpin, T.,. Bloesch, A. (1999). Data modeling in UML and ORM:. Comparison. *Journal of Database Management*, *10*(4), 4–13.

Han, J., Pei, J., Dong, G.,. Wang, K. (2001). Efficient Computation of Iceberg Cubes with Complex Measures. *ACM SIGMOD Conference* (pp. 1-12).

Hann, H., Hui, K. L., Lee, S. Y. T.,. Png, I. P. L. (2008). Consumer privacy and marketing avoidance:. static model. *Management Science*, *54*(6), 1094–1103. doi:10.1287/mnsc.1070.0837

Hares, J. S. (1992). *Information engineering for the advanced practitioner*. Chichester, UK: Wiley.

Harinarayan, V., Rajaraman, A.,. Ullman, J. (1996). Implementing Data Cubes Efficiently. ACM *SIGMOD Conference* (pp. 205-216).

Harmsen, A. F. (1997). *Situational Method Engineering*. Utrecht, The Netherlands: Moret Ernst. Young Management Consultants.

He, B., Luo, Q.,. Choi, B. (2006). Cache-conscious automata for xml filtering. *IEEE Transactions on Knowledge and Data Engineering*, *18*(12), 1629–1644. doi:10.1109/TKDE.2006.184

Henderson-Sellers, B. (2002). Process Metamodelling and Process Construction: Examples Using the OPEN Process Framework (OPF). *Annals of Software Engineering*, *14*(1-4), 341–362. doi:10.1023/A:1020570027891

Henderson-Sellers, B.,. Serour, M. K. (2005). Creating. Dual-Agility Method: The Value of Method Engineering. *Journal of Database Management*, *16*(4), 1–24. doi:10.4018/jdm.2005100101

Hirsch, M. (2002). Making RUP agile. In *OOPSLA 2002 Practitioners Reports*. Seattle, Washington.

Ho, C., Agrawal, R., Megiddo, N.,. Srikant, R. (1997). Range Queries in OLAP Data Cubes. *ACM SIGMOD Conference* (pp. 73-88).

Hong, M., Demers, A. J., Gehrke, J., Koch, C., Riedewald, M.,. White, W. M. (2007, Jun). Massively multi-query join processing in publish/subscribe systems. In *Proceedings of the acm sigmod international conference on management of data* (pp. 761–772). Beijing, China: ACM.

Hristidis, V.,. Papakonstantinou, Y. (2002). *DISCOVER: Keyword search in Relational Databases*, In Proc. VLDB'02.

Hristidis, V., Koudas, N.,. Papakonstantinou, Y. (2001). PREFER:. system for the efficient execution of multi-parametric ranked queries. *Proc. ACM SIGMOD Int'l Conf. Management of Data (SIGMOD'01)*. 259–270.

Hu, K., Dong, Y.,. Xu, L. (2002). DCA-Tree:. High Performance Structure for Incremental Update Cube on MDDW. *International Conference on Machine Learning and Cybernetics 2002*, *4*, 2069-2072.

Huang, M. H. (2003). Modeling virtual exploratory and shopping dynamics: an environmental psychology approach. *Information. Management*, *1*(41), 39–47. doi:10.1016/S0378-7206(03)00024-7

Huang, C.-H., Chuang, T.-R., Lu, J. J.,. Lee, H.-M. (2006, Sep). Xml evolution:. two-phase xml processing model using xml prefiltering techniques. In *Proceedings of the 32nd international conference on very large data bases* (pp. 1215–1218). Seoul, Korea: ACM.

Huh, S.-Y.,. Lee, J.-W. (2001). Providing approximate answers using. knowledge abstraction database. *Journal of Database Management*, *12*(2), 14–24. doi:10.4018/jdm.2001040102

Huo, H., Wang, G., Hui, X., Zhou, R., Ning, B.,. Xiao, C. (2006, Apr). Efficient query processing for streamed xml fragments. In *Proceedings of the 11th international conference on database systems for advanced applications* (pp. 468–482). Singapore: Springer.

Ilyas, I. F., Aref, W. G., Elmagarmid, A. K., Elmongui, H. G., Shah, R.,. Vitter, J. S. (2006). adaptive rank-aware query optimization in relational databases. *ACM Transactions on Database Systems*, *31*(4), 1257–1304. doi:10.1145/1189769.1189772

Ilyas, I. F., Beskales, G.,. Soliman, M. A. (2008).. survey of top-k query processing techniques in relational database systems. *ACM Computing Surveys*, *40*(4), 11. doi:10.1145/1391729.1391730

Ilyas, I. F., Aref, W. G.,. Elmagarmid, A. K. (2002). Joining ranked inputs in practice. *Proc. 28th Int'l Conf. Very Large Data Bases (VLDB'02)*, 950–961.

Ilyas, I. F., Aref, W. G.,. Elmagarmid, A. K. (2003). Supporting top-k join queries in relational databases. *Proc. 29th Int'l Conf. Very Large Data Bases (VLDB'03)*, 754-765.

Im, K. S., Dow, K. E.,. Grover, V. (2001). Research report:. reexamination of it investment and the market value of the firm. an event study methodology. *Information Systems Research*, *1*(12), 103–117. doi:10.1287/isre.12.1.103.9718

International Organization for Standardization. (2005, April). *ISO/IEC 19501:2004 -- Unified Modeling Language (UML)*. Retrieved from http://www.iso.org.

Jacobson, I., Booch, G.,. Rumbaugh, J. (1999). *The Unified Software Development Process*. Reading, MA: Addison Wesley.

Jacobson, I., Ericsson, M.,. Jacobson, A. (1994). *The Object Advantage: Business Process Reengineering with Object Technology*. Reading, MA: Addison-Wesley.

Jacobson, I. (1992). *Object-oriented software engineering:. use case driven approach*. Wokingham, MA: Addison-Wesley.

Jagadish, H. V.,. Patel, J. M. (2006). TIMBER. *University of Michigan*. Retrieved from: http://www.eecs.umich.edu/ db/timber/

Jagadish, H. V., Lakshmanan, L. V. S., Srivastava, D.,. Thompson, K. (2001, September). TAX:. Tree Algebra for XML. In Proceedings of the 8th international workshop of database programming languages (DBPL). Frascati, Italy.

Jahng, J. J., Jain, H.,. Ramamurthy, K. (2002). Personality traits and effectiveness of presentation of product information in e-business systems. *European Journal of Information Systems, 3*(11), 181–195. doi:10.1057/palgrave.ejis.3000431

Jarke, M.,. Koch, J. (1984). Query optimization in database systems. *ACM Computing Surveys, 16*(2), 111–152. doi:10.1145/356924.356928

Jensen, C.,. Potts, C. (2004, April). Privacy policies as decision-making tools: an evaluation of online privacy notices. *Proceedings of the SIGCHI conference on Human factors in computing systems CHI '04, ACM Press.*

Jensen, C., Sarkar, C., Jensen, C.,. Potts, C. (2007). Tracking website data-collection and privacy practices with the iWatch web crawler. *Proceedings of the 3rd Symposium on Usable Privacy and Security*, Pittsburgh, Pennsylvania. 29-40.

Jiang, H., Wang, W., Lu, H.,. Yu, J. X. (2003, September). Holistic Twig Joins on Indexed XML Documents. In Proceedings of the 29th international conference on very large data bases (VLDB)(p. 273-284). Berlin, Germany.

Johnson, R. (2002). Object-Oriented System Development:. Review of Empirical Research. *Communications of the Association for Information Systems, 8*, 65–81.

Johnson, R. E.,. Fotte, B. (1988). Designing Reusable Classes. *Journal of Object-Oriented Programming, 1*(2), 22–35.

Johnson, T.,. Shasha, D. (1997). Hierarchically split cube forests for decision support: descriotion and tuned design, 1996. *Bullettin of Technical Committee on Data Engineering, 20*(1).

Kache, H., Han, W., Markl, V., Raman, V.,. Ewen, S. (2006). POP/FED: progressive query optimization for federated queries in DB2. In *Proceedings of the 32nd international Conference on Very Large Data Bases*. U. Dayal, K. Whang, D. Lomet, G. Alonso, G. Lohman, M. Kersten, S. K. Cha, and Y. Kim, Eds. Very Large Data Bases. VLDB Endowment, 1175-1178.

Kane, G. C., Fichman, R. G., Gallaugher, J.,. Glaser, J. (2009). Community Relations 2.0: With the rise of real-time social media, the rules about community outreach have changed. *Harvard Business Review, 87*(11), 45–50.

Karlsson, F.,. Ågerfalk, P. J. (2004). Method Configuration: Adapting to Situational Characteristics while Creating Reusable Assets. *Information and Software Technology, 46*(9), 619–633. doi:10.1016/j.infsof.2003.12.004

Karlsson, F.,. Wistrand, K. (2006). Combining method engineering with activity theory: theoretical grounding of the method component concept. *European Journal of Information Systems, 15*, 82–90. doi:10.1057/palgrave.ejis.3000596

Karlsson, F. (2005). Method Configuration. A Systems Development Project Revisited. In A. G. Nilsson, R. Gustas, W. Wojtkowski, W. G. Wojtkowski, S. Wrycza,. J. Zupancic (Eds.), *The Fourteenth International Conference on Information Systems Development (ISD 2005)*. Karlstad, Sweden: Springer.

Karlsson, F.,. Ågerfalk, P. J. (2007). Multi-Grounded Action Research in Method Engineering: The MMC Case. In J. Ralyté, S. Brinkkemper,. B. Henderson-Sellers (Eds.), *Proceedings of IFIP WG8.1 Working Conference on Situational Method Engineering: Fundamentals and Experiences* (pp. 19–32): Springer.

Karlsson, F.,. Wistrand, K. (2004, 7-8 June). *MC Sandbox: Tool Support for Method Configuration*. Paper presented at the Ninth CAiSE/IFIP8.1/EUNO International Workshop on Evaluation of Modeling Methods in Systems Analysis and Design (EMMSAD'04), Riga, Latvia.

Karlsson, F., Ågerfalk, P. J.,. Hjalmarsson, A. (2001, 4–5 June). *Process Configuration with Development Tracks and Generic Project Types*. Paper presented at the 6th CAiSE/IFIP8.1 International Workshop on Evaluation of Modelling Methods in Systems Analysis and Design (EMMSAD'01), Interlaken, Switzerland.

Katz, H. (2005). XQEngine version 0.69. *Fatdog Software*. Retrieved from: http://www.fatdog.com/. Engine downloaded from: http://sourceforge.net/ projects/xqengine

Kay, M. (1999) DTDGenerator. A tool to generate XML DTDs, http://users.breathe.com/mhkay/saxon/dtdgen.html

Kepser, S. (2003).. *Simple Proof for the Turing-Completeness of XSLT and XQuery*. Paper presented at the Proceedings: ACM SIGACT-SIGMOD-SIGART Symposium on Principles of Database Systems.

Khatri, V., Vessey, I., Ramesh, V., Clay, P.,. Park, S.-J. (2006). Understanding Conceptual Schemas: Exploring the Role of Application and IS Domain Knowledge. *Information Systems Research, 17*(1), 81–99. doi:10.1287/isre.1060.0081

Klein, H. K.,. Myers, M. D. (1999).. Set of Principles for Conducting and Evaluating Interpretive Field Studies in Information Systems. *Management Information Systems Quarterly, 1*, 67–94. doi:10.2307/249410

Klettke, M., Schneider, L.,. Heuer, A. (2002). Metrics for XML document collections. *Akmal Chaudri and Rainer Unland, XMLDM Workshop, pages 162-176, Prague, Czech Republic.*

Knublauch, H., Musen, M.,. Rector, A. (2002). *Editing Description Logic Ontologies with the Protégé OWL Plugin. Technical discussion for logicians*. CA: Stanford University.

Kobryn, C. (1999).. Standardization Odyssey. *Communications of the ACM, 42*(10), 29–38. doi:10.1145/317665.317673

Kobsa, A. (2007). Privacy-enhanced Personalization. *Communications of the ACM, 50*(8), 24–33. doi:10.1145/1278201.1278202

Koch, C., Scherzinger, S., Schweikardt, N.,. Stegmaier, B. (2004, Aug). Schema-based scheduling of event processors and buffer minimization for queries on structured data streams. In *Proceedings of the thirtieth international conference on very large data bases* (pp. 228–239). Toronto, Canada: Morgan Kaufmann.

Koch, C., Scherzinger, S., Schweikardt, N.,. Stegmaier, B. (2004a, September). FluXQuery: An Optimizing XQuery Processor for Streaming XML Data. In Proceedings of the 30th international conference on very large data bases (VLDB)(p. 1309-1312). Toronto, Canada.

Koch, C., Scherzinger, S., Schweikardt, N.,. Stegmaier, B. (2004b). Schema-based Scheduling of Event Processors and Buffer Minimization for Queries on Structured Data Streams. In Proceedings of the 30th international conference on very large data bases (VLDB)(p. 228-239).

Koike, Y. (2001).. Conversion Tool from DTD to XML Schema. http://www.w3.org/2000/04/schema_hack/.

Kolp, M., Giorgini, P.,. Mylopoulos, J. (2002). *Information systems development through social strcutures.* Paper presented at the International Conference on Software Engineering and Knowledge Engineering SEKE.

Koops, B.-J., Leenes, R., Meints, M., van der Meulen, N.,. Jaquet-Chiffelle, D.-O. (2009, February).. Typology of Identify-Related Crime: Conceptual, Technical, and Legal Issues. *Information Communication and Society, 12*(1), 1–24. doi:10.1080/13691180802158516

Kossmann, D. (2000). The state of the art in distributed query processing. *ACM Computing Surveys, 32*(4), 422–469. doi:10.1145/371578.371598

Krompass, S., Kuno, H., Dayal, U.,. Kemper, A. (2007). Dynamic workload management for very large data warehouses. Juggling feathers and bowling balls. *Proceedings of 33rd International Conference on Very Large Databases (VLDB 2007)*, Vienna Austria, 1105-1115.

Kuhn, T. (1996). *The structure of scientific revolutions.* Chicago, IL: The University of Chicago Press.

Kumar, K.,. Wellke, R. J. (1992). Methodology Engineering:. proposal for situation specific methodology construction. In Cotterman, W. W.,. Senn, J. A. (Eds.), *Challenges and Strategies for Research in Systems Development* (pp. 257–269). Washington, DC: John Wiley. Sons.

Kwok, S. H.,. Zhao, J. L. (2006). Content-based object organization for efficient image retrieval in image databases. *Decision Support Systems, 42*(3), 1901–1916. doi:10.1016/j.dss.2006.04.013

Kwon, J., Rao, P., Moon, B.,. Lee, S. (2005, Aug–Sep). Fist: Scalable xml document filtering by sequencing twig patterns. In *Proceedings of the 31st international conference on very large data bases* (pp. 217–228). Trondheim, Norway: ACM.

Lakshmanan, L., Pei, J.,. Han, J. (2002). Quotient cube: How to summarize the semantics of. data cube. *VLDB conference* (pp. 766-777).

Lakshmanan, L., Pei, J.,. Zhao, Y. (2003). Qctrees: An efficient summary structure for semantic olap. *ACM SIGMOD Conference* (pp. 64-75).

Le Hors, A., Le Hegaret, P., Wood, L., Nicol, G., Robie, J., Champion, M., et al. (2004). Document Object Model (DOM) Level. Core Specification. Retrieved from http://www.w3.org/TR/2004/REC-DOM-Level-3-Core-20040407/

Lee, D. W.,. Chu, W. W. (2000). Comparative Analysis of Six XML Schema Languages. *SIGMOD Record, 29*(3). doi:10.1145/362084.362140

Lee, D. W., Mani, M.,. Chu, W. W. (2003). *Schema Conversion Methods between XML and Relational Models*. Knowledge Transformation for the Semantic Web.

Lee, D. W.,. Chu, W. W. (2000). Constraints-Preserving Transformation from {XML} Document Type Definition to Relational Schema. *International Conference on Conceptual Modeling. the Entity Relationship Approach, pp 323-338.*

Levy, A. Y. (1999, June). Logic-Based Techniques in Data Integration. In Workshop on logic-based artificial intelligence. College Park, Maryland.

Levy, A. Y., Rajaraman, A.,. Ordille, J. J. (1996). Querying Heterogeneous Information Sources Using Source Descriptions. In *Proceedings of the 22th international Conference on Very Large Data Bases*. T. M. Vijayaraman, A. P. Buchmann, C. Mohan, and N. L. Sarda, Eds. Very Large Data Bases. Morgan Kaufmann Publishers, San Francisco, CA, 251-262.

Li, C. (2003). Computing complete answers to queries in the presence of limited access patterns. *The VLDB Journal, 12*(3), 211–227. doi:10.1007/s00778-002-0085-6

Li, C.,. Chang, E. (2000). Query Planning with Limited Source Capabilities. In *Proceedings of the 16th international Conference on Data Engineering*, ICDE, IEEE Computer Society, Washington, DC, 401.

Li, C., Chang, K. C.-C., Ilyas, I. F.,. Song, S. (2005). RankSQL: Query algebra and optimization for relational topk queries. *Proc. ACM SIGMOD Int'l Conf. Management of Data (SIGMOD'05)*, 131-142.

Li, C., Chang, K. C.,. Ilyas, I. F. (2006). Supporting ad-hoc ranking aggregates. *Proc. ACM SIGMOD Int'l Conf. Management of Data (SIGMOD'06)*, 61-72.

Li, Q.,. Moon, B. (2001, September). Indexing and Querying XML Data for Regular Path Expressions. In Proceedings of the 27th international conference on very large data bases (VLDB)(p. 361-370). Roma, Italy.

Li, X.,. Agrawal, G. (2005, Aug–Sep). Efficient evaluation of xquery over streaming data. In *Proceedings of the 31st international conference on very large data bases* (pp. 265–276). Trondheim, Norway: ACM.

Li, X., Han, J.,. Gonzalez, H. (2004). High-Dimensional OLAP:. Minimal Cubing Approach. *VLDB Conference* (pp. 528-539).

Li, Y., Yu, C.,. Jagadish, H. (2004). *Schema-Free XQuery*, In Proc. VLDB'04.

Lillis, K.,. Pitoura, E. (2008, June). Cooperative XPath Caching. In Proceedings of the ACM SIGMOD International Conference on Management of Data (p. 327-338). Vancouver, Canada.

Lind, M.,. Goldkuhl, G. (2006). How to develop. Multi-Grounded Theory: The Evolution of. Business Process Theory. *Australian Journal of Information Systems, 13*(2), 69–85.

Lindland, O. I., Sindre, G.,. Solvberg, A. (1994). Understanding quality in conceptual modeling. *IEEE Software, 11*(2), 42–49. doi:10.1109/52.268955

Liu, C., Arnett, K. P., Capella, L.,. Beatty, B. (1997). Web sties of the fortune 500 companies: facing customers through home pages. *Information. Management, 1*(31), 335–345. doi:10.1016/S0378-7206(97)00001-3

Liu, C., Marchewka, J. T., Lu, J.,. Yu, C.-S. (2005). Beyond concern—a privacy-trust-behavioral intention model of electronic commerce. *Information. Management, 42*(2), 289–304. doi:10.1016/j.im.2004.01.003

Lo, T.,. Douglas, M. (1986). The evolution of workload management in data processing industry:. survey. *Proceedings of 1986 Fall Joint Computer Conference*, Dallas, TX, USA, 768-777.

Lomet, D. B.,. Salzberg, B. (1990). The hB-tree:. multi-attribute indexing method with good guaranteed performance. *ACM Transactions on Database Systems*, *15*(4), 625–658. doi:10.1145/99935.99949

Lu, S., Sun, Y., Atay, M.,. Fotouhi, F. (2003).. New Inlining Algorithm for Mapping XML DTDs to Relational Schemas. *Proc. Of the First International Workshop on XML Schema and Data Management, in conjunction with the 22nd ACM International Conference on Conceptual Modeling (ER2003)*.

Lynne, D. (1999). Web site stats: tracking hits and analyzing traffic. *Database*, *3*(22), 87–87.

Mackworth, A. K. (1977). Consistency in networks of relations. *Artificial Intelligence*, 99–118. doi:10.1016/0004-3702(77)90007-8

Mainsah, E. (2002). Autonomic computing: the next era of computing. *Electronics. Communication Engineering Journal*, *14*(1), 2–3. doi:10.1049/ecej:20020105

Mann, H. B.,. Whitney, D. R. (1947). On. test of whether one of two random variables is stochastically larger than the other. *Annals of Mathematical Statistics*, *18*, 50–60. doi:10.1214/aoms/1177730491

Mannino, M. V., Chu, P.,. Sager, T. (1998). Statistical profile estimation in database systems. *ACM Computing Surveys*, *29*(2), 191–221.

Manolescu, I., Florescu, D.,. Kossmann, D. (2001). Answering XML Queries on Heterogeneous Data Sources. In Proceedings of the 27th international conference on very large data bases (VLDB)(p. 241-250). San Francisco, CA, USA.

Manolescu, I., Florescu, D., Kossmann, D., Xhumari, F.,. Olteanu, D. (2000). Agora: Living with xml and relational. In Proceedings of the 26th international conference on very large data bases (VLDB)(p. 623-626).

Marian, A., Bruno, N.,. Gravano, L. (2004). Evaluating top-*k* queries over web-accessible databases. *ACM Transactions on Database Systems*, *29*(2), 319–362. doi:10.1145/1005566.1005569

Martin, P., Powley, W., Zheng, M.,. Romanufa, K. (2005). Experimental Study of. Self-Tuning Algorithm for DBMS Buffer Pools. *Journal of Database Management*, *16*(2), 1–20. doi:10.4018/jdm.2005040101

Mathiassen, L. (2002). Collaborative Practice Research. *Information Technology. People*, *15*(4), 321–345. doi:10.1108/09593840210453115

Mayer, R. (1989). Models for Understanding. *Review of Educational Research*, *59*(1), 43–64.

Mayer, R. (2009). *Multimedia Learning* (2nd ed.). New York: Cambridge University Press.

Mayer, S., Grust, T., van Keulen, M.,. Teubner, J. (2004). An Injection of Tree Awareness: Adding Staircase Join to PostgreSQL. In Proceedings of the 30th international conference on very large data bases(VLDB).

McIlroy, M. D. (1968). *Mass Produced Software Components*. Paper presented at the North Atlantic Treaty Organisation (NATO) Conference on Software Engineering, Garmisch-Partenkirchen, Germany.

McKnight, D. H., Choudhury, V.,. Kacmar, C. (2002). Developing and validating trust measures for e-commerce: An integrative typology. *Information Systems Research*, *3*(13), 334–359. doi:10.1287/isre.13.3.334.81

McLeod, R.,. Rogers, J. C. (1982). Marketing information systems: uses in the fortune 500. *California Management Review*, *25*(3), 106–118.

Mello, R.,. Heuser, C. (2001).. Rule-Based Conversion of. {DTD} to. Conceptual Schema. *Lecture Notes in Computer Science, 2224,*. doi:10.1007/3-540-45581-7_12

Mellor, S. (2002). Make models be assets. *Communications of the ACM*, *45*(11), 76–78. doi:10.1145/581571.581597

Menascé, D. A. (2004). Performance and availability of internet data centers. *IEEE Internet Computing*, *8*(3), 94–96. doi:10.1109/MIC.2004.1297280

Menascé, D. A.,. Almeida, V. A. F. (1998). *Capacity Planning for Web Performance: Metrics, Models, and Methods*. Upper Saddle River, NJ: Prentice Hall.

Menascé, D. A., Ruan, H.,. Gomaa, H. (2007). QoS management in service-oriented architectures. *Performance Evaluation, 64*(7-8), 646–663. doi:10.1016/j.peva.2006.10.001

Meso, P.,. Jain, R. (2006). Agile Software Development: Adaptive System Principles and Best Practices. *Information Systems Management, 23*(5), 19–29. doi:10.1201/1078.10580530/46108.23.3.20060601/93704.3

Micallef, J. (1988). Encapsulation, Reusability, and Extensibility in Object-Oriented Programming Languages. *Journal of Object-Oriented Programming, 1*(1), 12–36.

Microsoft. (2007). Query Governor cost limit option. Retrieved February 15, 2008. [Online]. Available: http://msdn2.microsoft.com/ en-us/library/ ms190419.aspx.

Microsoft. (2009). Managing SQL Server Workloads with Resource Governor. Retrieved December 12, 2009. [Online]. Available: http://msdn.microsoft.com/ en-us/library/ bb933866.aspx

Mignet, L., Barbosa, D.,. Veltri, P. (2003, May). The xml web:. first study. In *Proceedings of the 12th international world wide web conference* (pp. 500–510). Budapest, Hungary: ACM.

Miller, G. (1956). The Magical Number Seven, Plus Or Minus Two: Some Limits On Our Capacity For Processing Information. *Psychological Review, 63*(2), 209–227. doi:10.1037/h0043158

Milne, G. R.,. Culnan, M. J. (2002). Using the content of online privacy notices to inform public policy:. longitudinal analysis of the 1998-3001 U.S. web surveys. *The Information Society,* (18): 345–359. doi:10.1080/01972240290108168

Milne, G. R.,. Gordon, M. E. (1993). Direct mail privacy-efficiency trade-offs within an implied social contract framework. *Journal of Public Policy. Marketing,* (12): 206–215.

Milo, T., Zur, T.,. Verbin, E. (2007, Jun). Boosting topic-based publish-subscribe systems with dynamic clustering. In *Proceedings of the acm sigmod international conference on management of data* (pp. 749–760). Beijing, China: ACM.

Min, J. K., Ahn, J. Y.,. Chung, C. W. (2003). Efficient extraction of schemas for XML documents. *Information Processing Letters, 85*(Issue 1),. doi:10.1016/S0020-0190(02)00345-9

Mirbel, I.,. Ralyté, J. (2006). Situational method engineering: combining assembly-based and roadmap-driven approaches. *Requirements Engineering, 11*(1), 58–78. doi:10.1007/s00766-005-0019-0

Moe, W. W.,. Fader, P. S. (2004). Dynamic conversion behavior at e-commerce sites. *Management Science, 3*(50), 326–335. doi:10.1287/mnsc.1040.0153

Moh. C., Lim, e.,& Ng, W.,(2000). DTD-Miner:. tool for mining DTD from XML documents. *Proceedings of the second International Workshop on Advanced Issues of E-Commerce.*

Morfonios, K.,. Ioannidis, Y. (2006). Cure for Cubes: Cubing Using. ROLAP Engine. *VLDB Conference* (pp. 379-390).

Moro, M. M., Vagena, Z.,. Tsotras, V. J. (2005, Aug–Sep). Tree-pattern queries on. lightweight xml processor. In *Proceedings of the 31st international conference on very large data bases* (pp. 205–216). Trondheim, Norway: ACM.

Motro, A. (1988). VAGUE:. user interface to relational databases that permits vague queries. *ACM Transactions on Office Information Systems, 6*(3), 187–214. doi:10.1145/45945.48027

Muralikrishna, M.,. DeWitt, D. J. (1988). Equi-depth histograms for estimating selectivity factors for multi-dimensional queries. *Proc. ACM SIGMOD Int'l Conf. Management of Data (SIGMOD '88),* 28-36.

Murthi, B. P. S.,. Sarkar, S. (2003). The role of the management sciences in research on personalization. *Management Science, 10*(49), 1344–1362. doi:10.1287/mnsc.49.10.1344.17313

Myers, M. (1995). Dialectical hermeneutics:. theoretical framework for the implementation of information systems. *Information Systems Journal, 5*, 51–70. doi:10.1111/j.1365-2575.1995.tb00089.x

Mylopoulos, J. (1992). Conceptual modeling and telos. In Locoupolos, P.,. Zicari, R. (Eds.), *Conceptual modeling, databases, and cases.* New York, NY: John Wiley. Sons, Inc.

Nah, F. F.-H., Siau, K.,. Tian, Y. (2005). Knowledge management mechanisms of financial service sites. *Communications of the ACM, 48*(6), 117–123. doi:10.1145/1064830.1064836

Nayak, R. (2008). Fast and effective clustering of XML data using structural information. *Knowledge and Information Systems, 14*(2), 197–215. doi:10.1007/s10115-007-0080-8

Nene, S. A.,. Nayar, S. K. (1997).. simple algorithm for nearest neighbor search in high dimensions. *IEEE Transactions on Pattern Analysis and Machine Intelligence, 19*(9), 989–1003. doi:10.1109/34.615448

Nepal, S.,. Ramakrishna, M. V. (1999). Query processing issues in image (multimedia) databases. *Proc. 15th Int'l Conf. Data Engineering (ICDE'99),* 22-29.

Ngai, E. W. T.,. Wat, F. K. T. (2002).. literature review and classification of electronic commerce research. *Information. Management, 5*(39), 415–429. doi:10.1016/S0378-7206(01)00107-0

Nievergelt, J., Hinterberger, H.,. Sevcik, K. (1984). The Grid File: An Adaptable Symmetric Multikey File Structure. *ACM Transactions on Database Systems, 9*(1), 38–71. doi:10.1145/348.318586

Nilsson, A. G. (1999). The Business Developer's Toolbox: Chains and Alliances between Established Methods. In Nilsson, A. G., Tolis, C.,. Nellborn, C. (Eds.), *Perspectives on Business Modelling: Understanding and Changing Organisations* (pp. 217–241). Heidelberg: Springer Verlag.

Niu, B., Martin, P., Powley, W., Bird, P.,. Horman, R. (2007). Adapting mixed workloads to meet SLOs in autonomic DBMSs. *Proceedings of 2007 IEEE 23rd International Conference on Data Engineering Workshops (2nd International Workshop on Self-Managing Database Systems),* Istanbul, Turkey, 478-484.

Niu, B., Martin, P., Powley, W., Horman, R.,. Bird, P. (2006). Workload adaptation in autonomic DBMSs. *Proceedings of CASCON 2006,* Toronto.

Noy, N. F.,. Hafner, C. D. (1997). The state of the art in ontology design:. survey and compartive review. *AI Magazine, 18*(3), 53–74.

O'Neil, P. E., O'Neil, E. J., Pal, S., Cseri, I., Schaller, G.,. Westbury, N. (2004, June). ORDPATHs: Insert-Friendly XML Node Labels. In Proceedings of the acm sigmod international conference on management of data. Paris, France.

O'Reilly, T. (2005). *What is web 2.0.* O'Reilly Media. (http://oreilly.com/web2/archive/ what-is-web-20.html)

Odell, J. J. (1996).. primer to method engineering. In S. Brinkkemper, K. Lyytinen. R. J. Welke (Eds.), *Method Engineering: Principles of method construction and tool support (IFIP TC8, WG8.7/8.2 Working conference on method engineering).* Atlanta, USA.

Olteanu, D. (2007). Spex: Streamed and progressive evaluation of xpath. *IEEE Transactions on Knowledge and Data Engineering, 19*(7), 934–949. doi:10.1109/TKDE.2007.1063

OMG. (2005). *Unified modeling language: Superstructure, version 2.0 (No. formal/05-07-04).* The Object Management Group.

Onizuka, M. (2003, Nov). Light-weight xpath processing of xml stream with deterministic automata. In *Proceedings of the 12th international conference on information and knowledge management* (pp. 342–349). New Orleans, LA: ACM.

Opdahl, A.,. Henderson-Sellers, B. (2001). Grounding the oml meta-model in ontology. *Journal of Systems and Software, 57*(2), 119–143. doi:10.1016/S0164-1212(00)00123-0

Opdahl, A.,. Henderson-Sellers, B. (2002). Ontological evaluation of the UML using the bunge-wand-weber model. *Software and Systems Modeling, 1*(1), 43–67.

Opdahl, A., Henderson-Sellers, B.,. Barbier, F. (1999). An ontological evaluation of the oml metamodel. In Falkenberg, E.,. Lyytinen, K. (Eds.), *Information system concepts: An integrated discipline emerging.* IFIP/Kluwer.

Oracle. (2001). Oracle Database Resource Manager. [Online]. Available: http://www.oracle.com/ technology/ products/ manageability/database/ pdf/9i_Resource_Mgr_TWP.pdf

O'Reilly, T. (2005). What is Web 2.0. Design Patterns and Business Models for the Next Generation of Software.

Orlandic, R.,. Yu, B. (2004). Scalable QSF-trees: retrieving regional objects in high- dimensional spaces. *Journal of Database Management*, *15*(3), 45–59. doi:10.4018/jdm.2004070103

Paivio, A. (1986). *Mental representations:. Dual Coding Approach*. Oxford, England: Oxford University Press.

Palmer, J. W. (2002). Web site usability, design, and performance metrics. *Information Systems Research*, *2*(13), 151–167. doi:10.1287/isre.13.2.151.88

Pang, H., Carey, M. J.,. Livny, M. (1995). Multiclass query scheduling in real-time database systems. *IEEE Transactions on Knowledge and Data Engineering*, *7*(4), 533–551. doi:10.1109/69.404028

Papakonstantinou, Y., Gupta, A.,. Haas, L. (1998). Capabilities-based query rewriting in mediator systems. *Distributed and Parallel Databases*, *6*(1), 73–110. doi:10.1023/A:1008646830769

Paparizos, S., Al-Khalifa, S., Jagadish, H., Niermann, A.,. Wu, Y. (2002).. *Physical Algebra for XML (Tech. Rep.)*. University of Michigan.

Pardede, E., Rahayu, J.,. Taniar, D. "On Using Collection for Aggregation and Association Relationships in XML Object-Relational Storage", *Proc. ACM SAC'04.*

Parekh, S., Rose, K., Hellerstein, J., Lightstone, S., Huras, M.,. Chang, V. (2004). Managing the performance impact of administrative utilities. In *Self Managing Distributed Systems* (pp. 130–142). Heidelberg: Springer Berlin.

Parsons, J.,. Wand, Y. (1997). Using objects for systems analysis. *Communications of the ACM*, *40*(12), 104–110. doi:10.1145/265563.265578

Parsons, J.,. Wand, Y. (1991). *The object paradigm. two for the price of one?* Paper presented at the Workshop on Information Technology and Systems WITS.

Pavlou, P. A. (2002). Institution-based trust in interorganizational exchange relationships: the role of online B2B marketplaces on trust formation. *The Journal of Strategic Information Systems*, *3-4*(11), 215–243. doi:10.1016/S0963-8687(02)00017-3

Peng, F.,. Chawathe, S. S. (2005). Xsq:. streaming xpath engine. *ACM Transactions on Database Systems*, *30*(2), 577–623. doi:10.1145/1071610.1071617

Peng, F.,. Chawathe, S. S. (2003, Jun). Xpath queries on streaming data. In *Proceedings of the acm sigmod international conference on management of data* (pp. 431–442). San Diego, CA: ACM.

Pentaris, F.,. Ioannidis, Y. (2006). Query optimization in distributed networks of autonomous database systems. *ACM Transactions on Database Systems*, *31*(2), 537–583. doi:10.1145/1138394.1138397

Petropoulos, M., Deutsch, A., Papakonstantinou, Y.,. Katsis, Y. (2007). Exporting and interactively querying web service-accessed sources: The CLIDE system. *ACM Transactions on Database Systems*, *32*(4), 22. doi:10.1145/1292609.1292612

Pfeffer, J.,. Salancik, G. R. (1978). *The external control of organizations:. resource dependency perspective*. Stanford, California: Stanford Business Classics, Stanford Business Books.

Piatetsky-Shapiro, G.,. Connell, C. (1984). Accurate estimation of the number of tuples satisfying. condition. *Proc. ACM SIGMOD Int'l Conf. Management of Data (SIGMOD'84)*, 256-276.

Pinker, E. J., Seidmann, A.,. Vakrat, Y. (2003). Managing online auctions: current business and research issues. *Management Science*, *11*(49), 1457–1484. doi:10.1287/mnsc.49.11.1457.20584

Pirahesh, H., Hellerstein, J. M.,. Hasan, W. (1992). Extensible/Rule Based Query Rewrite Optimization in Starburst. In Sigmod conference (p. 39- 48).

Poosala, V.,. Ioannidis, Y. E. (1997). Selectivity estimation without the attribute value independence assumption. *Proc. 23rd Int'l Conf. Very Large Data Bases (VLDB'97)*, 486- 495.

Poosala, V., Ioannidis, Y. E., Haas, P. J.,. Shekita, E. J. (1996). Improved histograms for selectivity estimation of range predicates. *Proc. ACM SIGMOD Int'l Conf. Management of Data (SIGMOD'96)*, 294-305.

Powley, W., Martin, P., Zhang, M., Bird, P.,. McDonald, K. (2010). Autonomic workload execution control using throttling. *Proceedings of 2010 IEEE 26th International Conference on Data Engineering Workshops (5th International Workshop on Self-Managing Database Systems)*, Long Beach, CA, USA.

Prasad, A. (2002). The contest over meaning: Hermeneutics as an interpretive methodology for understanding texts. *Organizational Research Methods, 5*, 12–33.

Preibusch, S., Hoser, B., Gürses, S.,. Berendt, B. (2007). Ubiquitous social networks. opportunities and challenges for privacy-aware user modeling. *Proceedings of the Data Mining for Knowledge Discovery Workshop.*

Press, W. H., Teukolsky, S. A., Vetterling, W. T.,. Flannery, B. P. (1992). *Numerical Recipes in C: The Art of Scientific Computing*. Cambridge University Press.

Ralyté, J., Deneckère, R.,. Rolland, C. (2003). Towards. Generic Model for Situational Method Engineering. In M. M. Johann Eder (Ed.), *Advanced Information Systems Engineering, 15th International Conference, CAiSE 2003 2681*, 95-110. Berlin: Springer.

Ramakrishnan, R.,. Gehrke, J. (2003). *Database Management Systems* (3rd ed.). McGraw-Hill.

Rao, P.,. Moon, B. (2004, Mar). Prix: Indexing and querying xml using prüfer sequences. In *Proceedings of the 20th international conference on data engineering* (pp. 288–300). Boston, MA: IEEE Computer Society.

Re, C., Simeon, J.,. Fernandez, M. F. (2006, April).. Complete and Efficient Algebraic Compiler for XQuery. In Proceedings of the 22nd international conference on data engineering (ICDE) (p. 14). Atlanta, GA, USA.

Reddy, N.,. Haritsa, J. R. (2005). Analyzing Plan Diagrams of Database Query Optimizers. In Proceedings of the 31st international conference on very large data bases (VLDB)(p. 1228-1240).

Reeves, W. (1999). *Learner-Centered Design:. Cognitive View of Managing Complexity in Product, Information, and Envirommental Design*. Sage Publications.

Reinhartz-Berger, I.,. Sturm, A. (2008). Enhancing UML models:. domain analysis approach. *Journal of Database Management, 19*(1). doi:10.4018/jdm.2008010104

Relaxng(2003). RELAX NG, http://www.relaxng.org/.

Ricoeur, P. (1976). *Interpretation theory: Discourse and the surplus of meaning*. Fort Worth, TX: The Texas Christian University Press.

Riemenschneider, C. K., Hardgrave, B. C.,. Davis, F. D. (2002). Explaining Software Developer Acceptance of Methodologies:. Comparison of Five Theoretical Models. *IEEE Transactions on Software Engineering, 28*(12), 1135–1145. doi:10.1109/TSE.2002.1158287

Rittinger, J. (2005). Pathfinder/MonetDB:. Relational Runtime for XQuery. Master thesis, Konstanz University.

Roberts, T. L. Jr, Gibson, M. L., Fields, K. T.,. Rainer, R. K. Jr. (1998). Factors that Impact Implementing. System Development Methodology. *IEEE Transactions on Software Engineering, 24*(8), 640–649. doi:10.1109/32.707699

Robie, J., Lapp, J.,. Schach, D. (1998). *XML Query Language*. XQL.

Roe, P. (2003). *Distributed xml objects.* Paper presented at the Joint Modular Languages Conference JMLC.

Roland, C., Souveyet, C.,. Moreno, M. (2006). An Approach for Defining Ways-of-Working. *Information Systems, 20*, 337–359. doi:10.1016/0306-4379(95)00018-Y

Rolland, C., Prakash, N.,. Benjamen, A. (1999).. Multi-Model View of Process Modelling. *Requirements Engineering, 4*(4), 169–187. doi:10.1007/s007660050018

Rolland, C.,. Prakash, N. (1996, 26–28 August). 1996).. Proposal For Context-Specific Method Engineering. In S. Brinkkemper, K. Lyytinen,. R. Welke (Eds.), Method Engineering: Principles of method construction and tool support (pp. 191–208). Chapman. Hall.

Ropponen, J.,. Lyytinen, K. (2000). Components of Software Development Risk: How to Address Them?. Project Manager Survey. *IEEE Transactions on Software Engineering, 26*(2), 98–112. doi:10.1109/32.841112

Rosemann, M.,. Green, P. (2000). Integrated process modelling: An ontological analysis. *Information Systems, 25*(2), 73–87. doi:10.1016/S0306-4379(00)00010-7

Rossi, M., Ramesh, B., Lyytinen, K.,. Tolvanen, J.-P. (2004). Managing Evolutionary Method Engineering by Method Rationale. *Journal of the Association for Information Systems, 5*(9), 356–391.

Rosson, M. B.,. Alpert, S. R. (1990). The Cognitive Consequences of Object-Oriented Design. *Human-Computer Interaction, 5*(4), 345–379. doi:10.1207/s15327051hci0504_1

Roth, M. T.,. Schwarz, P. M. (1997). Don't scrap it, wrap it!. wrapper architecture for legacy data sources. In *Proceedings of the 23rd international Conference on Very Large Data Bases*. M. Jarke, M. J. Carey, K. R. Dittrich, F. H. Lochovsky, P. Loucopoulos, and M. A. Jeusfeld, Eds. Very Large Data Bases. Morgan Kaufmann Publishers, San Francisco, CA, 266-275.

Rozen, S.,. Shasha, D. (1989). Using. relational systm on wall street: The good, the bad, the ugly, and the ideal. *Communications of the ACM, 32*(8), 988–993. doi:10.1145/65971.65977

Rumbaugh, J., Blaha, M., Premerlani, W.,. Lorensen, W. (1991). *Object-Oriented Modeling and Design*. Englewood Cliffs, NJ: Prentice Hall.

Rumbaugh, J. (1991). *Object oriented modeling and design*. Englewood Cliffs, NJ: Prentice Hall.

Sahuguet, A.,(2000). Everything You Ever Wanted to Know About DTDs, But Were Afraid to Ask. *WebDB-2000*.

Sakr, S. (2007). Cardinality-Aware and Purely Relational Implementation of an XQuery Processor. Phd thesis, University of Konstanz. (http://www.ub.uni-konstanz. de/ kops/volltexte/2007/3259/)

Salehie, M.,. Tahvildari, L. (2005). Autonomic computing: Emerging trends and open problems. *Proceedings of Workshop on Design and Evolution of Autonomic Application Software (DEAS 2005)*, St. Louis Missouri, 82-88.

Salton, G.,. McGill, M. J. (1983). *Introduction to Modern Information Retrieval*. McGraw-Hill.

Sarathy, R.,. Robertson, C. J. (2003). Strategic and ethical considerations in managing digital privacy. *Journal of Business Ethics, 46*(2). doi:10.1023/A:1025001627419

Sartiani, C.,. Albano, A. (2002, July). Yet Another Query Algebra For XML Data. In Proceedings of the international database engineering. applications symposium (IDEAS) (p. 106-115). Edmonton, Canada.

Schmidt, A. R., Waas, F., Kersten, M. L., Florescu, D., Manolescu, I., Carey, M. J.,. Busse, R. (2002). The XML Benchmark Project. *Technical Report INS-R0103, CWI*. Retrieved from: http://www.xml-benchmark.org/.

Schroeder, B., Harchol-Balter, M., Iyengar, A., Nahum, E.,. Wierman, A. (2006). How to Determine. Good Multi-Programming Level for External Scheduling. *Proceedings of the 22nd International Conference on Data Engineering*, Atlanta, GA, USA.

Schwaber, K.,. Beedle, M. (2002). *Agile Software Development with Scrum*. Upper Saddle River, NJ: Prentice-Hall.

Semistructured Databases. *Very Large Data Bases, Proceedings of the 23rd International Conference on Very Large Data Bases*).

Sengupta, A.,. Mohan, S. (2003, March). *Formal and conceptual models for XML structures. the past, present and future*.

Seshadri, P. (2003, Jun). Building notification services with microsoft sqlserver. In *Proceedings of the acm sigmod international conference on management of data* (pp. 635–636). San Diego, CA: ACM.

Shanmugasundaram, J., Shekita, E., Kiernan, J., Krishnamurthy, R., Viglas, E., Naughton, J.,& Shematron(2008). Schematron, http://www.schematron.com/.

Shanmugasundaram, J., Fayyad, U.,. Bradley, P. (1999). Compressed Data Cubes for OLAP Aggregate Query Approximation on Continuous Dimensions. *Knowledge Discovery and Data Mining Conference* (pp. 223-232).

Sheetz, S. (2002). Identifying the Difficulties of Object-Oriented Development. *Journal of Systems and Software, 64*(1), 23–36. doi:10.1016/S0164-1212(02)00019-5

Sheth, A. P.,. Larson, J. A. (1990). Federated database systems for managing distributed, heterogeneous, and autonomous databases. *ACM Computing Surveys, 22*(3), 183–236. doi:10.1145/96602.96604

Shin, M. K., Huh, S. Y., Park, D.,. Lee, W. (2008). Relaxing queries with hierarchical quantified data abstraction. *Journal of Database Management, 19*(4), 47–61. doi:10.4018/jdm.2008100103

Shiren, Y., Xiujun, G., Zhongzhi, S.,&Bing, W.,(2001). Tree's Drawing Algorithm and Visualizing Method, *CAD/ Graphics '2001*.

Shiu, H.,. Fong, J. (2008). Reverse engineering from an xml document into an extended dtd graph. *Journal of Database Management*, *19*(4), 62–80. doi:10.4018/jdm.2008100104

Shiu, H. (2006). Reverse Engineering Data Semantics from Arbitrary XML document, *Computer Science department, City University of Hong Kong, M.Phil dissertation, September 2006.*

Shoval, P.,. Kabeli, J. (2005) Essentials of Functional and Object-Oriented Methodology. *Encyclopedia of Information Science and Technology II*, 1108-1115.

Shukla, A., Deshpanda, P., Naughton, J.,. Ramasamy, K. (1996). Storage Estimation for Multidimensional Aggregates in the Presence of Hierarchies. *VLDB Conference* (pp. 522-531).

Siau, K.,. Cao, Q. (2001). Unified Modeling Language (UML). a complexity analysis. *Journal of Database Management*, *12*(1), 26–34. doi:10.4018/jdm.2001010103

Siau, K., Erickson, J.,. Lee, L. (2005). Theoretical vs. Practical Complexity: The Case of UML. *Journal of Database Management*, *16*(3), 40–57. doi:10.4018/jdm.2005070103

Siau, K.,. Cao, Q. (2001). Unified Modeling Language (UML) --. Complextiy Analysis. *Journal of Database Management*, *12*(1), 26–34. doi:10.4018/jdm.2001010103

Siau, K.,. Loo, P.-P. (2006). Identifying Difficulties in Learning UML. *Information Systems Management*, *23*(3), 43–51. doi:10.1201/1078.10580530/46108.23.3.20060601/93706.5

Siau, K.,. Long, Y. (2006). Using social development lenses to understand e-government development. *Journal of Global Information Management*, *14*(1), 47–62. doi:10.4018/jgim.2006010103

Siau, K.,. Shen, Z. (2006). Mobile healthcare informatics. *Informatics for Health. Social Care*, *31*(2), 89–99. doi:10.1080/14639230500095651

Siau, K., Sheng, H.,. Nah, F. F.-H. (2006). Use of. classroom response system to enhance classroom interactivity. *IEEE Transactions on Education*, *49*(3), 398–403. doi:10.1109/TE.2006.879802

Sismanis, Y., Roussopoulos, N., Deligianannakis, A.,. Kotidis, Y. (2002). Dwarf: Shrinking the Petacube. *ACM SIGMOD Conference* (pp. 464–475).

Smith, B.,. Welty, C. (2001). *Ontology: Towards. new synthesis.* Paper presented at the Second International conference on Formal Ontology and Information Systems FOIS, Qgunquit, Maine.

Smolander, K.,. Rossi, M. (2008). Conflicts, compromises, and political decisions: Methodological challenges of enterprise-wide e-business architecture creation. *Journal of Database Management*, *19*(1). doi:10.4018/jdm.2008010102

Smolander, K.,. Rossi, M. (2008). Conflicts, compromises and political decisions: Methodological challenges of enterprise-wide e-business architecture. *Journal of Database Management*, *19*(1), 19–40. doi:10.4018/jdm.2008010102

Snoeck, M. (1998). Dedene, G. "Existence Dependency: The key to semantic integrity between structural and behavioral aspects of object types. *IEEE Transactions on Software Engineering*, *24*(24), 233–251. doi:10.1109/32.677182

Soffer, P., Golany, B., Dori, D.,. Wand, Y. (2001). Modelling off-the-shelf information systems requirements: An ontological approach. *Requirements Engineering*, *6*(3), 183–199. doi:10.1007/PL00010359

Somani, A., Choy, D.,. Kleewein, J. C. (2002). Bringing together content and data management systems: Challenges and opportunities. *IBM Systems Journal*, *41*(4), 686–696. doi:10.1147/sj.414.0686

Son, J. Y.,. Kim, S. S. (2008). Internet users' information privacy-protective responses:. taxonomy and. nomological model. *Management Information Systems Quarterly*, *32*(3), 503–529.

Sperberg-MCQueen. C.,& Thompson,H.,(2000). W3C XML Schema,http://www.w3.org/XML/Schema.

Stevens, P.,. Pooley, R. (2006). *Using UML: Software Engineering with Objects and Components*. Essex, England: Addison Wesley.

Stewart-Schwaig, K., Kane, J.,. Storey, V. C. (2005). Privacy, fair information practices and the fortune 500: the virtual reality of compliance. *Database*, *36*(1), 49–63.

Stolterman, E. (1991). *Designarbetets dolda rationalitet: en studie av metodik och praktik inom systemutveckling.* Doctoral Dissertation in Swedish, Umeå University, Umeå, Sweden.

Stolterman, E.,. Russo, N. L. (1997). *The Paradox of Information Systems Methods: Public and Private Rationality.* Paper presented at the The British Computer Society 5th Annual Conference on Methodologies, Lancaster, England.

Straub, D., Weill, P.,. Schwaig, K. S. (2008). Strategic dependence on the IT resource and outsourcing:. test of the strategic control model. *Information Systems Frontiers, 10*(2), 195–210. doi:10.1007/s10796-008-9064-9

Strauss, A. L.,. Corbin, J. M. (1998). *Basics of qualitative research: techniques and procedures for developing grounded theory* (2nd ed. ed.). Thousand Oaks, CA: SAGE.

Stumpf, R.,. Teague, L. (2005). *Object-Oriented Systems Analysis and Design with UML.* Pearson Prentice Hall.

Su, H., Jian, J.,. Rundensteiner, E. A. (2003, Nov). Raindrop:. uniform and layered algebraic framework for xqueries on xml streams. In *Proceedings of the 12th international conference on information and knowledge management* (pp. 279–286). New Orleans, LA: ACM.

Su, H., Rundensteiner, E. A.,. Mani, M. (2004, Aug–Sep). Semantic query optimization in an automata-algebra combined xquery engine over xml streams. In *Proceedings of the thirtieth international conference on very large data bases* (pp. 1293–1296). Toronto, Canada: Morgan Kaufmann.

Su, H., Rundensteiner, E. A.,. Mani, M. (2005, Aug–Sep). Semantic query optimization for xquery over xml streams. In *Proceedings of the 31st international conference on very large data bases* (pp. 277–288). Trondheim, Norway: ACM.

Suciu, D. (2002). Distributed query evaluation on semistructured data. *ACM Transactions on Database Systems, 27*(1), 1–62. doi:10.1145/507234.507235

Swire, P. P. (1997). *Markets, self-regulation, and government enforcement in the protection of personal information. Privacy and Self-Regulation in the Information Age* (pp. 3–20). Washington, D.C.: U.S. Department of Commerce.

Tabrizi, M., Collins, C., Ozan, E.,. Li, K. (2004). Implementation of Object-Orientation Using UML in Entry Level Software Development Courses. *Proceedings of the 5th Conference on Information Technology Education,* (pp. 128-131).

Taha, K.,. Elmasri, R. (2007), *XPCache: An Efficient Query Processor for Client-Server Architecture,* In Proc. SWOD'07.

Tang, Z. L., Hu, Y.,. Smith, M. D. (2008). Gaining trust through online privacy protection: Self-regulation, mandatory standards, or Caveat Emptor. *Journal of Management Information Systems, 24*(4), 153–173. doi:10.2753/MIS0742-1222240406

Tao, Y., Xiao, X.,. Pei, J. (2007). Efficient skyline and top-k retrieval in subspaces. *IEEE Transactions on Knowledge and Data Engineering, 19*(8), 1072–1088. doi:10.1109/TKDE.2007.1051

Tatarinov, I. (2001).. general technique for querying XML documents using. relational database system. *SIGMOD Record, 30*(3), 261–270.

Teo, T. S. H.,. Pian, Y. (2004).. model for web adoption. *Information. Management, 4*(41), 457–468. doi:10.1016/S0378-7206(03)00084-3

Teubner, J. (2006). Pathfinder: XQuery Compilation Techniques for Relational Database Targets. PHD doctoral dissertation, Technical University of Munich.

The Apache XML Project. (2007). *Xerces2 Java Parser.* The Apache Software Foundation. (http://xerces.apache.org/xerces2-j/)

Thiran, P., Hainaut, J., Houben, G.,. Benslimane, D. (2006). Wrapper-based evolution of legacy information systems. *ACM Transactions on Software Engineering and Methodology, 15*(4), 329–359. doi:10.1145/1178625.1178626

Thiran, P. H.,. Estiévenart, F. Hainaut. JL.,& Houben, GJ.,(2004). Exporting Databases in XML. A Conceptual and Generic Approach, *Proceedings of CAiSE Workshops (WISM'04).*

Thuraisingham, B. (2005). Privacy-preserving data mining: development and directions. *Journal of Database Management, 16*(1), 75–87. doi:10.4018/jdm.2005010106

Tian, F., Reinwald, B., Pirahesh, H., Mayr, T.,. Mylly-maki, J. (2004, Jun). Implementing. scalable xml publish/ subscribe system using. relational database system. In *Proceedings of the acm sigmod international conference on management of data* (pp. 479–490). Paris, France: ACM.

Tomasic, A., Raschid, L.,. Valduriez, P. (1998). Scaling access to heterogeneous data sources with DISCO. *IEEE Transactions on Knowledge and Data Engineering, 10*(5), 808–823. doi:10.1109/69.729736

Tombros, A., Malik, S.,. Larsen, B. (2005). *Report on the INEX 2004 Interactive Track*. ACM SIGIR Forum, Vol. 39 No. 1.

Trujillo, J.,. Luján-Mora, S. (2004). Applying UML and XML for Designing and Interchanging Information for Data Warehouses and OLAP Applications. *Journal of Database Management, 15*(Issue 1), 41–72. doi:10.4018/ jdm.2004010102

Tsaparas, P., Palpanas, T., Kotidis, Y., Koudas, N.,. Srivastava, D. (2003). Ranked join indices. *Proc. 19th Int'l Conf. Data Engineering (ICDE'03)*, 277-288.

Turing, A. (1936). On Computable Numbers, with an Application to the Entscheidungsproblem. *Proceedings of the London Mathematical Society, 42*, 230–265. doi:10.1112/ plms/s2-42.1.230

Uchiyama, H., Onizuka, M.,. Honishi, T. (2005, Apr). Distributed xml stream filtering system with high scalability. In *Proceedings of the 21st international conference on data engineering* (pp. 968–977). Tokyo, Japan: IEEE Computer Society.

Uschold, M.,. Gruninger, M. (1996). Ontologies: Principles, methods, and applications. *The Knowledge Engineering Review, 11*(2). doi:10.1017/S0269888900007797

UW Database Group. (2002). *XML Data Repository.* UW CSE, University of Washington. (http://www. cs.washington.edu/ research/xmldatasets/)

Valentin, G., Zuliani, M., Zilio, D. C., Lohman, G. M.,. Skelley, A. (2000). DB2 Advisor: An Optimizer Smart Enough to Recommend Its Own Indexes. In Proceedings of the 22nd international conference on data engineering (ICDE).

Van den Bussche, J.,. Vossen, G. (1993). *An Extension of Path Expressions to Simplify Navigation in Object-Oriented Queries*. Paper presented at the Proceedings of the third international conference on Deductive and Object-Oriented Databases (DOOD).

Van der Heijden, H. (2002). Factors influencing the usage of websites: The case of. generic portal in the Netherlands. *Information. Management, 40*(6), 541–549. doi:10.1016/ S0378-7206(02)00079-4

Van Hentenryck, P. (1989). *Consistency techniques in logic programming*. Cambridge, MA: MIT Press.

van Slooten, K.,. Hodes, B. (1996). Characterizing IS development projects. In Brinkkemper, S., Lyytinen, K.,. Welke, R. (Eds.), *Method Engineering: Principles of method construction and tool support* (pp. 29–44). Chapman. Hall.

Vessey, I.,. Galletta, D. (1991). Cognitive Fit: An Imperical Study of Information Acquisition. *Information Systems Research, 2*, 63–84. doi:10.1287/isre.2.1.63

Visual Paradigm International. (2006). Retrieved from Visual Paradigm for UML: http://www.visual-paradigm. com.

Vitter, J.,. Wang, M. (1999). "Approximate Computation of Multidimensional Aggregates of Sparse Data Using Wavelets". *ACM SIGMOD Conference* (pp. 193- 204).

W3C(1998). Schema for Object-oriented XML, http:// www.w3.org/TR/1998/NOTE-SOX-19980930/

W3C(2003). Document Object Model DOM. http://www. w3.org/DOM.

W3C(2004). Simple API for XML, SAX. http://www. saxproject.org/.

Wand, Y., Storey, V.,. Weber, R. (1999). An ontological analysis of the relationship construct in conceptual modeling. *ACM Transactions on Database Systems, 24*(4), 494–528. doi:10.1145/331983.331989

Wand, Y.,. Weber, R. (1993). On the ontological expressiveness of information systems analysis and design grammars. *Journal of Information Systems, 3*, 217–237. doi:10.1111/j.1365-2575.1993.tb00127.x

Wand, Y.,. Weber, R. (1995). On the deep structure of information systems. *Information Systems Journal*, (5): 203–223. doi:10.1111/j.1365-2575.1995.tb00108.x

Wand, Y.,. Weber, R. (1989). An ontological evaluation of systems analysis and design methods. In Falkenberg, E.,. Lindgreen, P. (Eds.), *Information system concepts: An in-depth analysis*. Elsevier Science Publishers, B.V.

Wand, Y. (1989).. proposal for. formal model of objects. In Kim, W.,. Lochovsky, F. (Eds.), *Object-oriented concepts, languages, applications and databases* (pp. 537–559). ACM Press/Addison-Wesley.

Wang, H., Park, S., Fan, W.,. Yu, P. S. (2003, Jun). Vist:. dynamic index method for querying xml data by tree structures. In *Proceedings of the acm sigmod international conference on management of data* (pp. 110–121). San Diego, CA: ACM.

Wang, S., Su, H., Li, M., Wei, M., Yang, S.,. Ditto, D. (2006, Sep). R-sox: Runtime semantic query optimization over xml streams. In *Proceedings of the 32nd international conference on very large data bases* (pp. 1207–1210). Seoul, Korea: ACM.

Wang, W., Lu, H., Feng, J.,. Yu, J. (2002). Condensed cube: An Effective Approach to Reducing Data Cube Size. *ICDE Conference* (pp. 155-165).

Warren, S.,. Brandeis, L. (1890). The right of privacy. *Harvard Law Review*, 5(4), 193–220. doi:10.2307/1321160

Weber, R.,. Zhang, Y. (1996). An analytical evaluation of niam's grammar for conceptual schema diagrams. *Information Systems Journal*, 6(2), 147–170. doi:10.1111/j.1365-2575.1996.tb00010.x

Weber, M. (1978). *Economy and society*. Berkeley, CA: University of California Press.

Wei, F., Moritz, S., Parvez, S.,. Blank, G. (2005).. Student Model for Object-Oriented Design and Programming. *Journal of Computing Sciences in Colleges*, 20(5), 260–273.

Welty, C. (1990). Human Factors Studies of Database Query Languages: SQL as. metric. *Journal of Database Administration*, 1(1), 2–10.

Welty, C.,. Stemple, D. W. (1981). Human Factors Comparison of. Procedural and. Nonprocedural Query Language. *ACM Transactions on Database Systems*, 6(4), 626–649. doi:10.1145/319628.319656

Westin, A. (1967). *Privacy and Freedom*. New York: Athenaeum.

Wheeler, B. C. (2002). NEBIC:. dynamic capabilities theory for assessing net- enablement. *Information Systems Research*, 13(2), 125–146. doi:10.1287/isre.13.2.125.89

Widjaya, N., Taniar, D.,. Rahayu, W. (2003). Aggregation Transformation of XML Schema to Object-Relational Databases. *Innovative Internet Community Systems, LNCS*, 2877, 251–262. doi:10.1007/978-3-540-39884-4_21

Widjaya, N., Rahayu, W. Association Relationship Transformation of XML Schemas to Object-Relational Databases, *iiWAS'02*.

Wiedenbeck, S., Fix, V.,. Scholtz, J. (1993). Characteristics of the Mental Representations of Novice and Expert Programmers: an Empirical Study. *International Journal of Man-Machine Studies*, 39(5), 793–812. doi:10.1006/imms.1993.1084

Wiedenbeck, S., Ramalingam, V., Sarasamma, S.,. Corritore, C. (1999).. Comparison of the Comprehension of Object-oriented and Procedural Programs by Novice Programmers. *Interacting with Computers*, 11(3), 255–282. doi:10.1016/S0953-5438(98)00029-0

Winter, S. J., Saunders, C.,. Hart, P. (2003). Electronic window dressing: impression management with websites. *European Journal of Information Systems*, 4(12), 309–322. doi:10.1057/palgrave.ejis.3000470

Wistrand, K.,. Karlsson, F. (2004). Method Components. Rationale Revealed. In A. Persson. J. Stirna (Eds.), *The 16th International Conference on Advanced Information Systems Engineering (CAiSE 2004)*, 3084, 189-201. Berlin: Springer.

Wu, Y., Patel, J. M.,. Jagadish, H. V. (2003b). Using histograms to estimate answer sizes for XML queries. *Information Systems*, 28(1-2), 33–59. doi:10.1016/S0306-4379(02)00048-0

Wu, Y., Patel, J. M.,. Jagadish, H. V. (2003a). Structural Join Order Selection for XML Query Optimization. In Proceedings of the 19th international conference on data engineering (ICDE) (p. 443-454).

Wyss, C. M.,. Van Gucht, D. (2001).. *Relational Algebra for Data/Metadata Integration in. Federated Database System*. Paper presented at the Proceedings of the 2001 ACM CIKM International Conference on Information and Knowledge Management.

Xiaou, R., Dillon, T., Feng, L. "*Modeling and Transformation of Object-Oriented Conceptual Models into XML Schema*", *DEXA'01*.

Xin, D., Han, J., Li, X.,. Wah, W. B. (2003). Star-cubing: Computing iceberg cubes by top-down and bottom-up integration. *VLDB Conference* (pp. 476-487).

Xiping, S.,. Osterweil, L. J. (1998). Engineering Software Design Processes to Guide Process Execution. *IEEE Transactions on Software Engineering, 24*(9), 759–775. doi:10.1109/32.713330

Xu, H., Teo, H. H., Tan, B. C. Y.,. Agarwal, R. (2009). The Role of Push-Pull Technology in Privacy Calculus: The Case of Location-Based Services. *Journal of Management Information Systems, 26*(3), 135–173. doi:10.2753/MIS0742-1222260305

Xu, W.,. Meral, Z. (2005, September). Rewriting XPath queries using materialized views. In Proceedings of the 31st international conference on very large data bases (VLDB)(p. 121-132). Trondheim, Norway.

Xu, X.,. Papakonstantinou, Y. (2005). *Efficient Keyword Search for Smallest LCAs in XML Databases,* In Proc. SIGMOD'05.

Yao, M. Z., Rice, R. E.,. Wallis, K. (2007). Predicting user concerns about online privacy. *Journal of the American Society for Information Science and Technology, 58*(5), doi:10.1002/asi.20530

Yin, X.,. Pedersen, T. B. (2006). Evaluating xml-extened olap queries based on physical algebra. *Journal of Database Management, 17*(2), 85–116. doi:10.4018/jdm.2006040105

Yoshikawa, M., Amagasa, T., Shimura, T.,. Uemura, S. (2001). XRel:. path-based approach to storage and retrieval of XML documents using relational databases. ACM Trans. *InternetTechn., 1*(1), 110–141.

Yu, C., Sharma, P., Meng, W.,. Qin, Y. (2001). Database selection for processing. nearest neighbors queries in distributed environments. *1st ACM/IEEE-CS Joint Conf. on DL*, 215-222.

Zadorozhny, V., Raschid, L., Vidal, M. E., Urhan, T.,. Bright, L. (2002). Efficient evaluation of queries in. mediator for web sources. In *Proceedings of the 2002 ACM SIGMOD international Conference on Management of Data*. SIGMOD '02. ACM, New York, NY, 85-96.

Zeller, H. (2003, Jun). Nonstop sql/mx publish/subscribe: Continuous data streams in transaction processing. In *Proceedings of the acm sigmod international conference on management of data* (pp. 636). San Diego, CA: ACM.

Zhang, J., Liu, H., Ling, T., Bruckner, R.,. Tija, A. (2006).. Framework for Efficient Association Rule Mining in XML Data. *Journal of Database Management, 17*(Issue 3), 19–40. doi:10.4018/jdm.2006070102

Zhang, H.,. Tompa, F. W. (2003, September). XQuery Rewriting at the Algebraic Level. Trends in XML Technology for the Global Information Infrastructure,. special issue of Journal of Computer Systems. *Science, and Engineering, 18*, 241–262.

Zhao, L.,. Siau, K. (2007). Information Mediation Using Metamodels: An Approach Using XML and Common Warehouse Metamodel. *Journal of Database Management, 18*(Issue 3), 69–82. doi:10.4018/jdm.2007070104

Zhao, Y., Deshpande, P.,. Naughton, J. (1997). An Array-based Algorithm for Simultaneous Multidimensional Aggregates. *ACM SIGMOD Conference* (pp. 159-170).

Zhou, Y., Salehi, A.,. Aberer, K. (2009). Scalable delivery of stream query results. *PVLDB, 2*(1), 49–60.

Zhu, K.,. Kraemer, K. L. (2002). E-commerce metrics for net-enhanced organizations: assessing the value of e-commerce to firm performance in the manufacturing sector. *Information Systems Research, 3*(13), 275–295. doi:10.1287/isre.13.3.275.82

Zipf, G. K. (1949). *Human Behavior and the Principle of Least Effort*. Addison-Wesley.

About the Contributors

Keng Siau is the E. J. Faulkner Professor of Management Information Systems (MIS) at the University of Nebraska-Lincoln (UNL), USA. He is currently serving as the editor-in-chief of the Journal of Database Management and co-editor-in-chief for Advances in Database Research. He is also the Director of the UNL-IBM Global Innovation Hub. In addition to being an internationally renowned database and systems analysis and design researcher, Professor Siau was ranked as one of the top ten e-commerce researchers in the world (Kim et al. 2006). He has won numerous research, teaching, and service awards –e.g., the IFIP Outstanding Service Award in 2006 and the IBM Faculty Award in 2006 and 2008. He received his PhD degree from the University of British Columbia (UBC), where he majored in management information systems and minored in cognitive psychology. His master and bachelor degrees are in computer and information sciences from the National University of Singapore. Professor Siau has more than 200 academic publications. He has published more than 100 refereed journal articles, and these articles have appeared (or are forthcoming) in journals such as Management Information Systems Quarterly, Journal of the Association for Information Systems, Communications of the ACM, IEEE Computer, Information Systems Journal, Journal of Strategic Information Systems, Information Systems, ACM SIGMIS's Database, IEEE Transactions on Systems, Man, and Cybernetics, IEEE Transactions on Professional Communication, IEEE Transactions on Information Technology in Biomedicine, IEICE Transactions on Information and Systems, Data and Knowledge Engineering, Journal of Information Technology, and International Journal of Human-Computer Studies. In addition, he has published more than 100 refereed conference papers, edited/co-edited more than 15 scholarly and research-oriented books, edited/co-edited ten proceedings, and written more than 25 scholarly book chapters. He served as the Organizing and Program Chairs of the International Conference on Evaluation of Modeling Methods in Systems Analysis and Design (EMMSAD) (1996–20005). Professor Siau served on the Organizing Committees of AMCIS 2005, ER 2006, AMCIS 2007, EuroSIGSAND 2007, EuroSIGSAND 2008, and ICMB 2009. He also serves on numerous advisory boards and journal editorial boards. For more information, please visit his Web site at http://www.cba.unl.edu/faculty/ksiau.html.

* * *

Anteneh Ayanso is an Assistant Professor of Information Systems at Brock University, Canada. He received his Ph.D. in Information Systems from the University of Connecticut in 2004. His research interests are in data management, electronic business, quantitative modeling and simulation in information systems and supply chains. His research has appeared in Communications of the AIS, Decision Support Systems, and European Journal of Operational Research.

Pär Ågerfalk holds the Chair in Computer Science in Intersection with Social Sciences at Uppsala University. He received his PhD in Information Systems Development from Linköping University and has held fulltime positions at Örebro University, University of Limerick, Jönköping International Business School and Lero – The Irish Software Engineering Research Centre, where he is also currently a Senior Research Fellow. His research on open source software, globally distributed and flexible software development, ISD methodology and conceptual modeling has appeared in a variety of IS journals and conferences and he is currently an associate editor of the European Journal of Information Systems and Systems, Signs and Actions.

Ryan Choi is a Ph.D. student in the School of Computer Science and Engineering at the University of New South Wales, Australia. He received a B.Eng. in Software Engineering with First Class Honours from the University of New South Wales. While working toward a Ph.D., he lectured, taught classes and reviewed conference proceedings. His research interests include XML database systems, query optimization, information retrieval, Web services, and visualization of query languages.

Kaushik Dutta is an Assistant Professor at in the College of Business at Florida International University. He has several years of professional and research experience in the fields of electronic commerce and enterprise IT infrastructure. Dr. Dutta has published articles in INFORMS Management Science, INFORMS Journal of Computing, ACM Transactions on Database Systems, European Journal of Operations Research, INFORMS Journal of Group Decision and Negotiation, IEEE Transactions on Systems, Man, and Cybernetics, VLDB Journal, IEEE Internet Computing and IEEE Transactions in Mobile Computing. Dr. Dutta also has several publications in various IEEE and ACM conference proceedings. He has received awards for conference papers and academic performance, and was a finalist in Pennsylvania State University's e-BRC Doctoral Proposal Award (2002). Dr. Dutta has received several college-wide research award at FIU. Prior to joining FIU, Dr. Dutta was Director of Engineering for Chutney Technologies, a software company that developed solutions to improve the scalability and performance of enterprise web applications. Dr. Dutta has almost a decade of experience in software product development in India, Europe and the U.S.

Joerg Evermann is with the Faculty of Business Administration at Memorial University of Newfoundland. Joerg received his PhD in MIS from The Sauder School of Business at The University of British Columbia. His research interests are in conceptual modeling and cognitive issues in knowledge representation. His research has been published in international journals such as IEEE Transactions on Software Engineering and Transactions on Knowledge and Data Engineering, Information Systems Journal, and Requirements Engineering.

Aykut Firat is an Assistant Professor in the Information, Operations, and Analysis group at Northeastern University. Professor Firat received his PhD in Management Science from MIT Sloan School of Management, his MSc in Systems Analysis from Miami University, OH, and BSc in Industrial Engineering from Bogazici University, Istanbul. Professor Firat has primary research interest in understanding the technology, strategy, and organizational factors in integrating information systems. In particular, he is interested in heterogeneous database integration, and achieving semantic interoperability among Web sources and services in the emerging area of Semantic Web.

Andrew Gemino is an Associate Professor in the Management Information Systems area in the Faculty of Business Administration at Simon Fraser University (SFU). His degrees include an M.A. in Economics and an M.B.A. from SFU and a Ph.D. in MIS from the University of British Columbia. His research interests include information technology project management and the effective communication of information system requirements. His research is currently funded by the Natural Sciences Research Council (NSERC) and the Social Sciences and Humanities Research Council (SSHRC) of Canada. Andrew is Vice President of the AIS Special Interest Group in System Analysis and Design (SIGSAND) and a member of the Surgeon Information System Working Group for the Provincial Surgical Oncology Council affiliated with the British Columbia Cancer Agency.

Paulo Goes is the Salter Distinguished Professor in Technology and Management, and Department Head of Management Information Systems, at the Eller College of Management, the University of Arizona. He received his Ph.D. from the University of Rochester in 1991. His research interests are in the areas of design and evaluation of models for e-business, emerging technologies, online auctions, database technology and systems, and technology infrastructure. His research has appeared in several journals including Management Science, MISQ, ISR, Journal of MIS, Operations Research, Decision Sciences, Decision Support Systems, INFORMS Journal on Computing, IEEE Transactions on Communications, IEEE Transactions on Computers. Dr. Goes is Senior Editor of Information Systems Research, and Associate Editor of Management Science, Decision Sciences, Journal of Management Information Systems, and the INFORMS Journal on Computing. In 2004 he co-chaired WITS, the Workshop on Information Technology and Systems, and was recently elected the WITS Organization President.

Wen-Chi Hou received the MS and Ph.D degrees in Computer Science and Engineering from Case Western Reserve University, Cleveland Ohio, in 1985 and 1989, respectively. He is presently a professor of Computer Science at Southern Illinois University at Carbondale. His interests include statistical databases, mobile databases, XML databases, and data streams.

Gerald Kane is an Assistant Professor of Information Systems at the Carroll School of Management at Boston College. His research interests include using collaborative technologies (e.g. Web 2.0/ Social Media) for knowledge creation and sharing, the strategic use of information technology (particularly social media) to create business value in firms, managing knowledge for organizational advantage, particularly healthcare organization, and the role of information systems in social networks. Prof Kane is a recent recipient of a CAREER Award from the National Science Foundation, the Foundation's "most prestigious award in support of junior faculty who exemplify the role of teacher-scholars through outstanding research, excellent education and the integration of education and research within the context of the mission of their organizations." His published research has appeared in Information Systems Research, MIS Quarterly, Organization Science, Harvard Business Review, DATABASE, Journal of Database Management, and Information & Management. Dr. Kane received his Ph.D. in Information Systems from the Goizueta Business School of Emory University.

Fredrik Karlsson is an Assistant Professor of Informatics at Örebro University. He received his PhD in Information Systems Development from Linköping University. His research about tailoring of systems development methods, system development methods as reusable assets, and CAME-tools has appeared in a number of IS journals and conferences. He is currently heading the Methodology Exploration Lab at Örebro University.

Cheng Luo received his PhD in Computer Science from Department of Computer Science at Southern Illinois University in 2007. He is currently an assistant professor in the Department of Mathematics and Computer Science at Coppin State University, Baltimore MD. His research interests are in databases and data mining.

Stuart Madnick is the John Norris Maguire Professor of Information Technology, Sloan School of Management and Professor of Engineering Systems, School of Engineering at the Massachusetts Institute of Technology. He has been a faculty member at MIT since 1972. He has served as the head of MIT's Information Technologies Group for more than twenty years. Dr. Madnick is the author or co-author of over 250 books, articles, or reports including the classic textbook, Operating Systems, and the book, The Dynamics of Software Development. His current research interests include connectivity among disparate distributed information systems, database technology, software project management, and the strategic use of information technology. He is presently co-Director of the PROductivity From Information Technology Initiative and co-Heads the Total Data Quality Management research program. He has been active in industry, as a key designer and developer of projects such as IBM's VM/370 operating system and Lockheed's DIALOG information retrieval system. He has served as a consultant to corporations, such as IBM, AT&T, and Citicorp. He has also been the founder or co-founder of high-tech firms, including Intercomp, Mitrol, and Cambridge Institute for Information Systems, iAggregate.com and currently operates a hotel in the 14th century Langley Castle in England. Dr. Madnick has degrees in Electrical Engineering (B.S. and M.S.), Management (M.S.), and Computer Science (Ph.D.) from MIT. He has been a Visiting Professor at Harvard University, Nanyang Technological University (Singapore), University of Newcastle (England), Technion (Israel), and Victoria University (Australia).

Patrick Martin is a Professor of the School of Computing at Queen's University. He holds a BSc from the University of Toronto, an MSc from Queen's University and a PhD from the University of Toronto. He is also a Visiting Scientist with IBM's Centre for Advanced Studies. His research interests include database system performance, Web services, pervasive computing and autonomic computing systems.

Kumar Mehta is an Assistant Professor of Management Information Systems at George Mason University's School of Management. He received his Ph.D. from University of Illinois at Chicago in 2002. His research interests include Data Mining, Information Retrieval and Agent-based Computational Modeling. His research has appeared in Decision Support Systems, Journal of Retailing, and Information Technology and Management.

Baoning Niu is an associate professor of the School of Computer and Software at Taiyuan University of Technology. He holds a BSc and an MSc from Taiyuan University of Technology and a PhD from the School of Computing at Queen's University. His research interests include: performance management for DBMSs, autonomic DBMSs.

Drew Parker is an Associate Professor in the Management Information Systems area in the Faculty of Business Administration at Simon Fraser University. He holds a B.Comm. and a M.B.A. degree from the University of Calgary, and a Ph.D. from the Ivey School of Business at the University of Western Ontario. He also holds the Information Systems Professional (I.S.P.) and Information Technology Certified Professional (ITCP) designation from the Canadian Information Processing Society and the International Professional Practice Partnership (IP3P) from the International Federation for Information Processing (IFIP). His current research interests originated to a large extent from work developing and delivering system analysis courses online internationally, and working on using telecommunications and the Internet to communicate and collaborate effectively.

Wendy Powley is a Research Associate and Adjunct Lecturer in the School of Computing at Queen's University. She holds a BA in psychology, a BEd, and an MSc in Computer Science from Queen's University. Her research interests include database systems, web services and autonomic computing.

Sherif Sakr received the B.Sc. degree in Computer Science from Information Systems Department, the Faculty of Computers and Information, Cairo University, Egypt, in 2000. He received his Master degree from the same department in March 2003. In 2007, Dr. Sherif Sakr received his PhD degree in Computer Science from Konstanz University, Germany. In 2008, He was a postdoctoral research fellow on National ICT Australia (NICTA). Currently, he is a postdoctoral research fellow in the Service Oriented Computing (SOC) research group at School of Computer Science and Engineering (CSE), University of New South Wales (UNSW), Australia. His research interests lie in the areas of relational database support for XML/XQuery processing, selectivity estimation of XML queries, XML compression techniques, graph data management, large scale and autonomous data sharing, process modeling and service oriented architectures for pervasive computing. His work has been published in international journals such as JDM, IJWIS, and JCSS, and conferences such as VLDB, SIGMOD, DASFAA, and DEXA.

Kathy Schwaig joined the faculty at Kennesaw State University in 2002 brining over twenty years of teaching and professional experience to the classroom. An authority on the topic of information privacy and policy formulation, her research has been published in some of the leading journals in the information systems field including Information Systems Research and Journal of Management Information System among others. She earned her BBA in Accounting and her MBA degree in Information systems from Baylor University and her PhD in Management Information Systems for the University of South Carolina. Currently, Dr. Schwaig is the Interim Dean in the Coles College of Business. In addition to her research and administrative responsibilities, Dr. Schwaig serves on the board of an Atlanta IT staffing firm as well as the Atlanta Care Center.

Arijit Sengupta is Associate Professor of Information Systems and Operations Management at the Raj Soin College of Business at Wright State University, Dayton, Ohio. He received his Ph.D. in Computer Science from Indiana University. Prior to joining Wright State, Dr.Sengupta served as faculty at Kelley School of Business at Indiana University and the Robinson College of Business at Georgia State University. Dr. Sengupta's current primary research interest is in the efficient use and deployment of RFID (Radio Frequency Identification) for business application. His other research interests are in databases and XML, specifically in modeling, query languages, data mining, and human-computer interaction. He has published over 30 scholarly articles in leading journals and conferences, as well as authored several books and book chapters.

Veda Storey is the Tull Professor of Computer Information Systems, College of Business Administration, and Professor of Computer Science, Georgia State University. She has Research interests in database management systems, intelligent systems, and Semantic Web, and ontology development. Her research has been published in ACM Transactions on Database Systems, IEEE Transactions on Knowledge and Data Engineering, Information Systems Research, Management Information Systems Quarterly, Data and Knowledge Engineering, Decision Support Systems, the Very Large Data Base Journal, and Information & Management. She has served on the editorial board of several journals including Information Systems Research, MIS Quarterly, DataBase, and Decision Support Systems. Dr. Storey was the program co-chair for the International Conference on Conceptual Modeling (ER 2000) and for the International Conference on Information Systems (ICIS 2001). Dr. Storey received her doctorate in Management Information Systems from the University of British Columbia, Canada. She earned a Master of Business Administration degree from Queen's University, Ontario, Canada, and a Bachelor of Science degree (with distinction) from Mt. Allison University, New Brunswick, Canada. In addition, she received her Associate of the Royal Conservatory of Music for flute performance from The University of Toronto, Canada.

Kamal Taha is a PhD candidate in the Department of Computer Science and Engineering at the University of Texas at Arlington. He has 7 referred publications that have appeared (or are forthcoming) in conferences and workshops proceedings, in addition to a book chapter. Kamal worked as Engineering Specialist for Seagate Technology (a leading computer disc drive manufacturer in the US) from 1995 to 2005. His research interests include XML Keyword and Loosely Structured Querying, Distributed XML Processing and Caching, Query Personalization, Web Modeling and Ontologies.

Debra VanderMeer is an Assistant Professor at in the College of Business at Florida International University. Her research interests focus on applying concepts developed in Computer Science and Information Systems to solve real-world problems. She is widely published in well-known journals, such as Management Science, ACM Transactions on Database Systems and IEEE Transactions on Knowledge and Data Engineering, as well as prestigious conference proceedings, including the International Conference on Data Engineering, International Conference on Distributed Computing Systems and the Very Large Database Conference. She also has significant professional experience in the software industry. She has served in software engineering and managerial roles in large companies, as well as early-stage venture-funded software enterprises.

Ramesh Venkataraman is Associate Professor in the Information Systems Department and Ford Motor Company Teaching Fellow at Indiana University's Kelley School of Business where he also serves as Director of the MS in Information Systems program. His research interests are in Data Modeling, Heterogeneous Databases, Virtual Teams and Groupware, Usability in Mobile Systems and Software Engineering. Ramesh has published over 25 papers in leading journals, book and conferences, such as /Communications of the ACM, Journal of Management Information Systems, ACM Transactions on Information Systems, Information Systems/ and /IEEE Expert/. His teaching interests include Database

Design, Object-oriented Design and Programming (Java and VB.NET), Web Applications Development (JSP/Servlets, ASP.NET), E-business Infrastructure.

Michael Wainer obtained his PhD in Computer and Information Science from the University of Alabama at Birmingham, in 1987 and is currently an associate professor of Computer Science at Southern Illinois University Carbondale. His research interests lie in the areas of software development, computer graphics and human computer interaction. He is particularly interested in interdisciplinary work which utilizes the computer as a tool for design and visualization.

Yair Wand is CANFOR Professor of MIS at the Sauder School of Business, the University of British Columbia, Canada, and a Professor at the MIS Department, Faculty of Social Sciences, Haifa University, Israel. He received his D.Sc. in Operations Research from The Technion (Israel Institute of Technology), his M.Sc. in Physics from the Weizmann Institute (Israel), and B.Sc. in Physics from the Hebrew University, Jerusalem. His research interests include theoretical foundations for information systems analysis and design, development and evaluation of systems analysis methods, and conceptual modelling. In particular, he has done work on the use of ontological concepts in information systems analysis and design. Presently he is on the editorial boards of the Journal of Data Semantics, Journal of Database Management, Requirements Engineering Journal, Applied Ontology, and Information Quality Research.

Chih-Fang Wang received his PhD in Computer Engineer at University of Florida in 1998. His current research interests include sequential, parallel and distributed algorithms, data structures, high performance computing, optical networks, quantum computing, DNA computing, bioinformatics, wireless/mobile security, data mining, and mobile agents and secure mobile agent platforms.

Raymond Wong is a Project Leader at National ICT Australia (NICTA). He is also an Associate Professor in the School of Computer Science and Engineering at the University of New South Wales, Australia. He received a B.Sc. in Computer Science from the Australian National University in 1993 and an M.Phil. and a Ph.D. in Computer Science from Hong Kong University of Science and Technology in 1994 and 1997, respectively. Before joining UNSW, he held academic and research positions at Stanford University, University of Sydney and Chinese University of Hong Kong.

Lynn Wu is a PhD candidate at MIT's Sloan School of Management. She is interested in studying the role of information and information technology in the productivity and performance of firms. Previously, she was a researcher at IBM. Lynn received a Bachelor and a Master degree from Electrical Engineering and Computer Science Department at MIT, along with a bachelor degree in Finance from the MIT's Sloan School of Management.

Feng Yu received his MS in Pure Mathematics in the School of Mathematics, Shandong University, China. He is currently a PhD student in the Department of Computer Science at Southern Illinois University, Carbondale IL, U.S.A . His interests include statistical databases, spatial databases, and query optimization.

Xiaoguang Yu received her MS from Department of Computer Science at Southern Illinois University in 2005.

Index

A

absolute privacy 82
accumulated knowledge 26
active system management (ASM) 160
ad-hoc query language 316, 317, 332, 336
admission control 158
AFilter 122, 126, 146
alternative flows 27
ANOVA analysis 11
application domain 37, 38, 39, 47, 53, 55
Array2D data set 300, 301, 302, 304, 306
Array3D data set 300, 301, 303, 304
assisted level 158
attributes 20, 29, 34
autonomic computing 154, 155, 158, 170
autonomic computing systems 155
autonomic workload management framework
        (AWMF) 155, 156, 157, 166, 167, 170

B

behaviors 21, 22
black-box model 163, 164
Bloom Filter 121, 125, 146
building expertise 26, 33
Bunge-Ontology 40
business process level metrics 156
business-to-consumer relationships 86, 87, 90

C

Cameleon# 63, 64, 65, 66, 70, 78
canonical trees graph (CTG) 184, 186, 187,
        188, 189, 190, 195, 196, 197, 198, 199,
        200, 201, 202, 203
capability restriction 62

Cartesian Product 247
Census2D data set 300, 302, 304
Census3D data set 300, 302, 303, 304
CHAOS report 2
child data element 175
CIA world fact book 63
class diagram 4
closed-feedback 159
cognitive complexity 20, 22, 23, 24, 25, 26, 27,
        29, 31, 32, 33, 34, 35
cognitive loads 22
cognitive theory of multimedia learning
        (CTML) 1, 3, 7, 8, 9, 12, 13, 14
commercial database systems 297, 299
communication of analysis information 2
communication plan component 231
component subqueries (CSQ) 70, 72, 74, 75
comprehension measures 11
ComputeInterconnectionIndex 178
conceptual modeling (CM) 1, 4, 5, 6, 15, 16,
        37
conceptual models 37, 38, 55, 56
conditionals 318
connect-the-dots metaphor 29
consumer information 82, 84, 86, 87, 89, 93,
        94
consumer-oriented privacy position 82
content subscriptions 120
context-driven search 174, 175, 176, 178, 181,
        182, 185, 212
cost-based range estimation 295, 296, 297,
        299, 300, 301, 306, 307

D

DAG plan 254